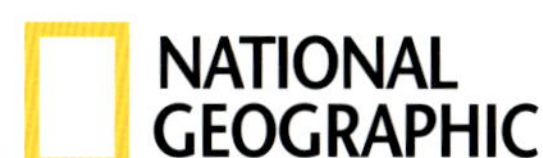

WORLD
FROM
ABOVE

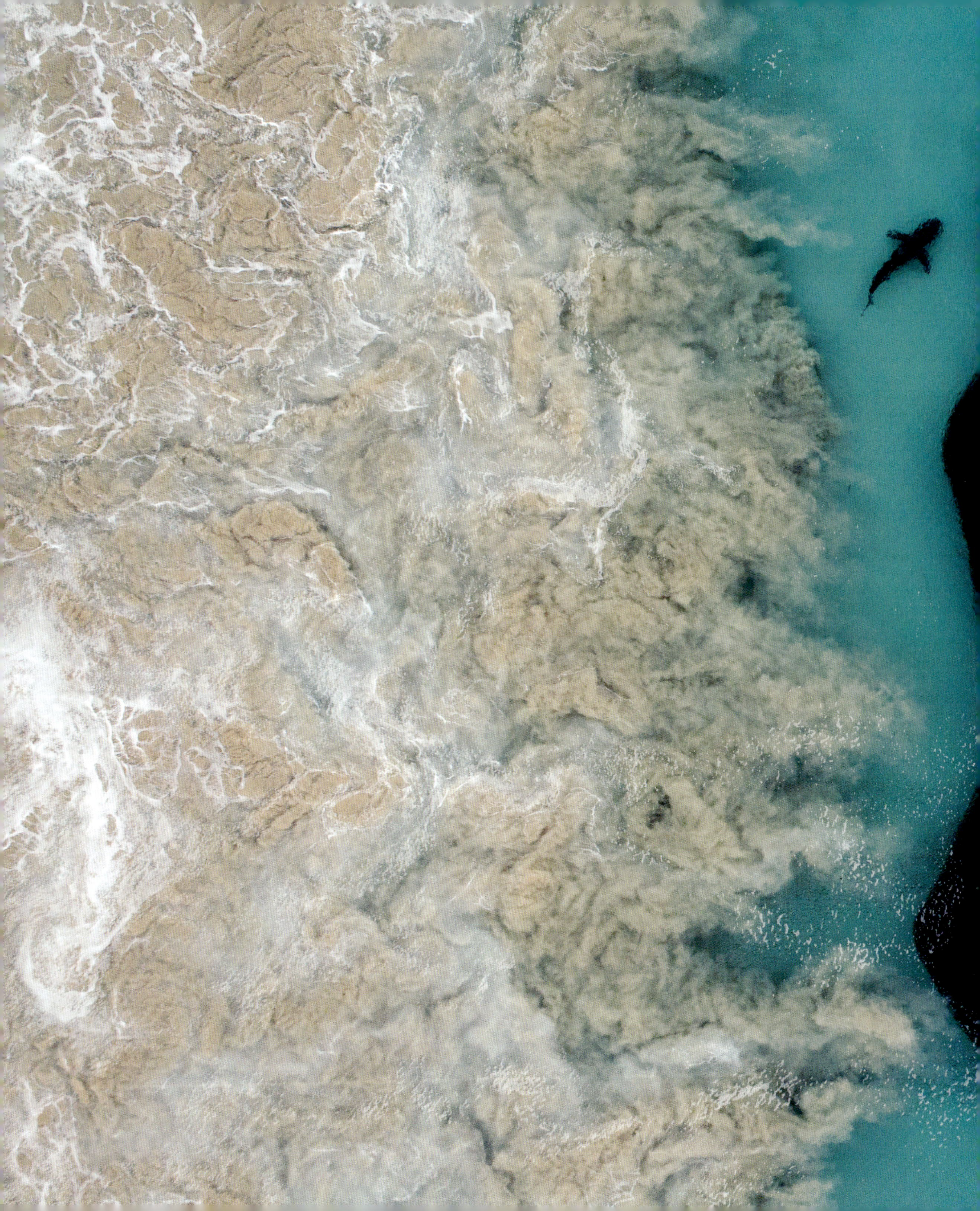

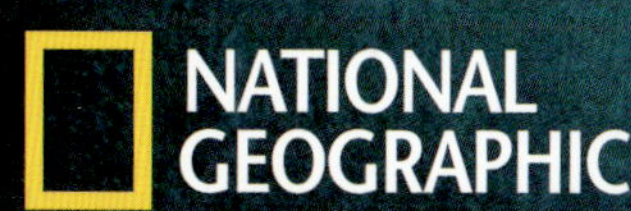

WORLD
FROM
ABOVE

JEFFREY KERBY

NATIONAL GEOGRAPHIC

WASHINGTON, D.C.

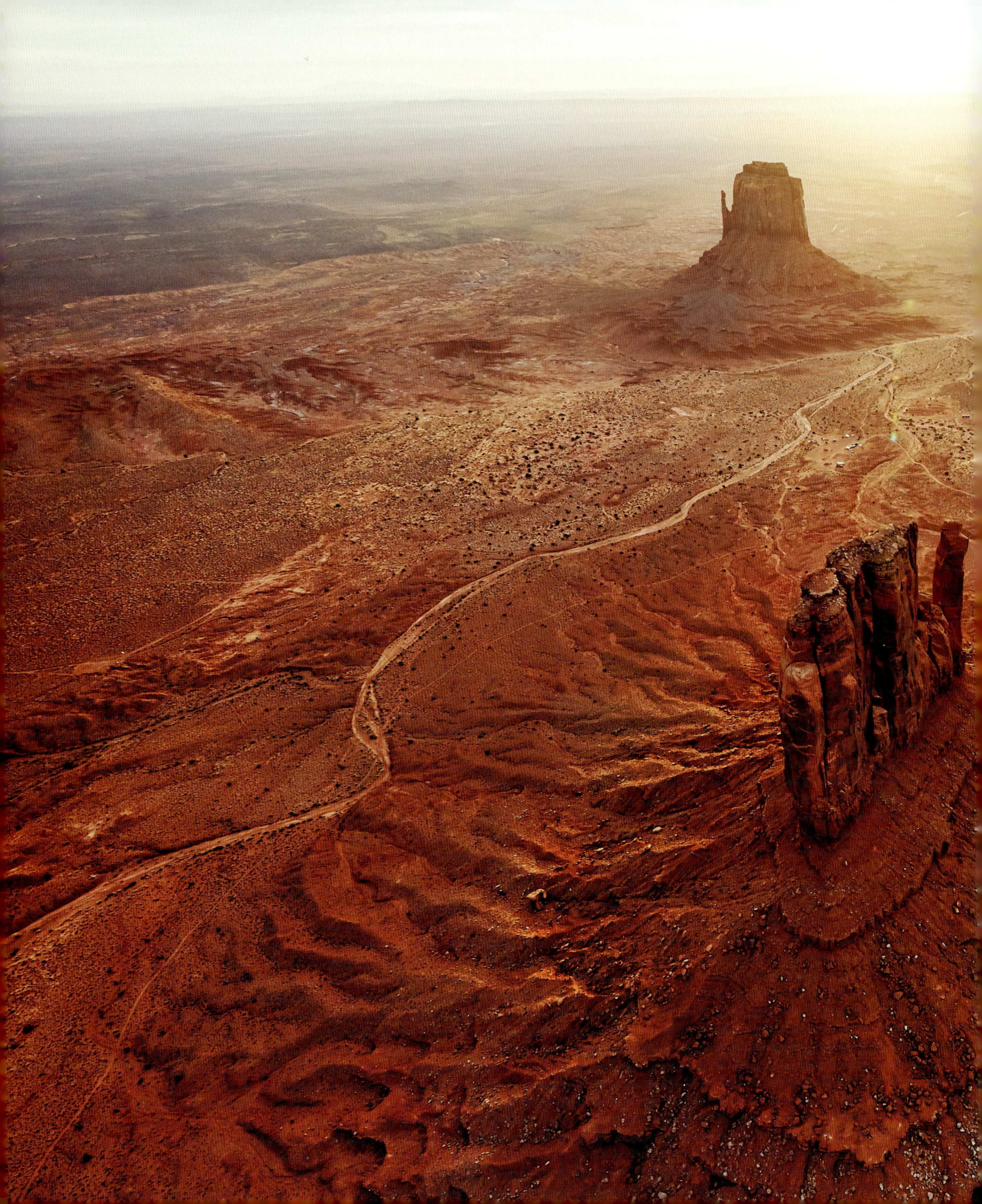

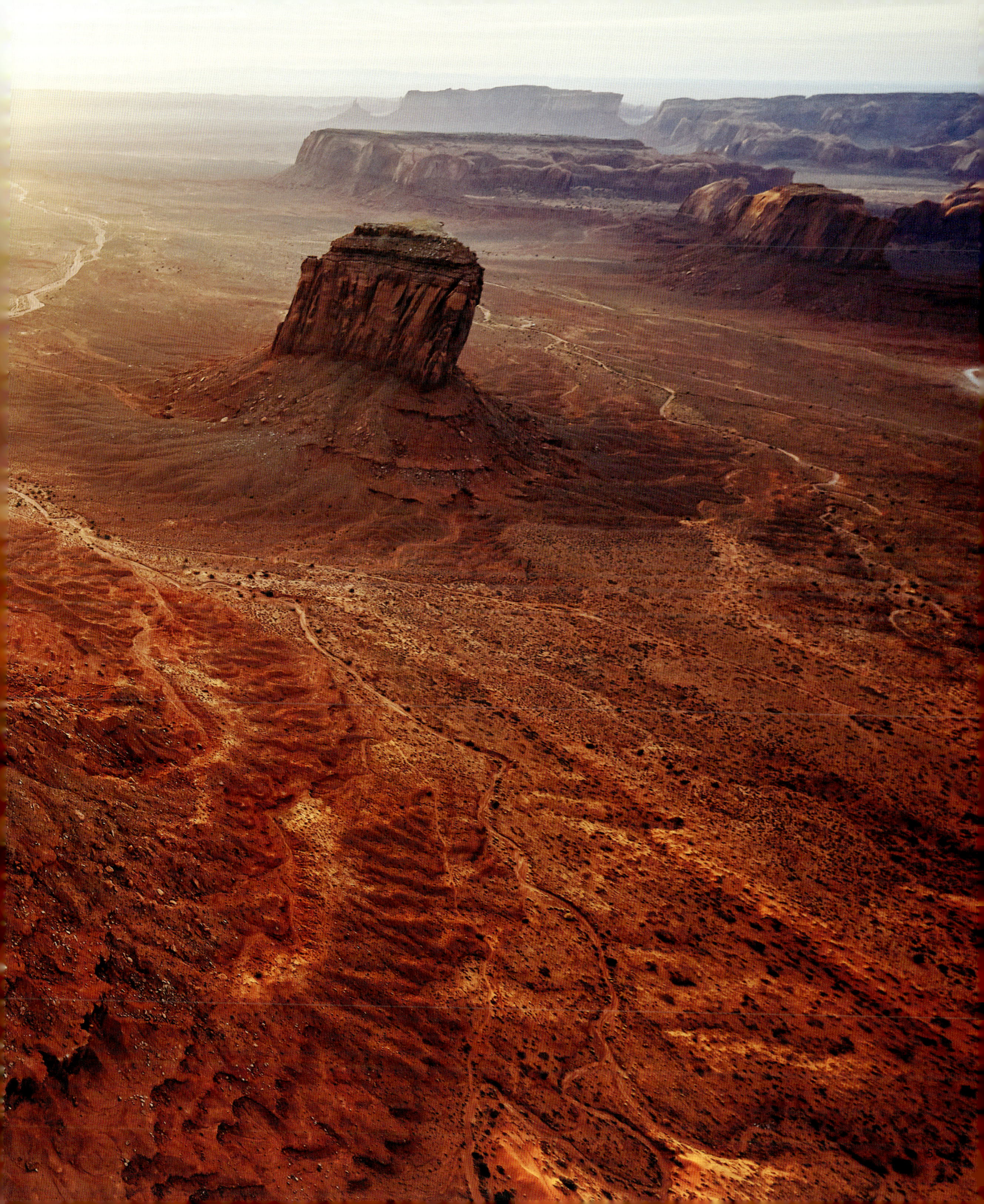

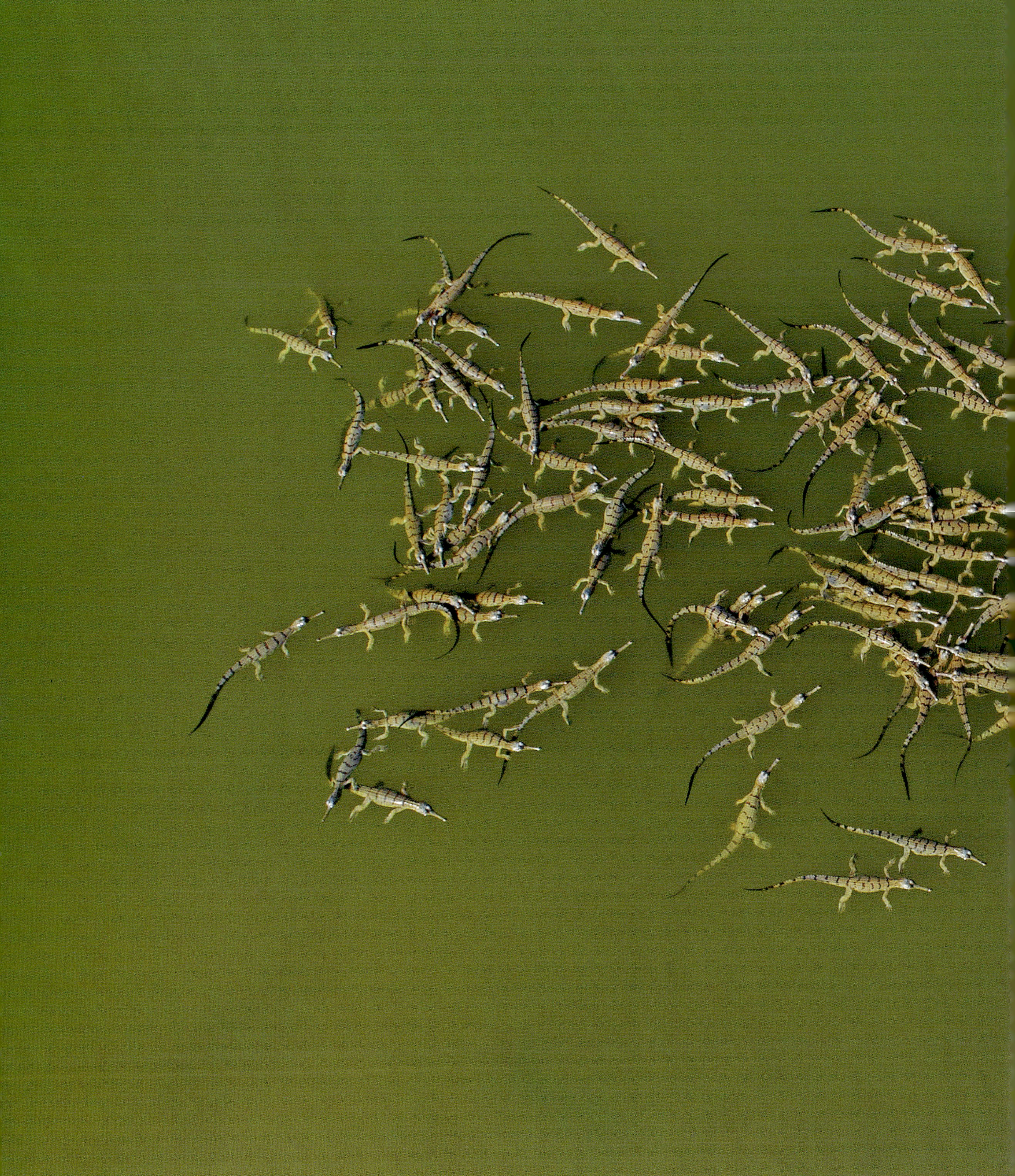

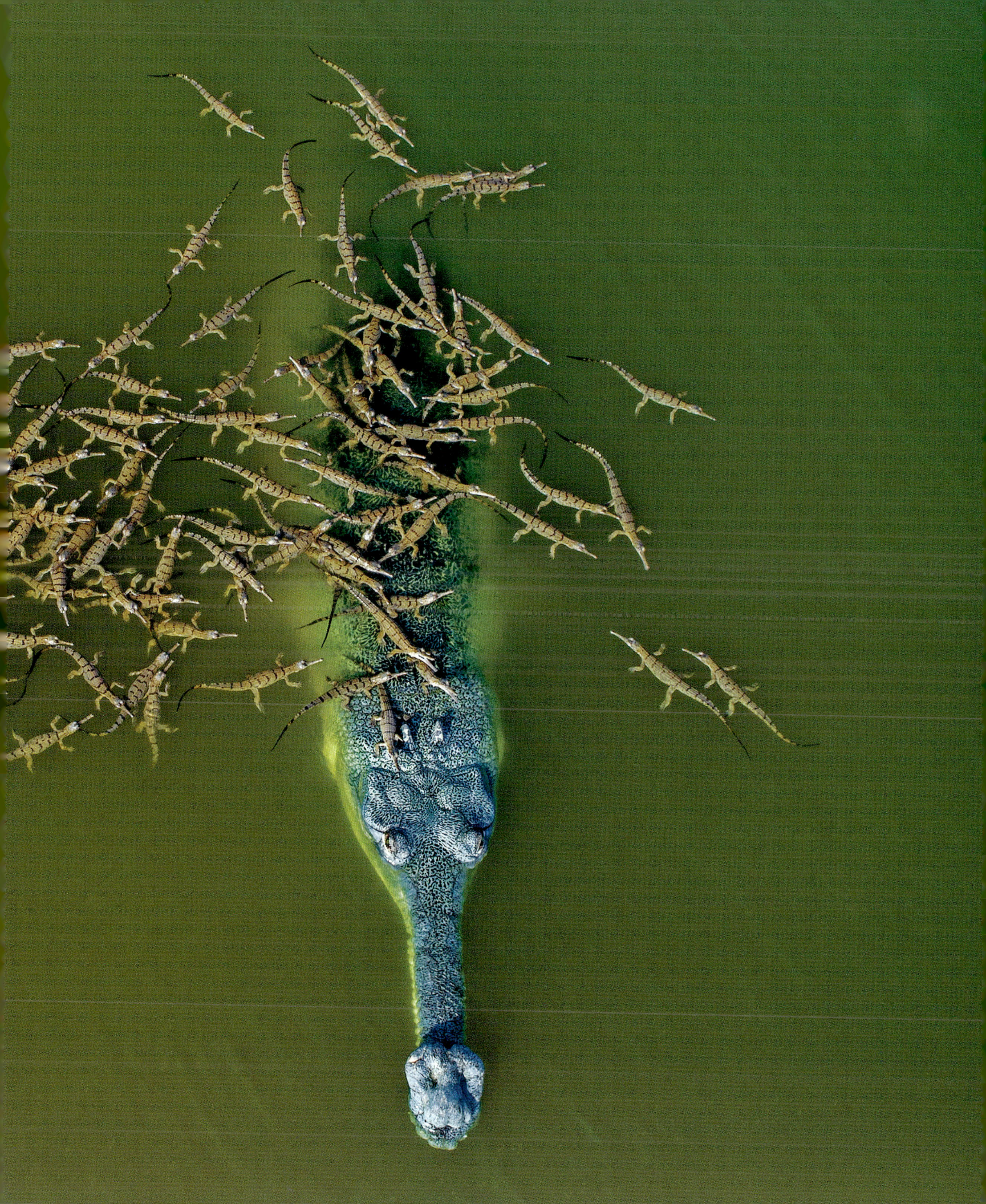

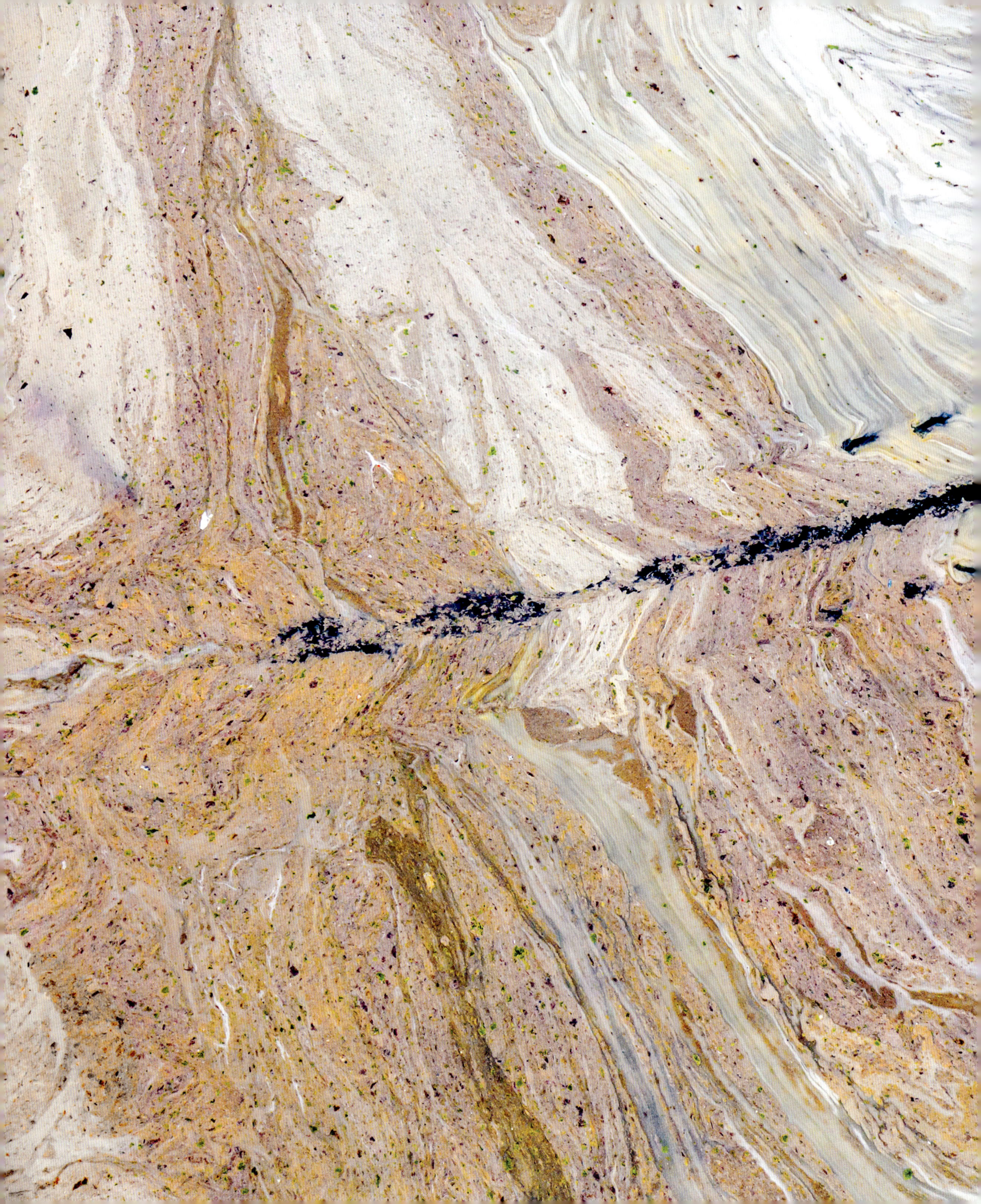

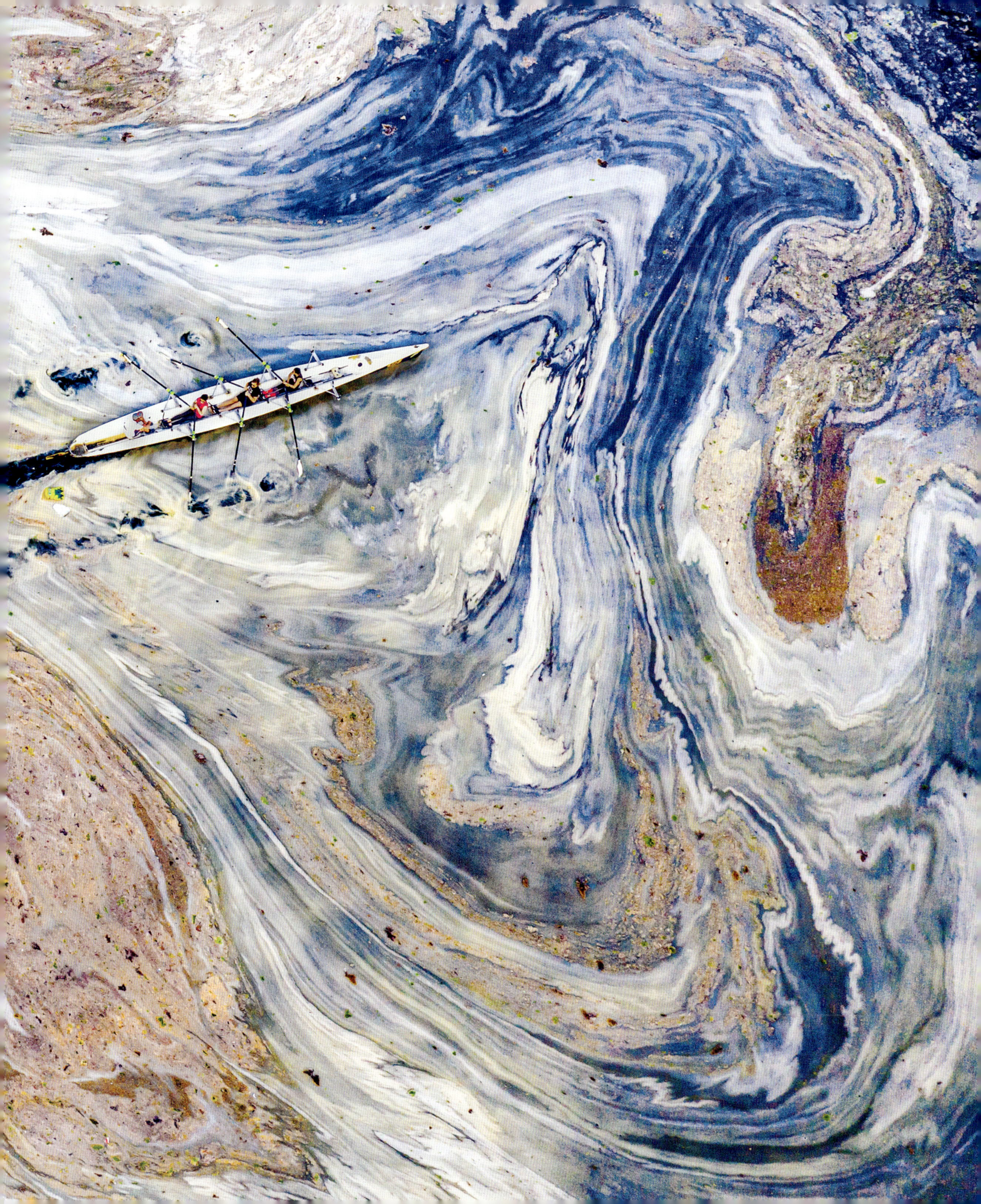

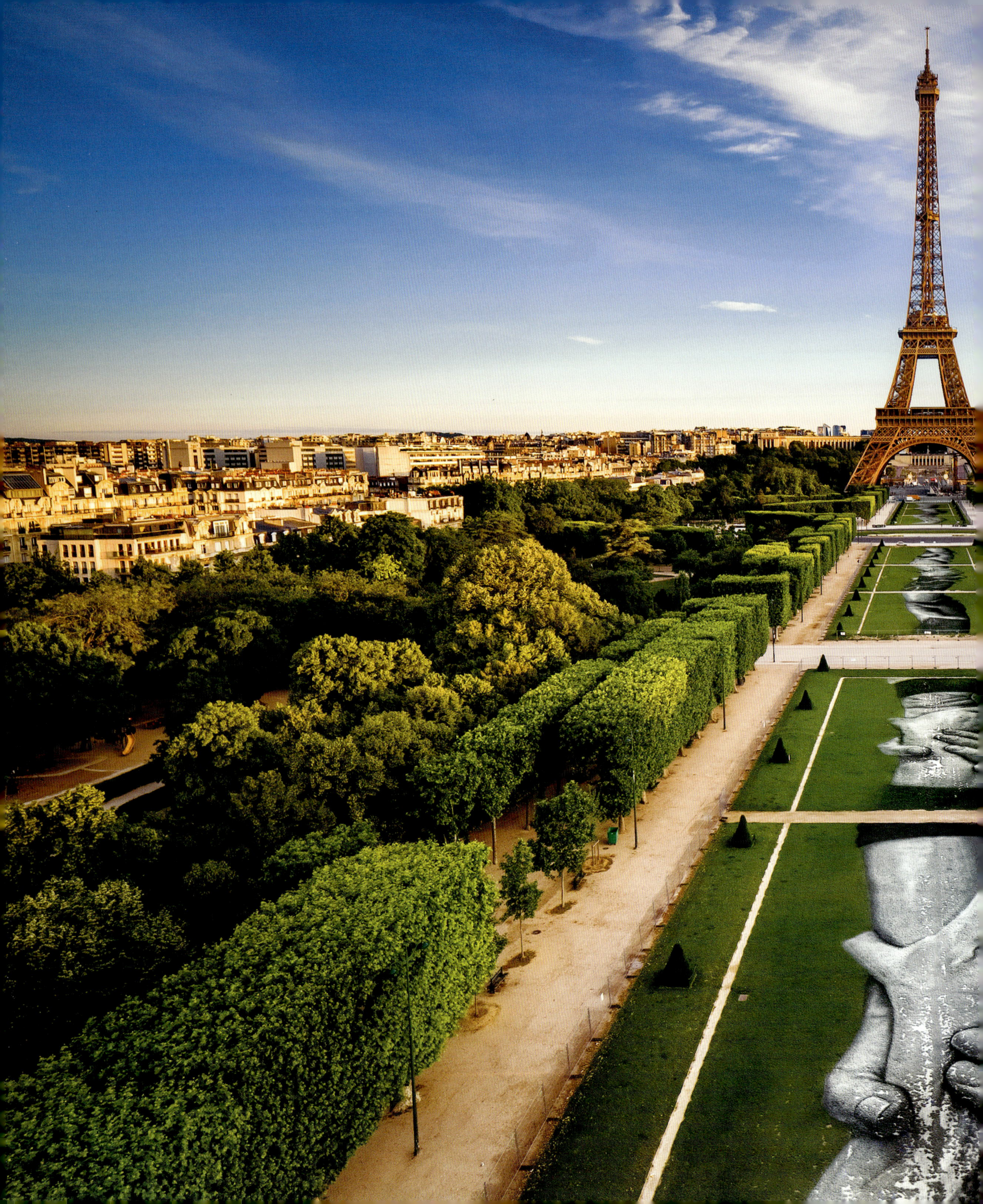

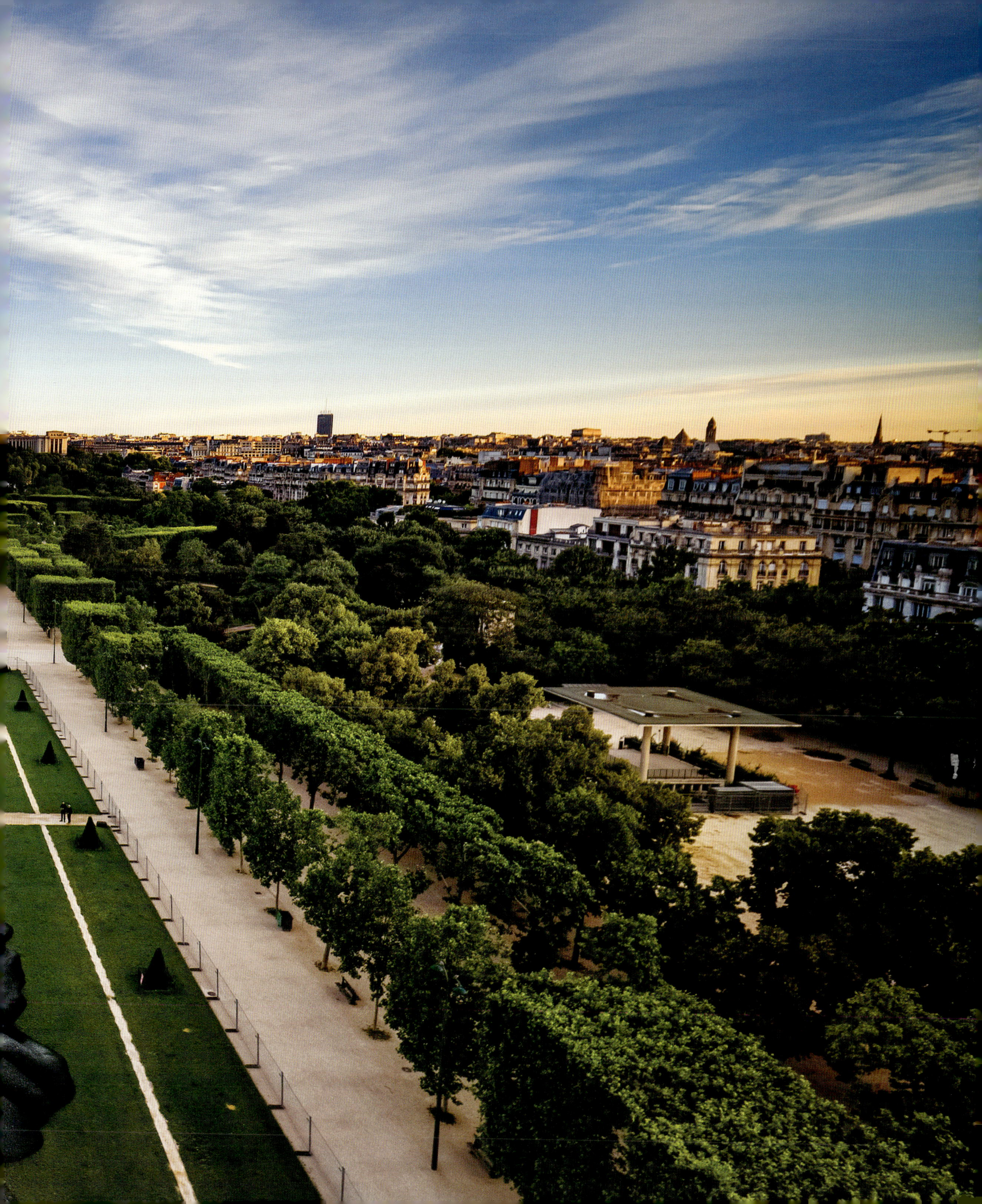

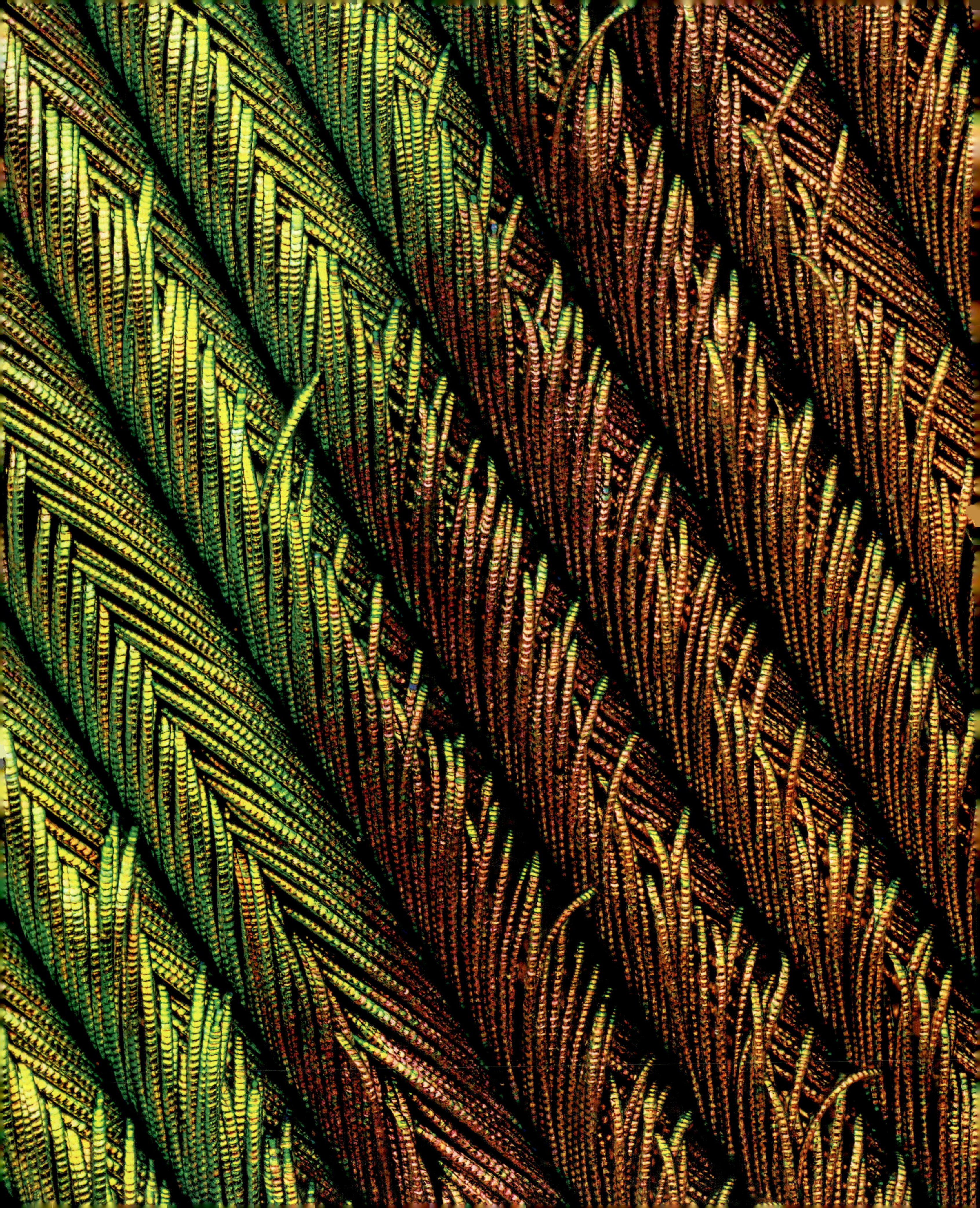

CONTENTS

CAN TUNÇER Detail of a peacock feather

Pages 2–3: **SEAN SCOTT** A shark approaches a bait ball of fish.

Pages 4–5: **CHRIS BURKARD** The eerie desertscape of Utah's Monument Valley

Pages 6–7: **DHRITIMAN MUKHERJEE** Hatchlings cling to a male gharial's back.

Pages 8–9: **KADIR TEZEL** Rowing through excess phytoplankton in Turkey's Sea of Marmara

Pages 10–11: **VALENTIN FLAURAUD FOR SAYPE** A biodegradable painting by artist Saype reaches toward Paris's Eiffel Tower.

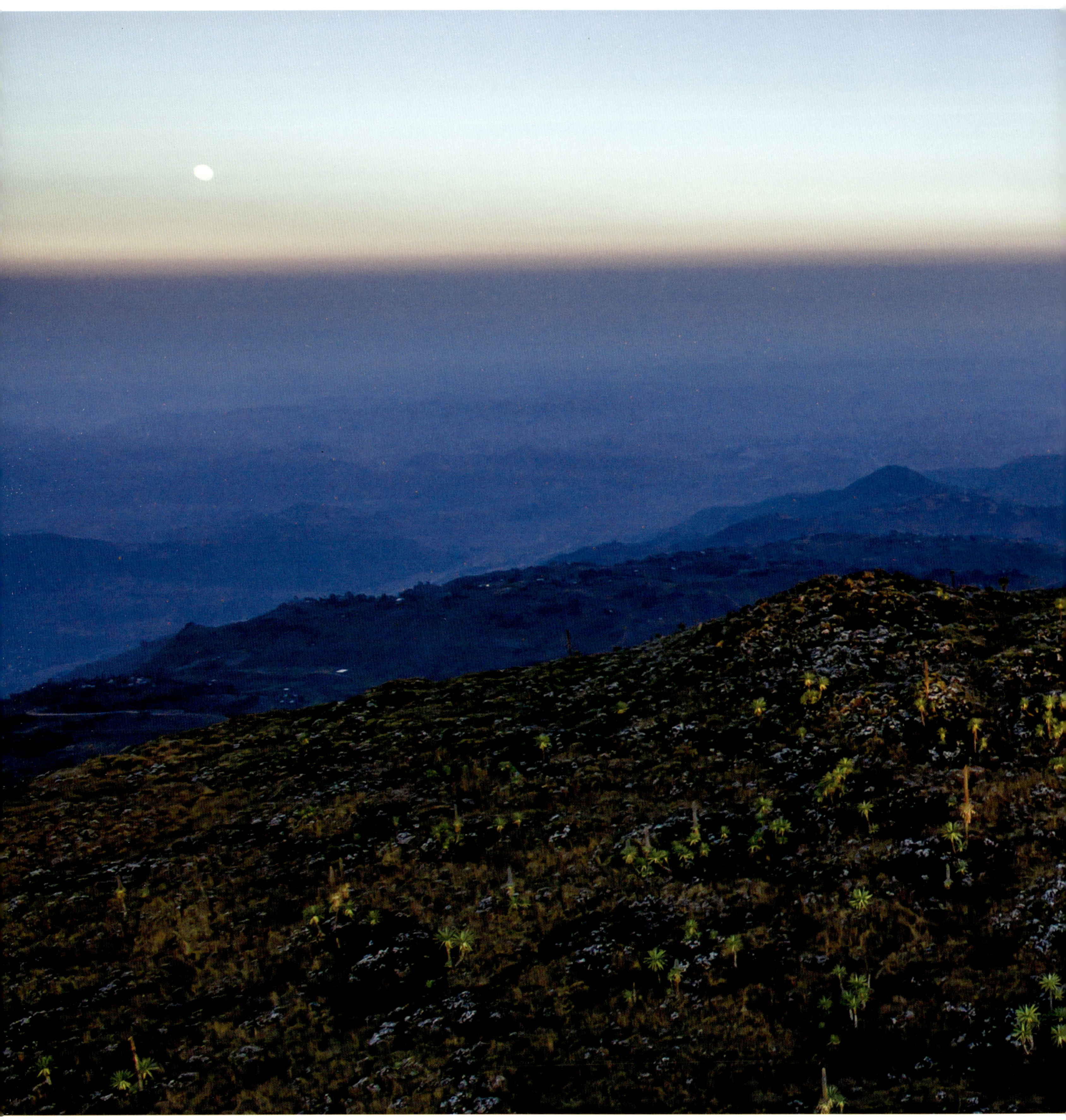

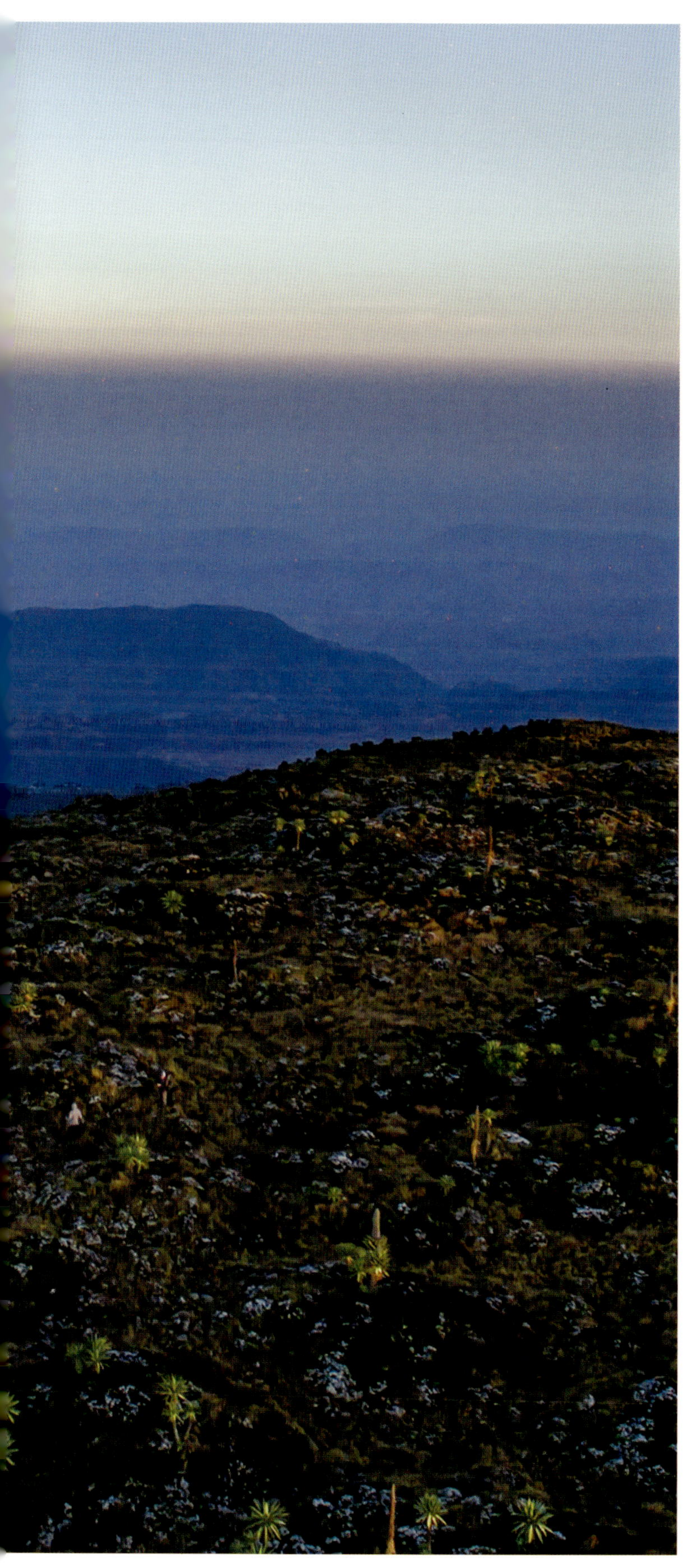

INTRODUCTION

I n my early 20s, I spent a year living on a mountaintop overlooking the Great Rift Valley in Ethiopia. Each day, I'd emerge from my tent and join hundreds of gelada monkeys as they swarmed across the alpine grasslands. Walking through the herd, I'd gaze down at the monkeys surrounding me, noting what they ate and who was healthy, popular, and having kids. Field biology is a unique mix of fun and boredom, but living in the middle of a monkey soap opera also had a purpose.

"Topanga ate an orange-colored berry" is not front-page news, but from thousands of similarly mundane notes on the monkeys' daily lives, a web of stories linking individual geladas to their complex society emerged. This knowledge is critical for wildlife conservation planning; it also provides a scaffolding for bigger questions. How can play, fear, and stress shape a society? Is grief uniquely human? Can we understand long-extinct species by studying their closest relatives? Not all big questions have clear answers, but sometimes simply searching for patterns can be a powerful lens to seeing the world differently.

That mountaintop was also the beginning of my journey as a serious photographer. Field biology taught me to be a keen observer, but I still didn't know how to effectively share these stories. That year I took thousands of photos, and very few of them were any good. I'd assumed photos of a beautiful and interesting place would speak for themselves, but instead they felt flat and disappointing. I was beginning to learn that effective photos are crafted, not just taken. A balancing of technique and intentions.

My big chance came a few years later, when I revisited the mountaintop on a National Geographic–supported

JEFFREY KERBY
A long view at dusk over the Great Rift Valley in Ethiopia

project led by my friend and fellow monkey researcher Vivek Venkataraman. We returned to do science, but I also had a secondary agenda: Make better photos. Before departing, I spent months looking through old photo essays in the magazine, asking myself questions like "How the hell did Nick Nichols do that?" Lots of trial and error with my digital camera followed as I attempted to replicate feelings or perspectives that moved me, and I came back from the mountains with a more effective portfolio. My photos still weren't great, but this time they had been made with intention. That helped crack open a door with a photo editor at *National Geographic,* and—after several more years of mentorship, failure, and learning—a feature photo story in the magazine.

That second trip to the mountains led to more than monkey stories and a crash course in photography; it changed the way I made observations. On clear evenings as the sun fell, I would watch a curtain of shadow grow from the base of cliffs thousands of feet below. It would accelerate across a patchwork of farmland, towns, and rivers until it was swallowed by a distant volcano on the horizon. The world of the monkeys seemed small from this perch, and my photos increasingly began to feature this broader environment as a character. The interwoven shapes, colors, textures, and sheer scale of the valley before me spoke to bigger stories of changing landscapes, centuries-old local conservation efforts, and the splitting of an immense geological fault line. Wildlife, people, and environment were woven together on a massive canvas. Looking down into the patterns of the Great Rift Valley helped me see and understand the patterns embedded in where I was living.

I've curated the images in this book to represent this "world from above" perspective, and to share the perspectives of other photographers on this theme. These images explore the ways photographers push our gaze downward to engage with the key elements of pattern: color, shape, scale, and texture. These are building blocks, and capturing them makes use of a variety of creative techniques on display in the pages that follow. In chapter 1, we see how colors can emphasize or obscure, even beyond what our eyes can perceive. Chapter 2 delves into familiar shapes in sometimes unfamiliar contexts. Chapter 3 reveals how scale confounds the human experience, dragging us from atoms to atmosphere. Chapter 4 allows our eyes to feel, itch, and embrace the many textures that we find below us.

While these images all share either a top-down perspective or highlight a feature coming from above, they express a wide range of intentions, choices, and patterns. I ask you to consider all these features with me. What was the photographer trying to say? How did they achieve this? Was this a photo visualized and planned months in advance? Does the story of the image come from its framing? Can a randomly snapped satellite image be considered art? Asking and thinking through these questions was both a challenge and a pleasure while curating these images, and it's a process I invite you to continue. What does the "world from above" mean to you? This book is my guide, but I encourage you to make the exploration your own.

My work as a photographer leans on my experiences as a scientist and vice versa. In recent years, both have focused on the Arctic as temperatures rise and ice vanishes. Every year I spend months at lower latitudes poring over satellite images to try to understand how the treeless tundra regions are changing. If I look at enough satellite images, even when some are blurry, cloudy, or obscured by the smoke of forest fires, places I've never visited begin to feel familiar and navigable. I start to believe that my view from far above tells me the full story of a place. Then I go to the field with my cameras and drones, and I speak to people who call these places home; they remind me that images from above are only one slice of reality. The sounds of birds and wind, the smell of thawing soils, memories shared of times long past—all of these add new meaning to my top-down assumptions. No view is all-encompassing, but from this diversity of perspectives comes a glimpse at a fuller story.

Aerial photos have long captured human attention by providing the experience of a bird's view of Earth. Advances in imaging can now give us aerial perspectives as seen by a flea, an astronaut, or a reindeer. Having this breadth of observations, seeing the patterns they reveal, opens up a well of curiosity for me—and, I hope, for you.

What we do with this curiosity is up to each of us. But when a photograph makes you stop, wonder, and ask a question, a journey is just beginning. ◼

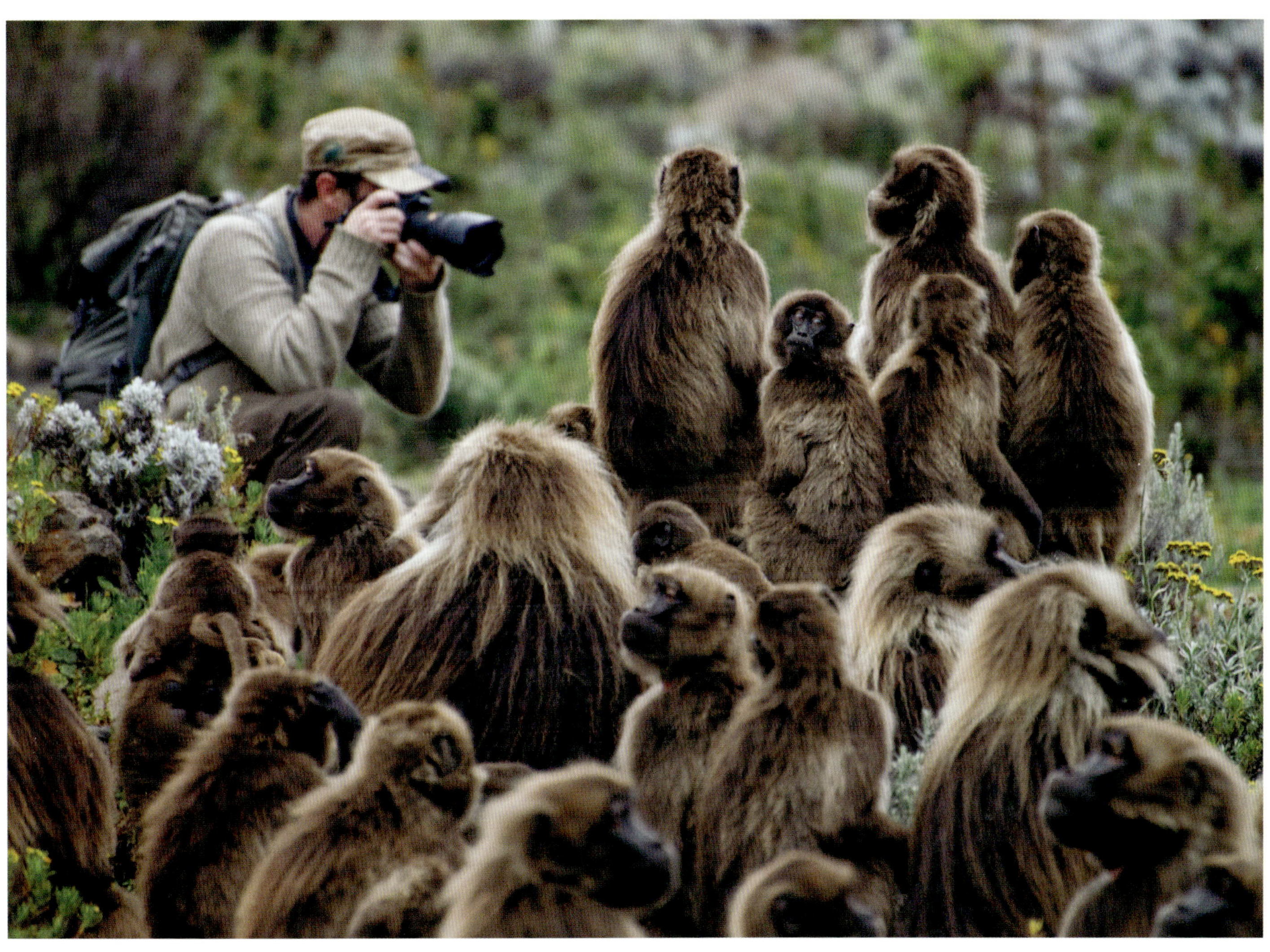

VIVEK V. VENKATARAMAN

Some pose, others ignore, as the author photographs a herd of gelada monkeys at the Guassa Community Conservation Area in Ethiopia.

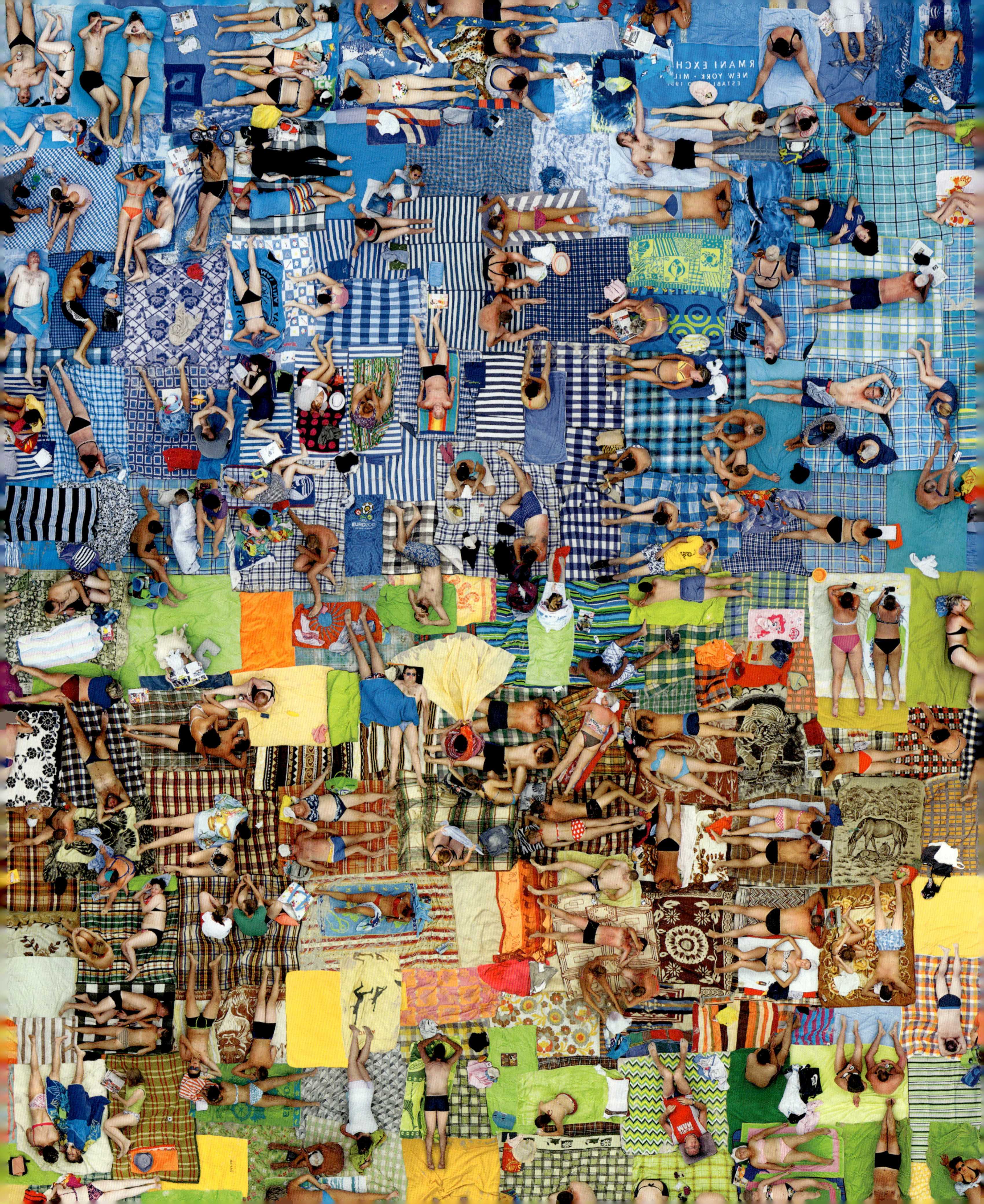

CHAPTER ONE

COLOR

The birds still
remember what
we have forgotten,
that the world
is meant to
be celebrated.

~TERRY TEMPEST WILLIAMS, *WHEN WOMEN WERE BIRDS*

The northernmost flower in the world looks a little ragged. Sitting just a few steps away from where the Arctic Ocean first meets land, it is hairy, a bit wrinkled, and a sickly yellow. But *National Geographic* hadn't sent our expedition team to northern Greenland to find the planet's most beautiful plant—just the one living closest to the world's northern edge. So, we walked, giants in a miniaturized landscape, with our heads turned down, scanning the rocky shoreline for other potential contenders to the northernmost title. Less than a step farther north of the flower, we found a small, green clump of moss, the ultimate winner. The longer we looked, the more the barren land began to fill with colorful signs of life. But within a few days, this micro-symphony of color would disappear under the white blanket of a July snowstorm.

I had expected the northern edge of land on Earth to be a drab rock garden, but even in the flat light of high-Arctic midsummer, a wide range of colors emerged. I shouldn't have been surprised. Arctic summers have been getting greener and greener as temperatures soar and ice retreats, not just in Greenland but all around the north. Peering down from above, satellites measure this and other changes in color across the planet's surface as they track crop growth, deforestation, water pollution, and more. In nature, a change in color can provide clues that bigger processes are afoot.

Color is everywhere around us, but the novelty of an aerial perspective helps us see patterns we might otherwise ignore or miss. A biologist might see indicators of some broader ecological processes. A painter might find mood and emotion. To an architect, signs of order and design. The photographers in this chapter make use of the color in patterns seen from above to emphasize, isolate, and surprise.

Prasenjeet Yadav's rare capture of a green meteor above the "sky islands" of India's Western Ghats (pages 52–53) draws a contrast to the amber glow of humanity at night. Galice Hoarau's subtly lit portrait of an eel larva (page 67) reveals that colors are omnipresent, even when they hover above the abyss in complete darkness. Sebastian Müller's carefully framed drone photo demands our attention, asking, "Why would a river run yellow?" (pages 42–43).

Whether color reveals a process, an intention, or some other facet of reality, it forms a key element of the patterns that populate any view from above, if you know how to capture it. ■

Page 18:
KACPER KOWALSKI
A composition of beach blanket images combined by the photographer to mirror the Ukrainian flag

Following pages:
GHEORGHE POPA
Chemical flow in Romania's Apuseni Mountains, waste from copper mining

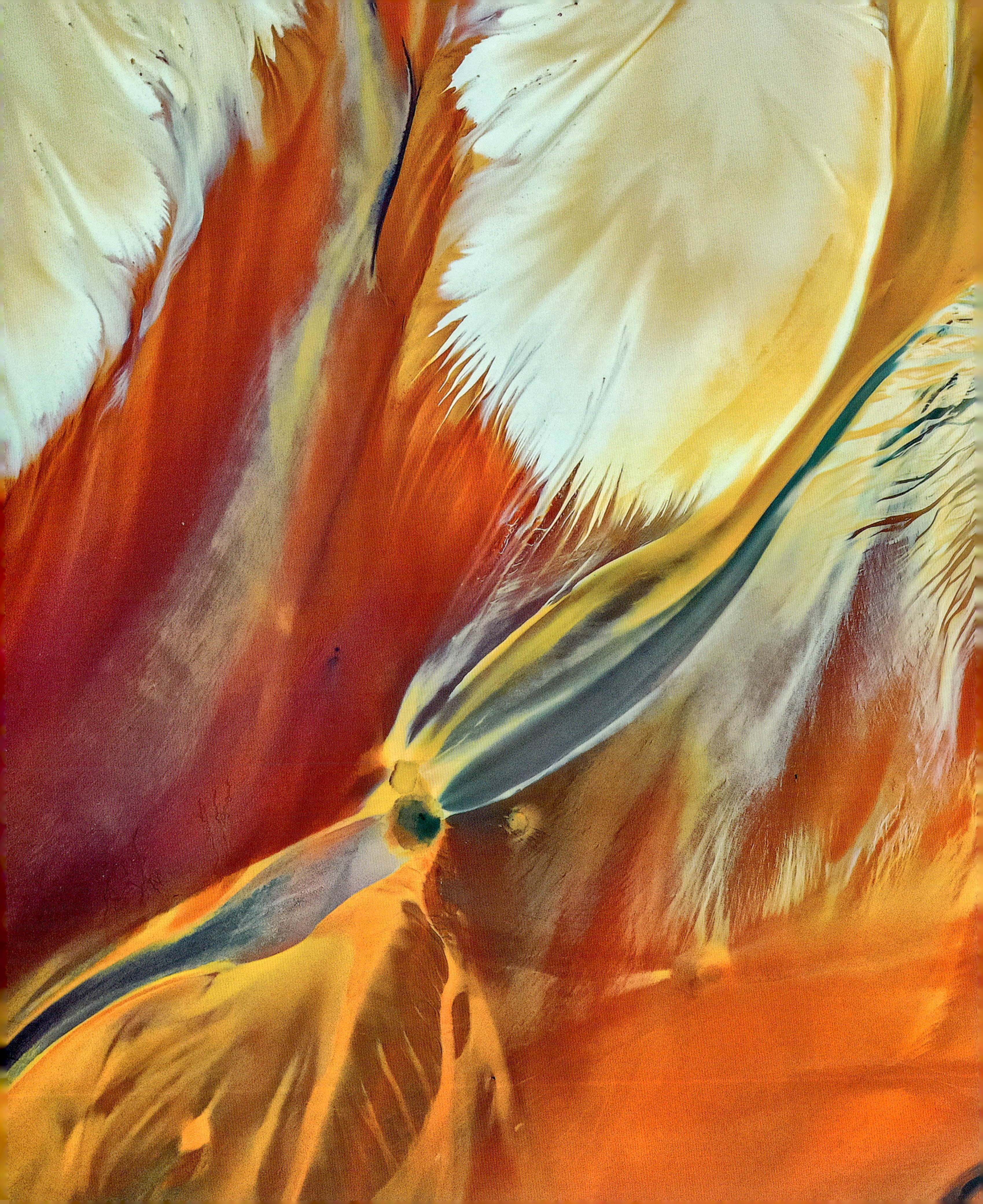

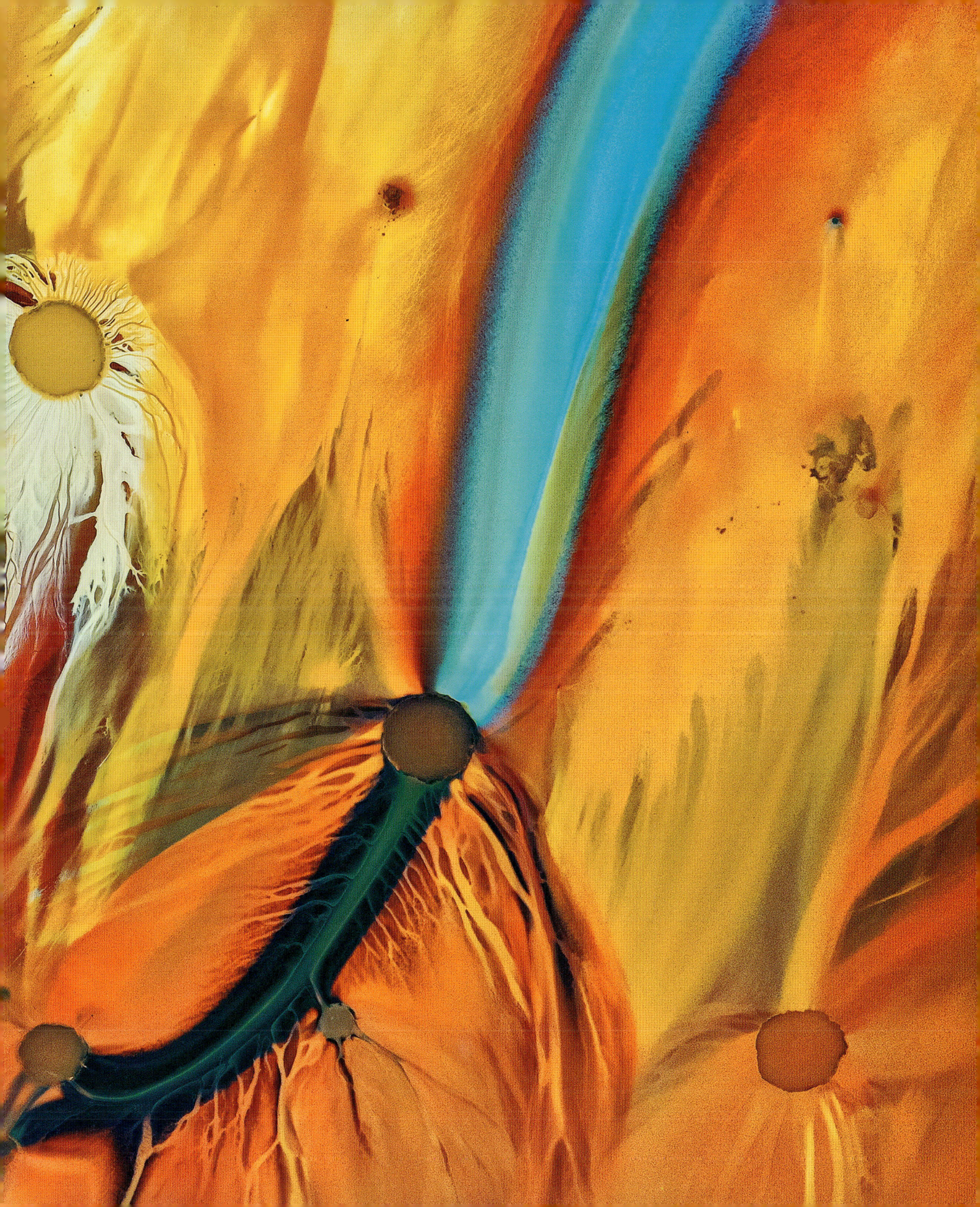

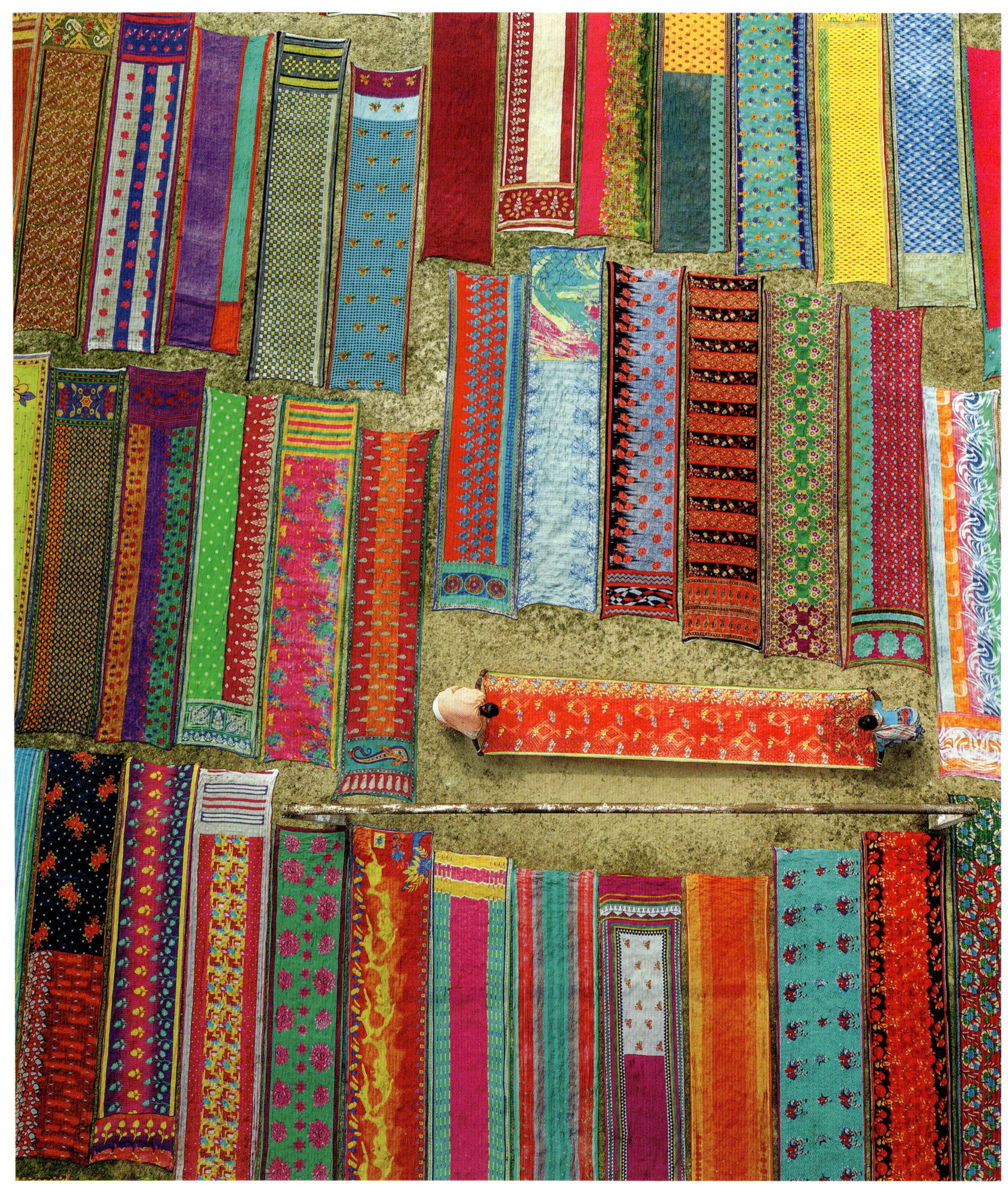

SHIBASISH SAHA
An array of colorful saris in Mumbai, India

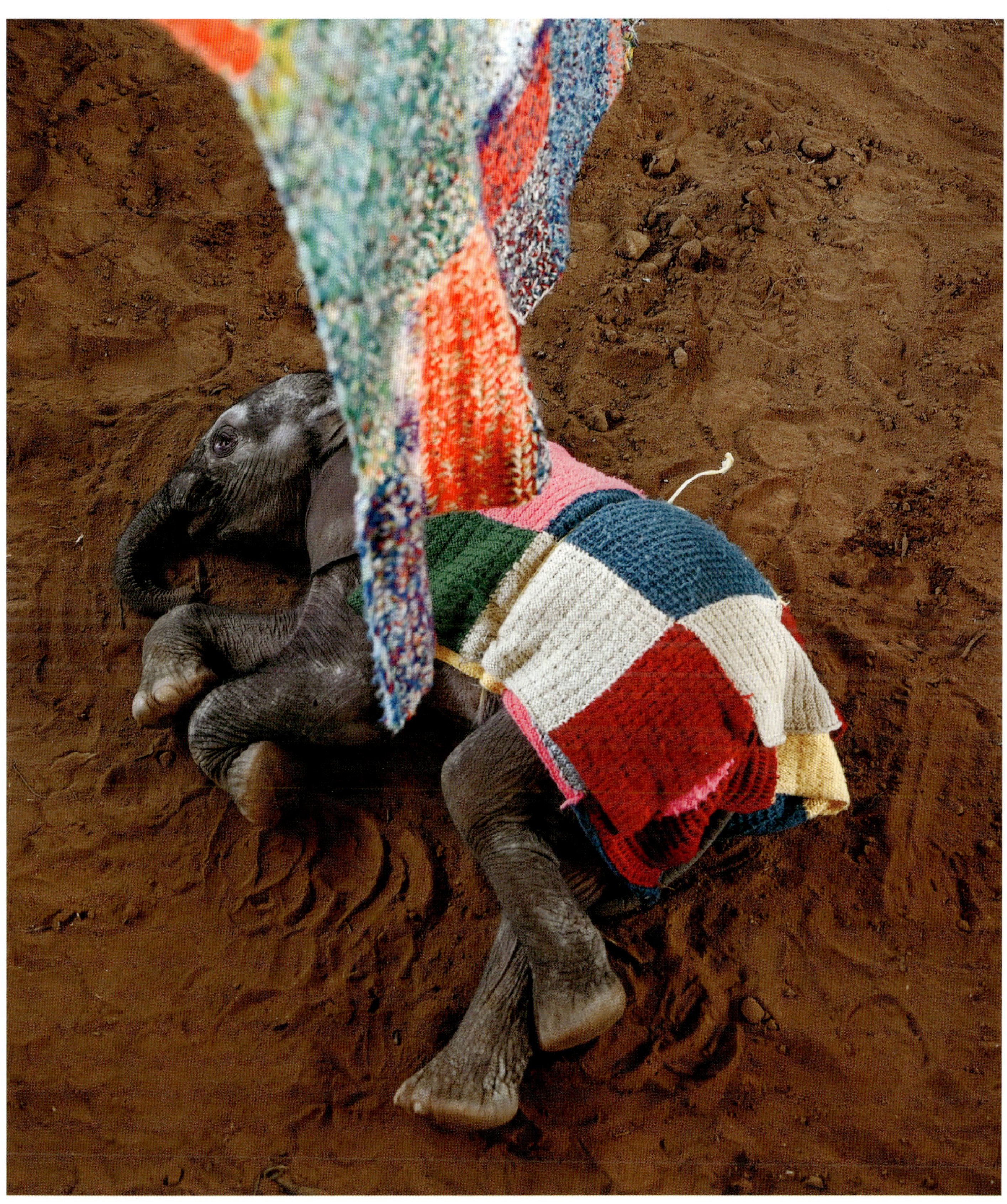

A blanket warms an orphaned elephant rescued from a fall into a well.

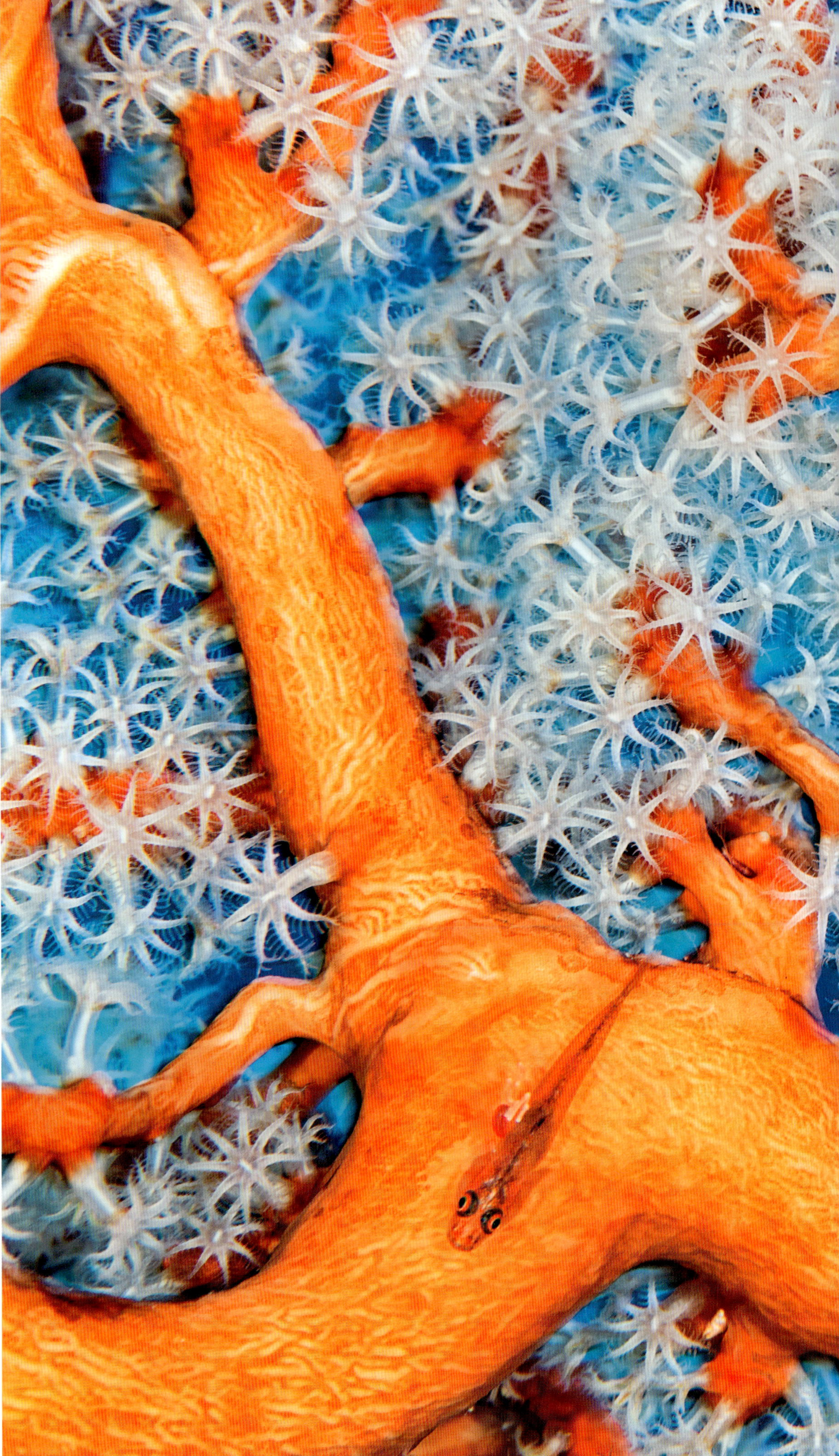

ALEX MUSTARD
Ghost gobies almost disappear against sea fan branches, their color so finely attuned to their surroundings in Indonesia's Lembeh Strait.

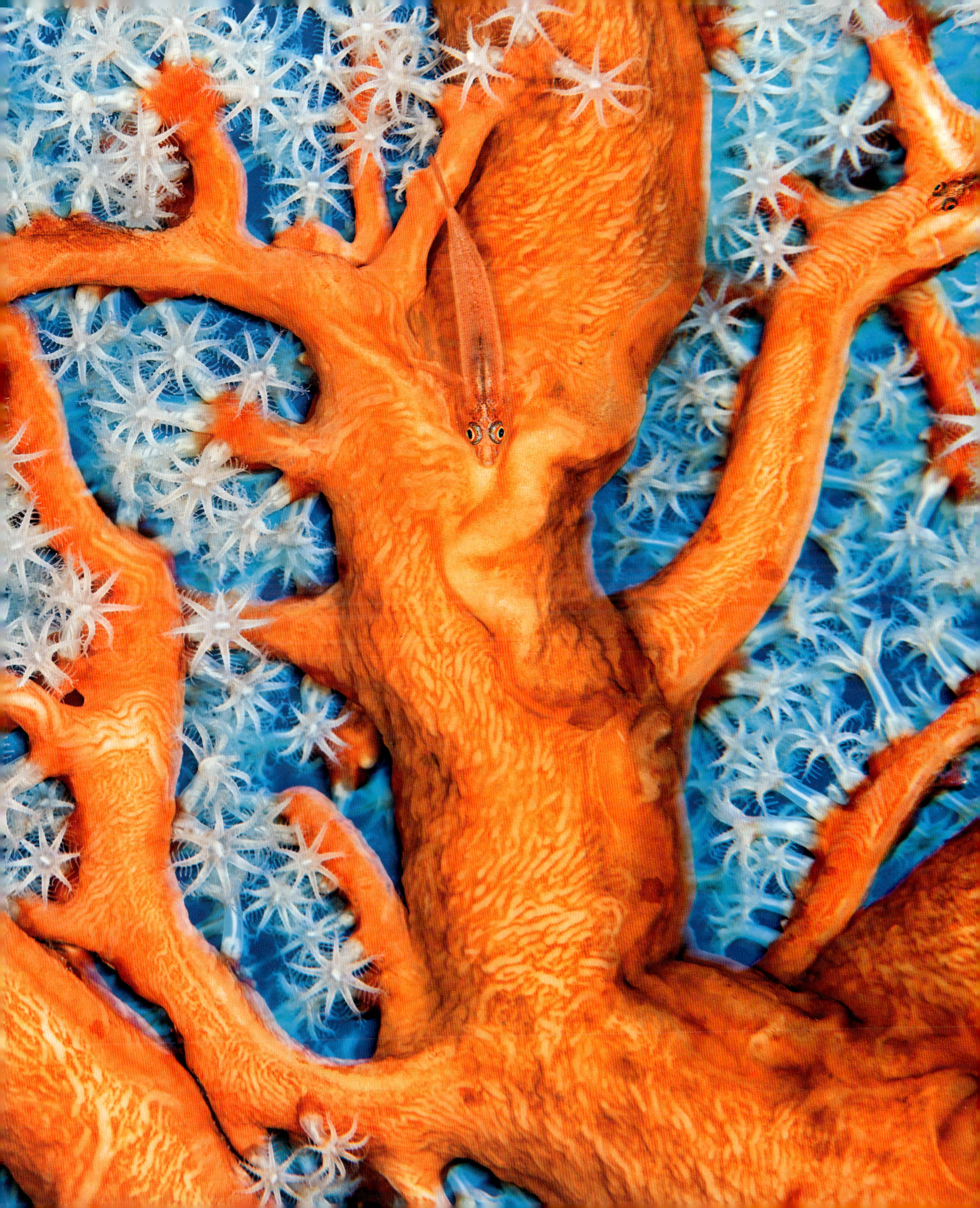

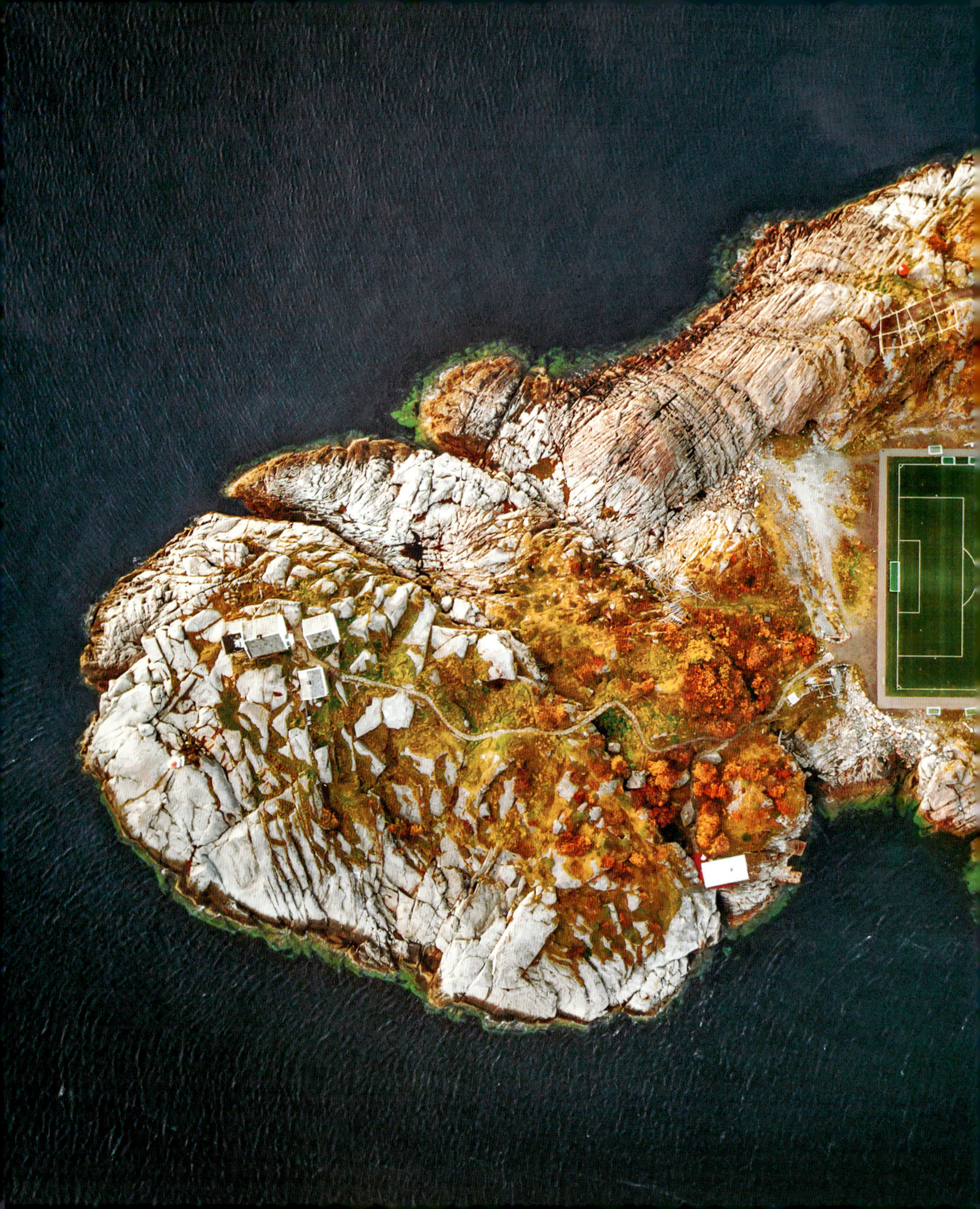

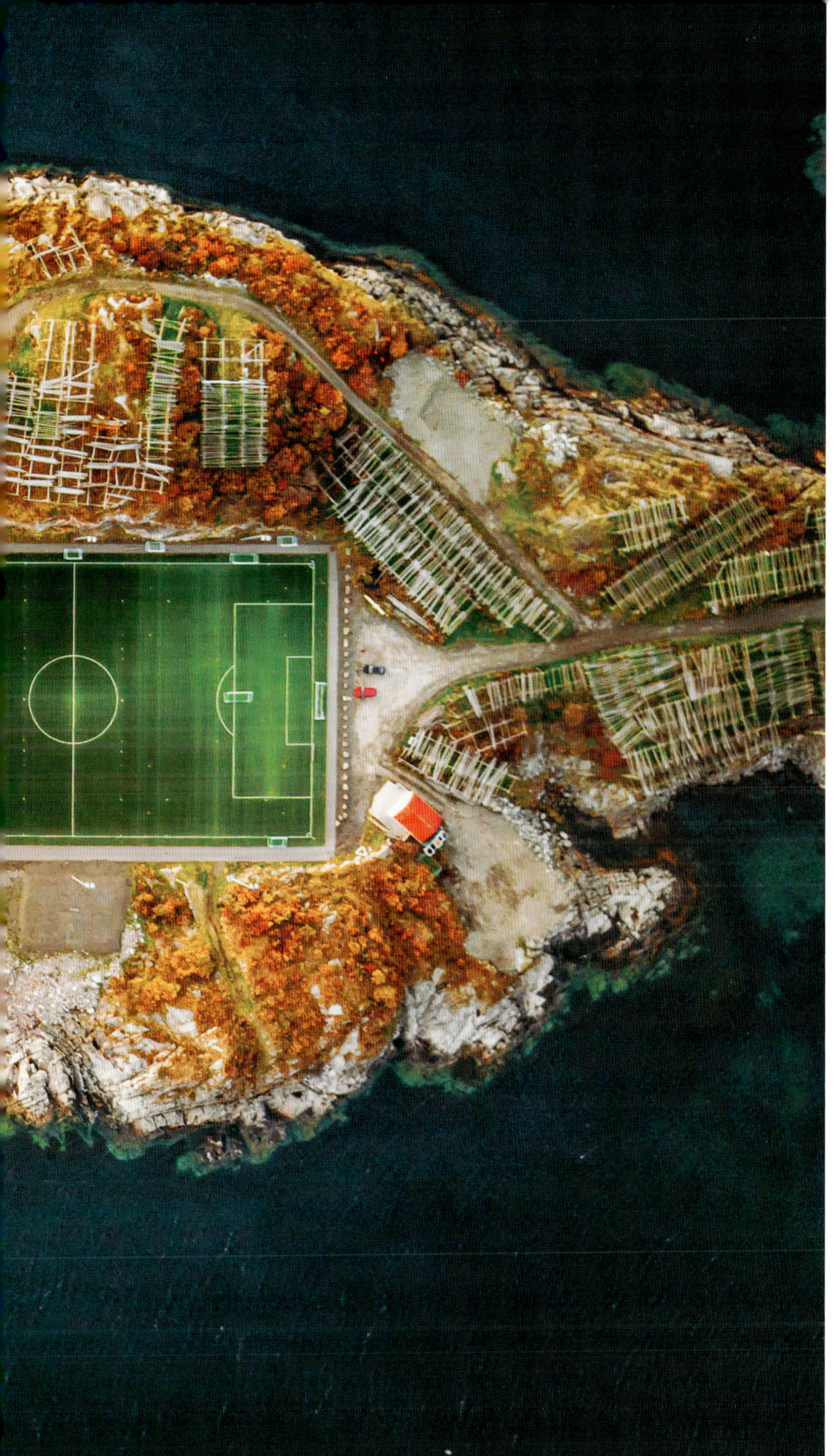

DIMITRI WEBER
Artificial turf doesn't change color with the seasons at Henningsvær soccer stadium, located in Norway's Lototen Islands.

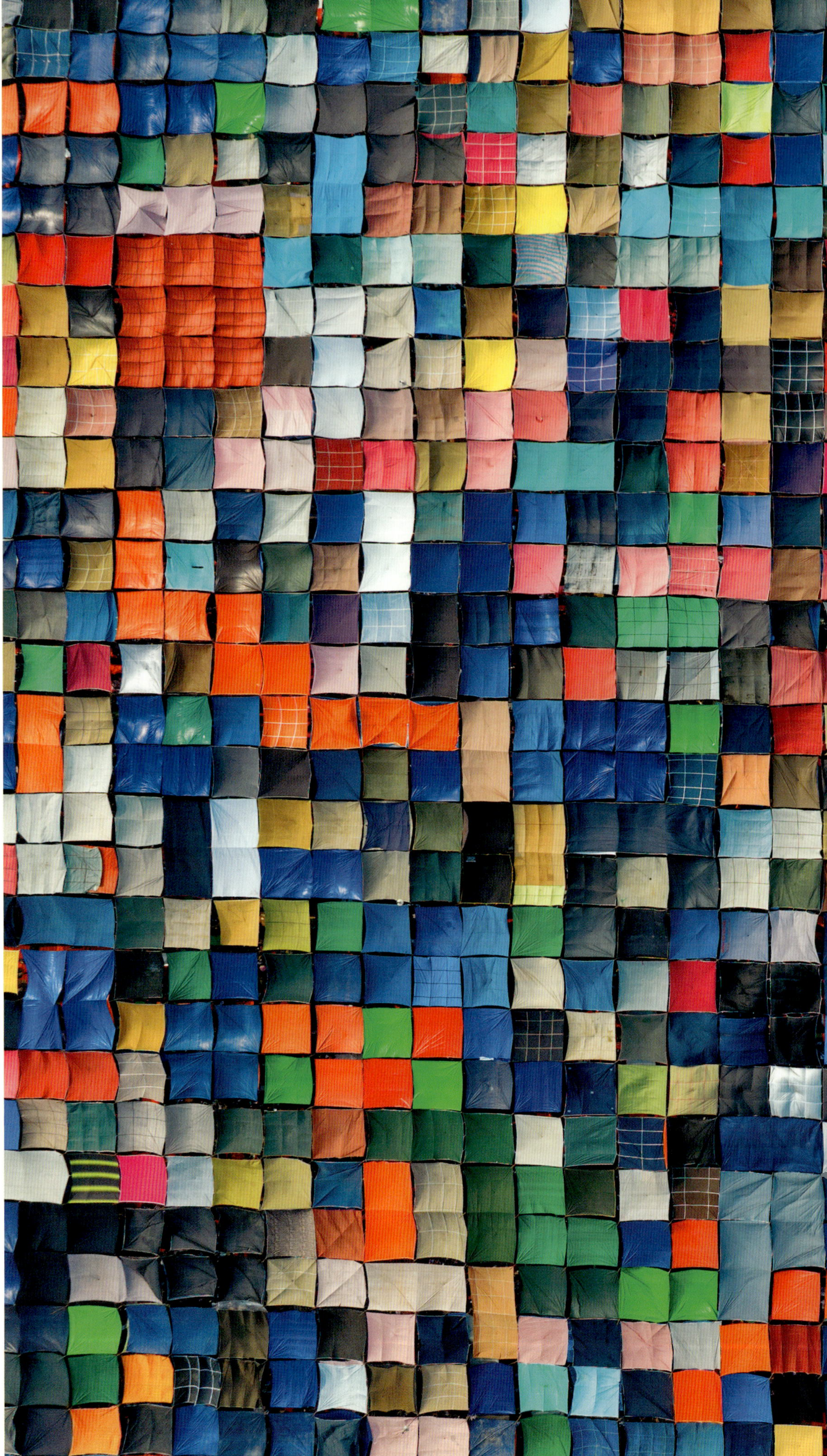

AZIM KHAN RONNIE
Colorful awnings cover the millions attending Bangladesh's Bishwa Ijtema, a Muslim gathering second only to the hajj in size.

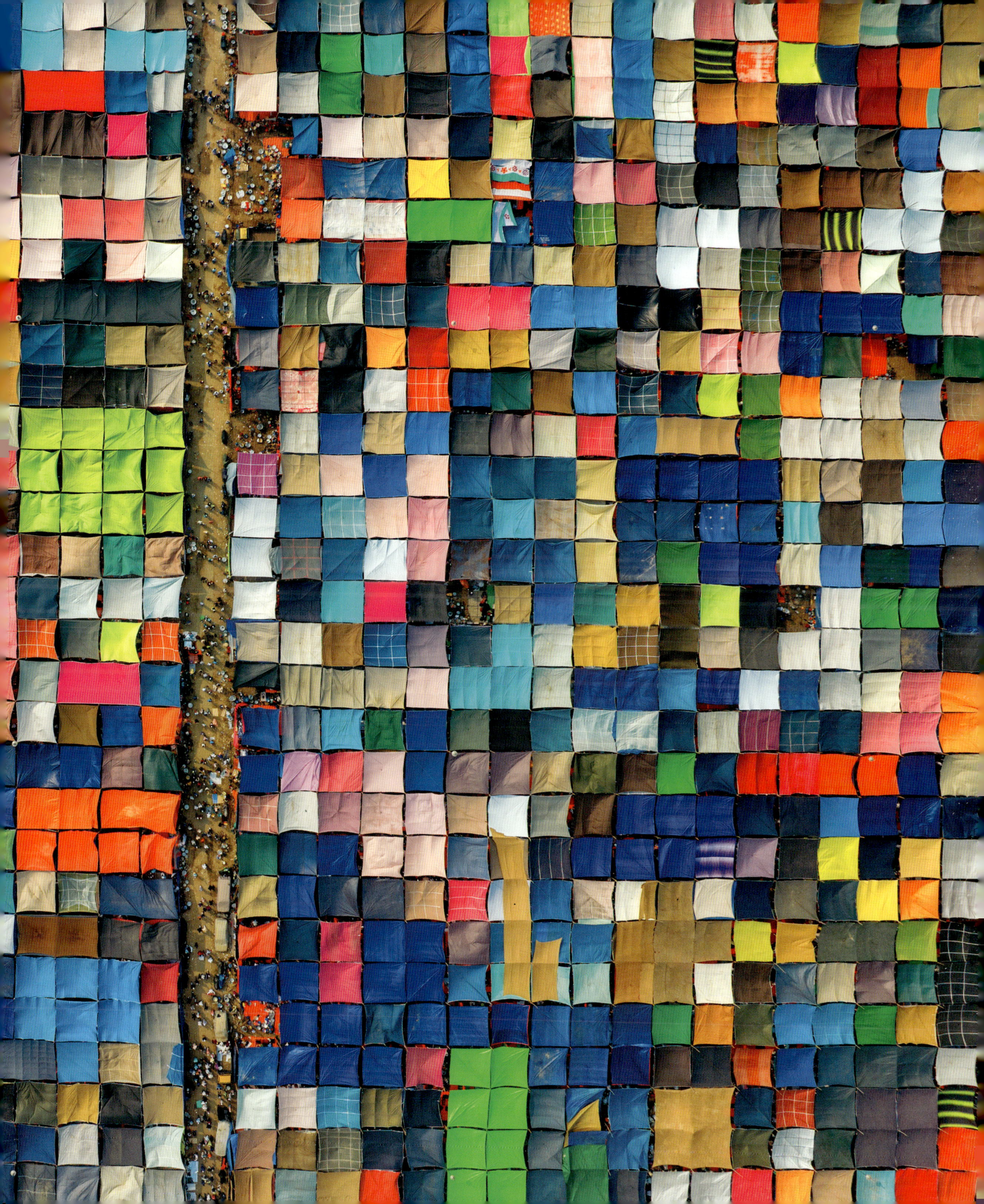

Your world is as
big as you make it. /
I know, for I used
to abide / In the
narrowest nest
in a corner

BARRY WEBB
The photographer uses focus stacking to isolate and reveal this colorful close-up of slime mold.

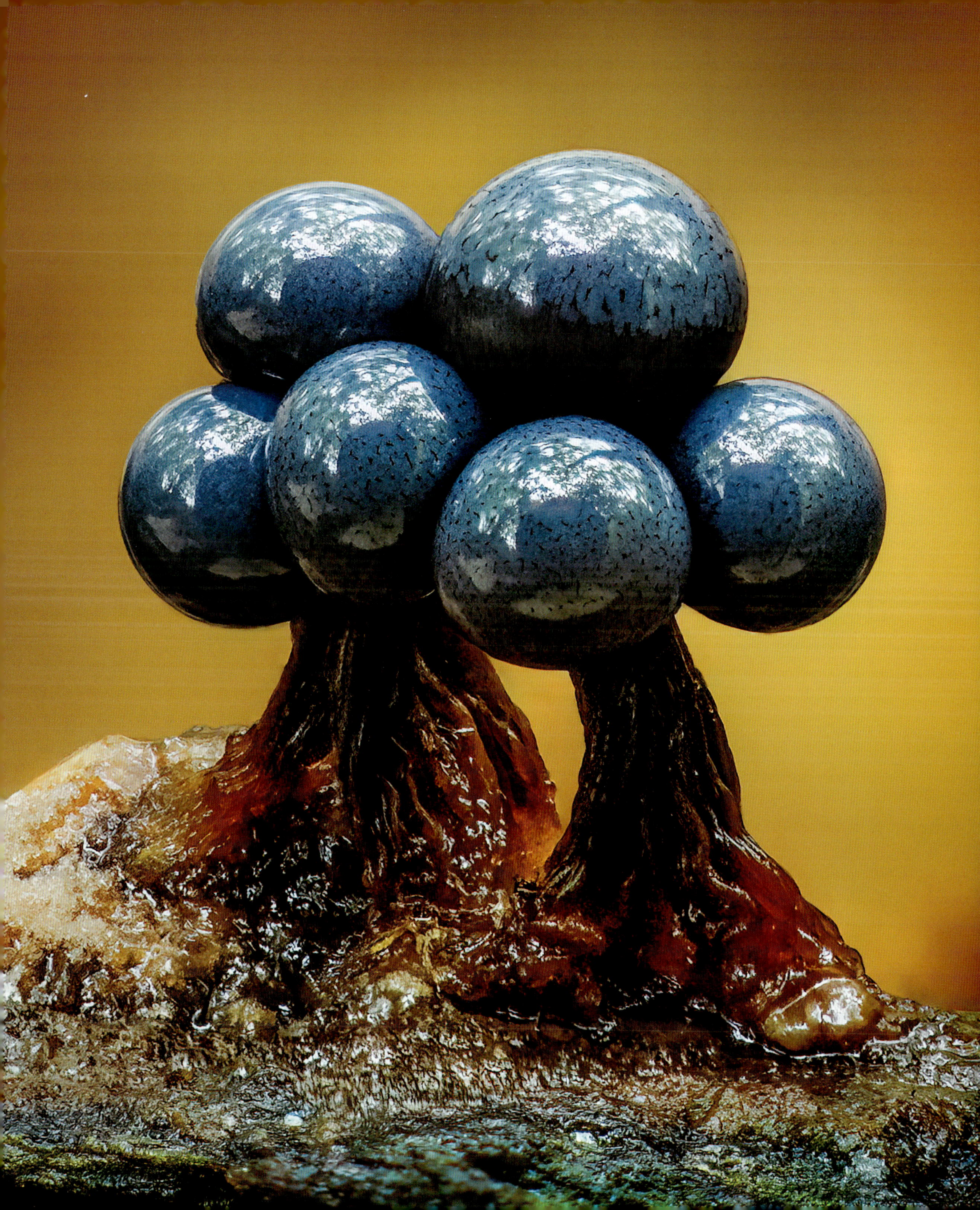

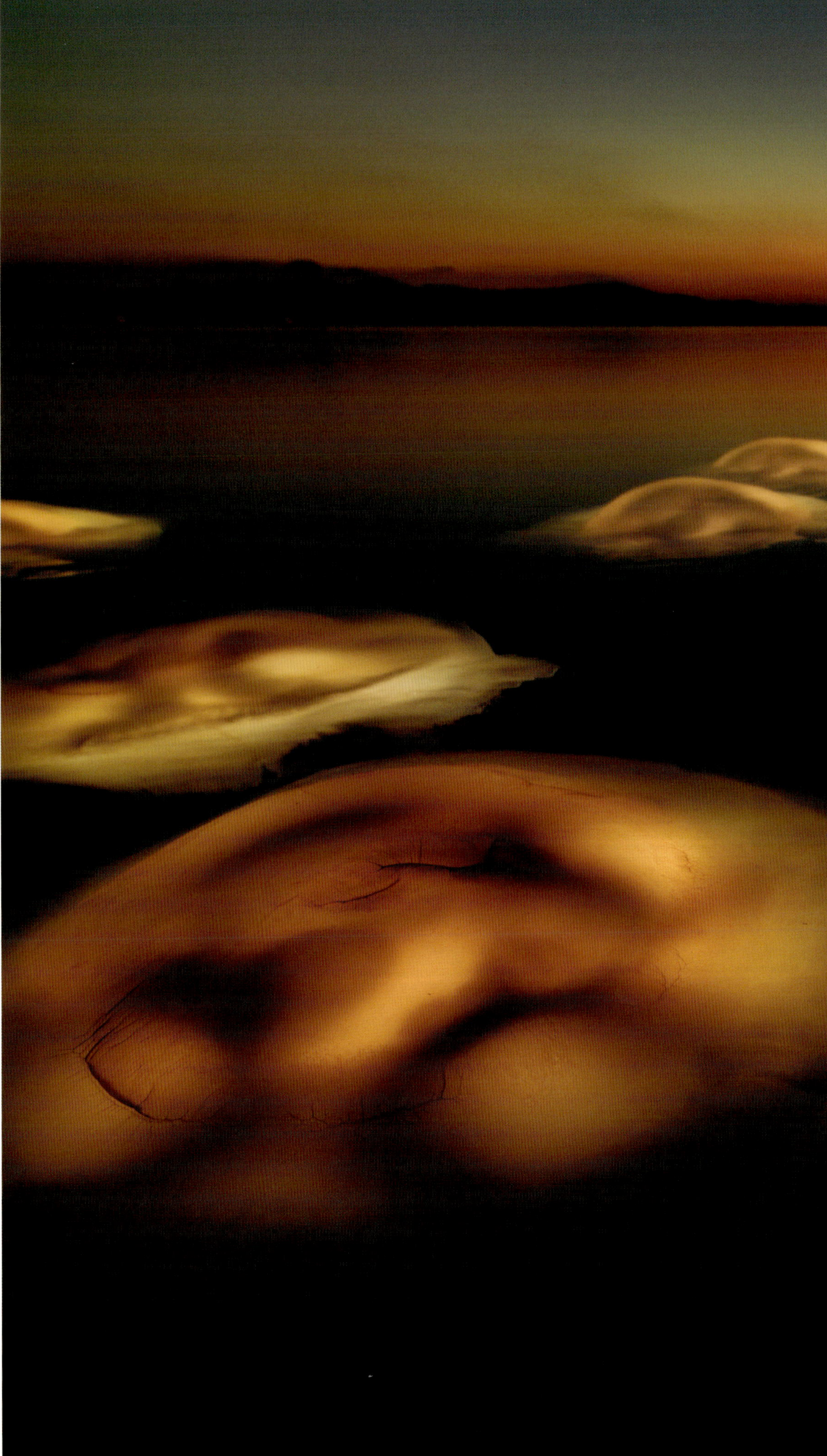

ANGEL FITOR
Two jellyfish in Spain's Mar Menor,
photographed through time with
multiple flashes to create the
impression of many more

Following pages:
TOM HEGEN
Beach chairs and umbrellas in
southern Florida create a colorful
geometry.

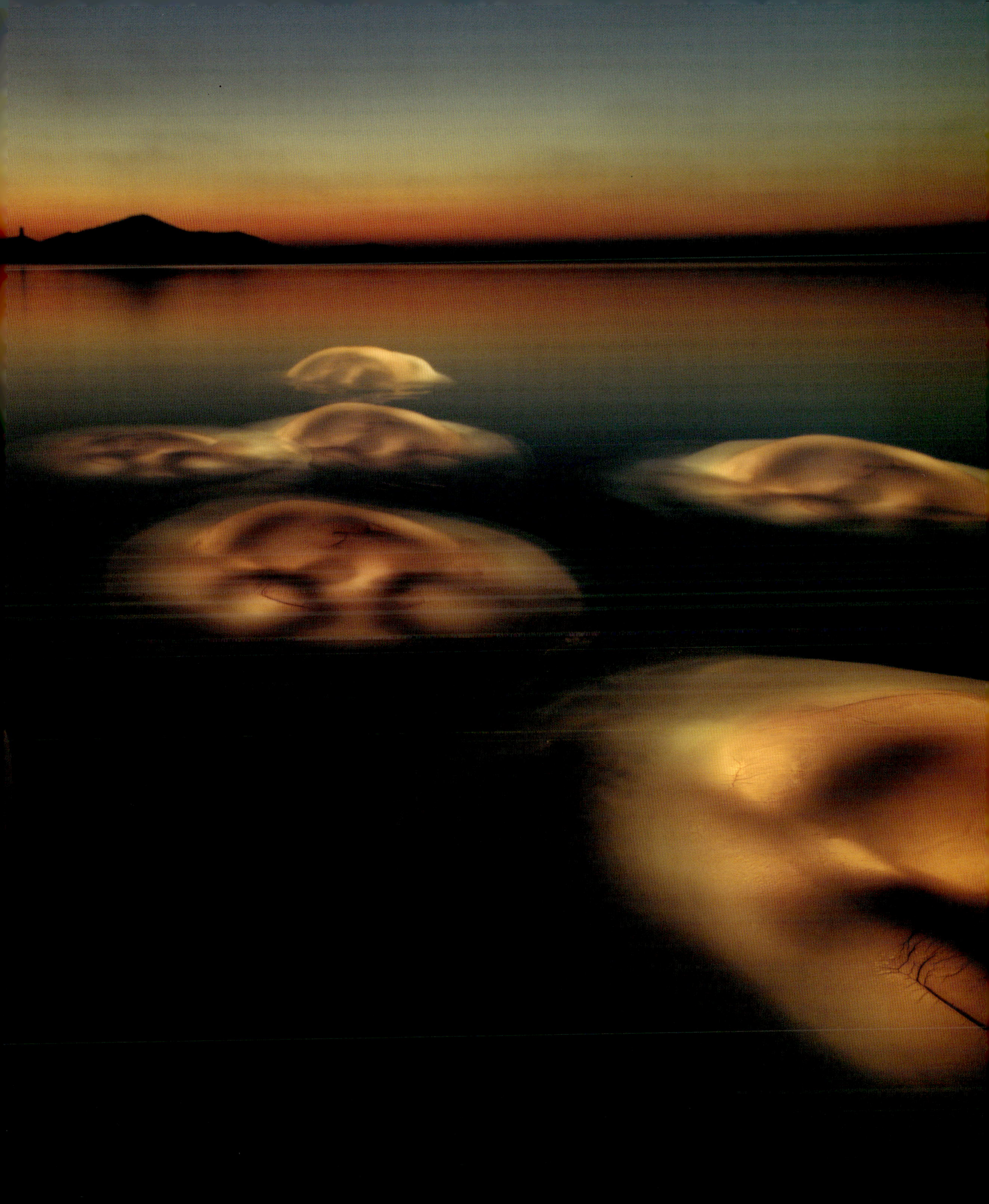

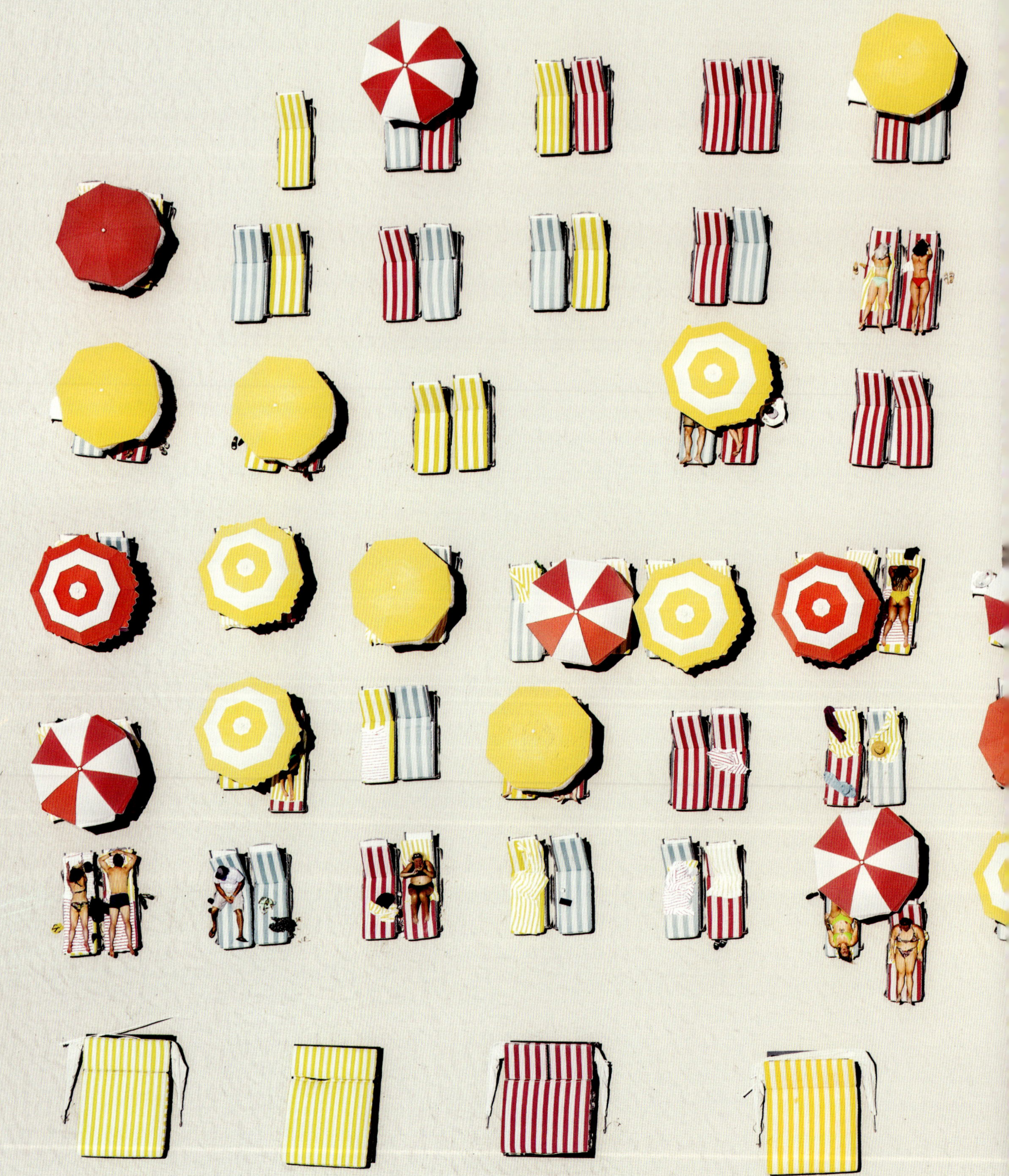

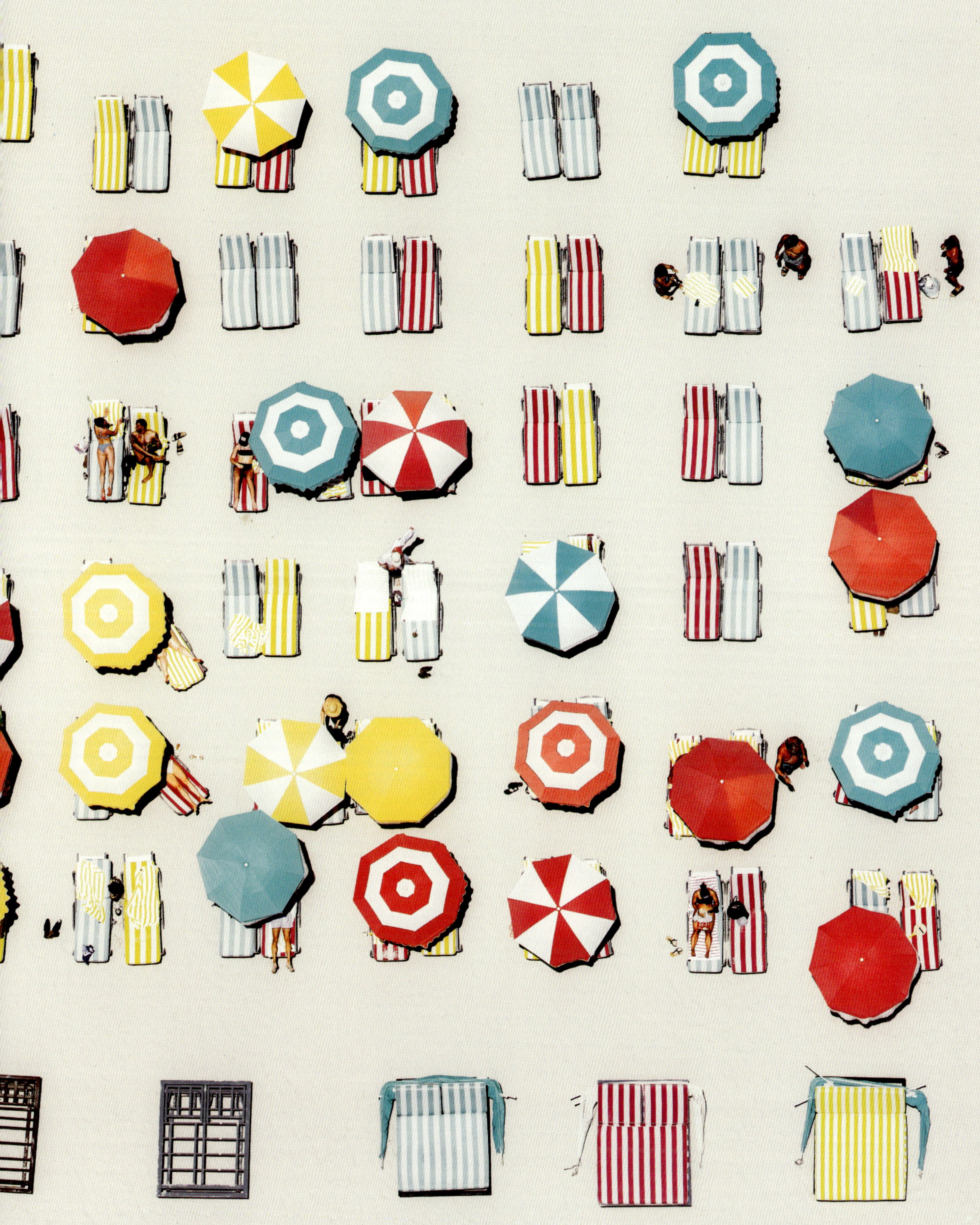

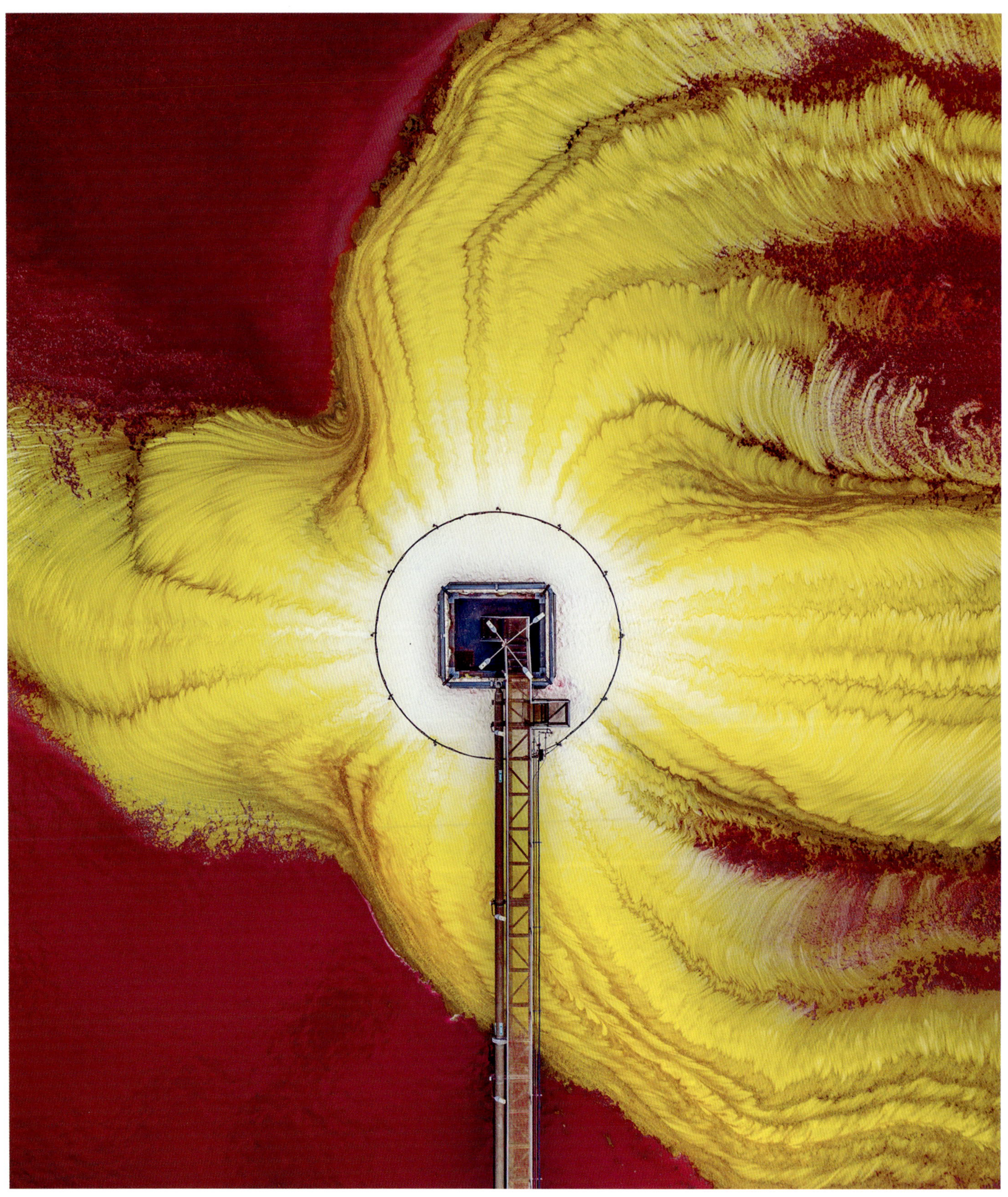

BOYAN ORTSE
A chemical drift infuses its color into one of Australia's pink lakes.

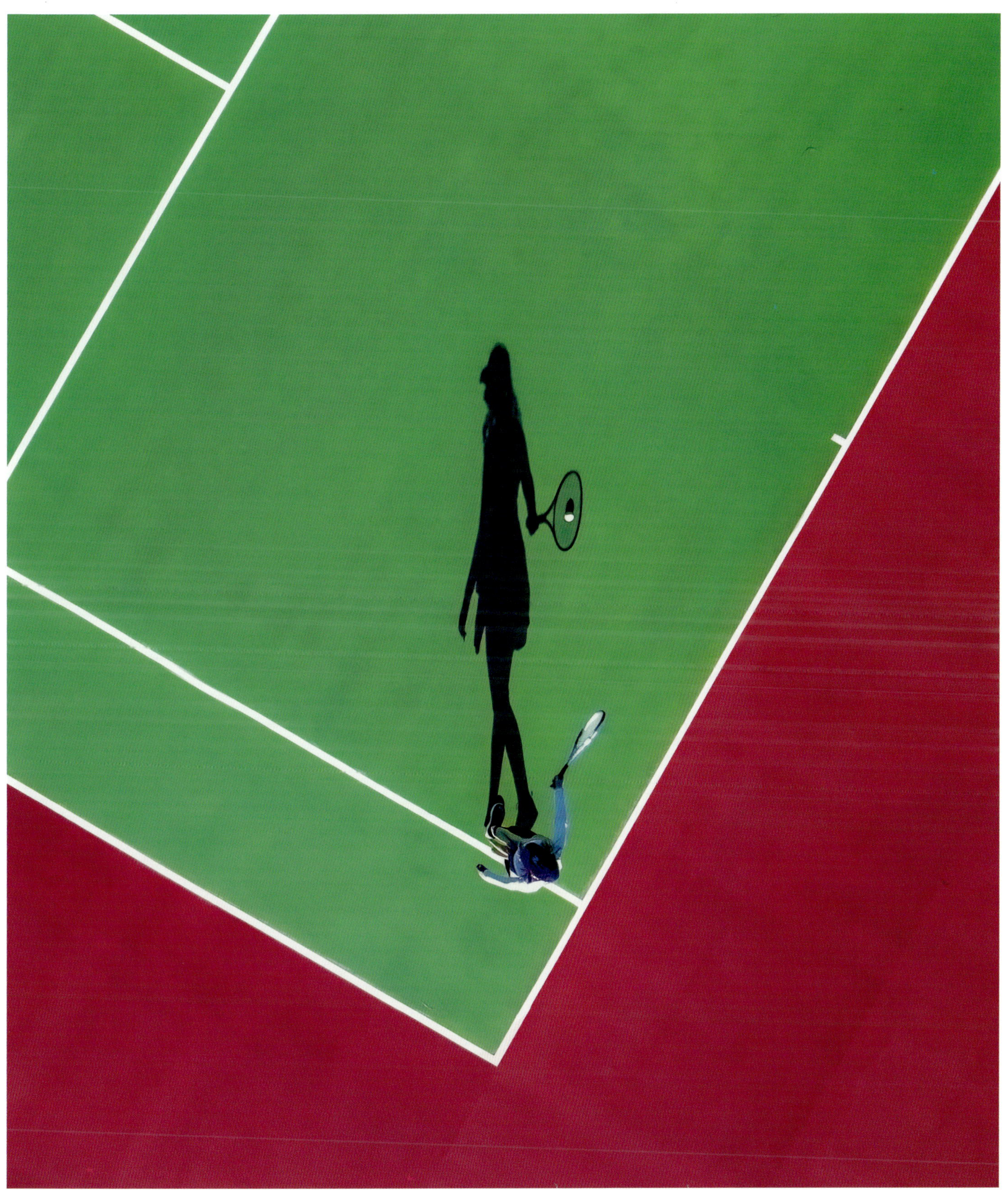

JOANNA L. STEIDLE
Shadow play on the tennis court in the Hamptons, Long Island, New York

How do you know
but ev'ry Bird that
cuts the airy way, / Is an
immense world of delight,
clos'd by your senses five?

~WILLIAM BLAKE, *THE MARRIAGE OF HEAVEN AND HELL*

MARK HARVEY
A Eurasian blue tit hovers, its wings outstretched.

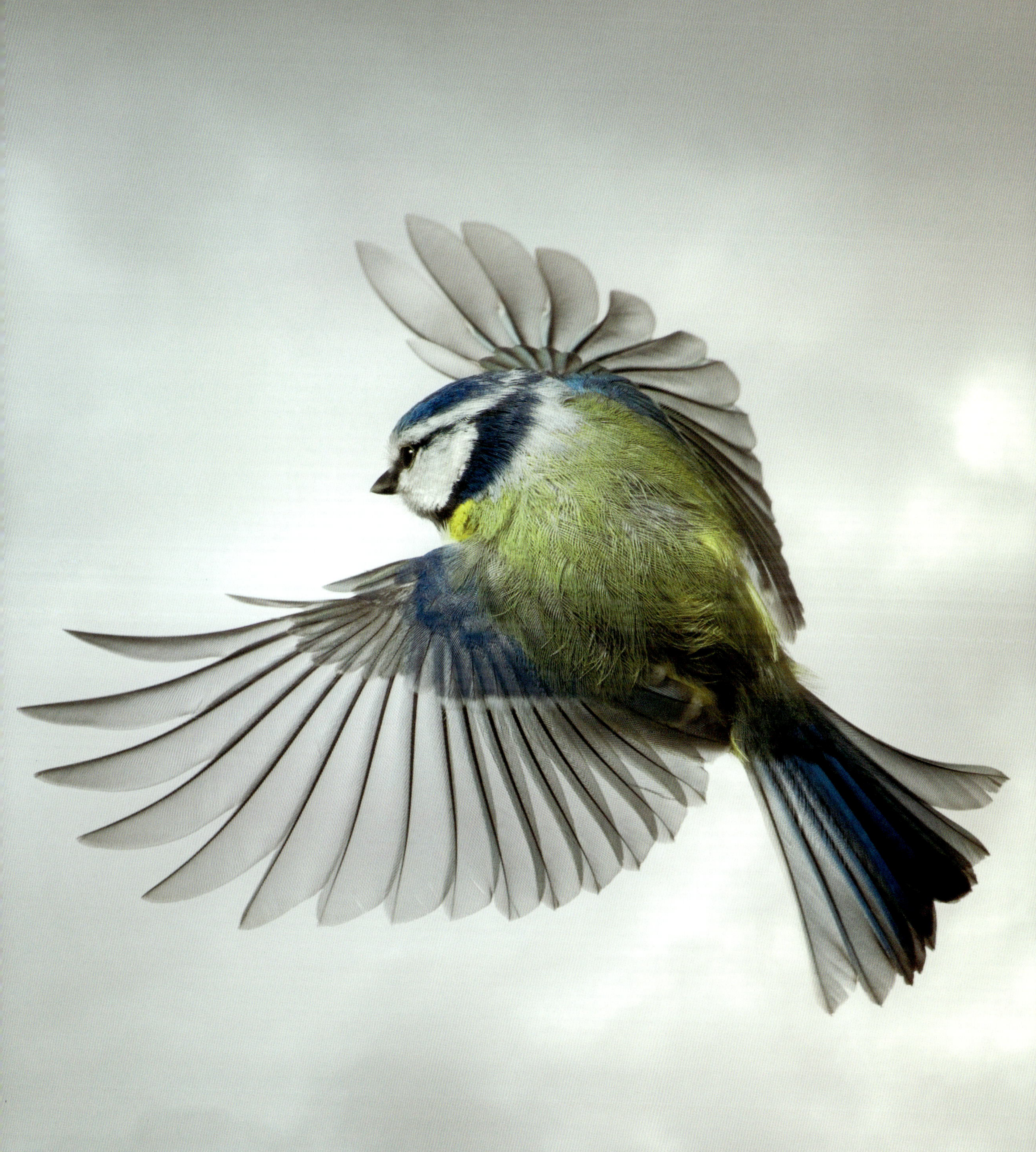

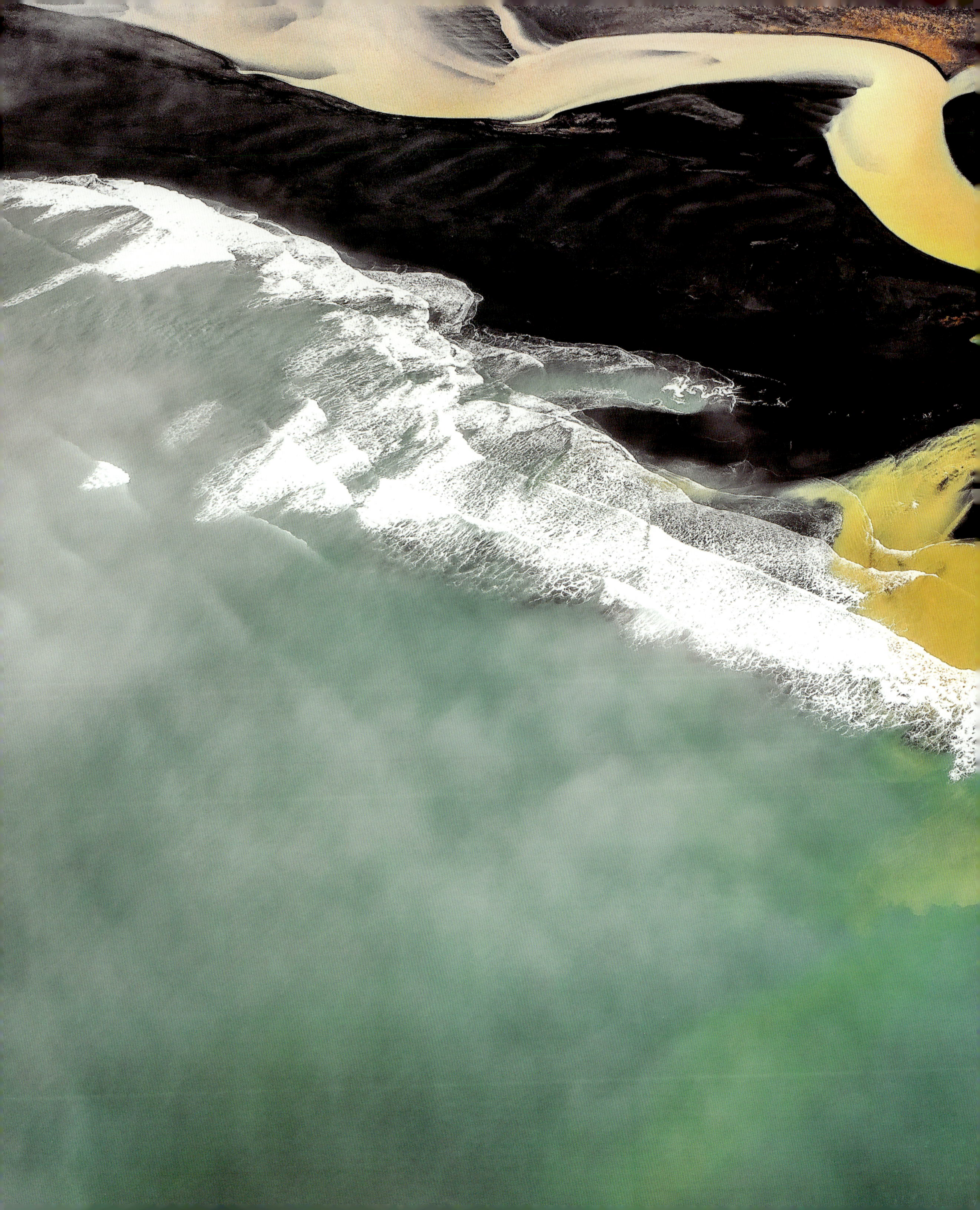

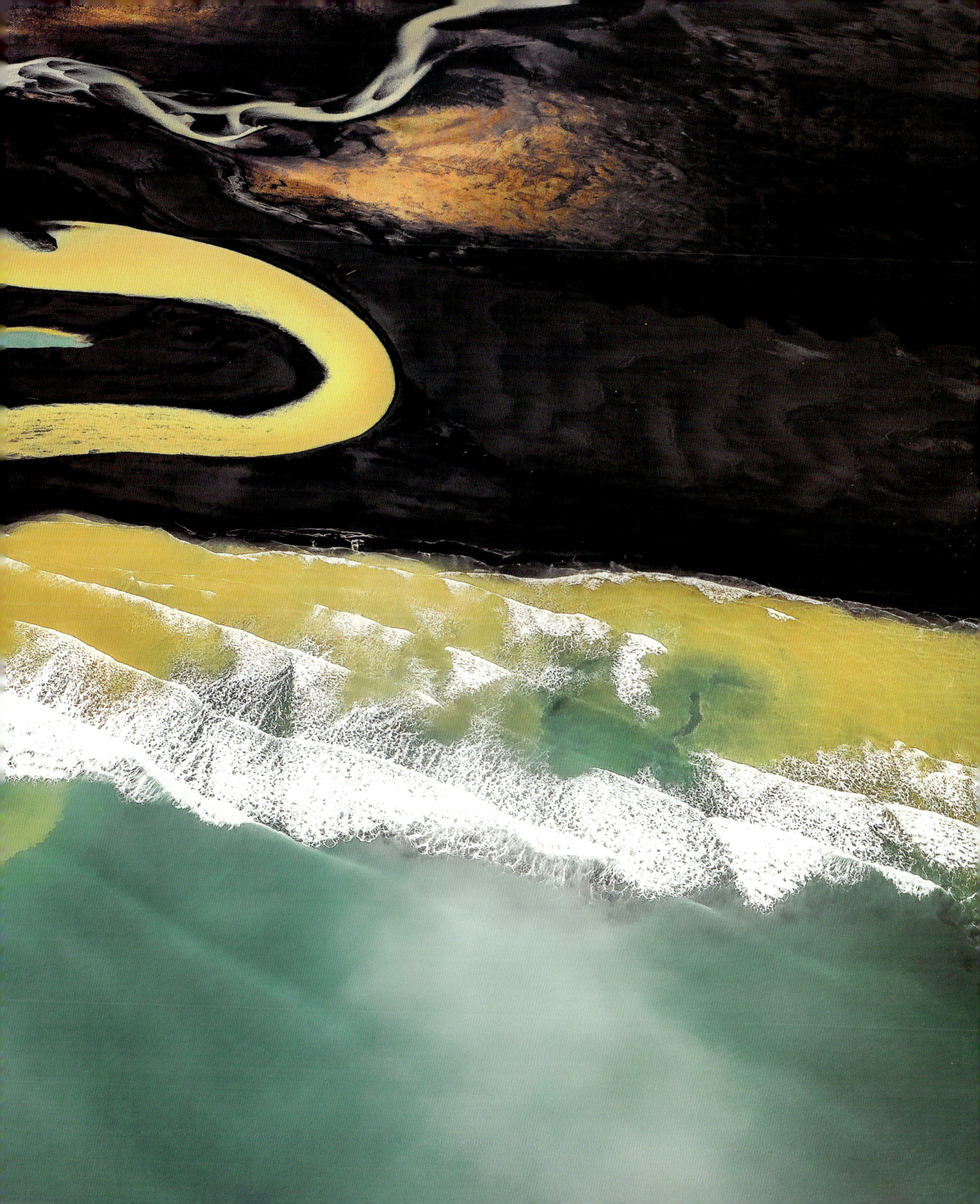

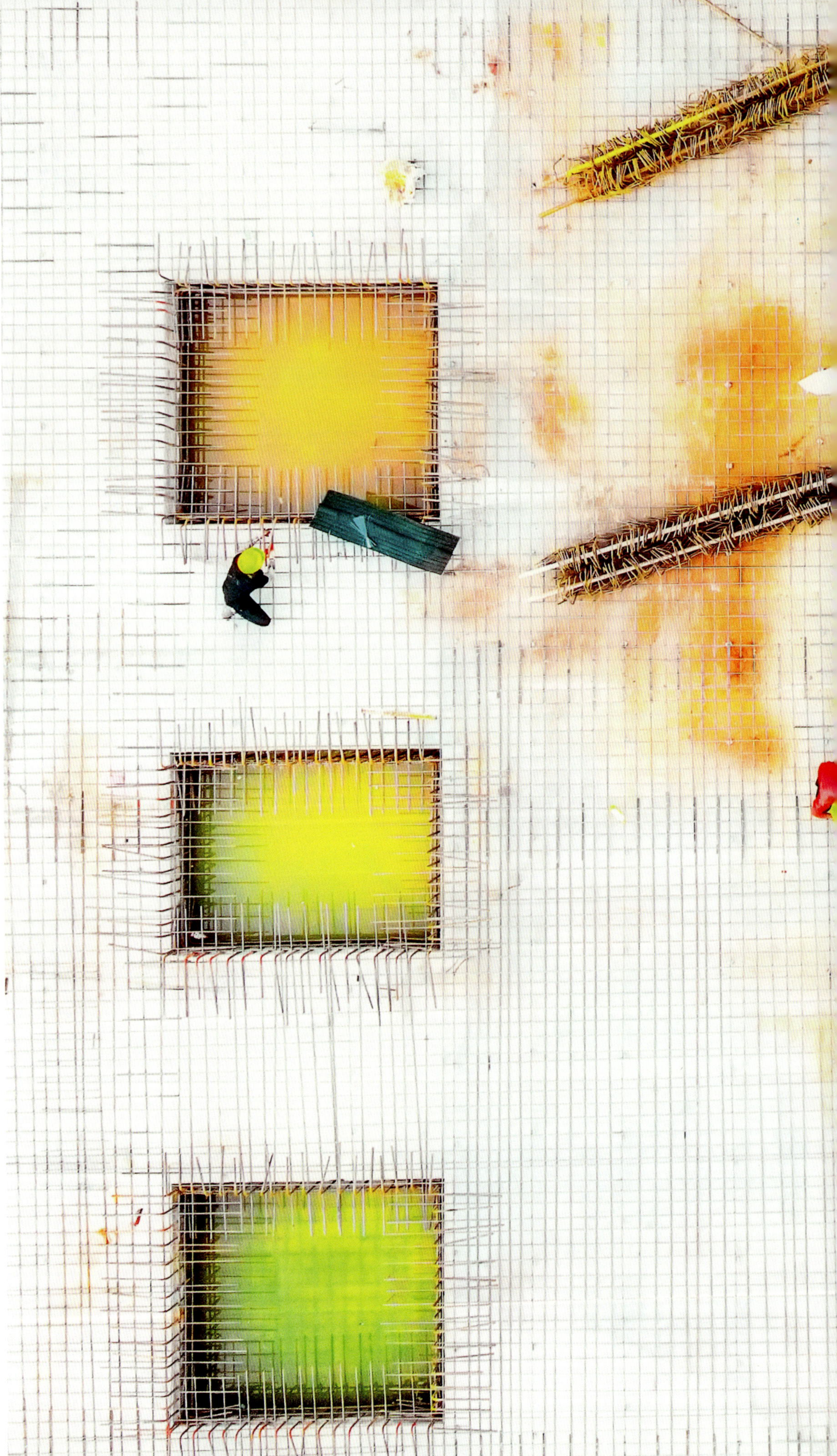

GU GUANGHUI
Workers build a high-rise in
Ninghai, China.

Previous pages:
SEBASTIAN MÜLLER
Black beach meets emerald sea
in southern Iceland, where a river
flows yellow due to volcanic
runoff.

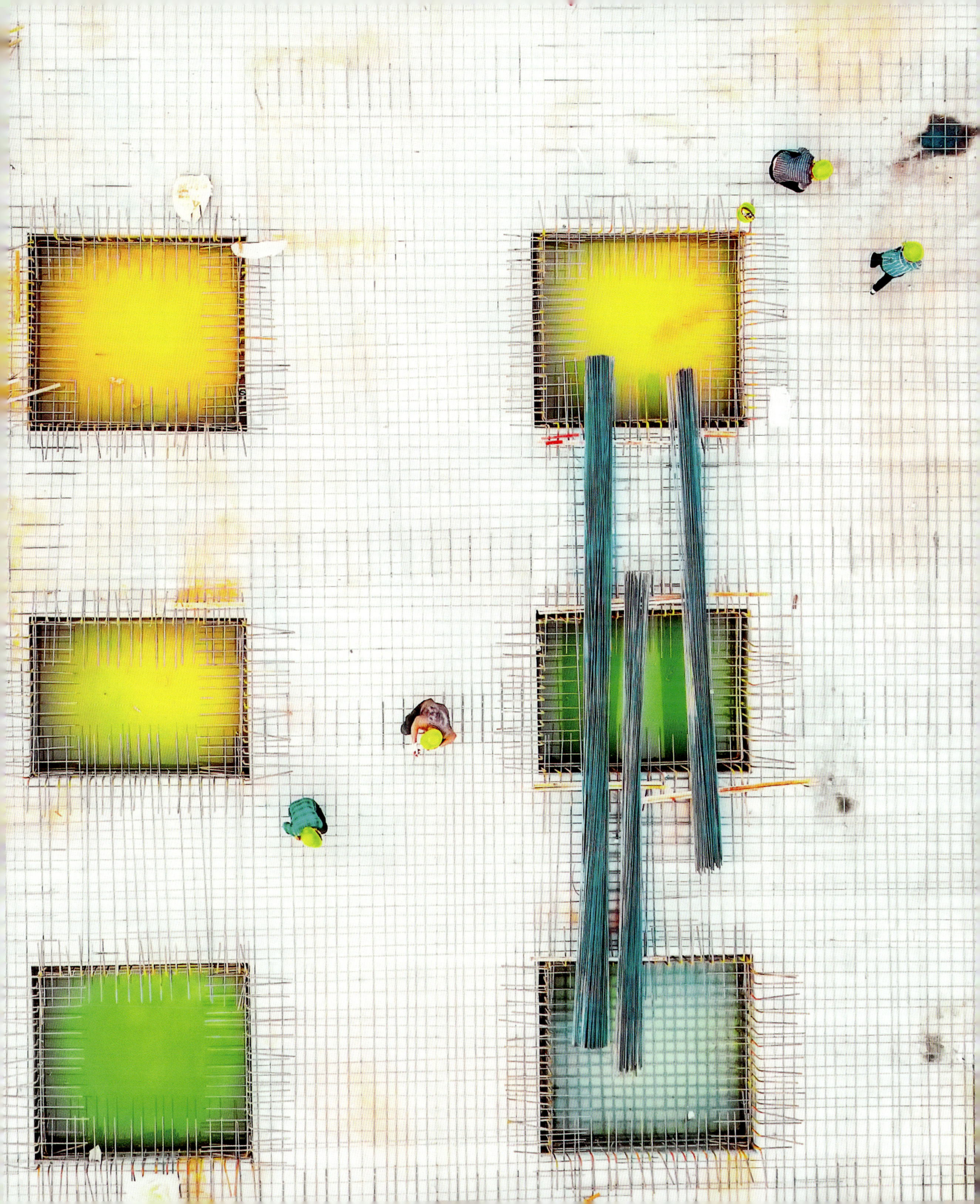

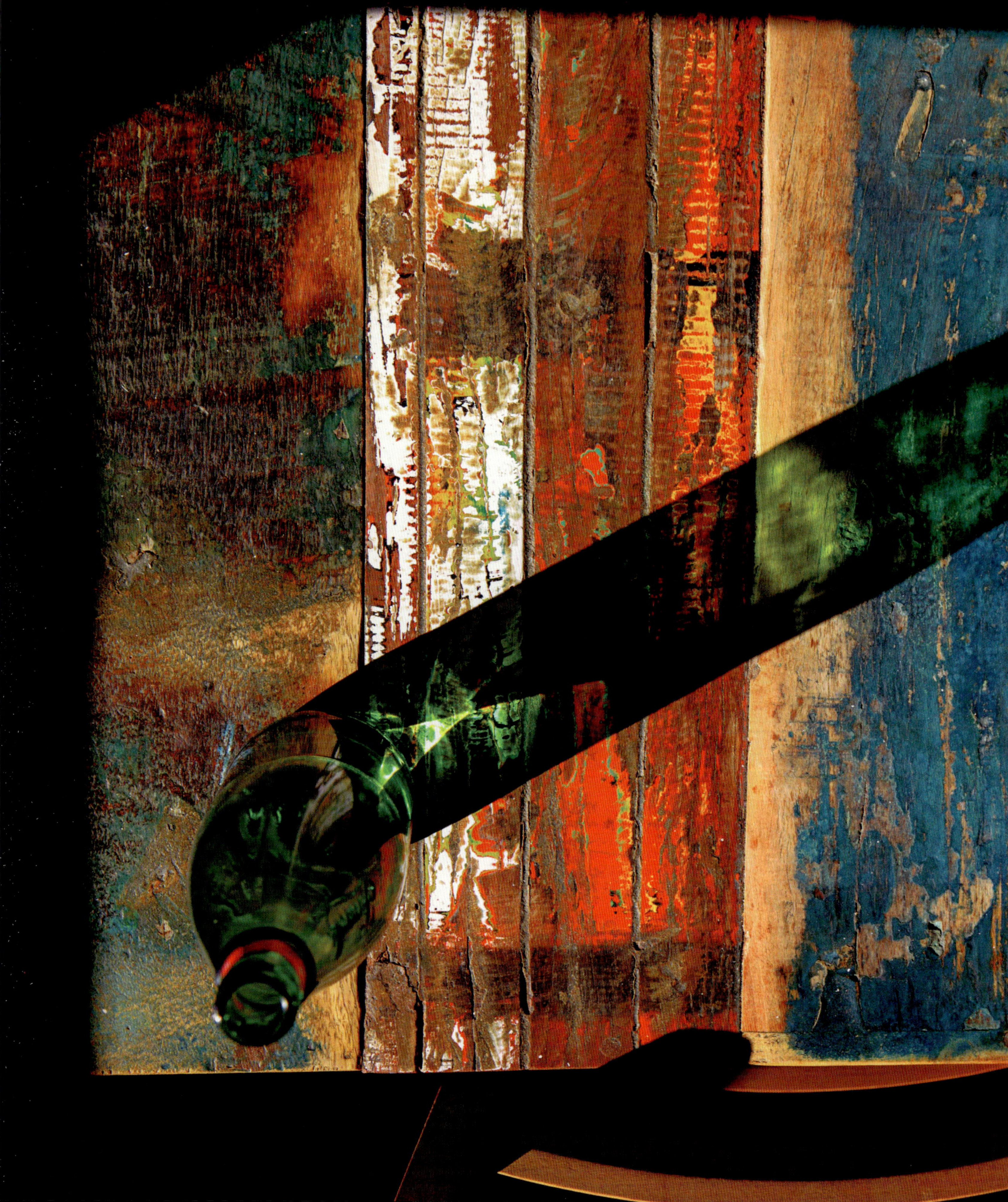

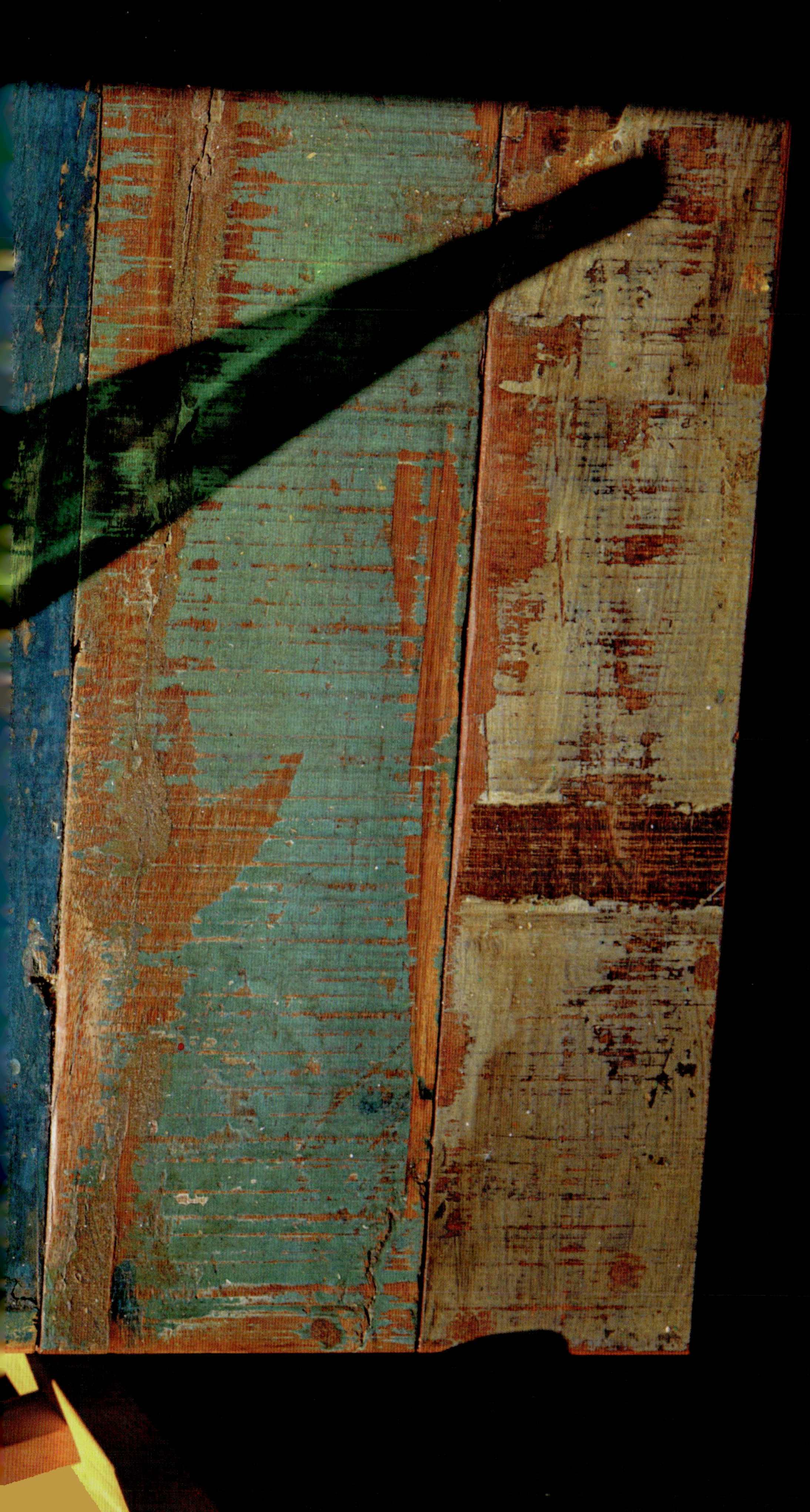

VERONIKA K KO
A green bottle casts a long
shadow onto a colorful table in
the ancient town of Anagni, Italy.

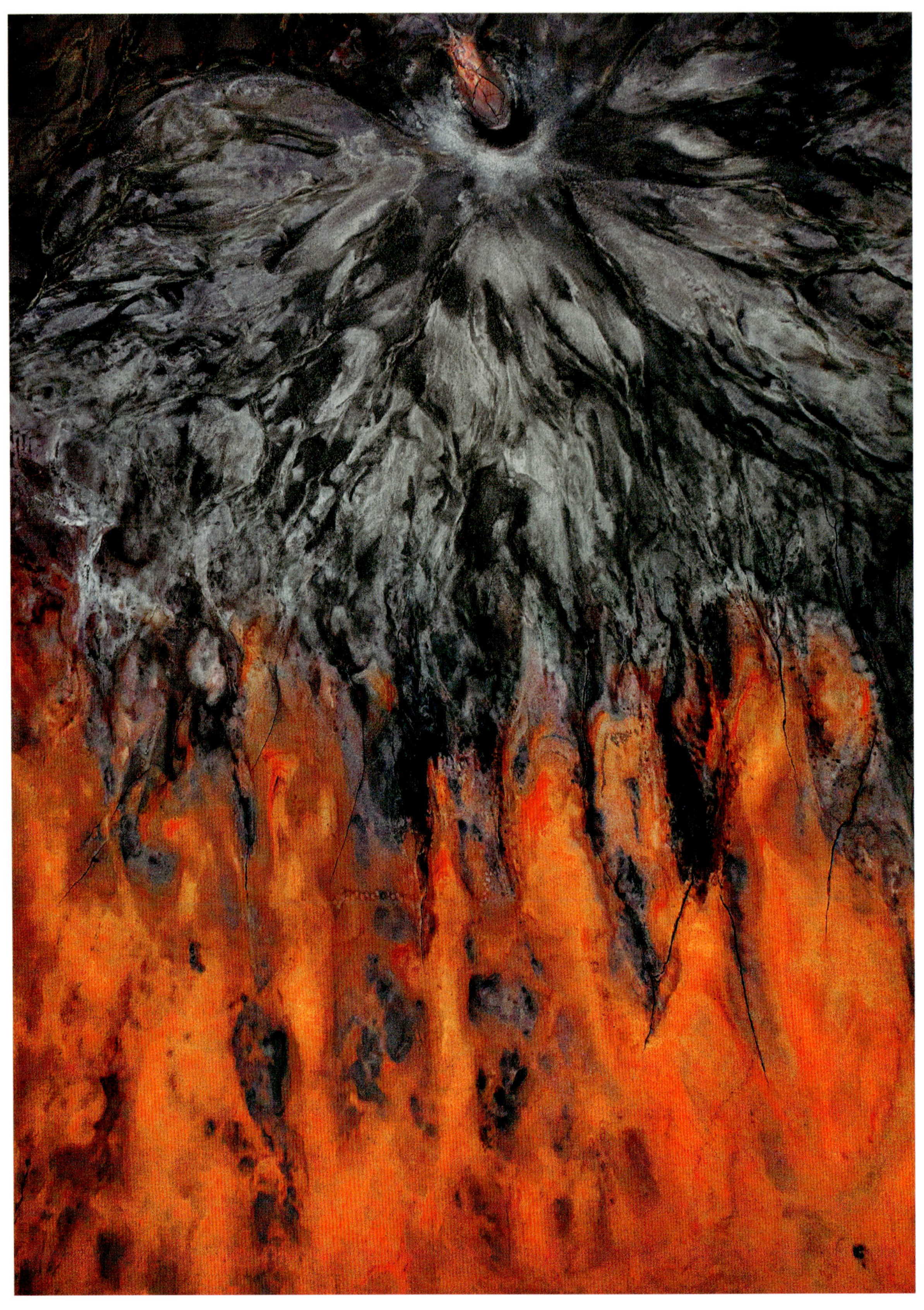

TIMOTHY MOON
Mineral tailings spill out over the land.

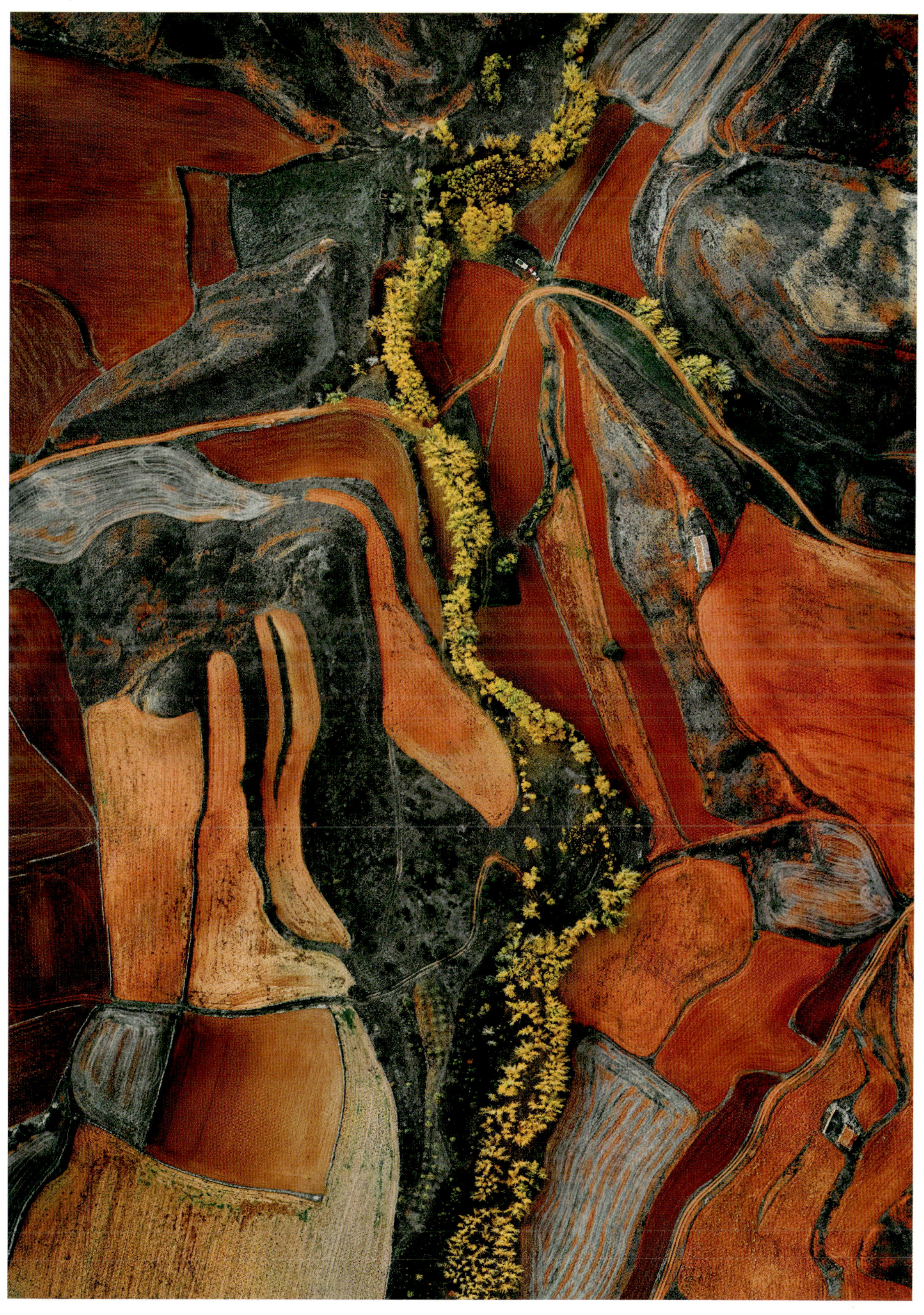

Roads, trees, houses, and fields create colorful patterns in this Spanish aerial landscape.

The senses transform
the coursing chaos
of the world into
perceptions and experiences—
things we can react
to and act upon.

~ED YONG, *AN IMMENSE WORLD*

A soap bubble's shimmering swirls and colors, made motionless in a photograph

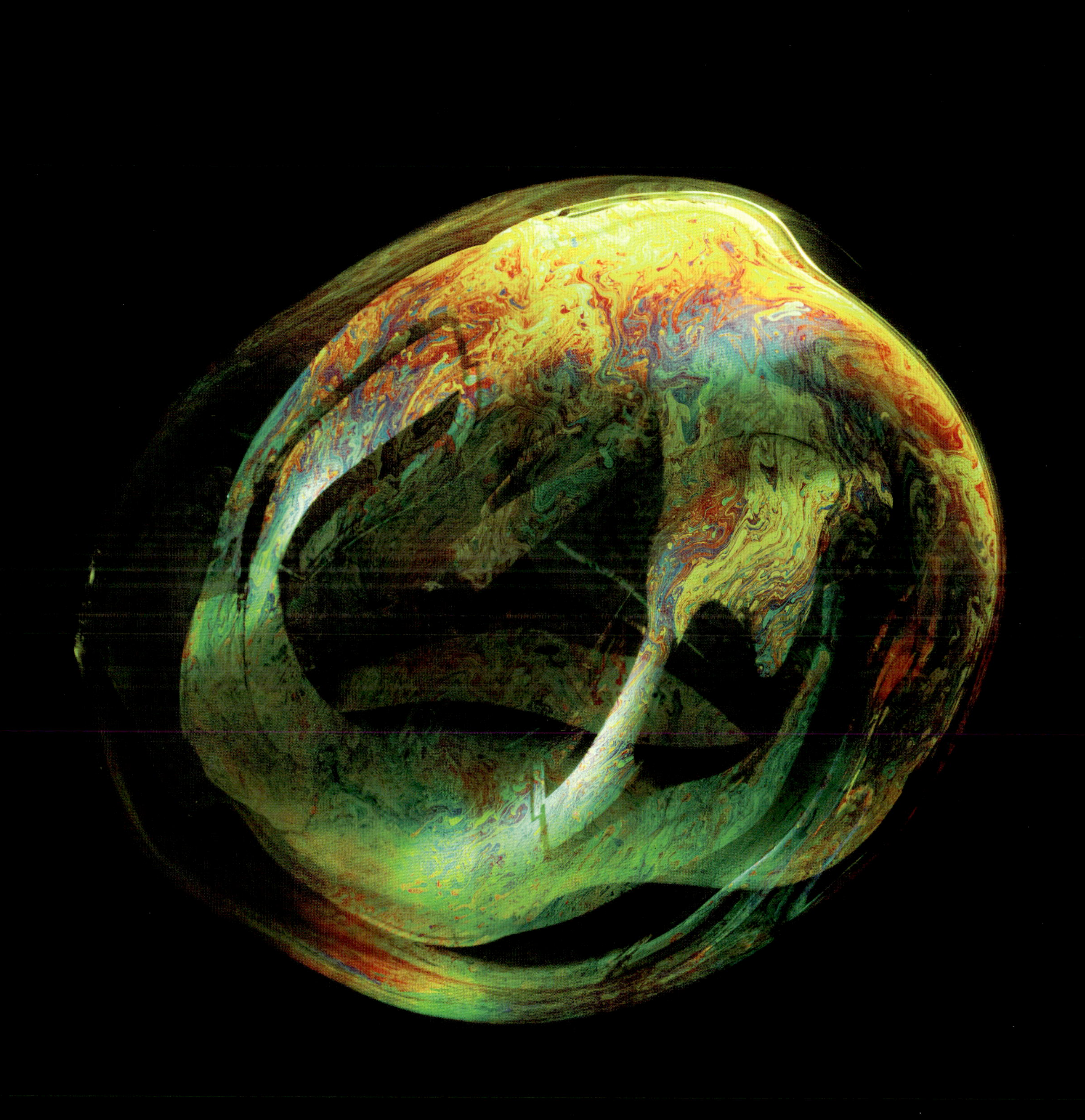

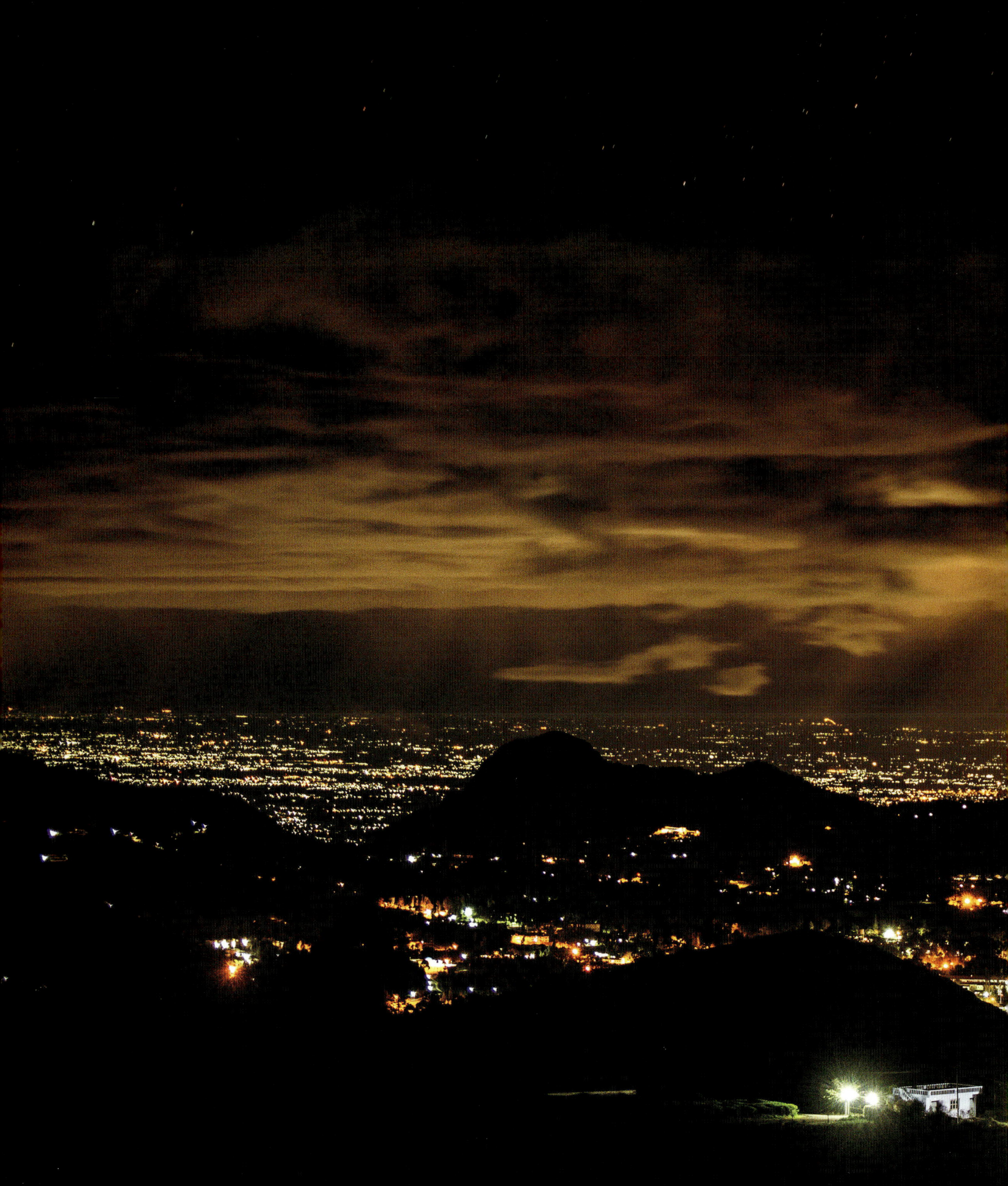

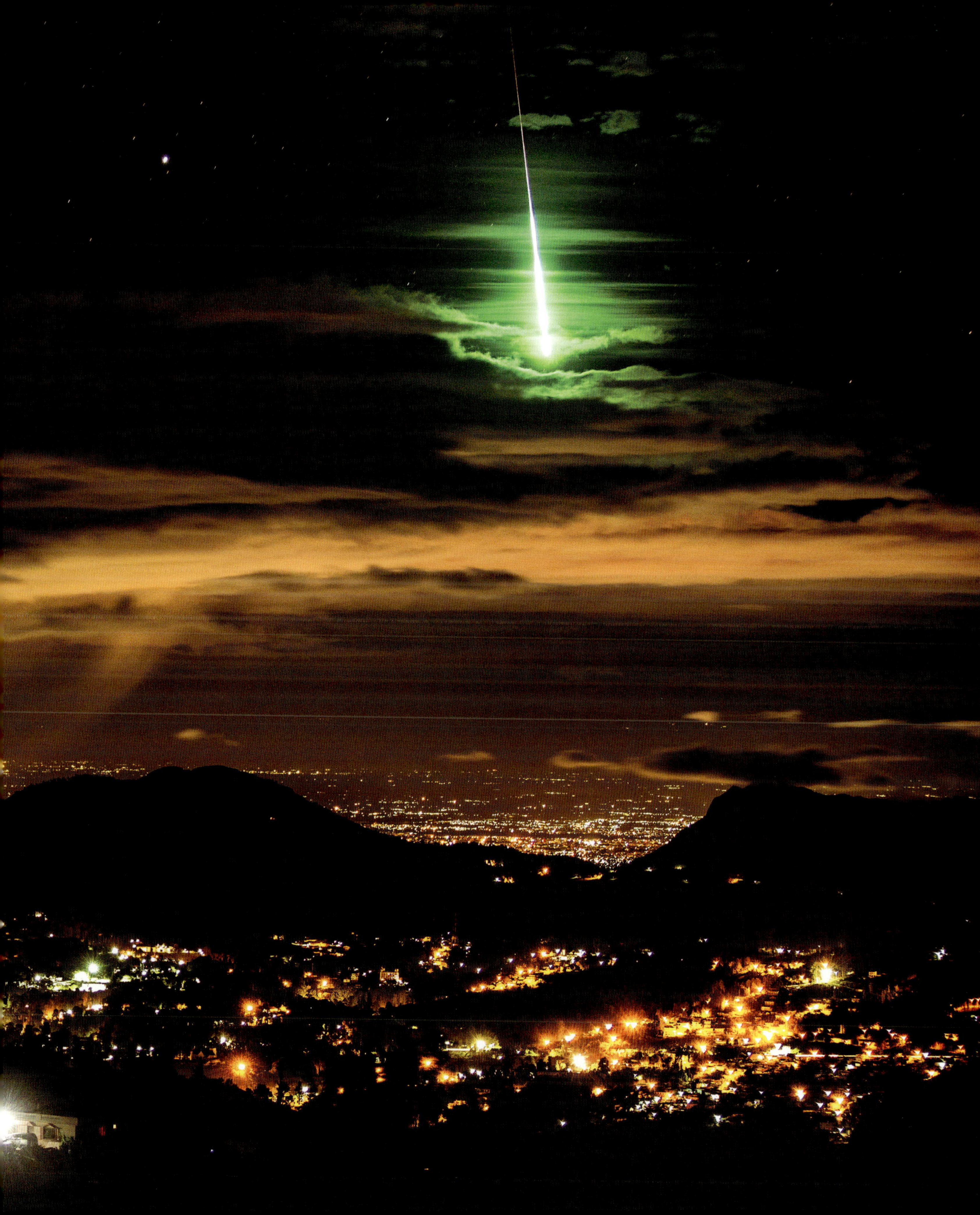

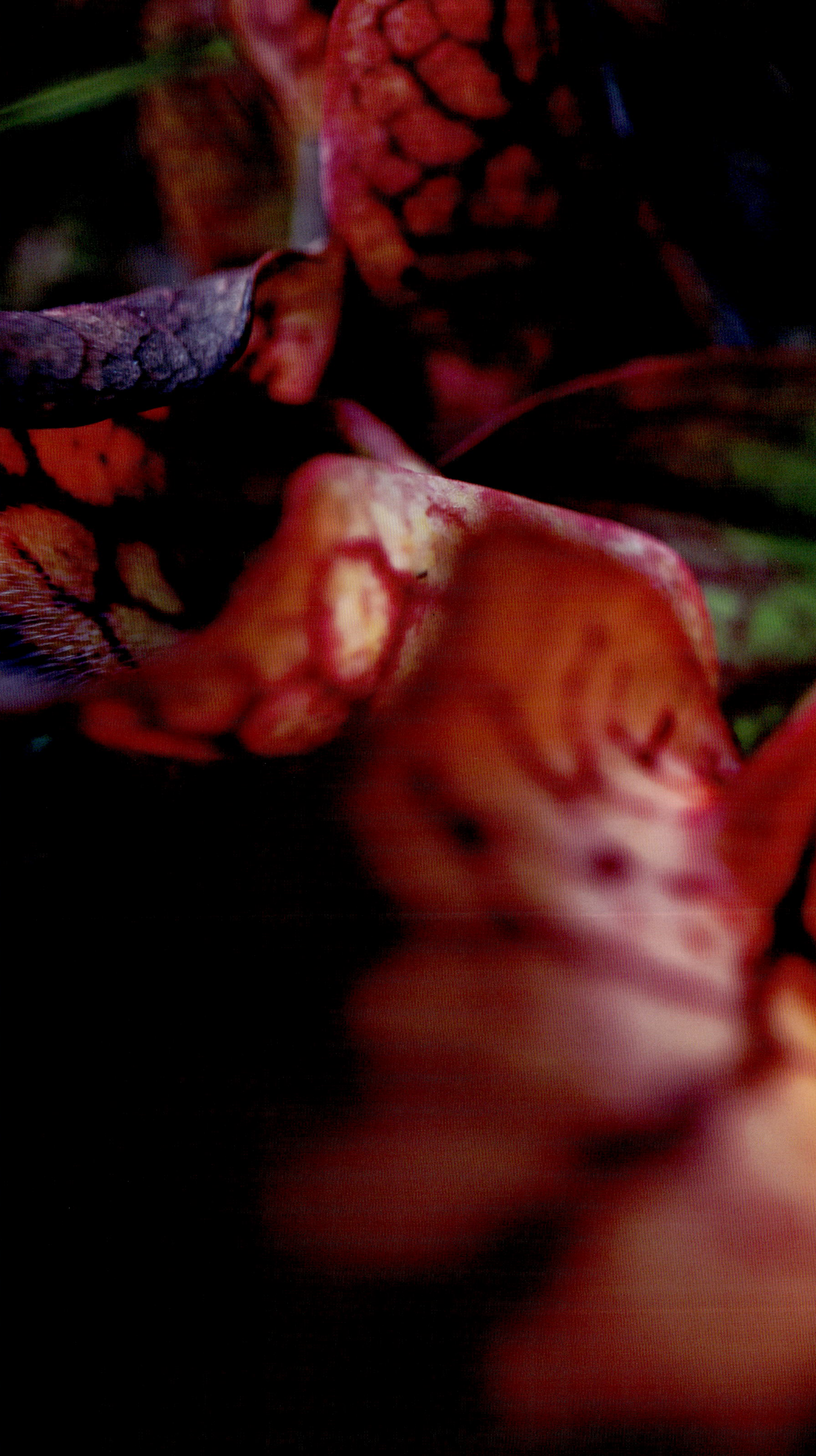

SAMANTHA STEPHENS
A carnivorous pitcher plant in Canada's Algonquin Provincial Park has captured two juvenile spotted salamanders.

Previous pages:
PRASENJEET YADAV
A meteor speeds over the "sky islands" of India's Western Ghats, its green flash appearing as its mineral content heats and vaporizes.

Following pages:
DHEERA VENKATRAMAN
By combining a black-and-white photo with a thermal one, captured with a camera that senses radiation emitted in the infrared range, the photographer shows a geothermal spring in Iceland.

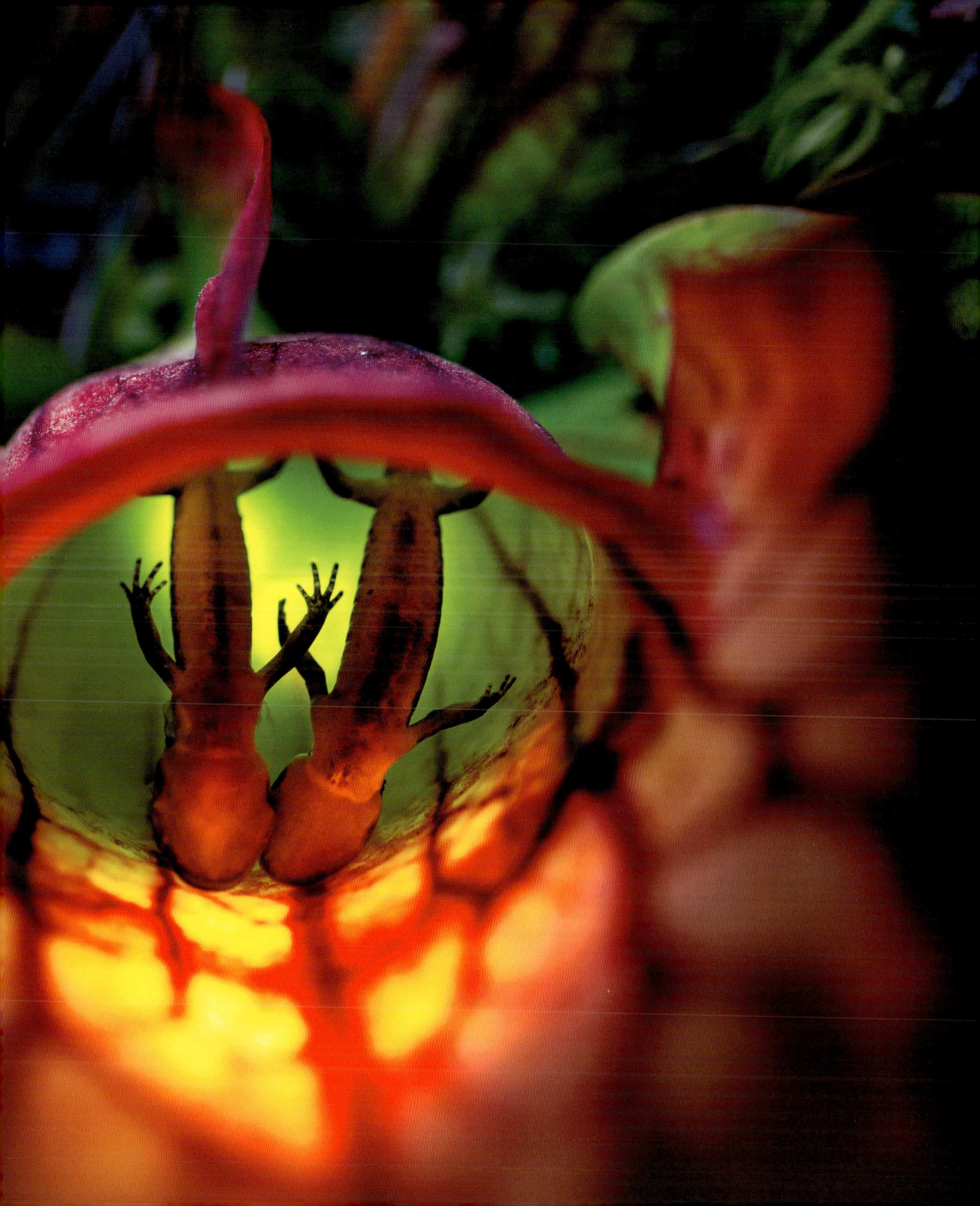

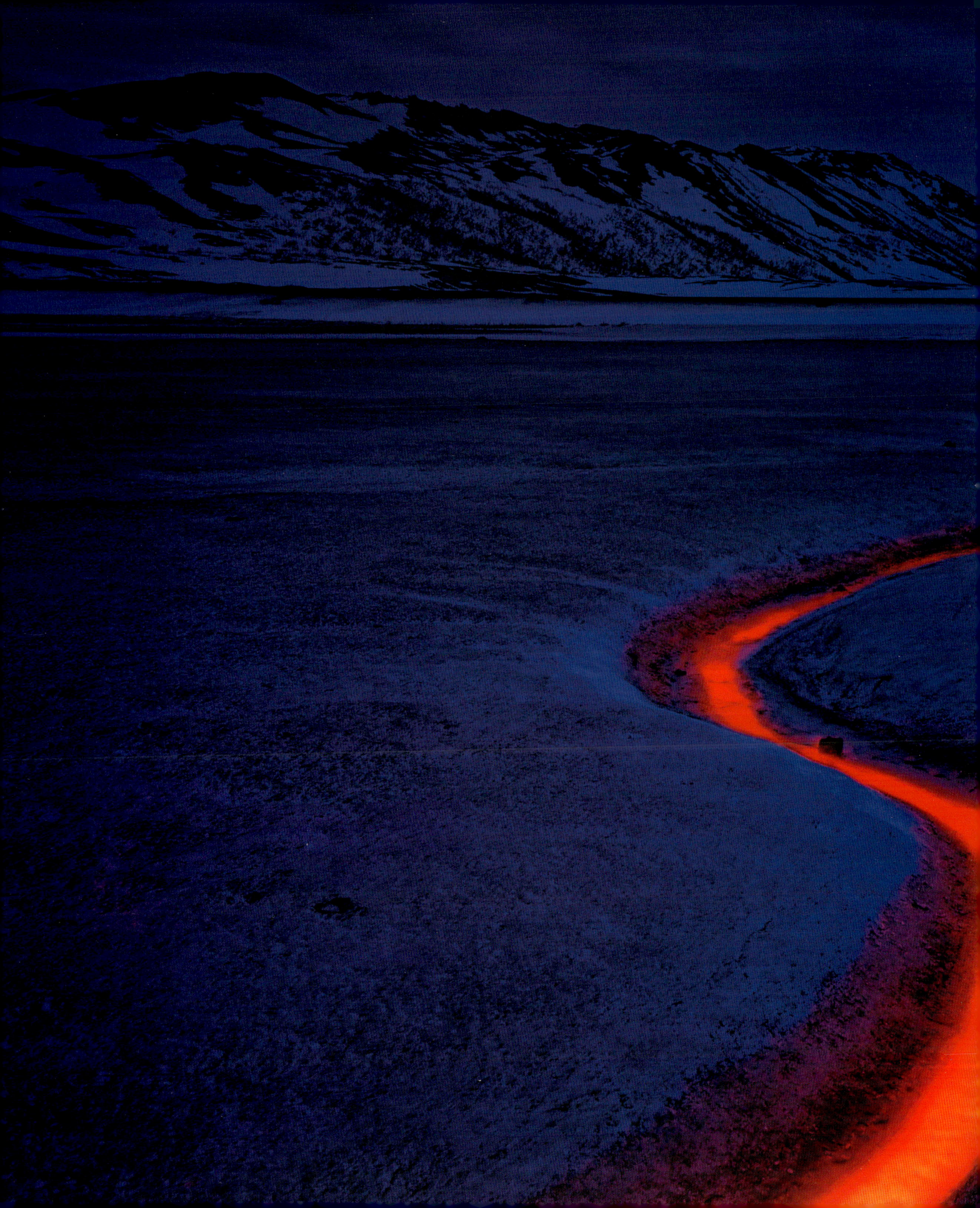

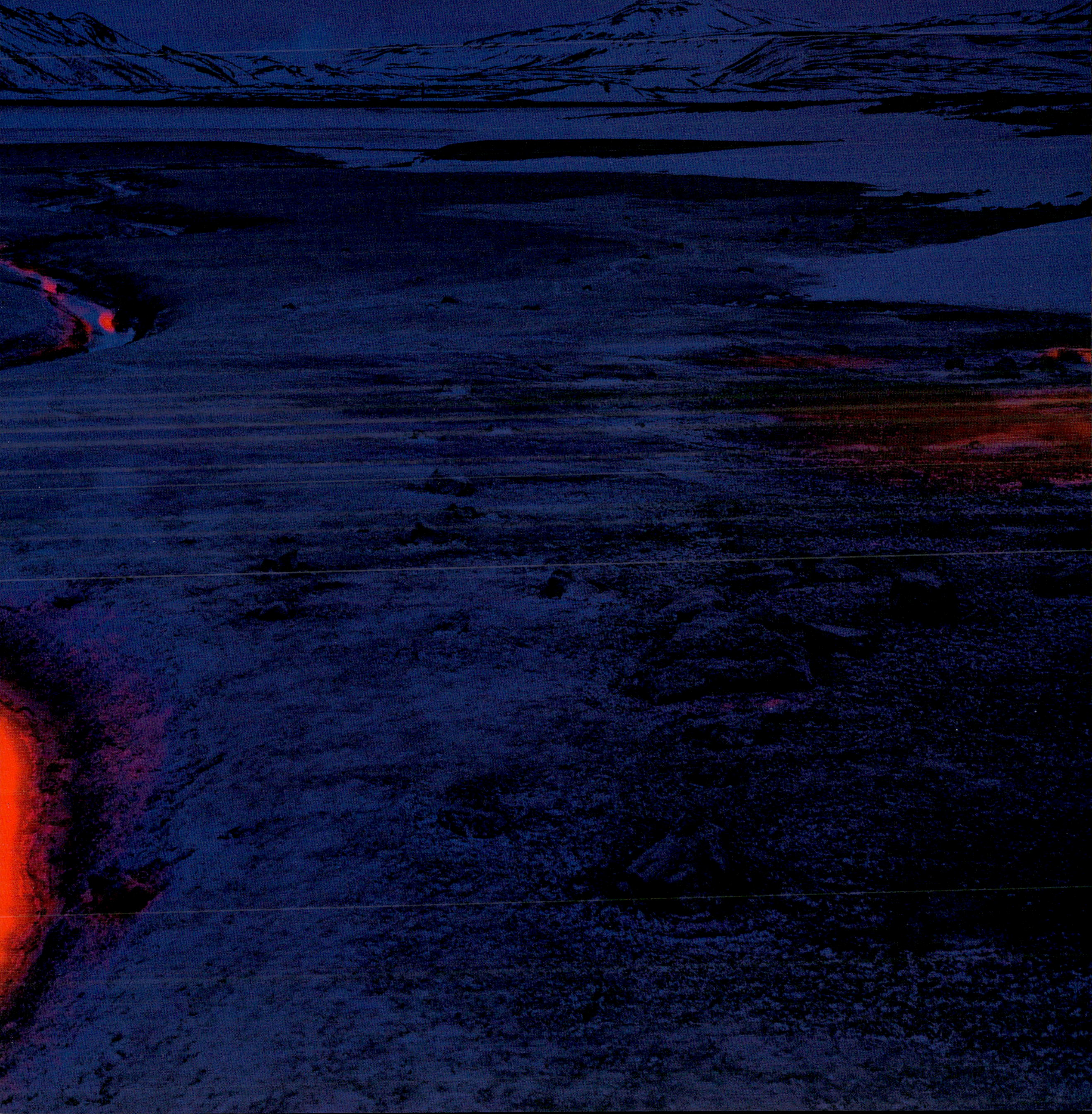

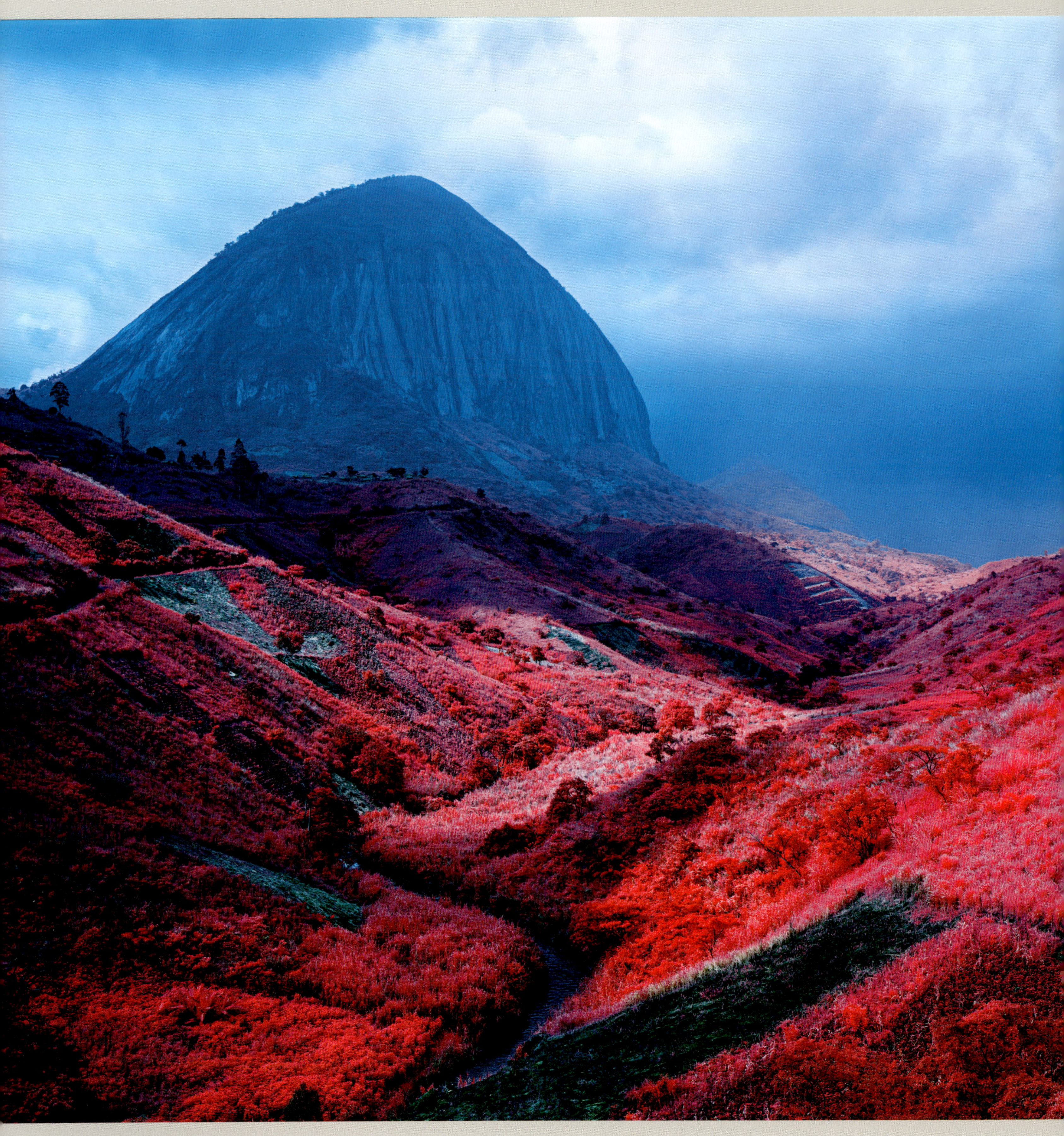

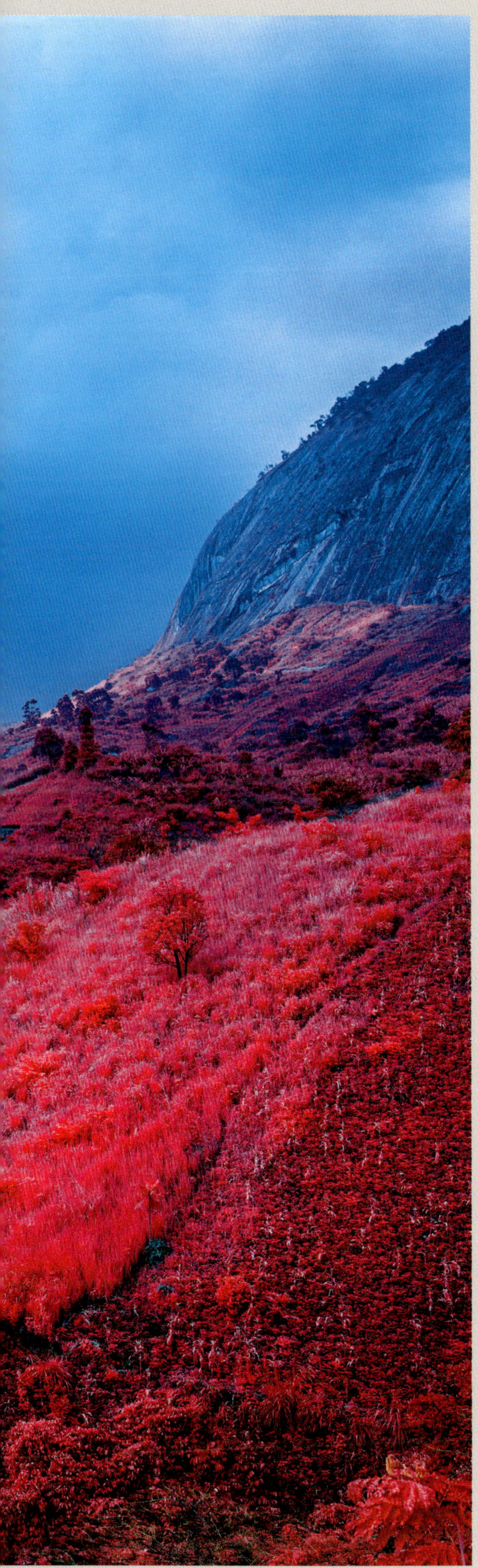

SPECTRA BEYOND THE VISIBLE

There is a world of color our eyes cannot see—but photography allows us to expand the limits of what we can perceive into hidden parts of the spectrum. In some cases, we're just catching up with the animals around us.

When Richard Mosse decided to document the rich, vegetated landscapes of the Democratic Republic of the Congo during the rainy season, he turned to Kodak Aerochrome infrared film. Originally developed by the U.S. military in the 1940s to reveal camouflage in aerial photography, it works by unleashing the full color of vegetation, and in so doing, making other green things in the environment stand out as dull voids. Plants look green to humans because they reflect green wavelengths of light very strongly. Our eyes can't see it, but plants are also wonderful at reflecting colors in the near-infrared part of the spectrum. The pink glow captured in Aerochrome manifests these invisible layers of infrared tones, drawing us into the vibrant, patchy vegetation above all else in this multilayered landscape.

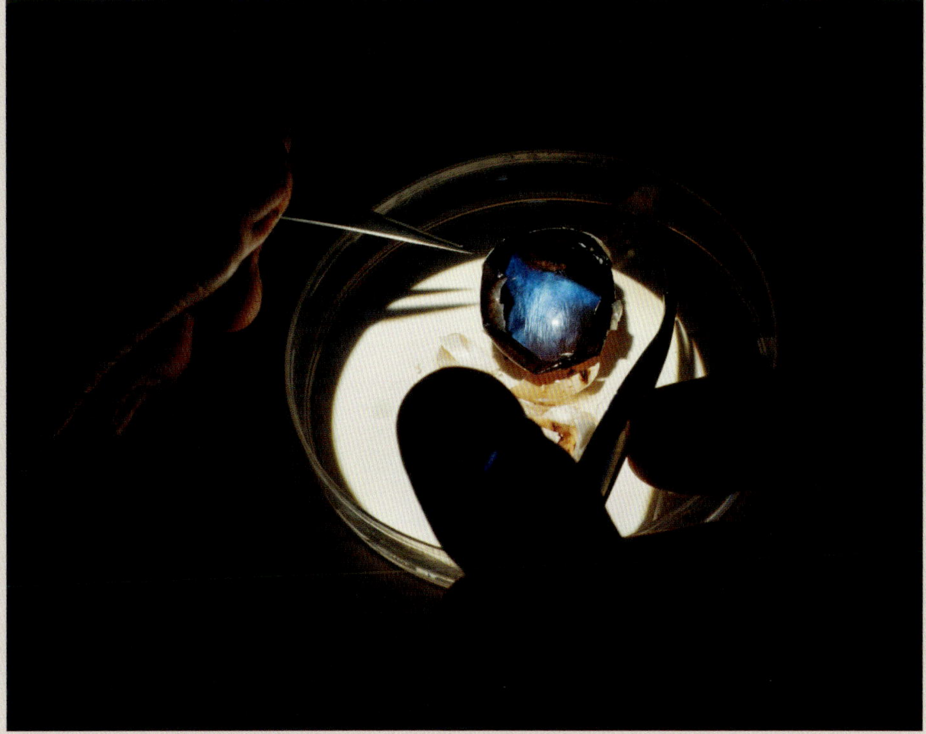

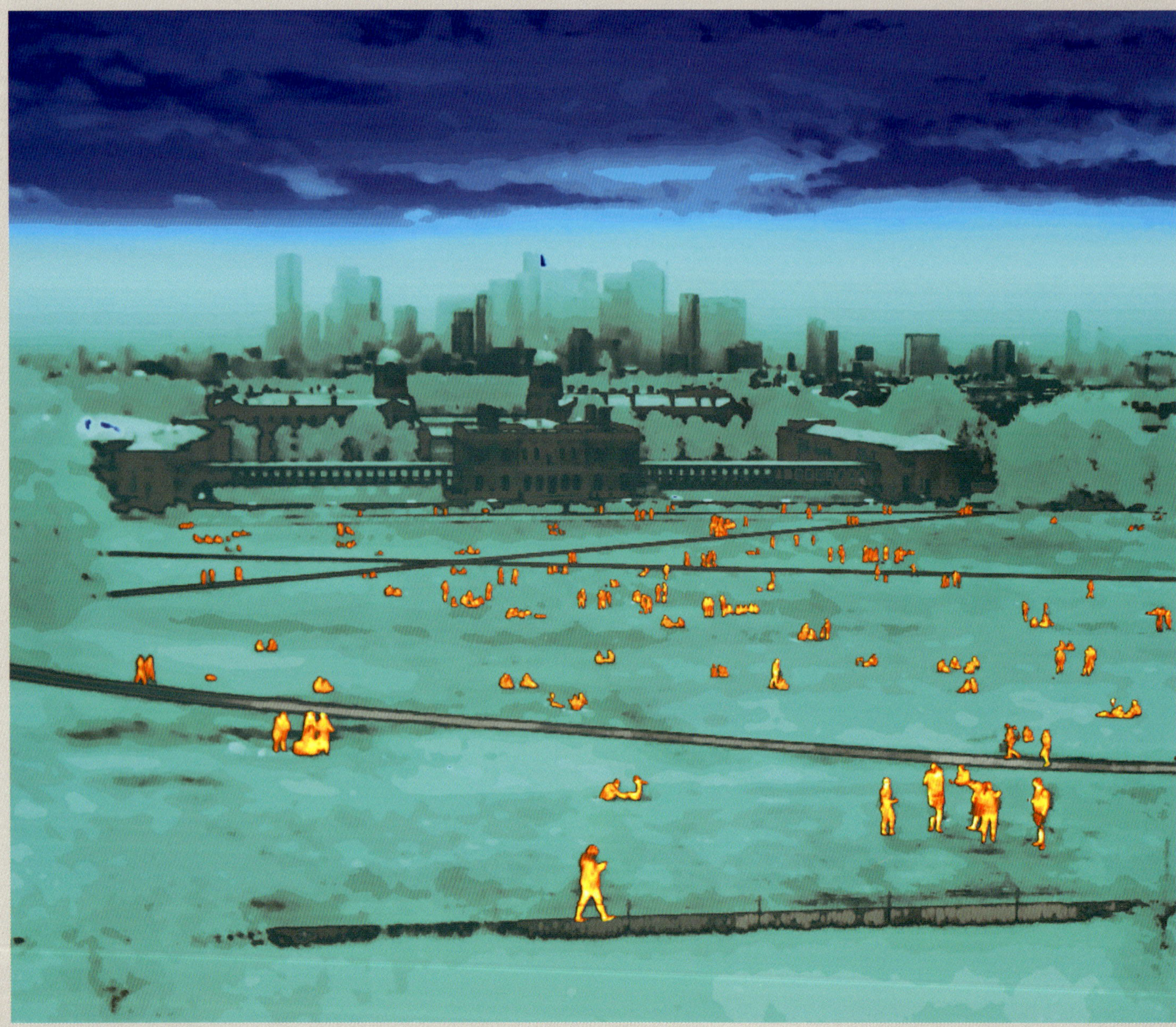

As the Arctic gets warmer, its tundra regions shine more strongly in near-infrared. Plants are flourishing as the region heats up, but rather than tracking greenness, scientists rely on changes in near-infrared to more accurately sense vegetation change with satellites. This is because colors like green and blue don't pass through Earth's atmosphere very well; they become scattered along the way, whereas near-infrared and red are much better at passing through the atmosphere without weakening.

Summers are bright in the Arctic, but the rest of the year is a long dusk followed by months of darkness. Reindeer eyeballs deal with this by changing with the seasons, allowing reindeer to extract maximal color information as lighting conditions change. In summer, their yellow eyes help them to navigate great distances and find tasty herbs. But in winter, when the sun sits below the horizon, their eyes turn a brilliant

GILES PRICE
An aerial infrared photograph singles out people as they stroll near the National Maritime Museum in Greenwich, United Kingdom.

Previous pages, left:
RICHARD MOSSE
In a photo made with film that senses infrared light, the forested hills of the eastern Democratic Republic of the Congo glow in vivid color.

Previous pages, right:
ROBERT FOSBURY
Dissecting a reindeer eyeball

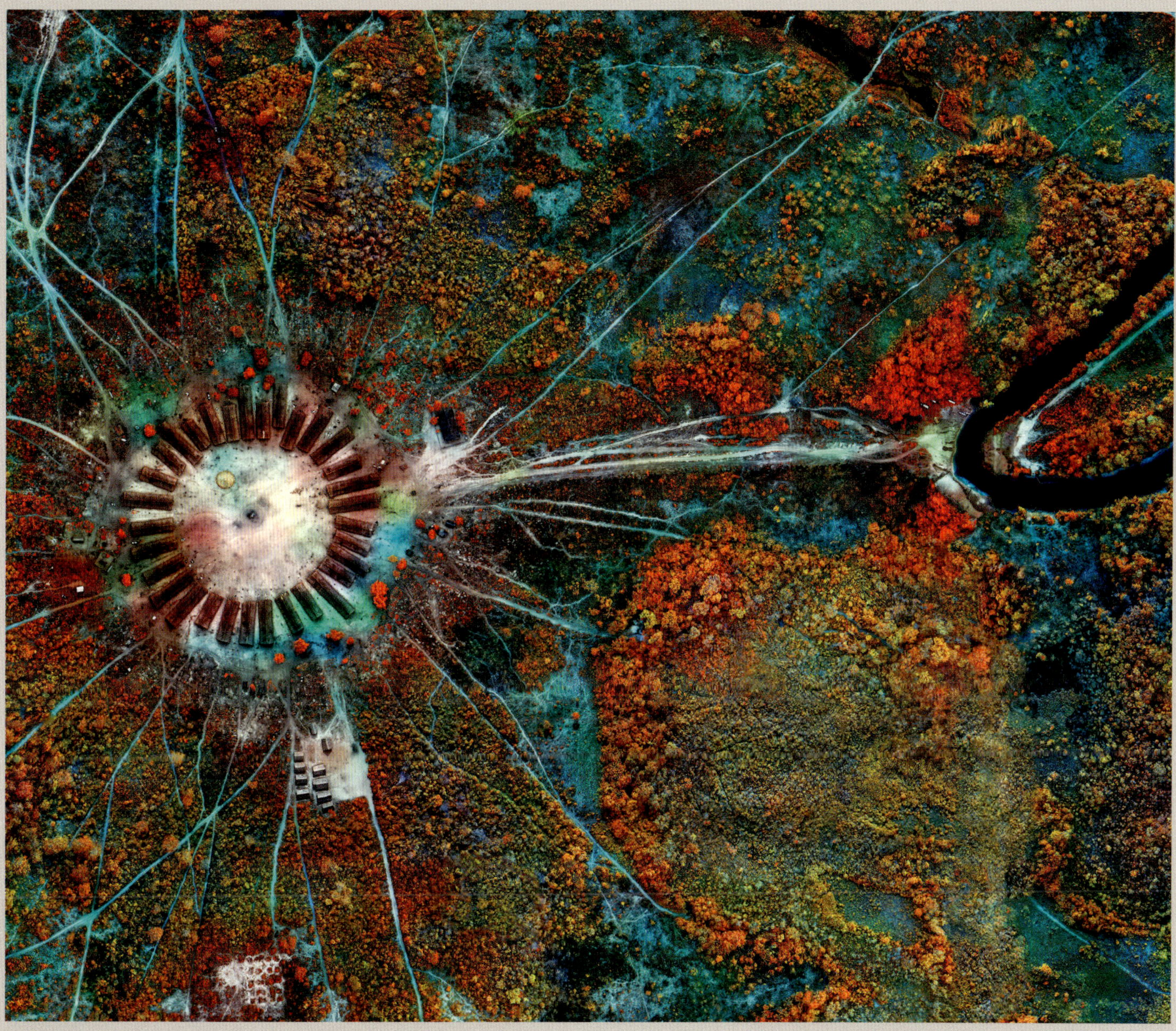

blue, becoming 100,000 times more sensitive to light in order to pick up the weakly scattered blues that have bounced back down to Earth off the ozone layer. Reindeer eyes can also detect beyond the visible spectrum where violet becomes ultraviolet. In this colorscape, a white polar bear on a snowy background might stand out as a contrasting black to reindeer.

Digital camera technology has also flourished in the color regions beyond the visible. Thermal images are essentially capturing the color of heat, allowing us to visualize patterns our eyes would miss, like body temperature or the presence of a geothermal-fed stream in a cold landscape (pages 56–57). Satellites can capture nuanced differences in colors, whether visible or not, which then allow humans to mix, emphasize, and reveal real contrasts in landscapes invisible to our limited human eyes.

RICHARD MOSSE
By layering bands of ultraviolet and infrared color captured by a multispectral aerial camera, the photographer evokes the interconnectedness of the Enawenê Nawê, Indigenous people of the southern Amazon, with their increasingly threatened environment.

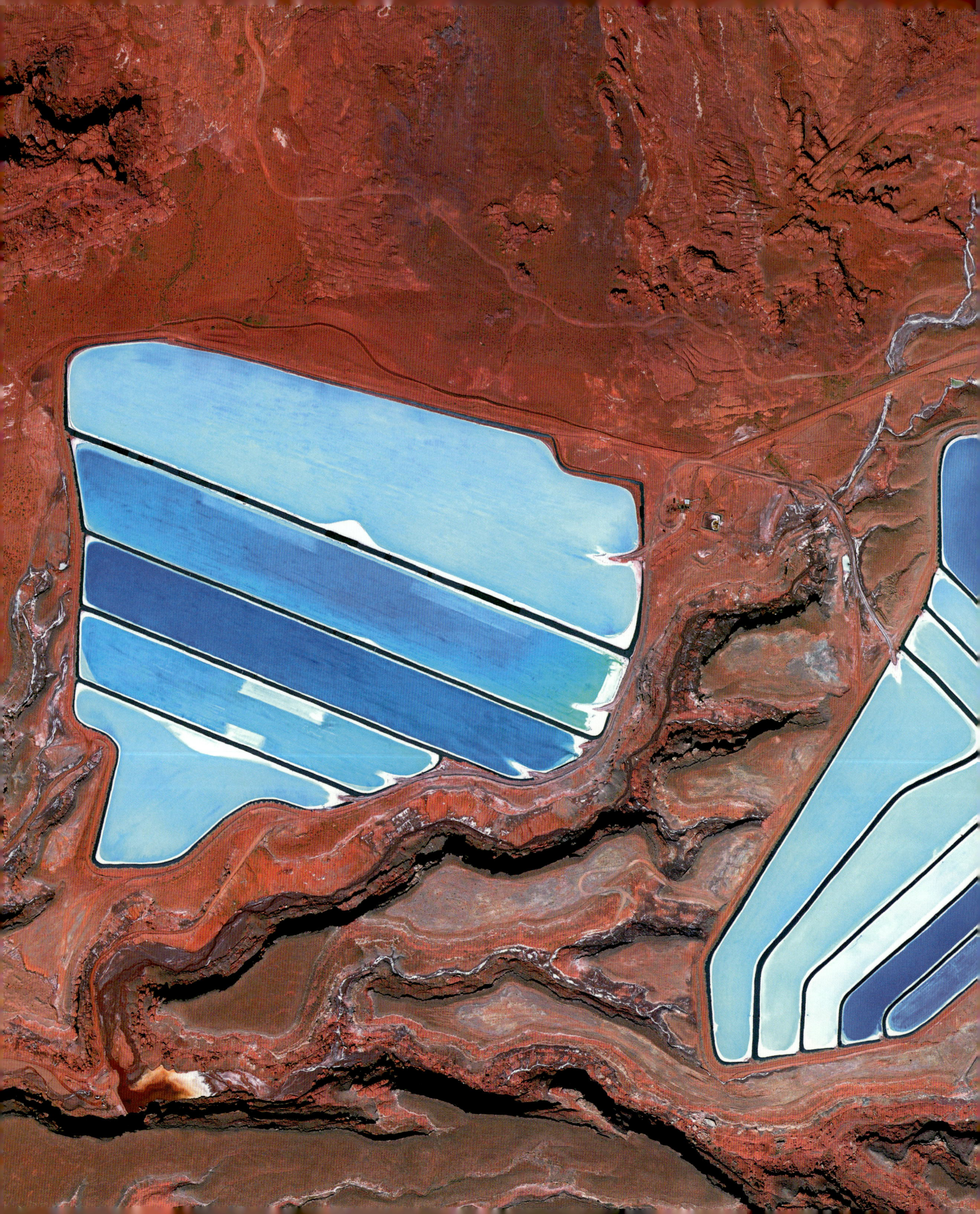

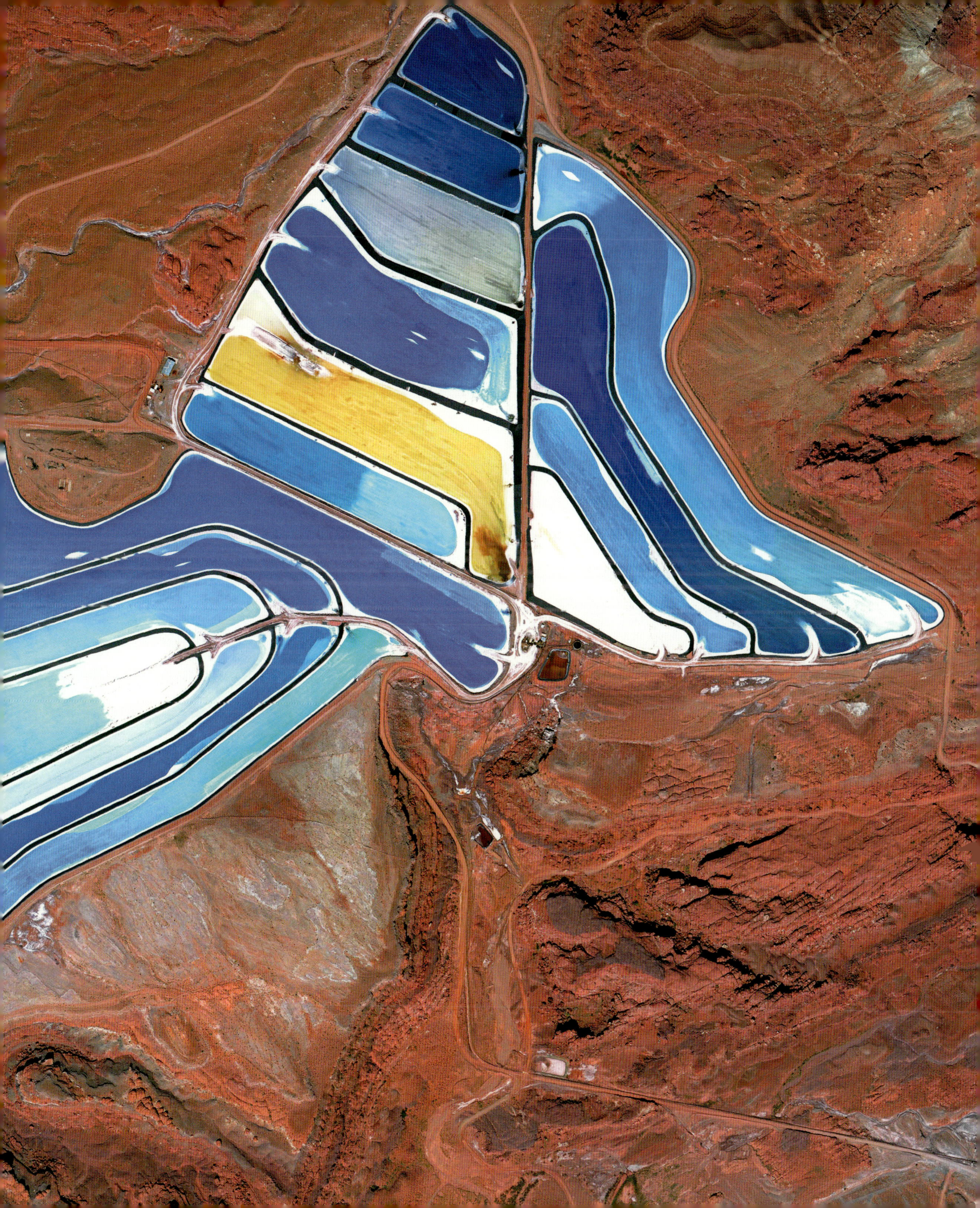

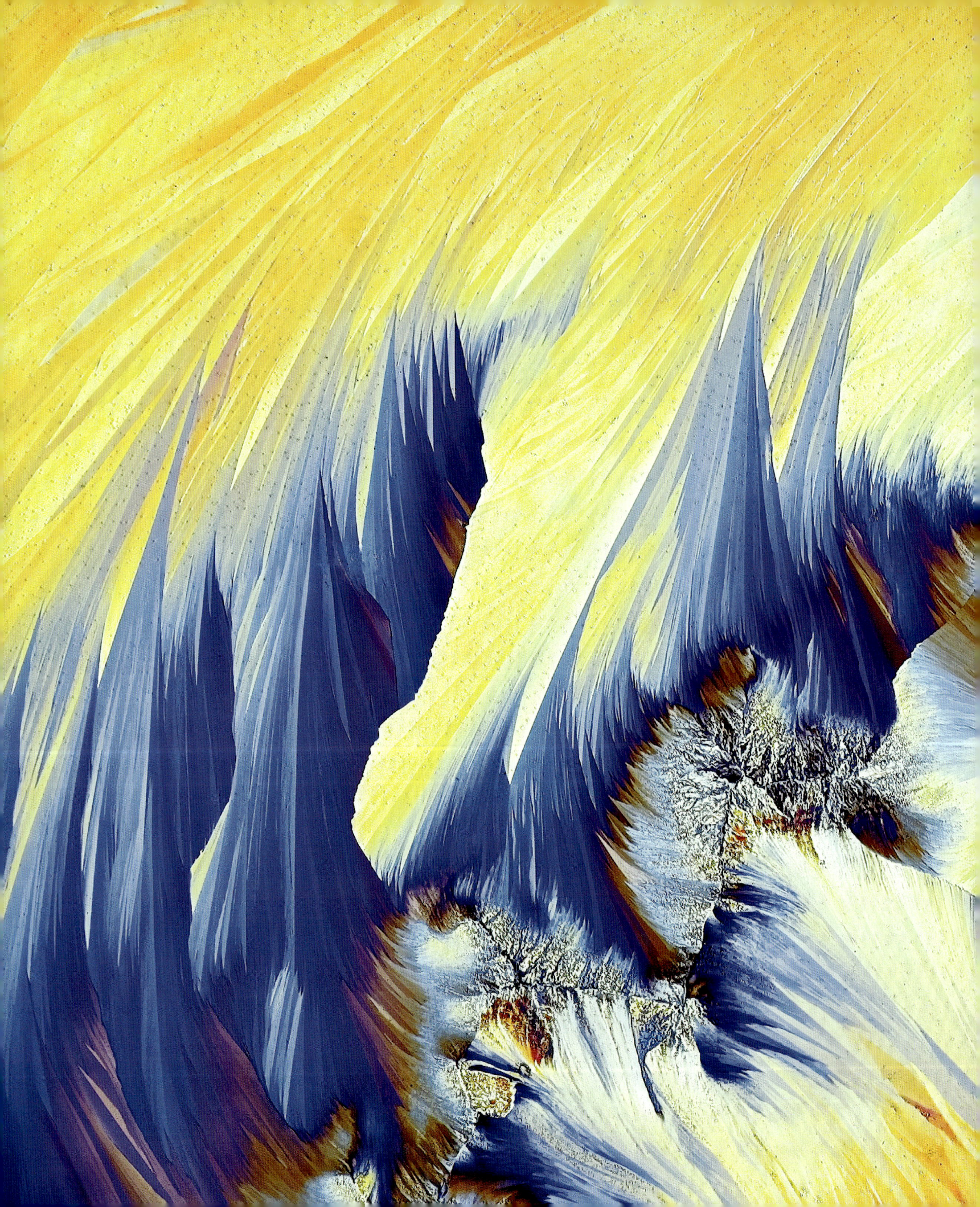

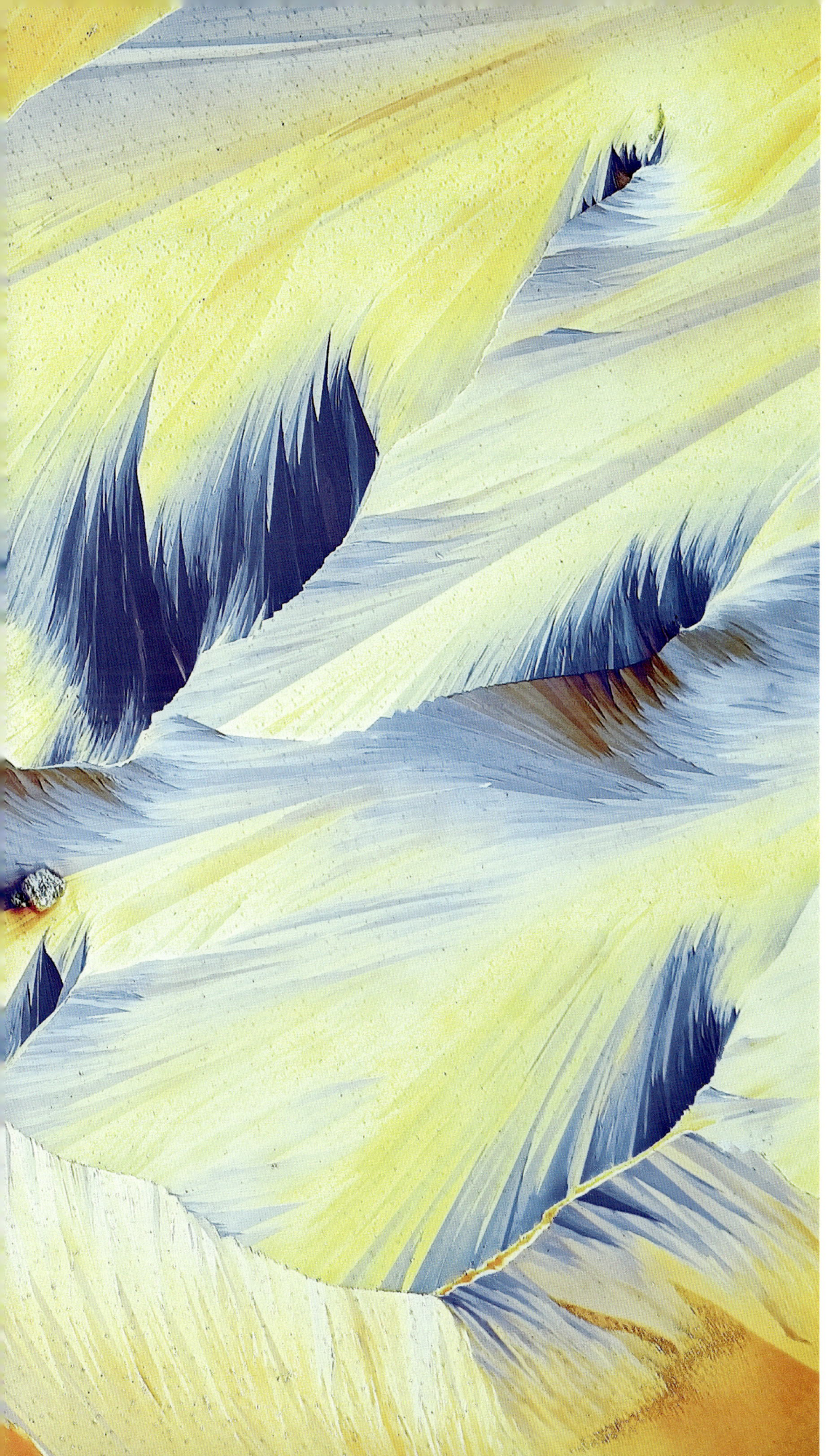

HENRI KOSKINEN
A microscopic view of
paracetamol crystals,
photographed in polarized light

Previous pages:
OVERVIEW
Potash evaporation ponds in
Moab, Utah, glow a vibrant blue.
The mineral-rich water is dyed
this dark color to absorb more
heat and light, so it will dry faster.

The Grass divides
as with a Comb, /
A spotted Shaft
is seen— / And then it
closes at your Feet /
And opens further on—

GALICE HOARAU
An eel larva makes its serpentine way through the inky water.

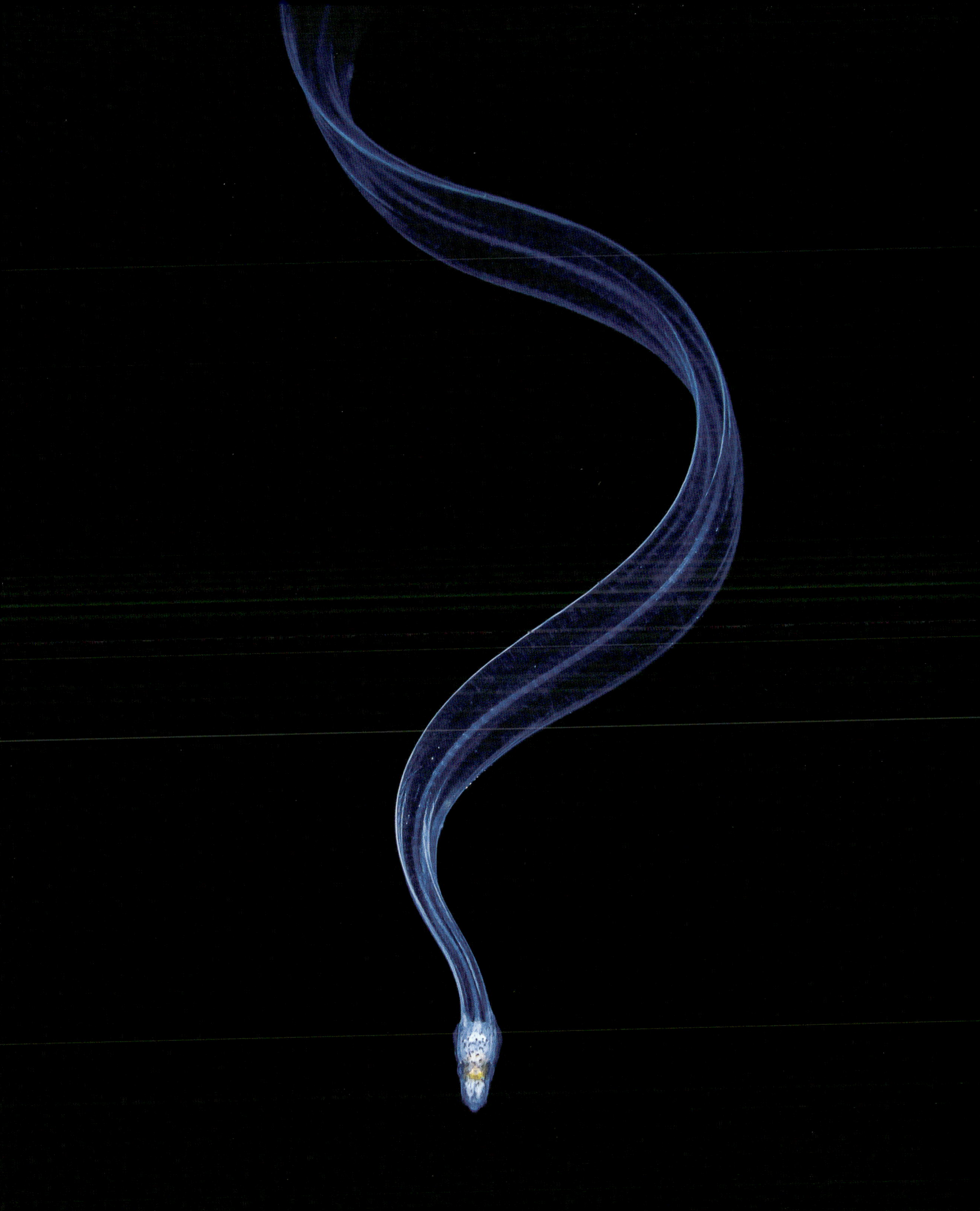

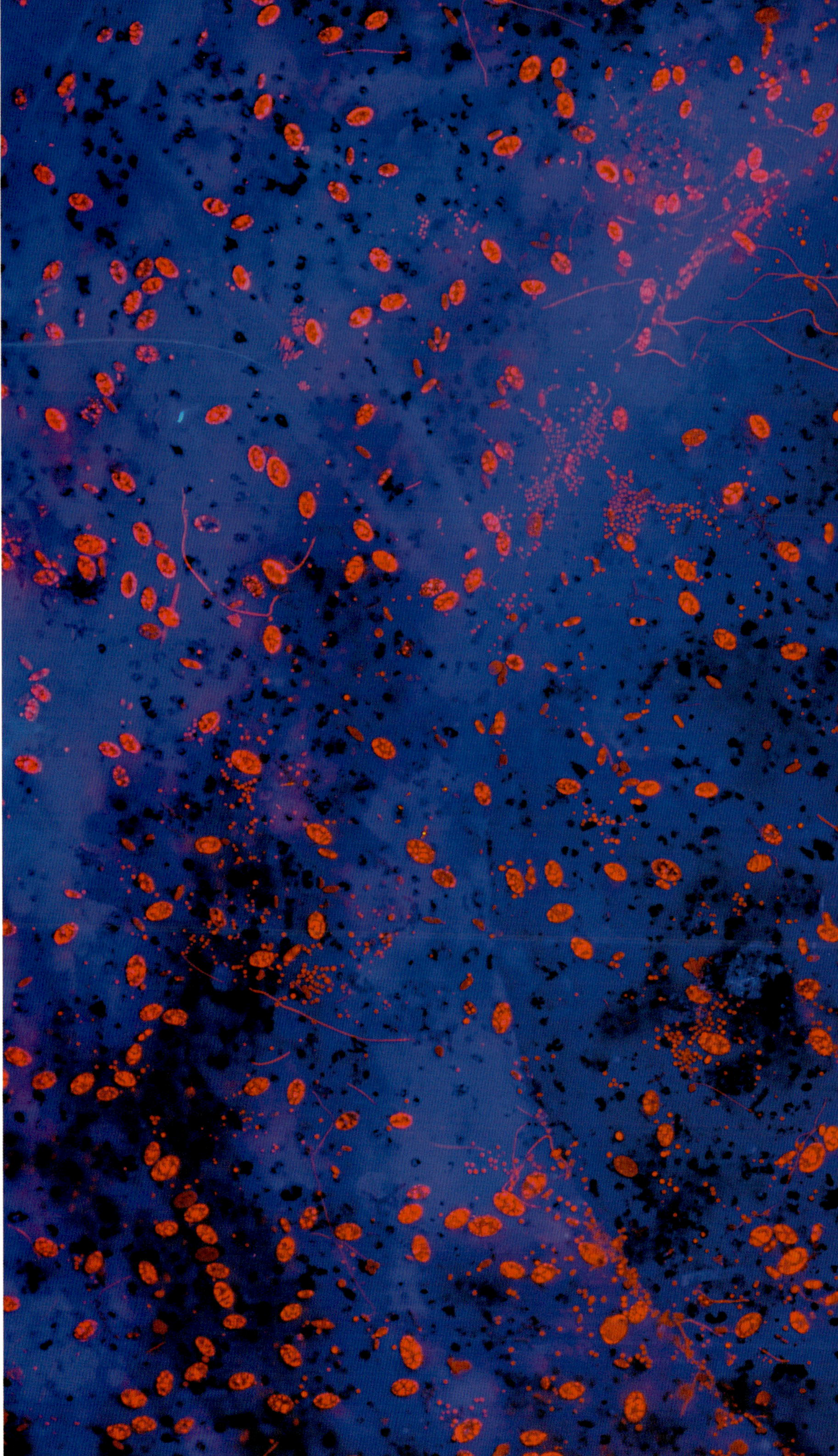

DAVID MAITLAND
Look deep into the film covering
a particular species of pond snail,
then cast fluorescent light on it,
and you see this galaxy of color:
The red is chlorophyll in resident
algae; the blue is the snail's
intestines.

Following pages:
DENNIS BORUP JAKOBSEN
Rainbow colors accentuate
the panoramic walkway of ARoS,
the contemporary art museum in
Aarhus, Denmark.

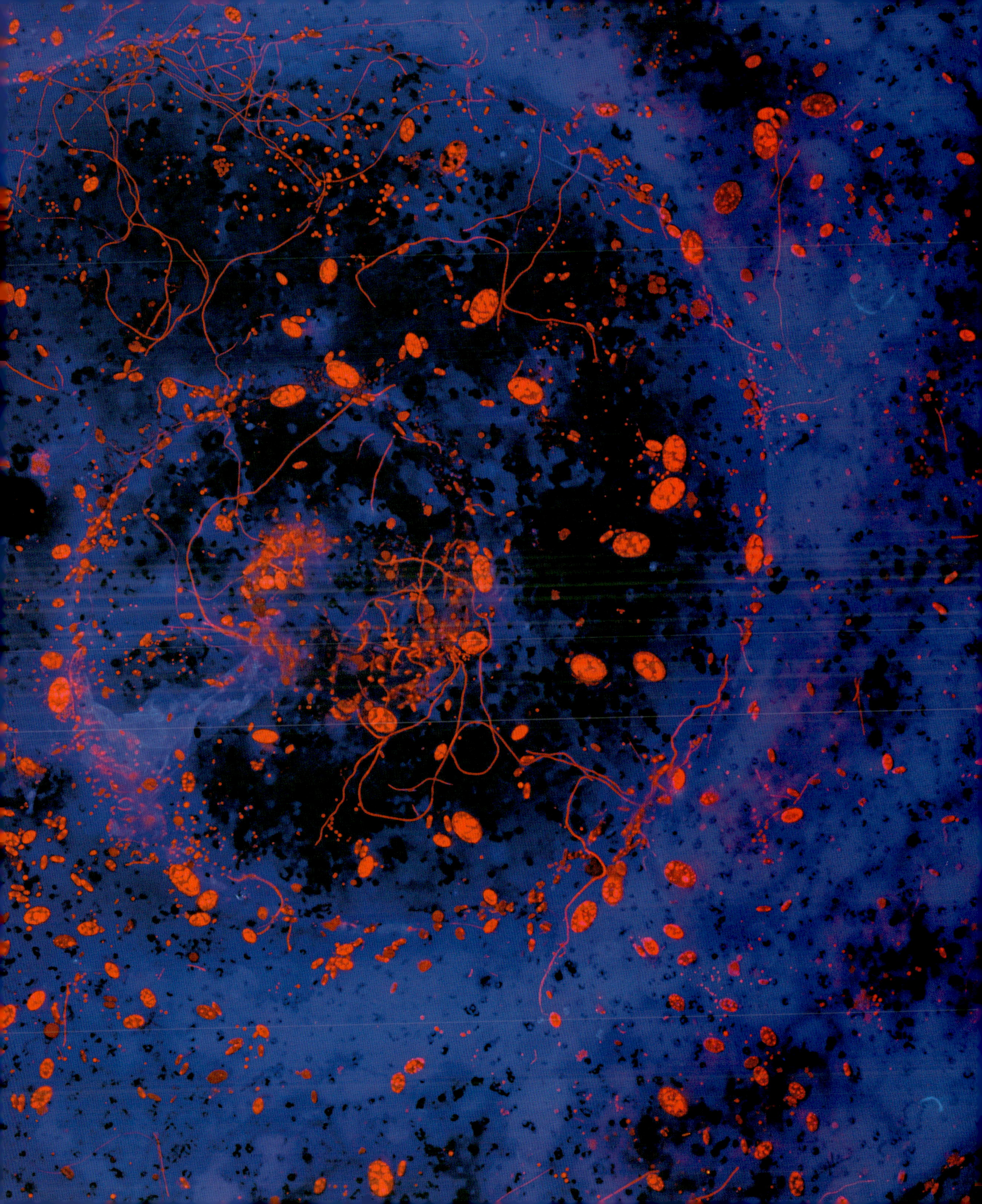

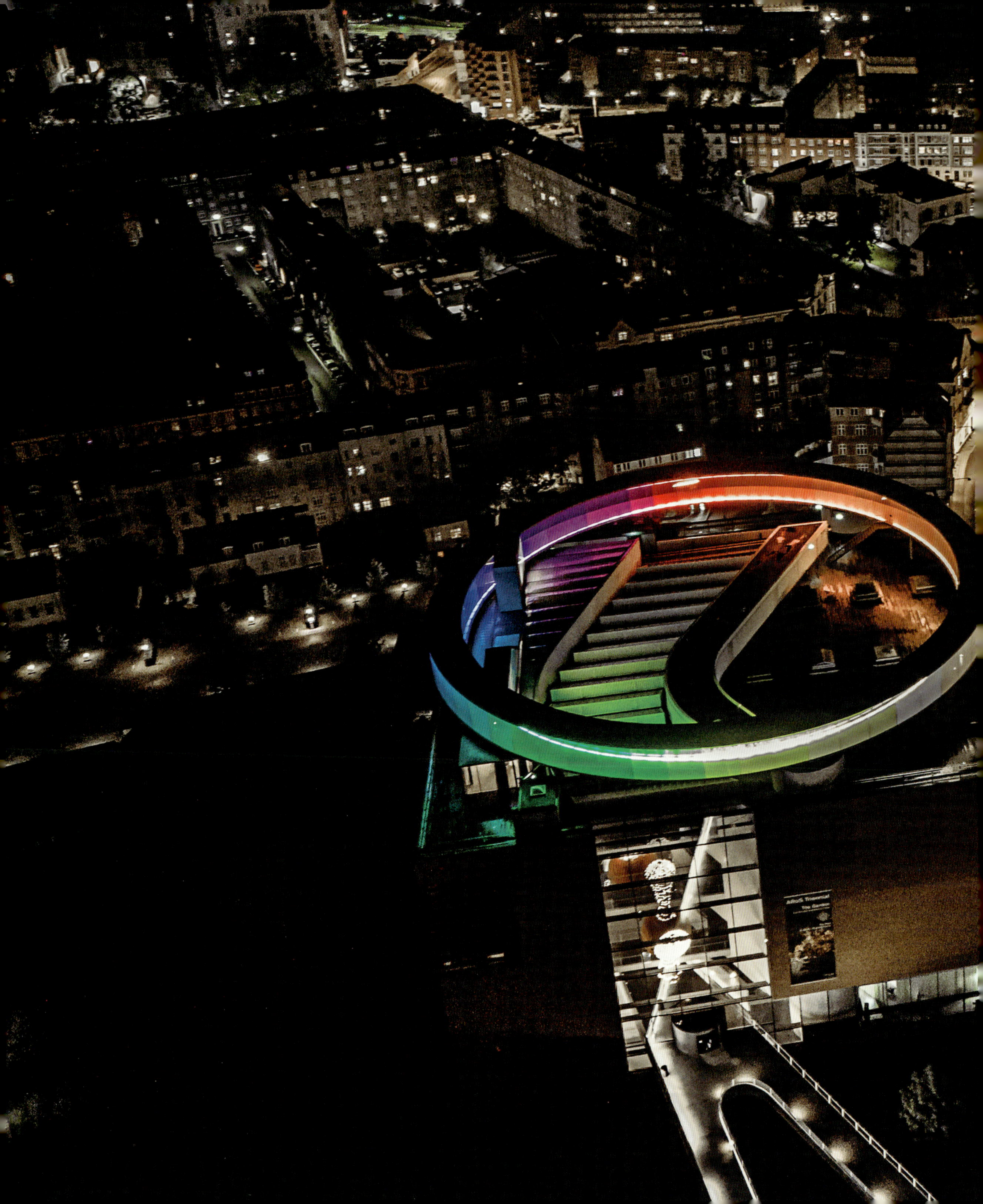

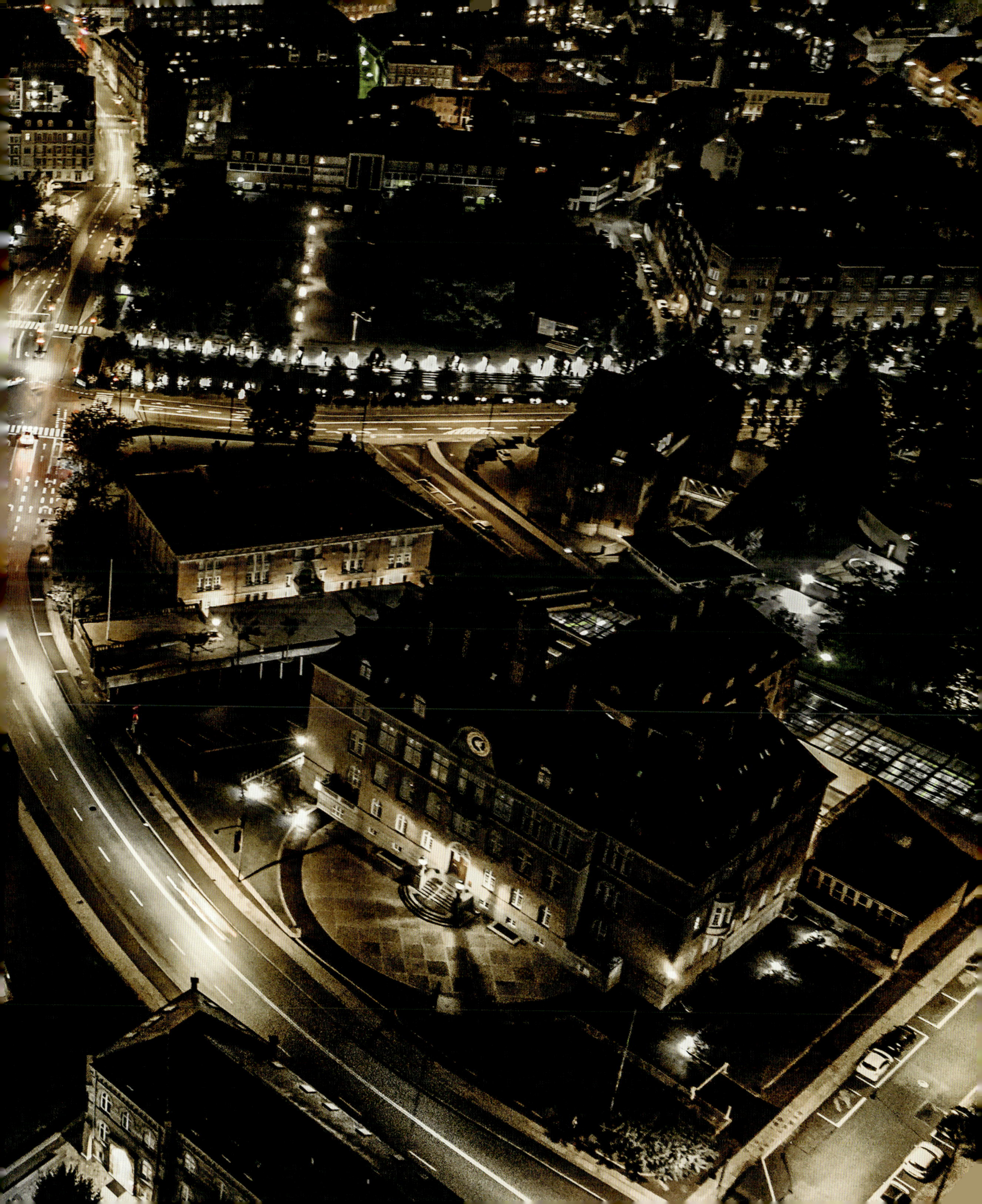

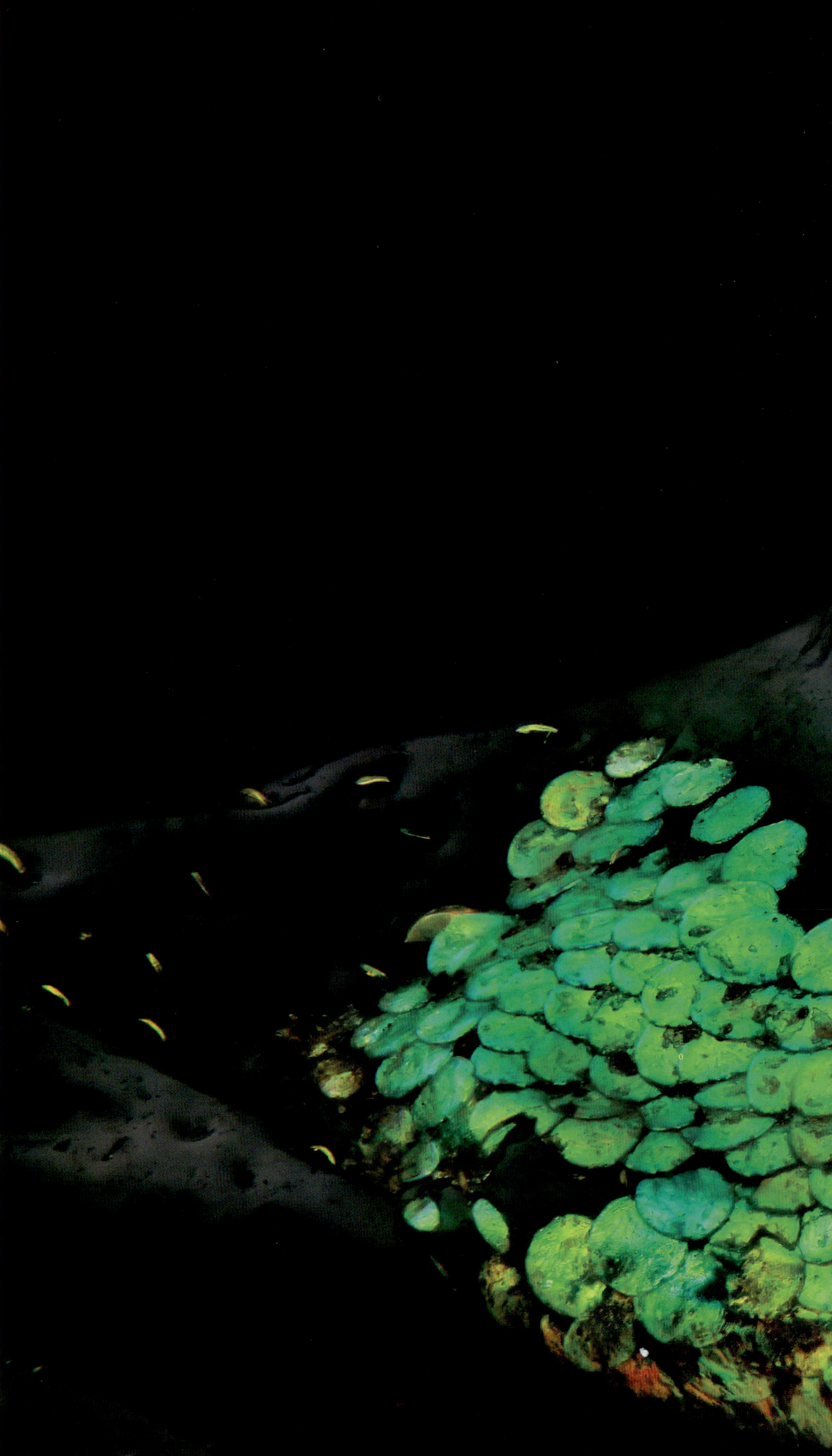

YOUSEF AL HABSHI
Scales around a weevil's multilens eye shine with a metallic color created not by pigments but by microscopic structures that interfere with visible light.

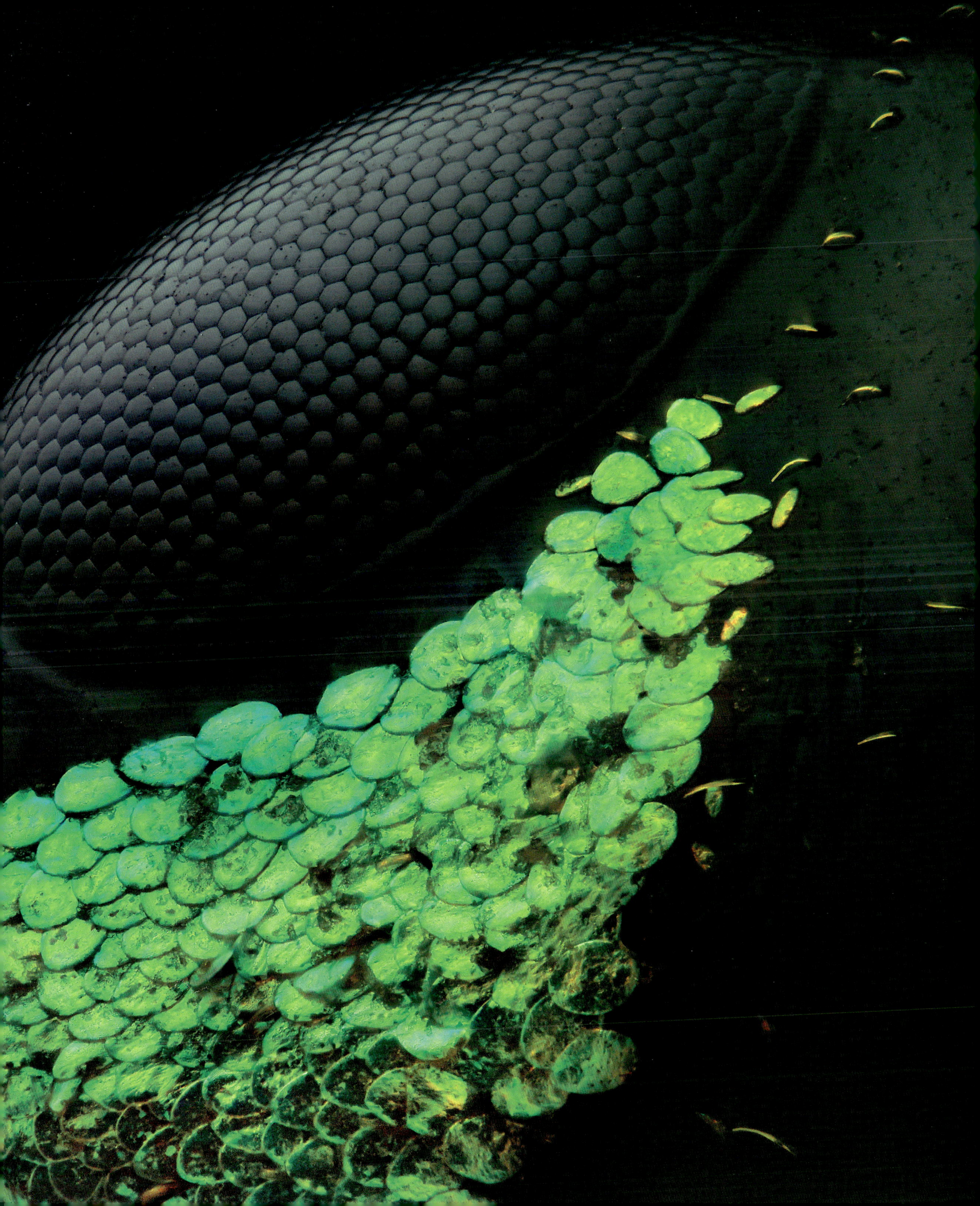

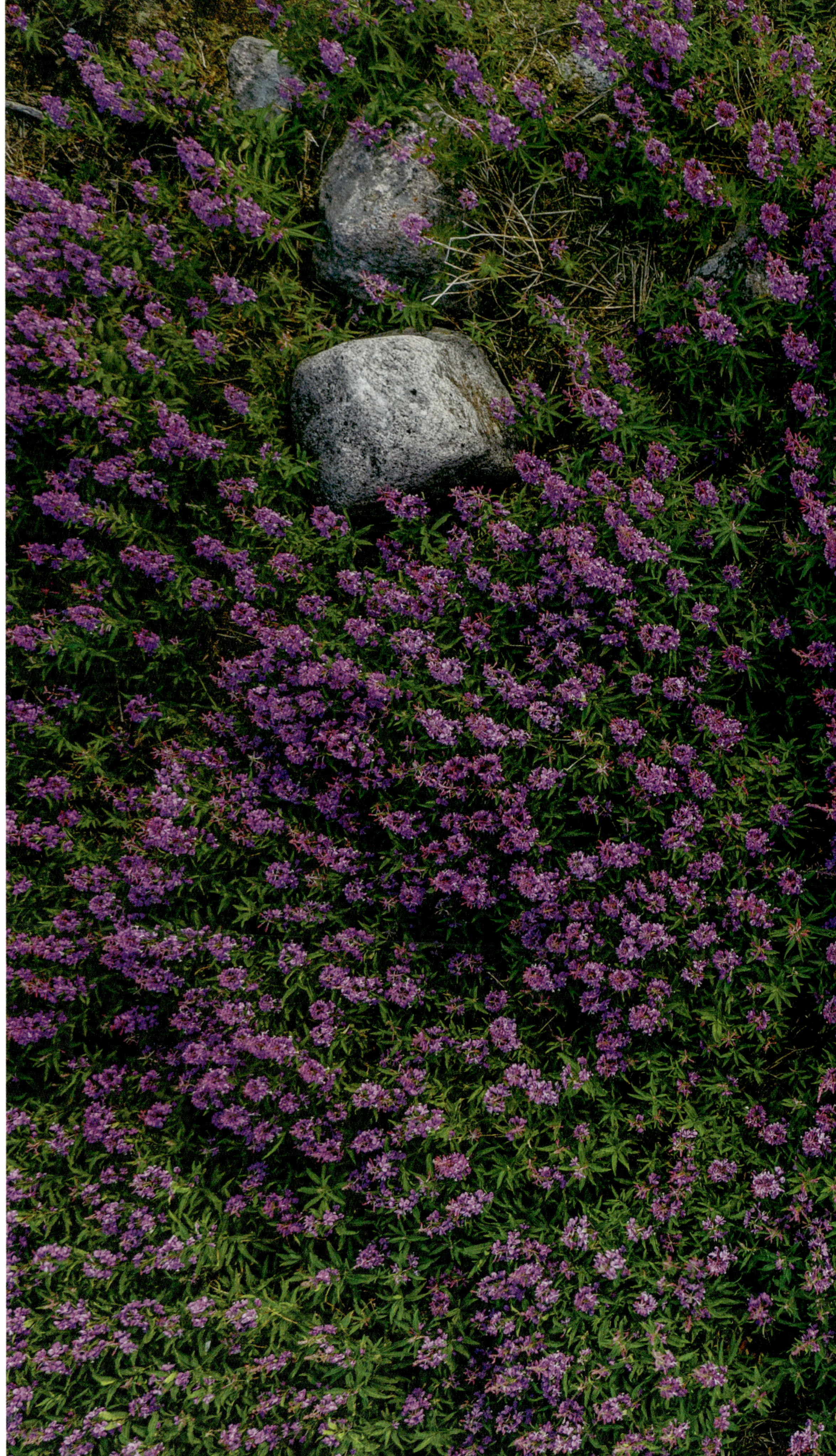

MARTIN GREGUS, JR.
Even a drone, hovering above to photograph this polar bear, did not disturb the animal's sleep amid purple fireweed blooms.

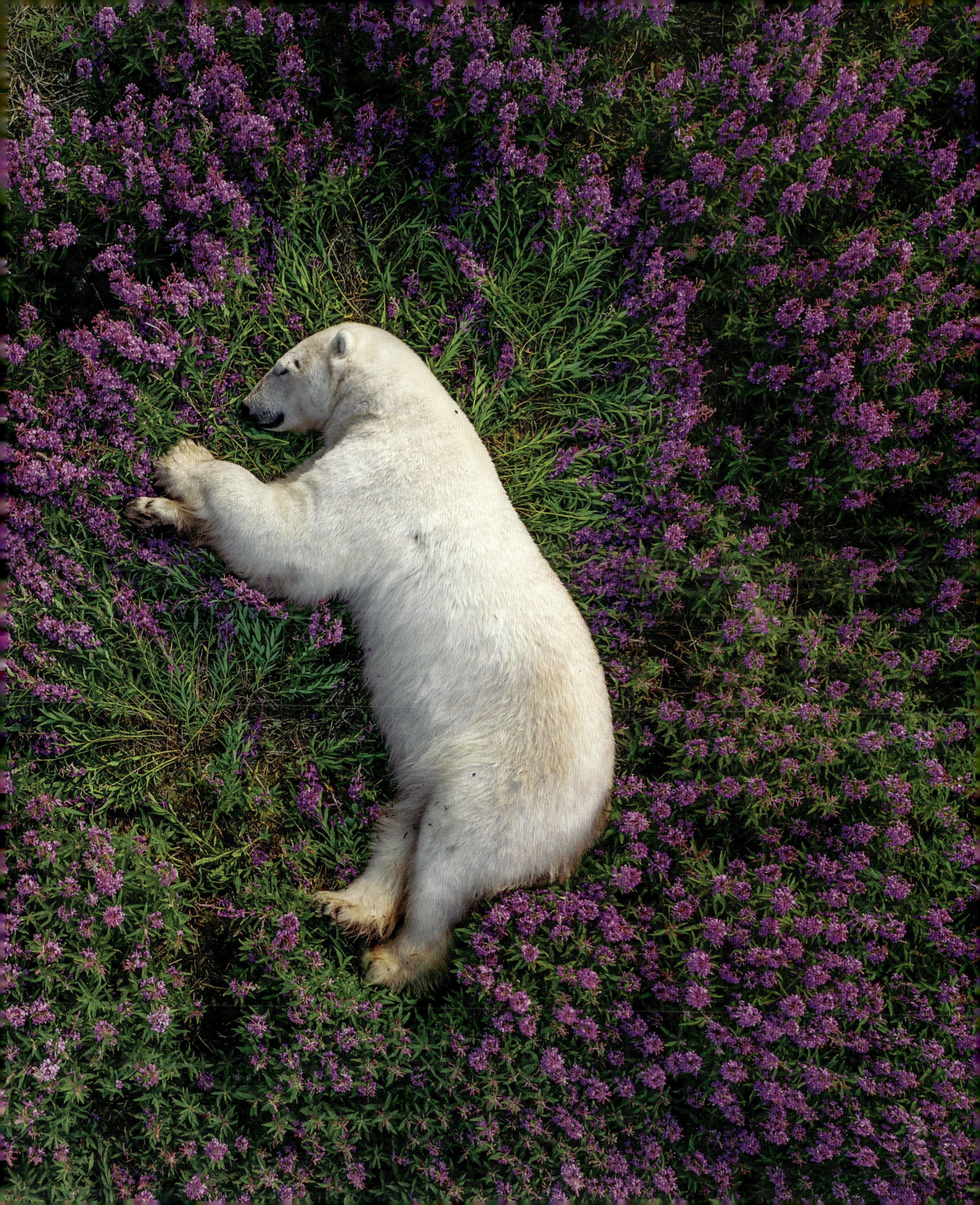

The only true voyage ... would be not to visit strange lands but to possess other eyes.

~MARCEL PROUST, *REMEMBRANCE OF THINGS PAST*

MAT PRICE
A boat transects the boundary between salt and fresh water.

Following pages:
RANDY OLSON
Colorfully dressed commuters swarm through the Churchgate railway station in Mumbai, India.

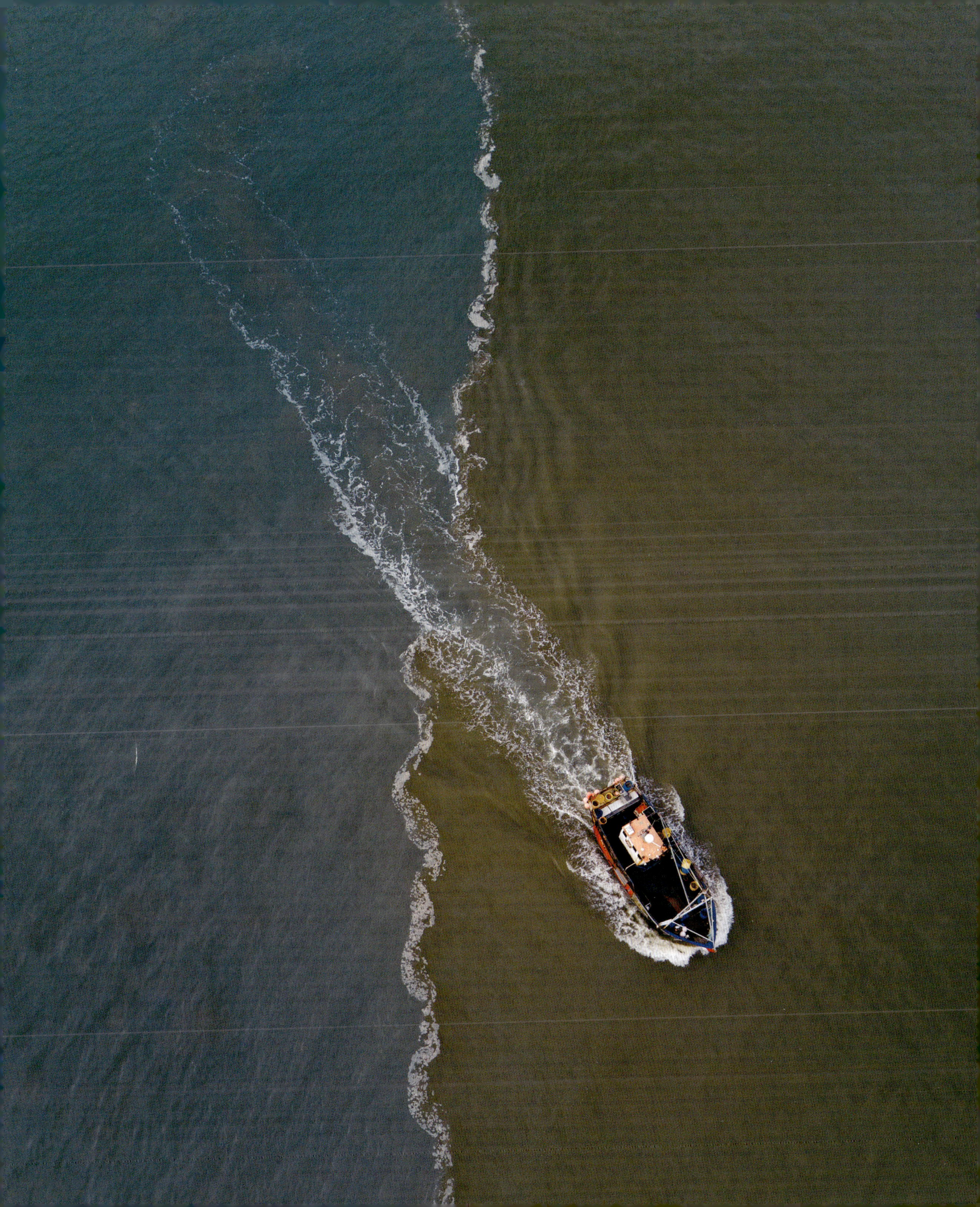

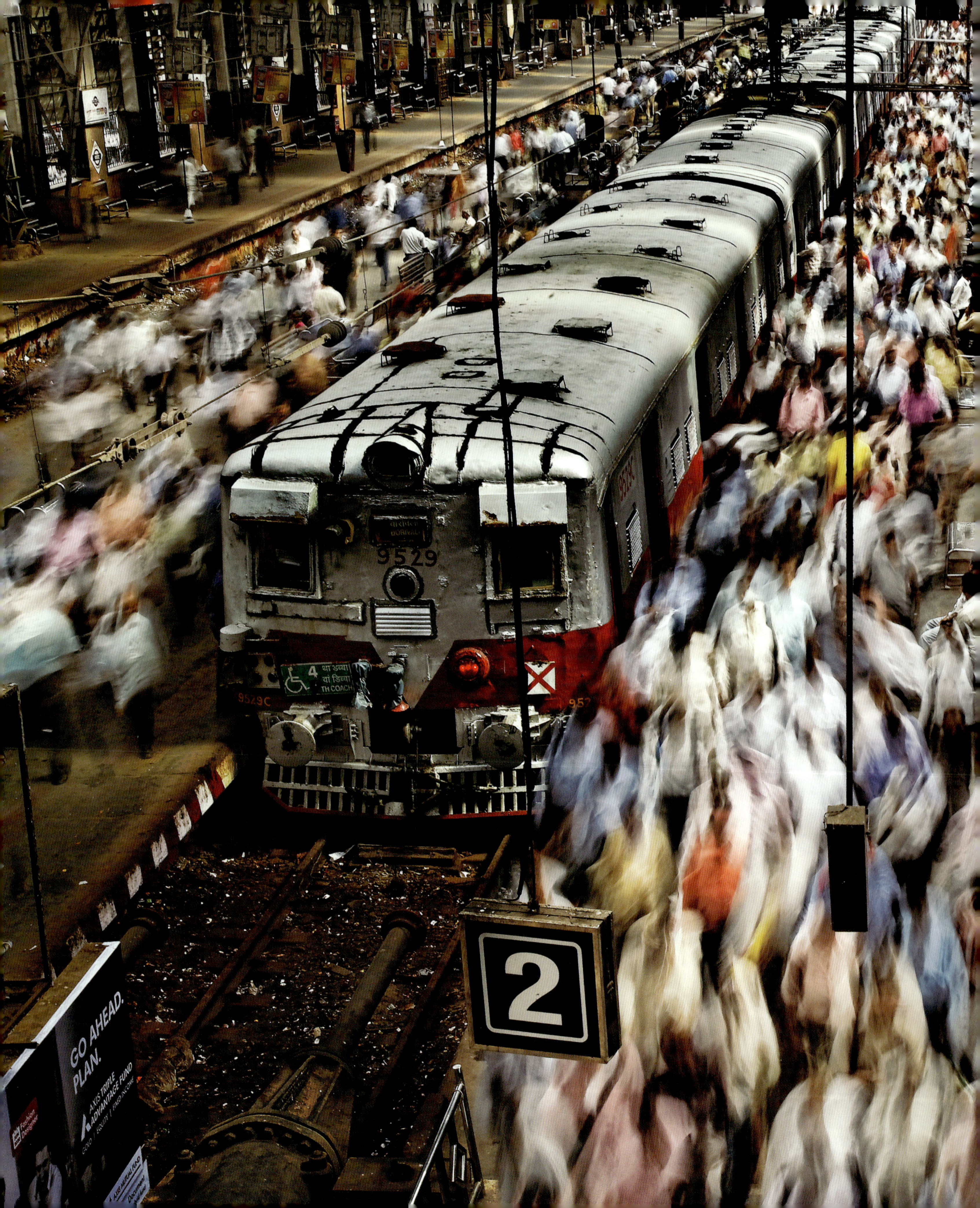
9529
4 था अध्या / था शिक्षा
TH COACH
9529C
2
GO AHEAD.
PLAN.
AXIS TRIPLE
ADVANTAGE FUND

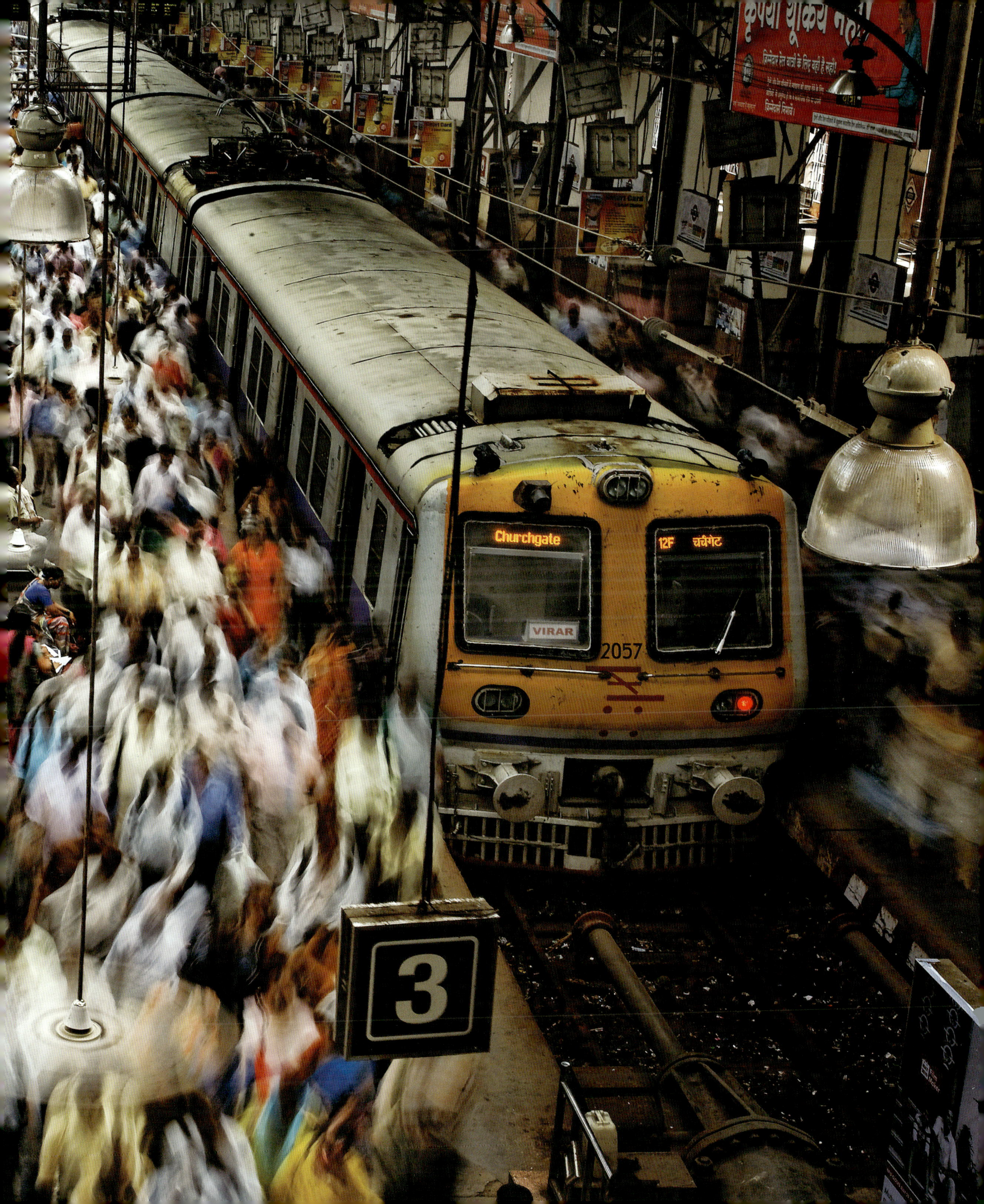

Churchgate
12F चर्चगेट
VIRAR
2057
कृपया रूकचय नल
3

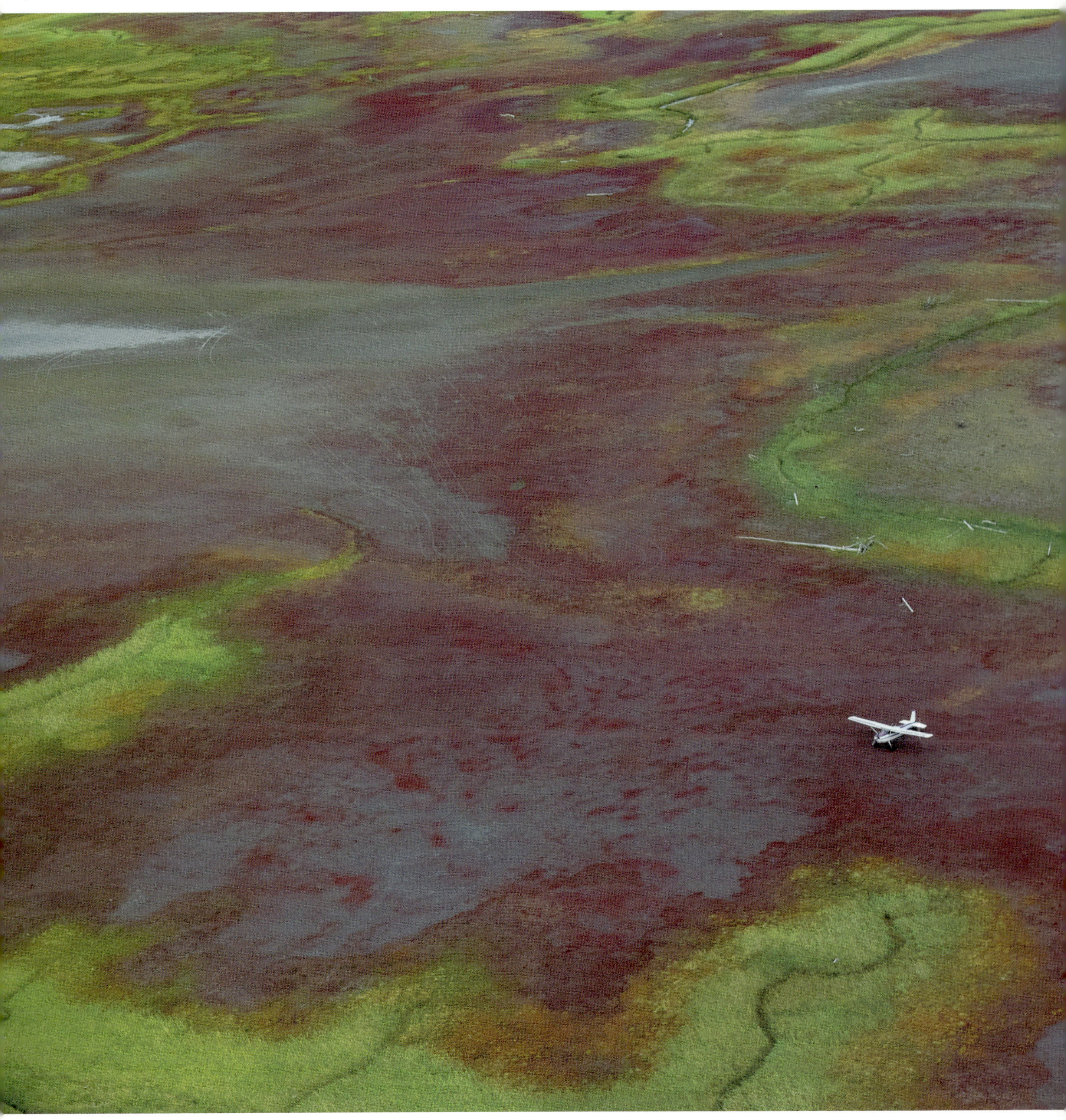

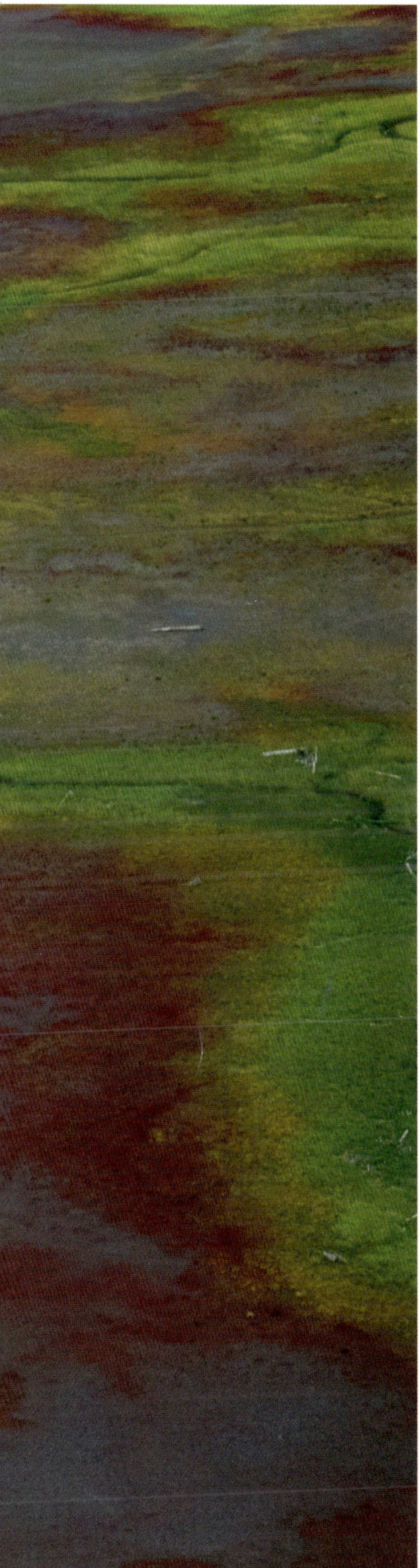

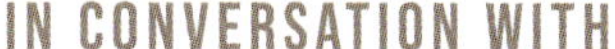

ACACIA JOHNSON

Acacia Johnson is an artist and photographer from Alaska who focuses on the environment, conservation, and the connections between people and place. She has made more than 50 expeditions to the Arctic and Antarctica as a photographer and a guide. Her photographs have been exhibited internationally and are housed in collections at the Anchorage Museum and the Smithsonian National Museum of American History.

JEFFREY KERBY: Has it always felt natural for you to pair photography with perspectives from above?

ACACIA JOHNSON: Definitely. I grew up in Anchorage, Alaska, where vast wilderness is all around us, and many people, including my family, fly small airplanes to get around. We have six times more pilots per capita than anywhere else in the United States. In a little plane over Anchorage, you can see mountains for what seems like eternity.

My parents were wilderness guides before I was born, so growing up, we often tried to get to places in Alaska that were very remote, where we would have these wonderful experiences connecting with the natural world. I chose photography over other mediums because you have to be there in person to take the picture. You have to have the experience. Part of photography for me is going into a place and translating the experience of being there into something that other people can see and feel. I feel very driven to make pictures of this Earth that make people stop and think: *Where's that? What is that?* And I can say: *This is right here. This is our Earth.* That's where a lot of my use of color comes in.

JK: You just said "making" a picture. Is there a difference between taking a picture and making a picture?

AJ: In my mind, there is. I found my voice as a photographer when I started using a 4x5 view camera and color film. The quality of the colors on the 4x5 negatives is dreamy, but it also made me work slowly and thoughtfully, because it's expensive and it takes a long time to set up a picture. I would go on trips to remote places in the north and essentially walk through the landscape until I encountered something I wanted to make into this tangible object, the color negative. It's about creating something with intention, which felt different to me than holding down the shutter on a digital camera that can take 20 frames per second. Now, when I work digitally, I try to hold on to that intentional mindset whenever possible.

JK: Thinking about my very limited experiences in small planes, that's a hard place to be methodical. There's a lot of constraints and overstimulation, and that pushes me into bad habits.

AJ: Oh yeah. That's one area where I've become a chronic overshooter. It's crazy.

ACACIA JOHNSON
A bush plane has landed in the multihued tidal flats along the coast of Alaska's Cook Inlet.

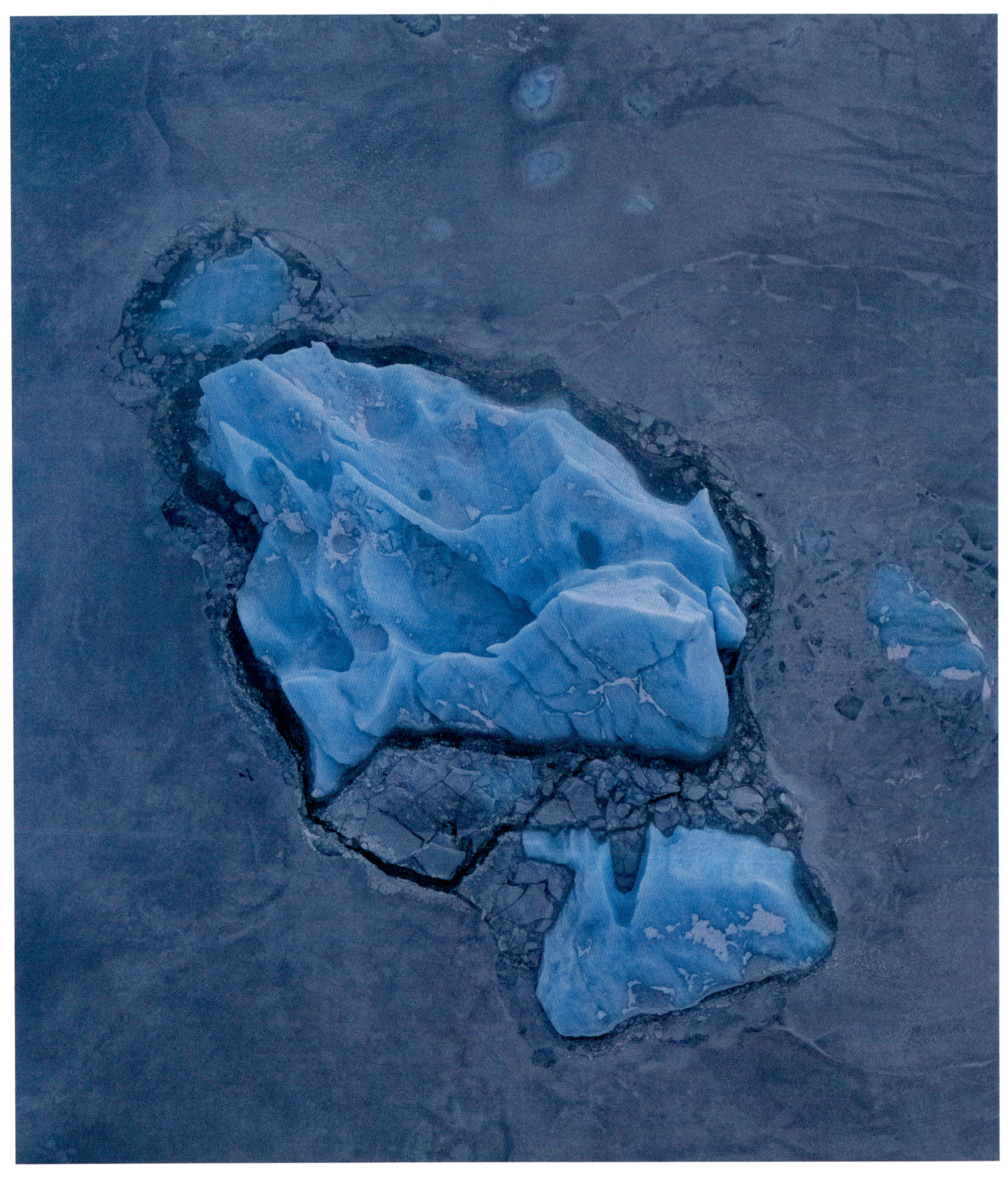

The brilliant blue of a recently calved iceberg differentiates it
from younger pack ice, darker in color.

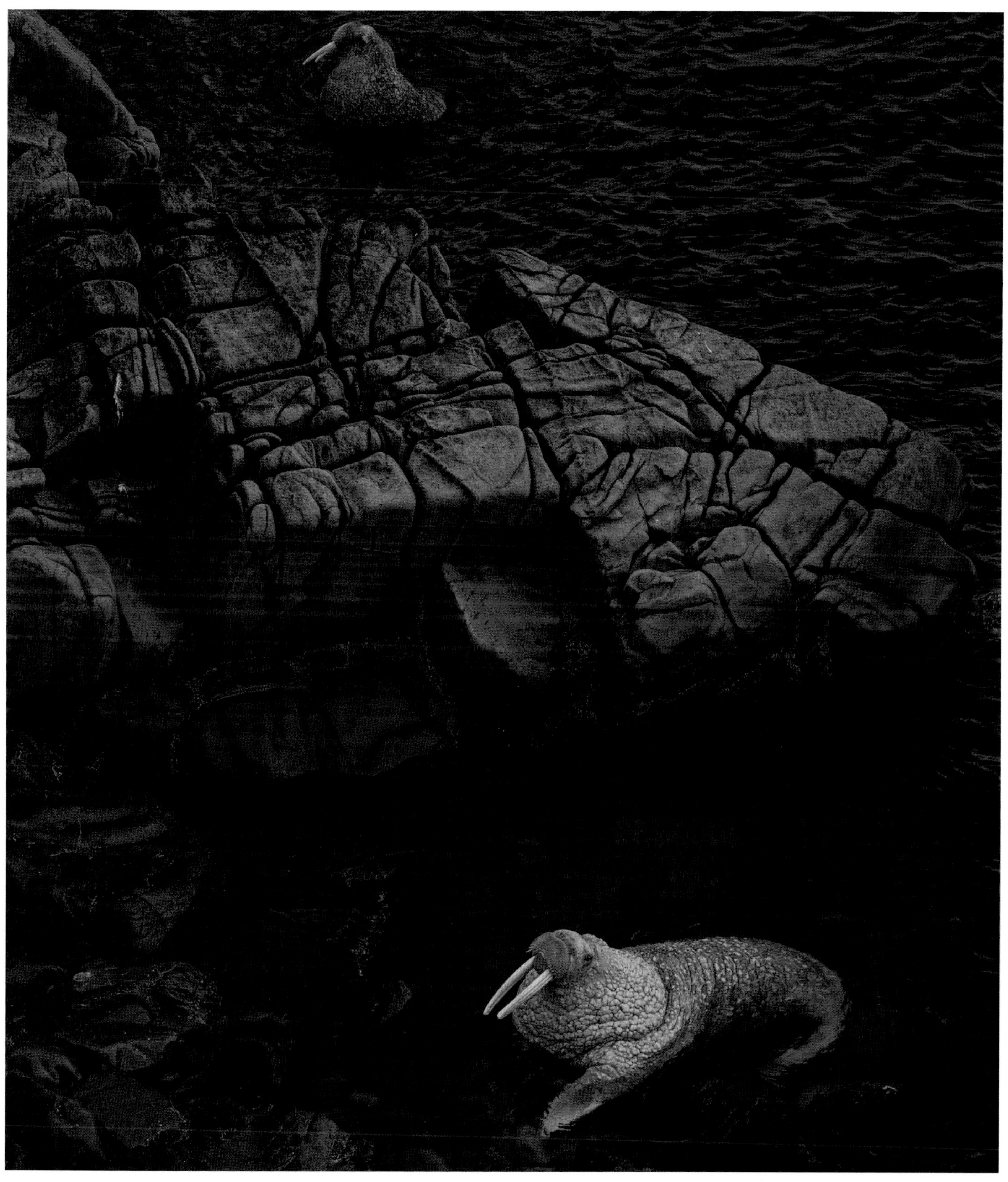

Blood flow during and after a dive into cold waters changes the color of a Pacific walrus,
such as these on Alaska's Round Island, from brown to white to lavender.

JK: So when you're in a plane, what's your process trying to make a photo in that situation?

AJ: What happens first is seeing the picture, something where you have to make a photo. But it's hard in a plane, because typically by the time you have had that moment, you have already passed the image. You have to ask the pilot to turn around and slow down so you can try to frame it up exactly as you perceived it, but it's not always the same. You often end up making several passes, usually with intense wind shuddering the camera, as you're leaning out the window and hoping you've got the frame. It can feel chaotic, but there are also times in the air when I feel deeply focused and connected to what I'm doing.

JK: What's going on in your picture of the Alaskan tundra? Those are some amazing colors. Why does it look like this?

AJ: This is a scene I came upon while out flying. Near Anchorage, the ocean is lined by huge expanses of mudflats created by glacial silt, as well as wetlands. The vegetation turns vivid colors in the late summer and fall. Somebody had landed their plane and was maybe out hunting or enjoying the landscape.

JK: So you can just land in places like this? Is that a runway?

AJ: No, it's not! A lot of the small planes in Alaska are equipped with extra-large tires called tundra tires to be able to land on natural surfaces. If you look toward the upper left quarter of the picture, you can see tracks where people have landed before. That's a good indicator that the ground there has been a safe consistency to land on. In the winter, a lot of people put their planes on skis to land on snow and ice.

JK: Would you say your work has given you a unique perspective on the color of winter?

AJ: You could say winter is every color. Living in northerly places, it's the time of year when everything is covered in snow, and when the weather is clear, the soft pastel light around sunrise and sunset lingers for a long time. The whole landscape just glows when that light reflects off the snow. The most pervasive color, I would say, is twilight dark blue, like the color of snow in shadow.

JK: How do you capture the feeling of that color in a picture?

AJ: I love dark pictures, which is funny to some people because I'm really not a dark person. But I'll go out when it's almost totally dark. To me, that's kind of the magic hour, or the blue hour, when I think things start looking different. If you go out right at twilight, things like flowers start to glow, and even the inanimate world takes on this otherworldly quality.

JK: Your walrus photo didn't have the colors that I expected, either. Why is this walrus pink?

AJ: Walruses have evolved to fill such a specific ecological niche, they can seem almost too weird to be real! They spend a lot of time in cold waters feeding on the seafloor, and during these long feeding forays, they conserve body heat by limiting blood flow to their exterior. When that happens, they can appear pale pink, lavender, or almost white. Looking down at them from above, I thought they looked like creatures from the moon. They're very dancerly and graceful, the way they move in the water, which I think is hard to appreciate from a ground perspective.

After the walruses come ashore and warm up, they need to regulate their body heat once again, so their blood flows to their skin to cool them down, and they turn this rosy sunburn color. They're unbelievably insulated animals. Their skin alone can be four inches

(10 cm) thick in places, not to mention their blubber, so they really need to cool down when they get on shore.

JK: How do you capture these photos? Do the walruses mind you being there?

AJ: Walruses are huge animals, but they're very sensitive to disturbance. They don't have very good eyesight, and they haul out in groups of hundreds or thousands. And if one gets spooked, they can all freak out and stampede into the water and crush each other in the process. The Walrus Islands State Game Sanctuary in Alaska has a public viewing program where you can sit up on these bluffs overlooking the haulouts for hours, so we just sat hidden in the tall grass and watched the walruses come and go. Eventually, the light would change and everything would line up for a perfect photo.

JK: How did you get that picture of the bear on the rock?

AJ: The cool thing about Alaska is there are many places where bears haven't learned to associate humans with danger, so there are places where you can go and, in a guided context, be close to bears in the wild. Growing up, we'd go to places where the bears reminded me of cows, lumbering around in meadows and munching on sedge grass. They're very dignified and intelligent animals. I became very comfortable around bears, so I hope some of my stories can challenge the stereotypes of bears being inherently dangerous.

When I took this photo in particular, I was actually having a hard day. I was standing on a tourist boardwalk at Brooks Falls, where people watch bears catch salmon that are jumping up a waterfall. It was crowded with people and cameras. I was struggling with burnout after a major project, and on top of that, it was pouring rain. I was not having it. But I looked away from the waterfall, down the river, where this blond bear was just glowing out of the forest. It was a gift. I pulled my camera out of my bag and took the photo, there among all the tourists. It was a reminder to me that you don't need to have it all together to make the best pictures, or have unusual access, or even be feeling good. You just have to be ready and receptive.

JK: It looks like a studio setup!

AJ: It's hardly edited at all. It's truly one of the more fortunate photographic moments I've had so far. It just fell out of the sky.

JK: How do you think the overhead perspective of your images has affected you, personally?

AJ: When I view the world from the air, I start to understand the patterns in which the natural world fits together. Many of the patterns in the landscape are similar to those inside of our bodies. For example, river deltas follow in a similar pattern as our blood veins, and if you've ever gone scuba diving, you can recognize the same pattern the waves make on the seafloor, magnified at a large scale in the shape of the landscape itself. It's wild. It makes you realize that everything is connected. It really changes the way you see things.

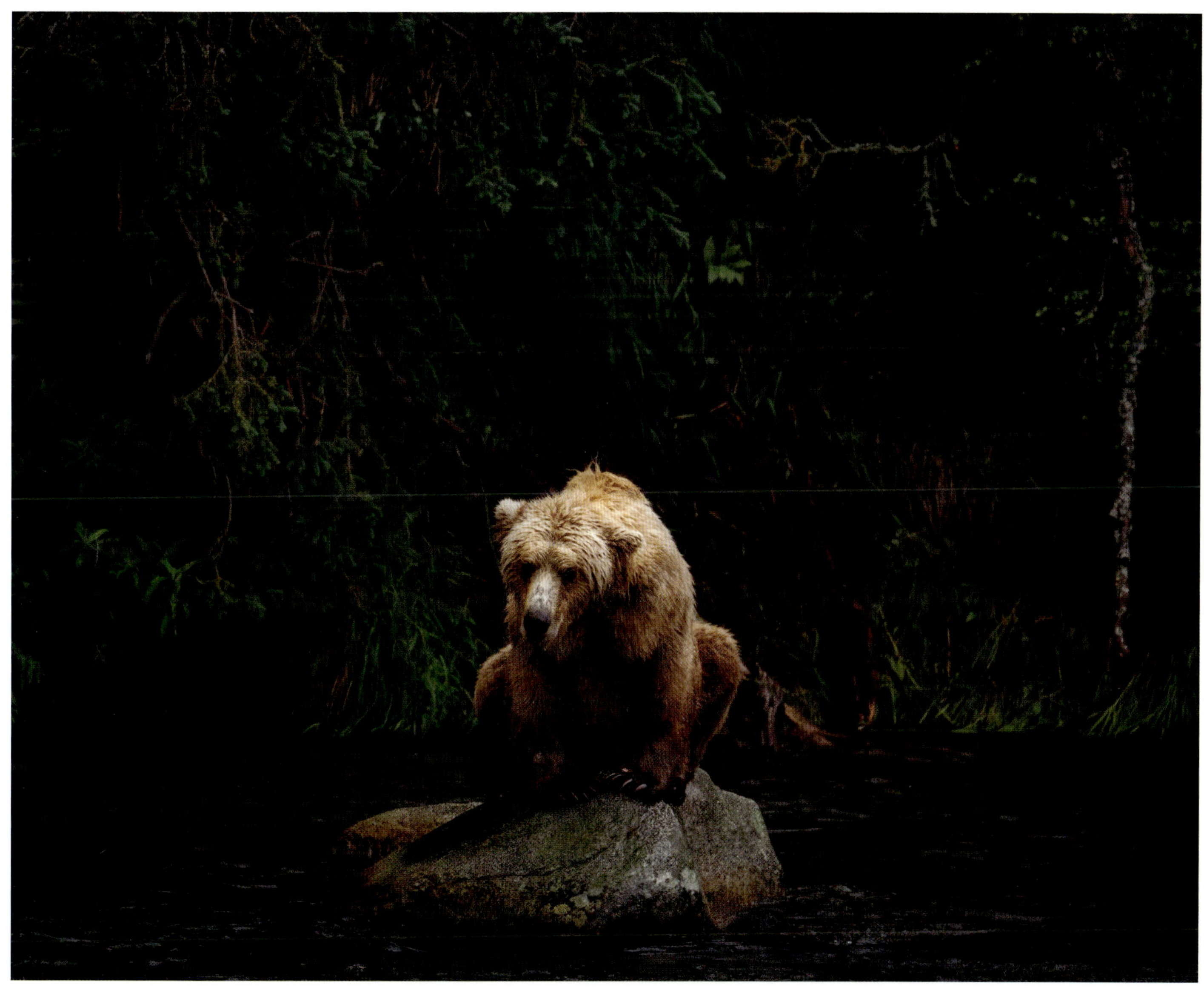

ACACIA JOHNSON
A ray of light illuminates a drenched grizzly bear as it hungrily monitors the salmon run in Alaska's Katmai National Park.

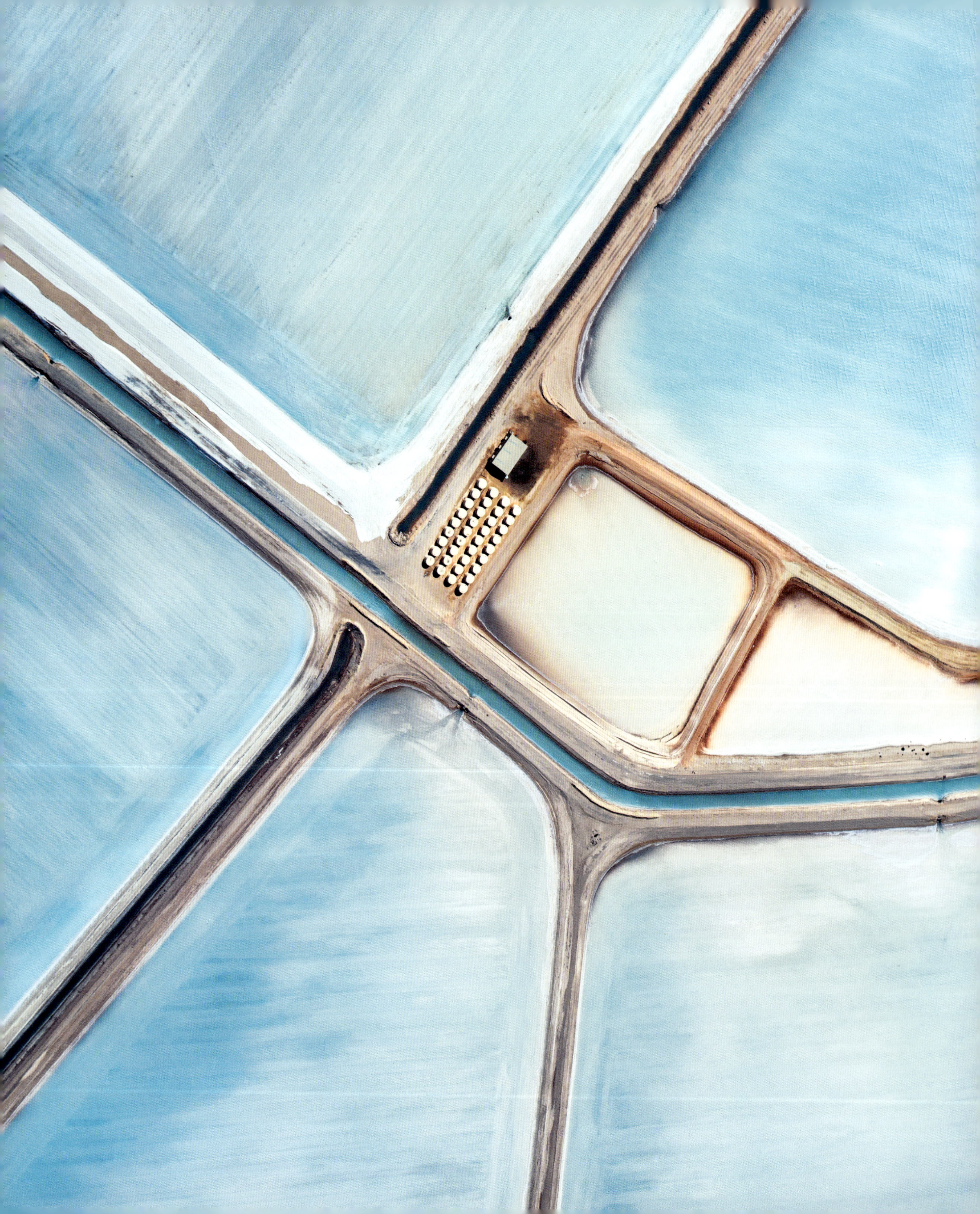

CHAPTER TWO

SHAPE

My noble friend,
geometry will draw
the soul towards truth,
and create the spirit
of philosophy ...

~PLATO, *THE REPUBLIC*

When the full aerial view of Yankicha Island (pages 110–11) emerged on my drone screen, my first thought was, *Surely that can't be real!* Then I vomited. The deck of a boat at dawn is just the right place to deal with the aftermath of seasickness while also getting the shot.

Nestled in a remote island chain off the east coast of Russia, this emerald ring of mountainous rock looks more like a James Bond villain's hideaway than a landscape formed by nature. The shape of this island fascinated me because it defied explanation—I'd truly never seen anything like it. Ask a geologist and this same shape may interest her for the opposite reasons; it's so obviously a collapsed and flooded volcano it could be in a textbook. We didn't have any geologists on this trip, but fortunately Vladimir Burkanov, a marine mammal biologist who has worked in this region for decades, was able to explain the histories of all the strangely shaped islands in this archipelago, even when the islands were covered with animals (pages 152–53). But the power of interesting or strange shapes in a landscape doesn't diminish with an explanation.

Intuitively our brains feel that straight lines indicate some sort of human creation, whereas squiggles or blobs are perhaps more expected in nature than in the middle of Manhattan. But with this intuition comes an opportunity for photographers to confound, challenge, or soothe by presenting shapes in or out of context.

In this chapter, we see photographers who find shapes through the perspectives of drones, microscopes, and more. Or they simply create shapes by combining shadows, perspective, and framing to provoke, amuse, or inspire.

Kacper Kowalski uses his training as an architect and his skills on a paraglider to contrast boxy vehicles with circular river ice pancakes in Poland (pages 100–101). Acacia Johnson turns her gaze downward to capture how dark seaweed melts its own shape into sea ice by absorbing more of the sun's heat than its surroundings (pages 108–109). Kateryna Polishchuk mixes shadows, timing, and the strong lines of organized sport to freeze a moment, and in so doing, our attention (pages 156–57).

In all of these images, shapes lead us to find a story in photos of the world below us. What other stories can you find? ▪

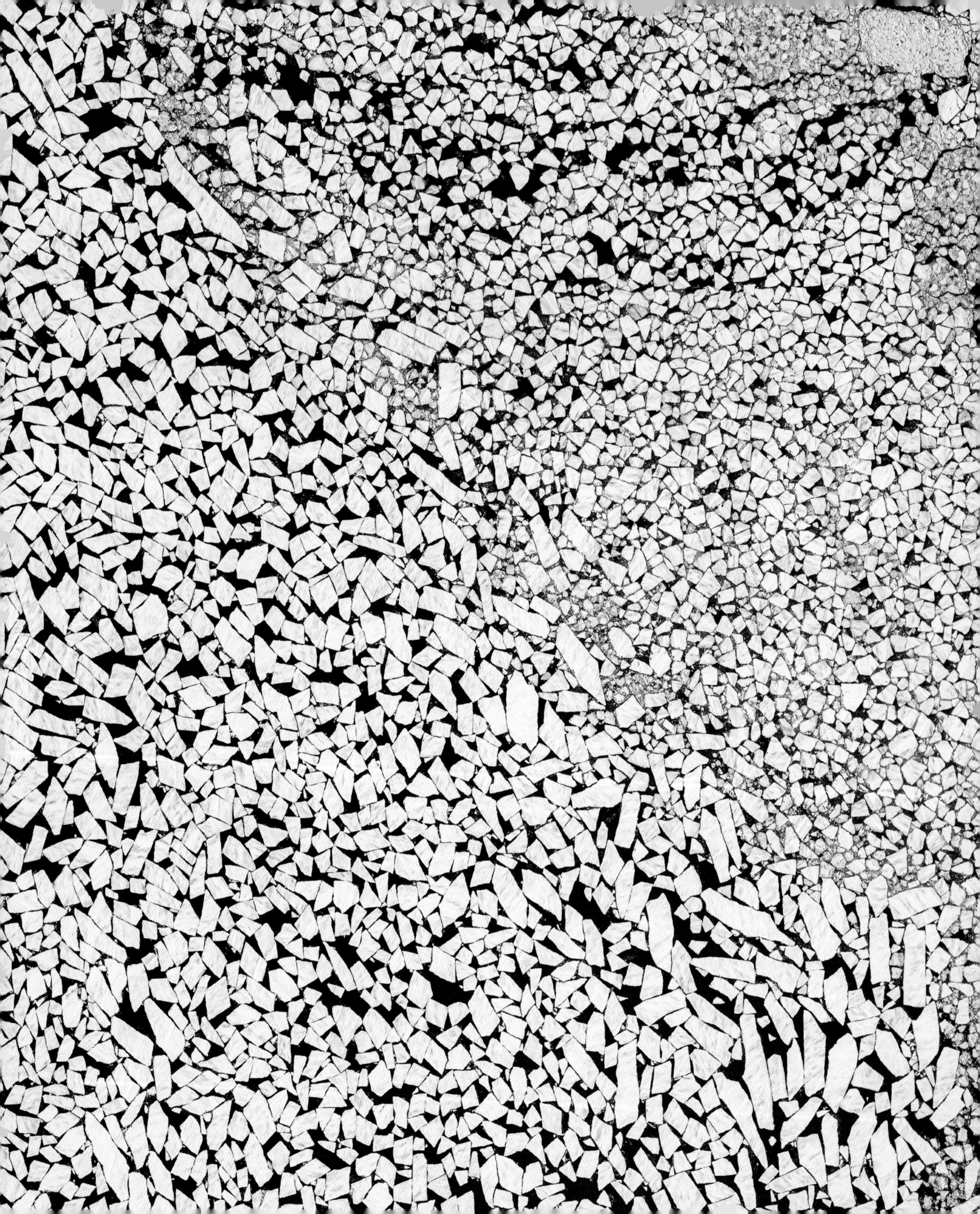

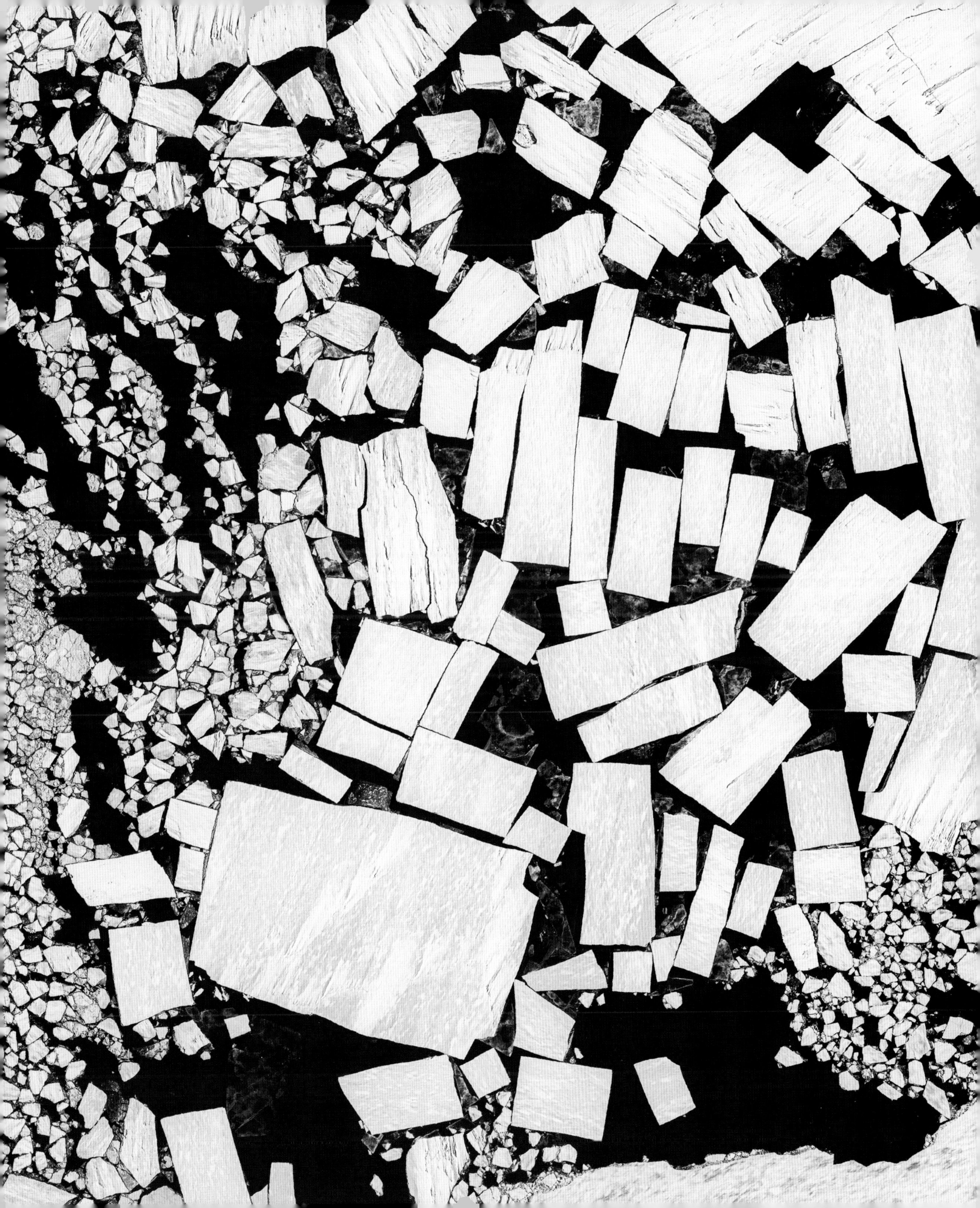

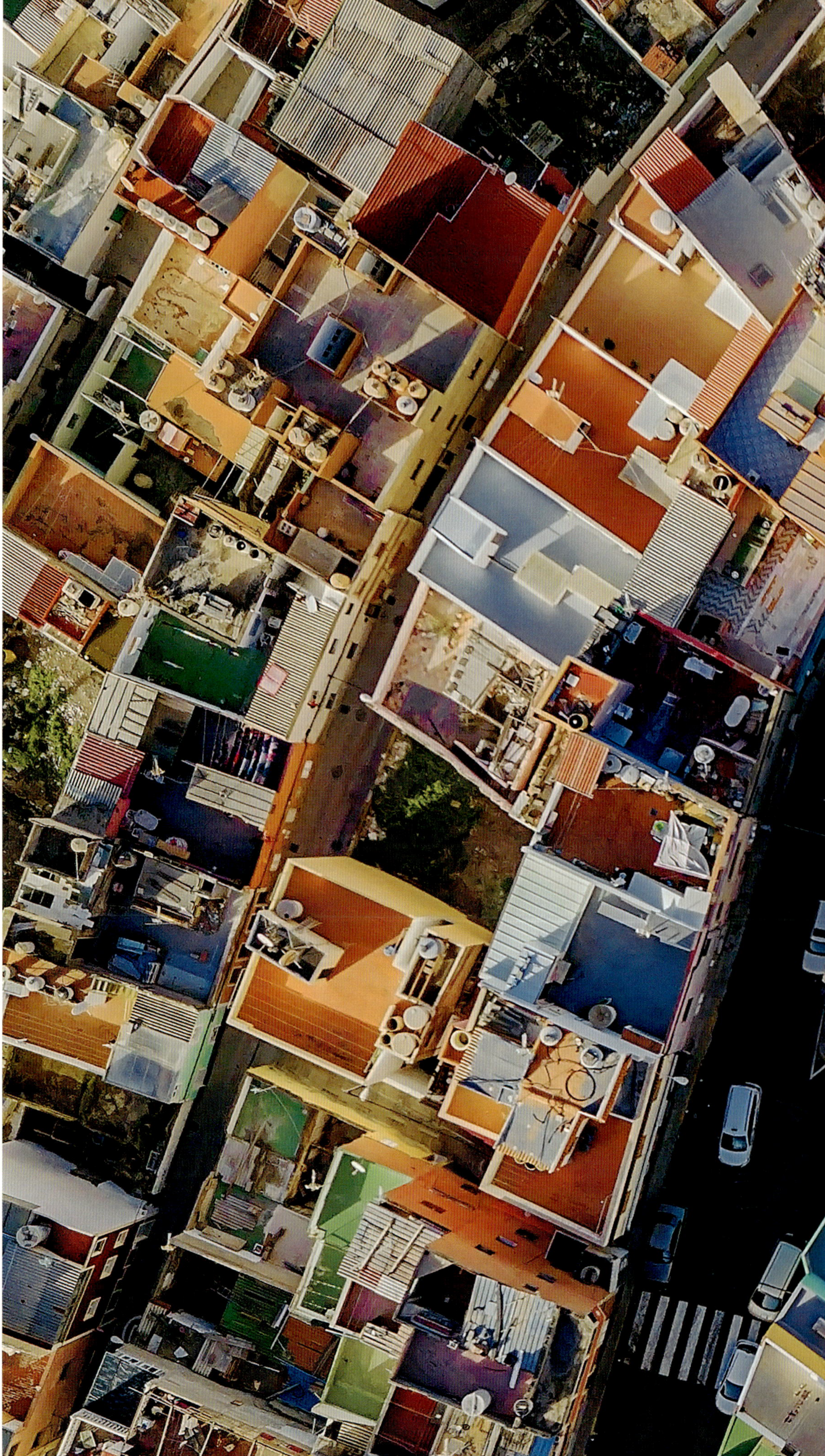

SÉBASTIEN NAGY
Looking down at life in Las
Palmas de Gran Canaria, largest
city of the Canary Islands

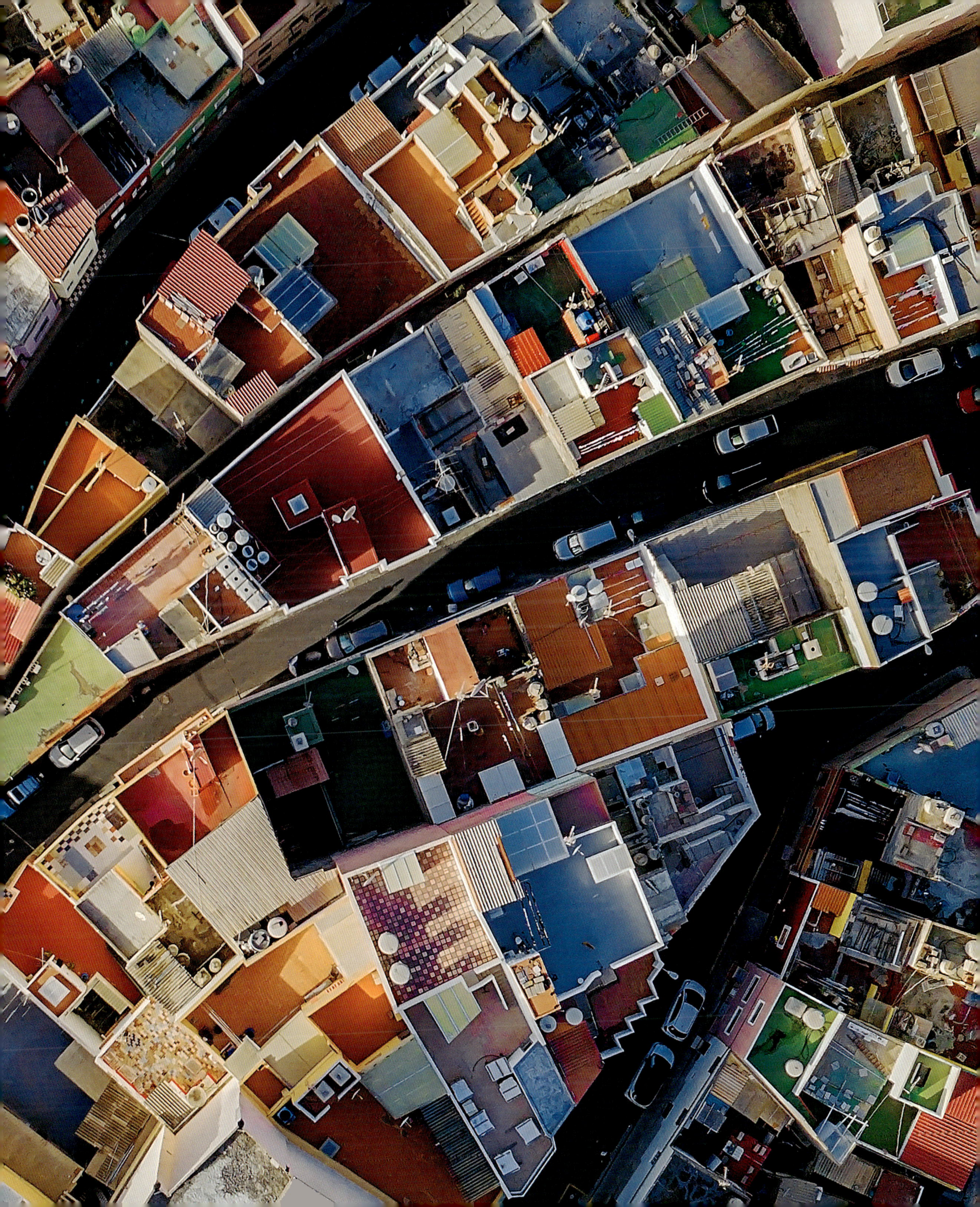

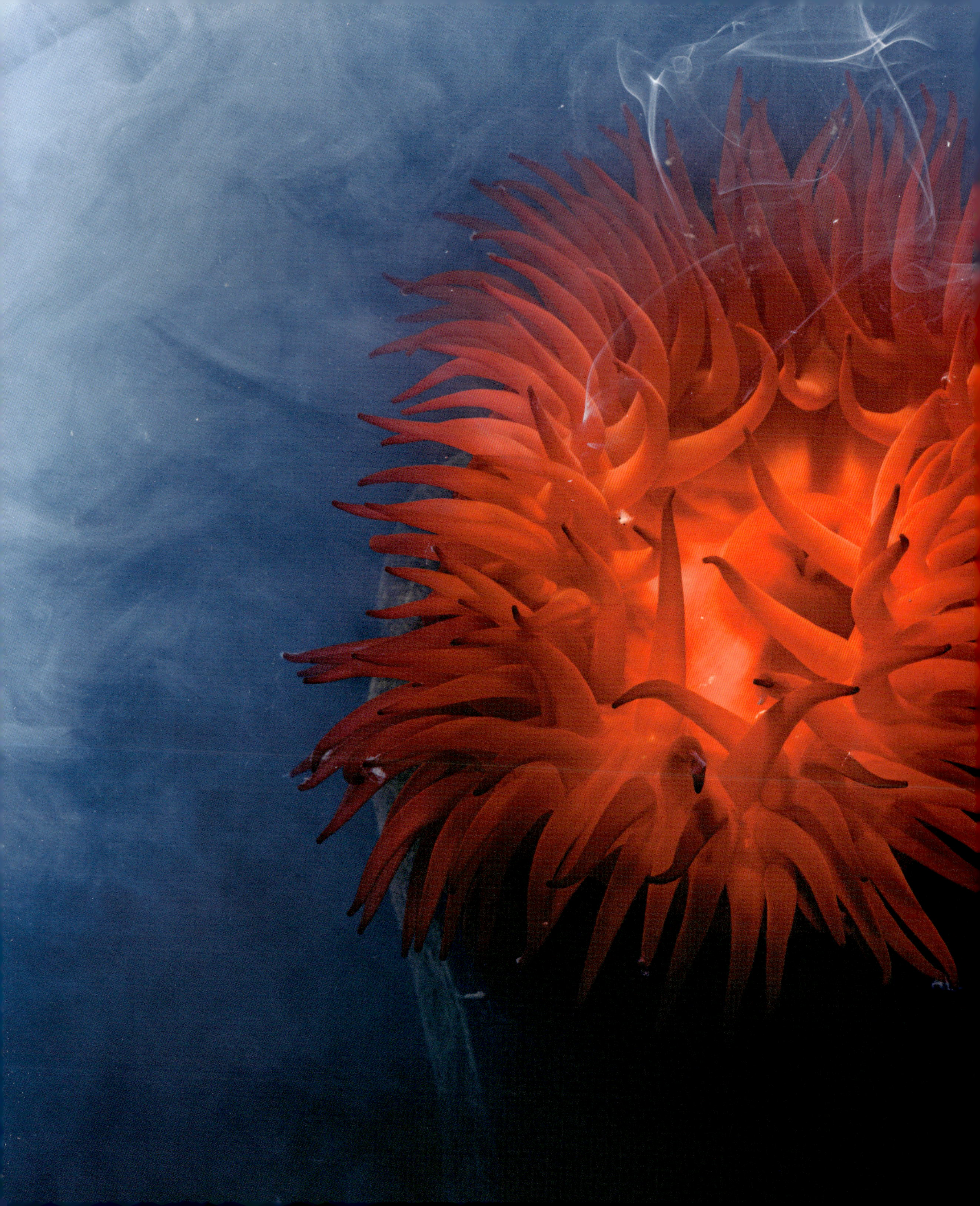

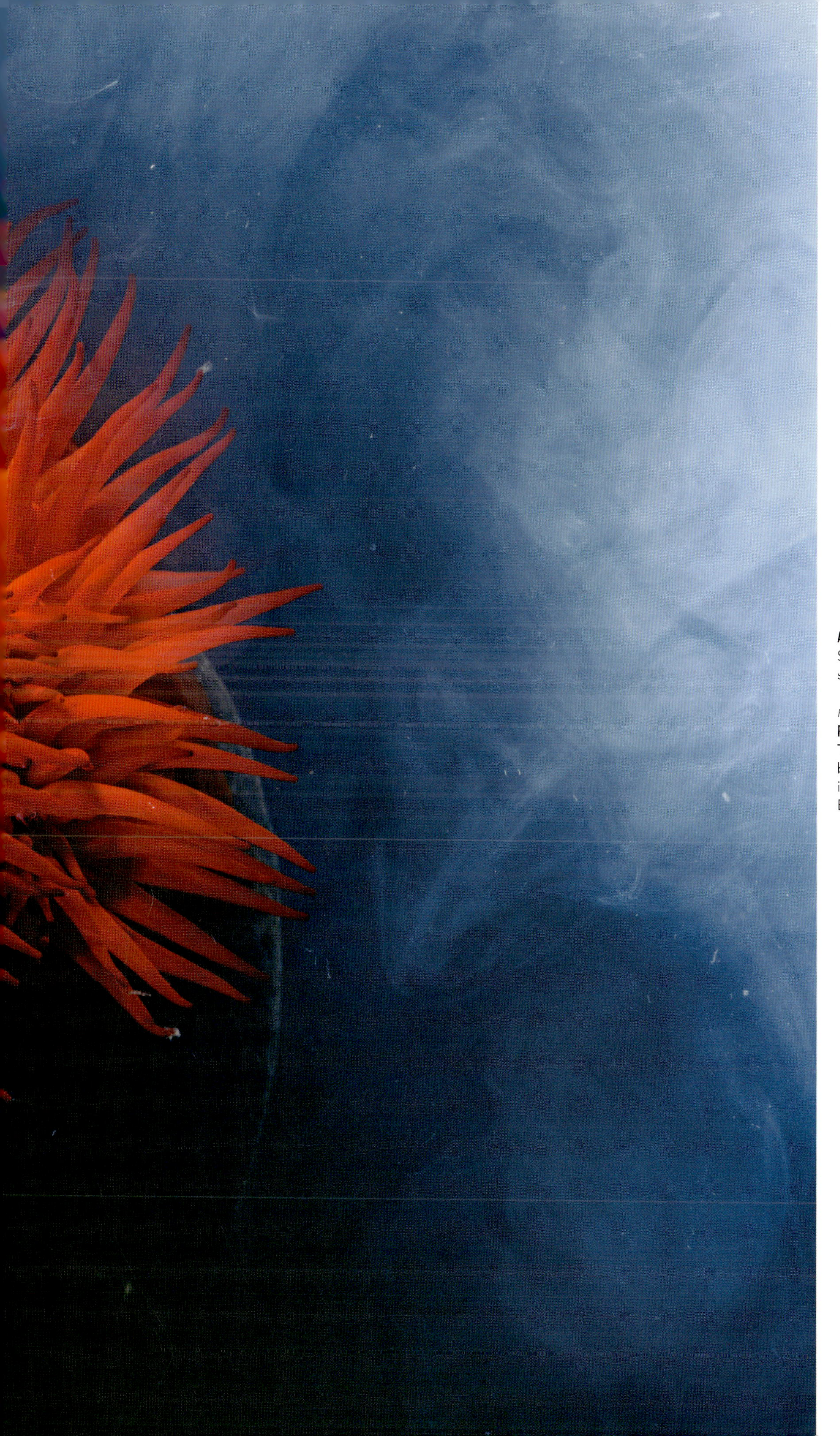

ANGEL FITOR
Sperm wafts from a laboratory
specimen of a beadlet anemone.

Following pages:
REUBEN WU
The path of a drone creates
brilliant angles that reveal the
intricate natural shapes of
Bolivia's vast salt flats.

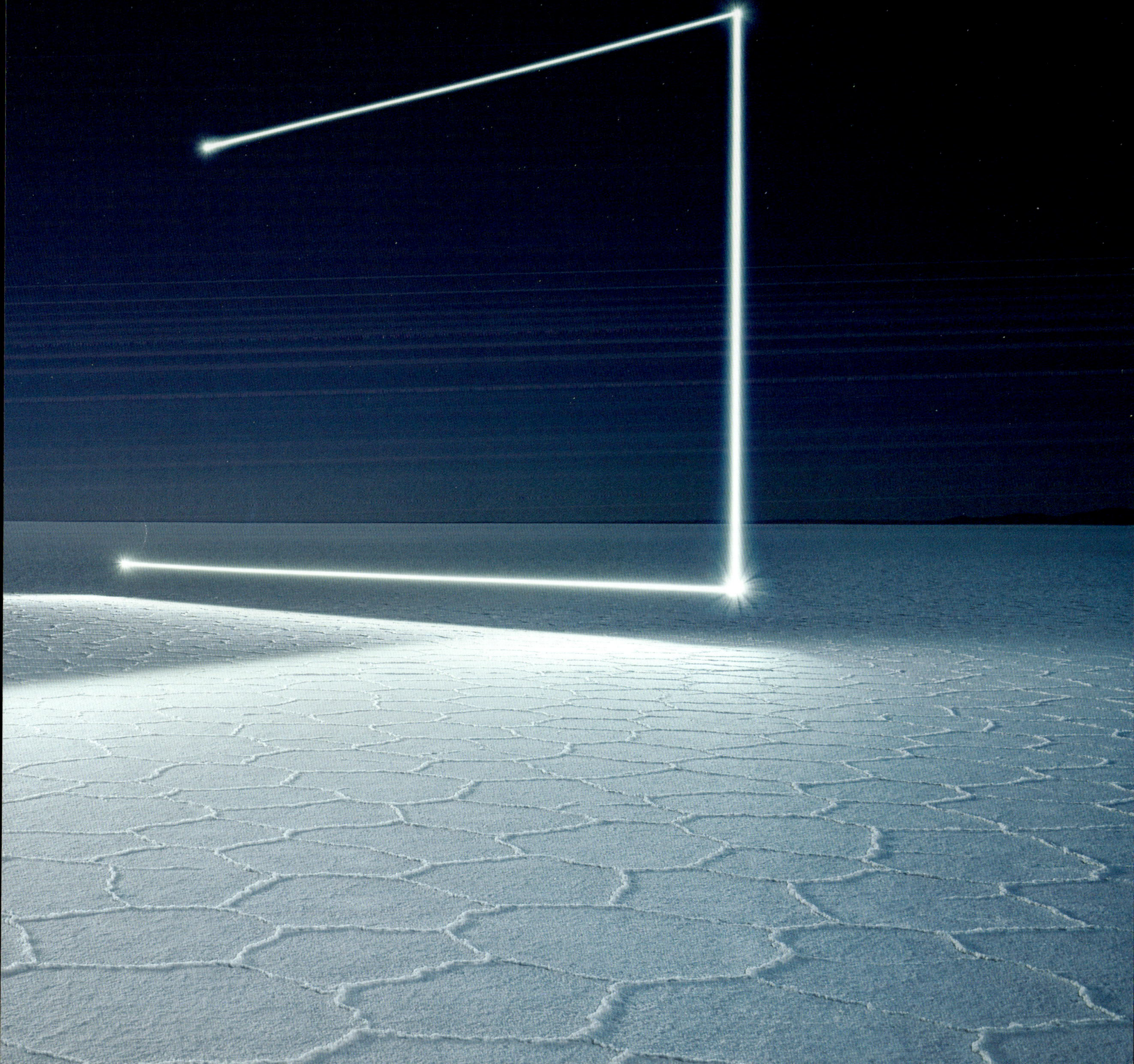

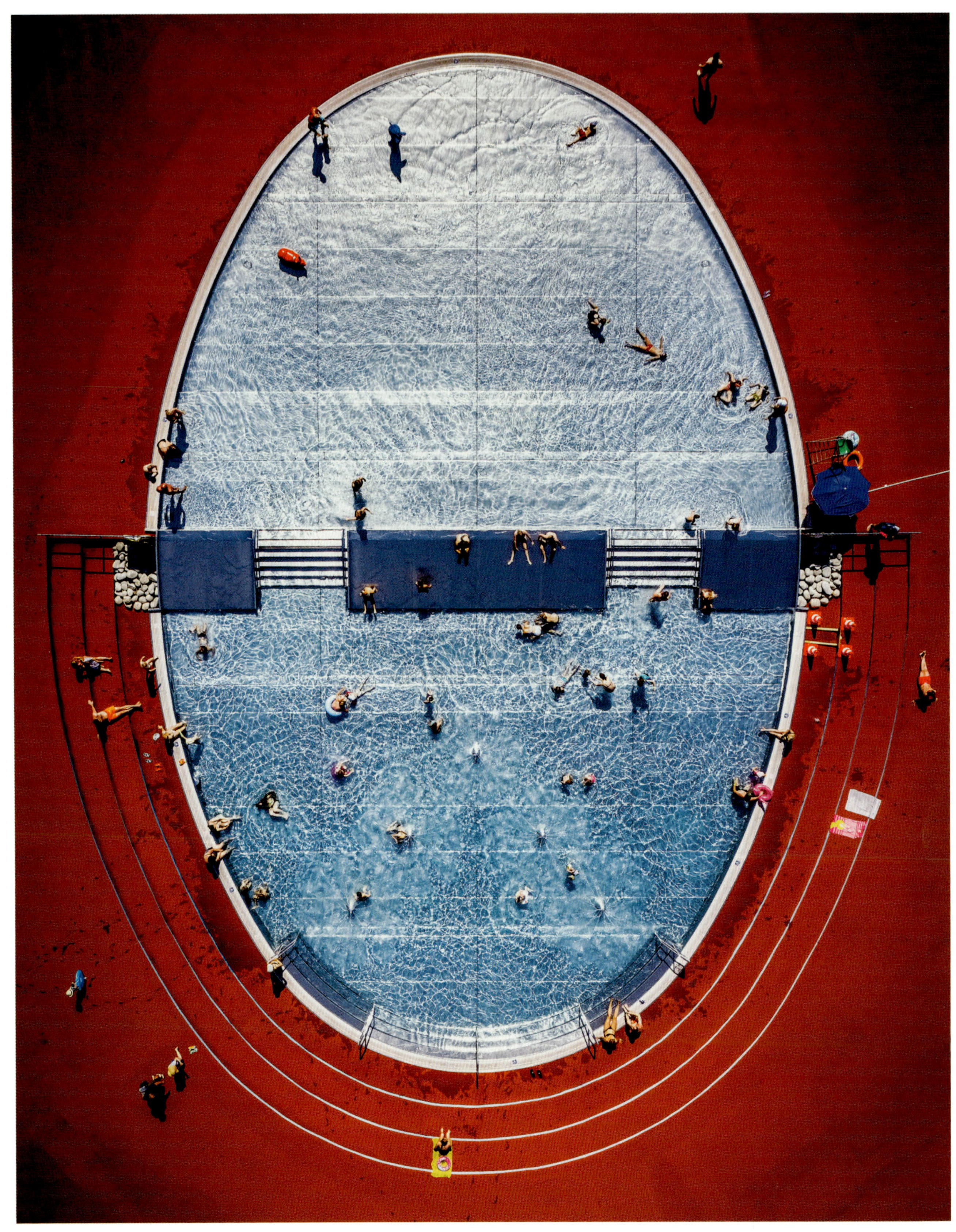

MARCIN GIBA
Swimmers frolic in an oval-shaped pool in Rybnik, Poland.

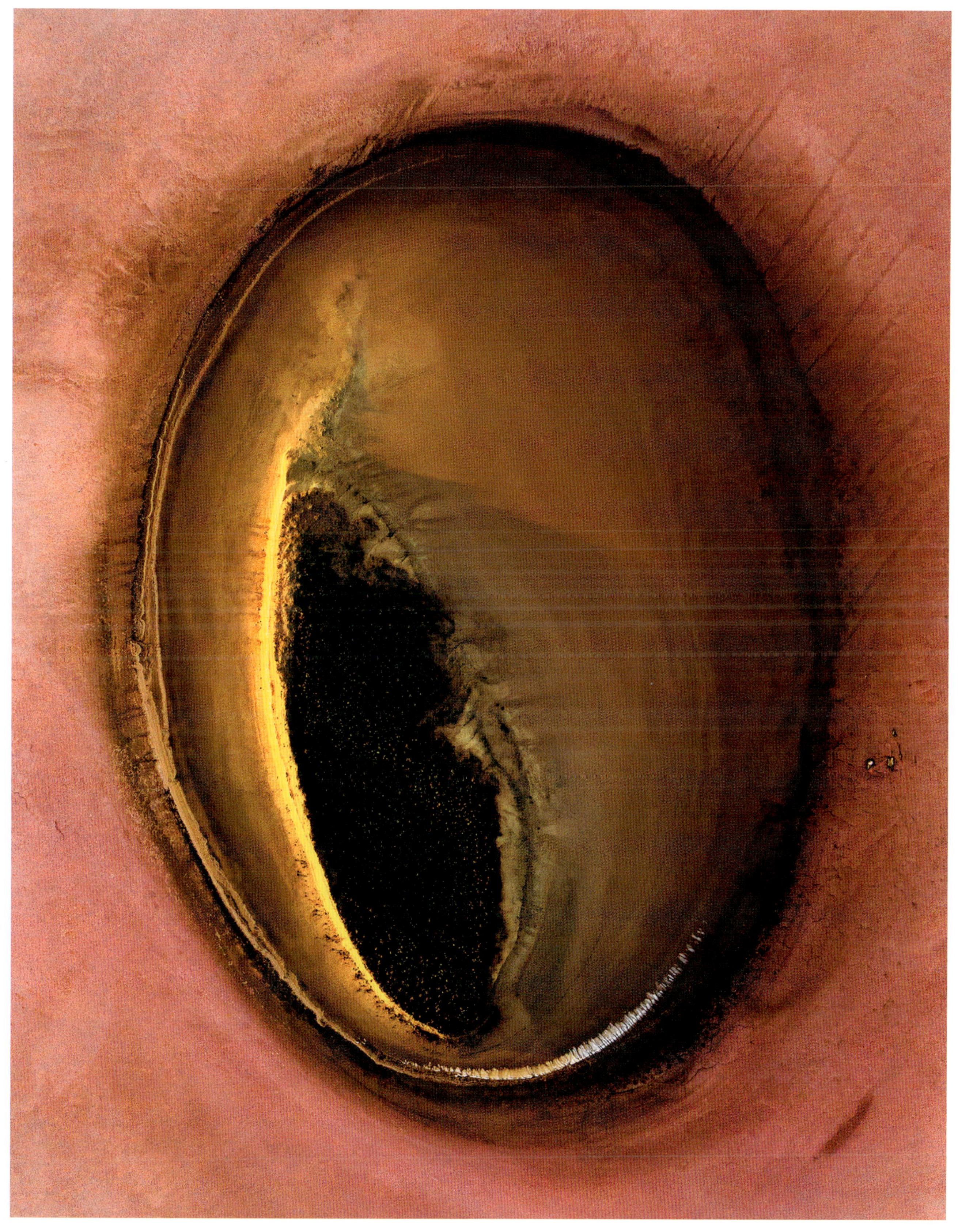

JIM PICÔT
A pink salt lake in Victoria, Australia

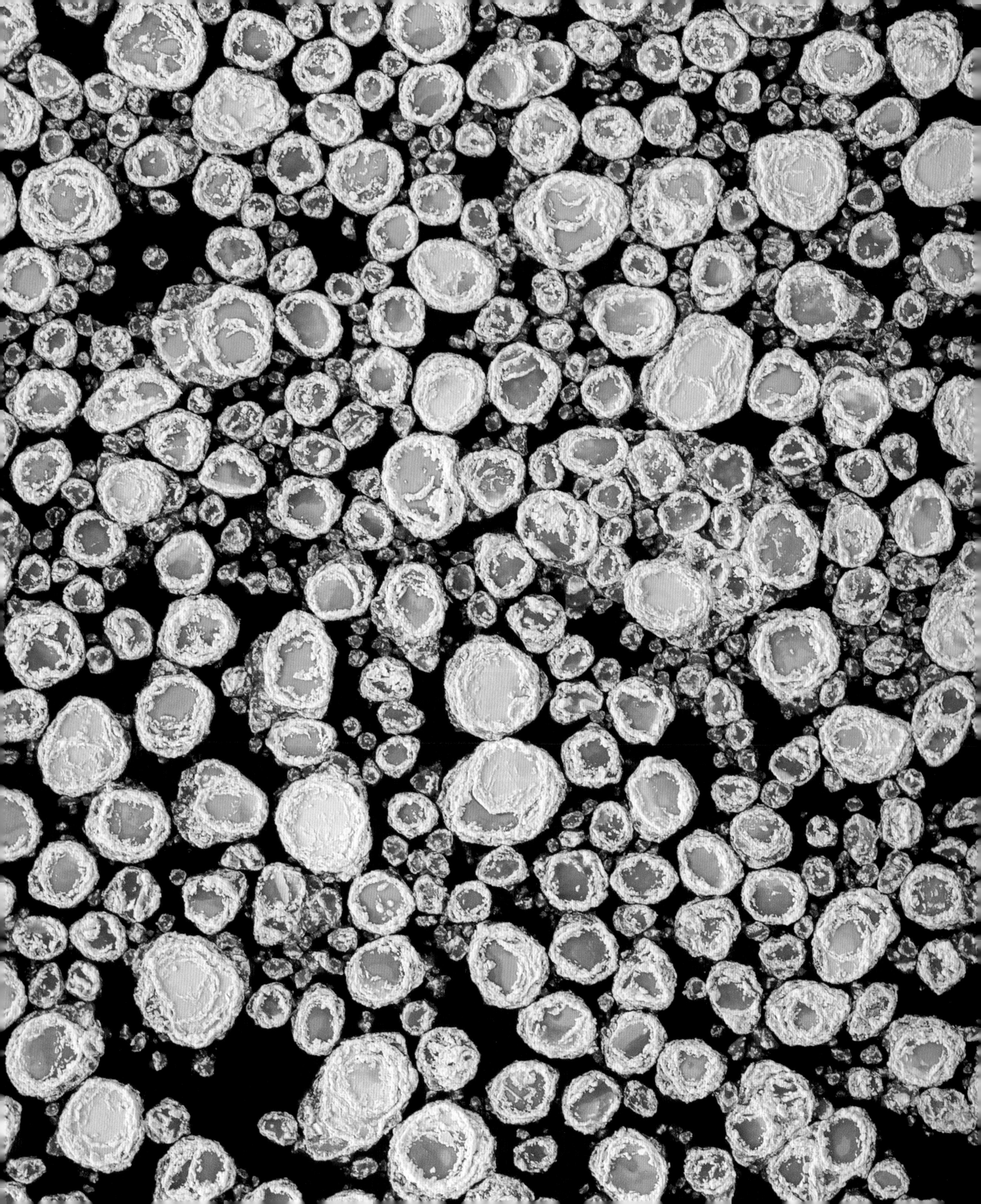

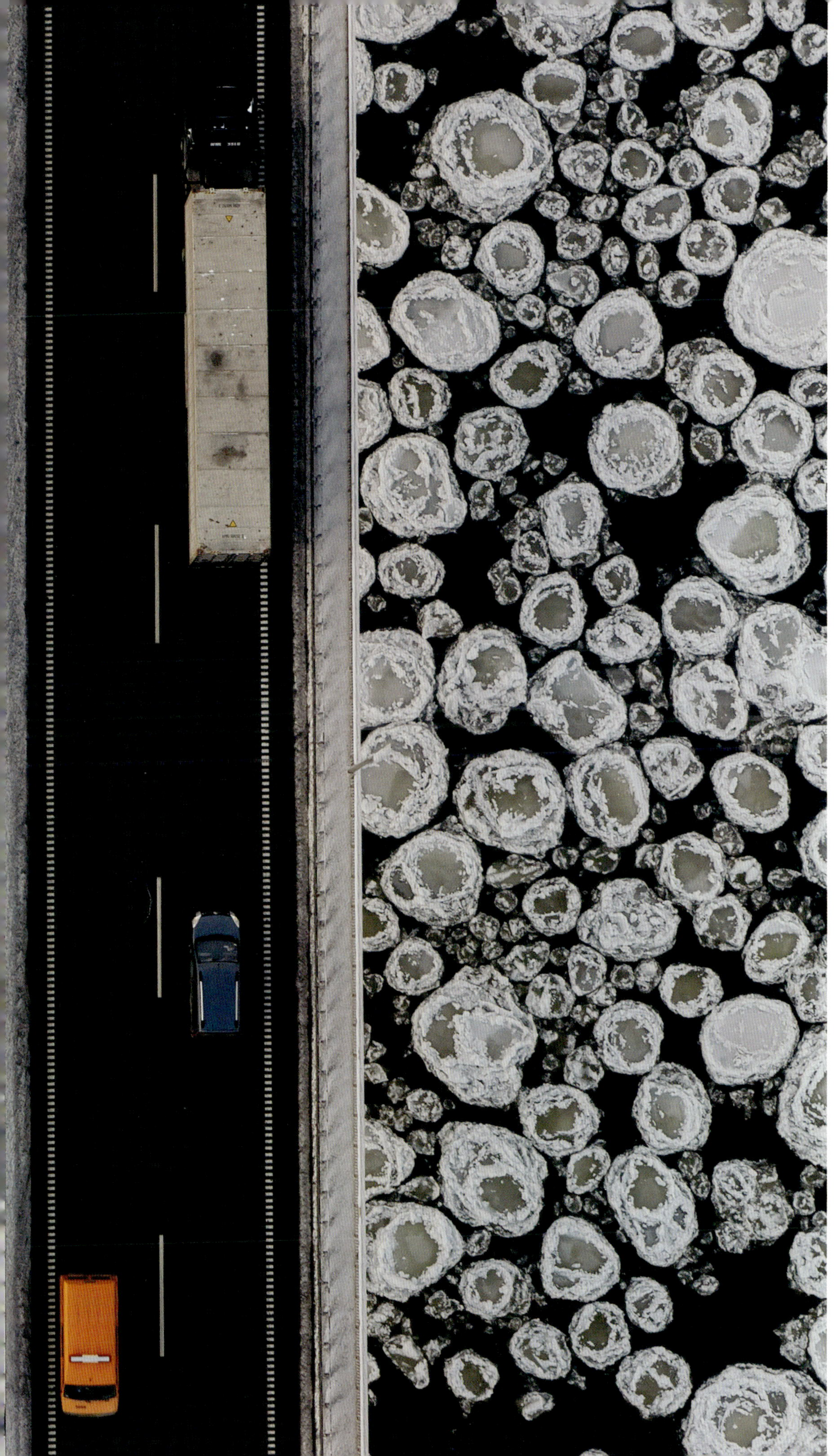

Traffic whizzes over the ice-covered Vistula River near Kiezmark, Poland.

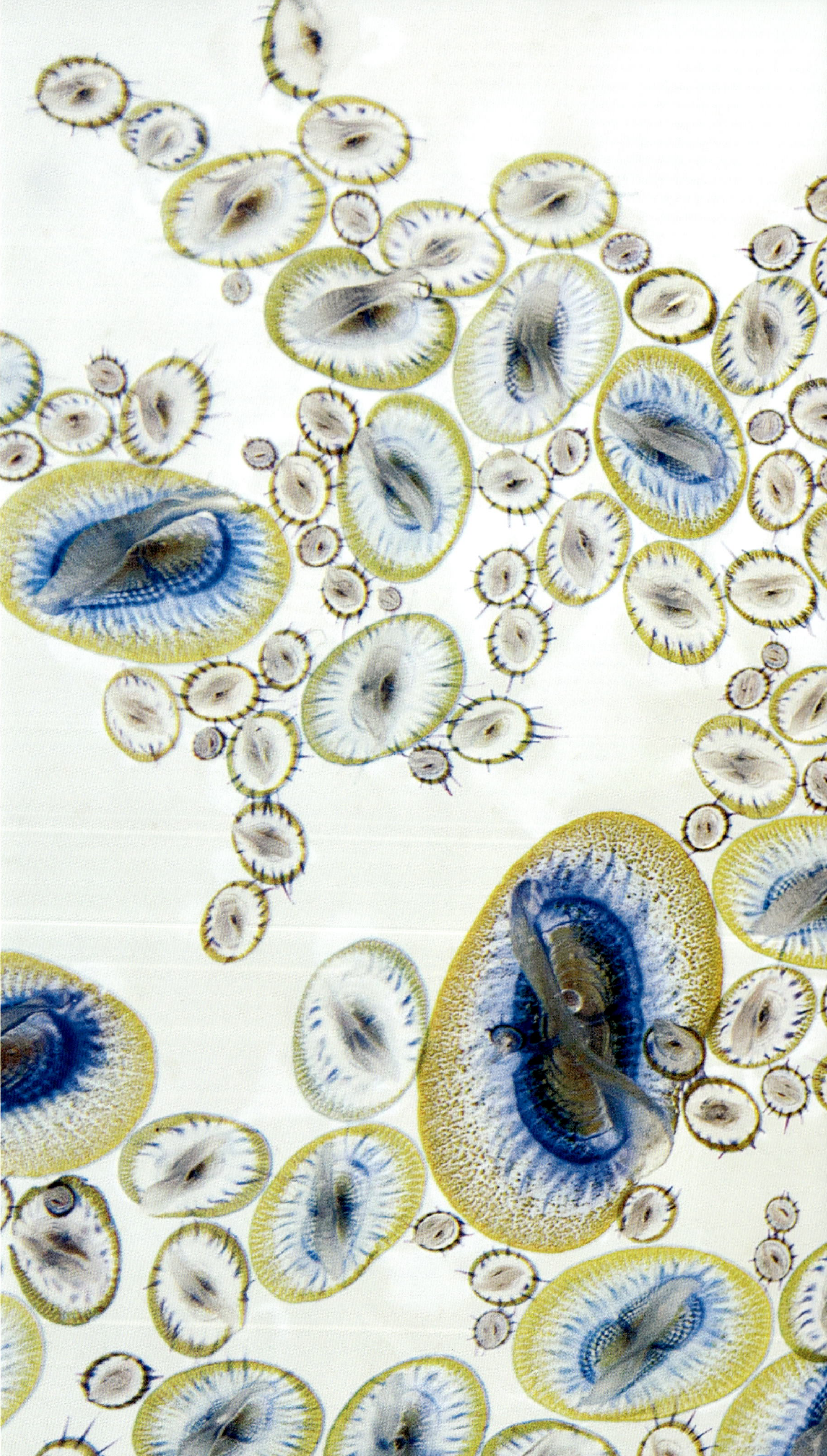

JODI FREDIANI
Gaze down into a bucketful of jellyfish, called by-the-wind sailors for their delicate vertical membranes.

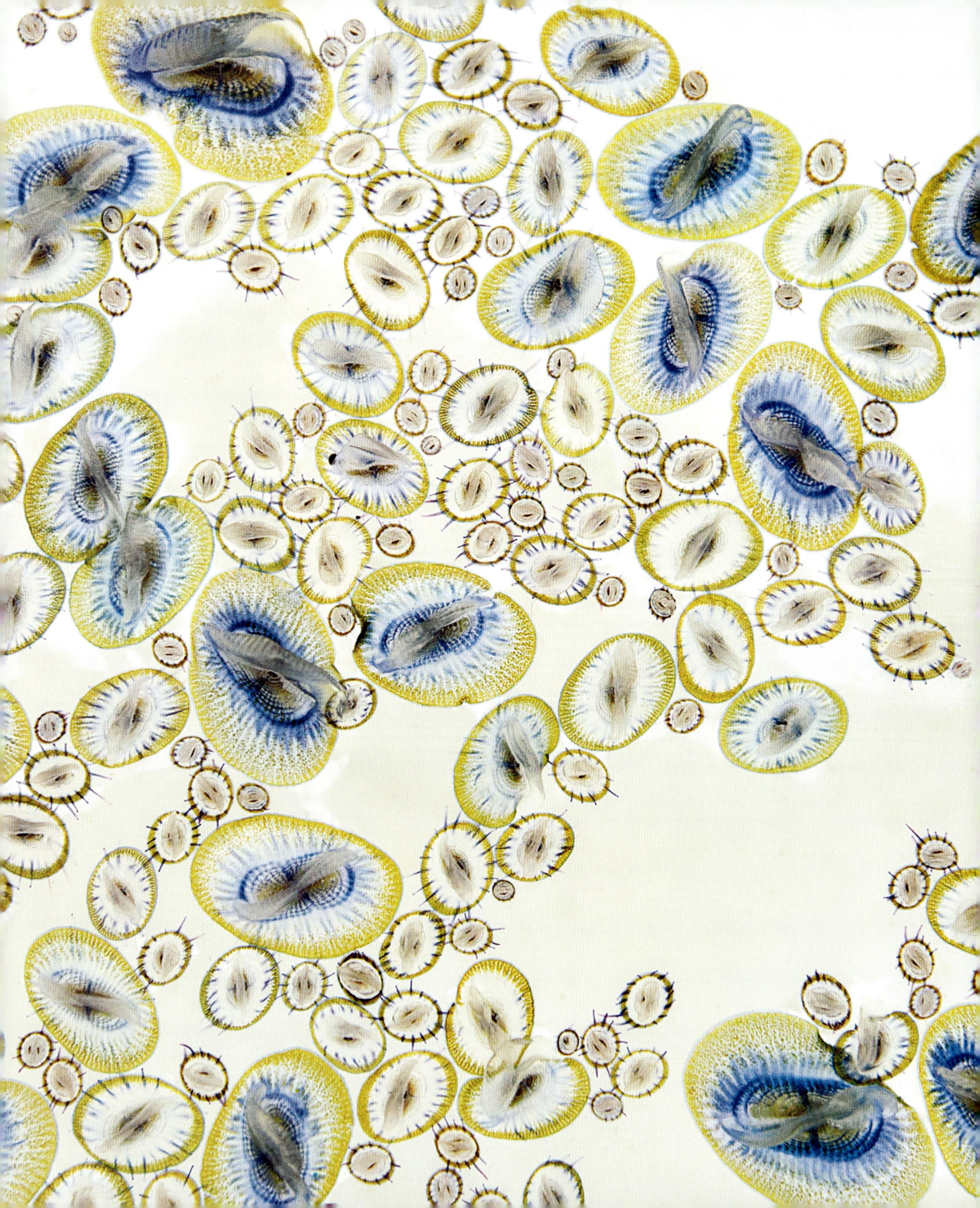

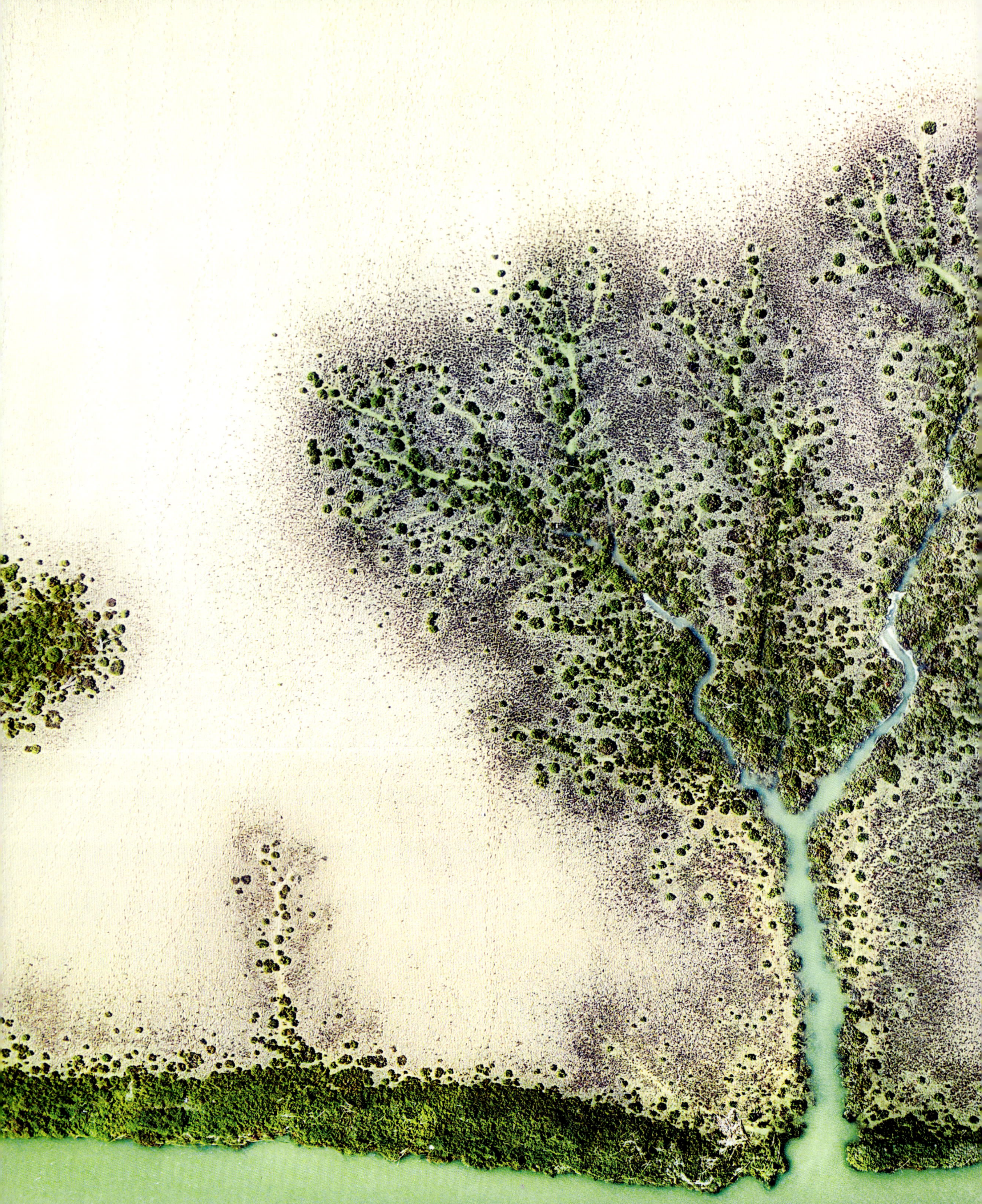

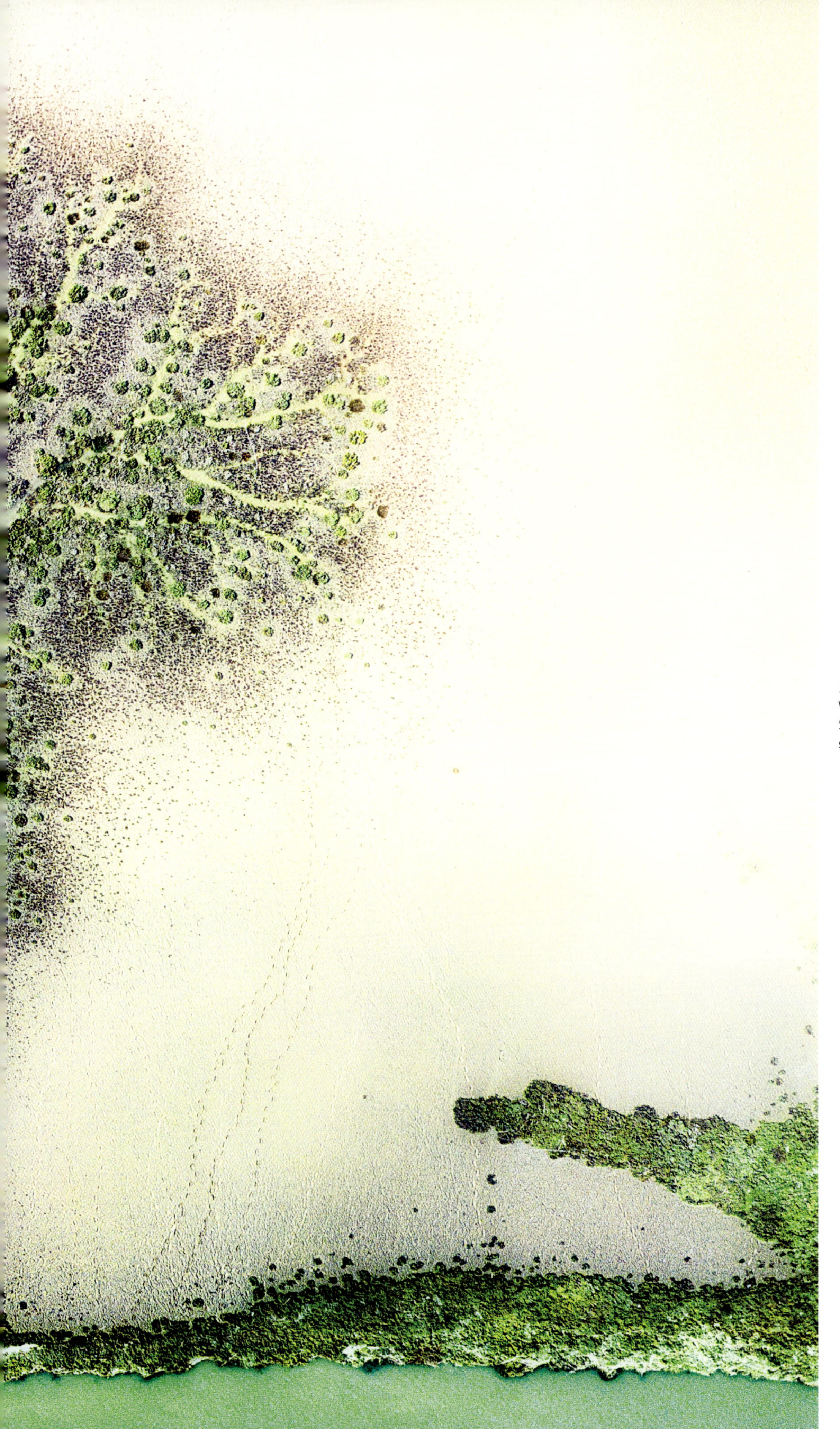

Water trickling through Andalusia, Spain, creates a silhouette suggesting a branching tree.

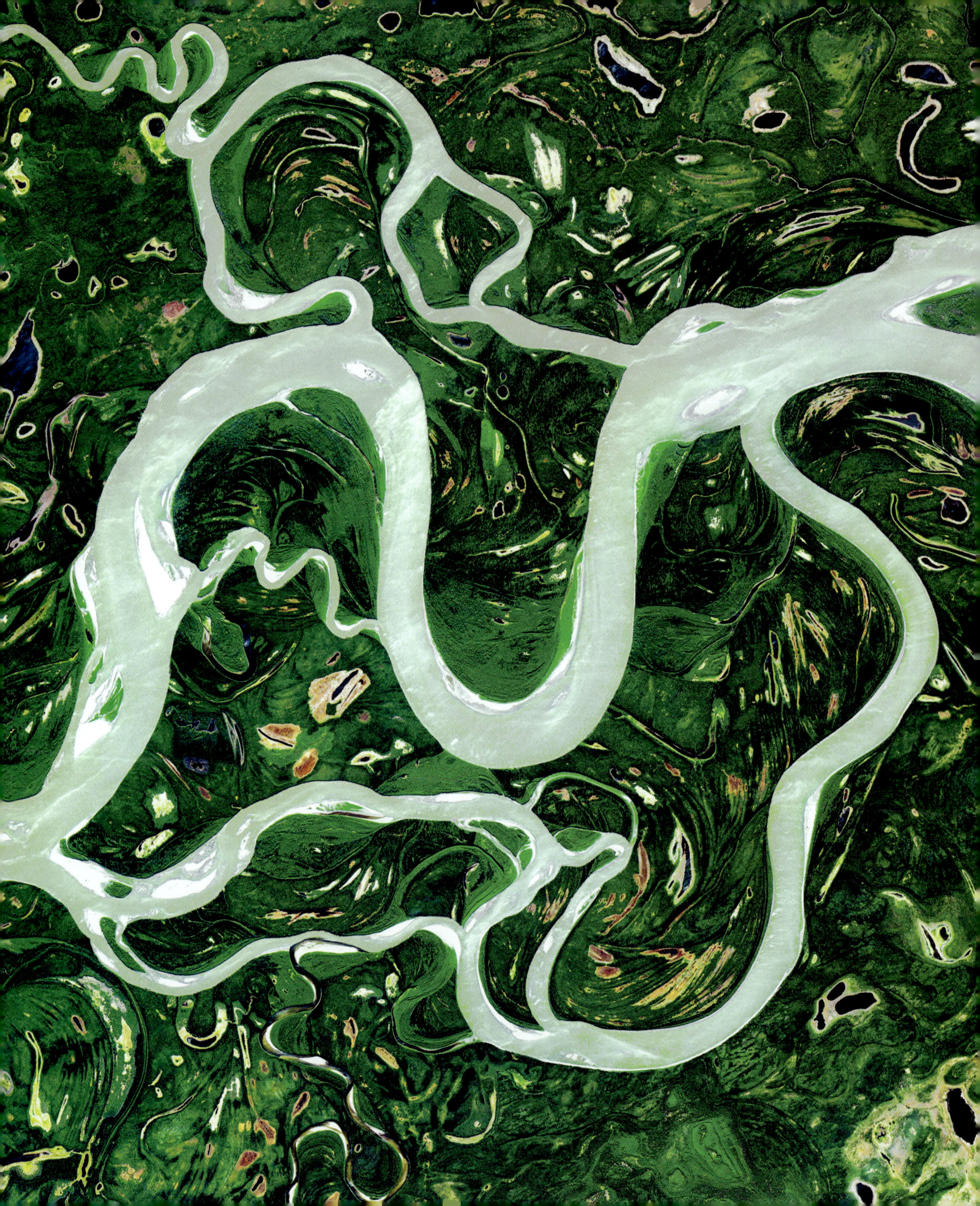

I wandered lonely
as a cloud /
That floats on
high o'er vales
and hills

OVERVIEW
A satellite image turns the Yukon River meandering near tiny Beaver,
Alaska, into an intricate array of twists and bends.

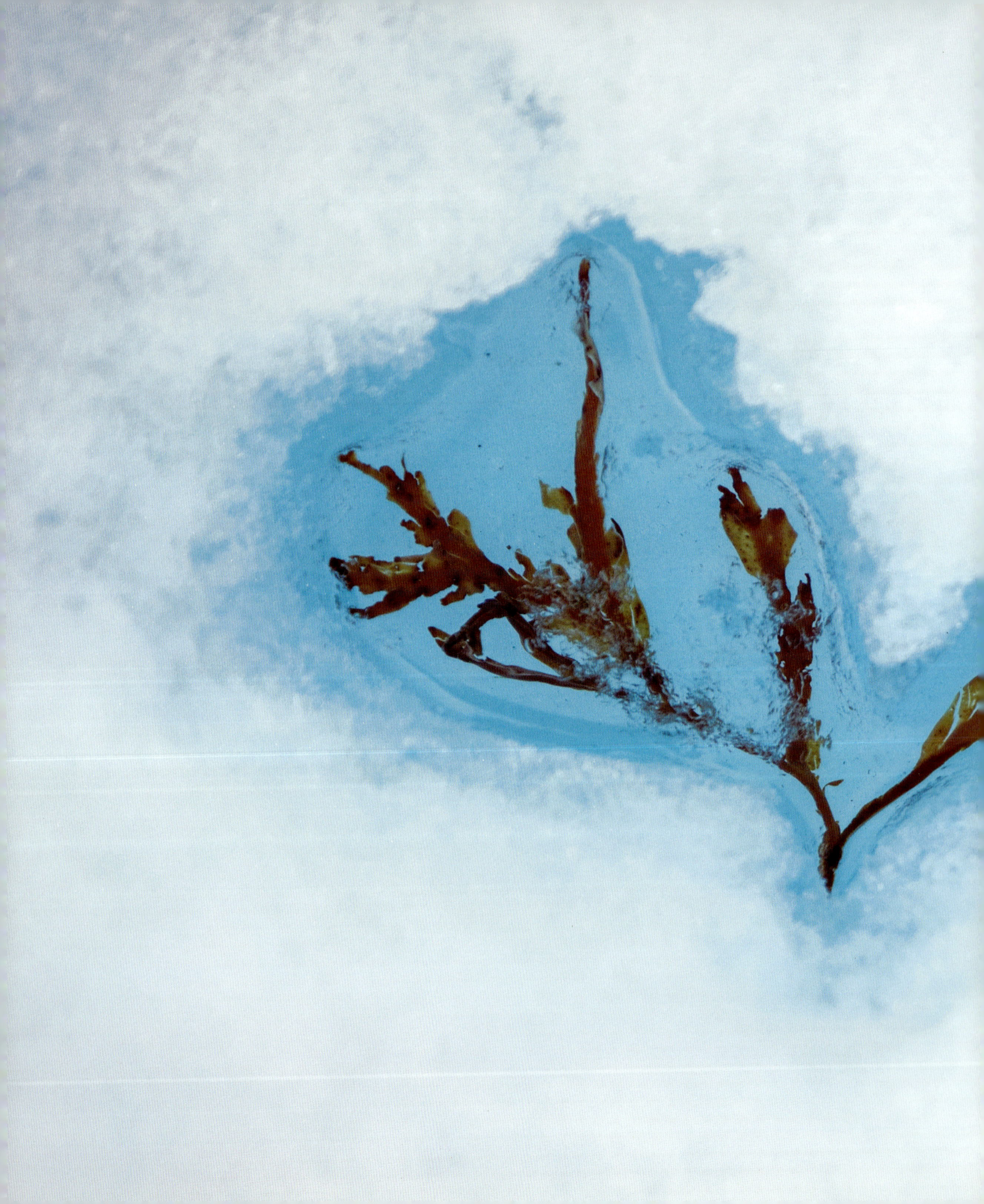

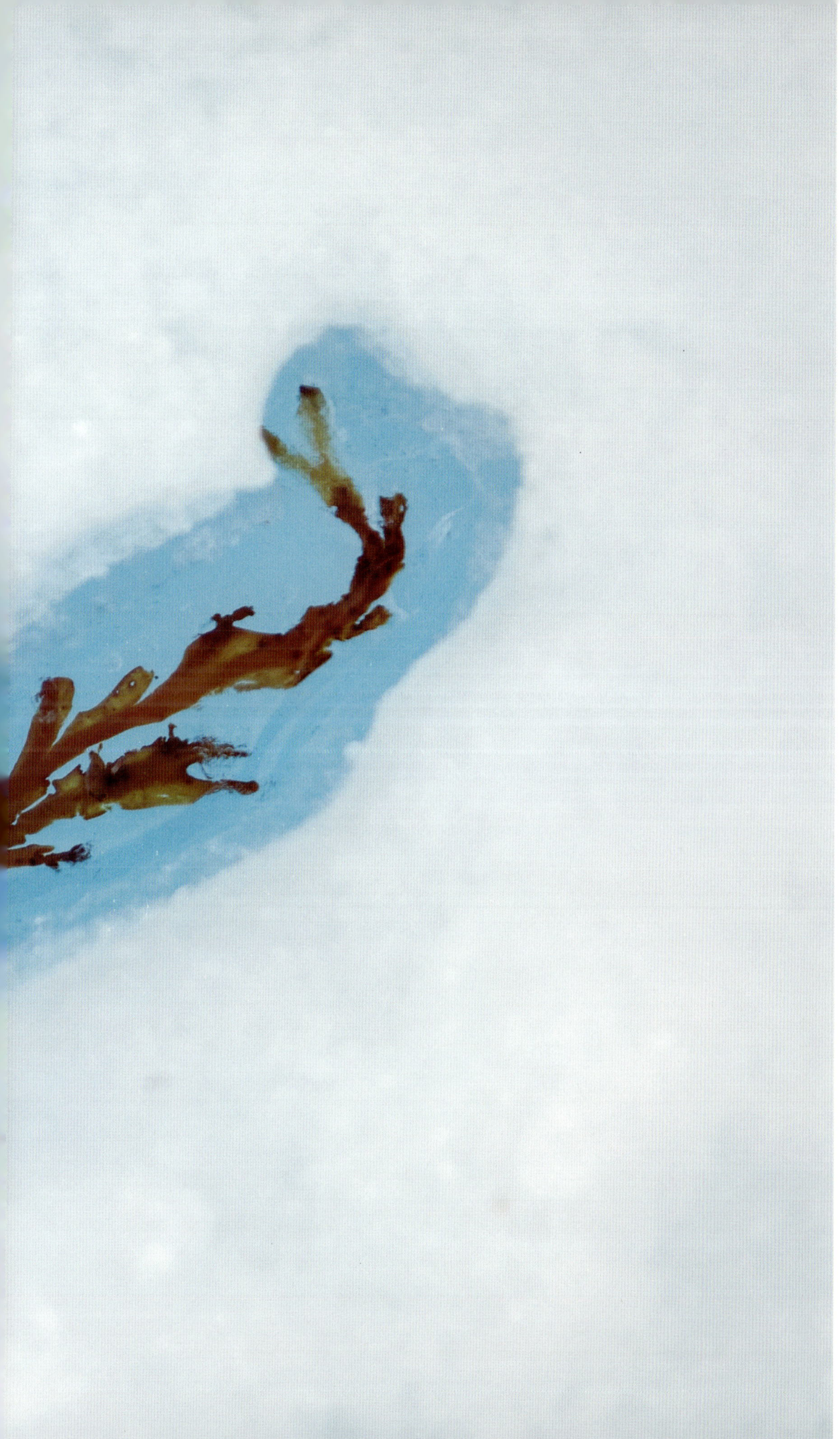

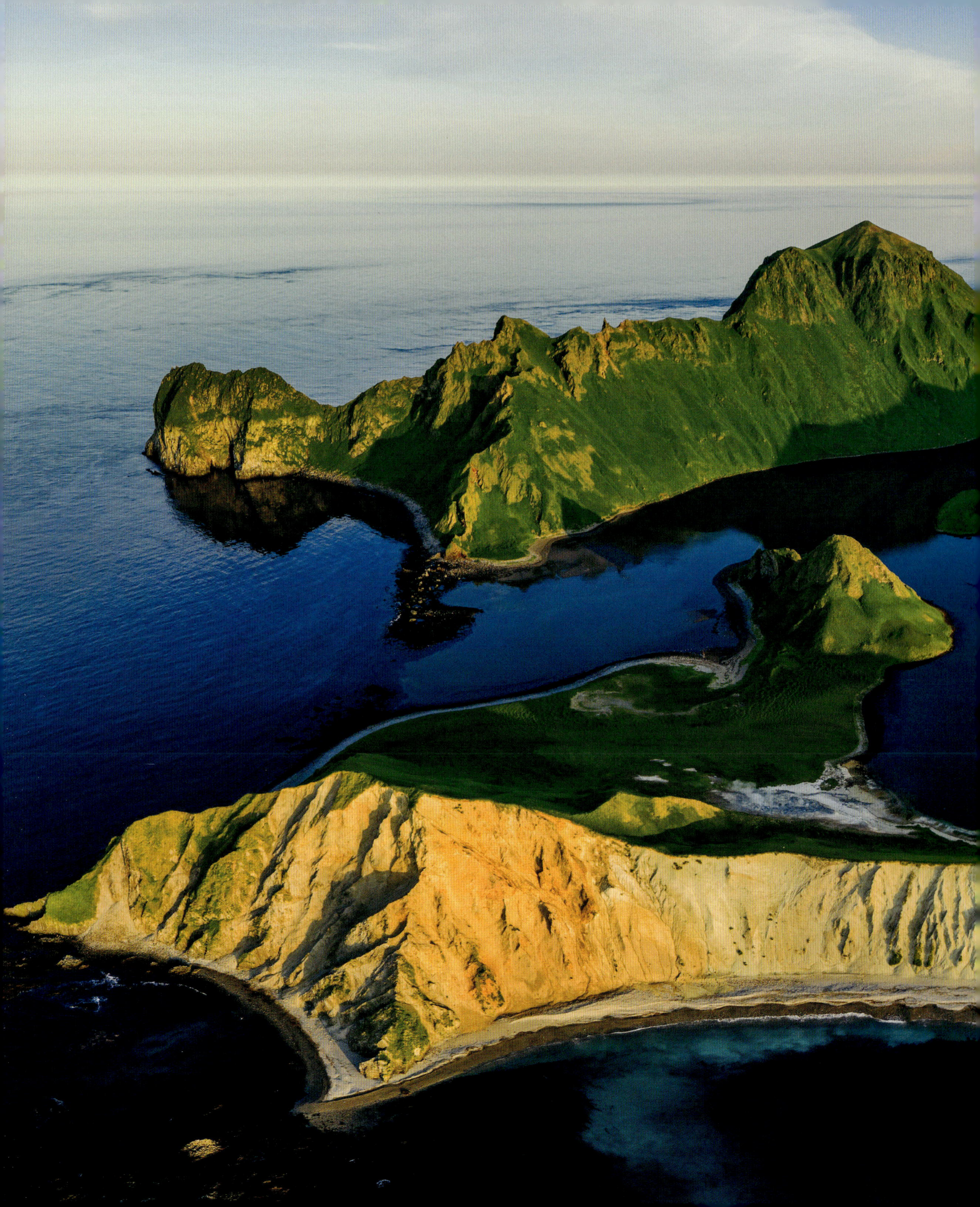

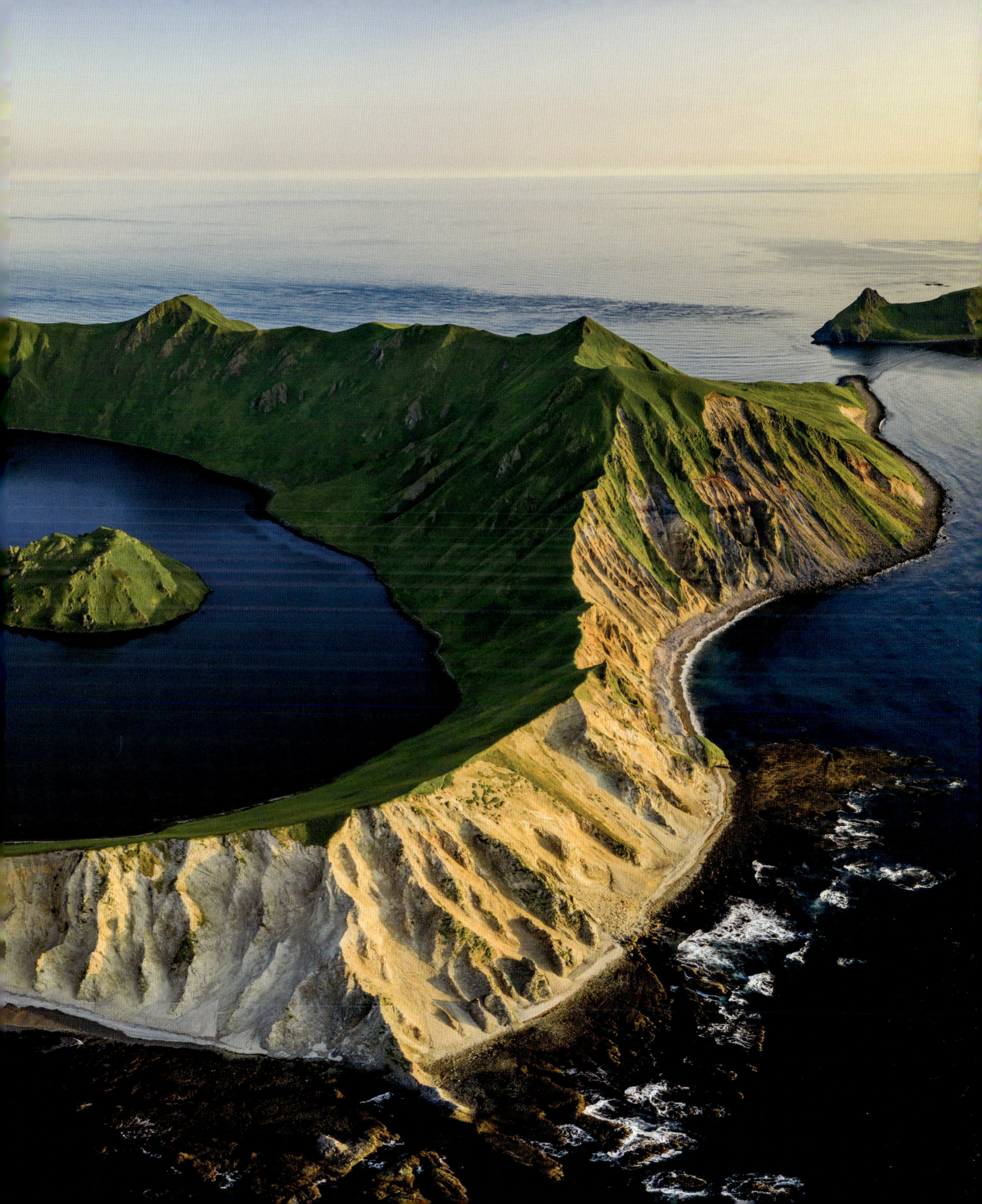

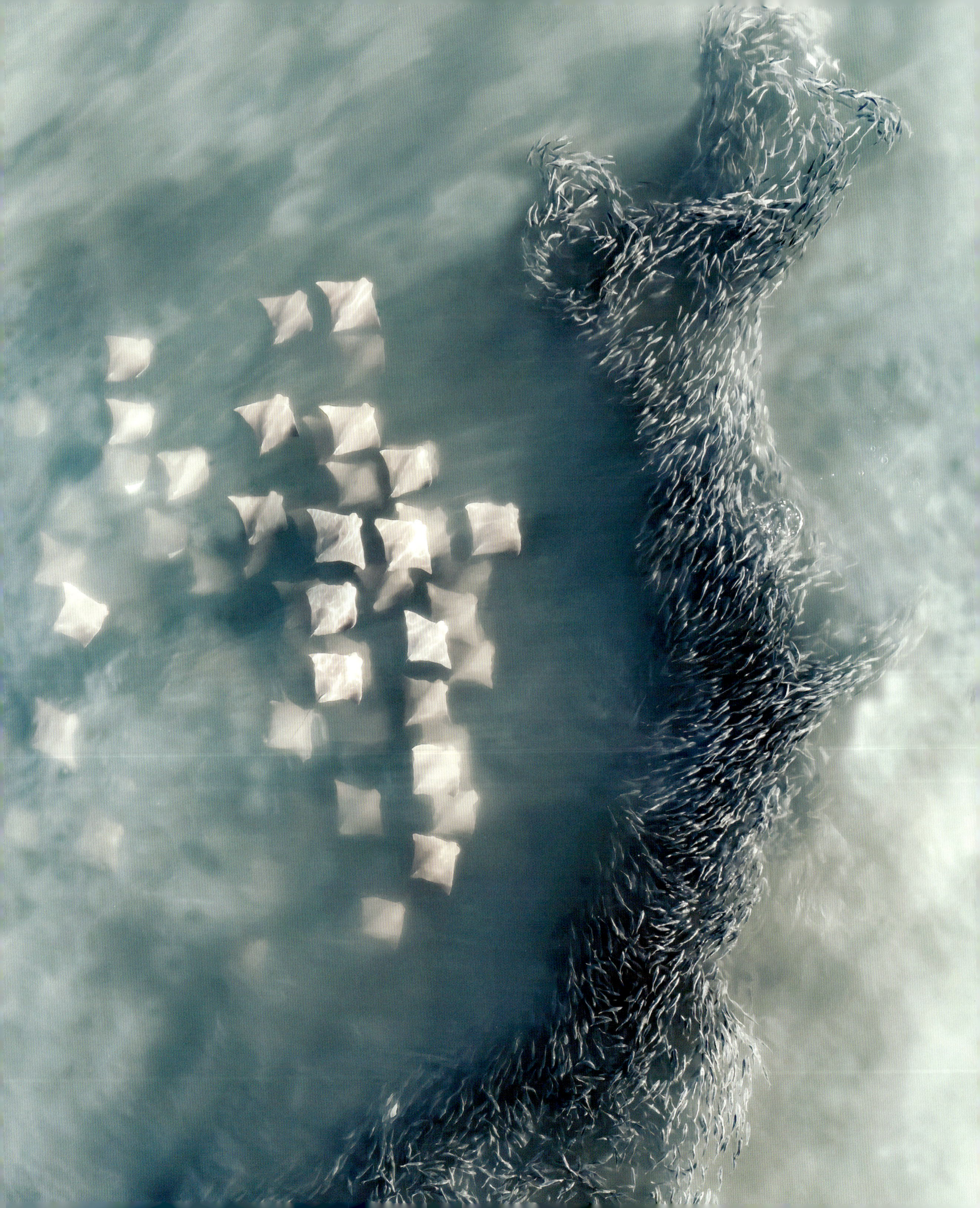

You catch a sight
of Nature, earliest, /
In full front sun-face,
and your eyelids wink /
And drop before
the wonder of 't

JOANNA L. STEIDLE
Cownose rays coordinate to assemble a school of menhaden,
their prey, off the coast of Long Island, New York.

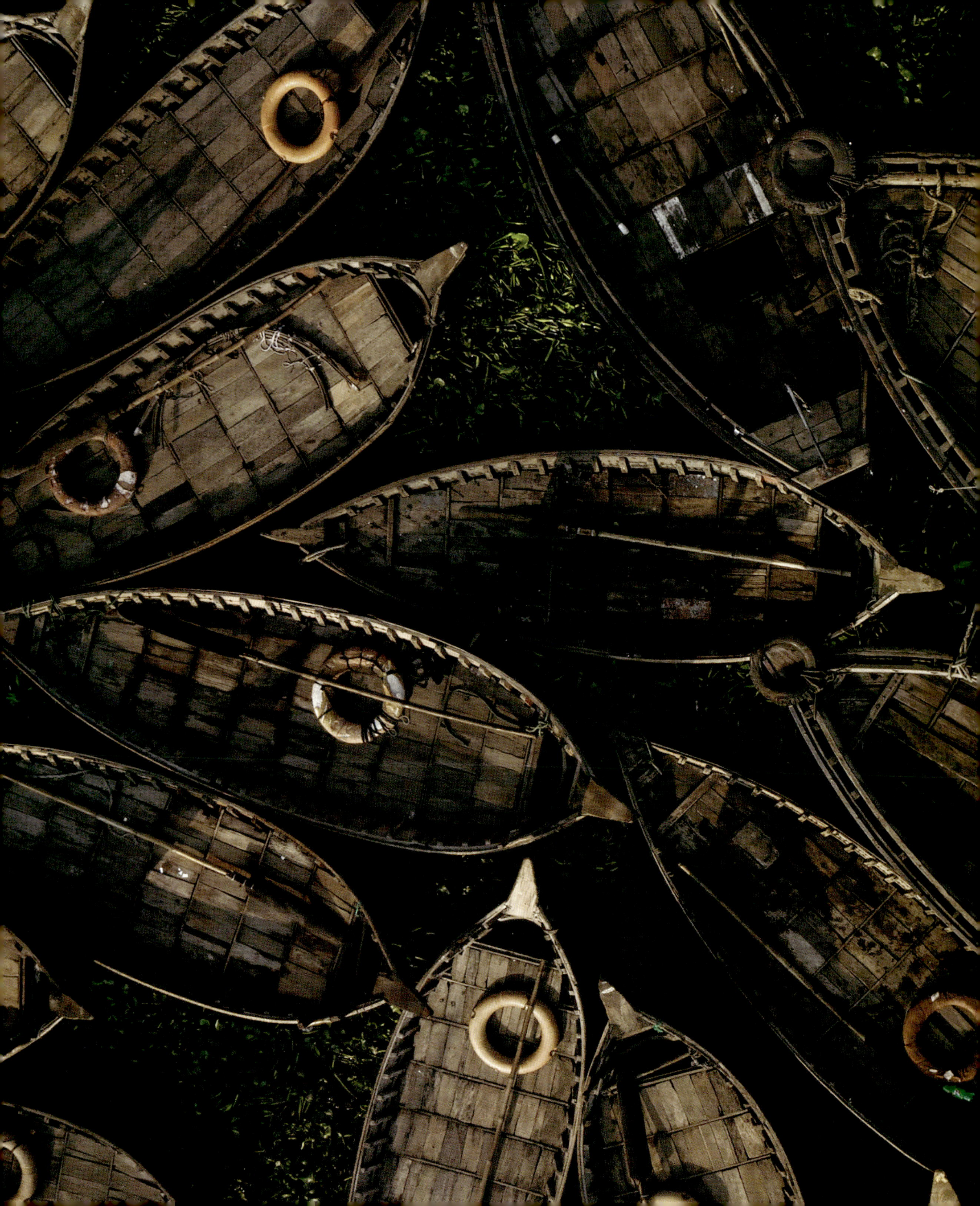

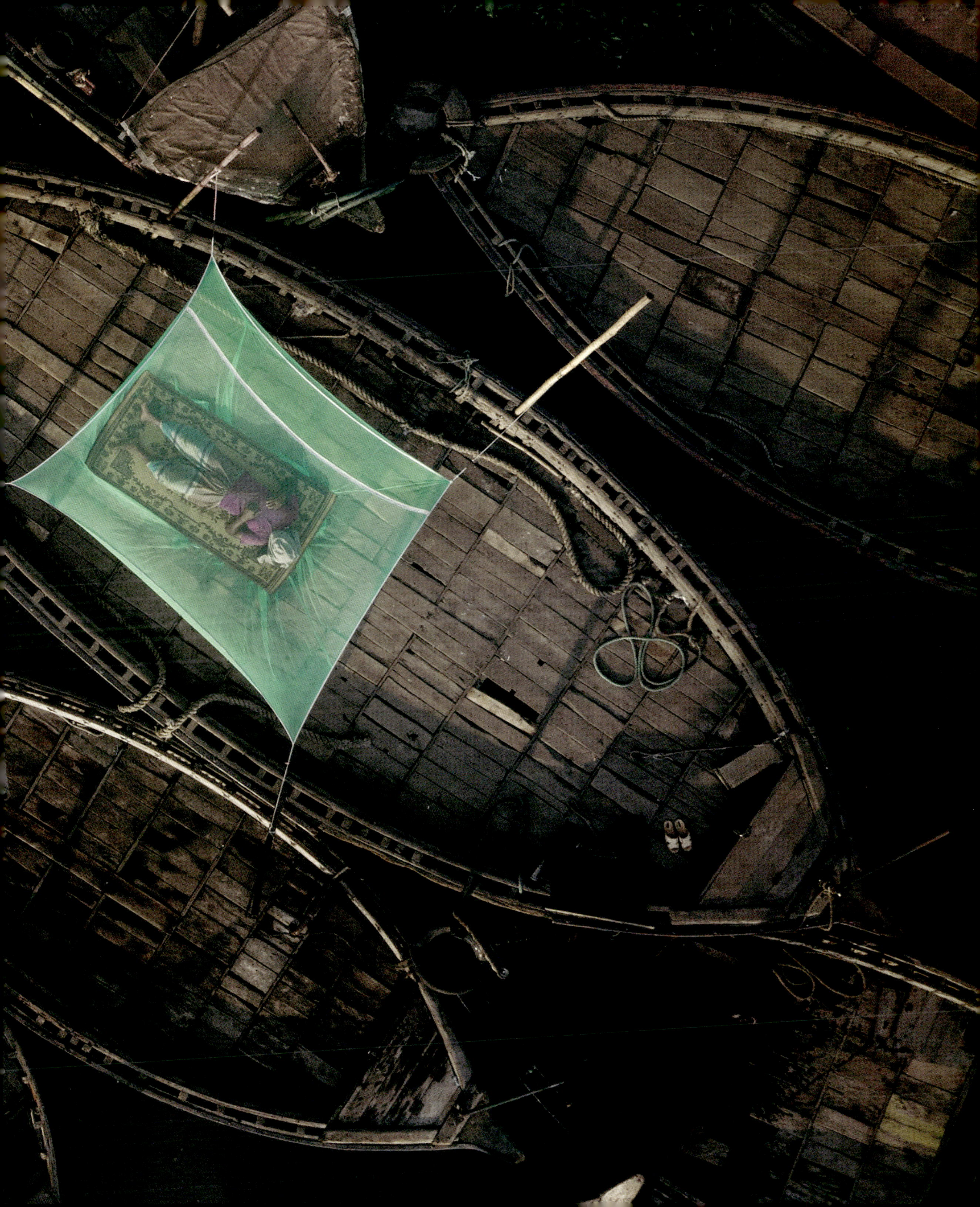

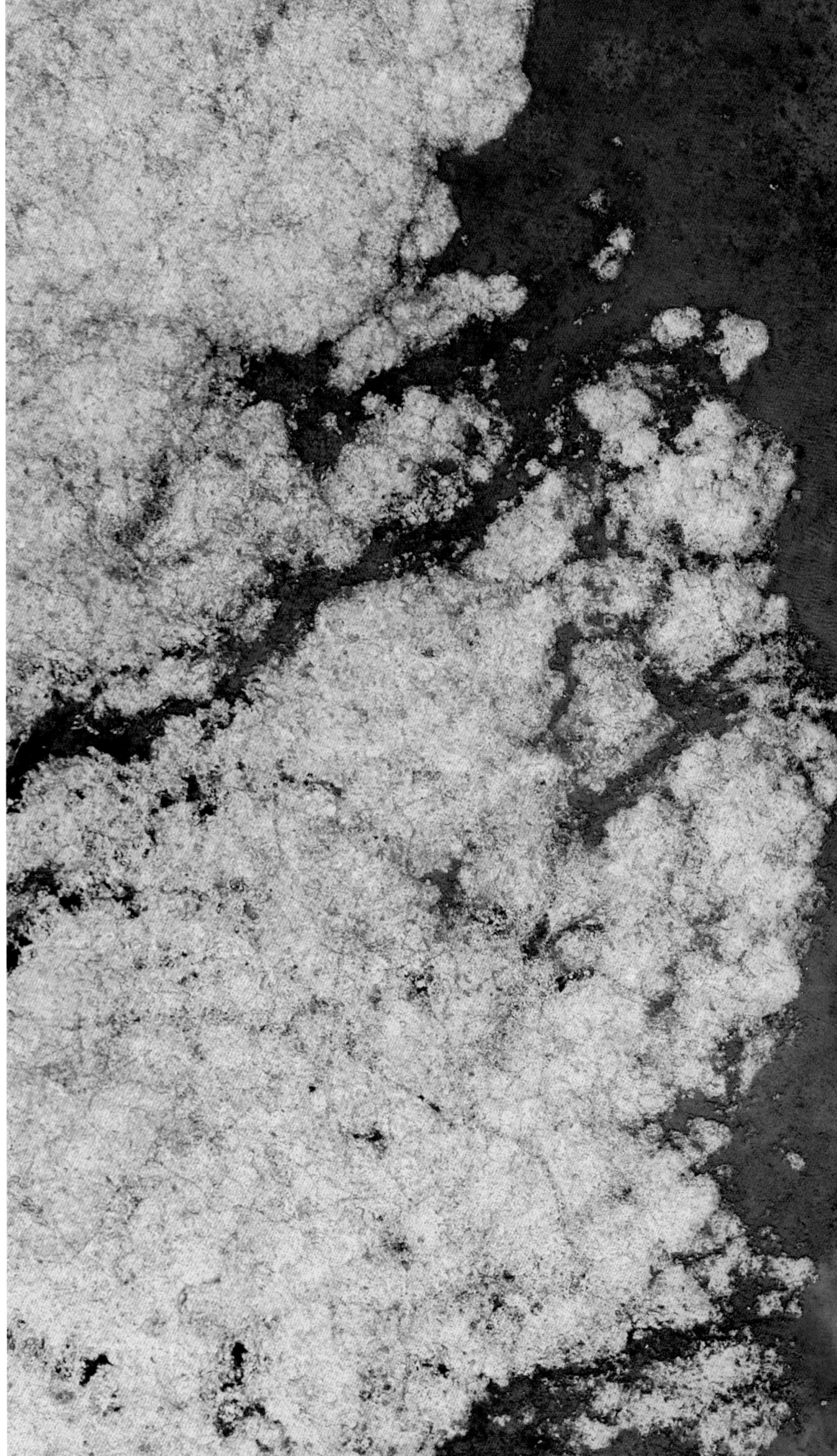

RAJ MOHAN
Flamingos converge as
they perform a suggestively
heart-shaped courtship dance
alongside a chartreuse algae
bloom.

Previous pages:
ANINDITA ROY
A boatsman snoozes under
a canopy stretched across one
of many riverboats in the harbor
of Dhaka, Bangladesh.

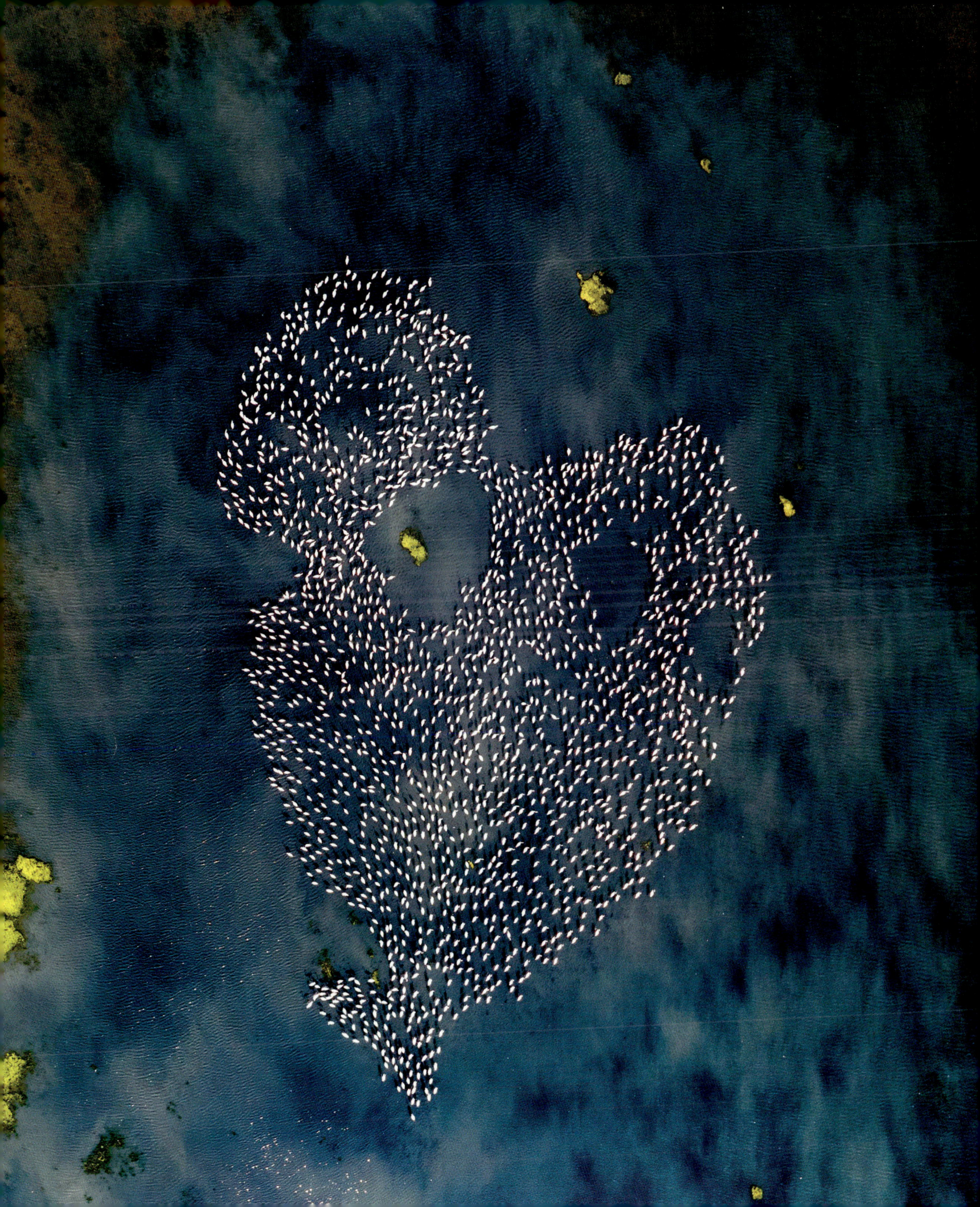

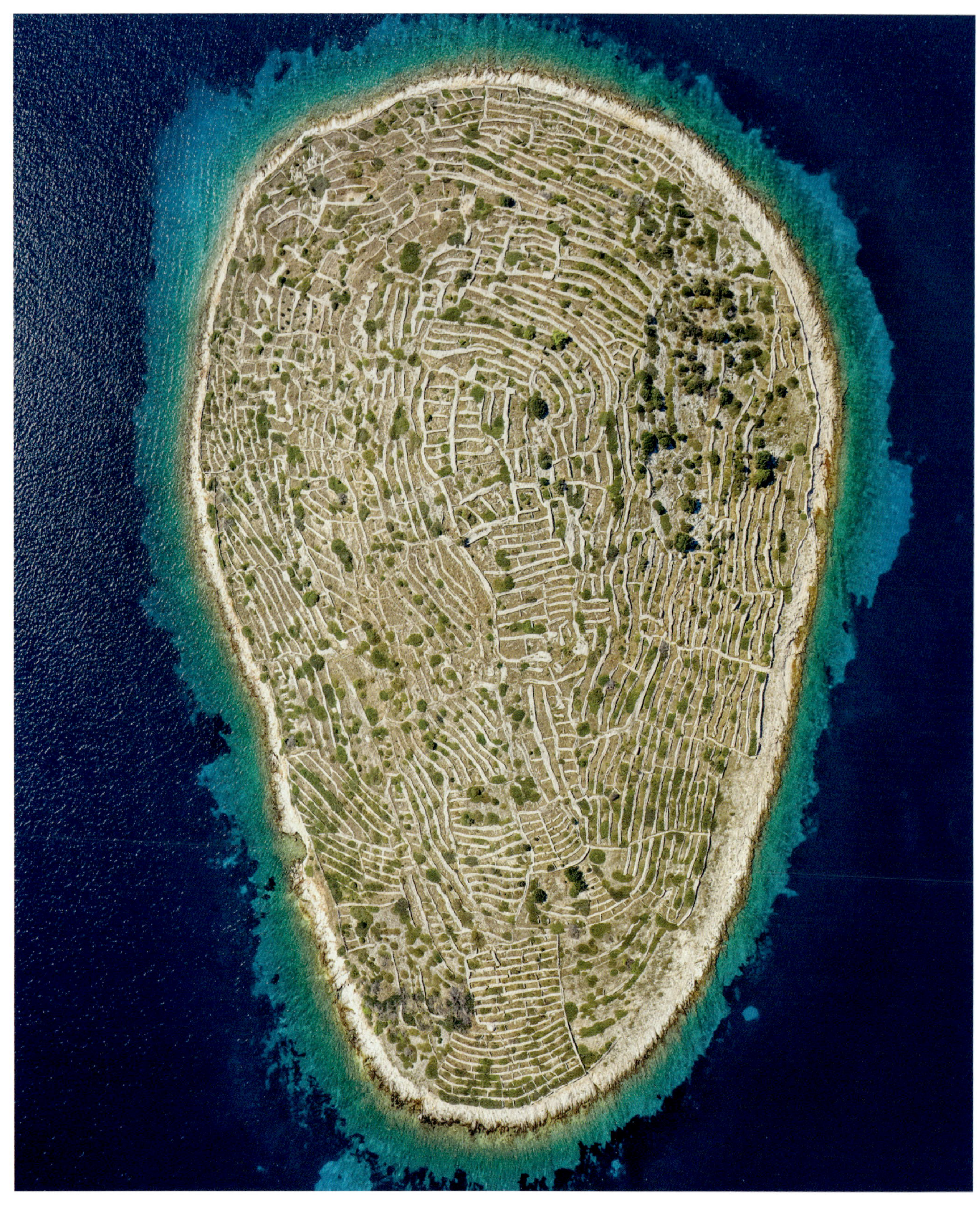

JULIEN DUVAL
Nearly 15 miles (23 km) of dry-stacked stone walls etch a story of fields and groves
on the island of Bavljenac, Croatia, now uninhabited.

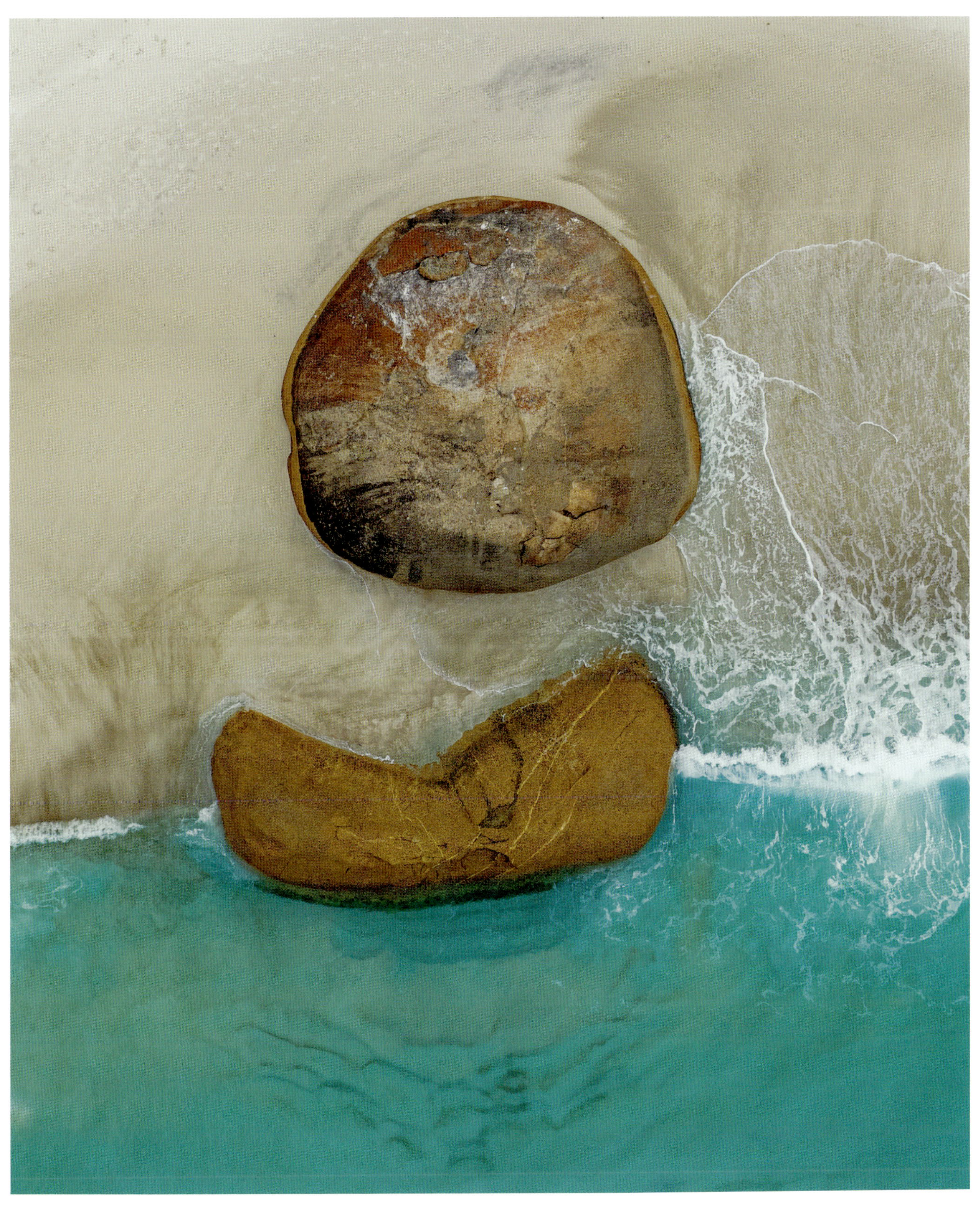

JUDE NEWKIRK
Rocks interrupt the shoreline of Little Beach in Nanarup,
Western Australia.

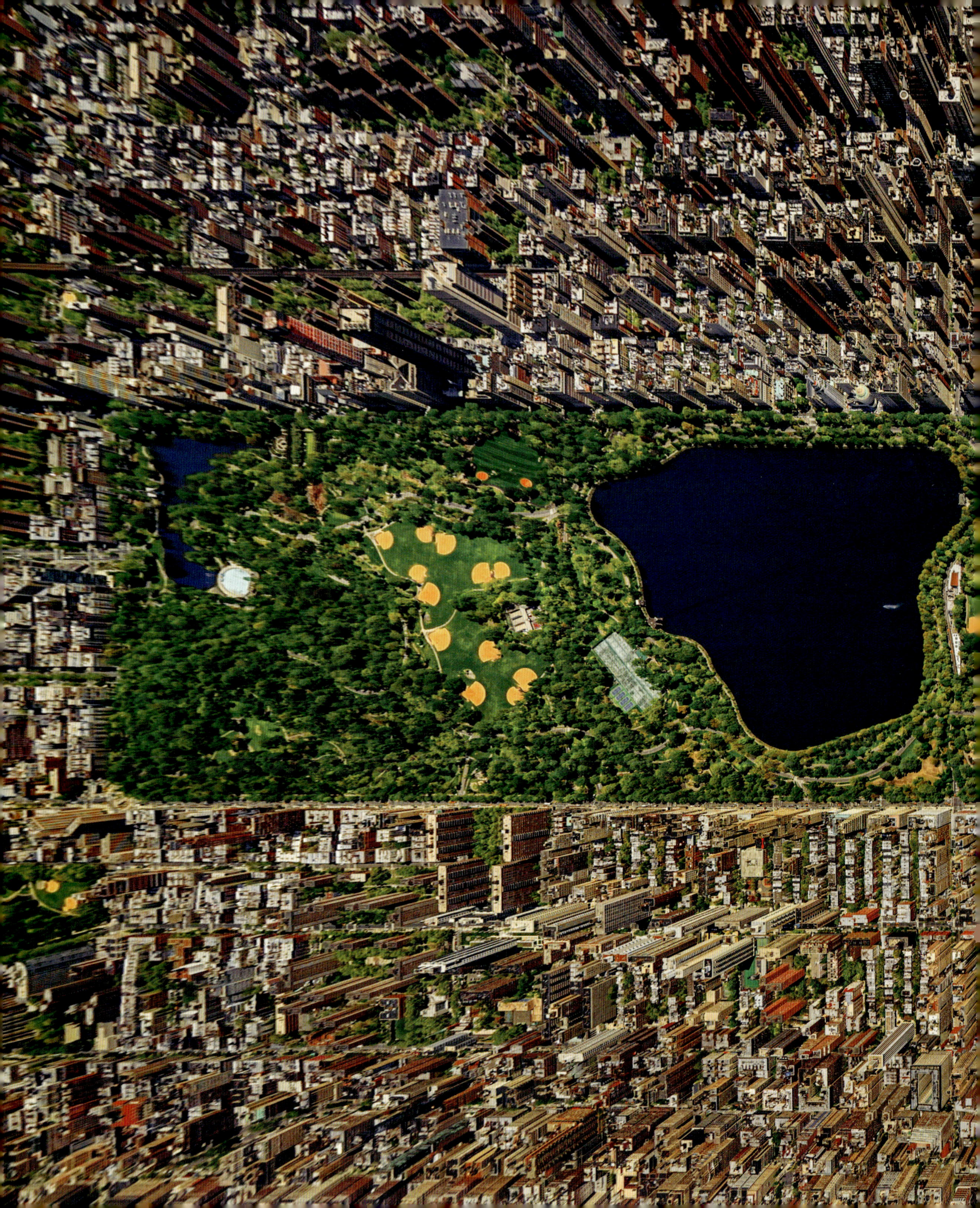

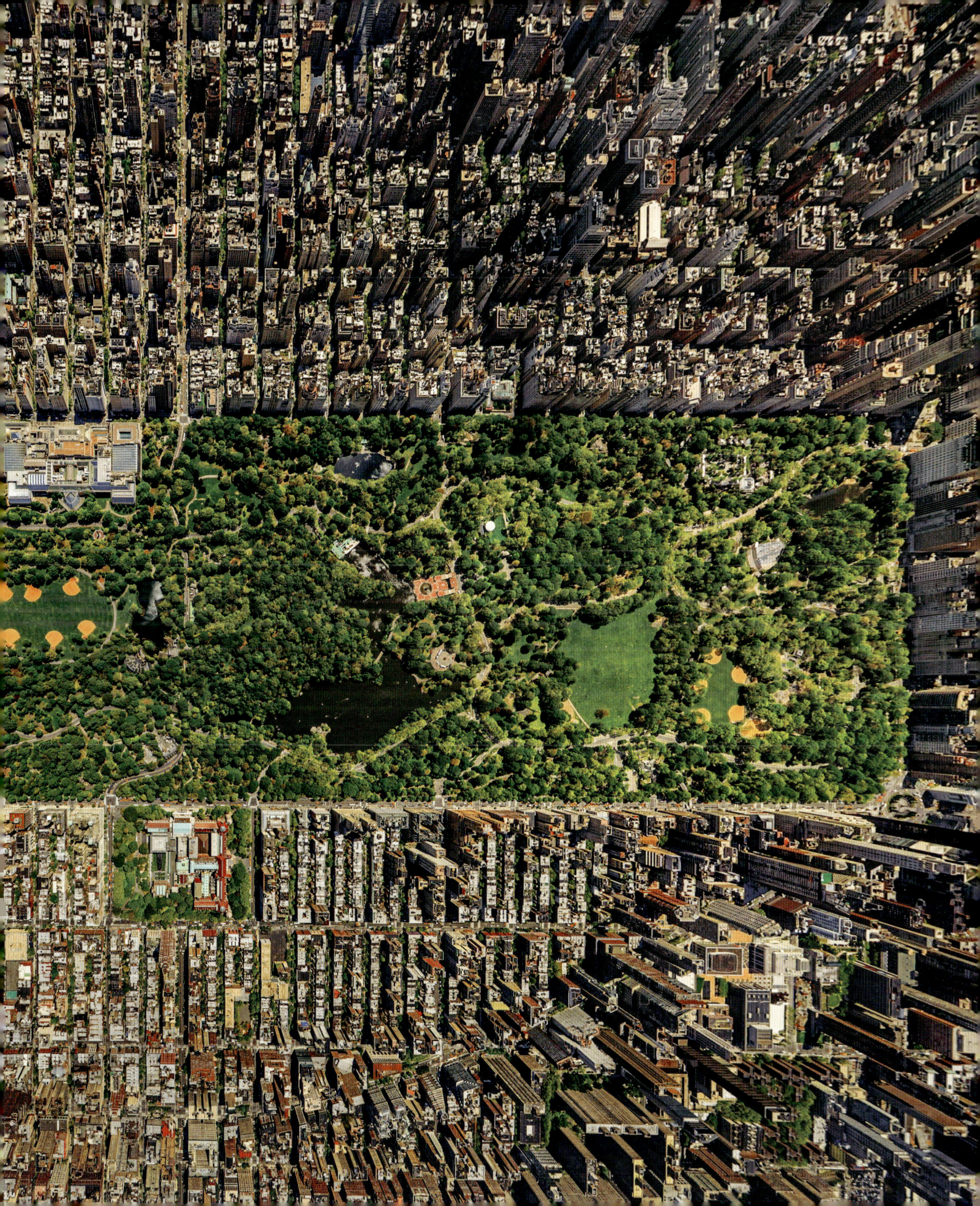

Art and nature shall always be wrestling until they mutually conquer each other.

KEITH LADZINSKI
The Cono de Arita, a natural pyramid, rises some 400 feet (122 m) above the Salar de Arizaro, a massive salt flat in Argentina.

Previous pages:
SERGEY SEMENOV
An aerial photograph takes in all of New York City's Central Park and many blocks of surrounding buildings.

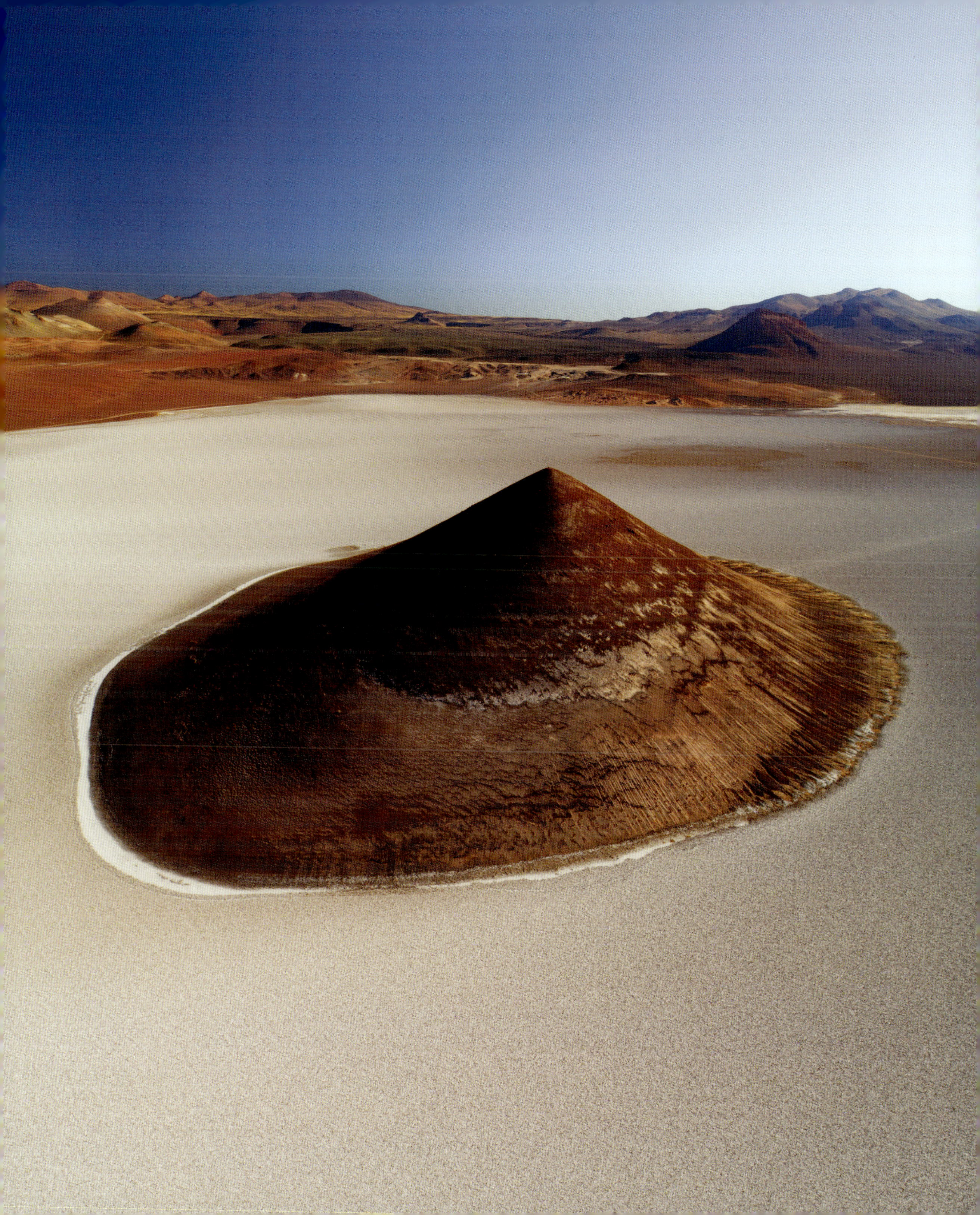

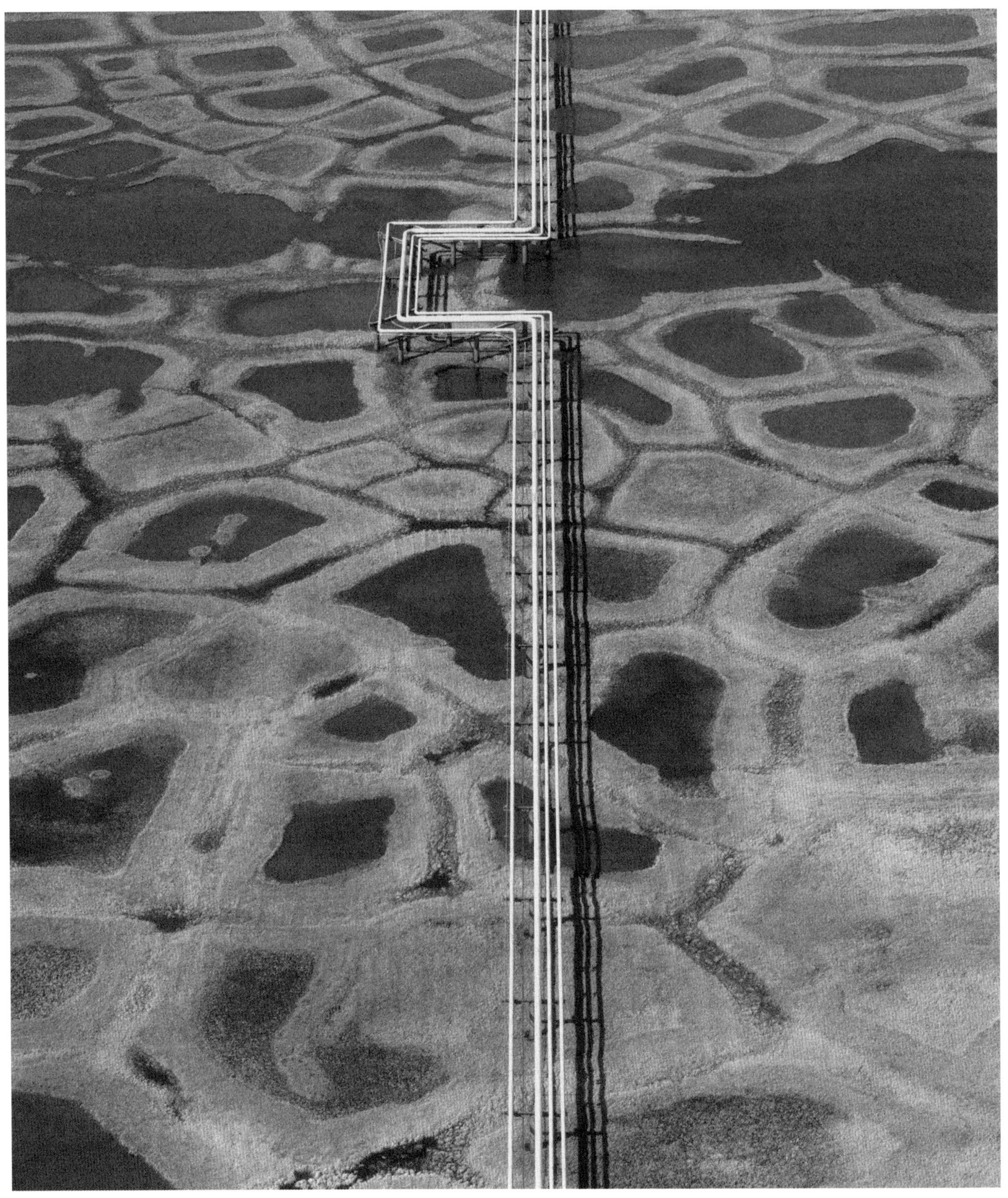

KILIII YUYAN
A pipeline on the National Petroleum Reserve takes sharp turns across the tundra west of Prudhoe Bay, Alaska.

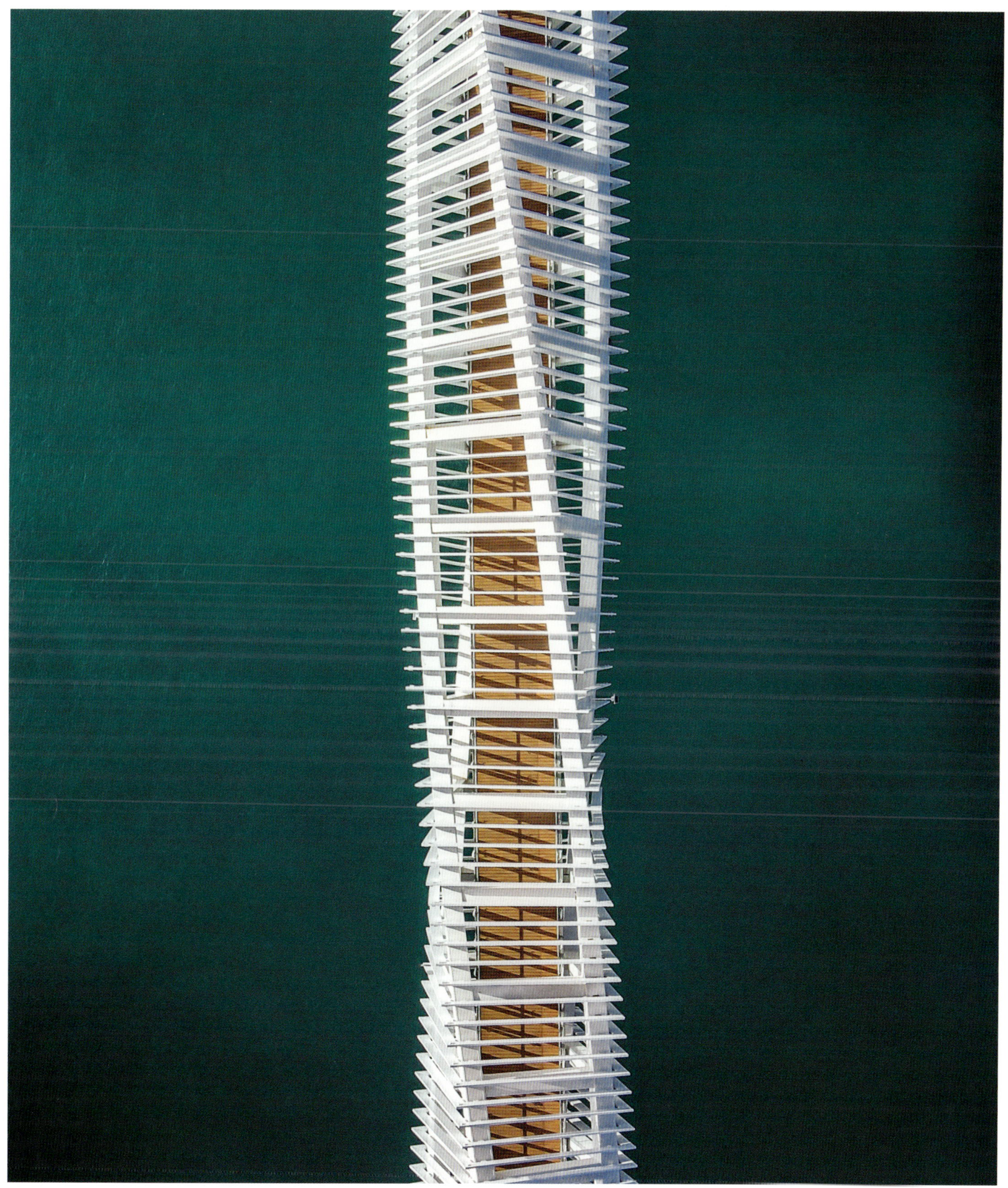

FLORIAN KRIECHBAUMER
A helical structure encases this pedestrian bridge over the Dubai Water Canal.

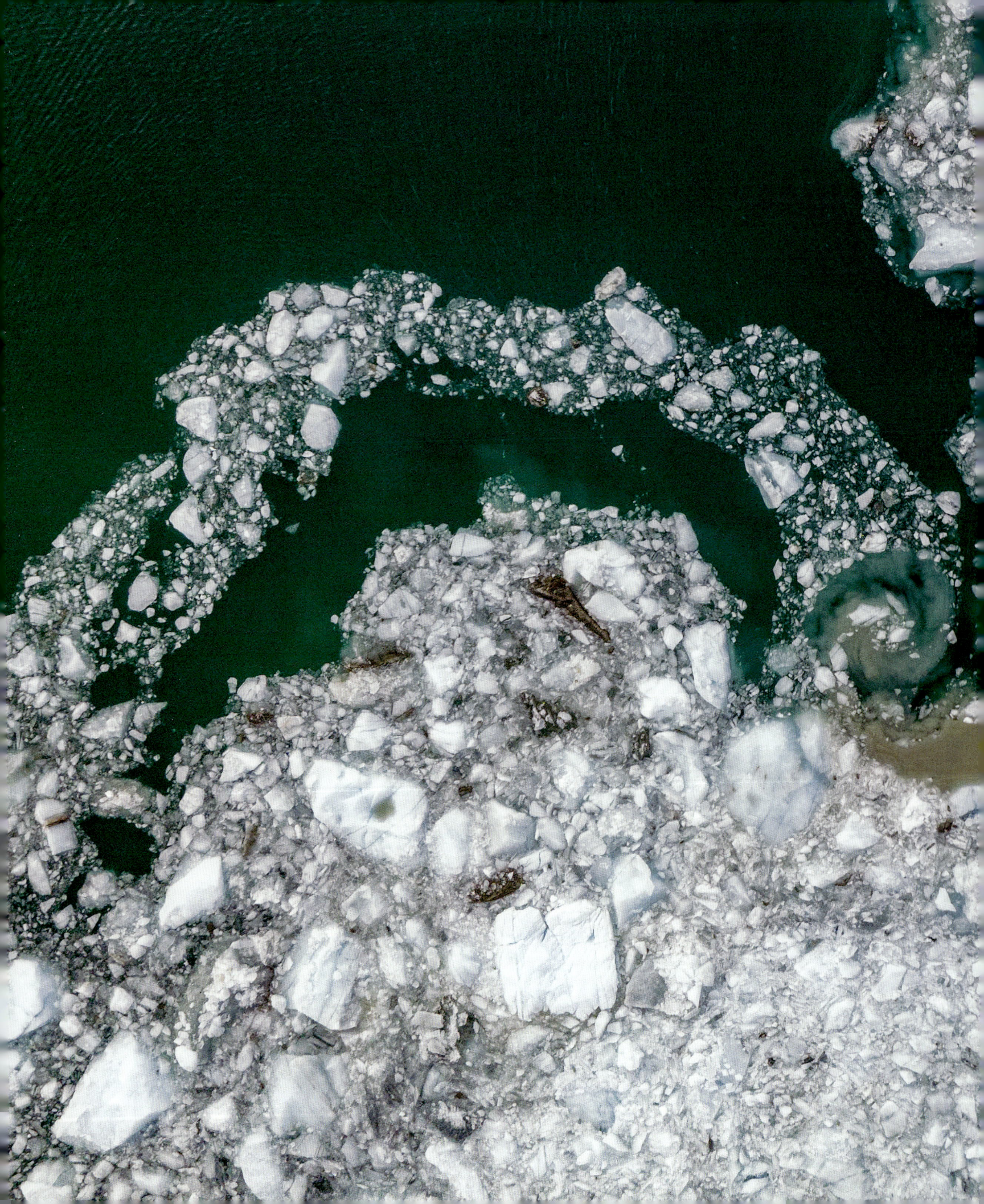

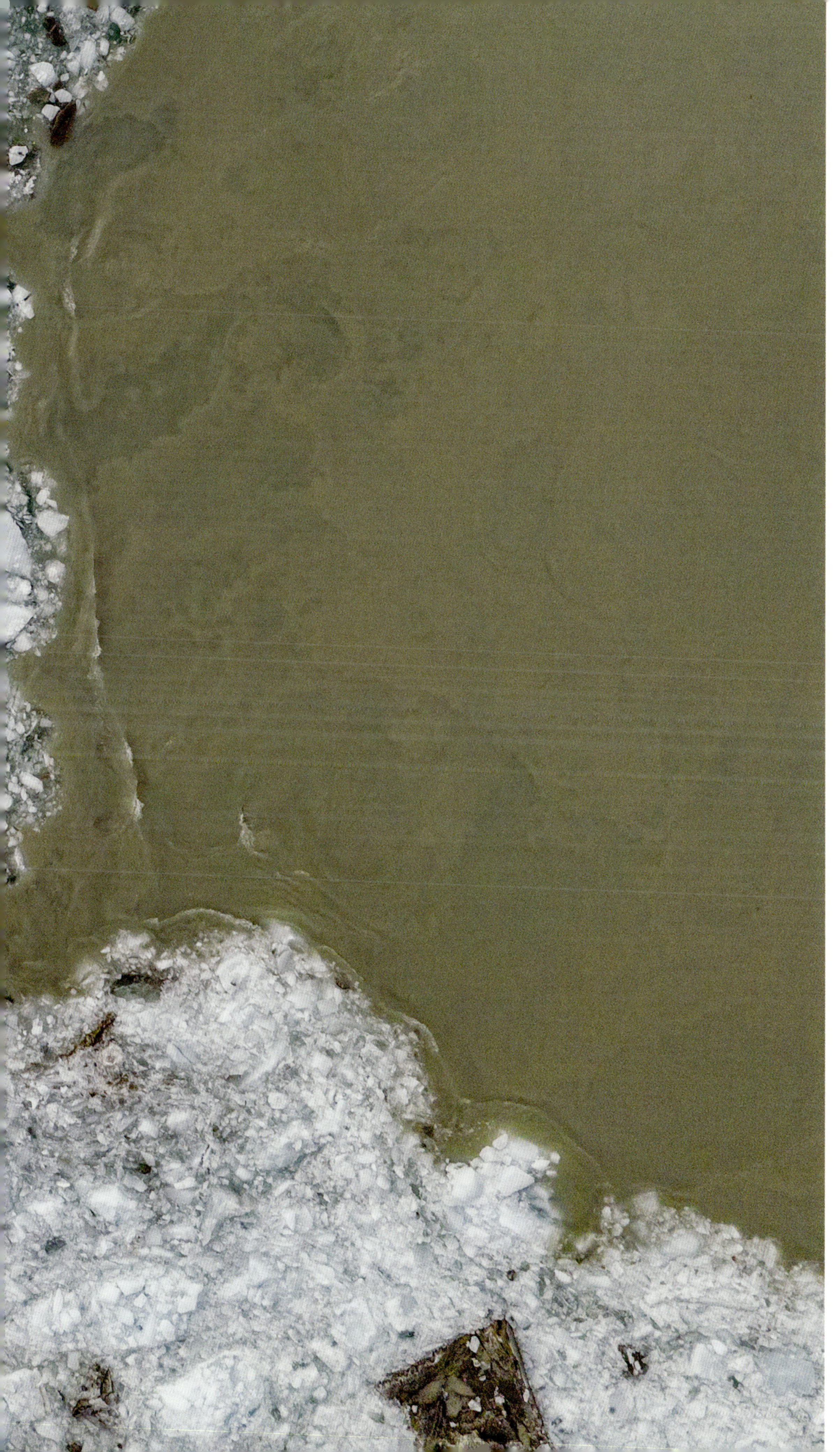

JEFFREY KERBY
An icy spiral forms after an ice
dam beneath a glacier bursts,
releasing brown fresh water into
Dickson Fjord in northeastern
Greenland.

Following pages:
JEFFREY KERBY
An Arctic stream cuts a twisting
canyon through unusual red rock
on Ymer Island in northeastern
Greenland.

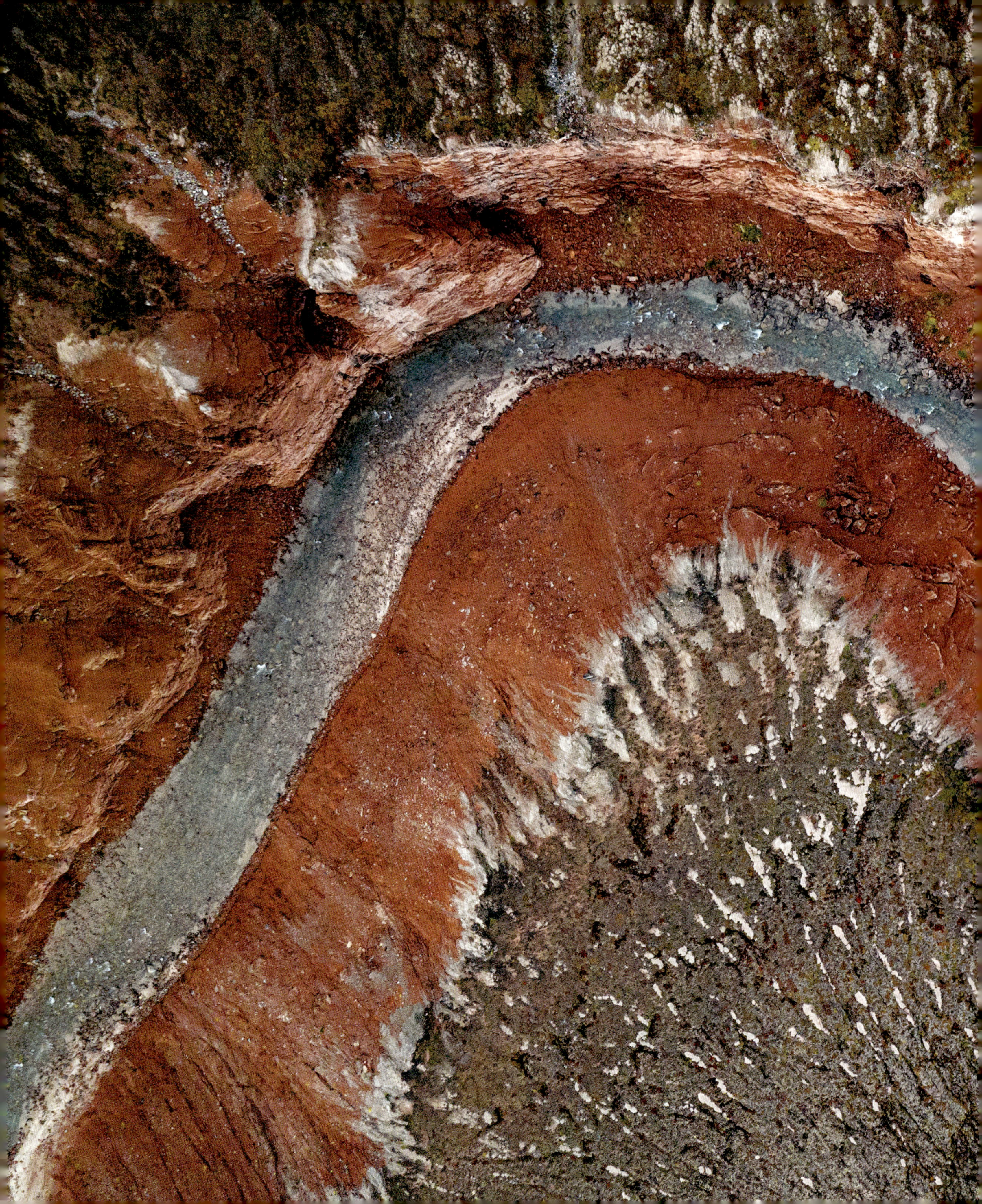

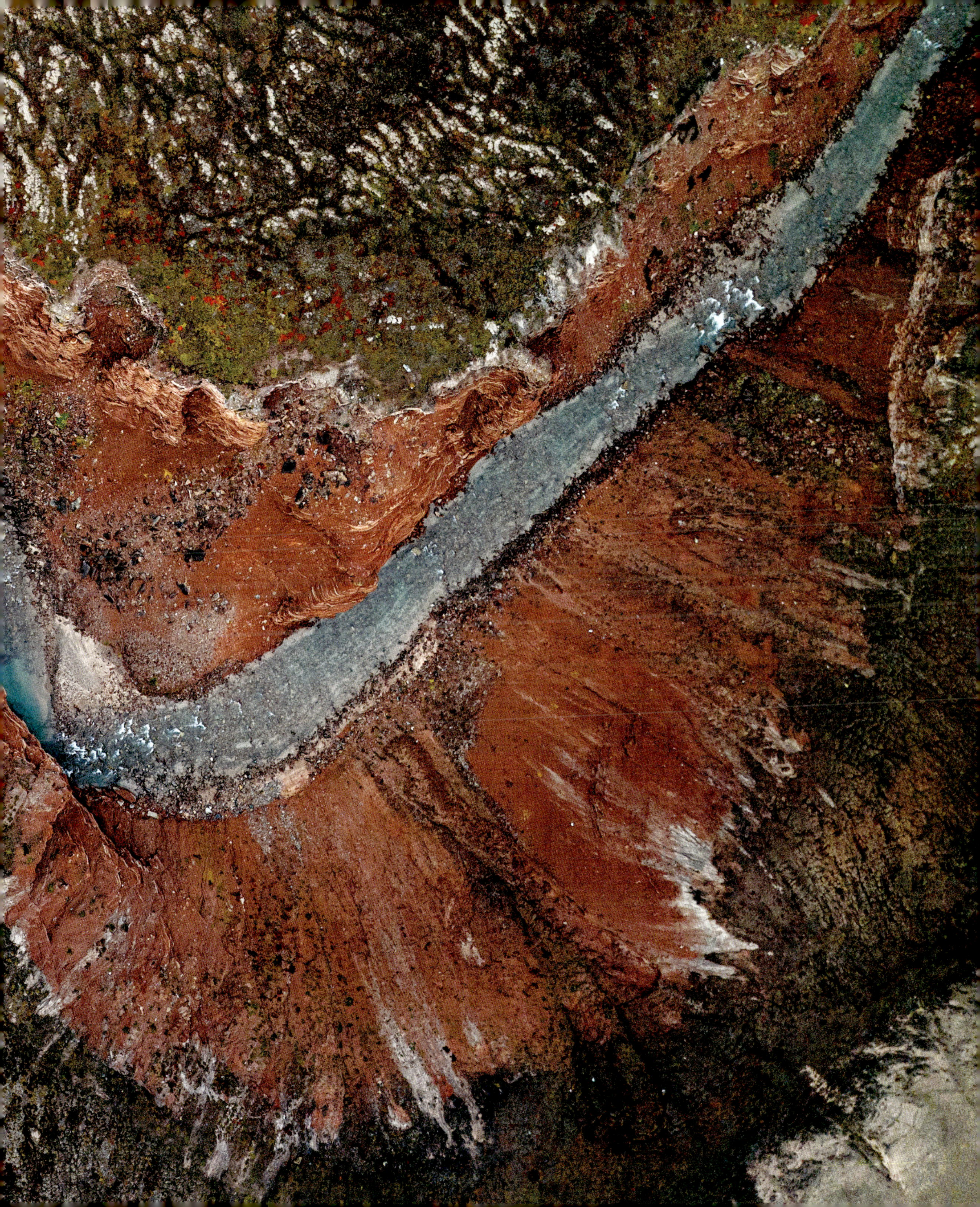

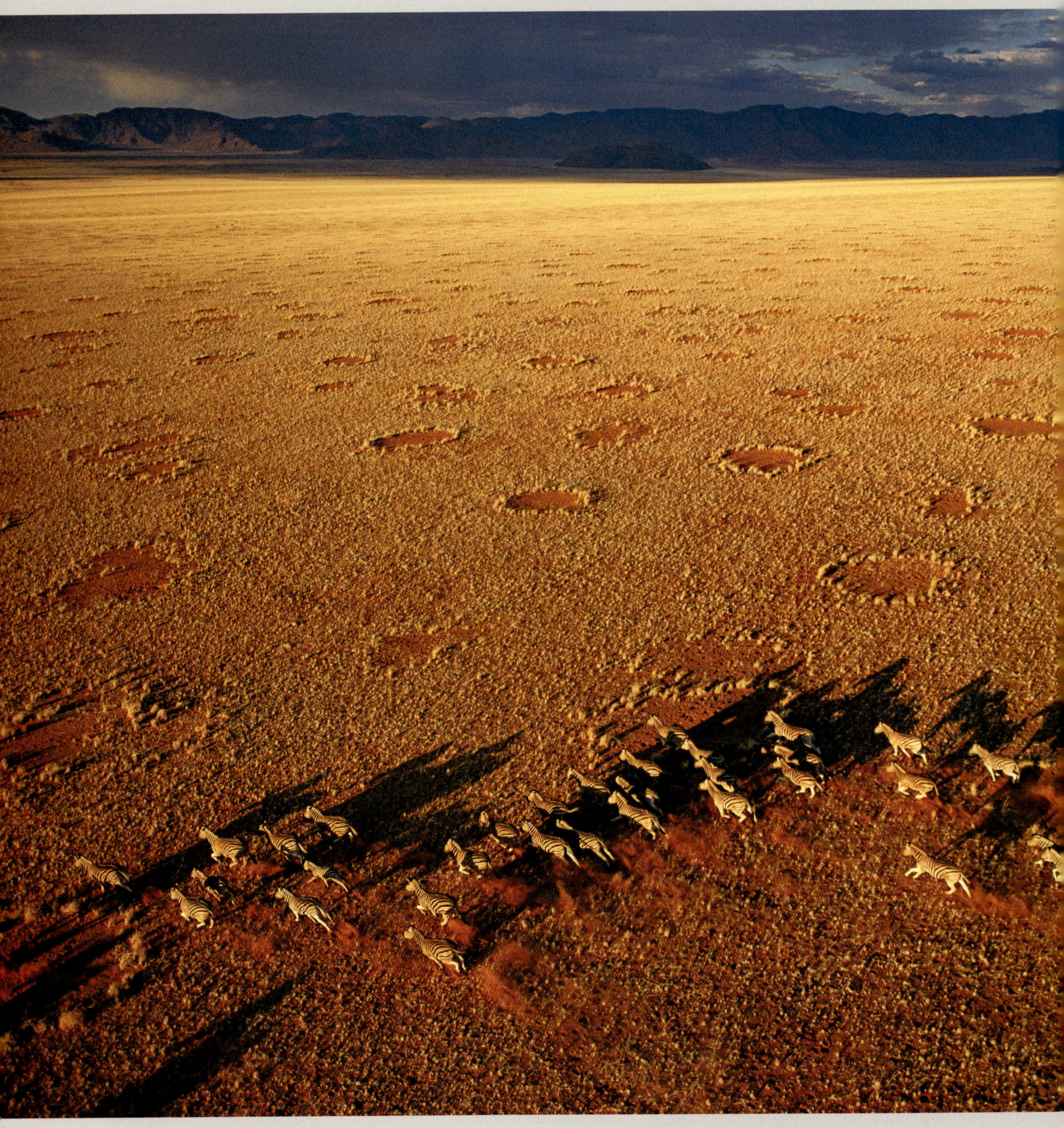

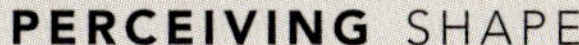

PATTERNS OF MYSTERY

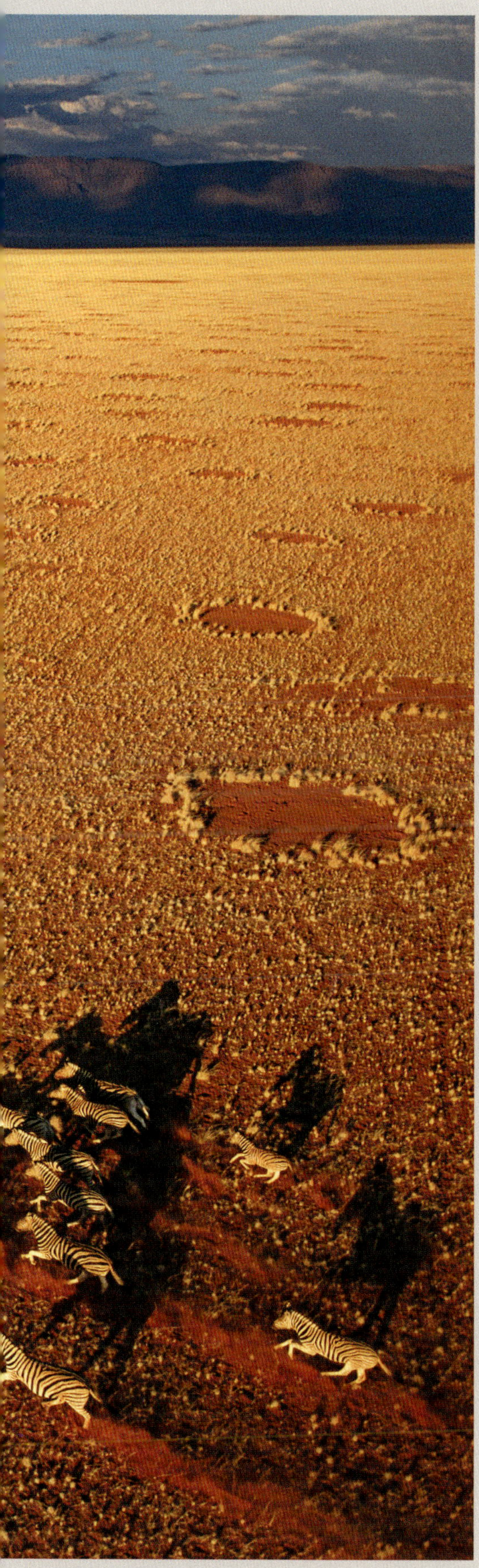

People love a good mystery, but sometimes a simple circle can cause decades of debate. Along the eastern edge of the Namib Desert, stretching from Angola to Namibia and into South Africa, drylands are speckled with circles of barren ground surrounded by vigorously growing grasses. Called "fairy circles," they range in size from a motorcycle to a garbage truck. Their symmetry, precision, and repeated pattern caught the attention of early naturalists and have long been discussed by local Indigenous peoples. They are also a favorite subject for aerial photographers, as in this photograph by renowned aerial photographer George Steinmetz (left). Theories explaining their origins include divine footprints, pockets of hydrogen gas seeping out of the ground, or even some association with Ice Age termites. Similar circular patterns have also been reported and discussed in drylands in Australia.

As far as we know, discovering what causes fairy circles is not critically urgent,

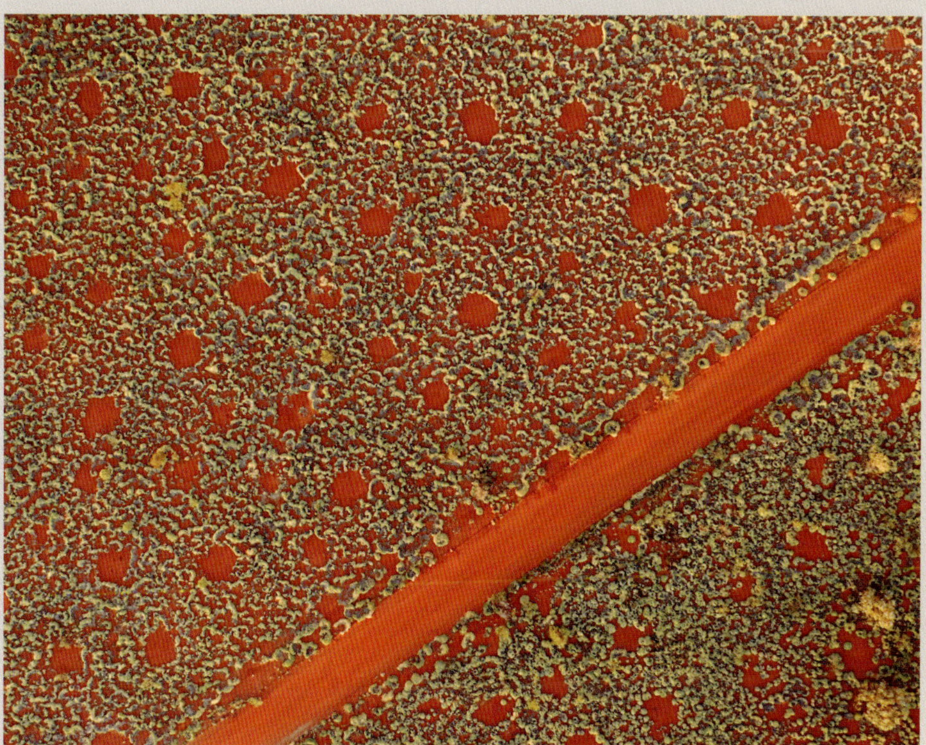

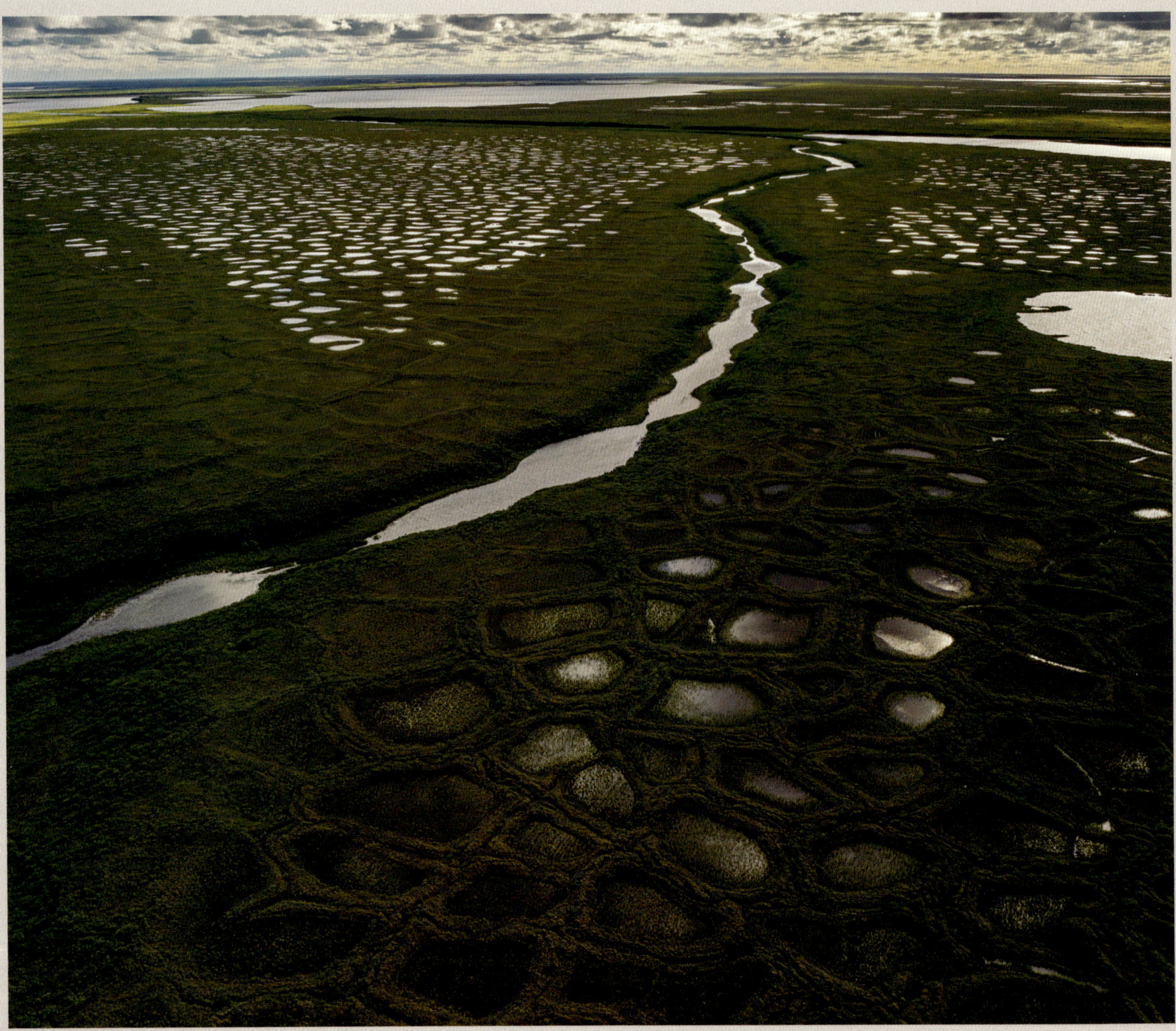

but the desire to find an explanation for such a strange and widespread pattern has many people hooked. By studying where patterns are located, their size, and their shape, scientists can begin to guess at the processes that create them. They can then look for evidence to support their ideas in the field, and if they're wrong, start the process over again with new ideas or a better description of the pattern.

Recently, researchers in Spain thought that maybe the fairy circle mystery wasn't fully described, and that perhaps a broader view from above might help clarify the debate. They reasoned that repeating circles in drylands are a weird enough pattern that artificial intelligence algorithms should be able to detect them in satellite imagery—what if they weren't just in the Namib and Australia? So, they set AI loose on high-resolution imagery taken from above all global drylands and discovered fairy circles, or at least patterns that looked like them, spread out

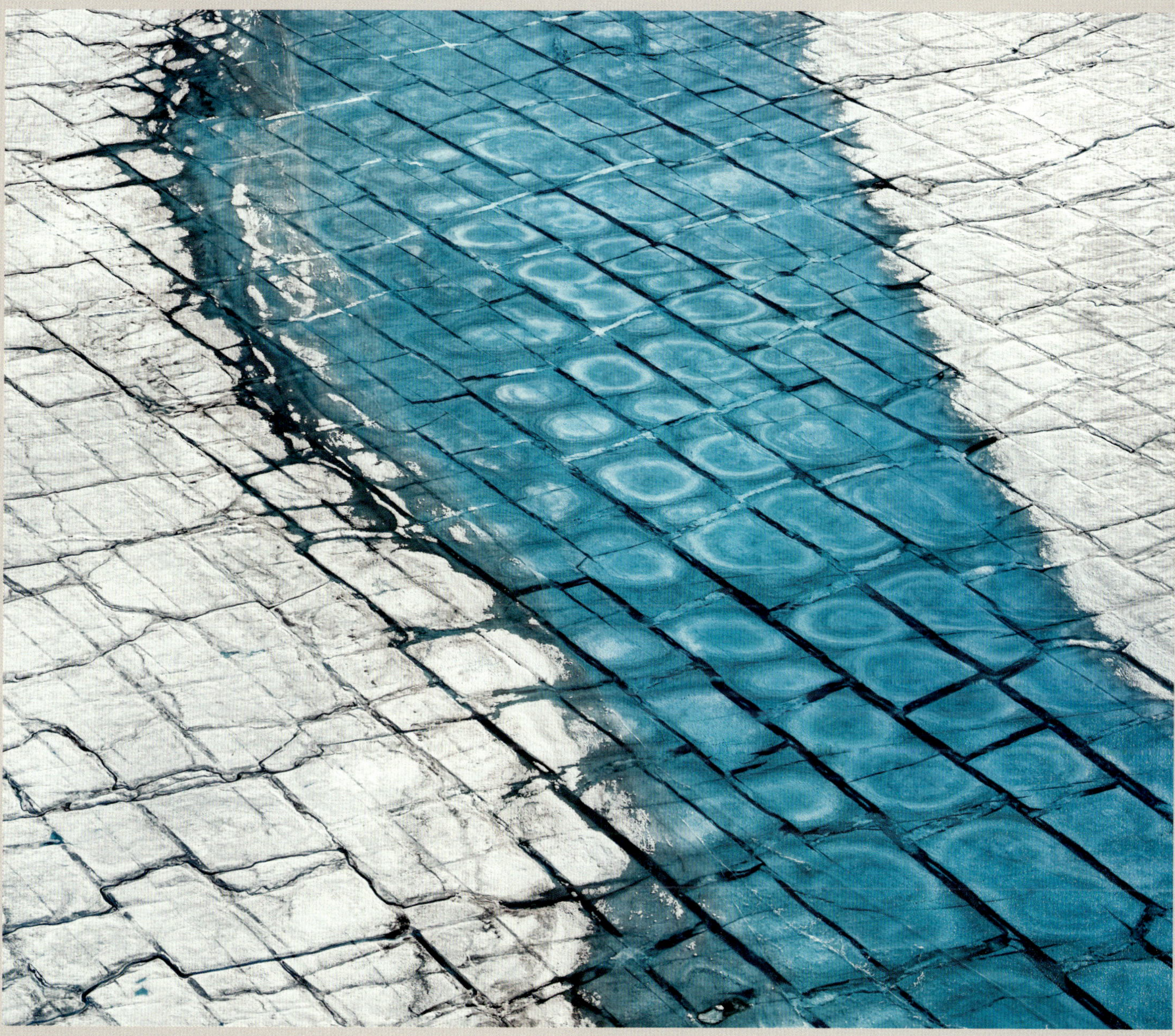

across 15 countries in three continents at 250 locations. Rather than solving the mystery, they made it bigger. In some sense, this is progress. It should help rule out ideas about the origin of fairy circles that are unique to the Namib or Australia. On the other hand, this might just be a mystery to watch unfold from on high for many more years to come.

Elsewhere, aerial photographs of strange-looking shapes in nature have helped yield more satisfying results.

Drone, airplane, and satellite images have all been used to describe and map shapes in thawing ground or melting ice that, as they change from year to year, reveal their origins in freeze-thaw cycles and the slow slide of landscapes.

Can strange shapes in an overlook give us clues to how the world works? Certainly. Have we figured out all the links between natural patterns of shapes and the processes that create them? Certainly not.

DANIEL BELTRÁ
Meltwater pools square up southeast of Ilulissat, within the Greenland ice sheet.

Following pages:
GEORGE STEINMETZ
A dormant volcano lords over the patchwork terrain of Terceira, one of the islands of the Azores.

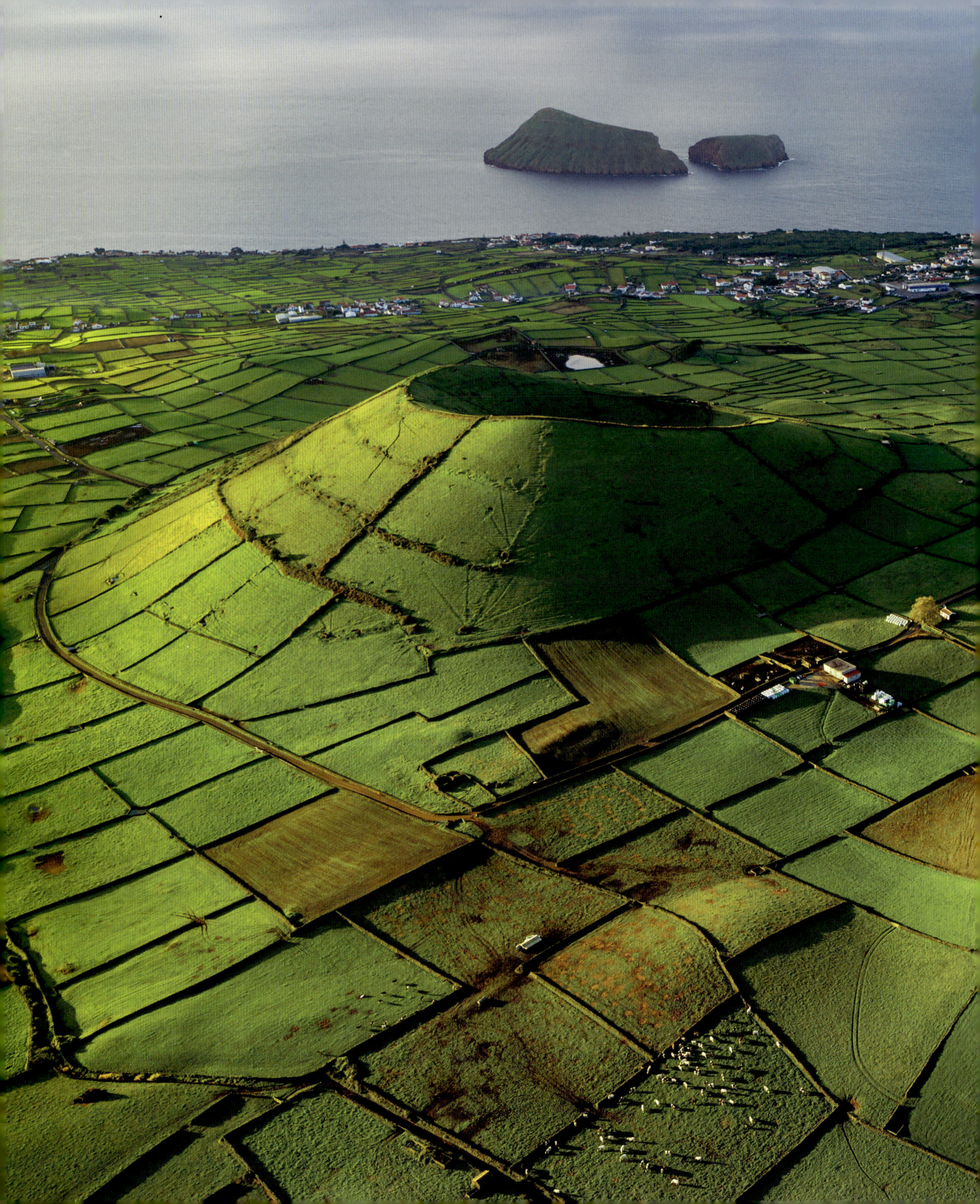

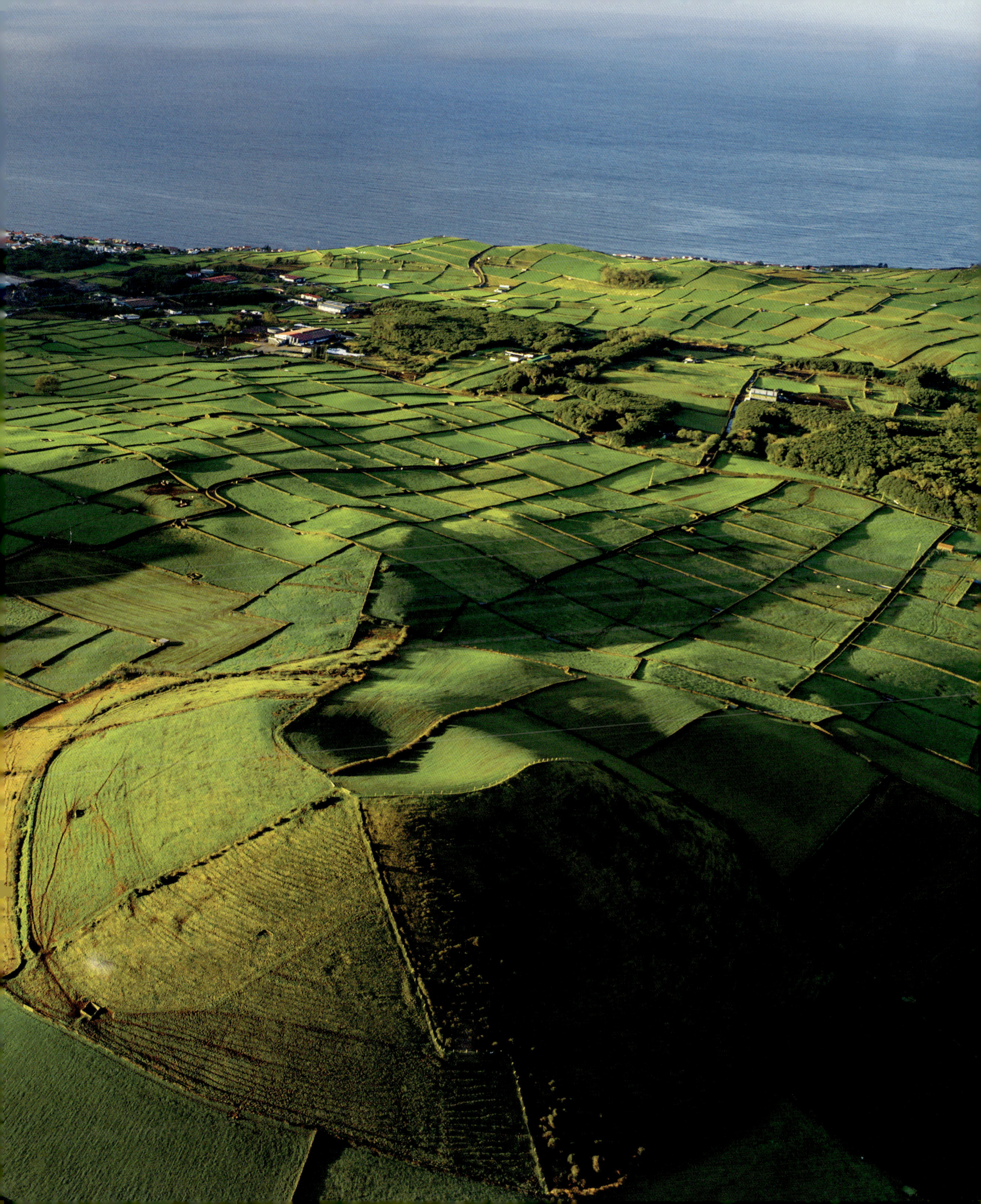

Lord,
but this
is a funny
world when
you get
to studying!

~GENE STRATTON-PORTER, *A GIRL OF THE LIMBERLOST*

ROB KESSELER
The seed of an Australian legume, *Medicago arborea*, curls in upon itself as it matures.

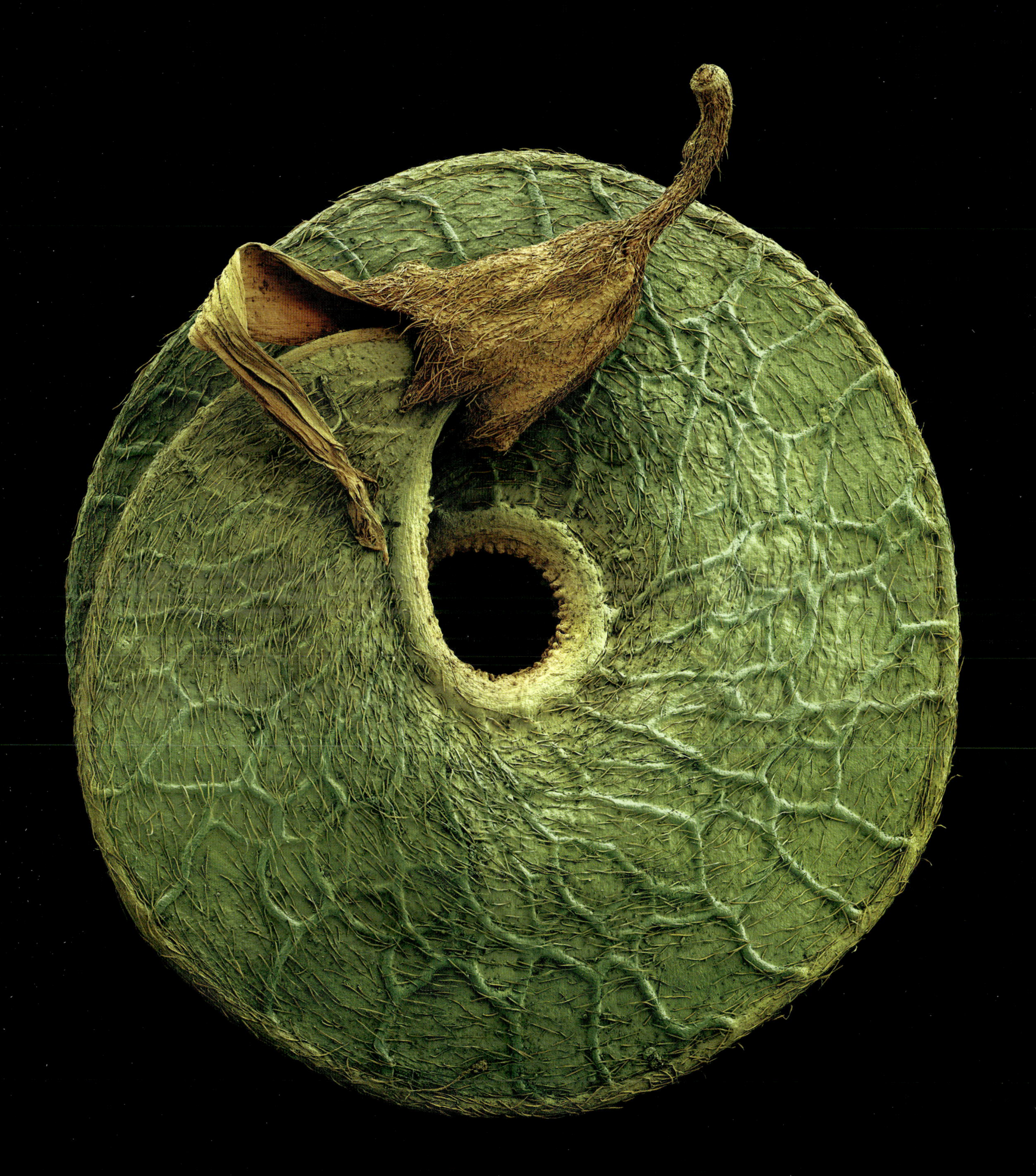

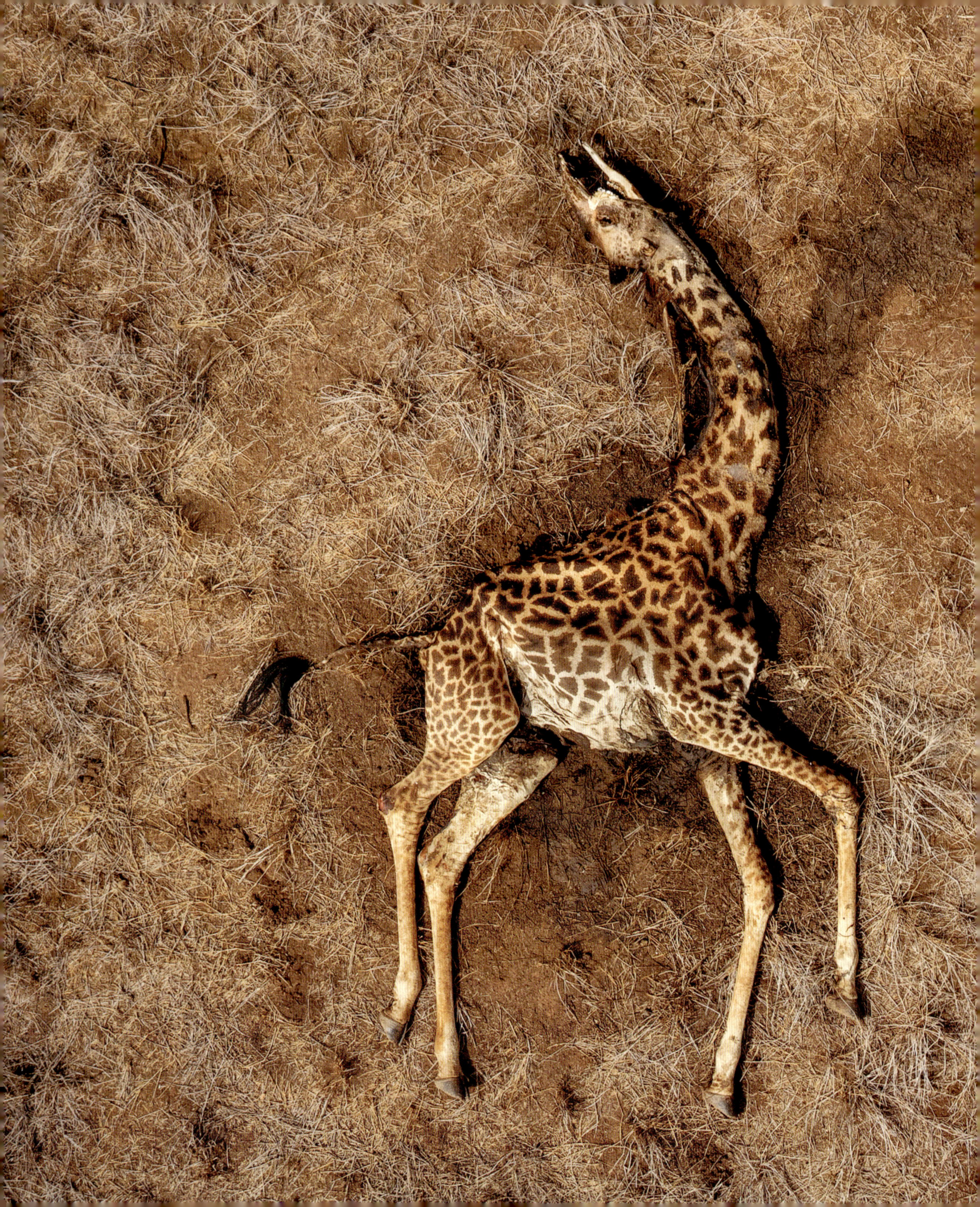

CHARLIE HAMILTON JAMES
A victim of a lengthy drought in southern Kenya, the corpse of a giraffe seems one with the parched earth.

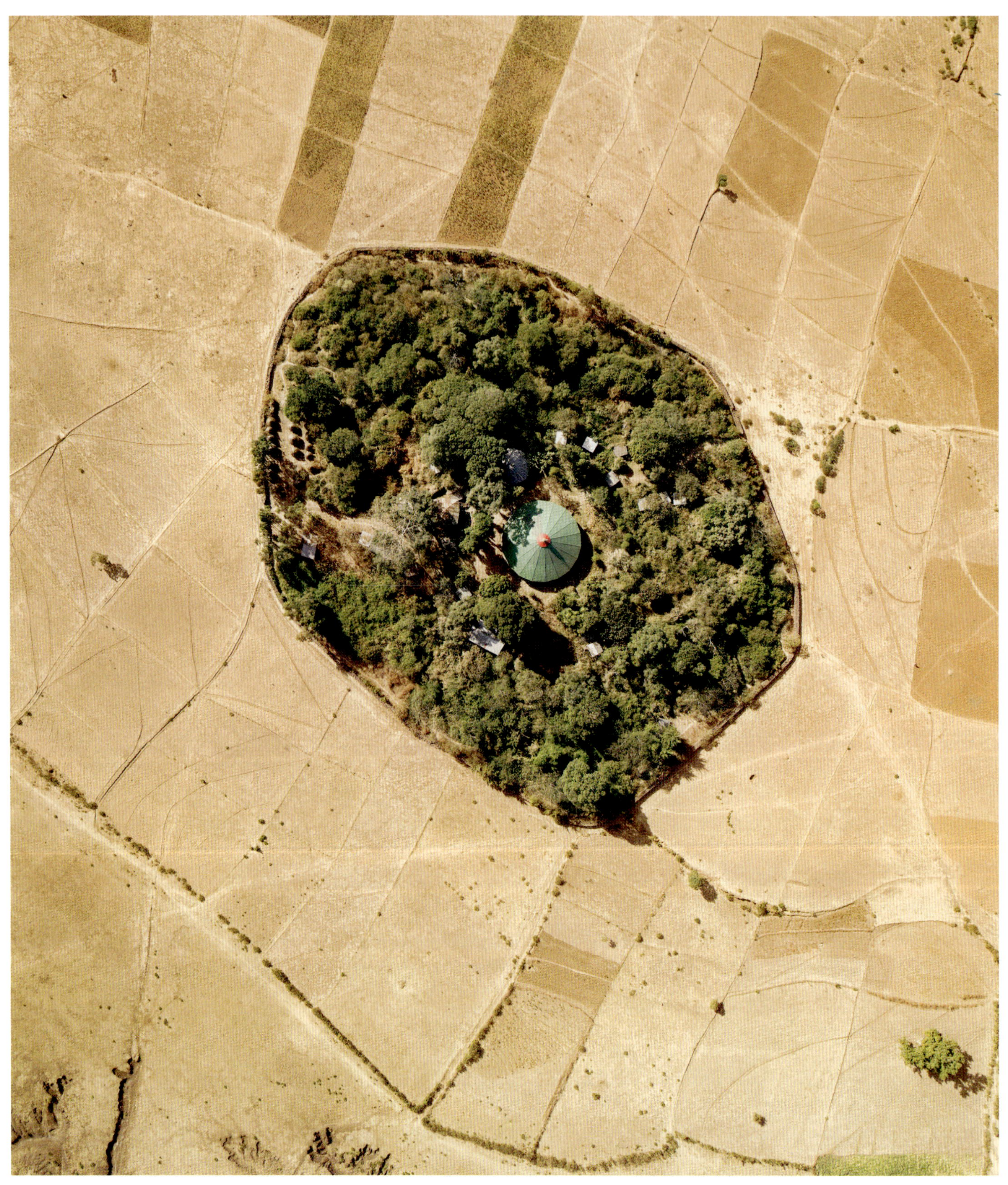

KIERAN DODDS
The keepers of the round Ethiopian Orthodox Tewahedo Church, an oasis both
literal and spiritual, tend to the trees that surround it as well.

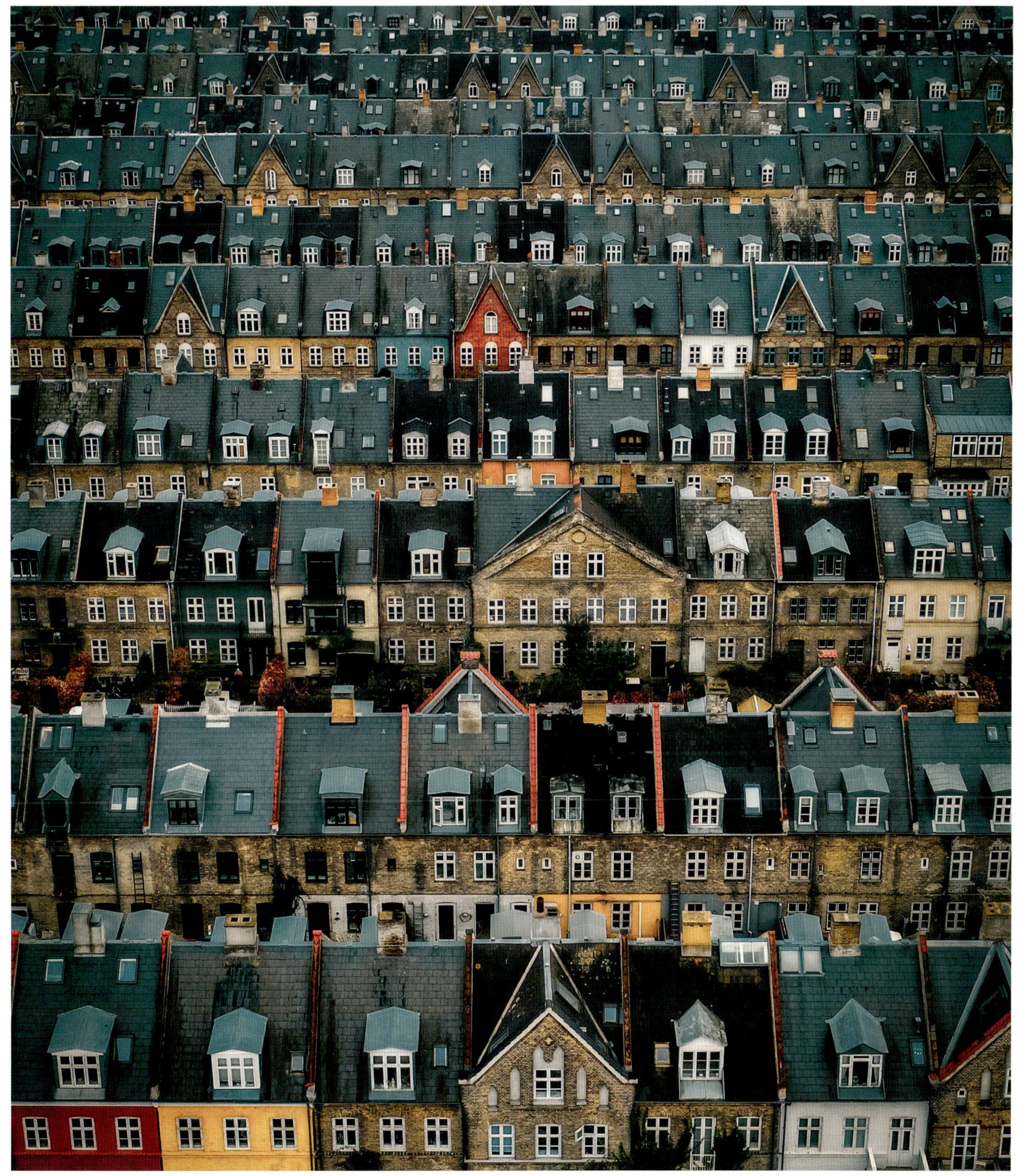

SERHIY VOVK
Elegant lines and symmetry characterize Kartoffelraekkerne,
a neighborhood in Copenhagen, Denmark.

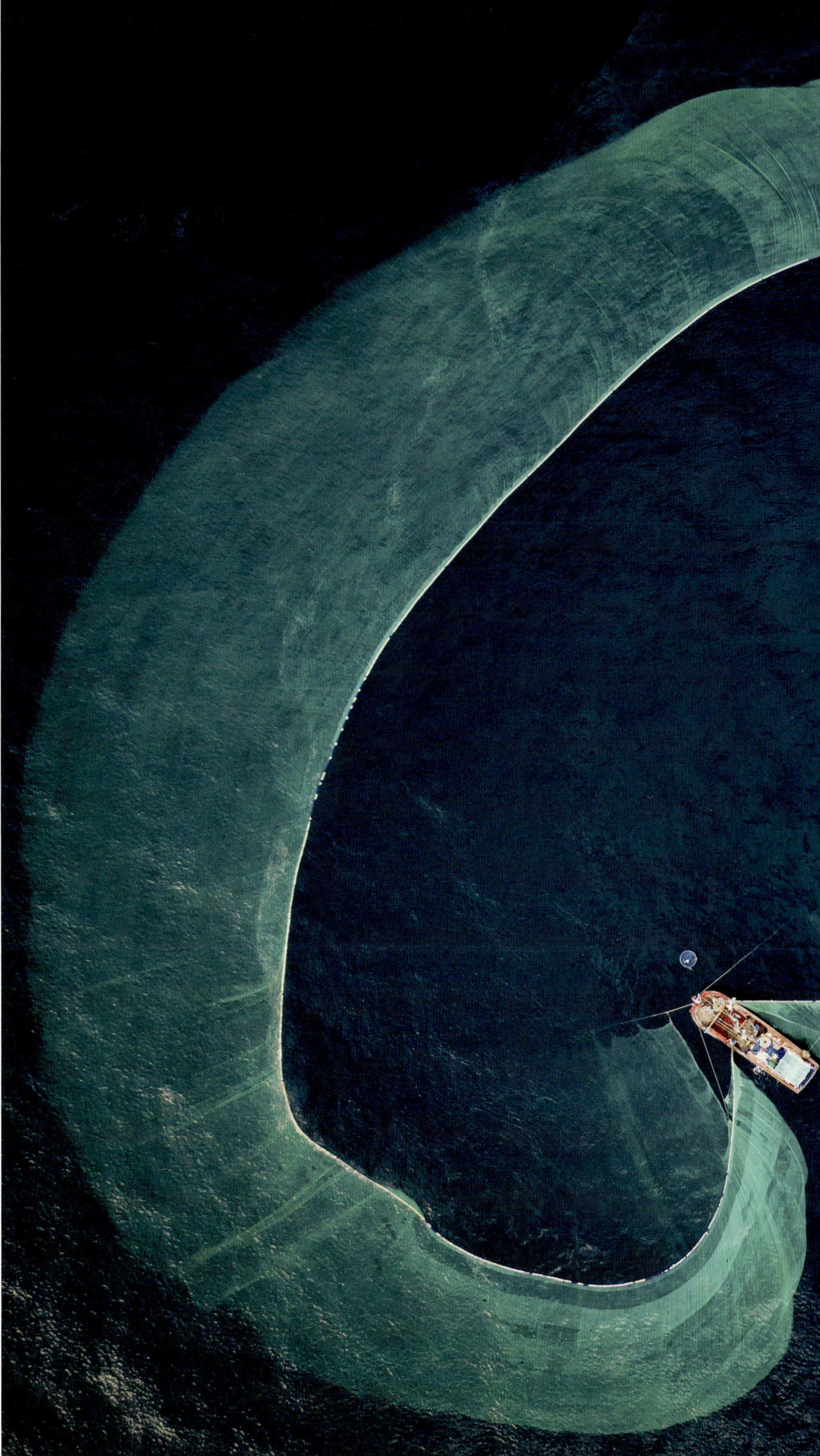

THIEN NGUYEN NGOC
Nets spread wide, fishers off Vietnam's Hon Yen coast seek anchovies, a key ingredient in local fish sauce.

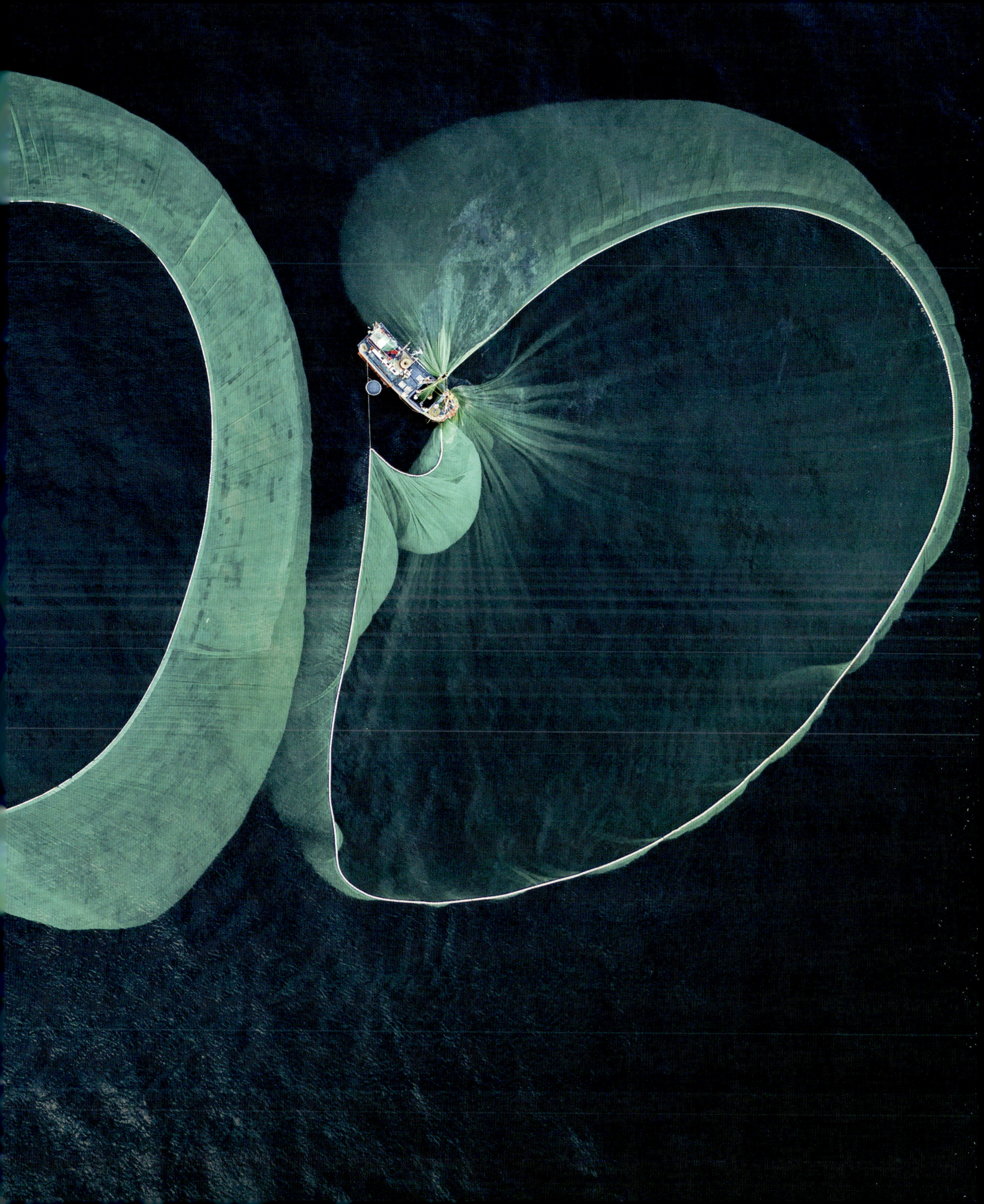

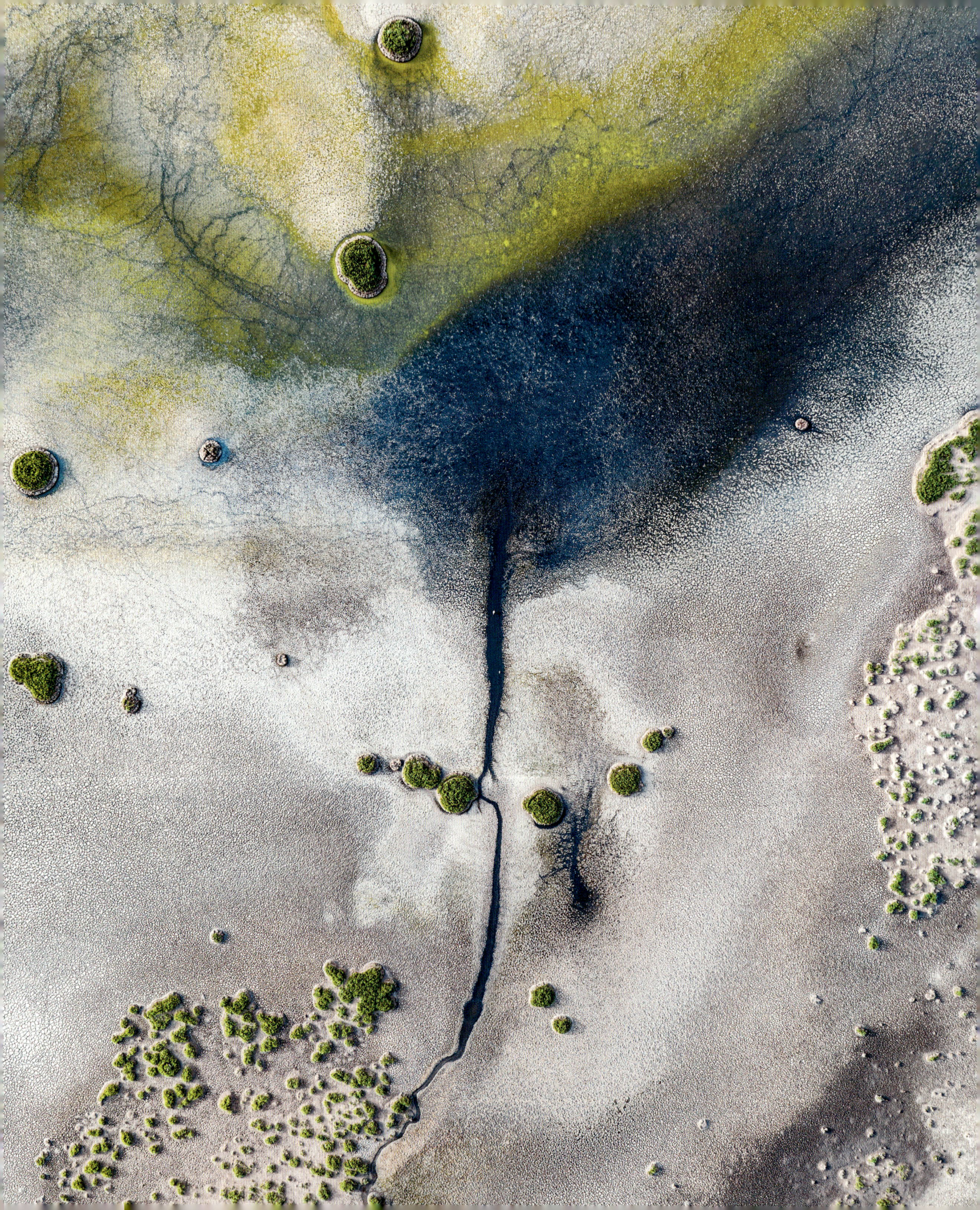

You are the deep
cool moss /
Rain-soaked, fresh. / ...
You are everything
that is young, /
And cool and beautiful.

ANDREA MARONGIU
Salt formations emerged amid 2022's severely dry summer,
creating rarely seen shapes and colors in Sardinia's Sinis Peninsula.

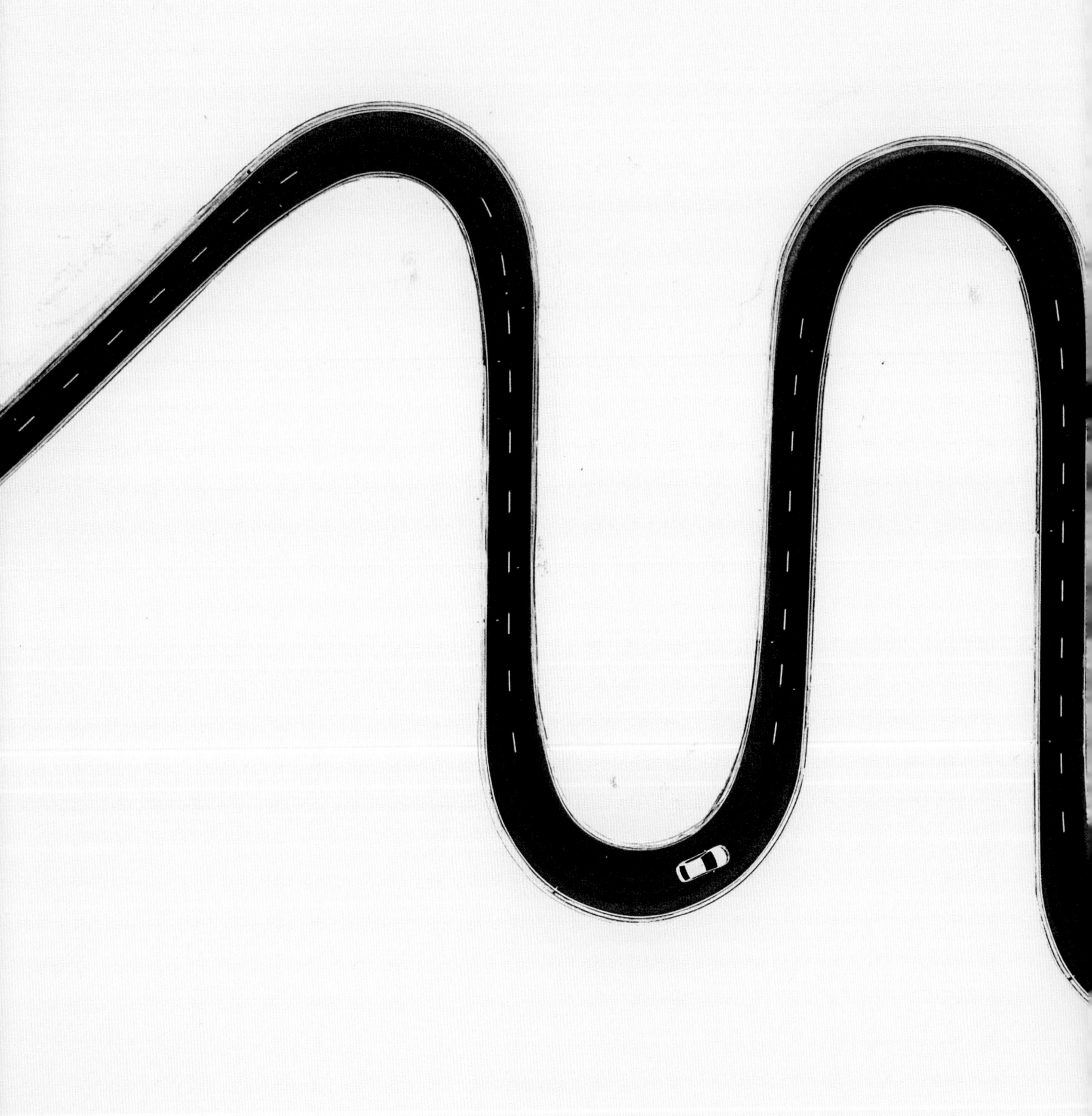

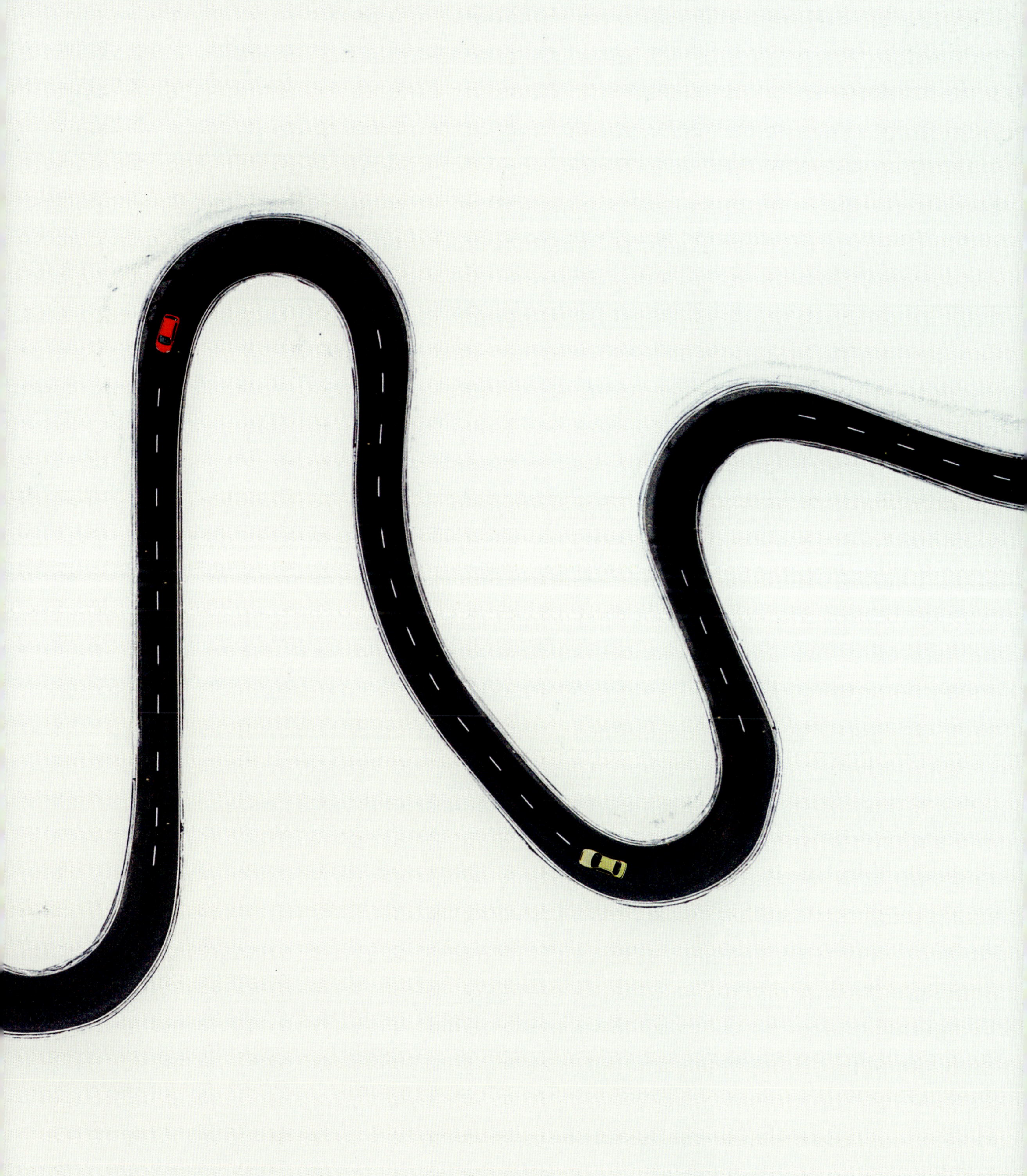

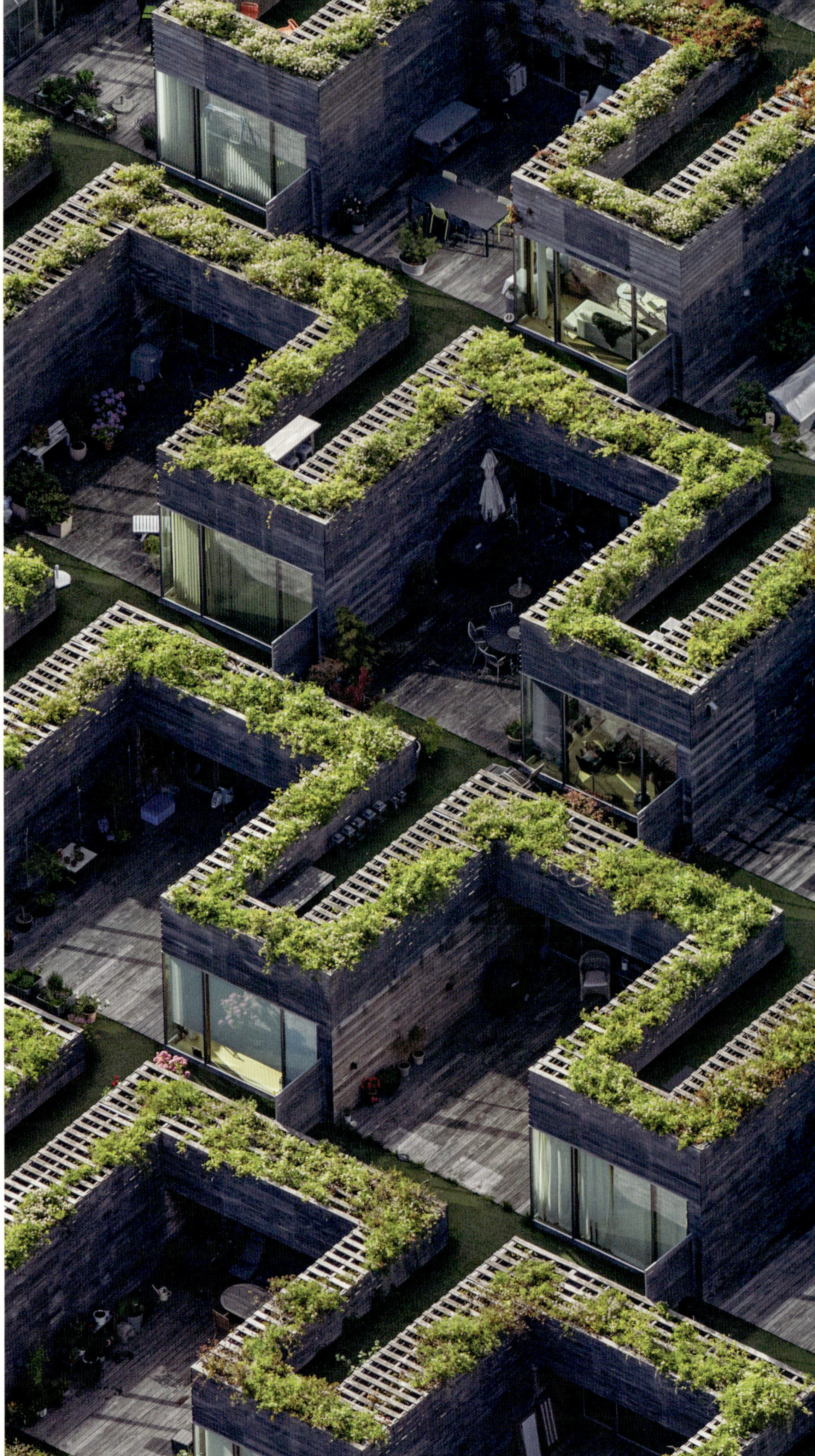

ALEX MACLEAN
Picture windows and rooftop gardens enhance this orderly neighborhood in Ørestad, Denmark.

Previous pages:
ROBERTO MOIOLA
Black road, white snow: Julier Pass, a beloved drive through the Albula range of the Swiss Alps

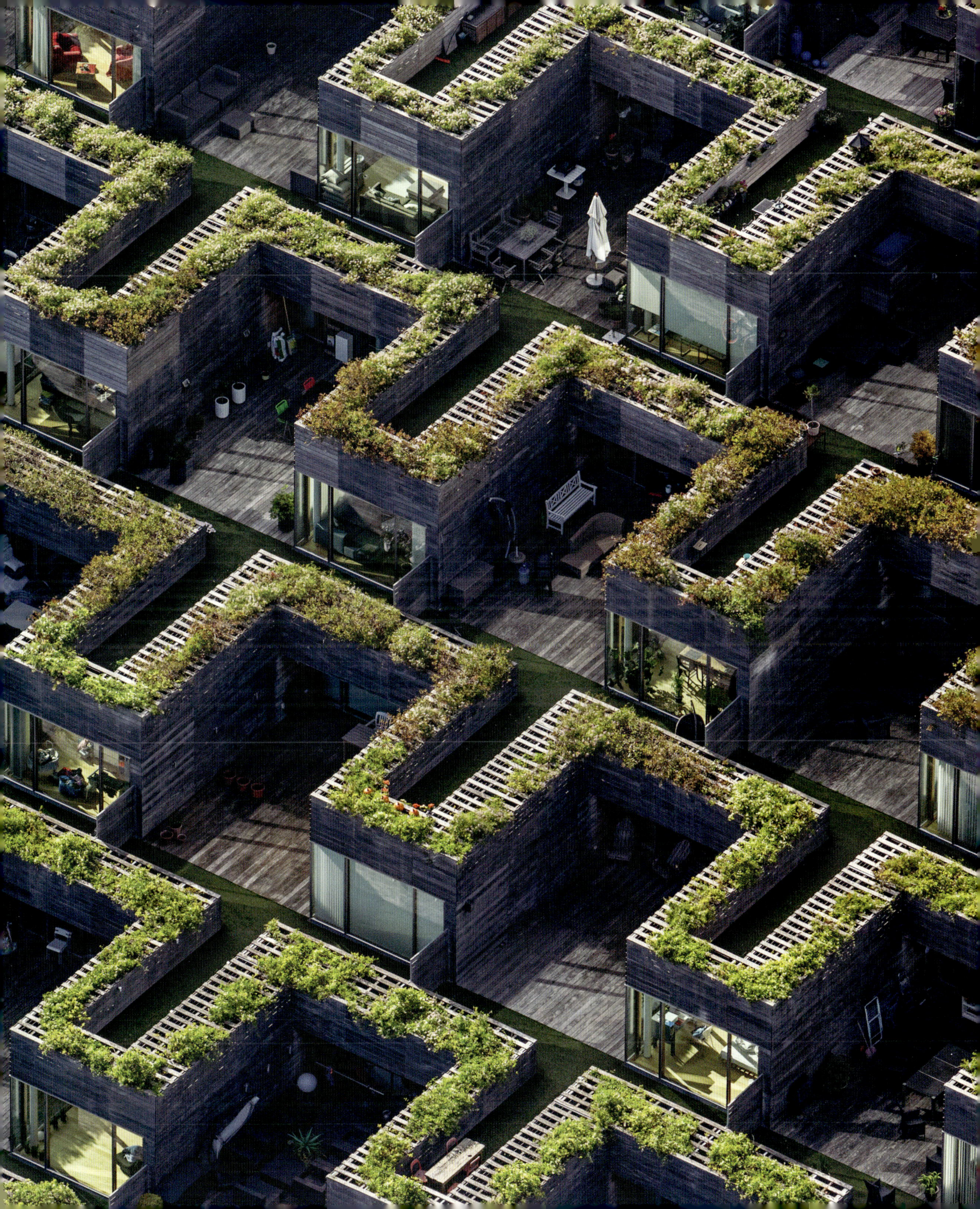

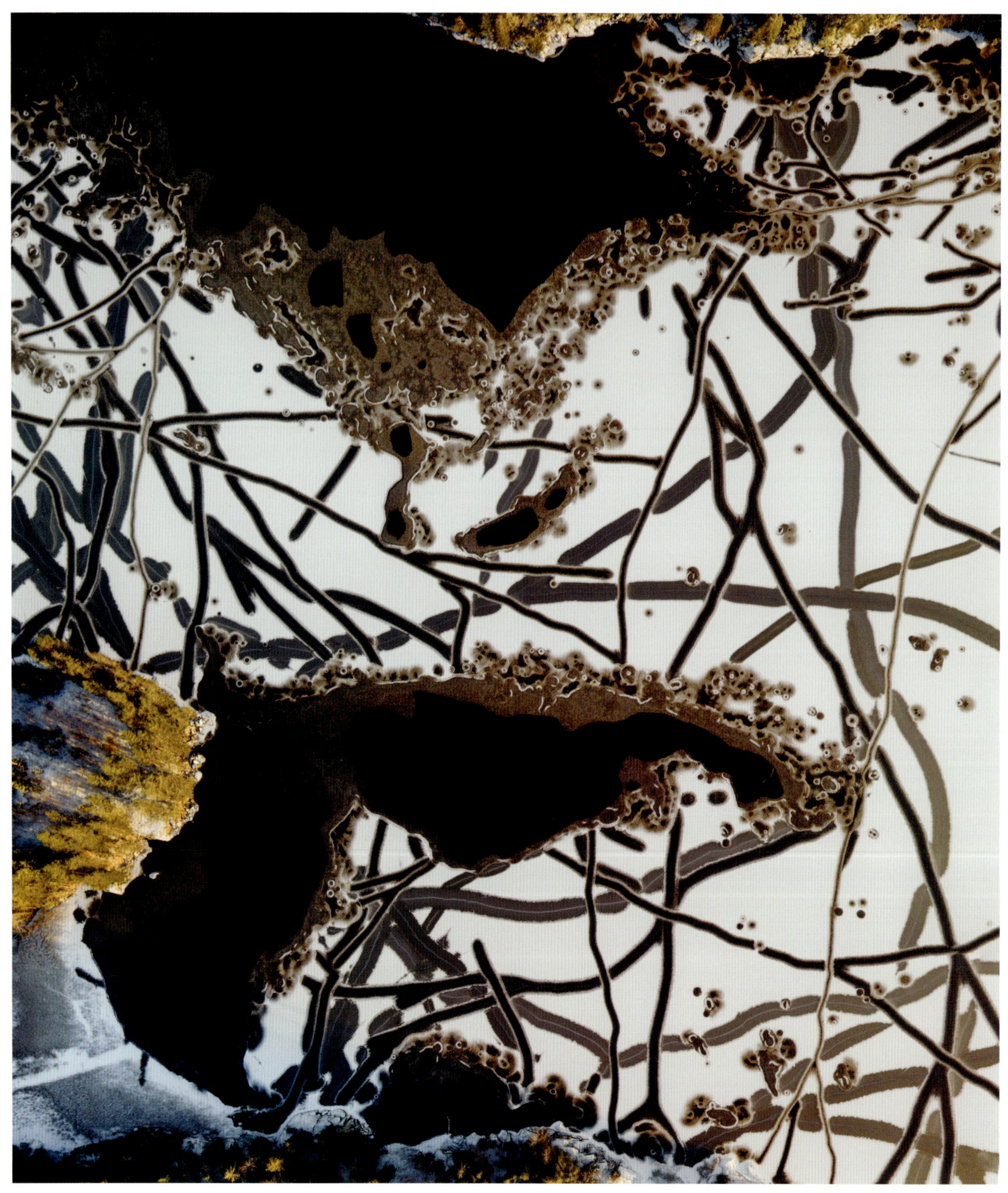

PÅL HERMANSEN
Thin ice begins to crack across a lake after the first snow in Follo, Norway.

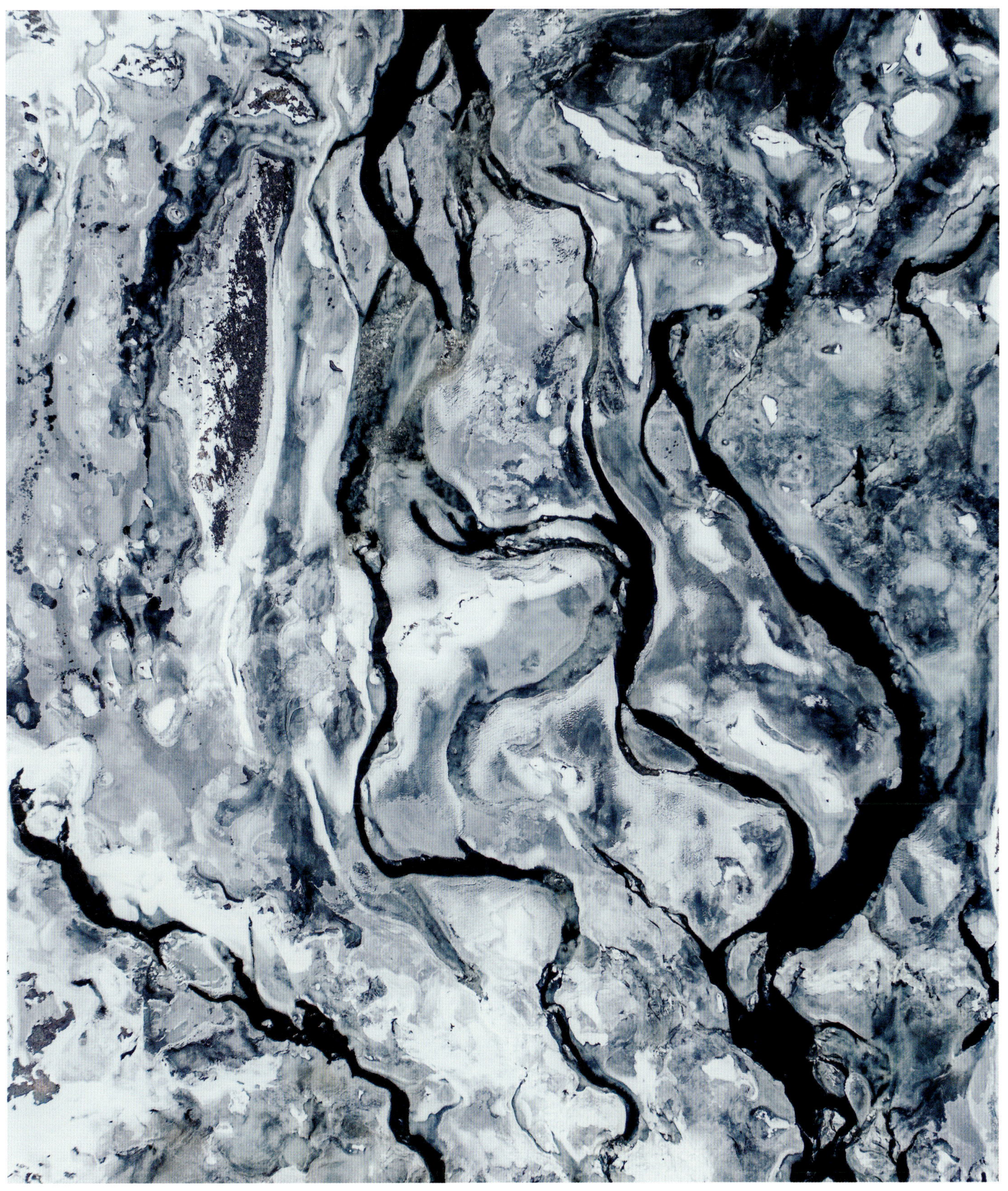

JULIA PERTEK
Icy intricacy as the Grimsá River cascades down the Laxfoss waterfall in western Iceland

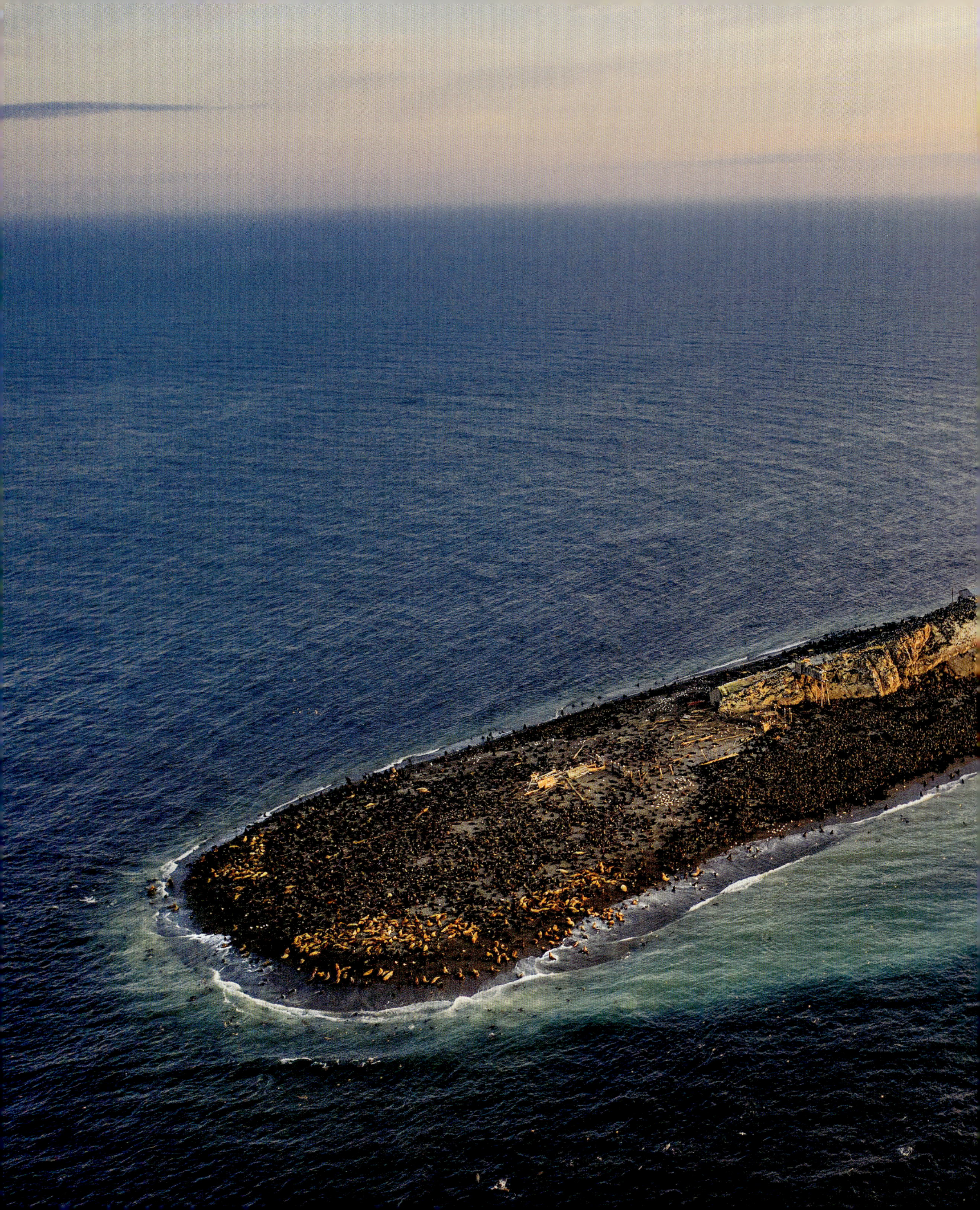

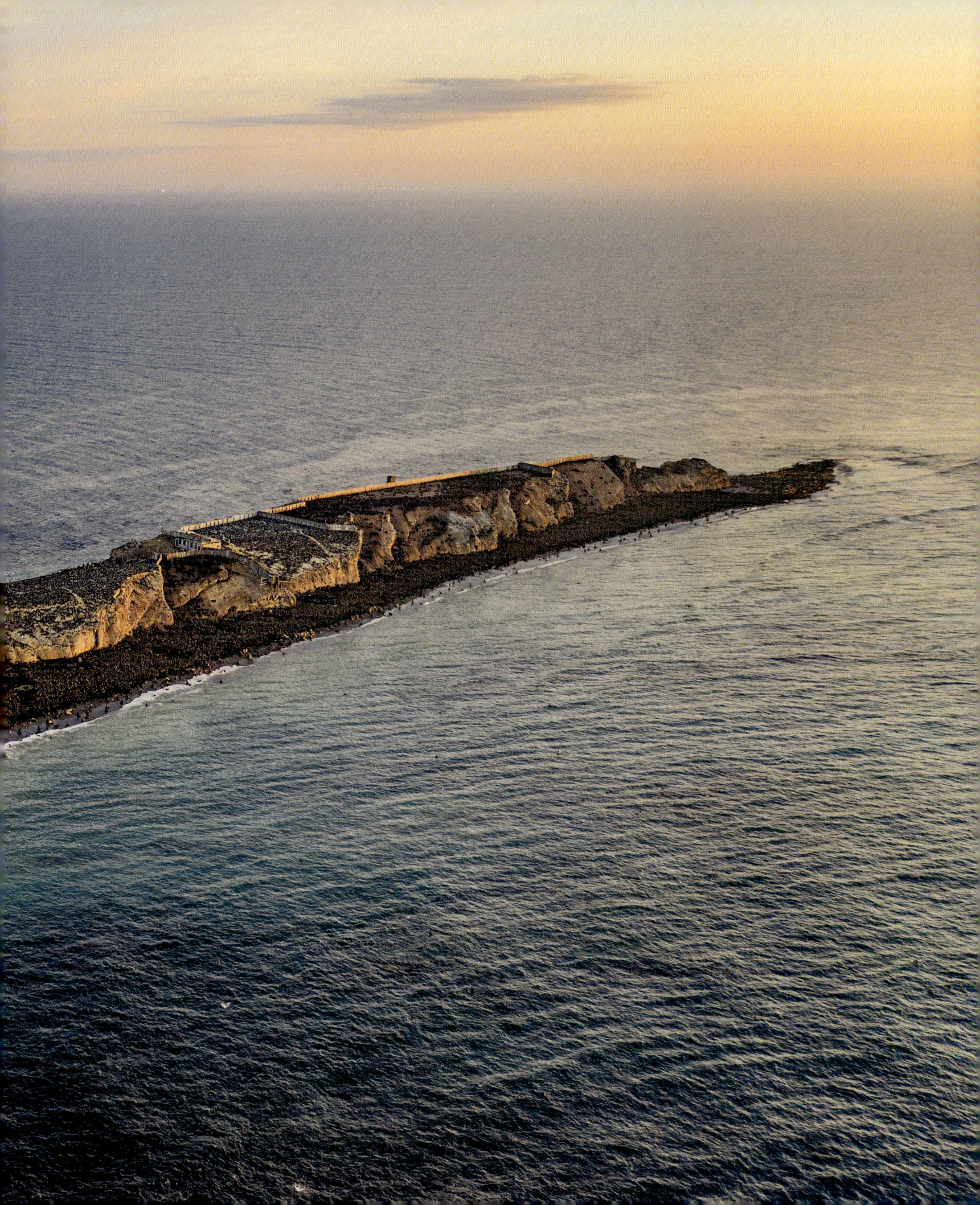

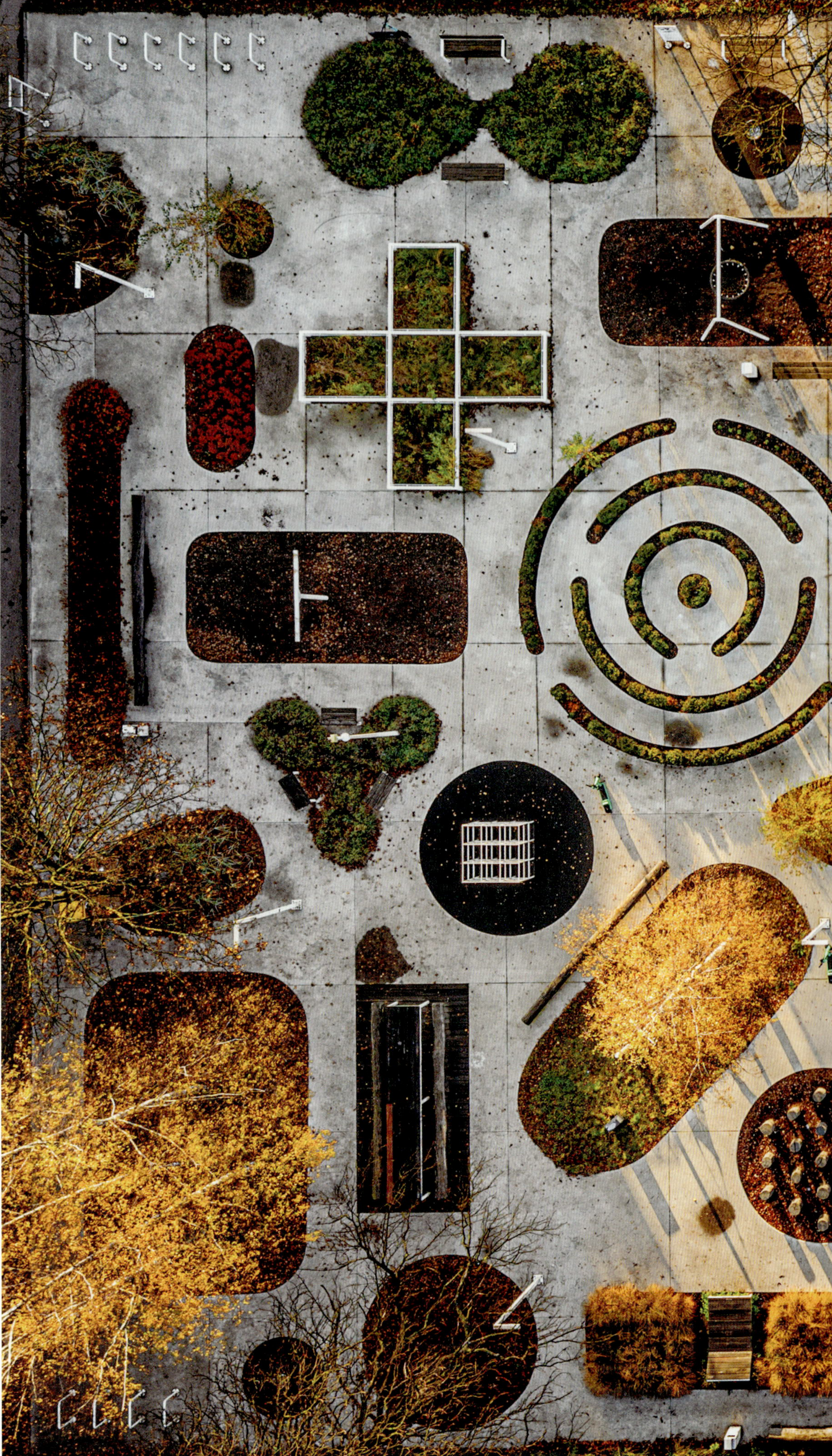

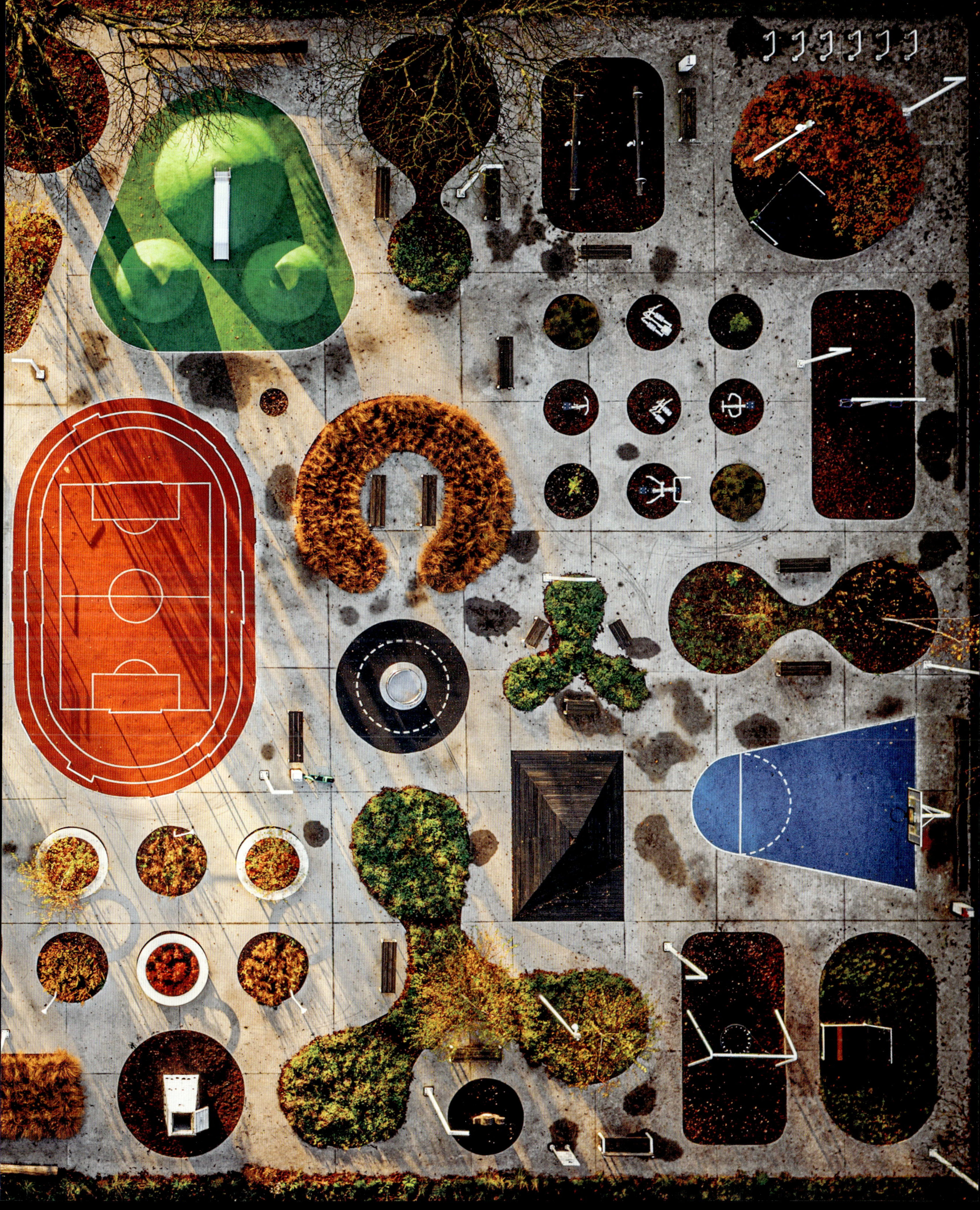

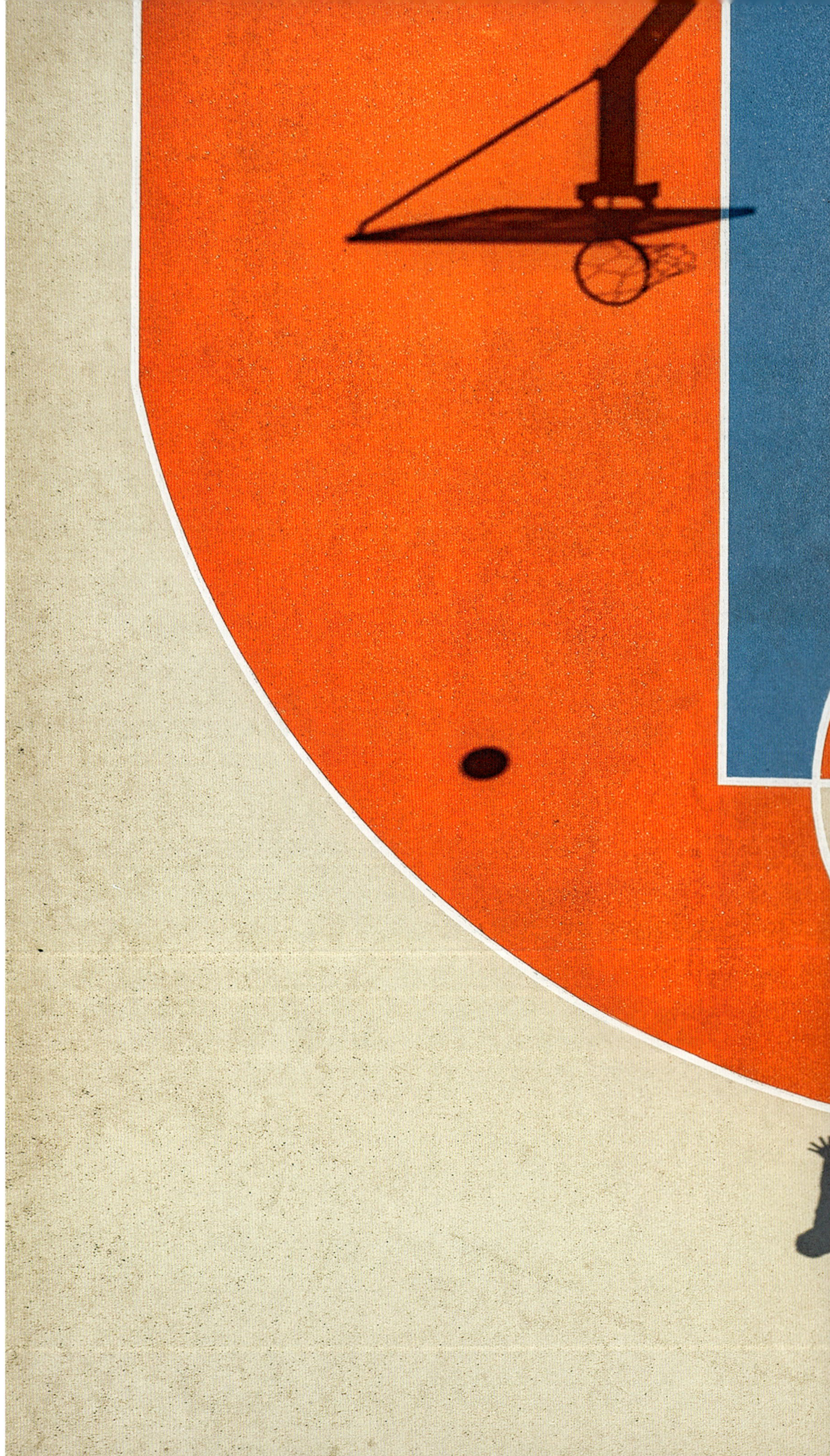

KATERYNA POLISHCHUK
Stop-action shadows break
the patterns of a basketball court
in Kharkiv, Ukraine.

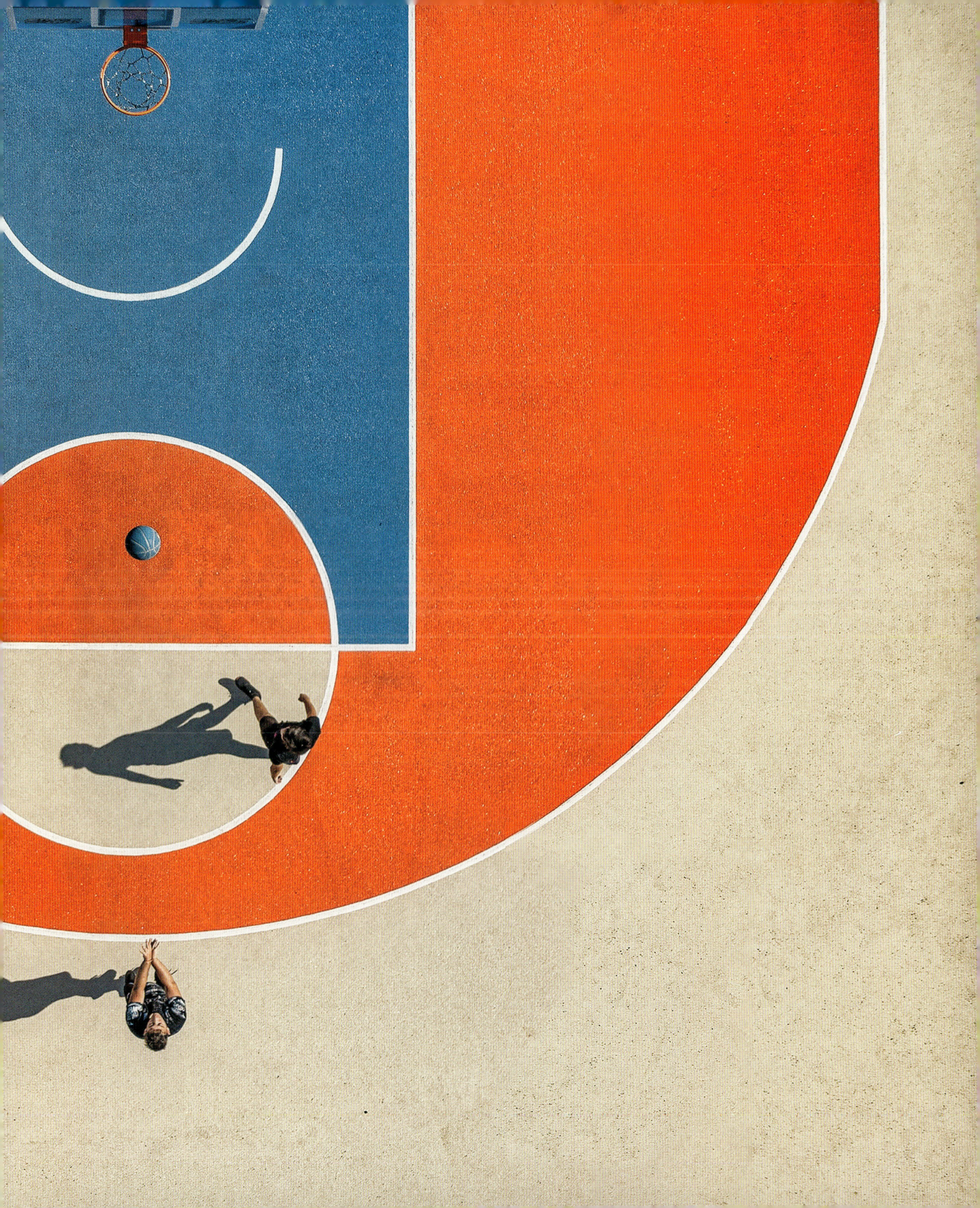

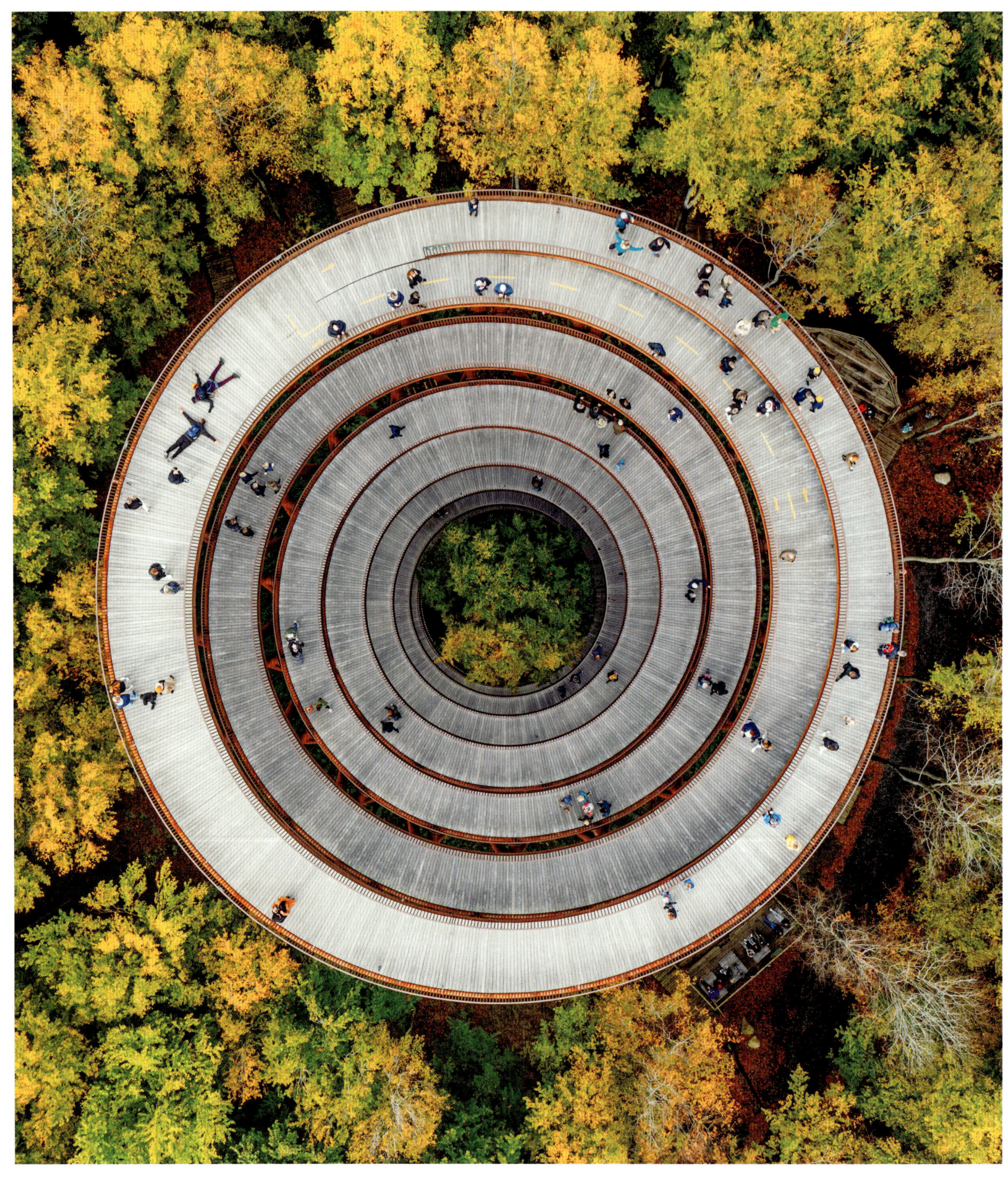

ORSOLYA HAARBERG
Spiraling into the treetops, a circular boardwalk invites visitors to commune with nature at
Camp Adventure near Copenhagen, Denmark.

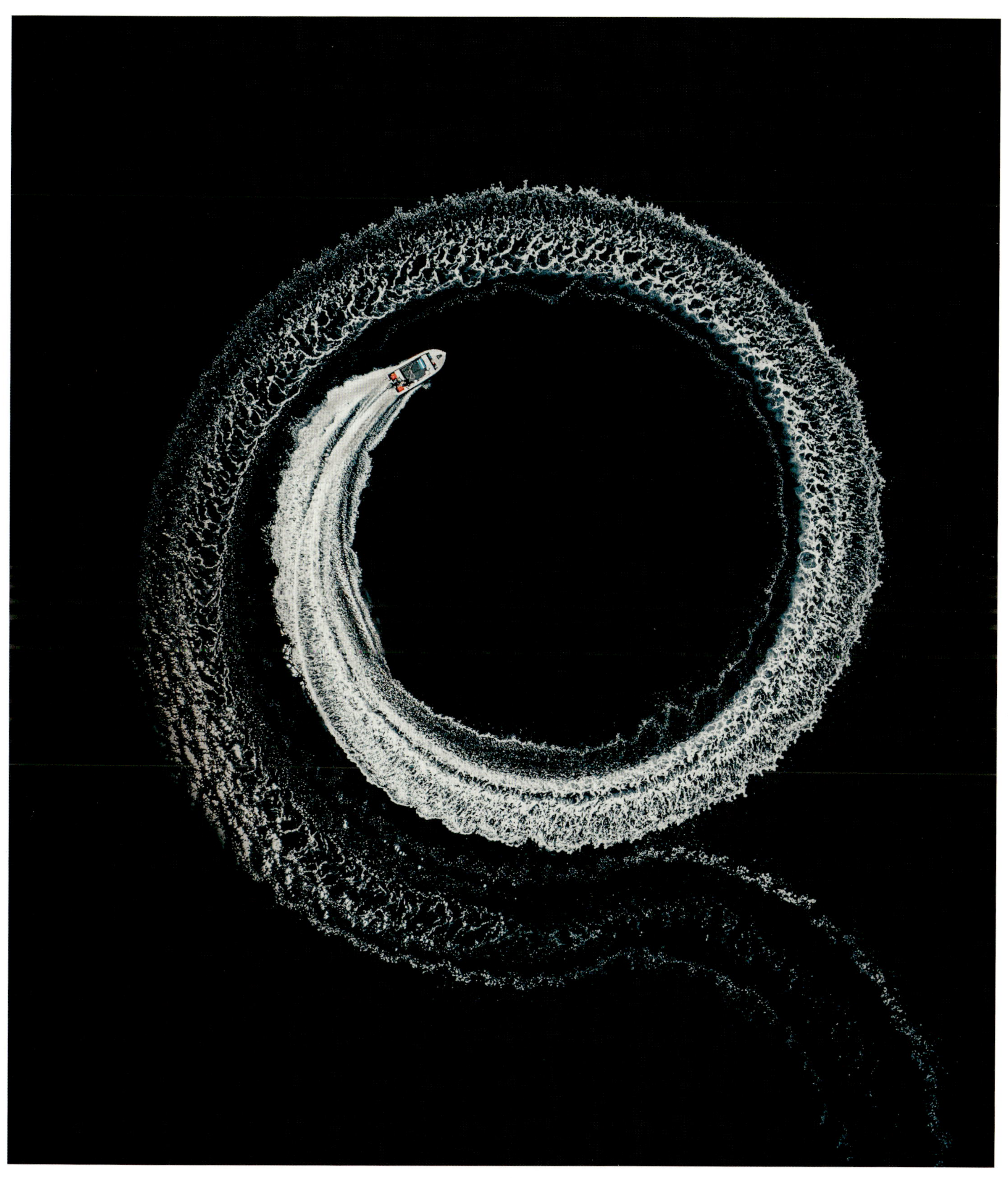

DEBBIE STEVENS
Boaters redefine the word "wheelie" in the waters of the Mandurah Estuary south of Perth,
Western Australia.

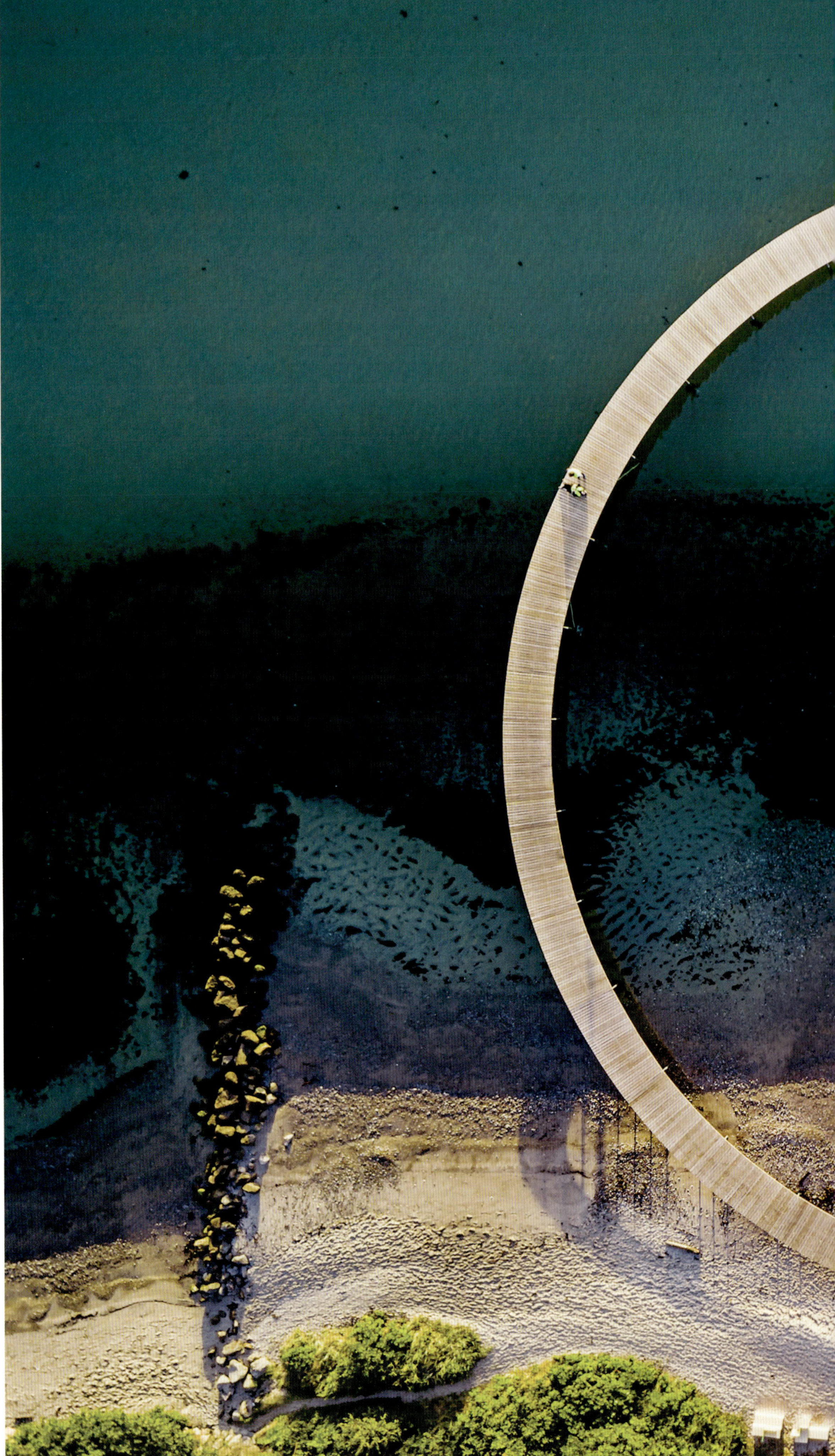

DENNIS BORUP JAKOBSEN
The Infinite Bridge imposes a
perfect circle on the water's edge
in Aarhus, Denmark.

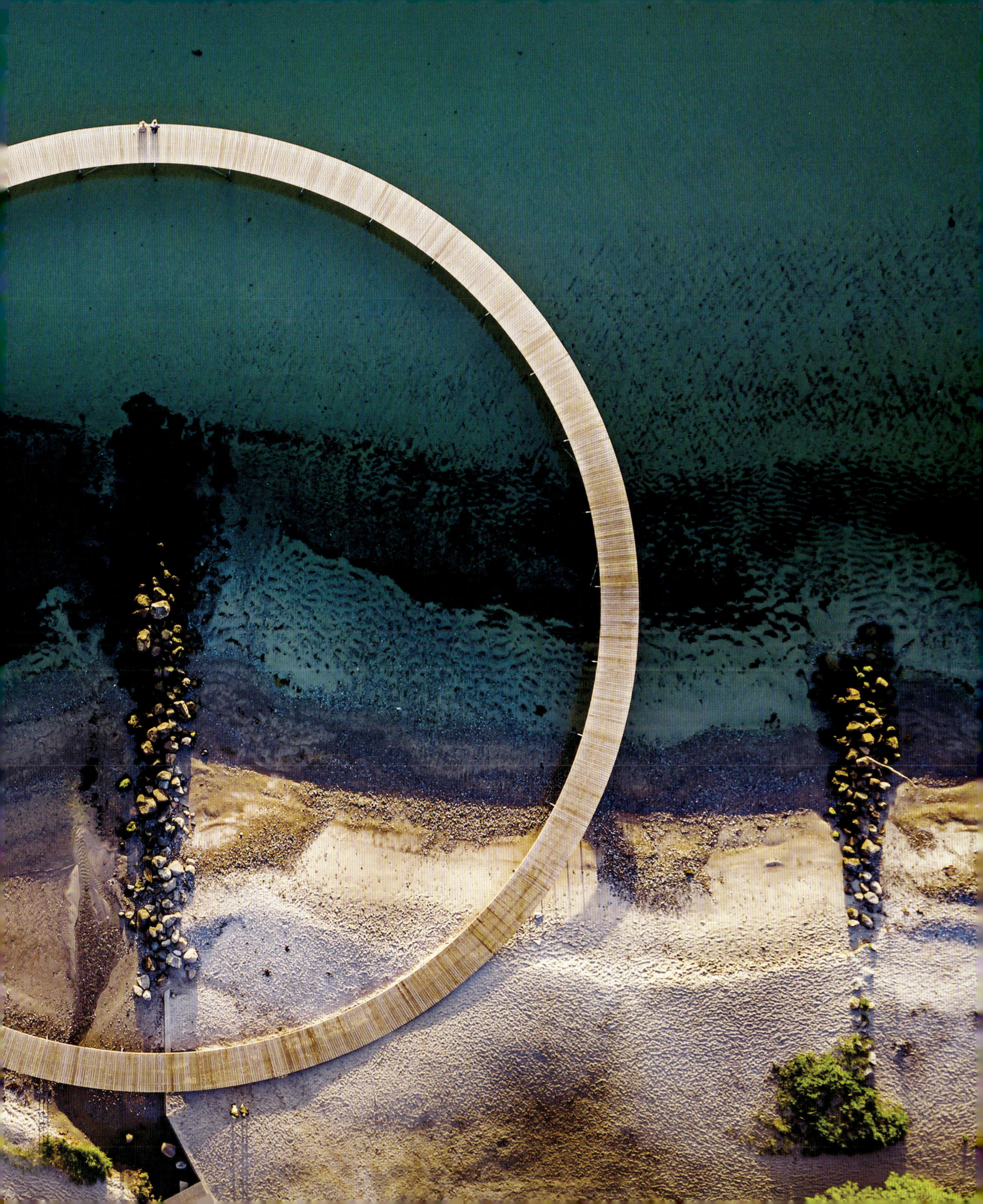

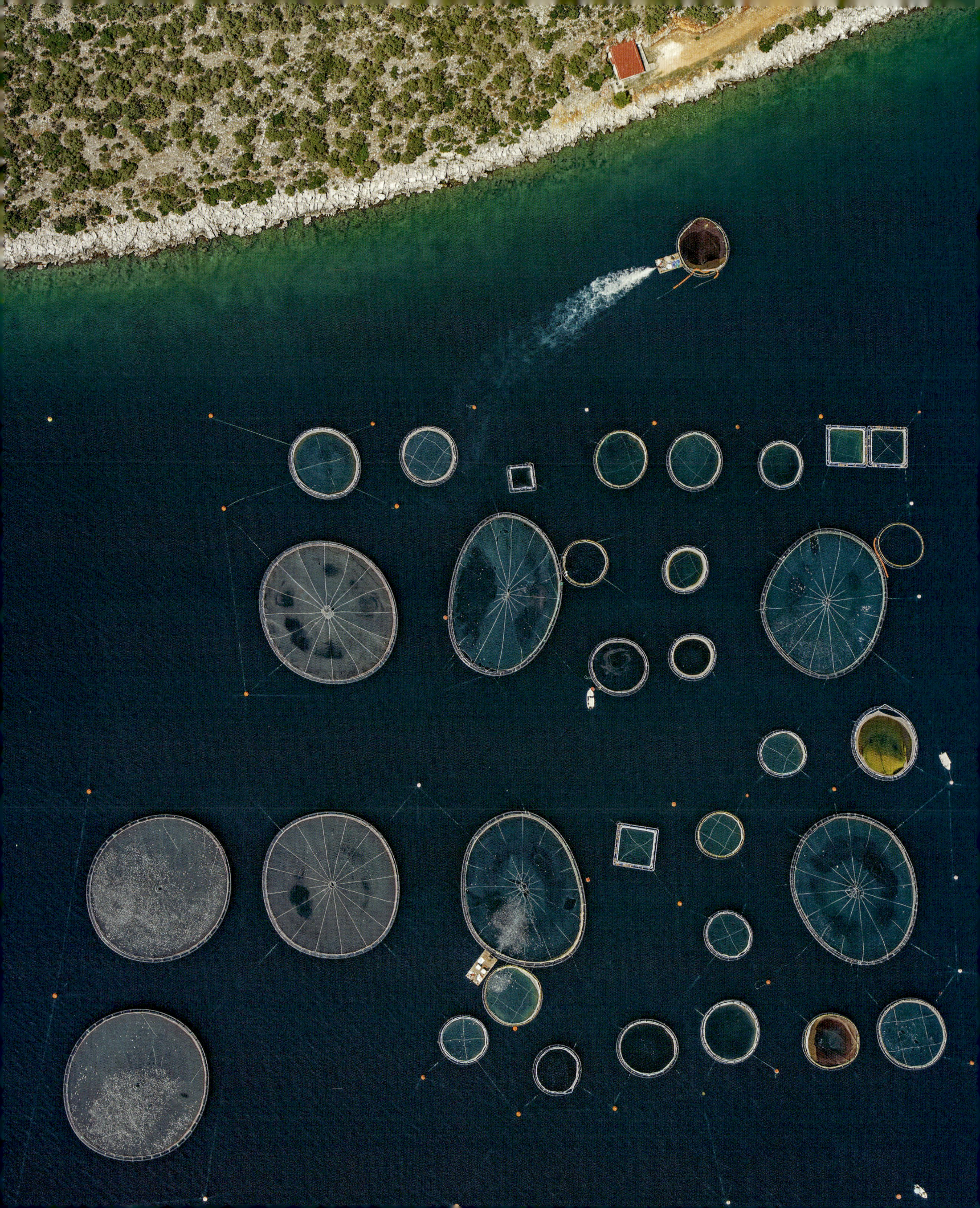

If anyone should come to
the top of the air ...
he could lift his head above it
and see, as fishes lift their
heads out of the water and
see the things in our world ...

~SOCRATES, AS REPORTED BY PLATO IN *PHAEDO*

BERNHARD LANG
Circular and square cages set to trap fish off the Greek coast:
One boat moves a trap toward shore to haul in the catch.

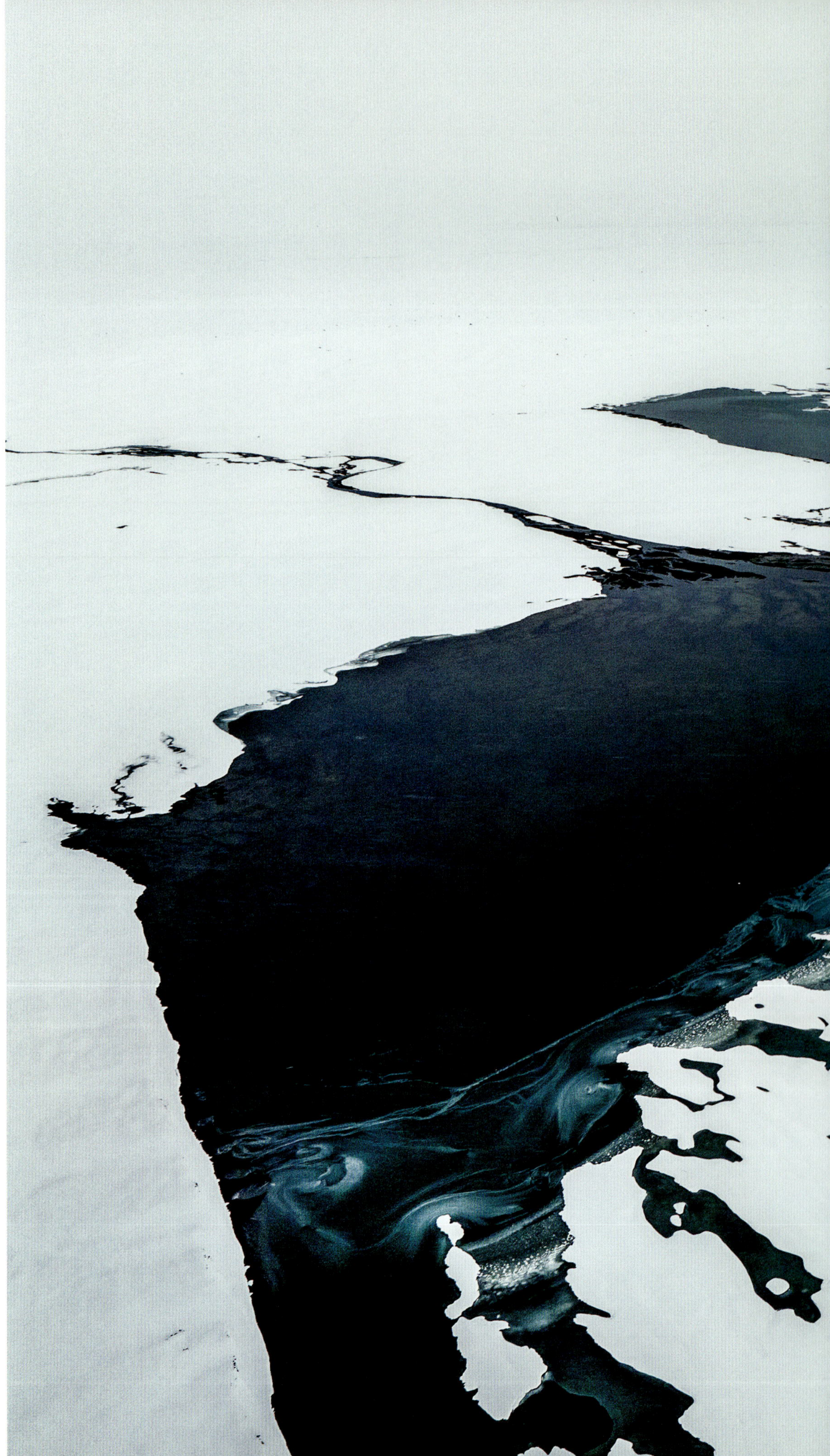

Land meets water meets ice during a summer snowstorm in Bliss Bay, on the north coast of Greenland.

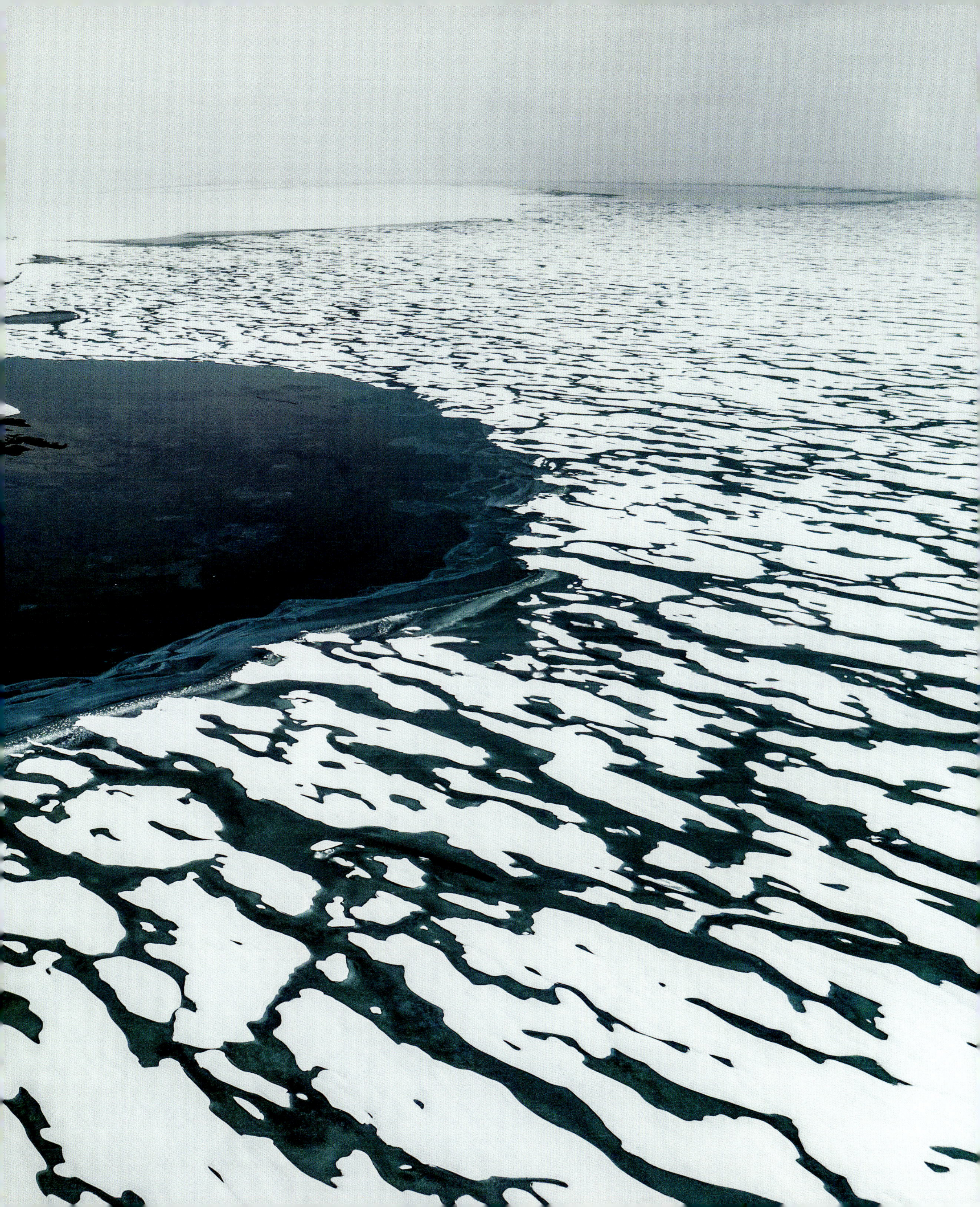

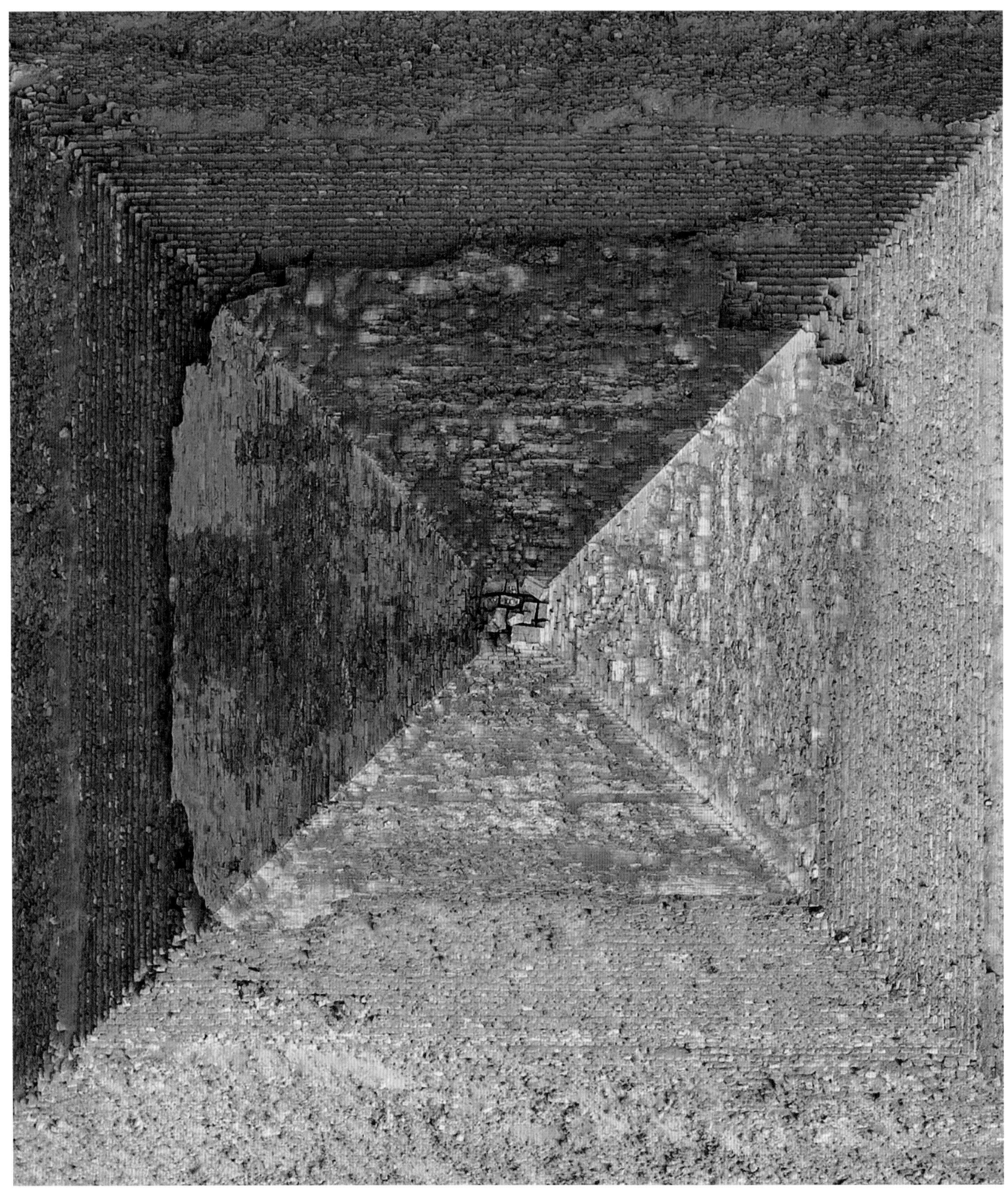

ISLAM MOAWAD
A top-down drone camera view of the pyramid of Khafre, a pharaoh who ruled circa 2500 B.C.E., in Giza, Egypt

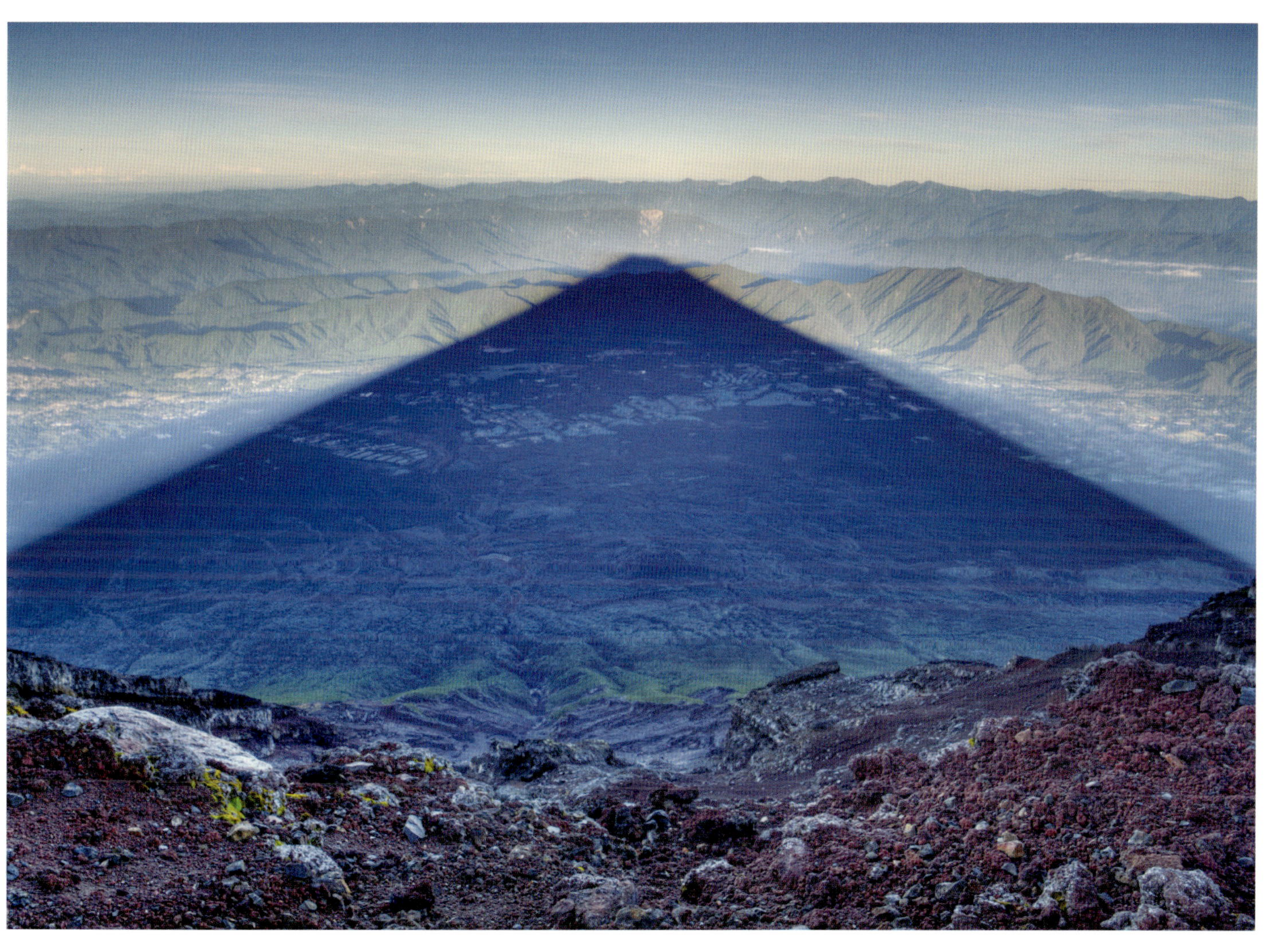

KRIS BOORMAN
Mount Fuji casts its shadow upon the nearby terrain of Honshu island, southwest of Tokyo, Japan.

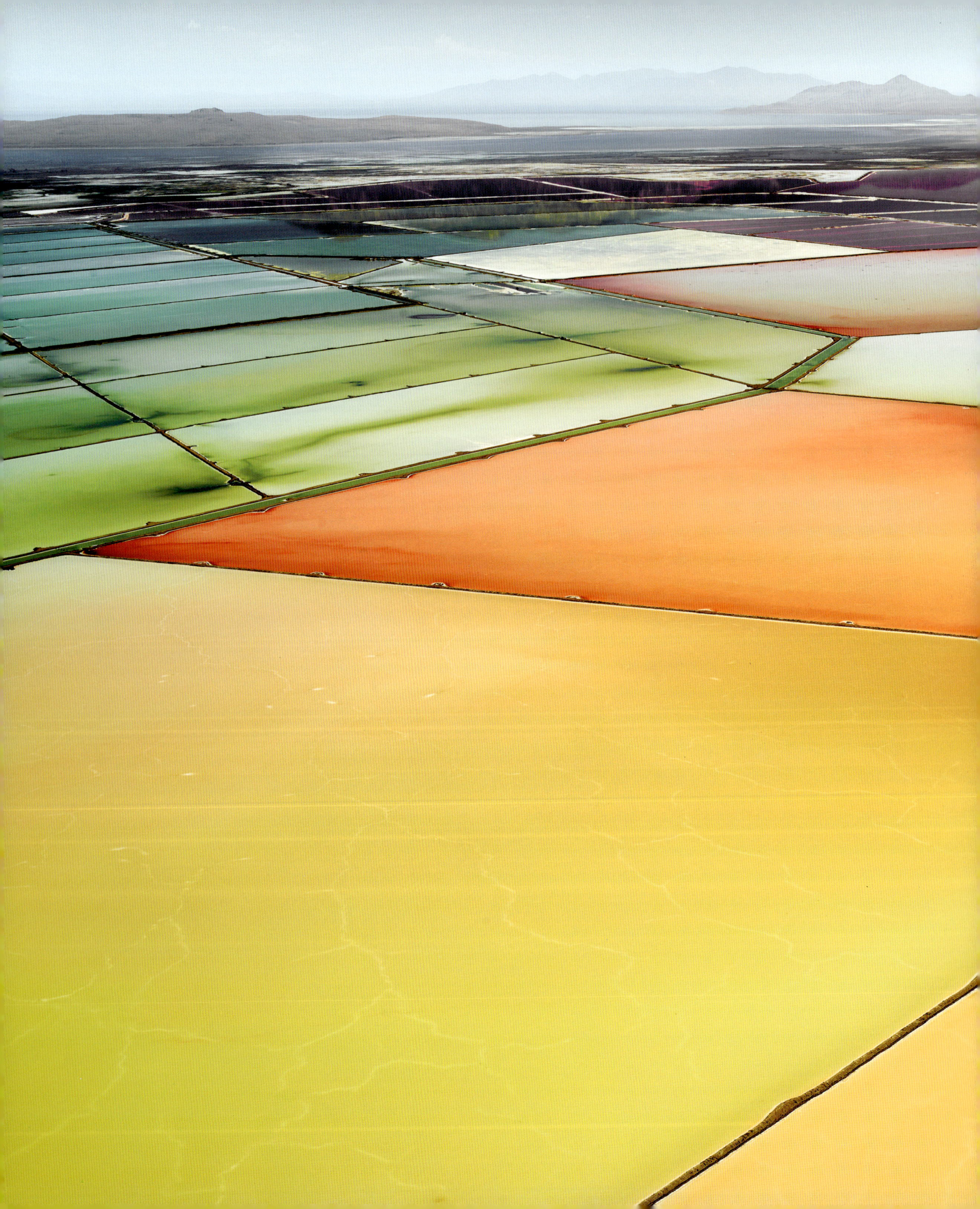

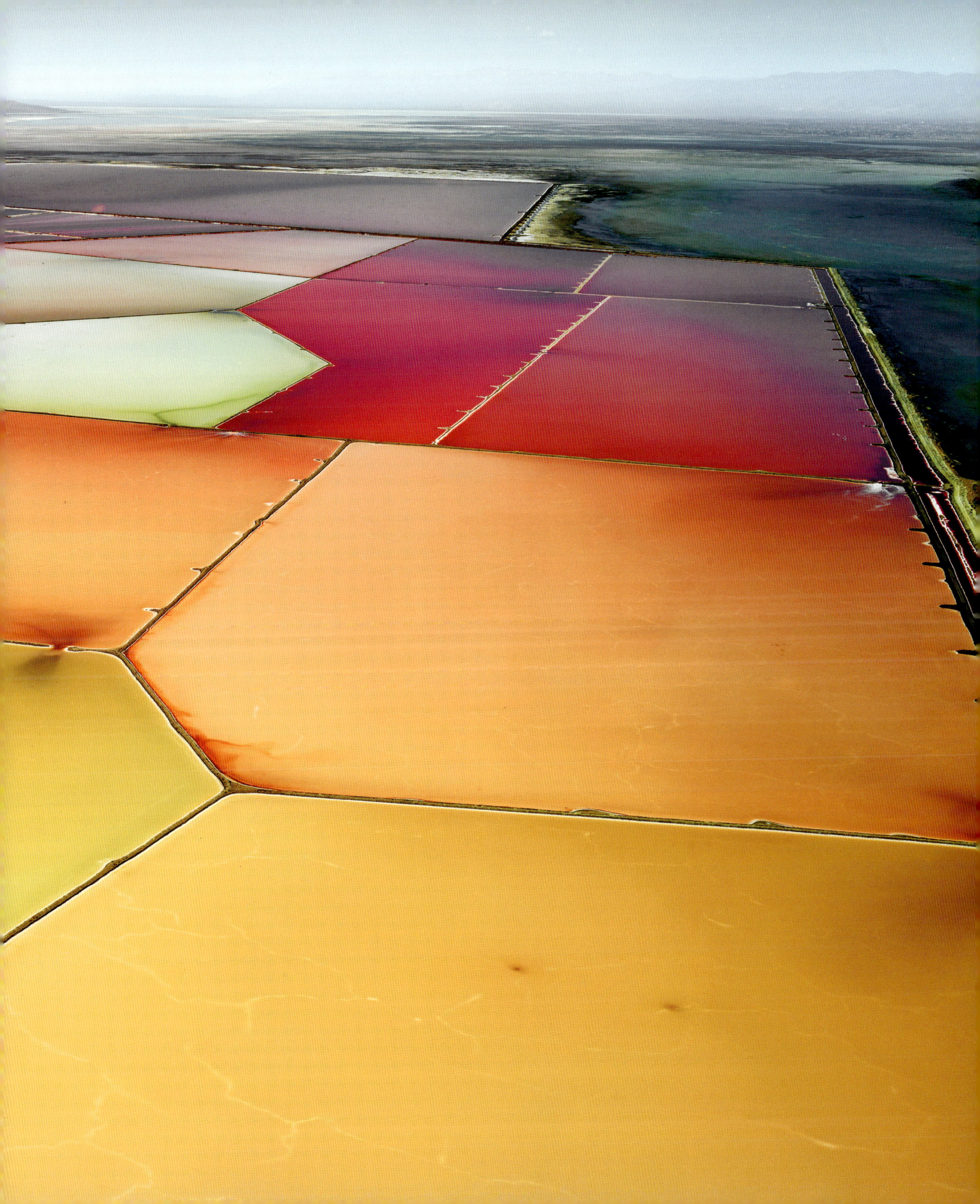

CARSTEN PETER
Tracing the path of least resistance, molten lava flows through the Canary Islands' La Palma during the 2021 eruption of Cumbre Vieja.

Previous pages:
DAVID BURDENY
Salt evaporation pans near Utah's Great Salt Lake glow with colors determined by varying concentrations of salt, bacteria, and algae.

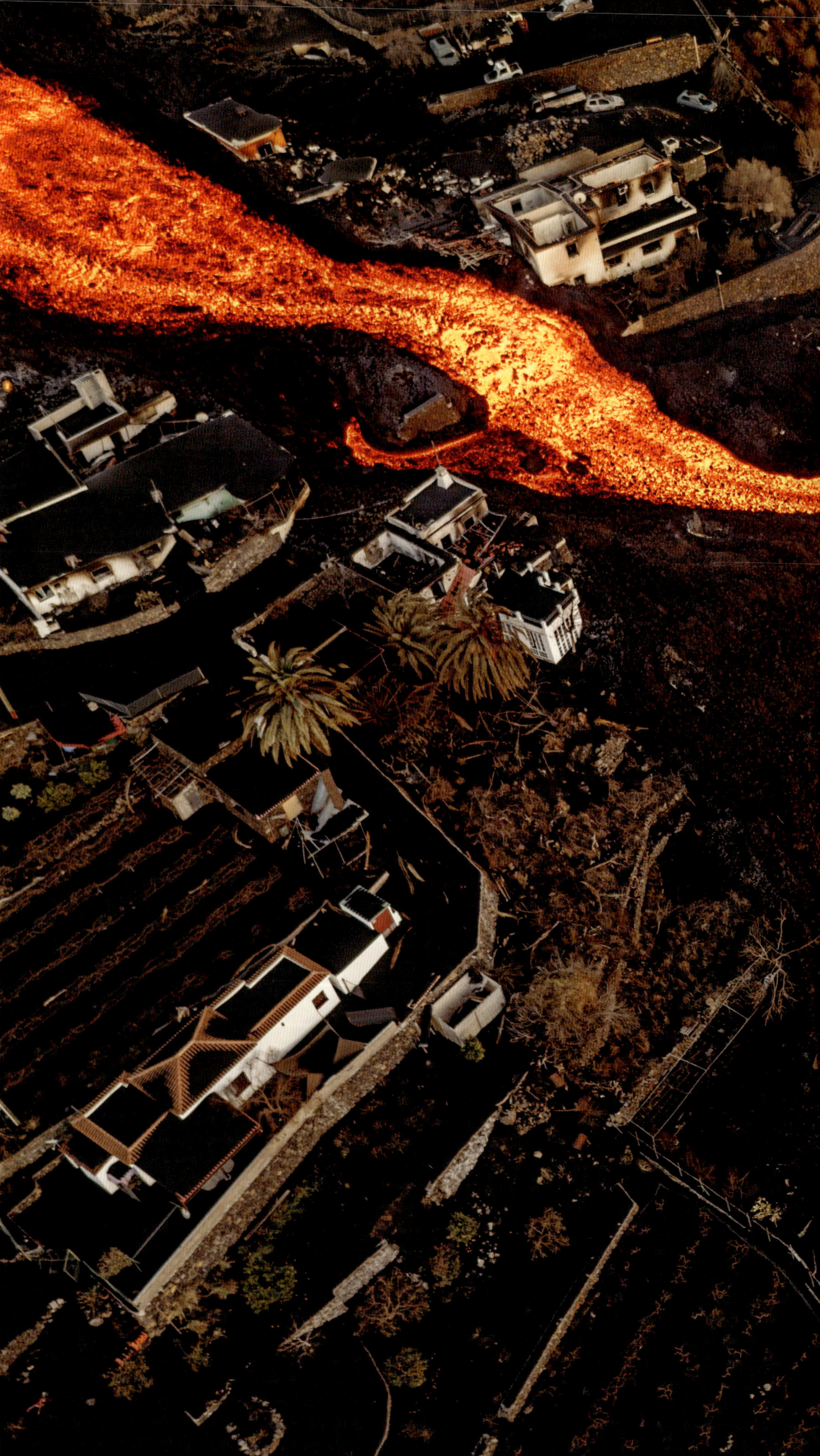

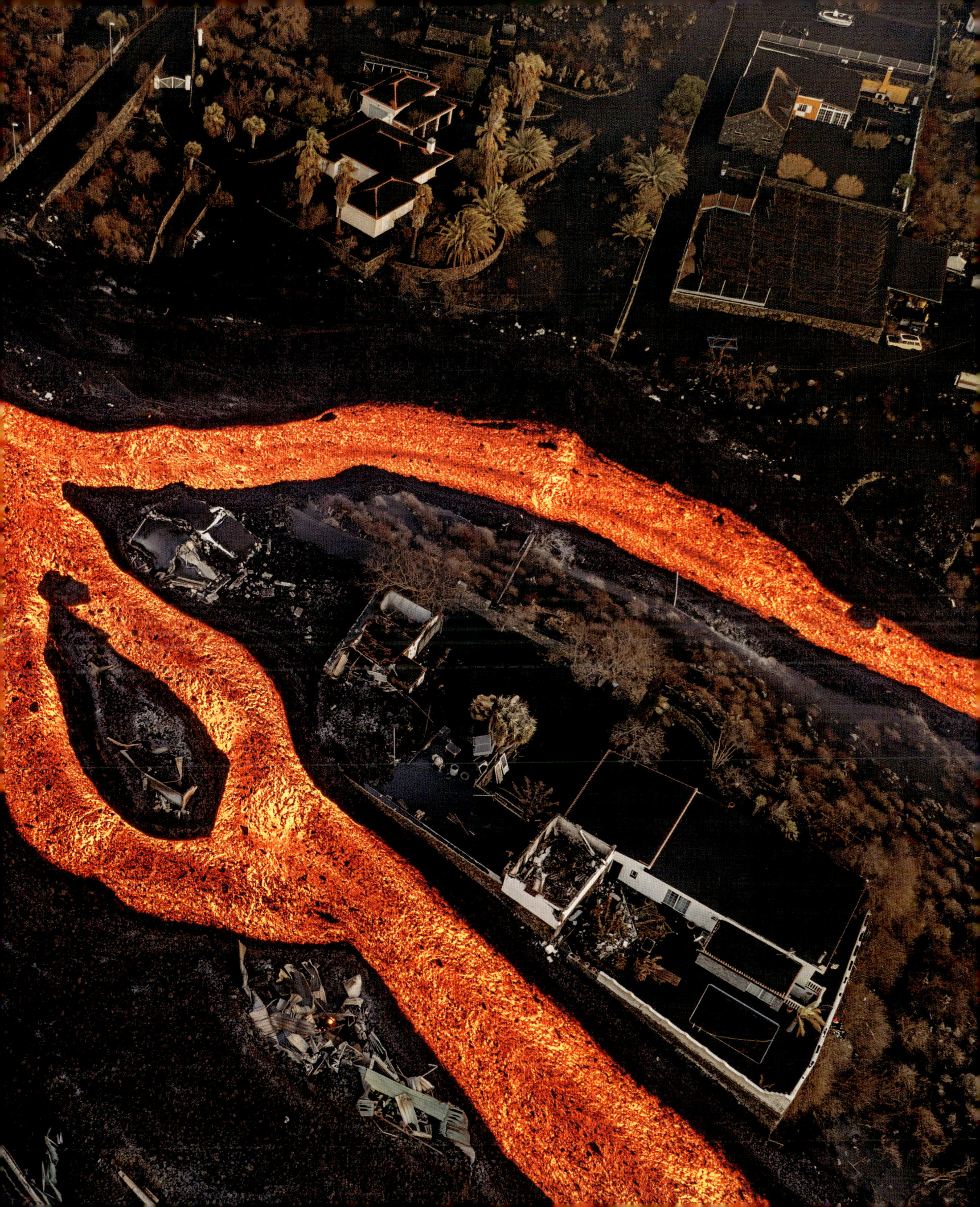

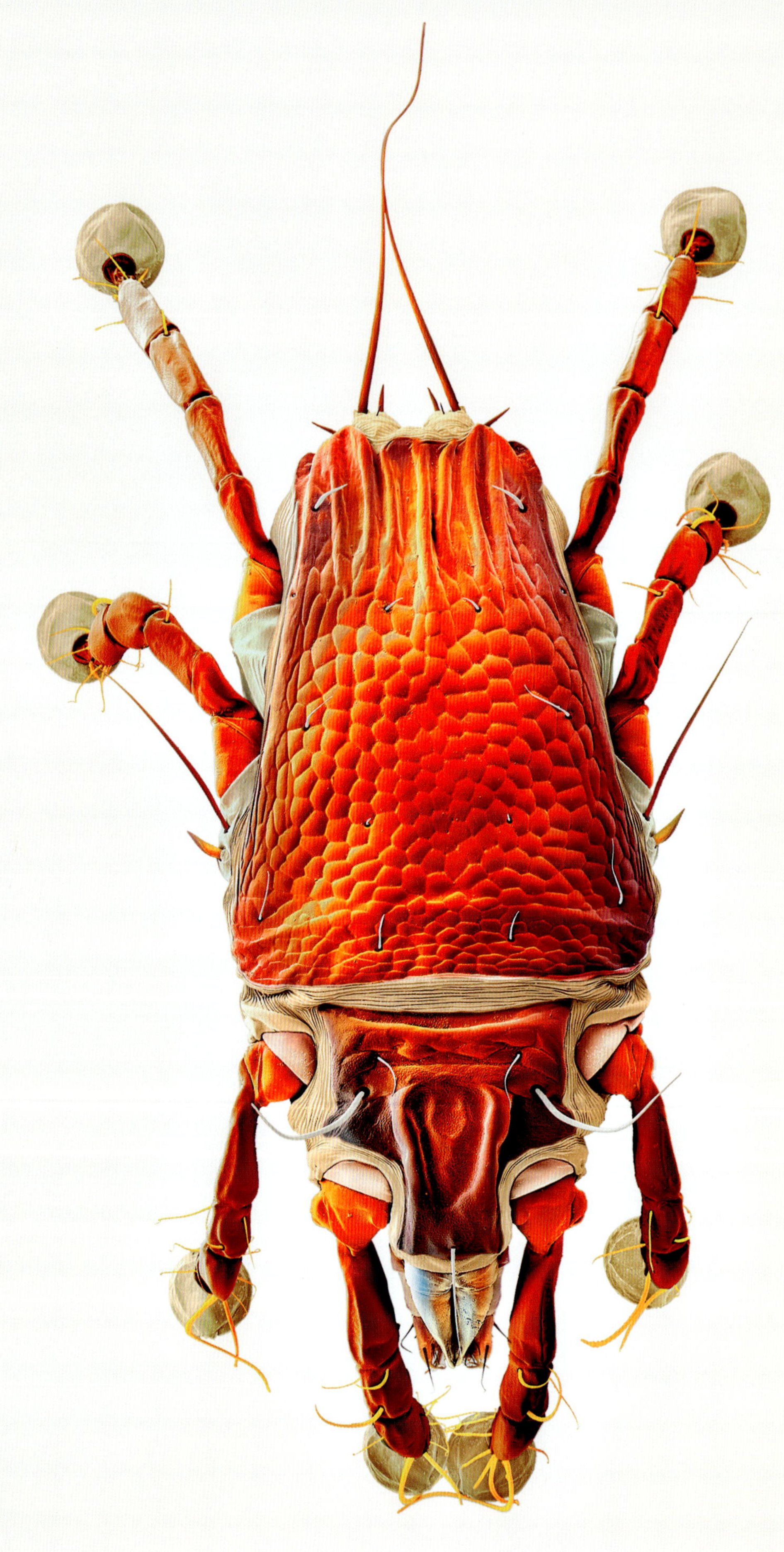

Our own experience provides the basic material for our imagination, whose range is therefore limited.

MARTIN OEGGERLI
A colorized photo taken through a scanning electron microscope
reveals the intricate anatomy of a mite.

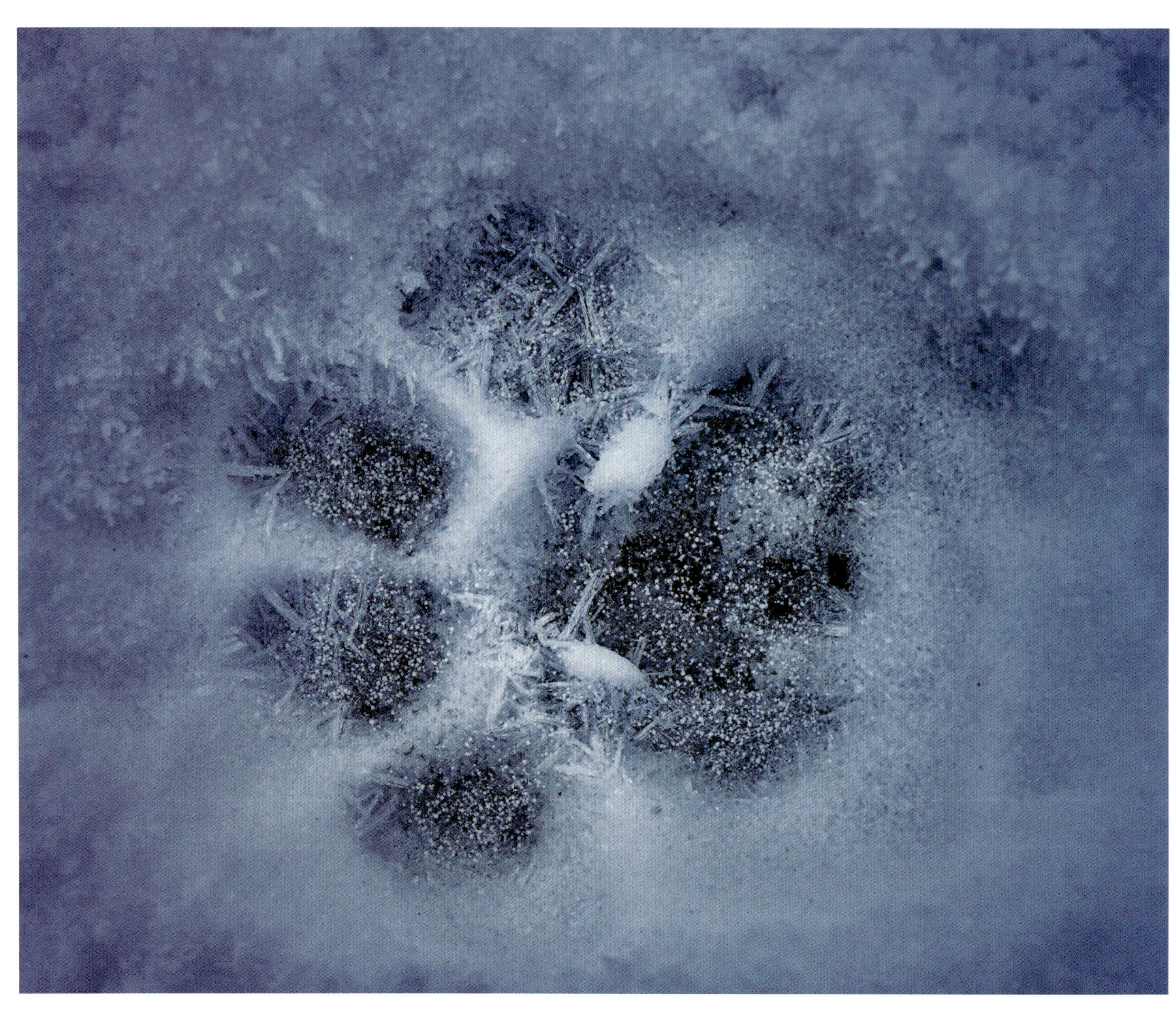

KEITH LADZINSKI
A long-gone puma has left its footprint,
now enshrined in ice.

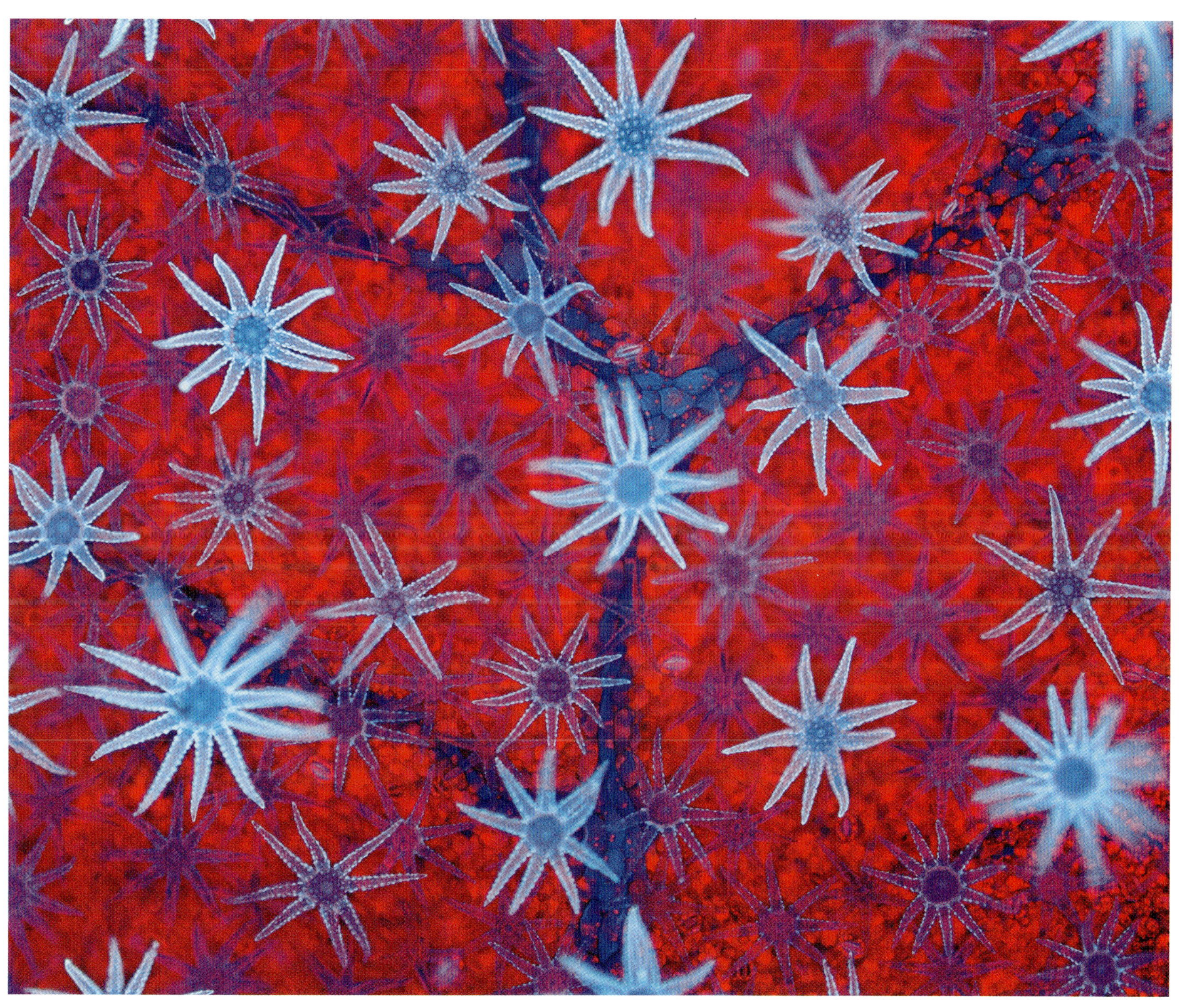

DAVID MAITLAND
Like blue stars glowing within a sky of red, defensive hairs on the leaf of a garden shrub
fluoresce after being exposed to ultraviolet light.

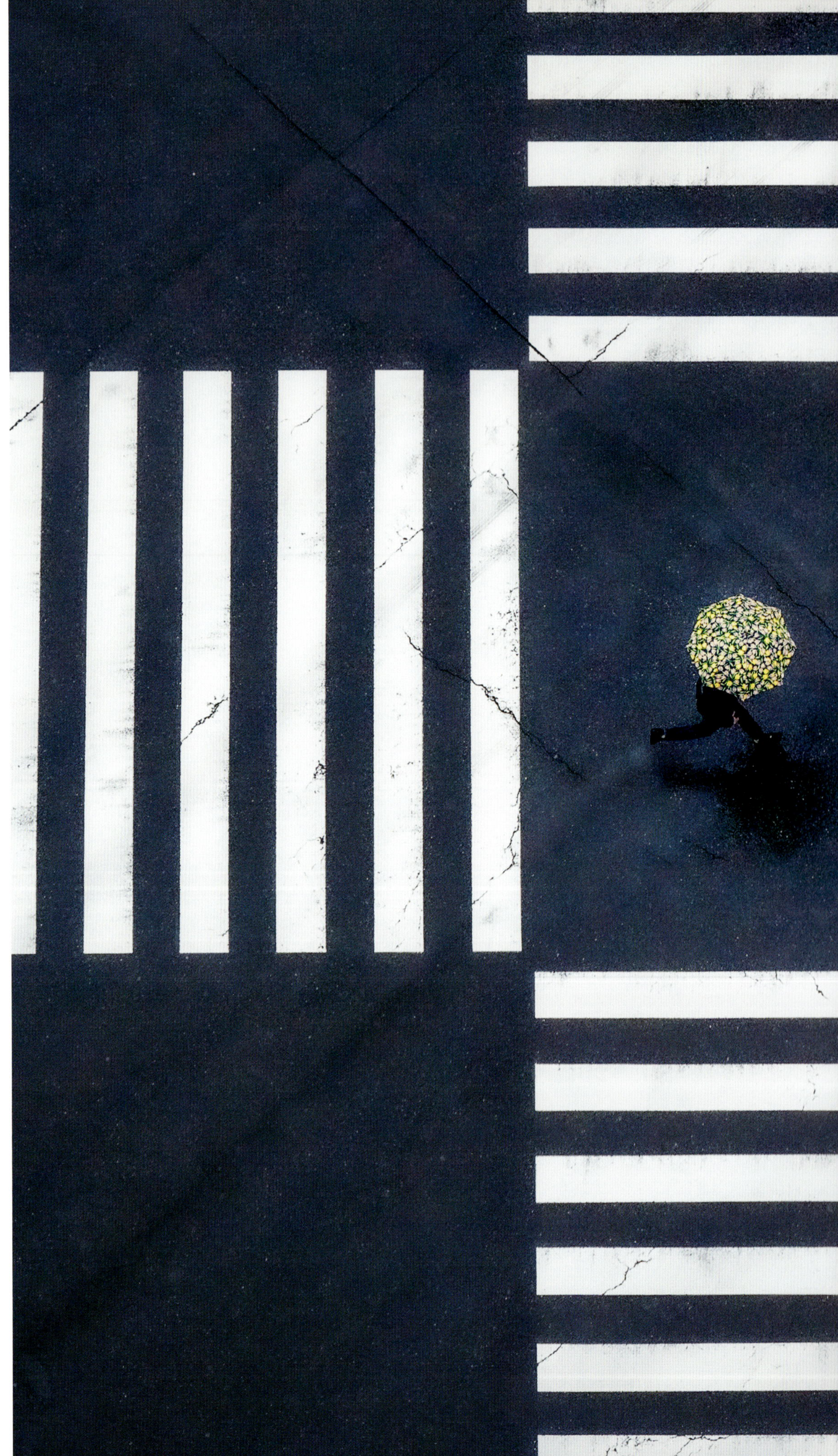

CHIN LEONG TEO
Geometrical passageway: An umbrella-bearing pedestrian dashes across a Tokyo traffic intersection.

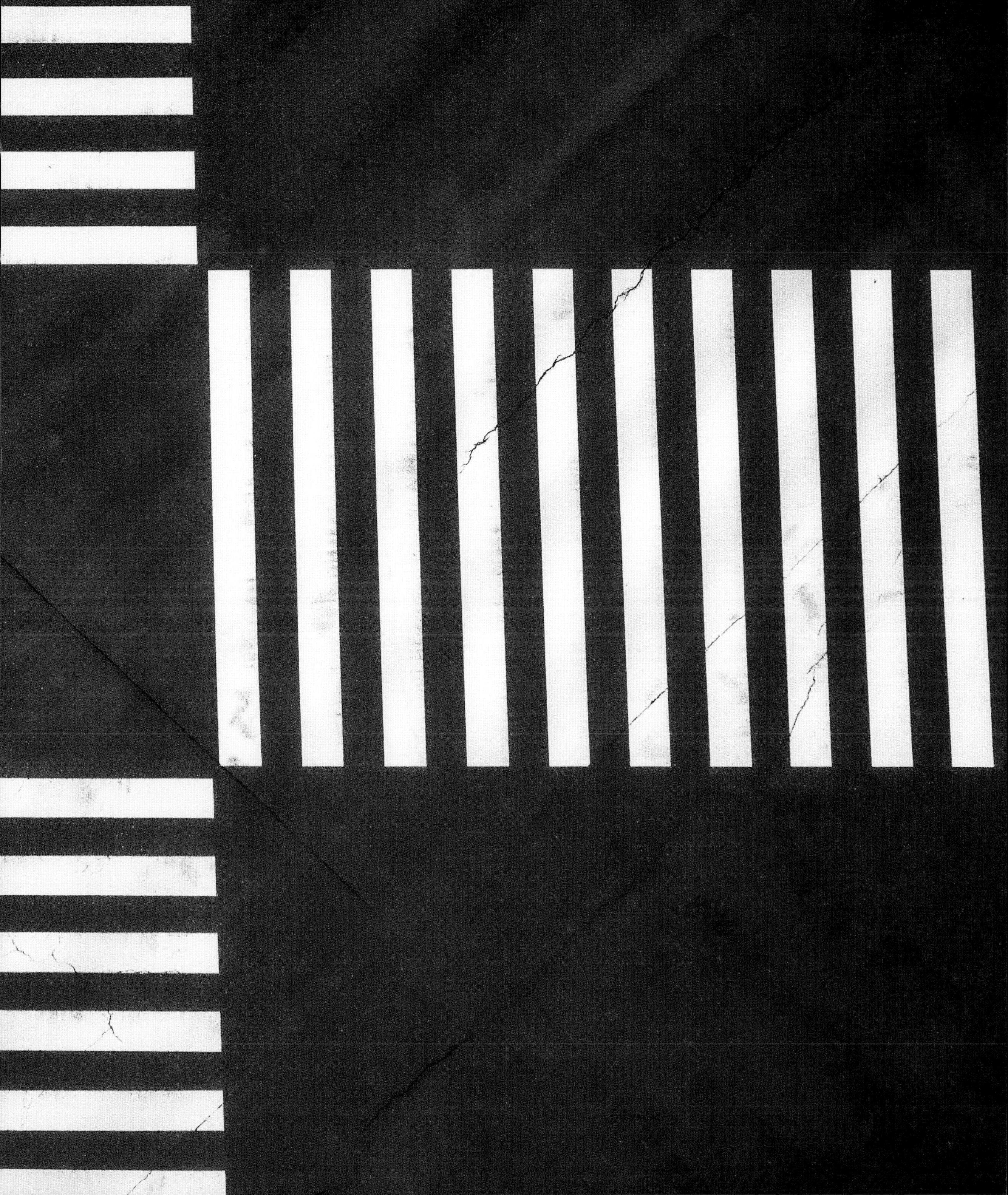

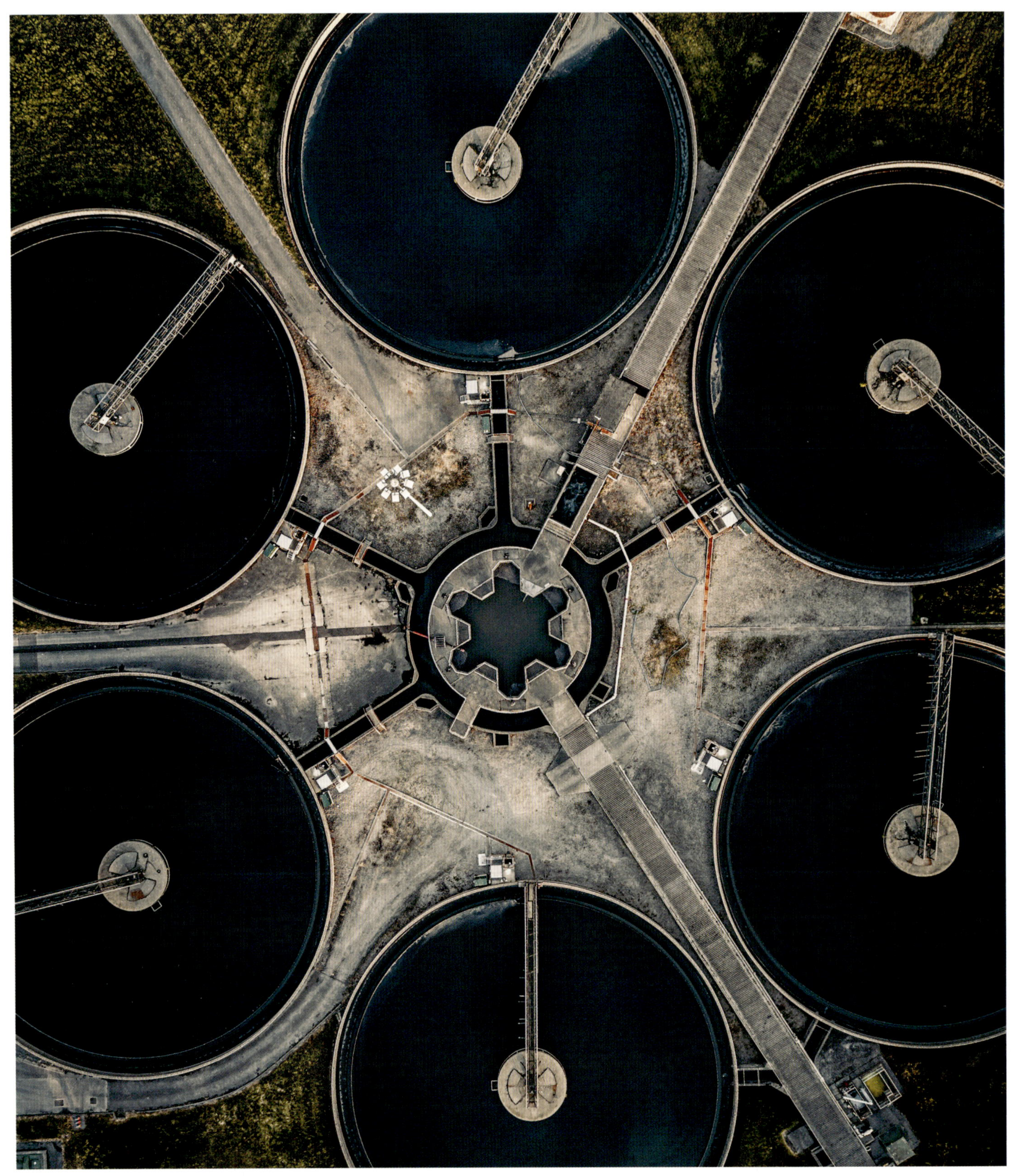

Geometric symmetry as seen from above,
a municipal sewage treatment center at ground level

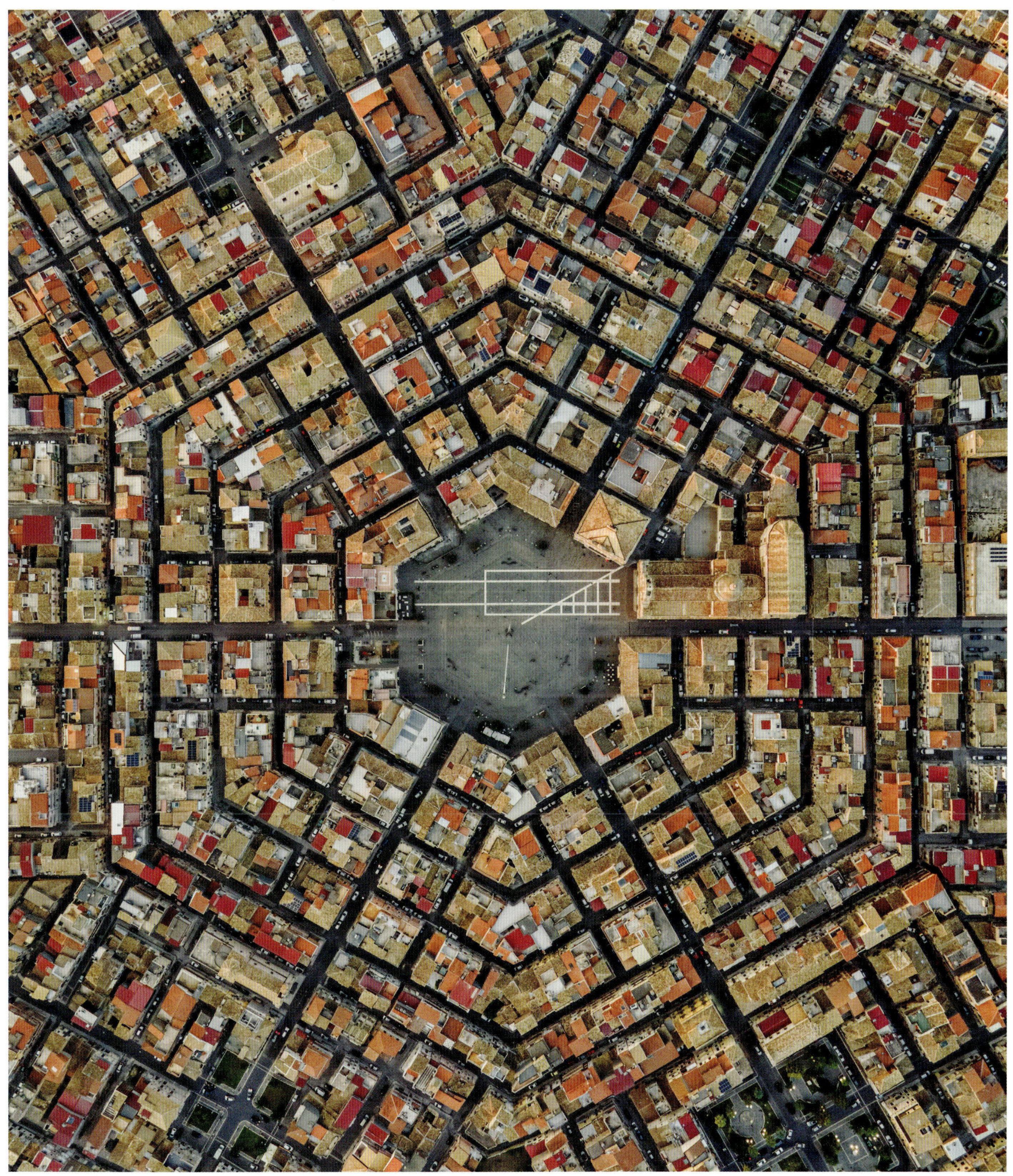

MICHELE RINALDI
Many roads in Grammichele, Sicily, lead to the town's piazza,
whose hexagonal shape propagates through the city.

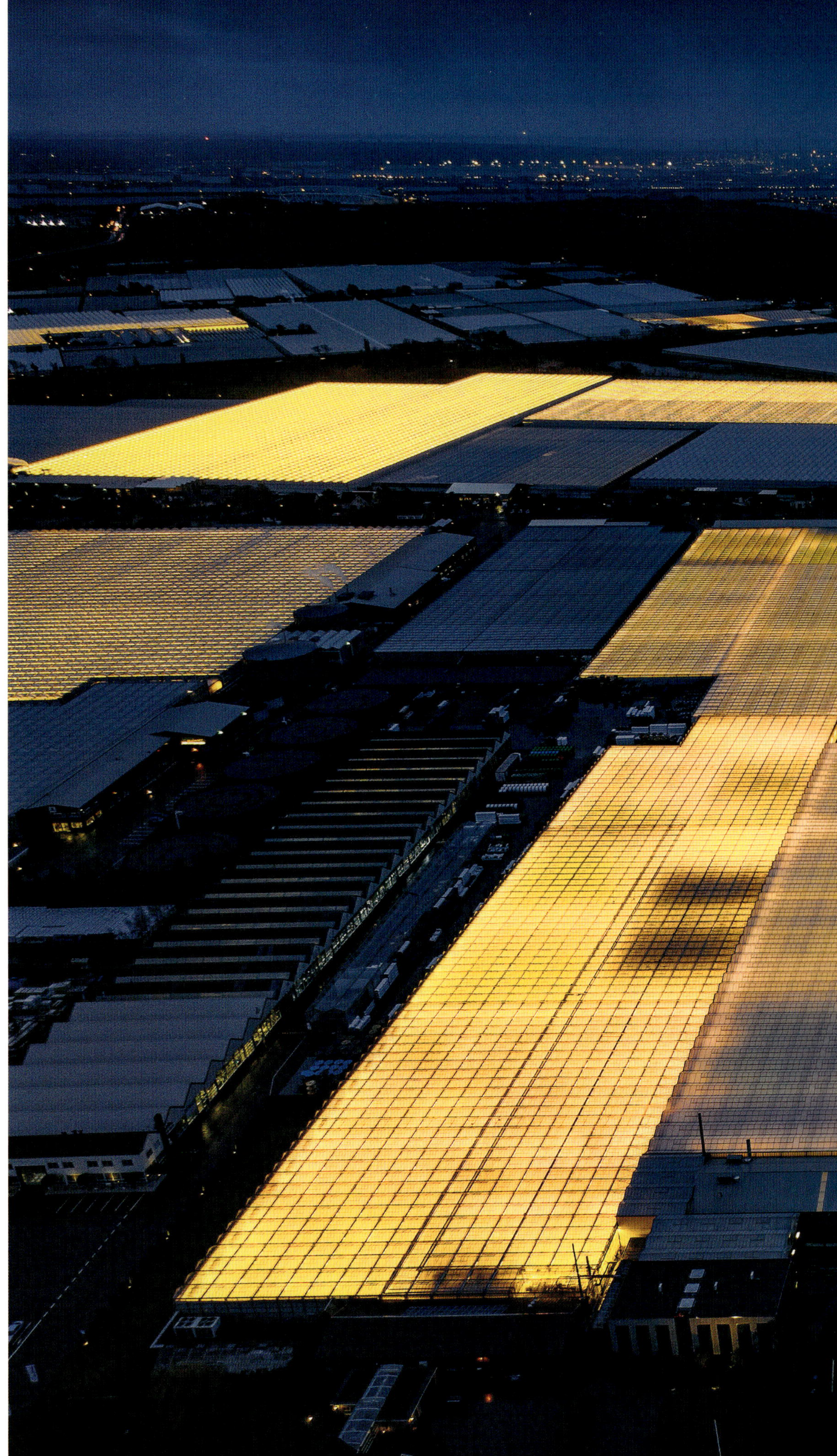

TOM HEGEN
Night lights keep plants growing
around the clock in massive
greenhouses in the Netherlands.

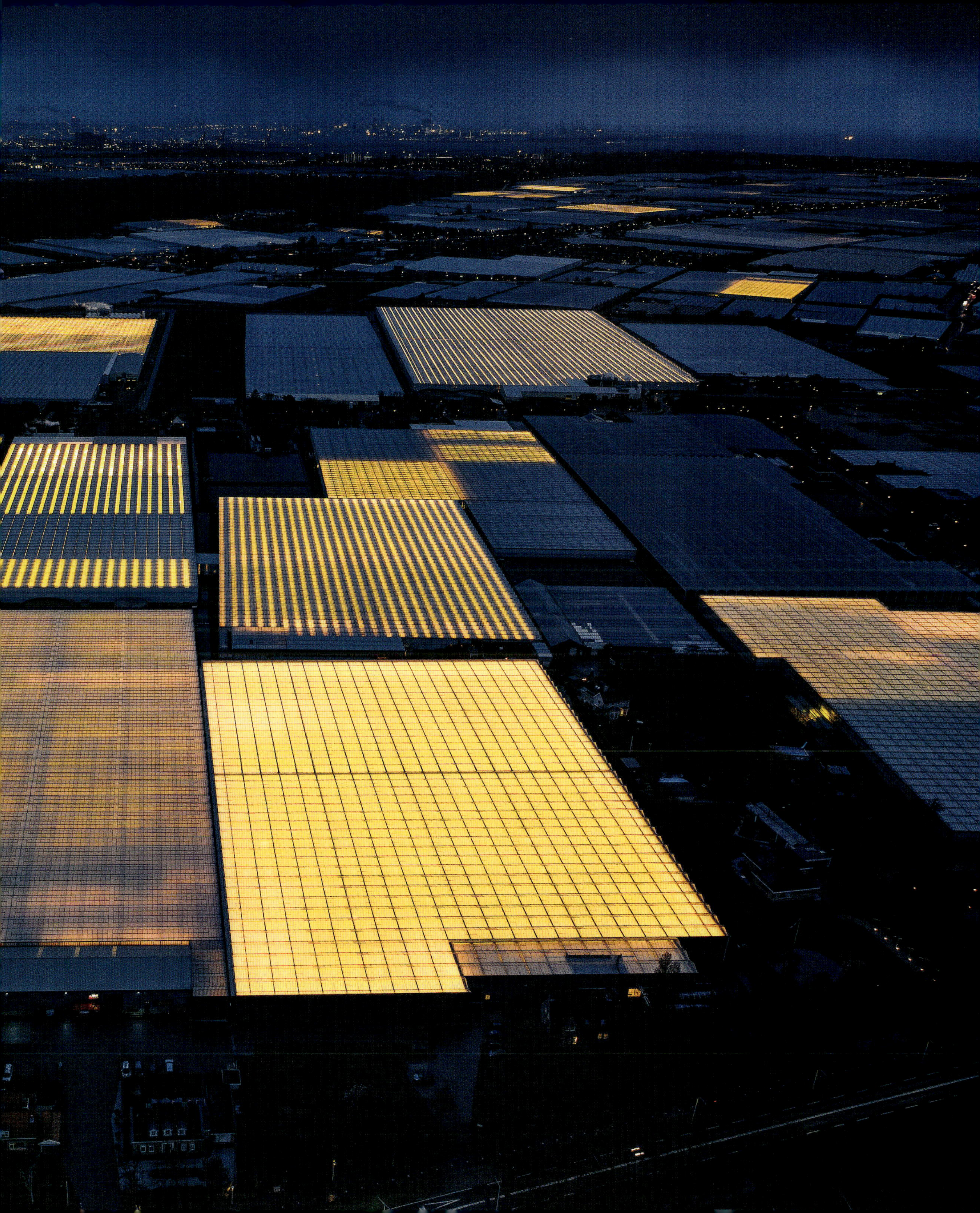

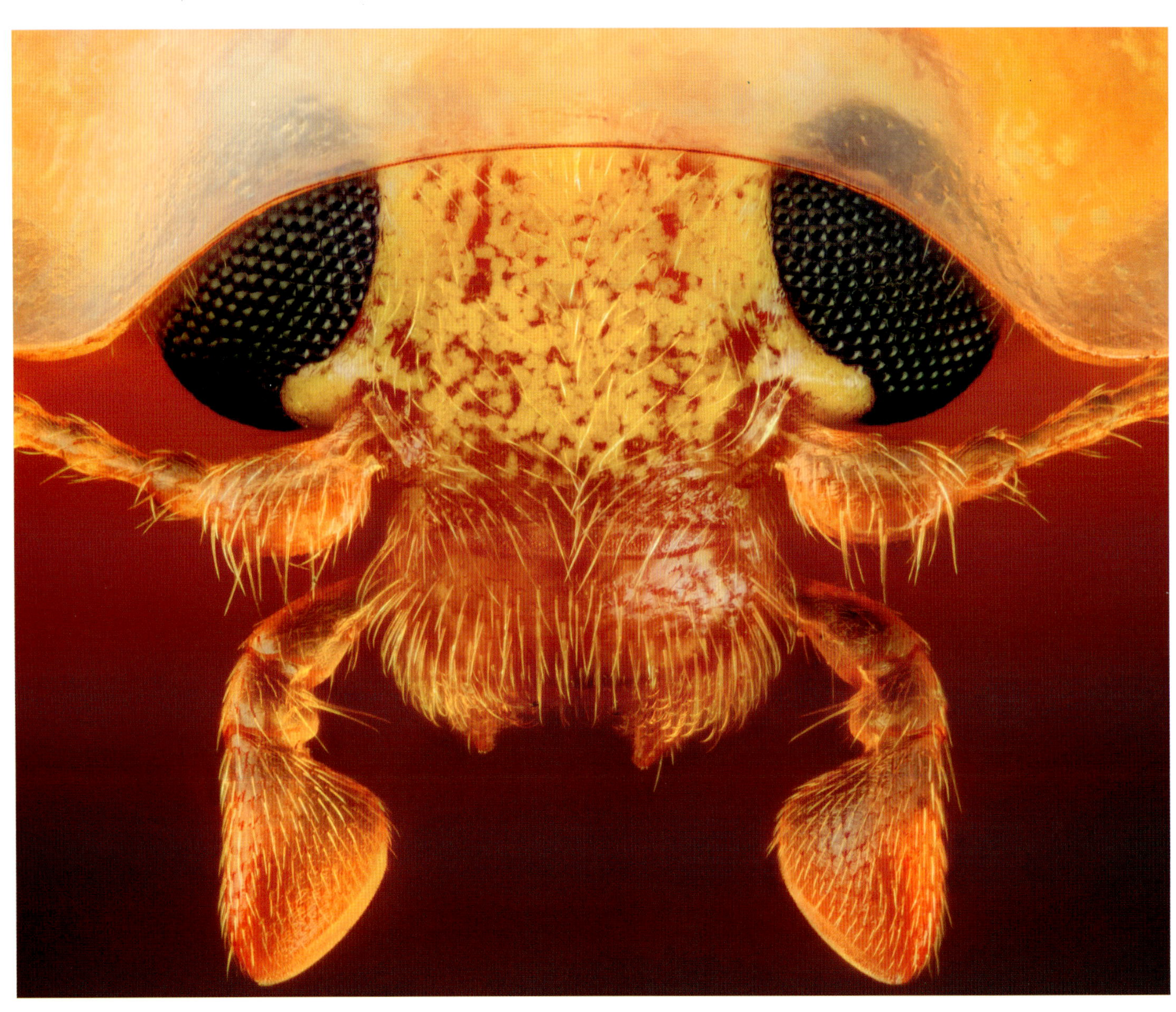

GEIR DRANGE
The compound eyes and complicated mouthparts of an orange ladybird

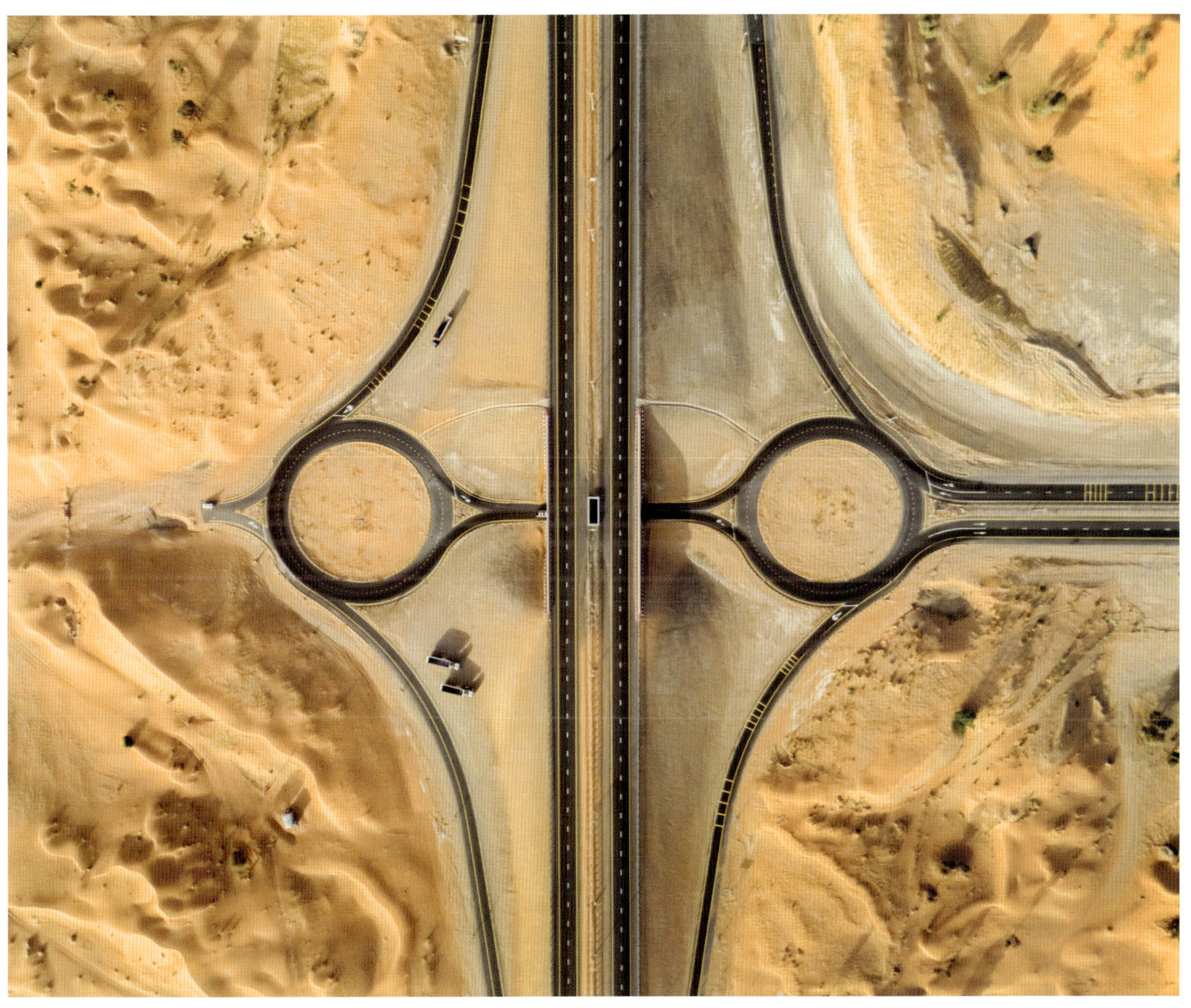

BACHIR MOUKARZEL
Roads and roundabouts weave through the desert of Umm Al Quwain in the United Arab Emirates.

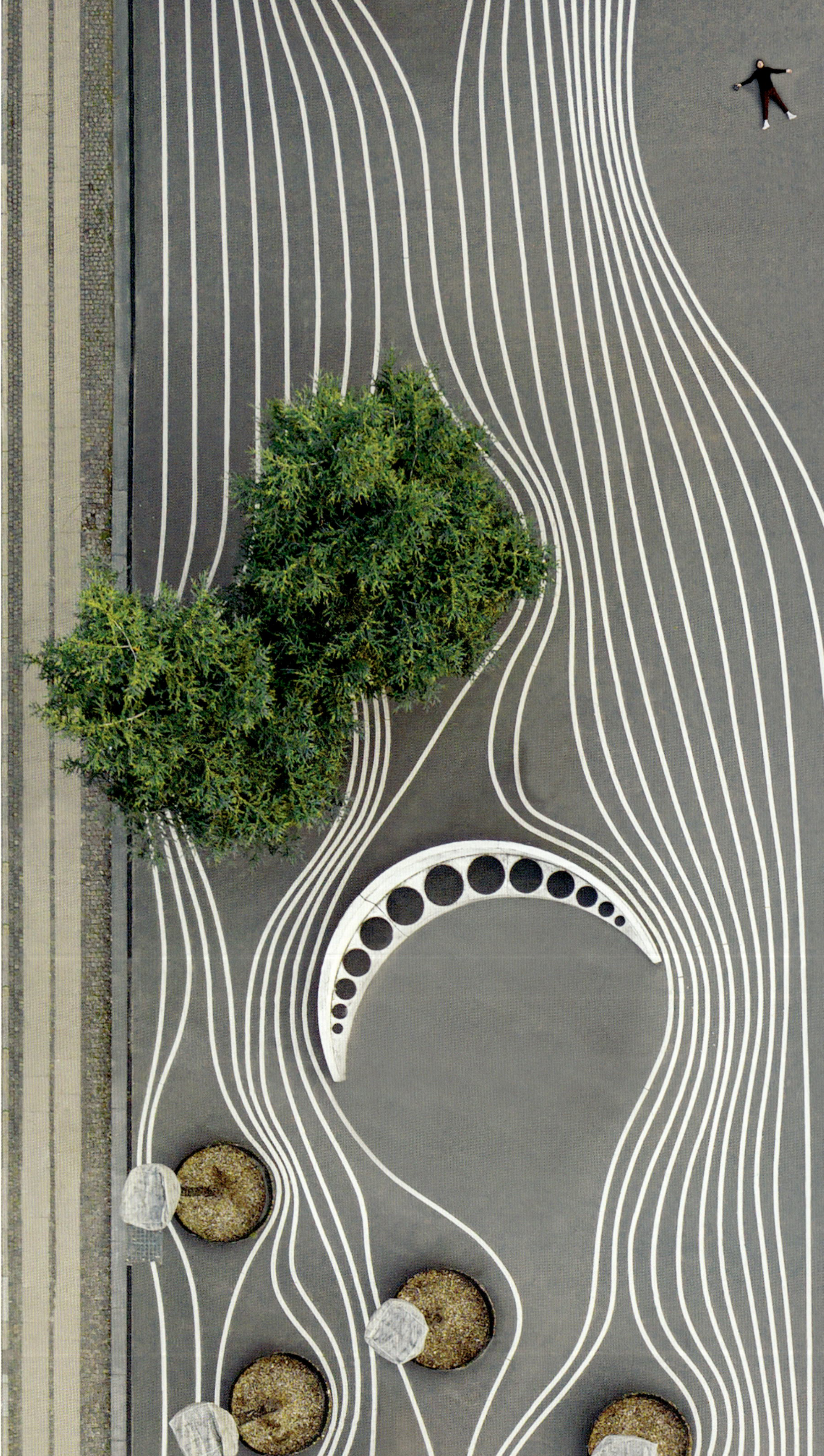

PIOTR BRATOSIEWICZ
Shapes and lines, trees and fountains invite people to congregate and relax in Superkilen Park in Nørrebro, Denmark.

Following pages:
JEFFREY KERBY
Sharp edges meet rounded shapes as sea ice breaks up near Ellesmere Island in northern Canada.

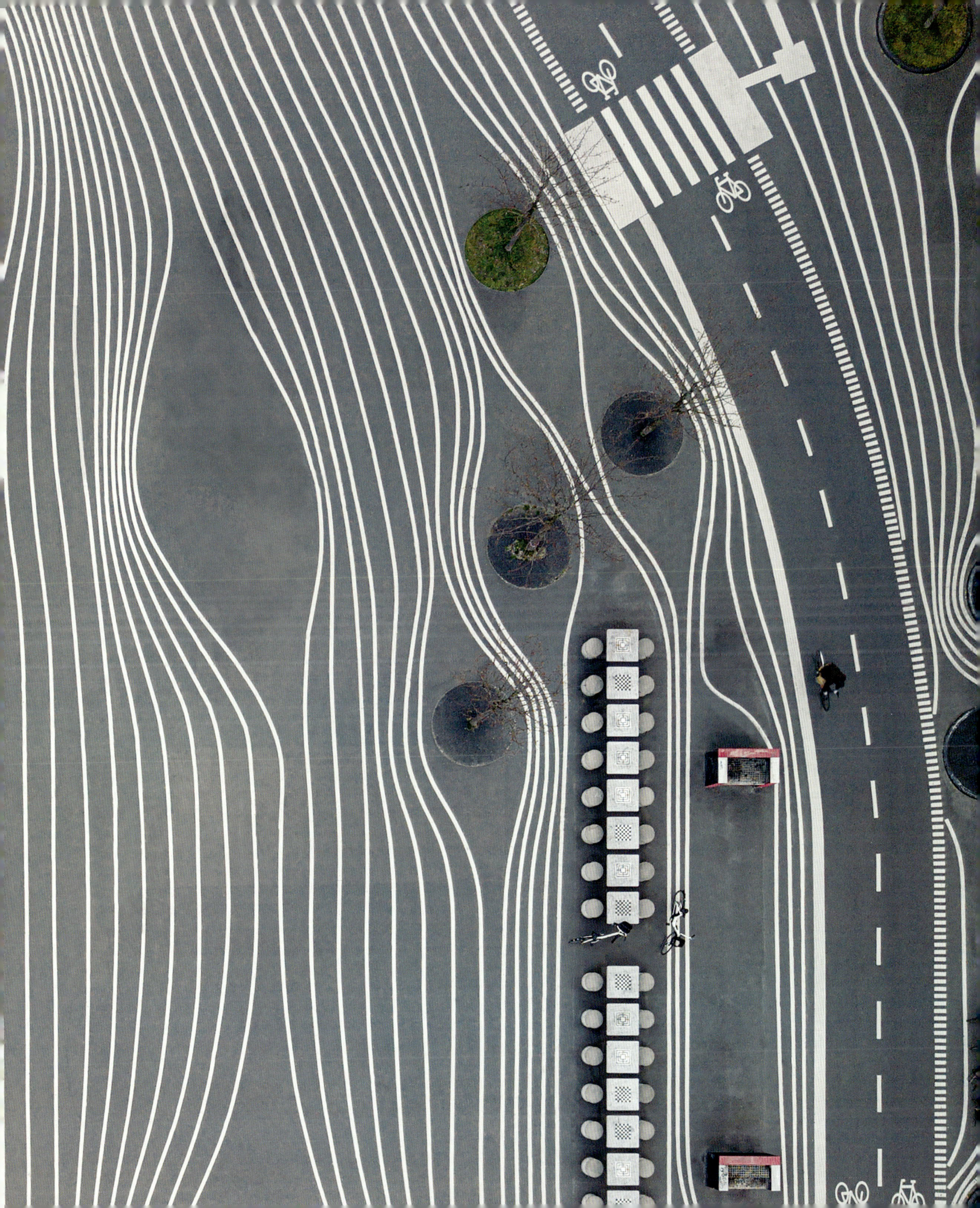

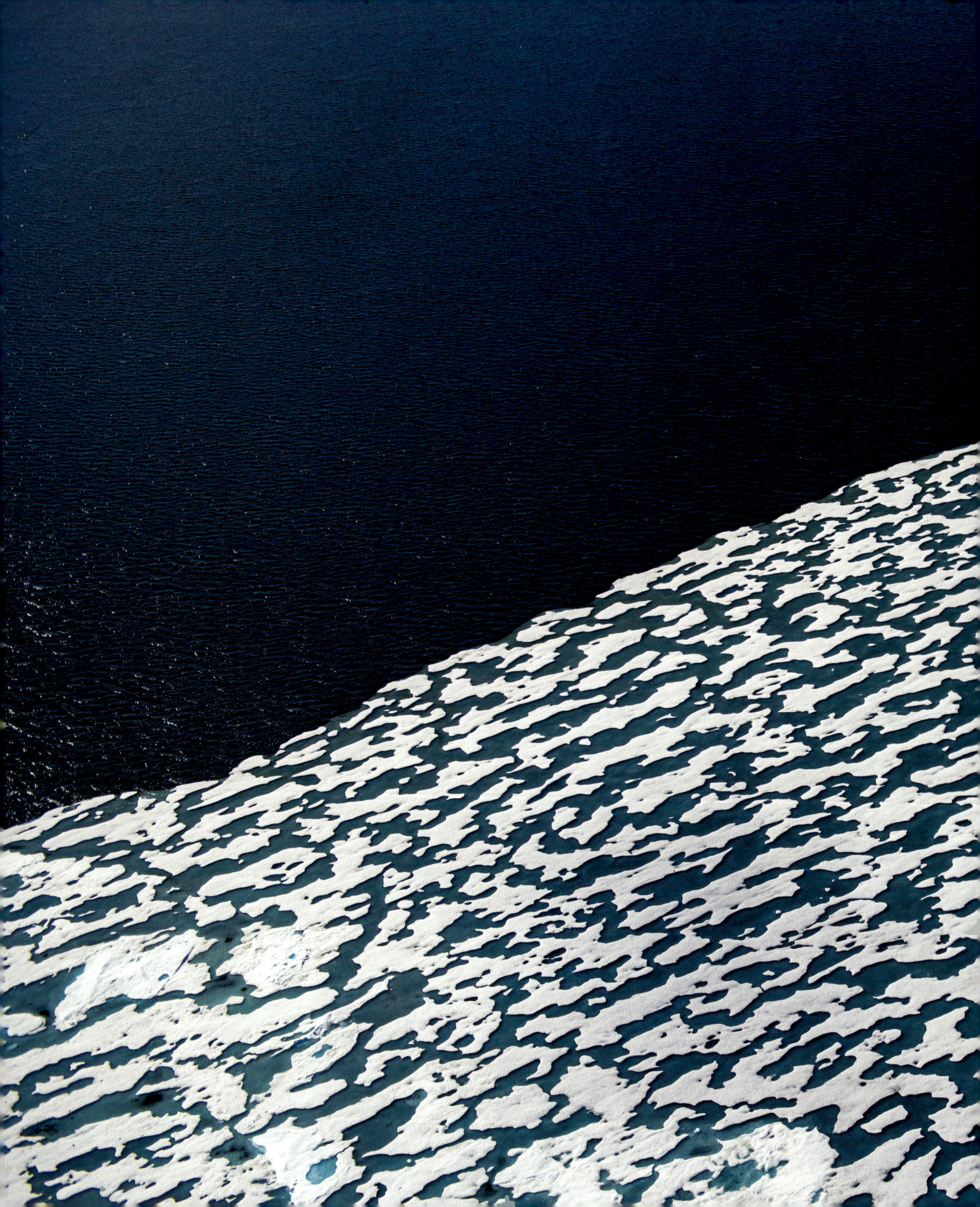

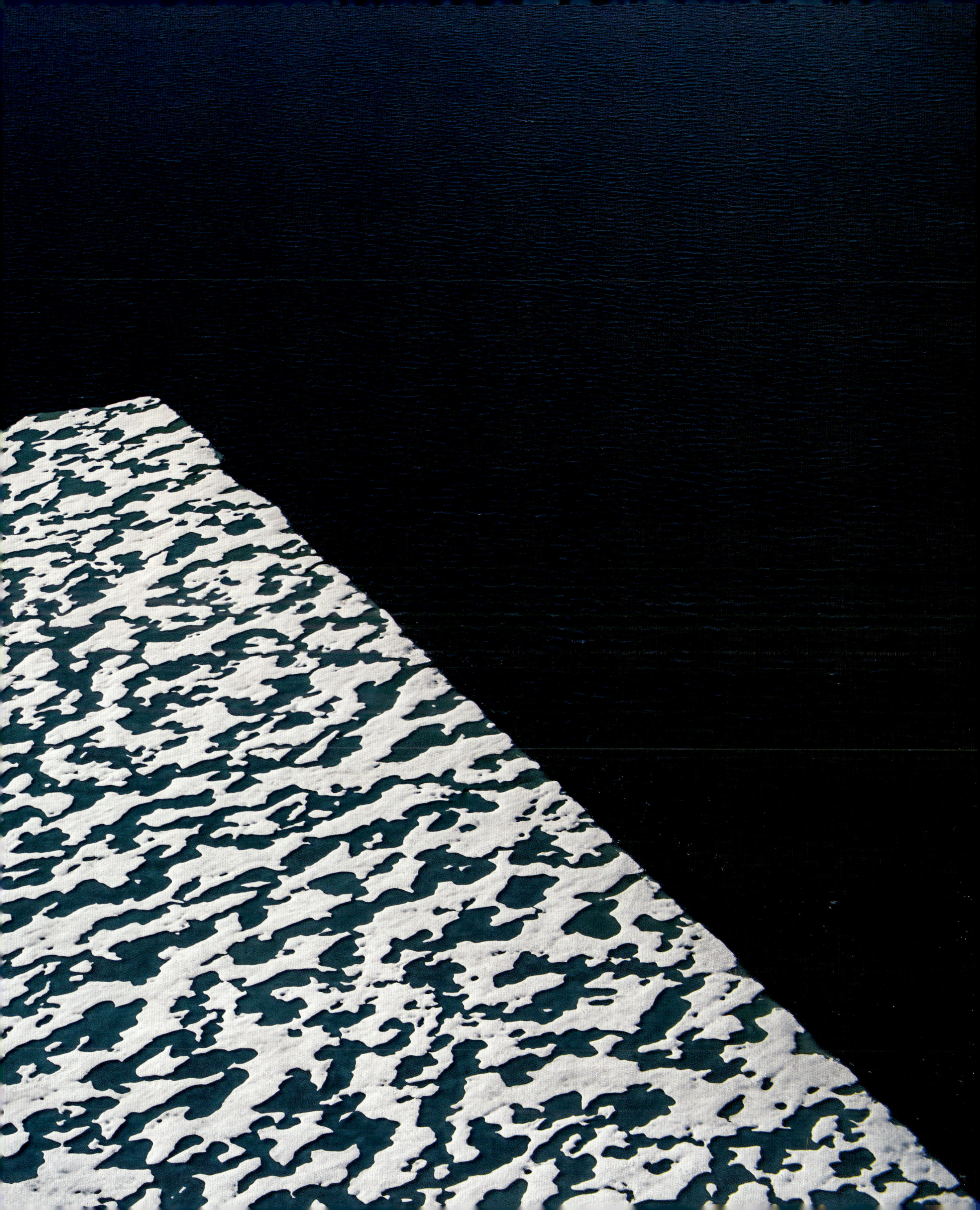

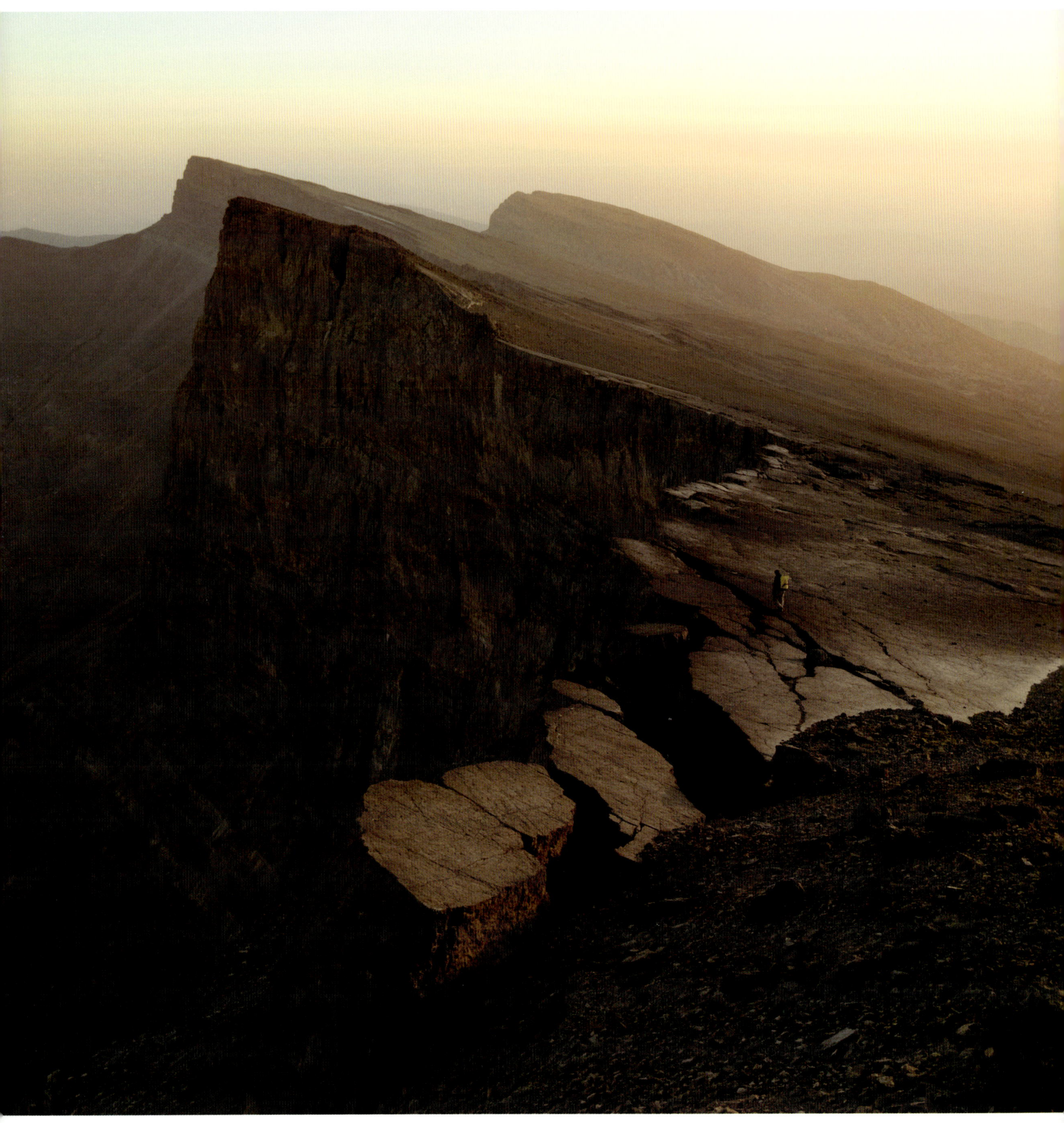

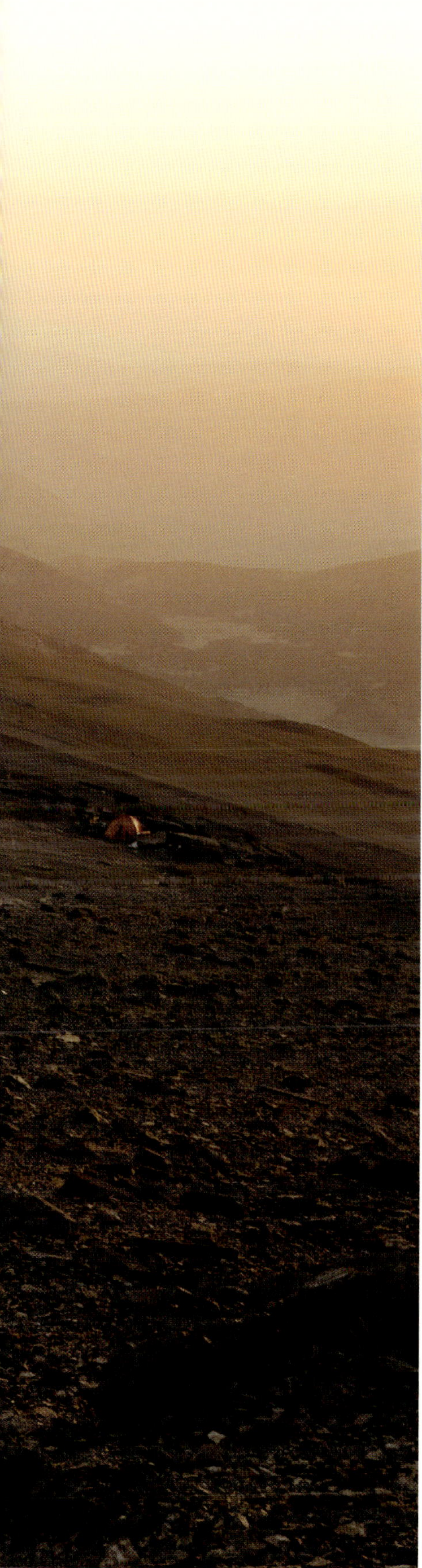

ROBBIE SHONE

Robbie Shone is a cave explorer and visual storyteller based in the Alpine town of Innsbruck, Austria. Over the past 20 years, his cave photography has taken him to the most remote parts of the world, including the deepest, largest, and longest known cave systems on Earth. He routinely operates in pitch-blackness, in places where natural light has never reached. His award-winning work has been featured in magazines, books, and IMAX films.

JEFFREY KERBY: Your career is full of cave superlatives—the deepest, the longest, the largest—but I'm curious about your introduction to caves. How did your photography and caves first meet?

ROBBIE SHONE: When I was 19, a friend of mine in my university fine arts course persuaded me to go with him to a cave in the Yorkshire Dales. I was reluctant up to the point of going underground, but honestly, it was love at first sight. Within 30 seconds I was feeling emotions that I'd never experienced before. The adrenaline and the lure of exploration were so impactful that they resonated right deep inside me. It was so intense that I wanted my art to be inside caves.

In school, I was painting big abstract floor paintings where you pushed around the paint with a brush and walked all over the canvas. But it wasn't practical to take paints and canvases into the caves, so I picked up the camera. Soon, I was in the U.K.'s Peak District caving every day. I wasn't in lectures for weeks on end, and my lecturer had to call my parents on one occasion. She said, "If you carry on in caves, I don't know if you're going to pass." I thought, well, that's telling it like it is, really. But I had to follow my heart, and I ended up pursuing caving.

JK: What were your early photographs like?

RS: I was literally playing around with lights. I was using candles and LEDs, magnesium flash powder, strobes, all sorts of little light sources that I could find. And I wrote down everything I did in a diary because it was all on film. Every time I took a photograph I would calculate the aperture, the f-stop of the lens, how far away the flash was from the wall, what the wall was coated in—if it was coated in sediment, it would absorb light; if it was washed with water, it would reflect light—I'd write it all down. These things kind of stuck to my brain, which is partly the reason why when I'm in a cave now, I don't really need to make any trial photographs.

JK: That suggests a lot of visualizing of the photo before you take it. When you go into a dark cave, do you see

ROBBIE SHONE
An expedition team braves a cliff edge en route to Dark Star, a cave system in Uzbekistan.

Following pages:
ROBBIE SHONE
The view straight down into Derbyshire's Titan, the United Kingdom's largest natural shaft at 475 feet (145 m) deep

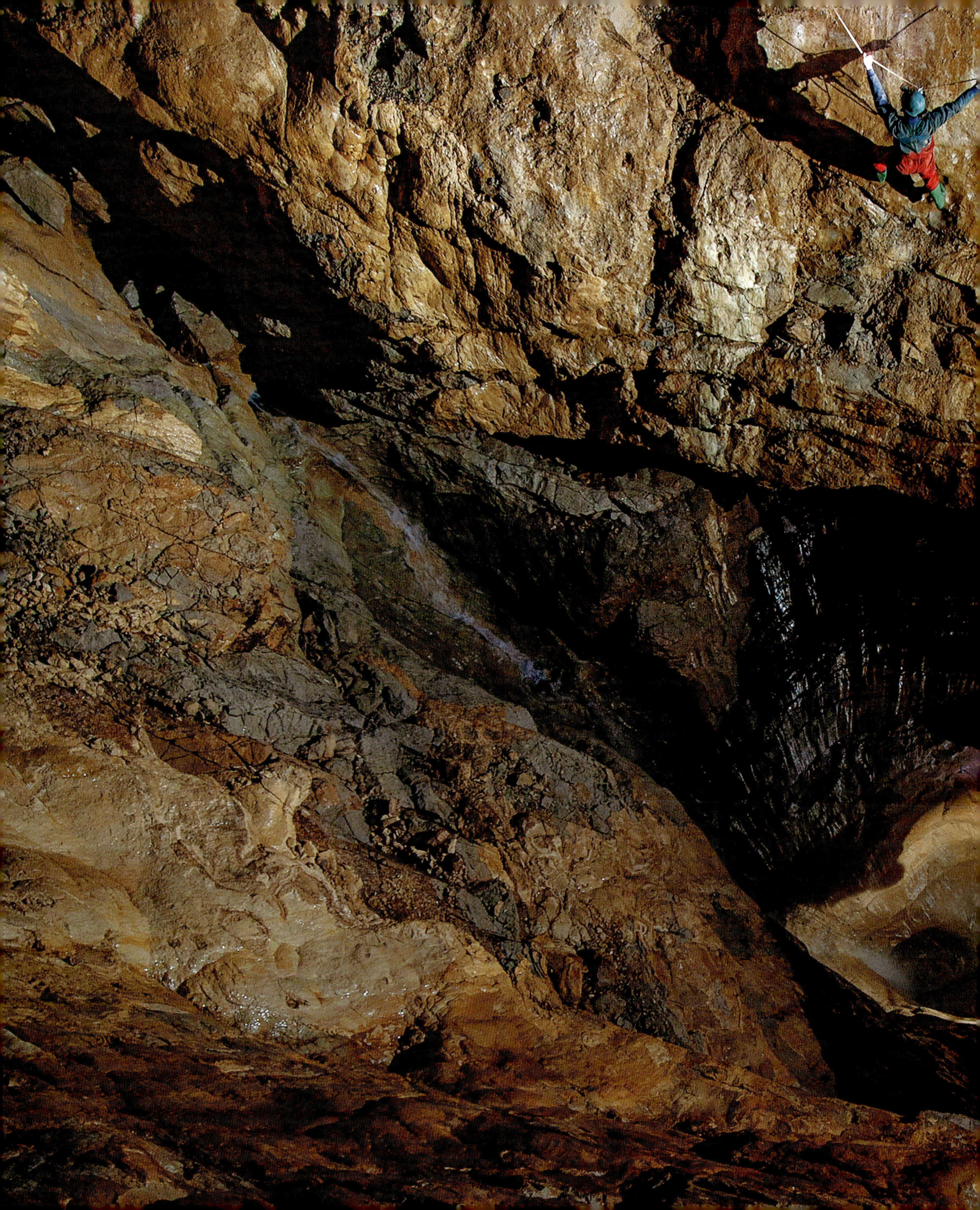

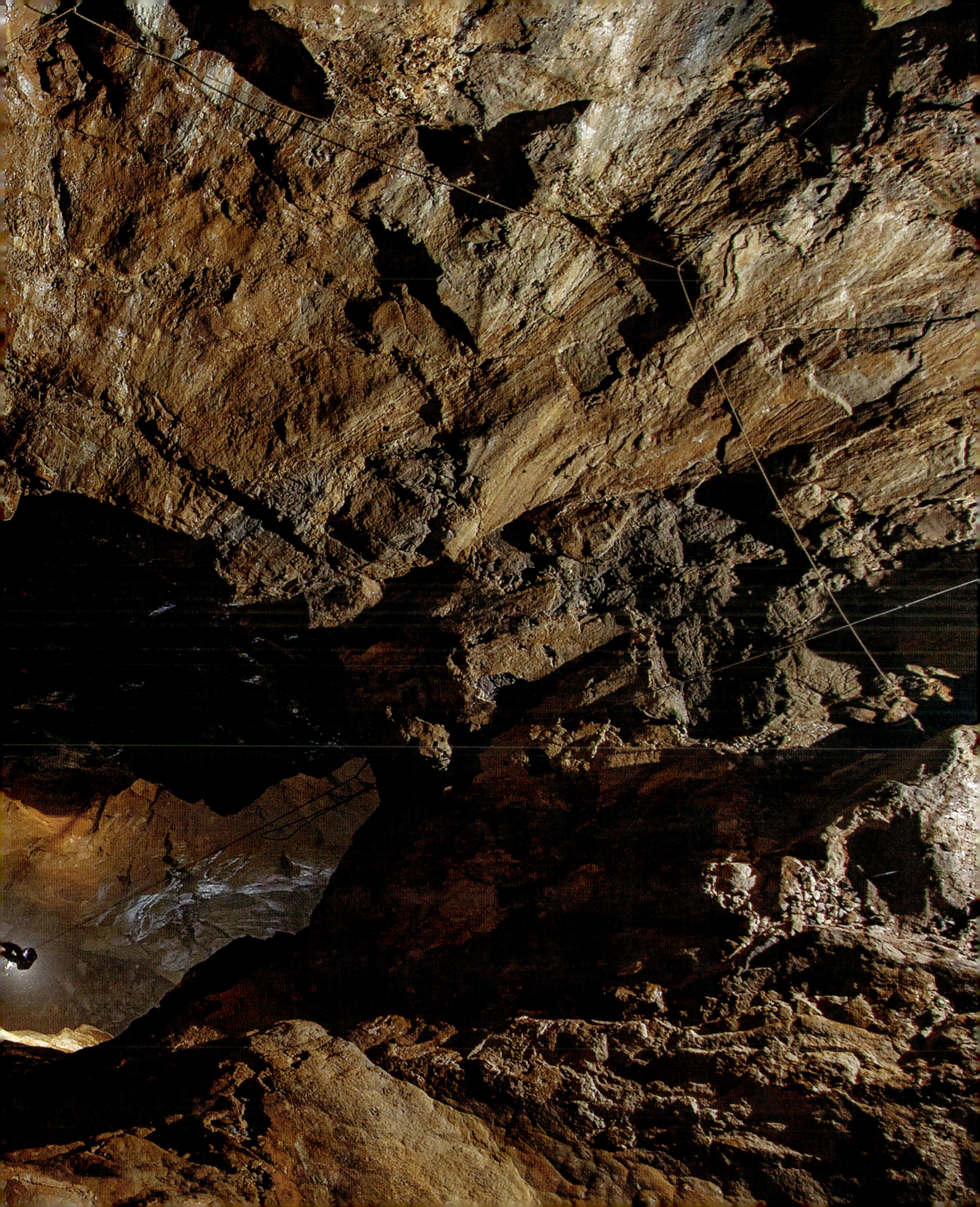

many versions of a photo and just pick between them? Or is there one that kind of pops out to you?

RS: When I go into a cave, the first thing I do before we start unpacking anything is go around the room, to all angles I can get to on the floor, and study the shape of the cave. I typically turn off my lights and watch my team members traversing around the cave, and slowly I'd build up a picture in my head. It takes so long to take one photograph, especially of really big rooms, that I can't really afford to take more than two or three. That's a whole day.

JK: Despite working underground, you often take pictures with a view from above, looking down a huge shaft or cavern, for example. How did you find this perspective?

RS: I was an industrial abseiler in London for about 10 years. You know all the guys who are cleaning windows on skyscrapers in Manhattan? That was me. Having spent so long working on the ropes, as we call it, I was fascinated with looking straight down at things: I'd see a river, tiny pedestrians. I love that view. Typically a lot of cave photographers go to the bottom of a cave and take a picture looking straight up, which is fine. But from my side I was thinking, *How can we reverse that process?* With these photographs looking straight down, you get different shapes from light sources that are fired up the shaft instead of down the shaft; you're getting a whole new atmosphere.

JK: Do you find yourself falling into patterns of what you think is best in a cave, or do you have to challenge yourself about what will look good?

RS: I don't know where this comes from—I call it second nature, or my eye—but when I go into these caves, everything just kind of clicks into place. I don't have a mental checklist. It just happens. I just know where I'm taking

the picture from. Sometimes it can be a completely new technique, even with the same old lights I've been using for 15 years. I'm just hanging them differently or taking the reflector off or using a different filter gel. It gives a whole new atmosphere to the same place.

JK: Does that translate to aboveground for you?

RS: You know, when we do the assignments for Nat Geo, you've got to get surface stuff as well, but I never feel that sense of *I've never seen that before.* It's often just another landscape shot. But in the cave, it's totally new. And maybe that's because these environments are so alien to us.

JK: As a painter, what photographic tool do you see more as your paintbrush: the lights or your camera?

RS: Oh, the lights. An old friend of mine wrote a book that was kind of my bible when I was younger. *Images Below,* by Chris Howes, it was called. And the line in his book that has stuck with me to this day says the trick to cave photography is knowing what *not* to light up. Some of the best photographs I've seen are ones where 80 percent of the photograph is black, and you just see a head torch on a rock in the distance. It's like, *Wow, how big is that room?* All that blackness is just so powerful. You don't need to light it all up sometimes.

JK: What can you tell me about Titan?

RS: Titan is the U.K.'s largest vertical shaft underground. But it's at the very far end of a cave system called Peak Cavern, which is about 12 miles (19 km) long. It's about a four-hour caving trip—very arduous, very technical, very demanding. I got involved with some explorers who were excavating a surface shaft to intercept Titan and make a "back door" into the cave system. I quickly grew fascinated with the cave

and wanted to make a photograph of Titan from the roof dome, looking straight down. It's about 400 feet (122 m) vertical all the way down to the bottom. It took lots and lots of trips. I had to fabricate a seat made from the same fiberglass rings we were using to line the surface shaft down into Titan, so all my weight was not in my harness. We used walkie-talkie radios to communicate, because of course our voices got lost in the big space. And then taking the photograph and having people fire the flashes at the right time was quite complicated. I used a film camera, too, so I couldn't see the picture until I developed it. My friends begged me to buy a digital camera so I could realize where I was going wrong and change it. In the end, I bought one, and it really caught the tiny, tiny imperfections I was making. Overall it took three years to perfect that photograph.

JK: How long did it take for the explorers to excavate Titan?

RS: Five years, and we were there every weekend. I would walk up this valley and meet the guys at 10 o'clock. We'd work till one o'clock, have lunch for an hour, and then we'd work till six. I didn't miss a weekend. We used these compressed air drills to drill giant holes, which we filled with gelignite explosives to blow the rock up. And these compressed air drills were so heavy that they gave me a hernia. I was out of action for six weeks, but I would still hobble up to the dig with two walking sticks just to watch them work. I was obsessed, Jeff, honestly. It was crazy. But it was the best time of my life. It really was.

JK: You use a fair amount of old technology. I've seen that some of the flashes you use are very old.

RS: There's a company in Ireland that's the only company in the world today that still manufactures these old flashbulbs that the paparazzi used to use to capture Marilyn Monroe and stuff back in the '40s, '50s and '60s. I love these bulbs. I have an attic full of them. They're so powerful, and they generate an enormous amount of light in a slightly longer burn time than a speed light—so they burn at a 60th of a second instead of a 250th of a second. And when you're working with water, they add a little bit more texture to the water itself. Instead of freezing it in the picture, you get this lovely blur. They can also be used underwater because they're sealed units, aren't they? So they burn underwater, which is great for these big lakes when you want to light up underwater and turn it blue.

JK: How much has time in these spectacular caves broadened your interest in the processes that make these caves?

RS: I would say for the first 10 years of this journey, I was fascinated by exploration and adventure. And that's what I was documenting, teams in pursuit of new uncharted worlds that nobody's ever seen before. Because ultimately that's what lured me into a cave. But then I met Gina [Moseley], a cave scientist who studies caves to answer questions about climate change and what the future is going to be like. Now, that kind of added something more meaningful to my journey. Don't get

me wrong, exploration is amazing. I love it and I always will, but I've sort of gone off the doing-it-for-kicks aspect. The science added this huge, and I say important, aspect to my photography, because we're now understanding what caves hold. There's nowhere else on the planet where you're going into a world that is like a time machine. You're going back to a point hundreds of thousands of years ago that is unchanged. I think that is such a powerful story to tell. And as a photographer, I can do that.

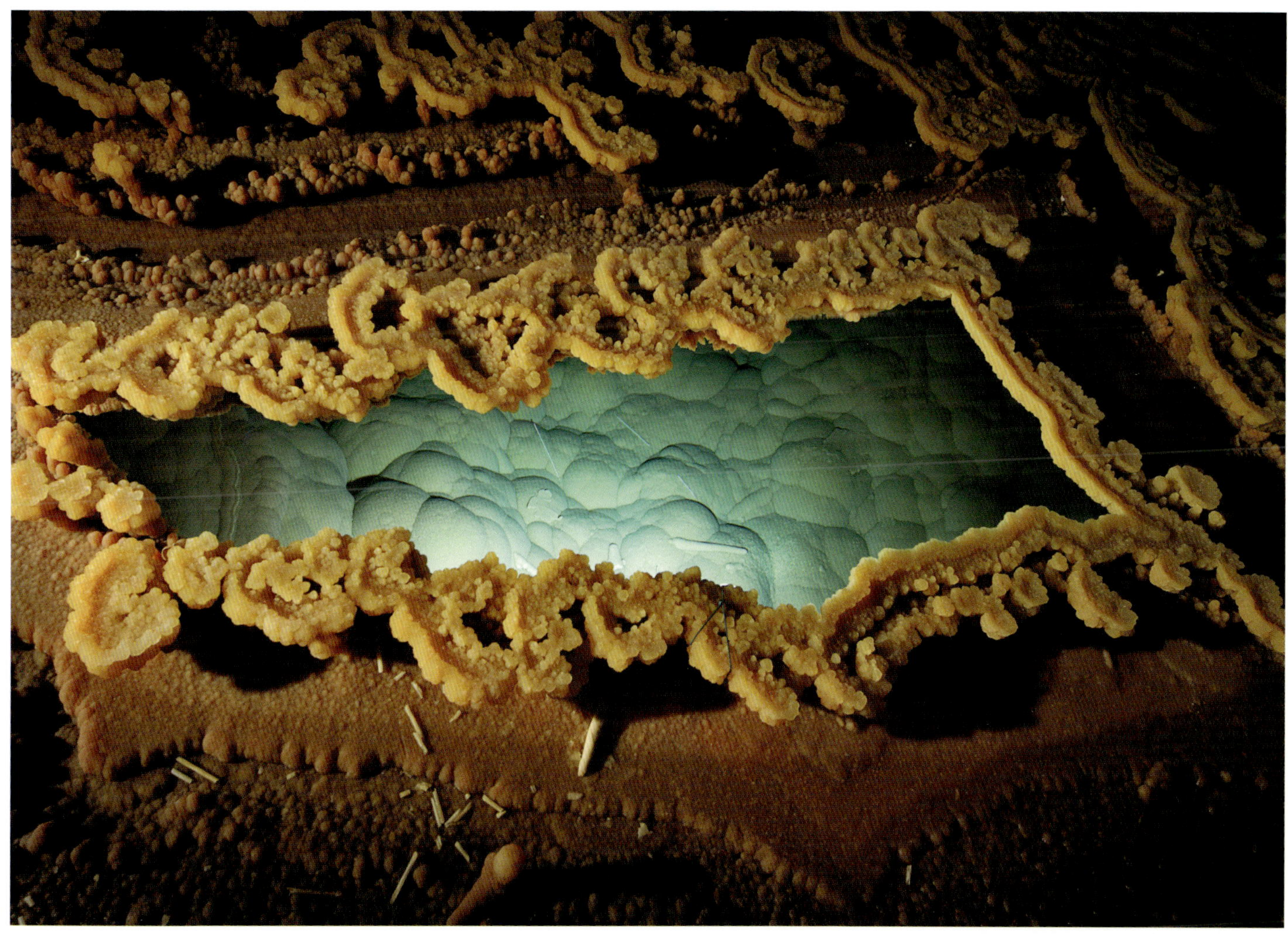

ROBBIE SHONE
A gnarled mineral edge frames an aquamarine pool inside Lechuguilla Cave in New Mexico's Carlsbad Caverns National Park.

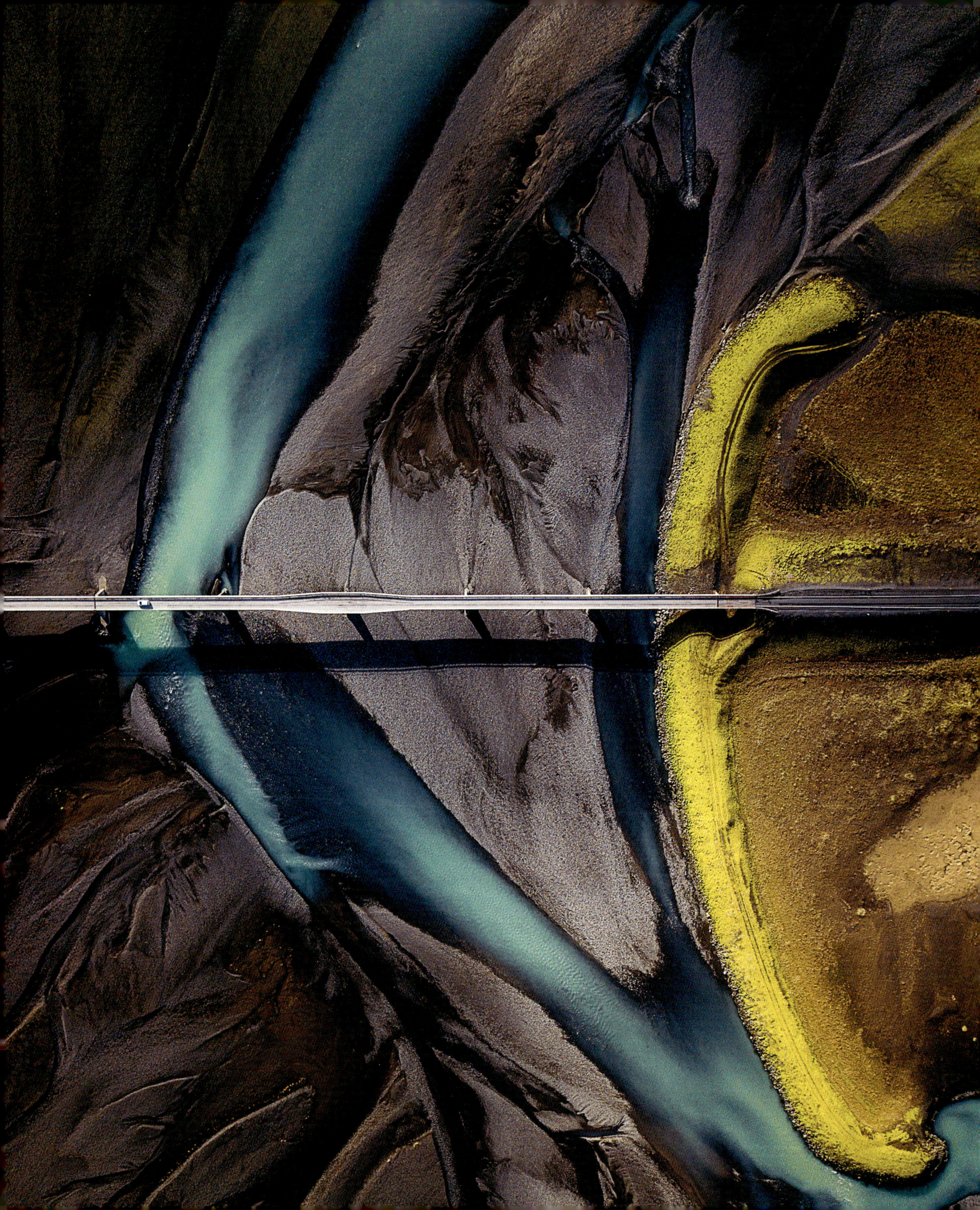

CHAPTER THREE

SCALE

Blinding,
joyous,
fearful
symmetry
surrounds me.

~TED CHIANG, "UNDERSTAND," *STORIES OF YOUR LIFE AND OTHERS*

ecently, while flying a drone over a large glacial front in north-east Greenland, I noticed a strange swirling pattern in the water where the snout of the ice met the fjord (pages 126–27). Brown water was pouring out from deep beneath the glacier, weakening it from below. Slowly, the glacier's front wall, as wide as a skyscraper tilted over on its side, began to rise out of the water of the fjord. I radioed the science team in the boat to warn them of what I was seeing through my drone, but they were already turning around to flee the impending tsunami. Eventually, the wall of ice ceased its rise, tilted over backward, and crashed into the fjord, sending ice and a wave of water more than six feet (2 m) tall in the direction of where the boat had been just moments before.

From my vantage point on a distant shore, watching something so big happen so slowly made me feel disconnected from reality. The boat, moving at full speed, seemed to crawl away from the glacier. As this was unfolding between mountainous cliffs more than half a mile (1 km) tall on either side, the scale of the glacial collapse seemed small from where I stood; yet through the lens of my drone camera, the tumult unleashed was both huge and frightening.

A sense of scale is hard to calibrate. We tend to measure it against our own experiences or perspectives—but these represent a small slice of reality. At the time, the experience I just described felt huge. However, a few weeks after I'd returned from this trip, a landslide near the top of one of those tall cliffs sent a mountain of debris and ice crashing into that same fjord. A tsunami more than 130 feet (40 m) tall spread across hundreds of miles of fjords, annihilating a few historic structures and the edge of a research base in this otherwise uninhabited region (the waves even swept up past the rock island in the delta on pages 252–53). The shock wave from the event was picked up by sensors as far away as New Zealand. What I thought was big turned out to be small. Scale is the ultimate head-scratcher. It perplexes human minds that are so used to experiencing the world on our own everyday terms.

The quest to capture tiny, rapid, or immense patterns and the juxtapositions of human-centered perspectives has spurred innovation in camera technology and technique since the dawn of photography. Early aerial photography was a notable entry point into this space, and it remains a reliable source of brain-tickling views.

With the photos selected in this chapter, I seek out those otherworldly feelings, often with a downward cast, that make us pause, look again, and try to recalibrate. Few are better at making little worlds feel immersive than Javier Aznar González de Rueda, who allows us to exist alongside a stingless bee as it protects a parade of treehopper nymphs (pages 256–57). Katie Orlinsky's drone shots transport us to a place where spruce trees appear miniature atop a massive cliff of thawing permafrost (page 262). And David Nadlinger's long exposure somehow makes a single atom visible and relatable to the scale of normal life as it reradiates absorbed laser light (page 251).

The human scale can be limiting, but thoughtful photographs from above can allow us to experience perspectives that our eyes and brains would otherwise struggle to accept. ■

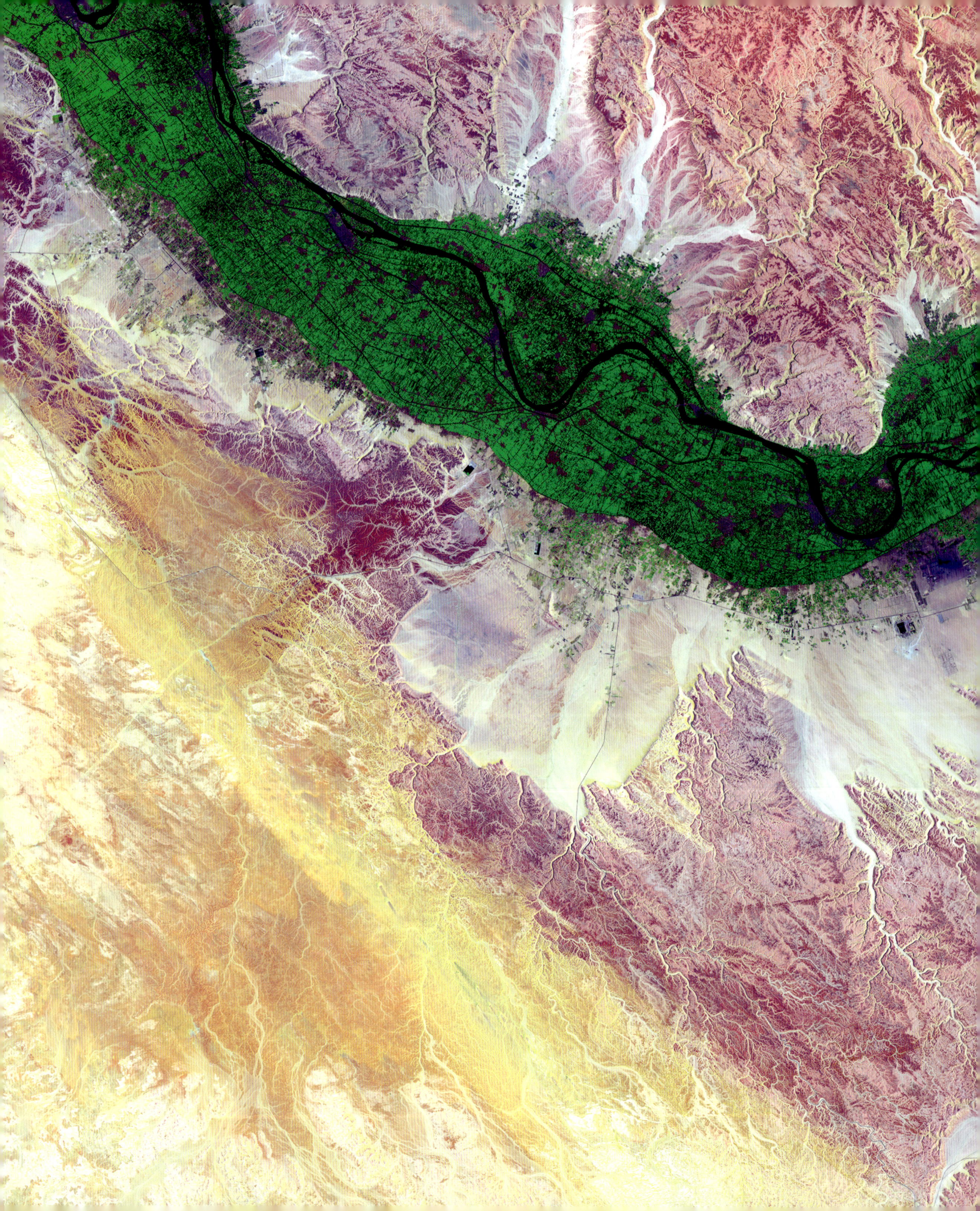

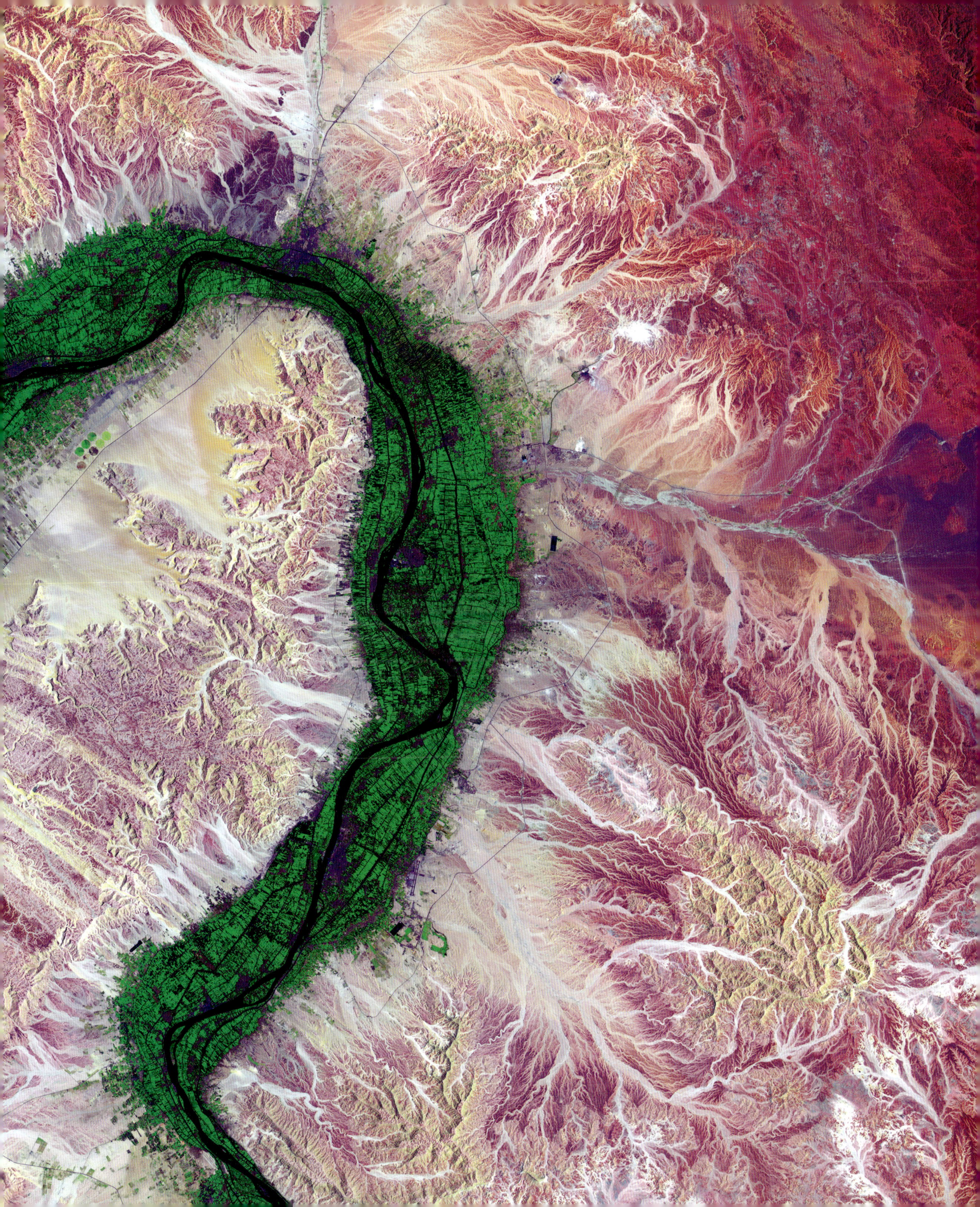

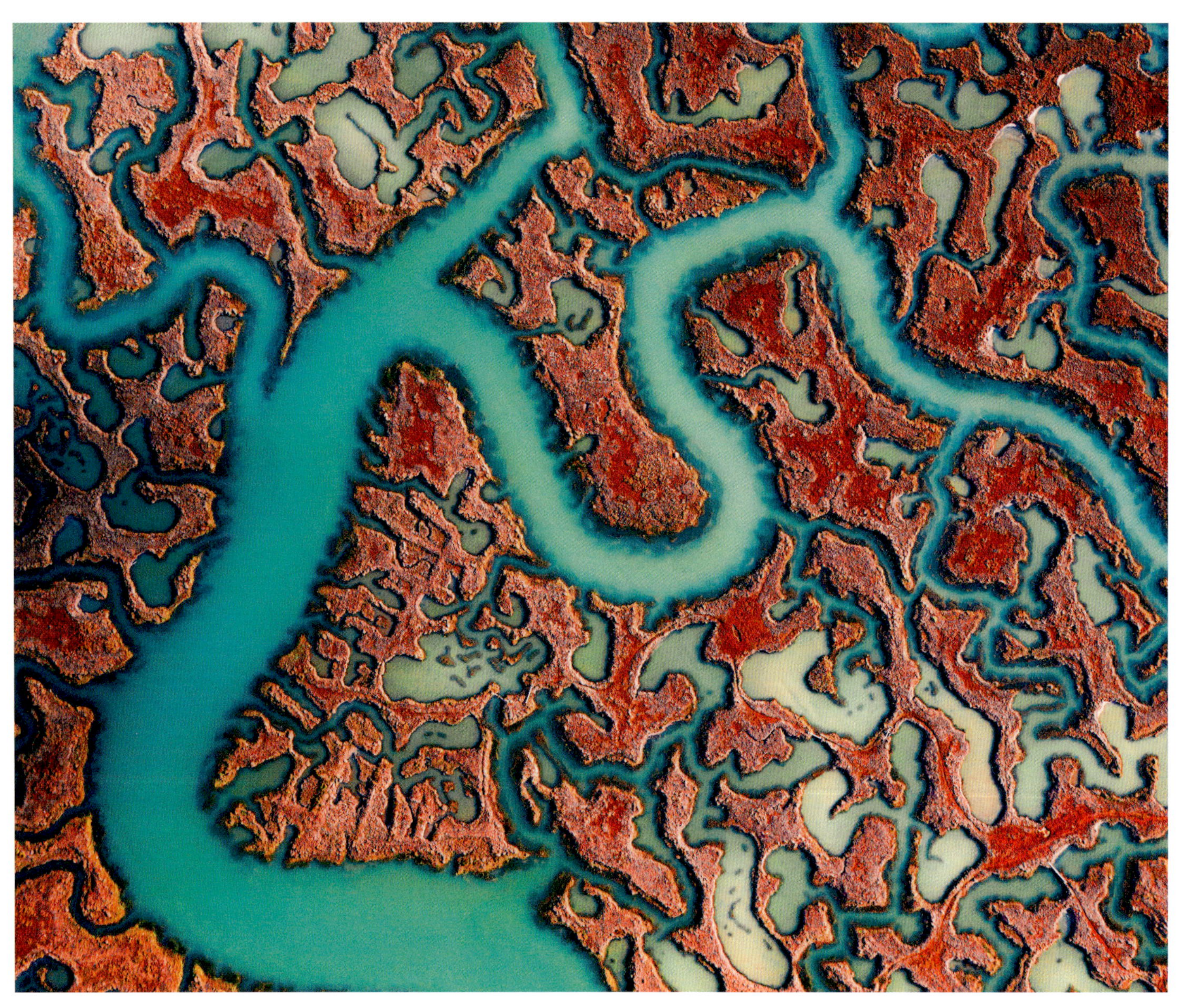

HUGO HEALY
A colorized infrared aerial of a river and tributary streams in the United Kingdom

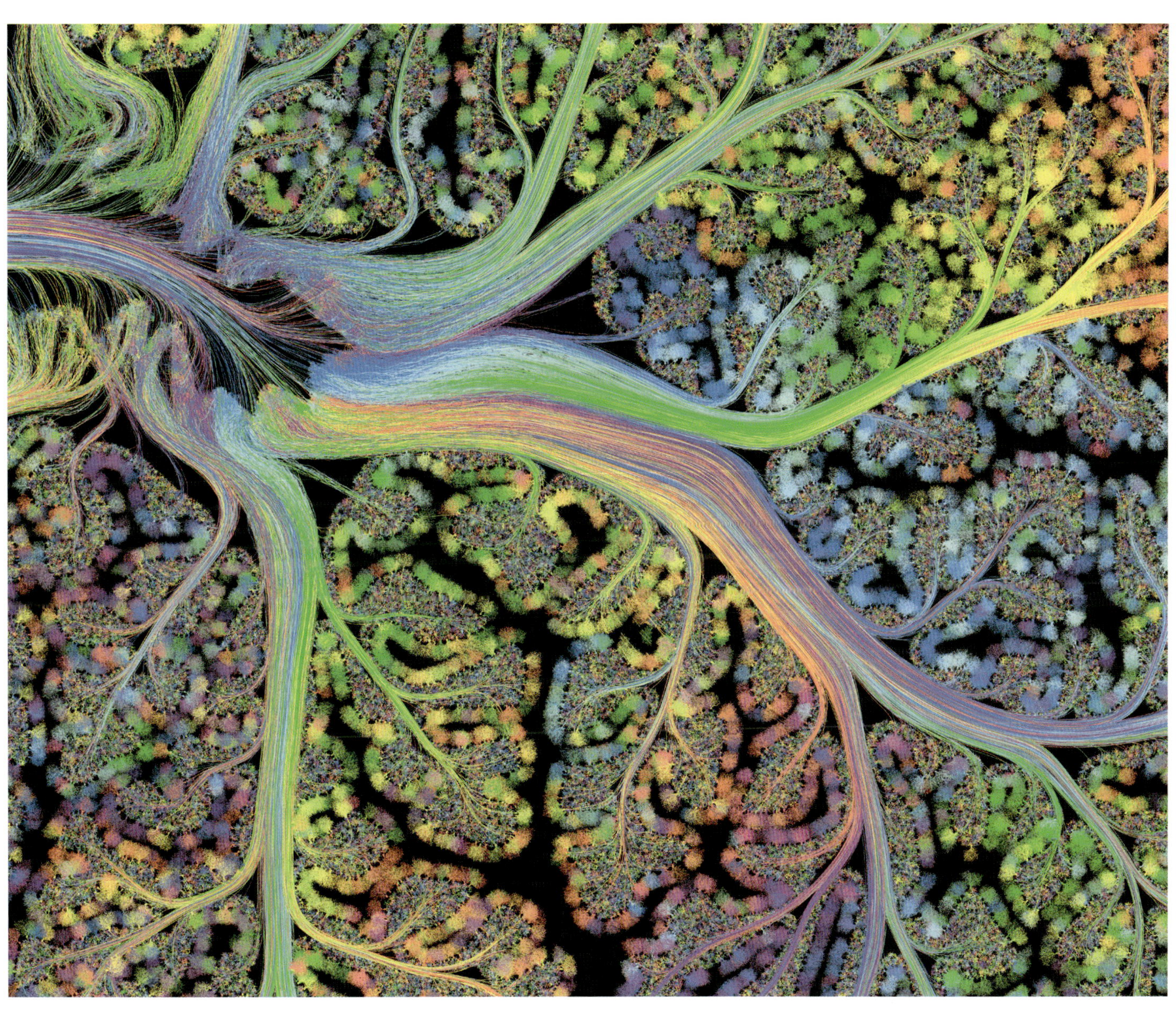

GREG DUNN AND BRIAN EDWARDS
A close-up cross section of brain tissue from a human cerebellum

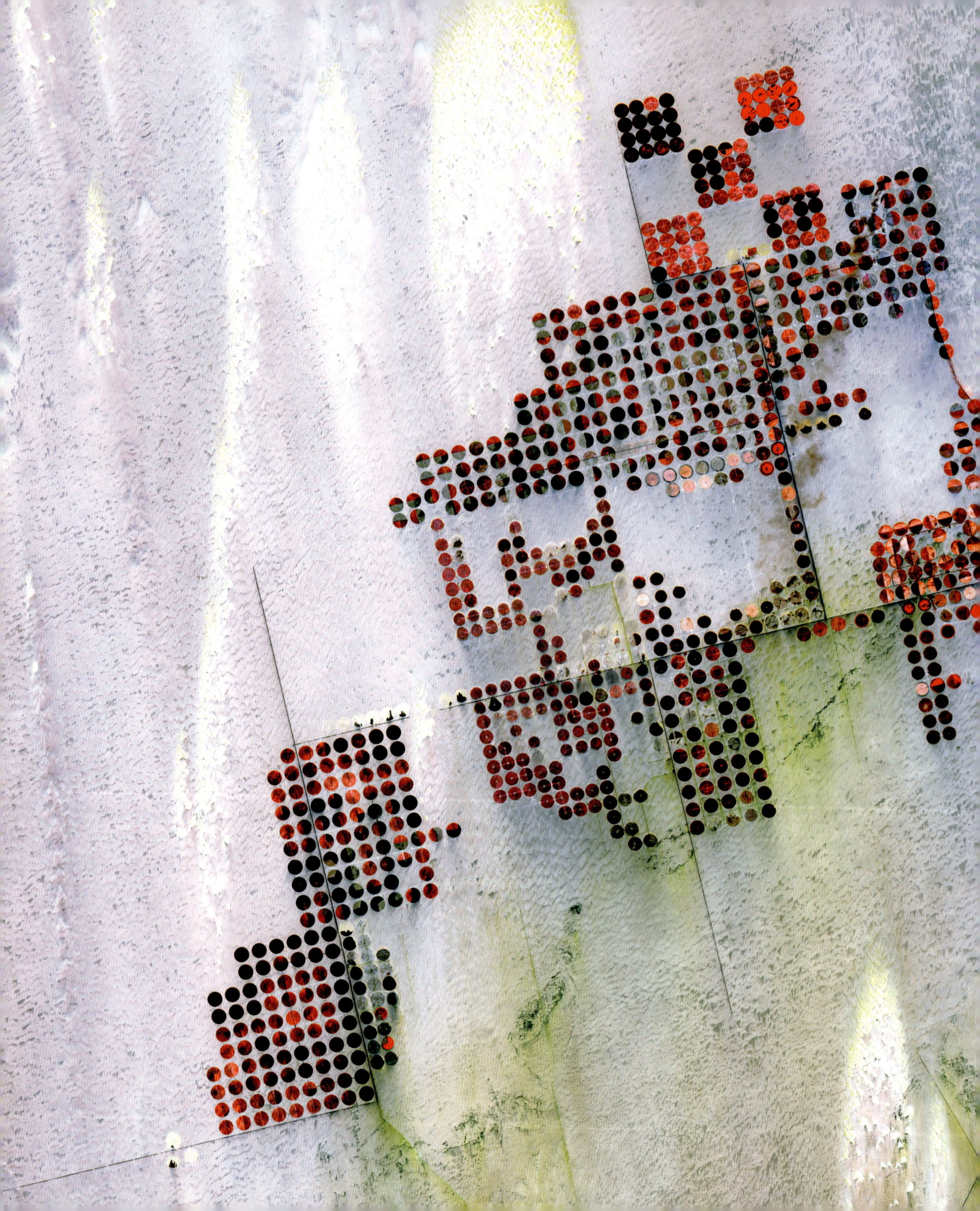

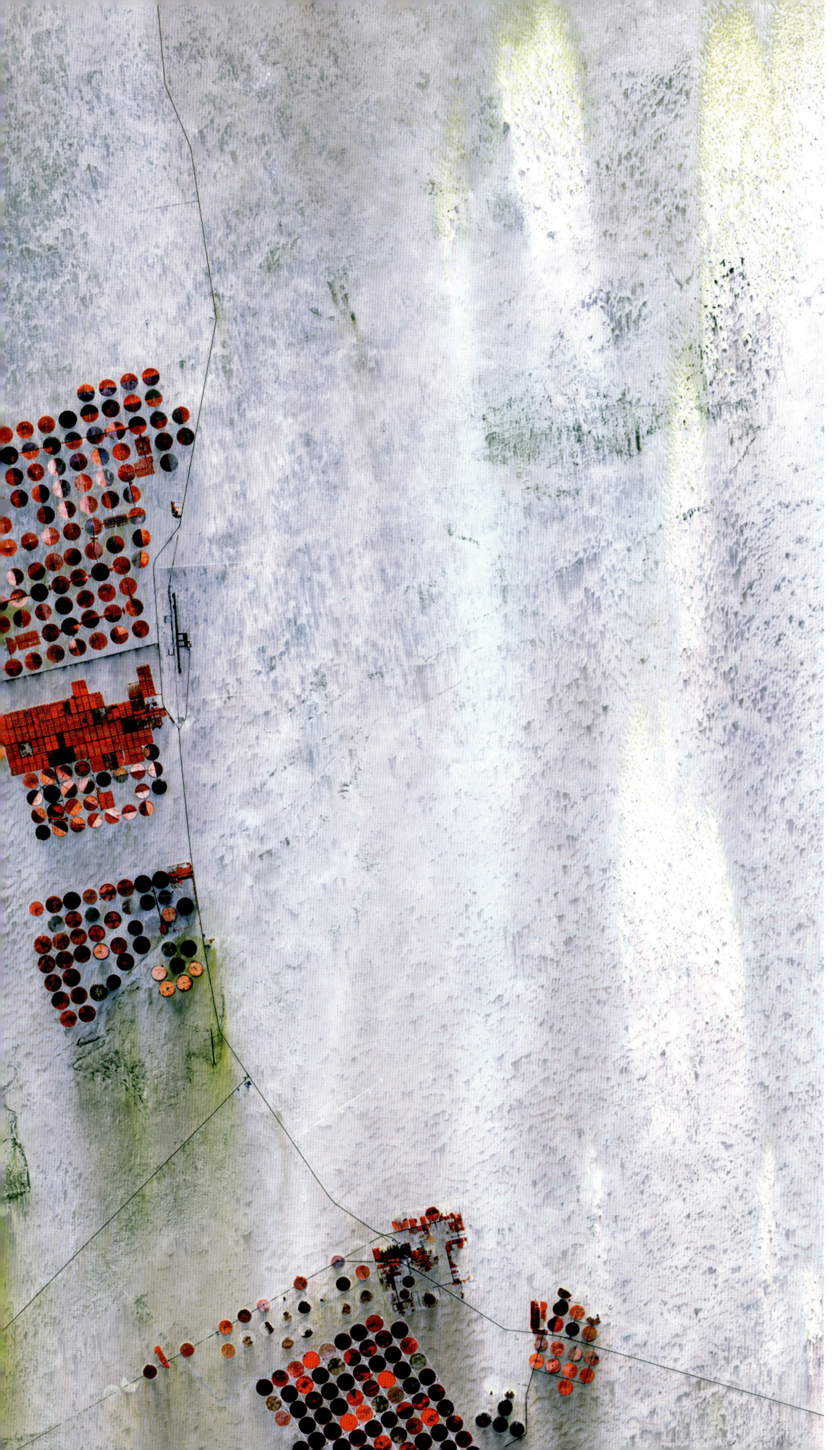

U.S. GEOLOGICAL SURVEY
Like tiny pieces on a game board,
center-pivot irrigation systems
dot a region of southern Egypt's
Sahara. Wells draw water from a
deep aquifer to allow agriculture
in this arid region.

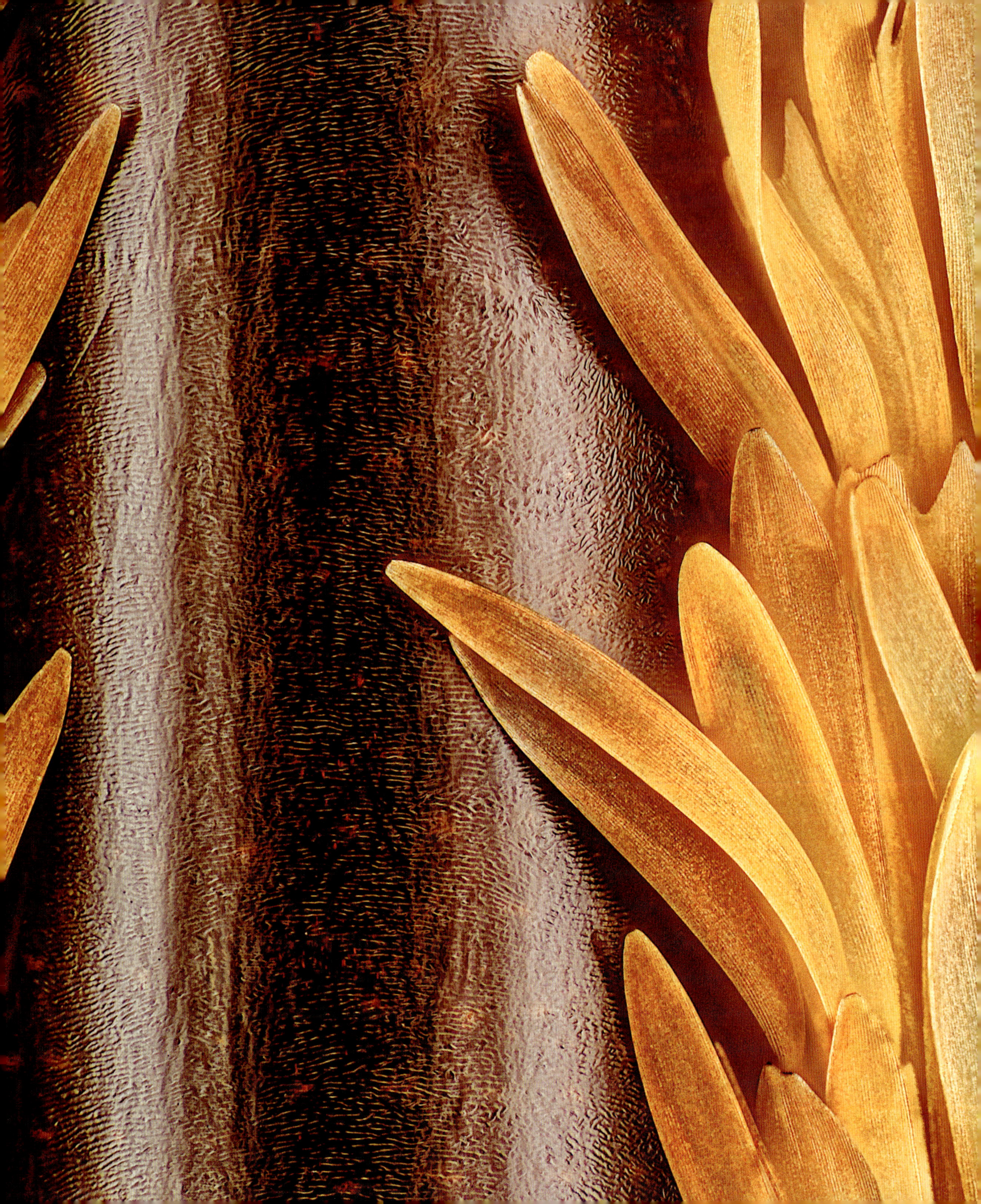

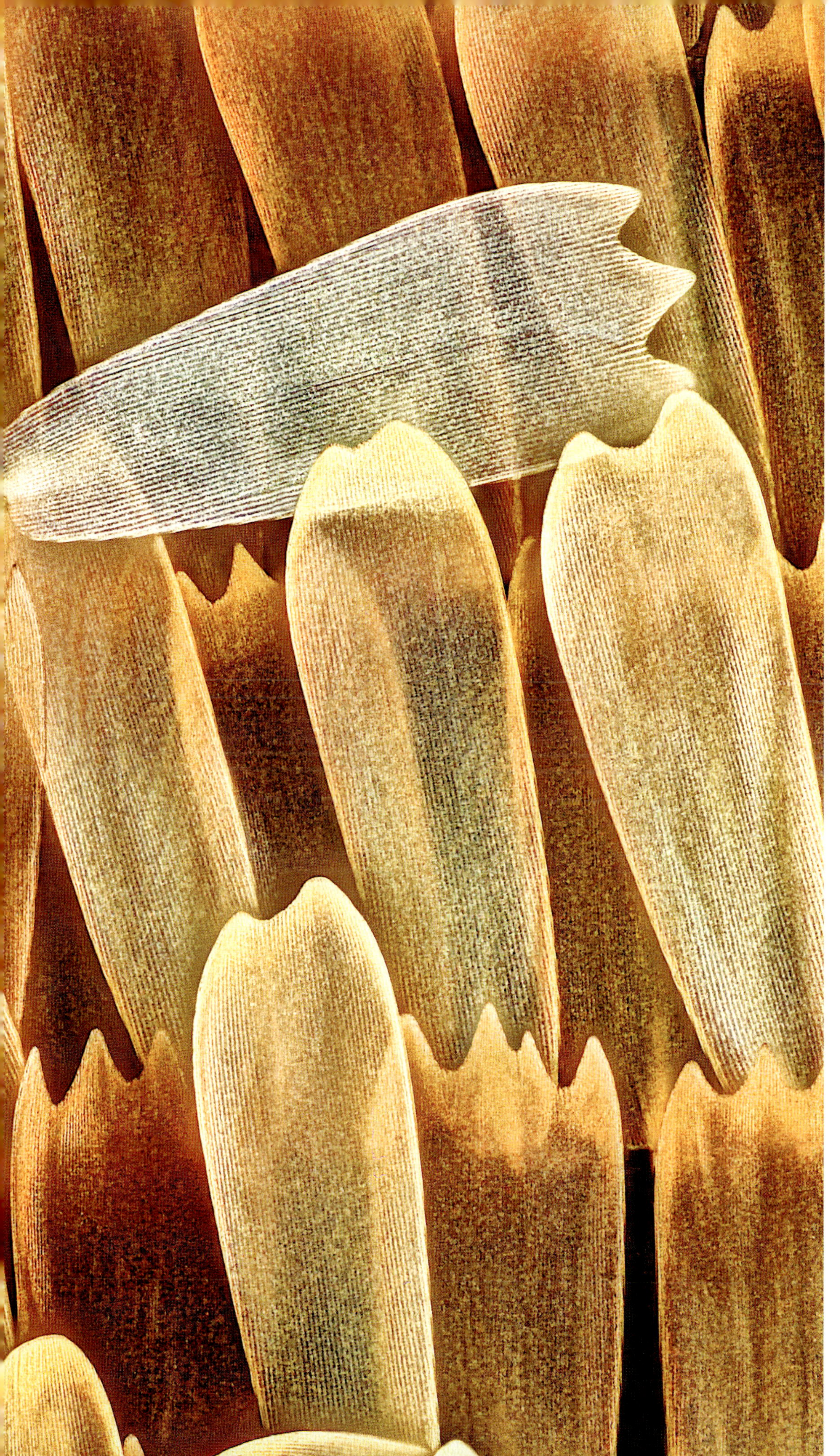

SÉBASTIEN MALO
A vein and scales on the wing of
a Morpho butterfly

Following pages:
CHRIS BURKARD
A bush plane casts a tiny shadow
where land meets river at the
southern edge of Iceland's
Vatnajökull glacier.

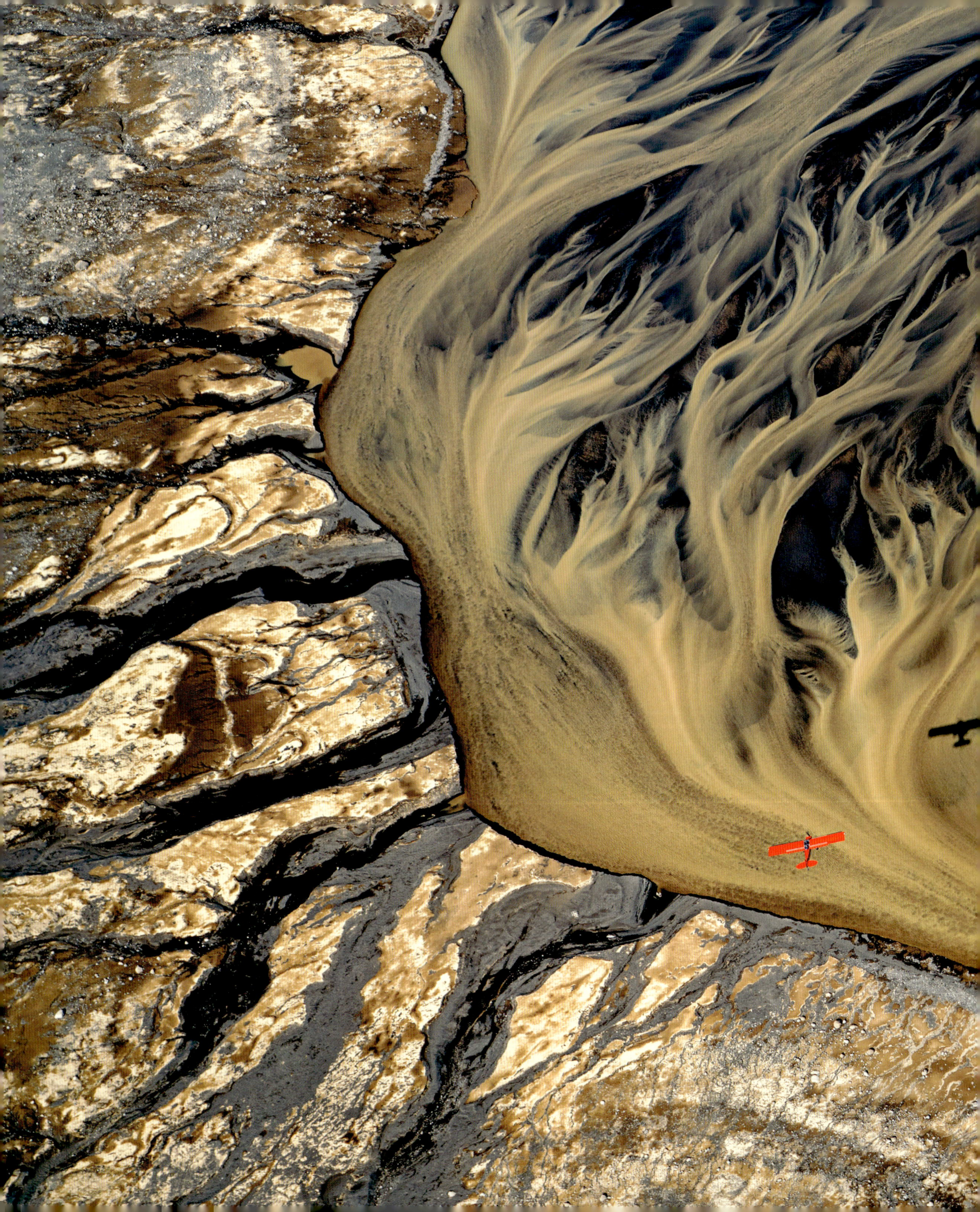

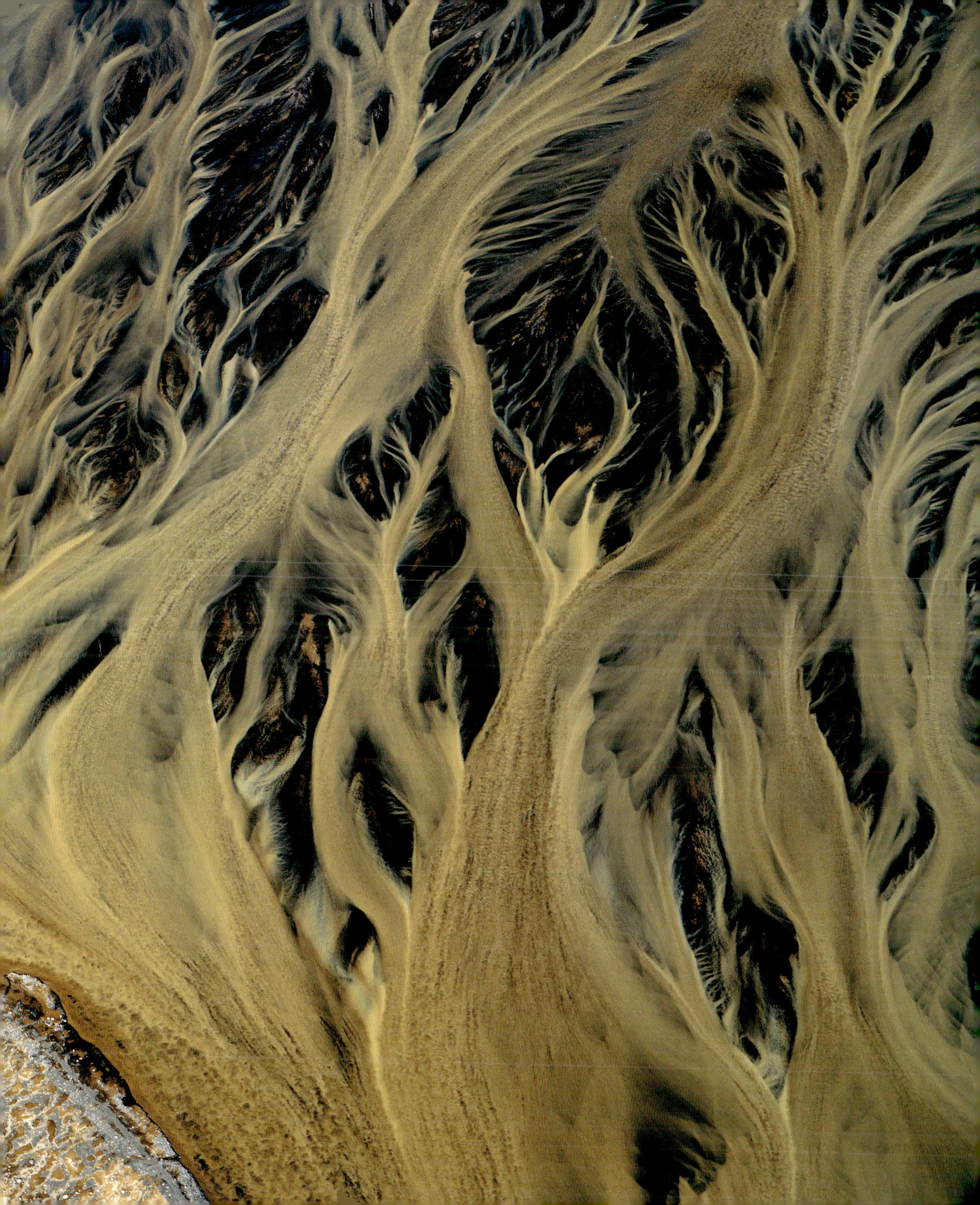

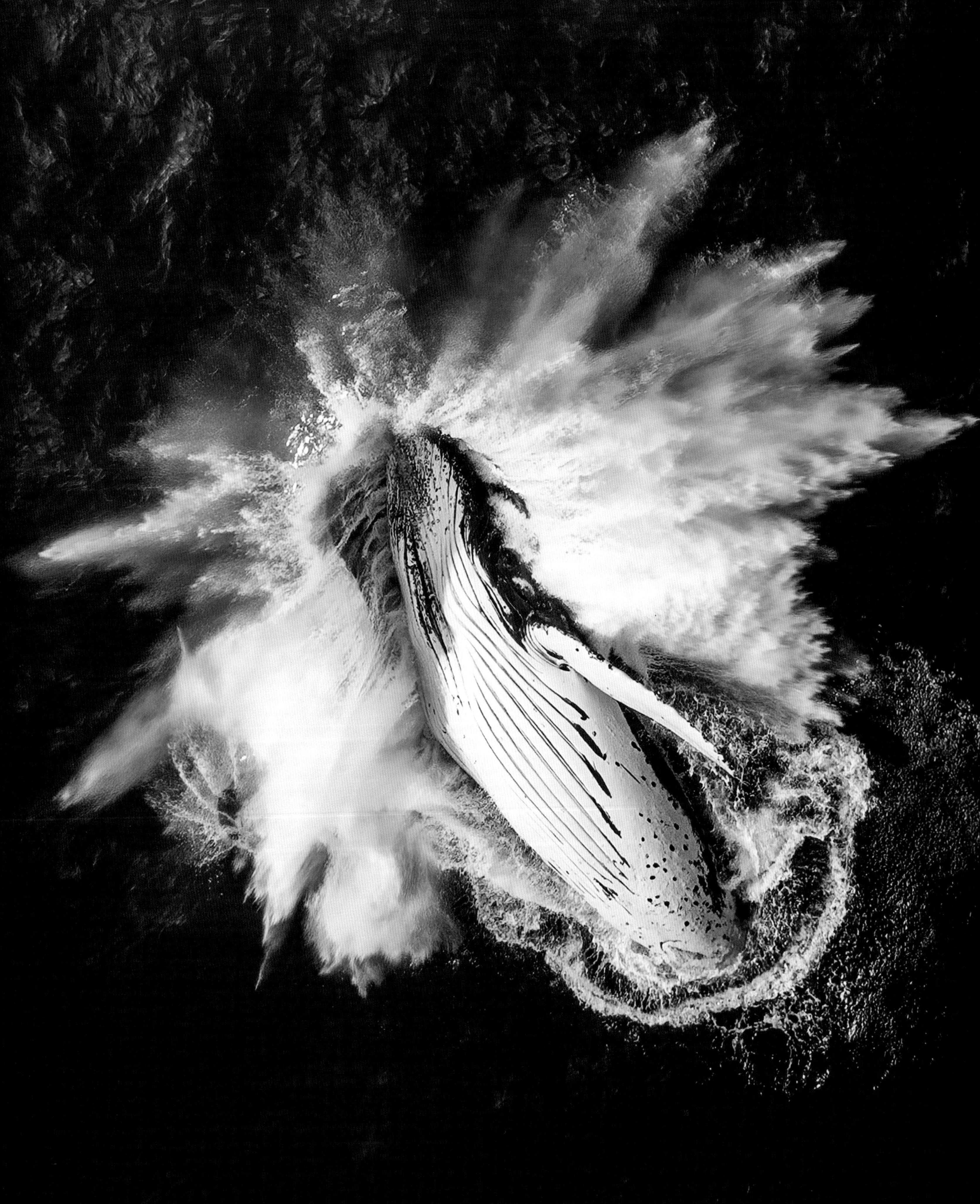

With an outward stroke
of power intense your
mighty arm goes forth, /
Cleaving its way through
waters that rise and roll ...

DAVID FAIRS
A massive whale breaches and splashes back into the waters of Illawarra, a coastal region in southeastern Australia.

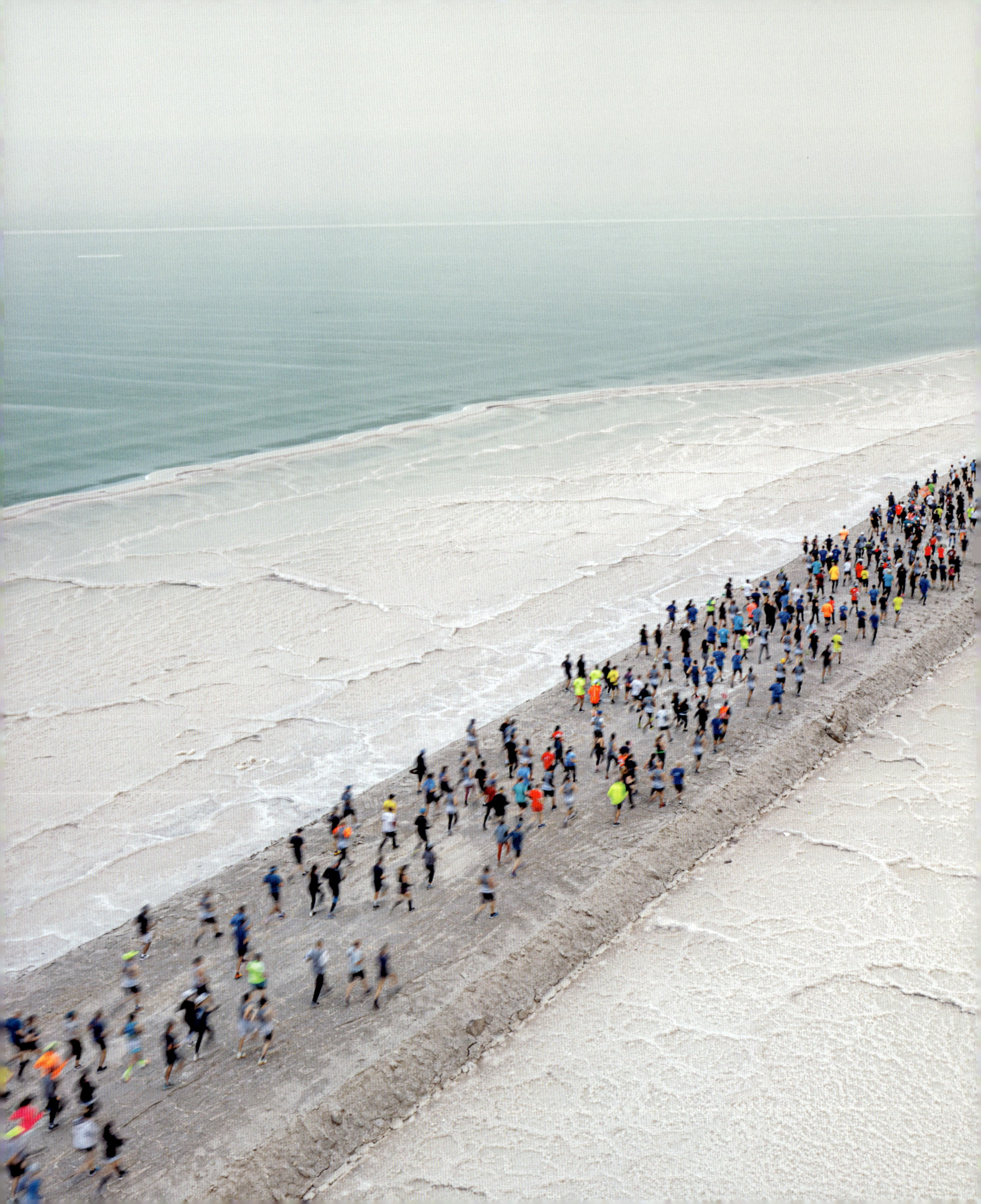

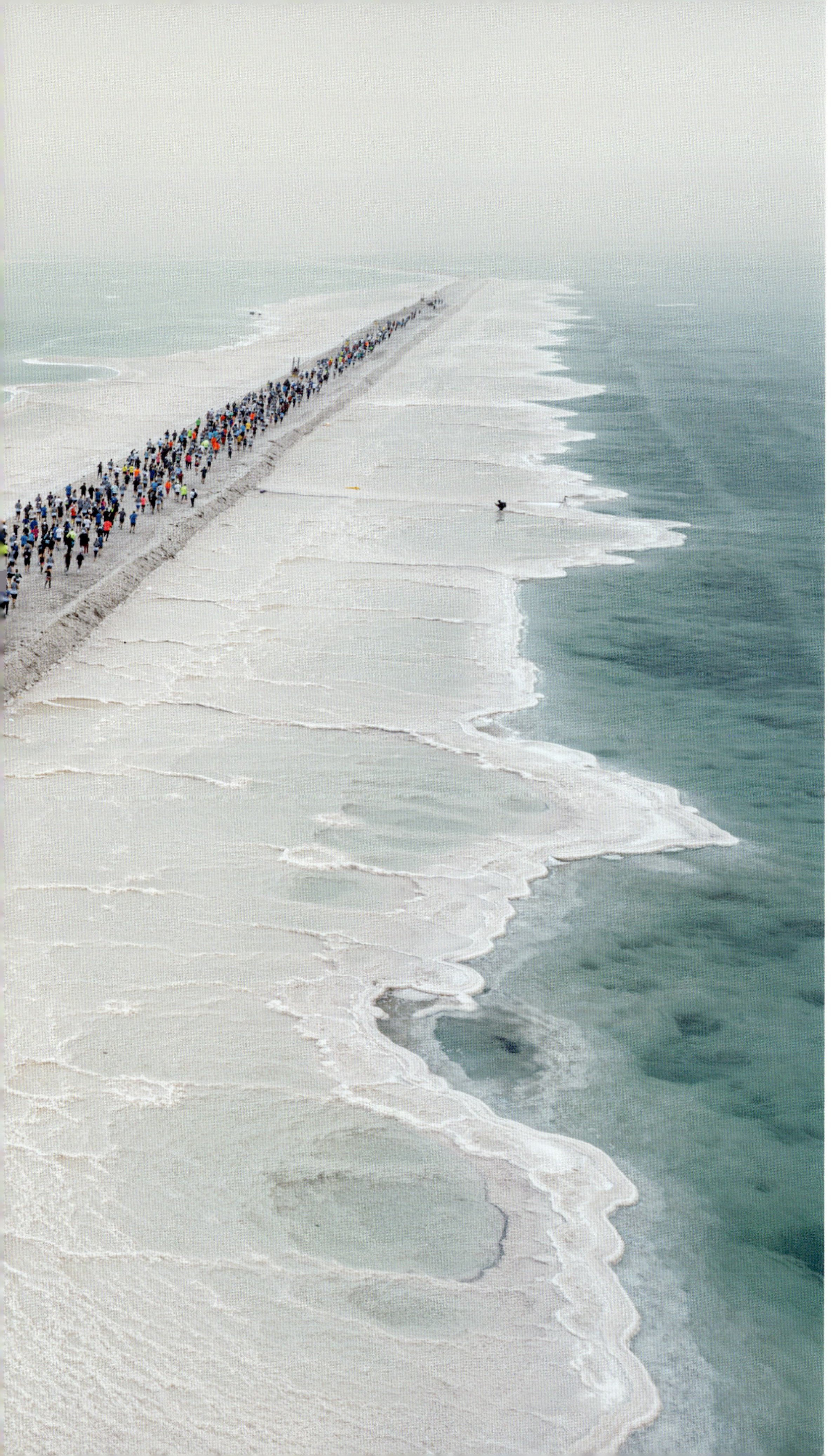

OREN ALON
Runners near Ein Bokek, Israel, approach the starting line of the Dead Sea Marathon, nicknamed "the lowest race in the world."

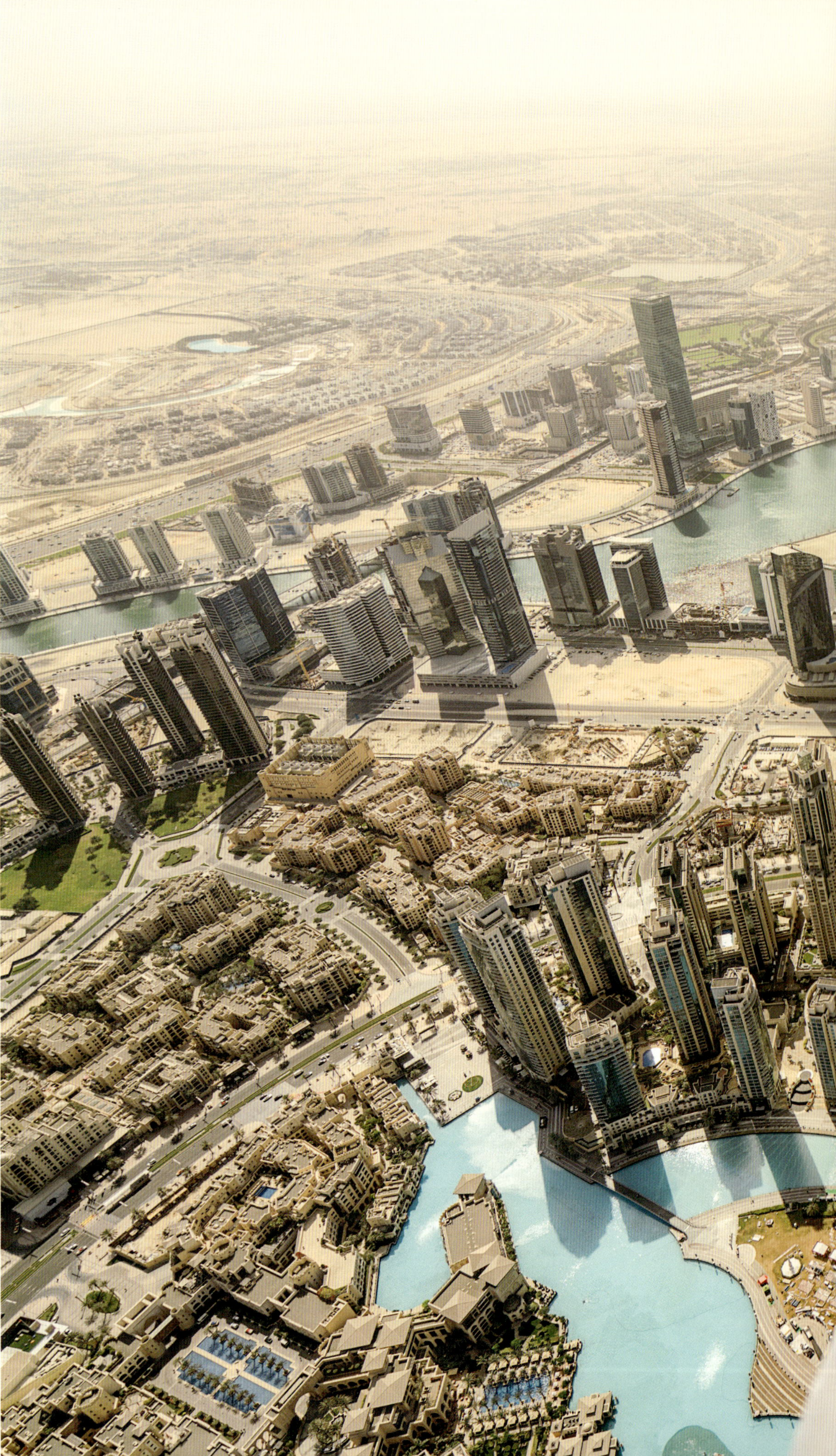

LUCA LOCATELLI
Like little Lego constructions, skyscrapers punctuate the cityscape of Dubai.

Following pages:
OVERVIEW
Once called Tire Mountain, Hudson's monofill near Denver, Colorado, contains 64 pits of used tires 15 feet (4.6 m) deep.

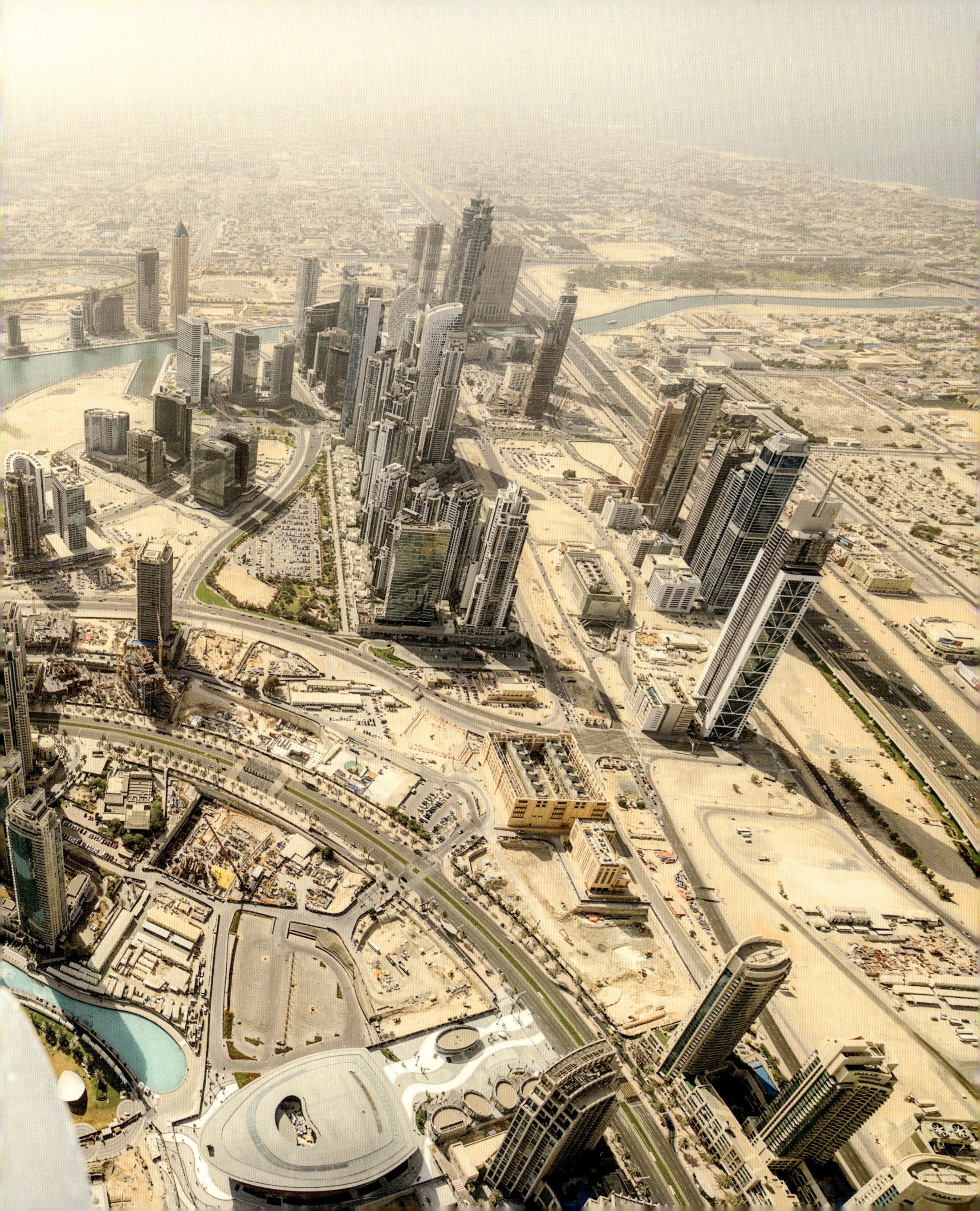

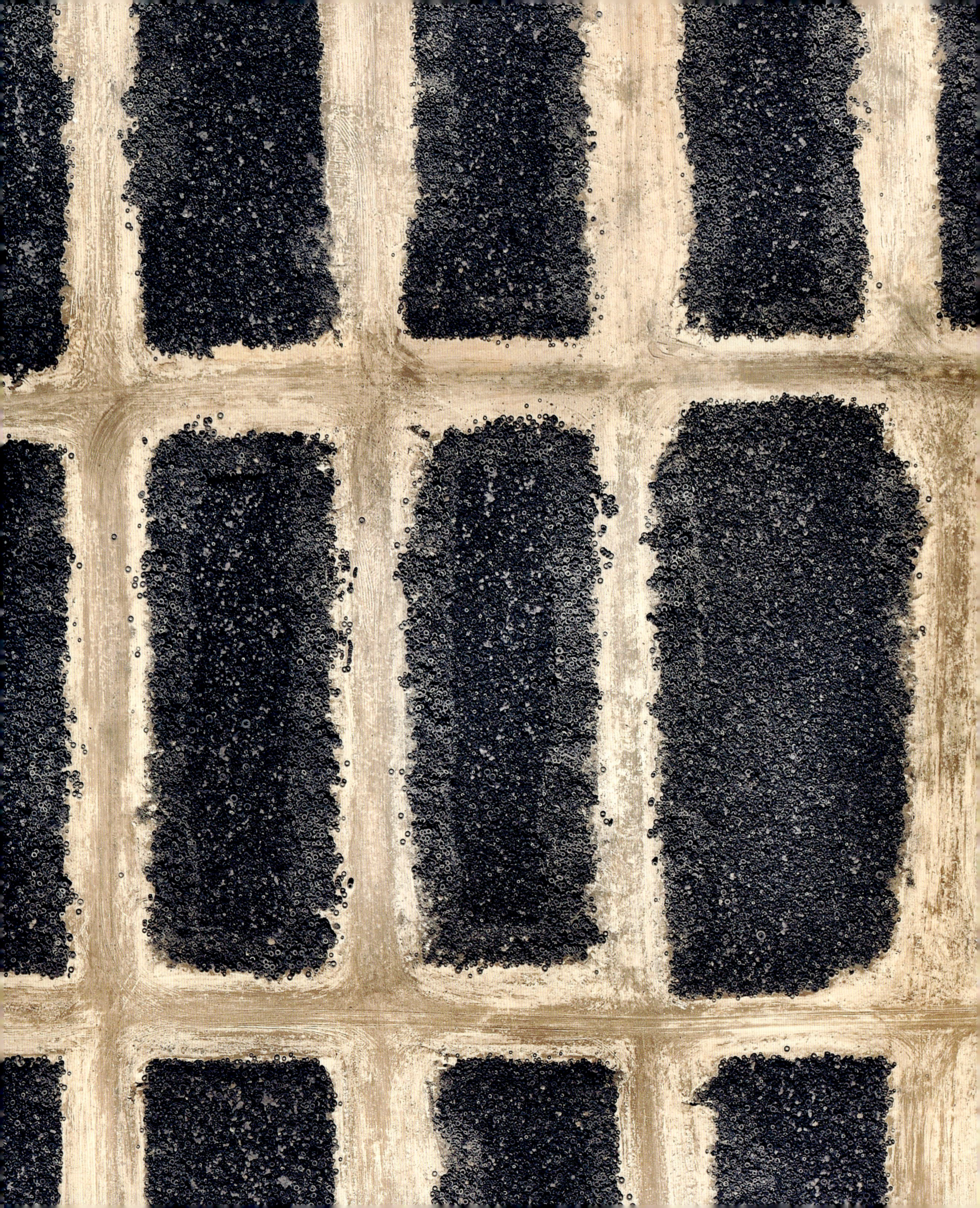

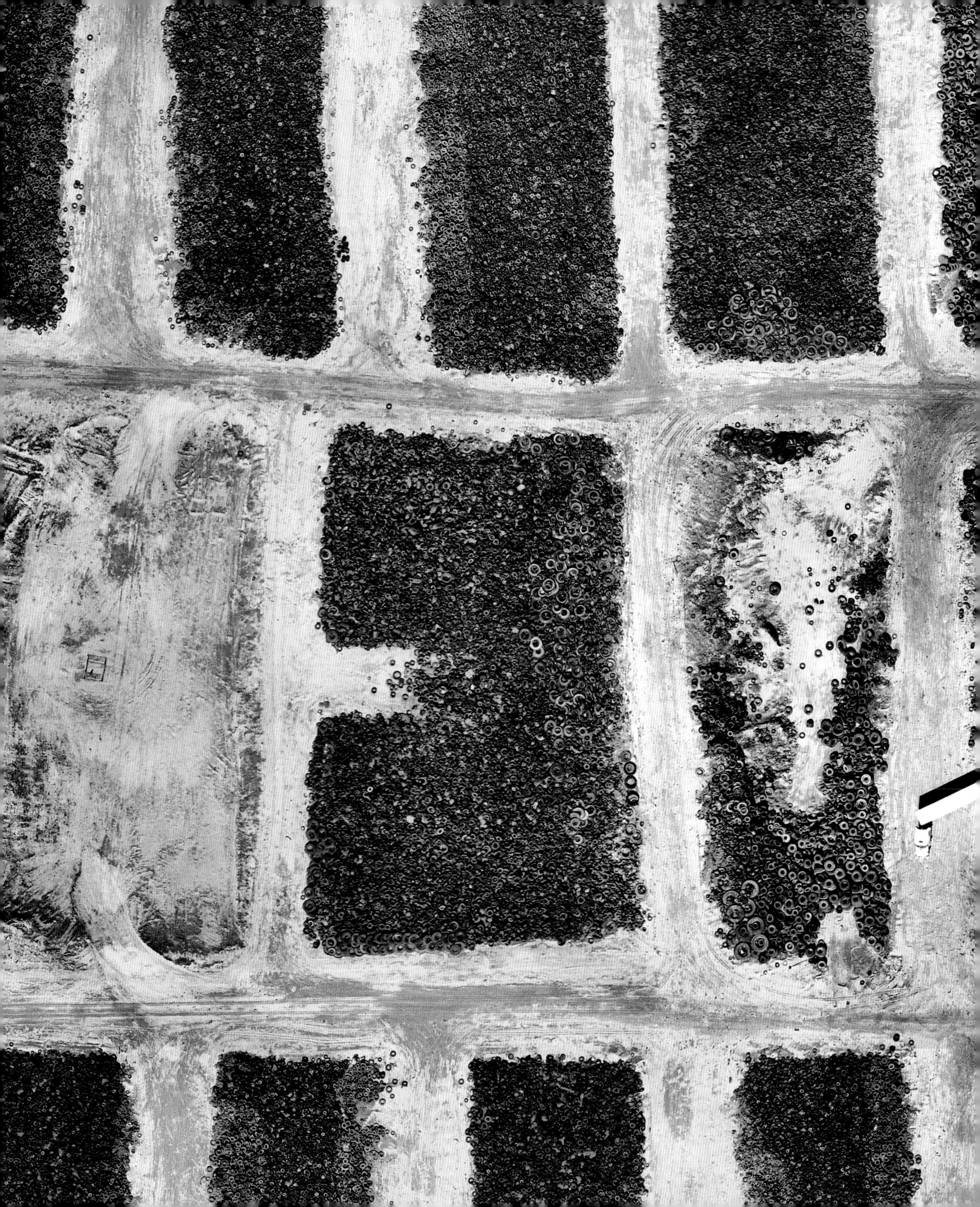

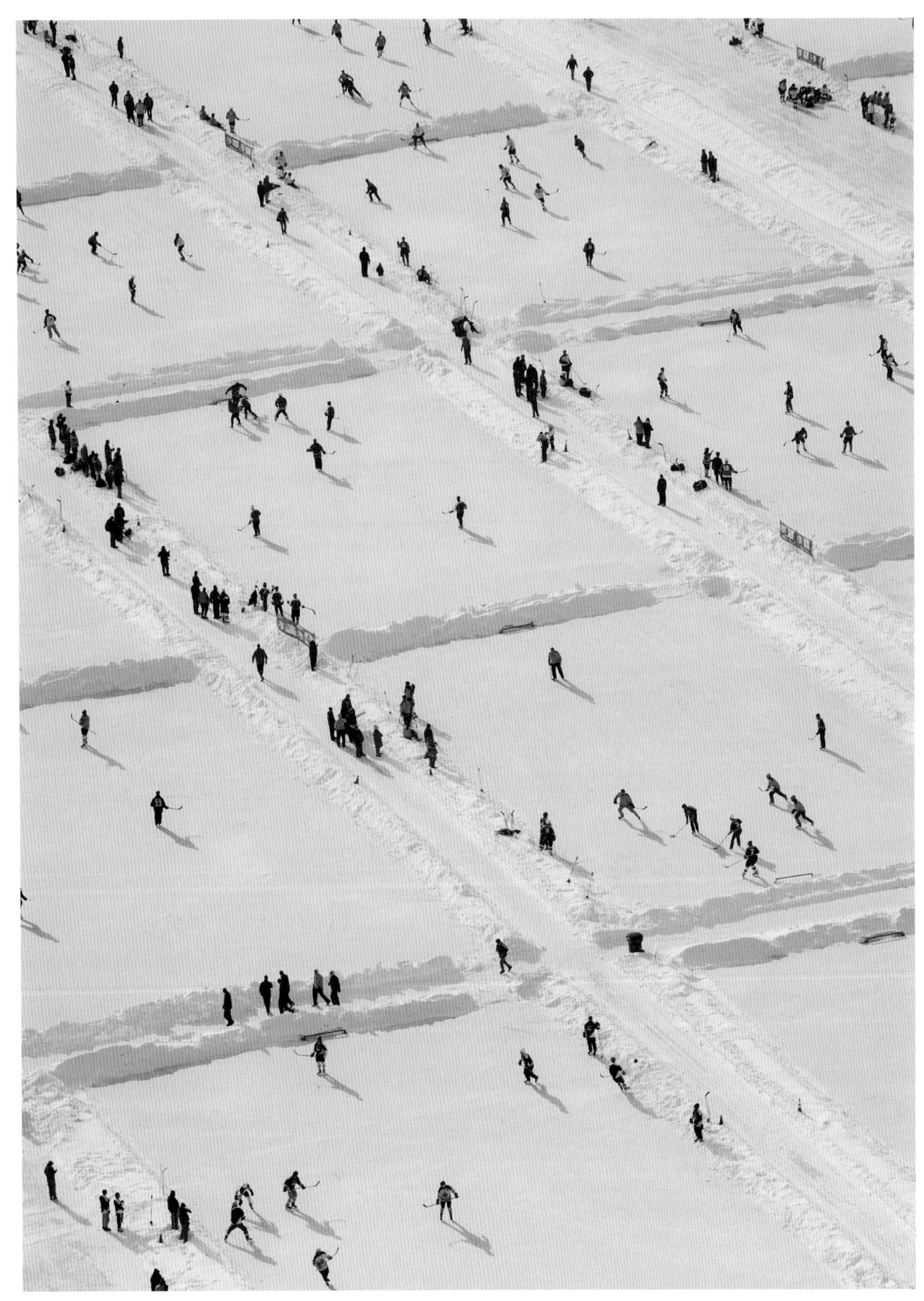

Hockey players gather for an outdoor competition on Wisconsin's Dollar Lake.

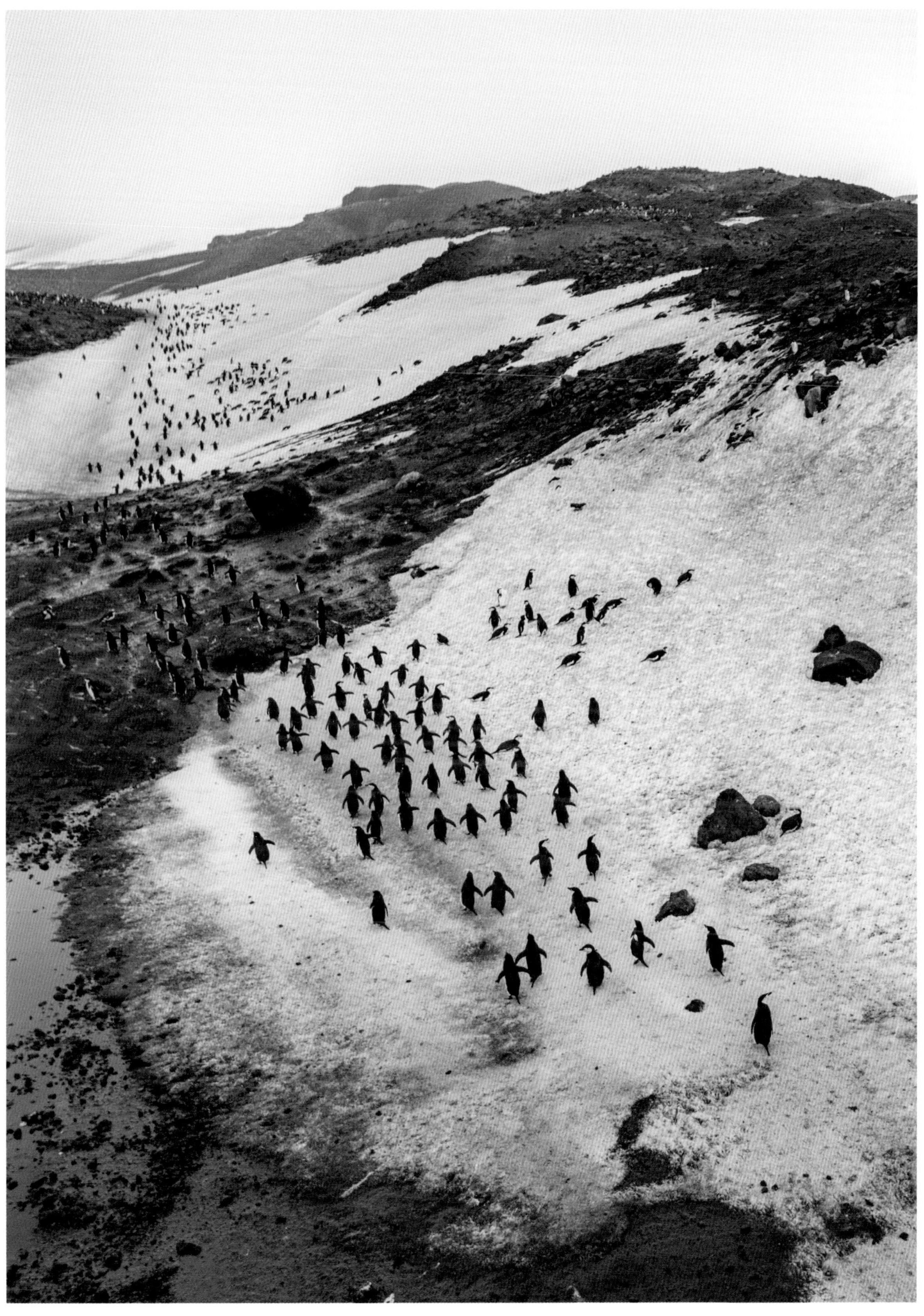

Chinstrap penguins in Antarctica commute from the sea to nesting sites, their excrement staining the snow pink.

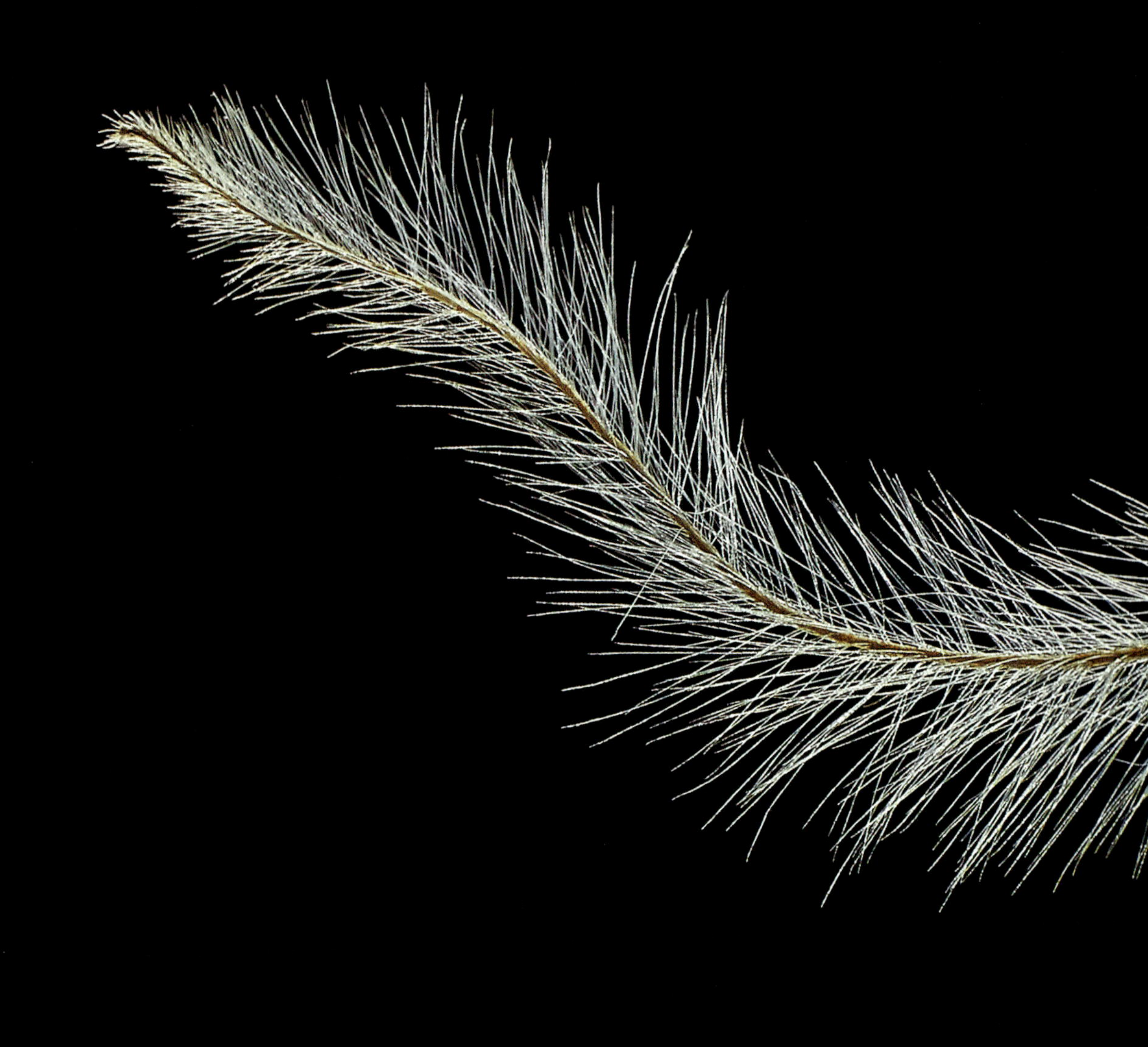

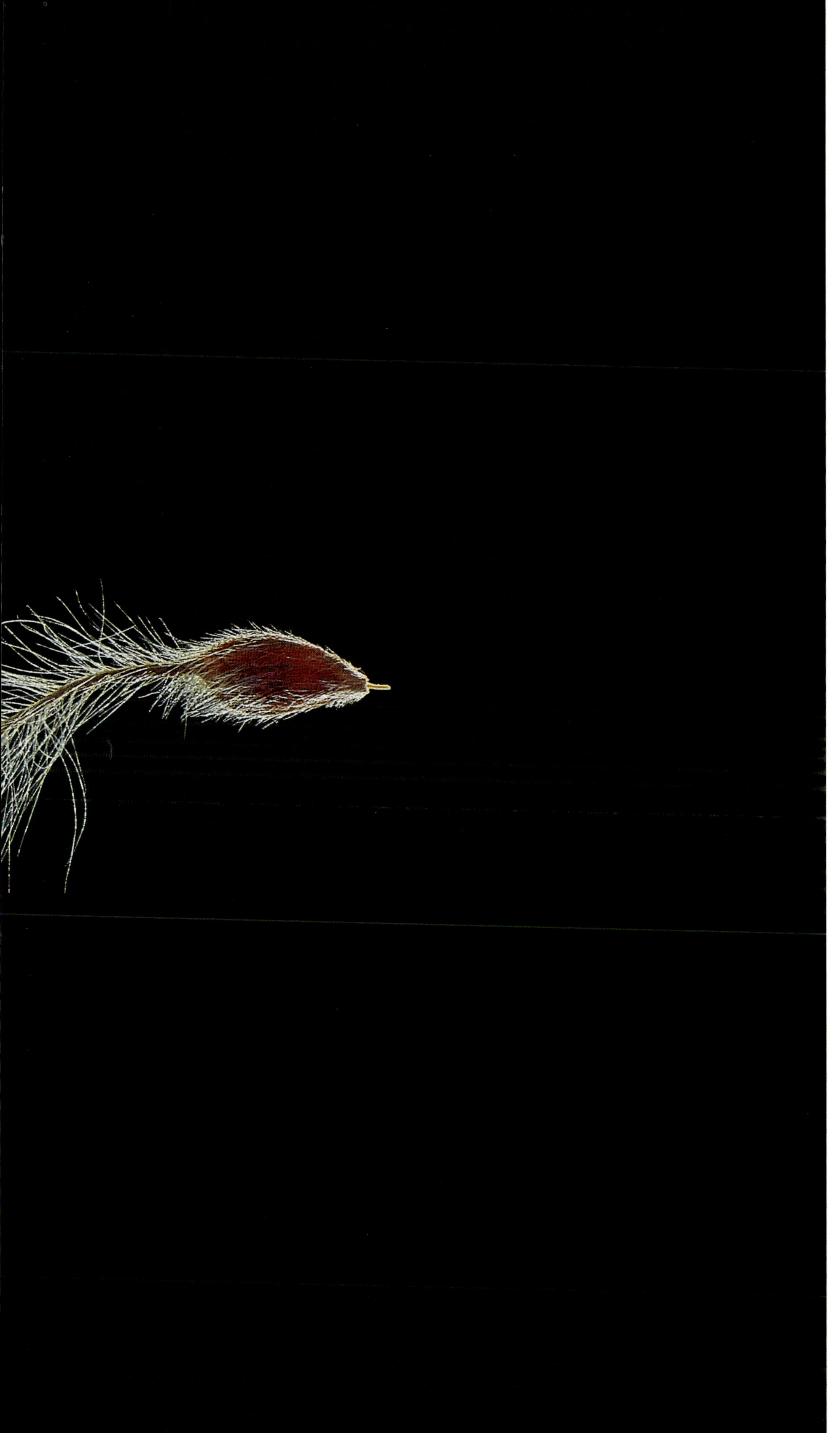

THIERRY ARDOUIN
A feathery tail helps send this clematis seed off to find a new place to germinate.

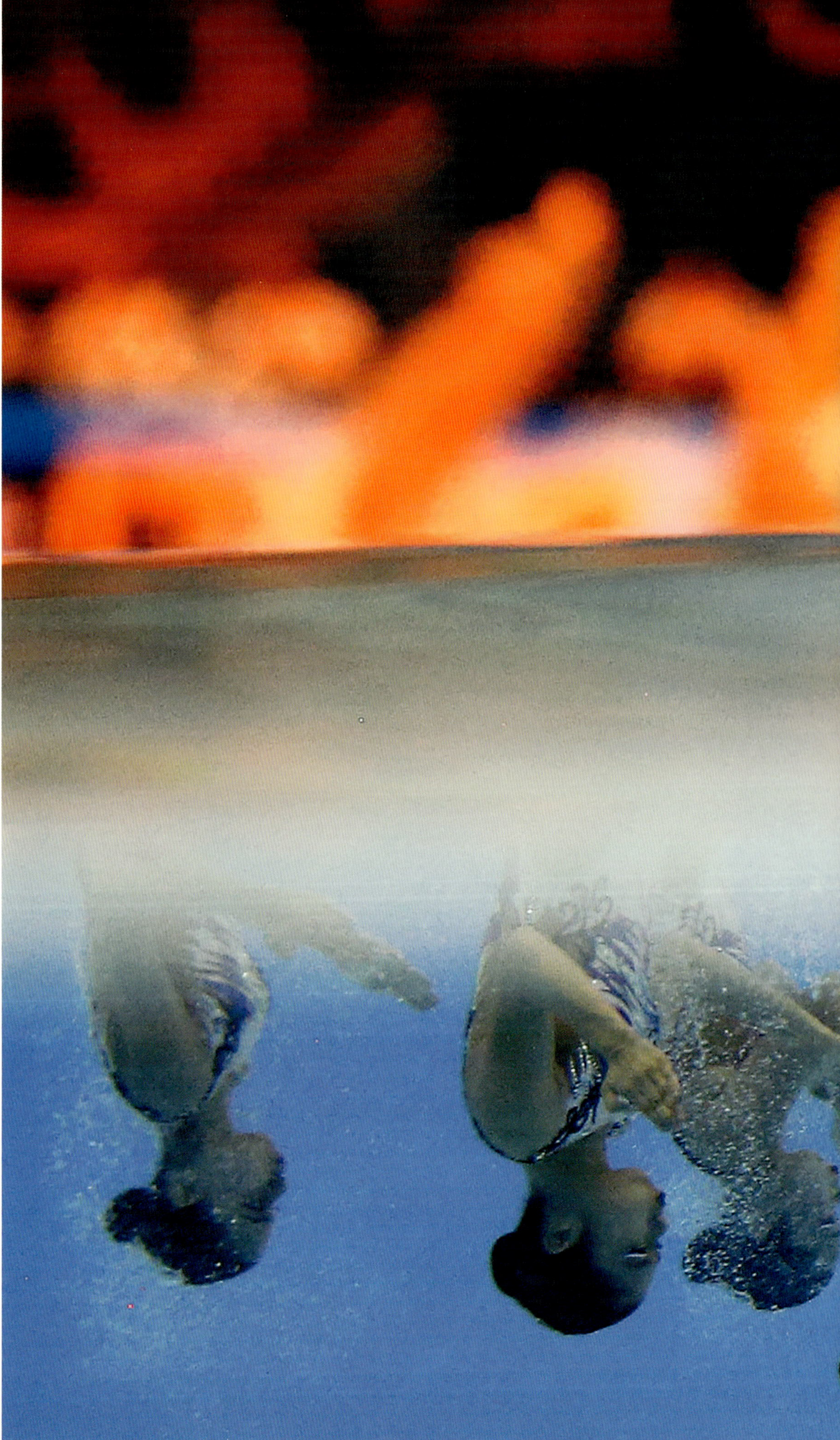

STEFAN WERMUTH
Heads down, feet up:
A synchronized swimming
team competes for world
championship placement.

Following pages:
ANAS ALDHEEB
Camels climb to the mountain-
tops after the rainy season in the
Dhofar Governorate of Oman.

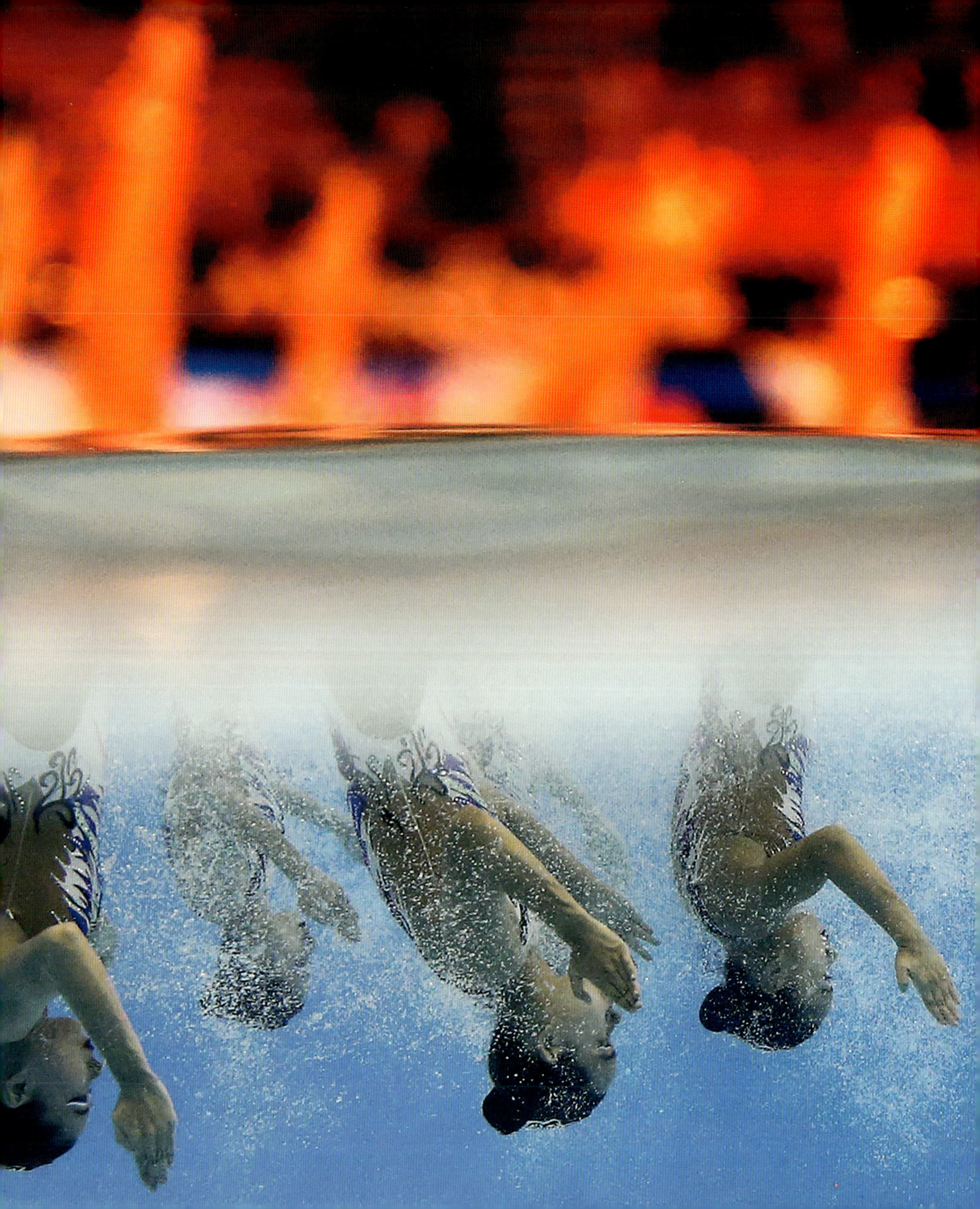

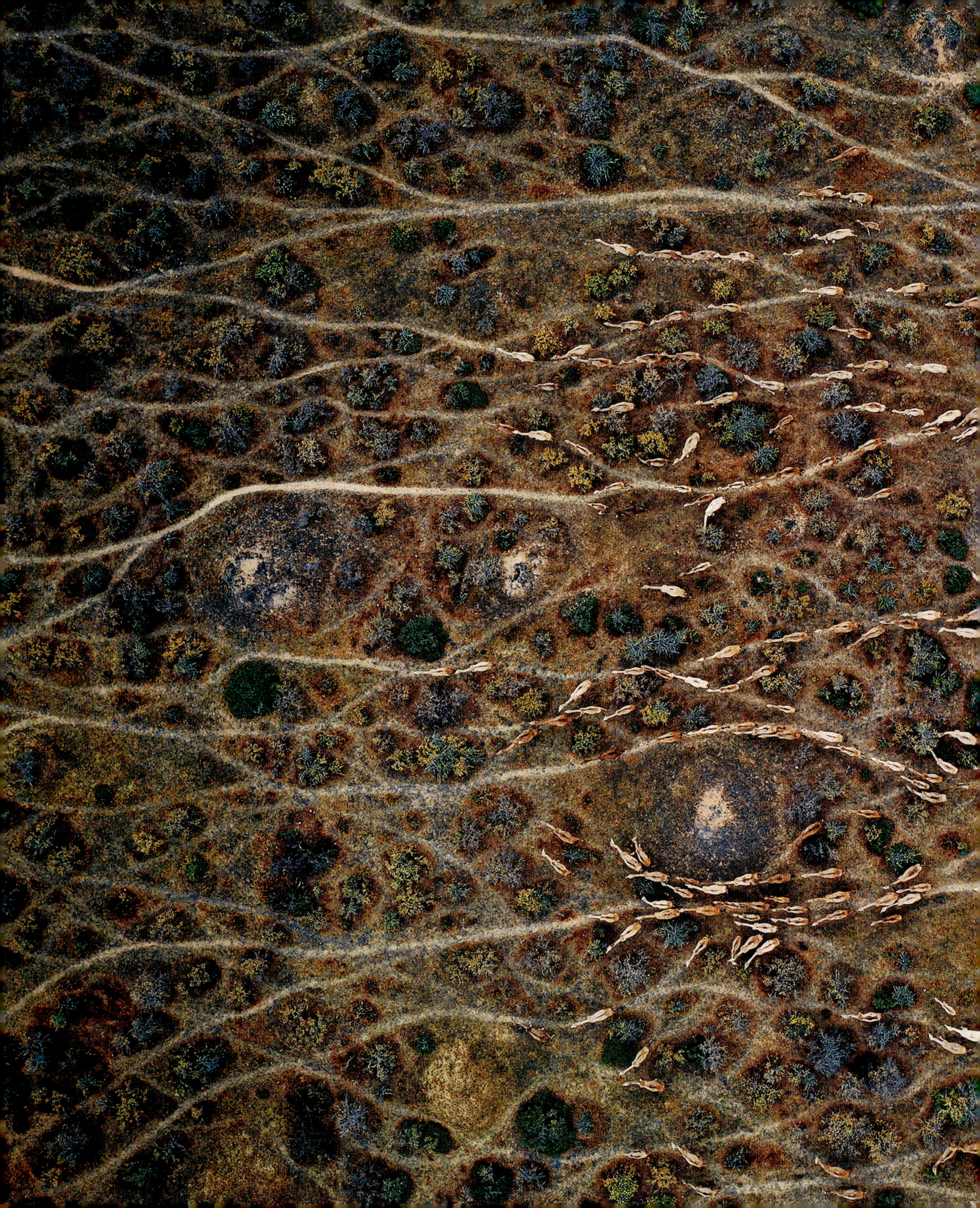

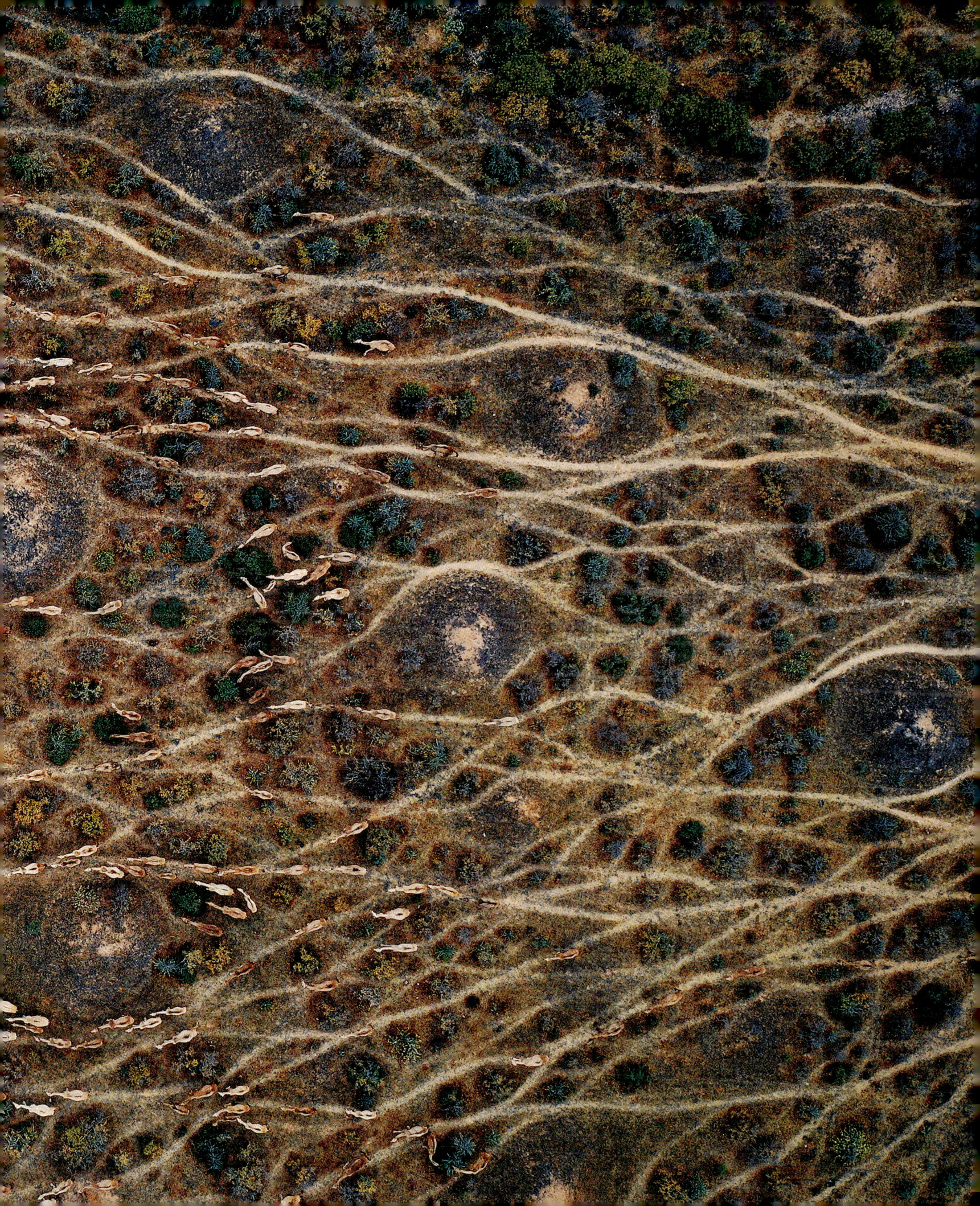

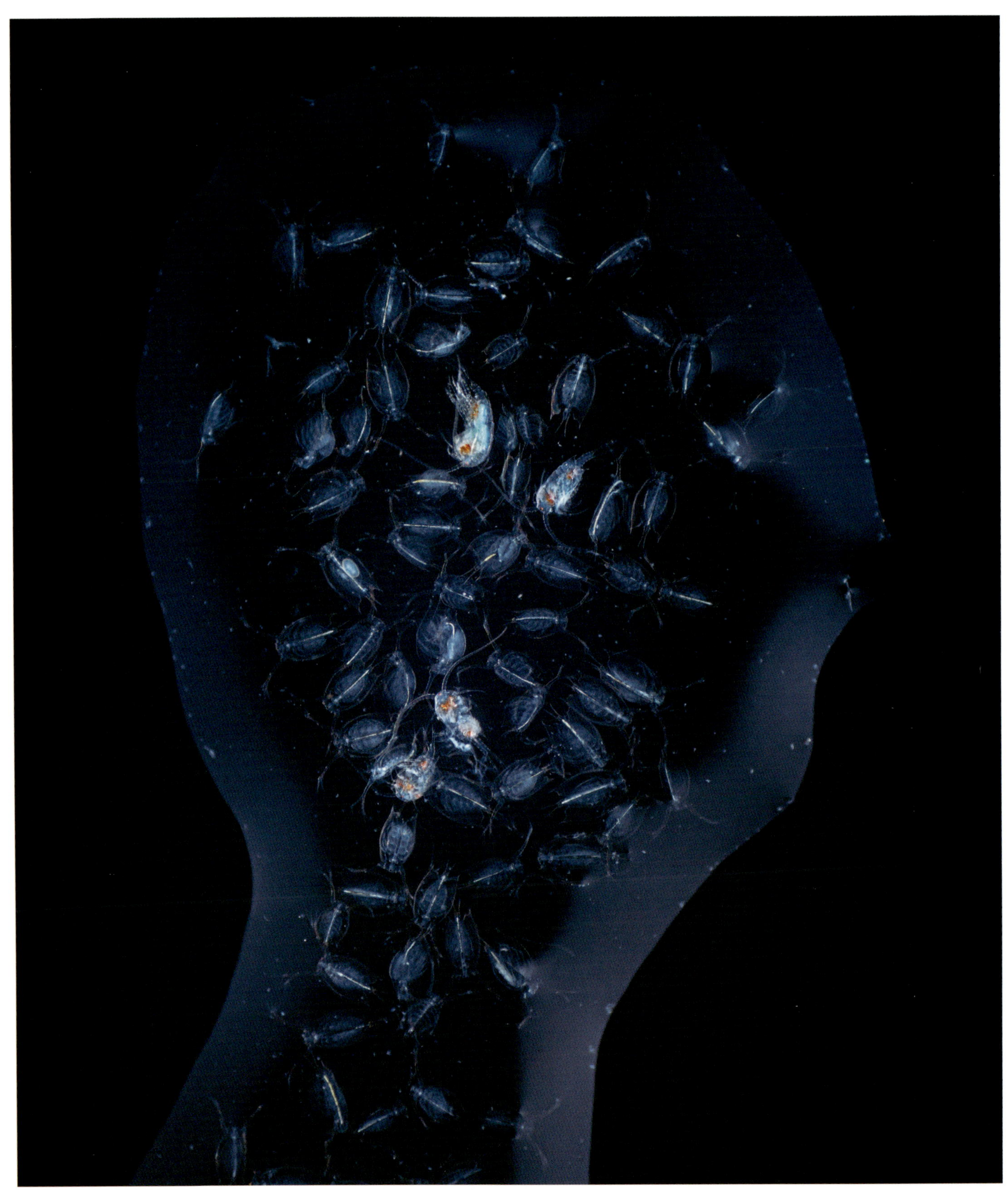

ANGEL FITOR

In drops of water from the Mediterranean Sea, daphnia plankton—the most colorful here—measure no more than five millimeters long.

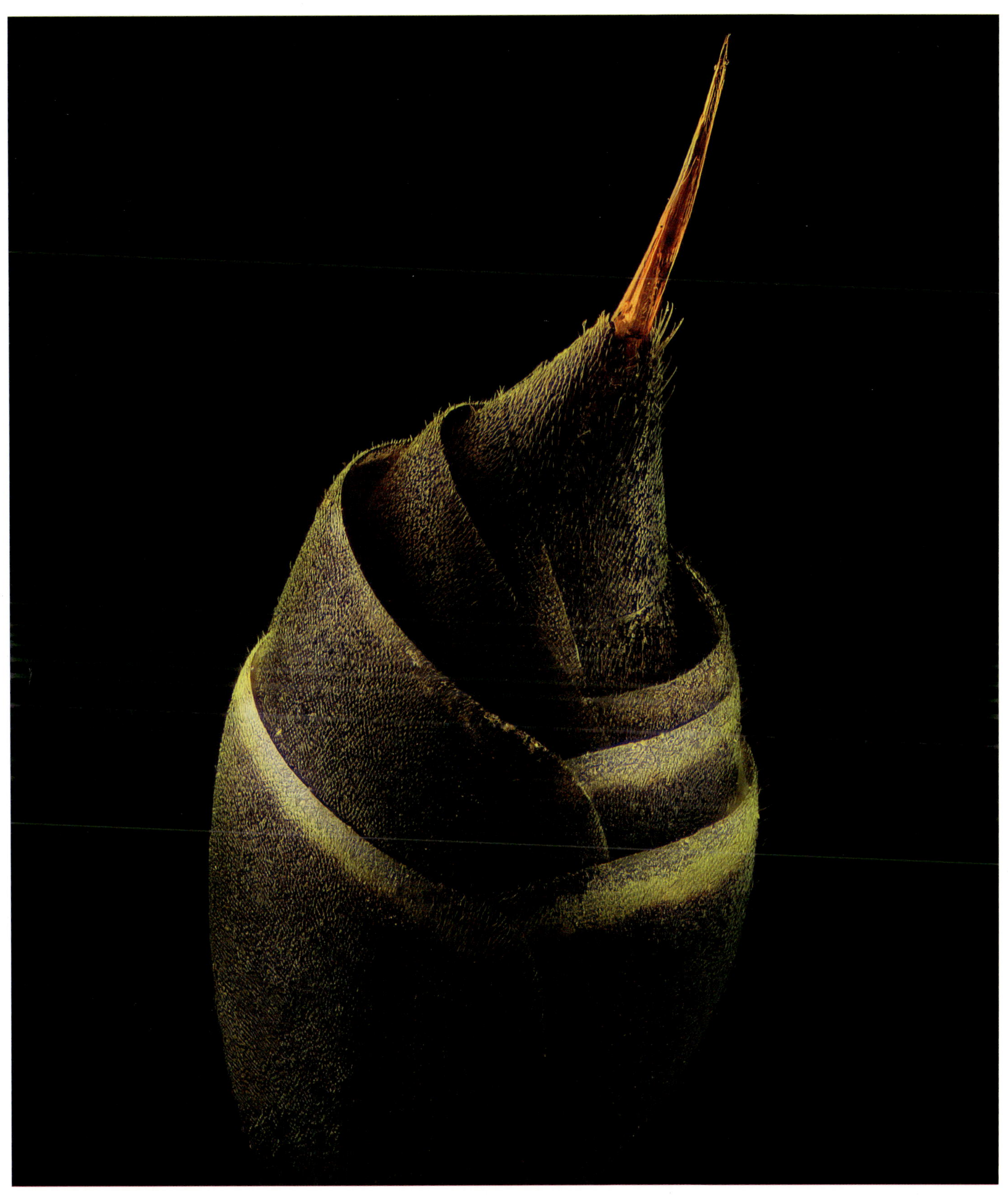

PABLO PIEDRA
The abdomen and stinger of a small paper wasp, magnified 12 times

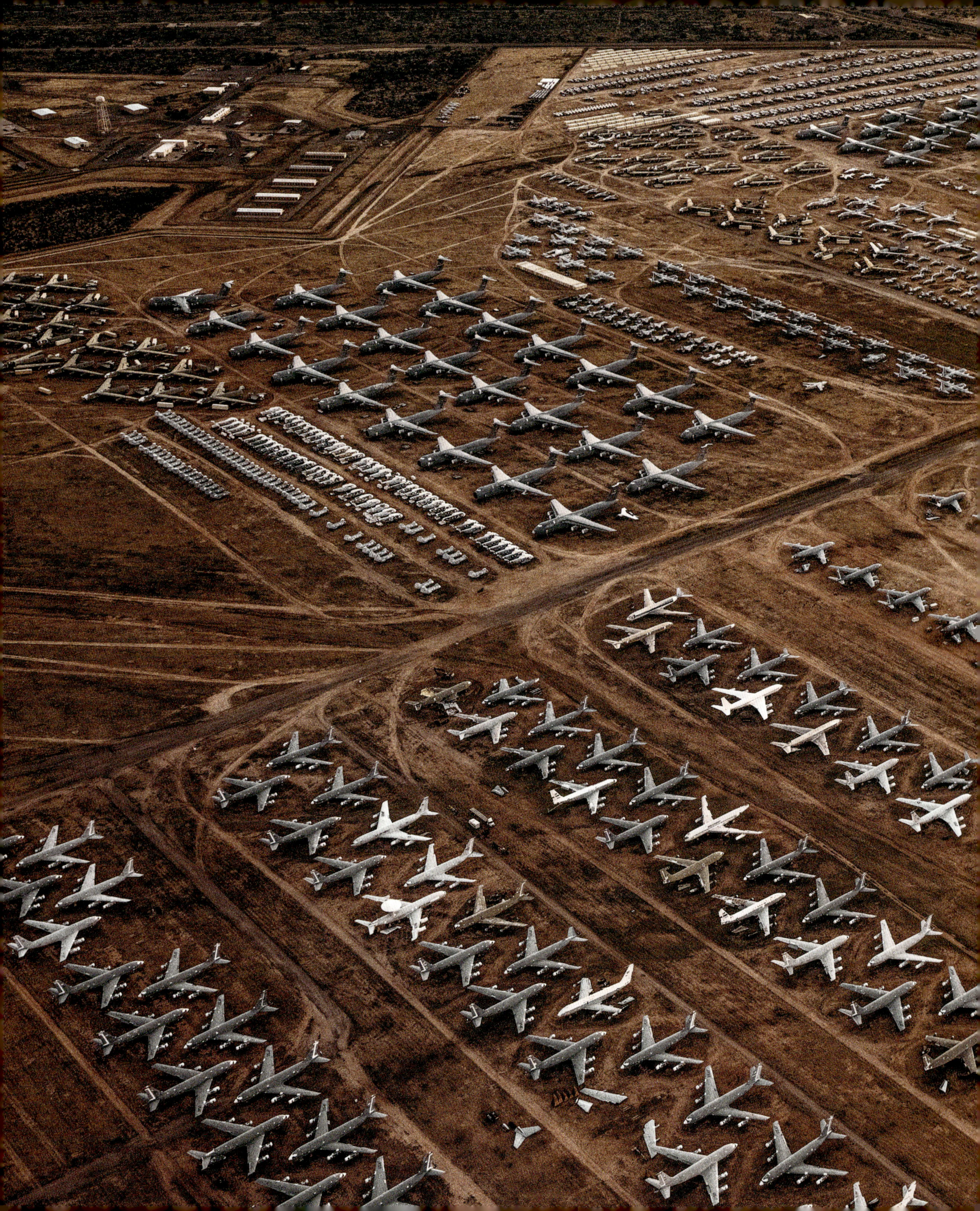

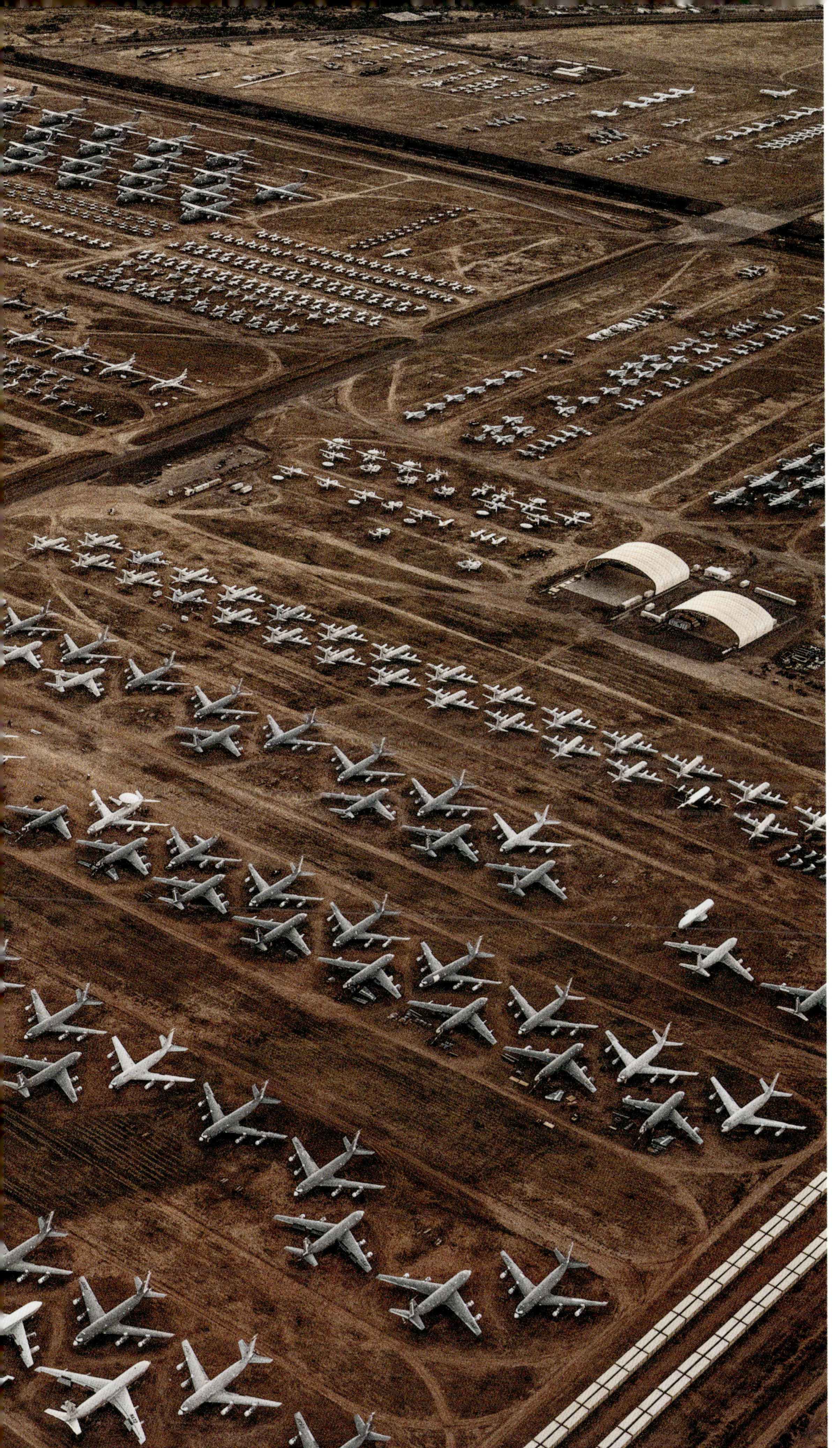

LUCA LOCATELLI
At Davis-Monthan Air Force Base in Tucson, Arizona, nearly 3,300 planes and helicopters, currently decommissioned, stand ready for repurposing.

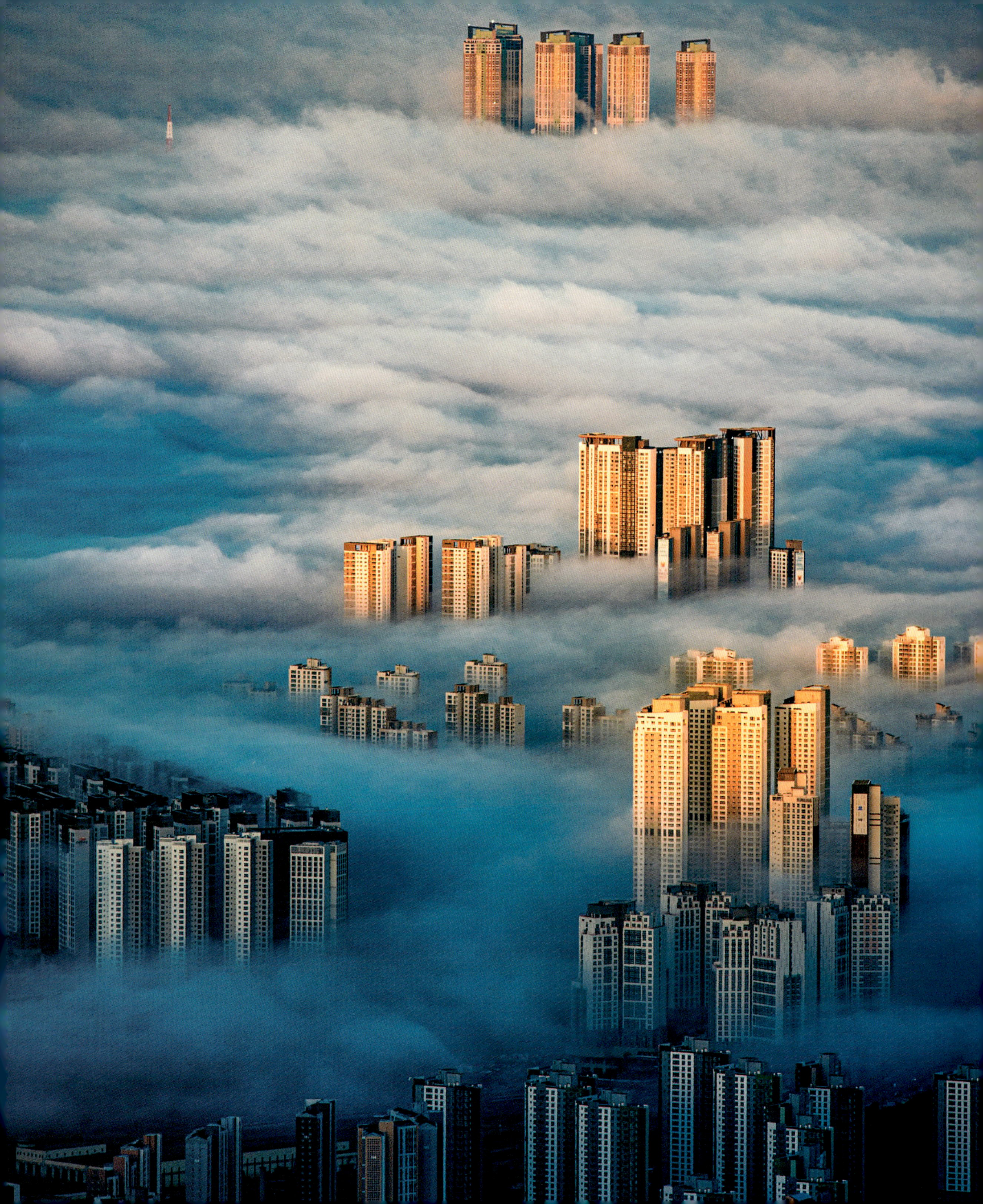

The silver queen
of night drew
back the blinds /
Of the eastern
void and kiss'd
the mournful pines.

~ALEXANDER LAWRENCE POSEY, "THE WARRIOR'S DREAM"

WONYOUNG (COCU) CHOI
Enveloping fog photographed from Bukhansan mountain in Seoul, South Korea, makes city skyscrapers look like mountains in the mist.

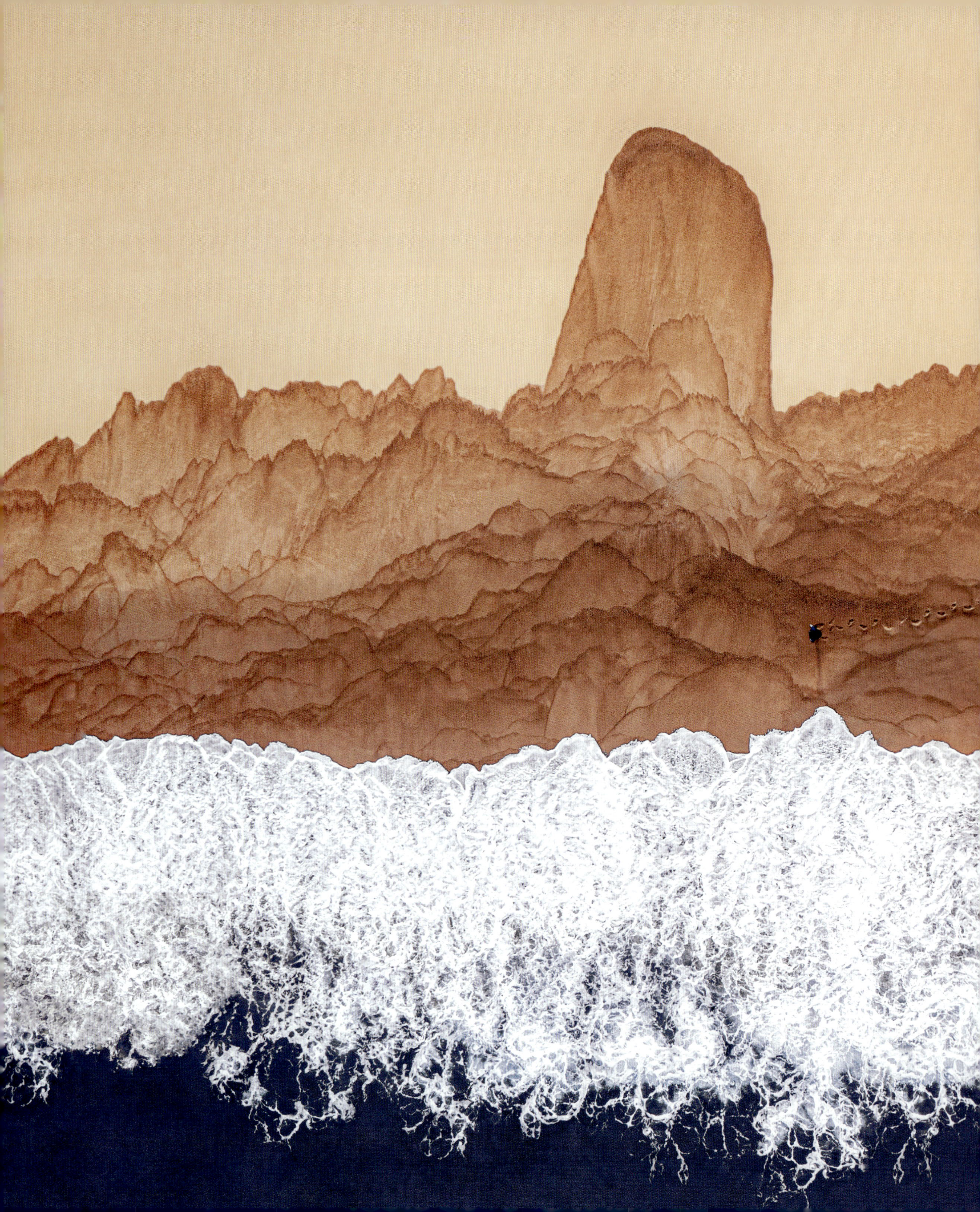

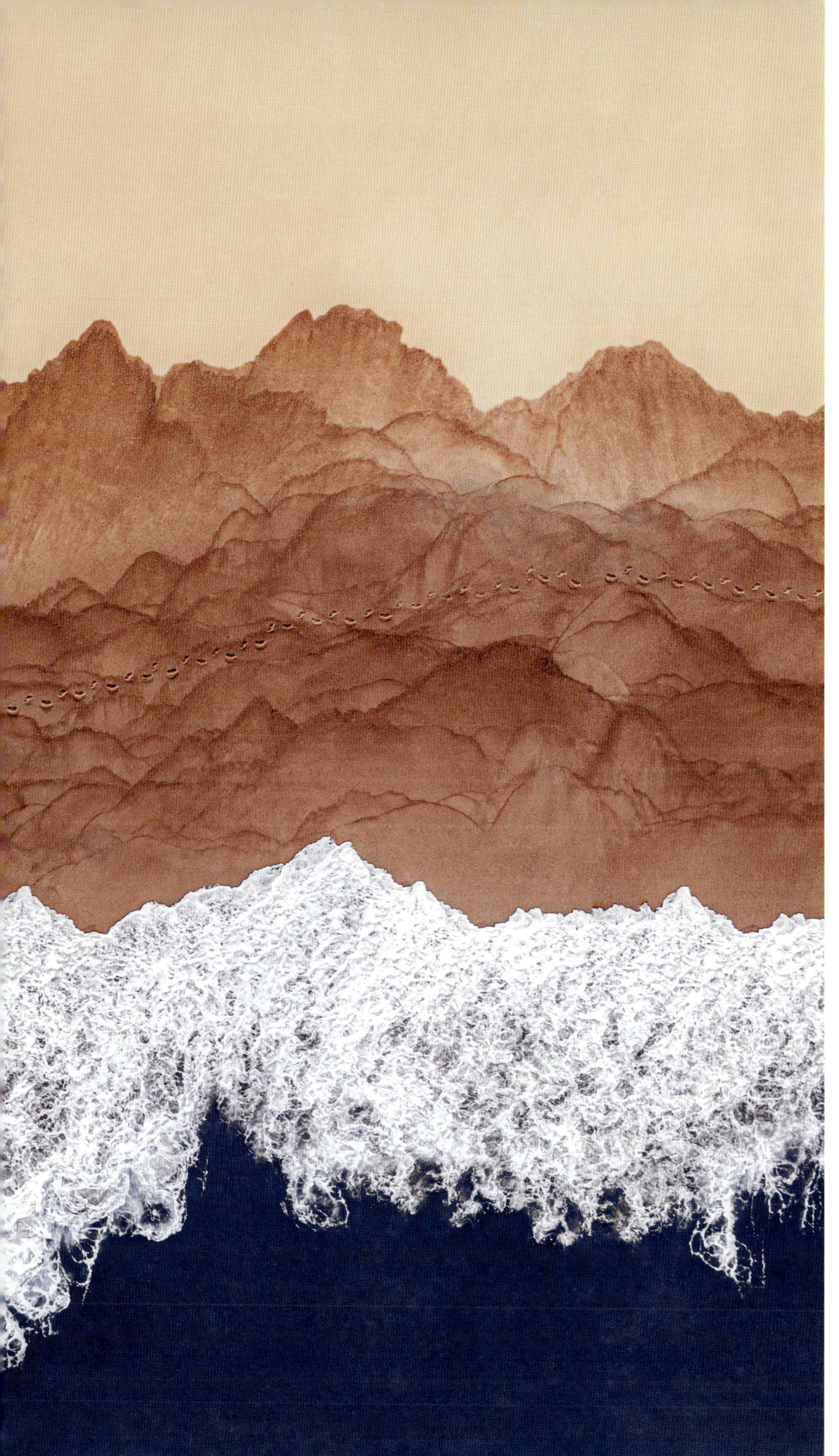

YUXUAN HOU
A solitary wanderer witnesses waves in the South China Sea carving shapes in the coastline sands.

Following pages:
RENAN OZTURK
Sandstone pillars and elevated plateaus distinguish Utah's Monument Valley.

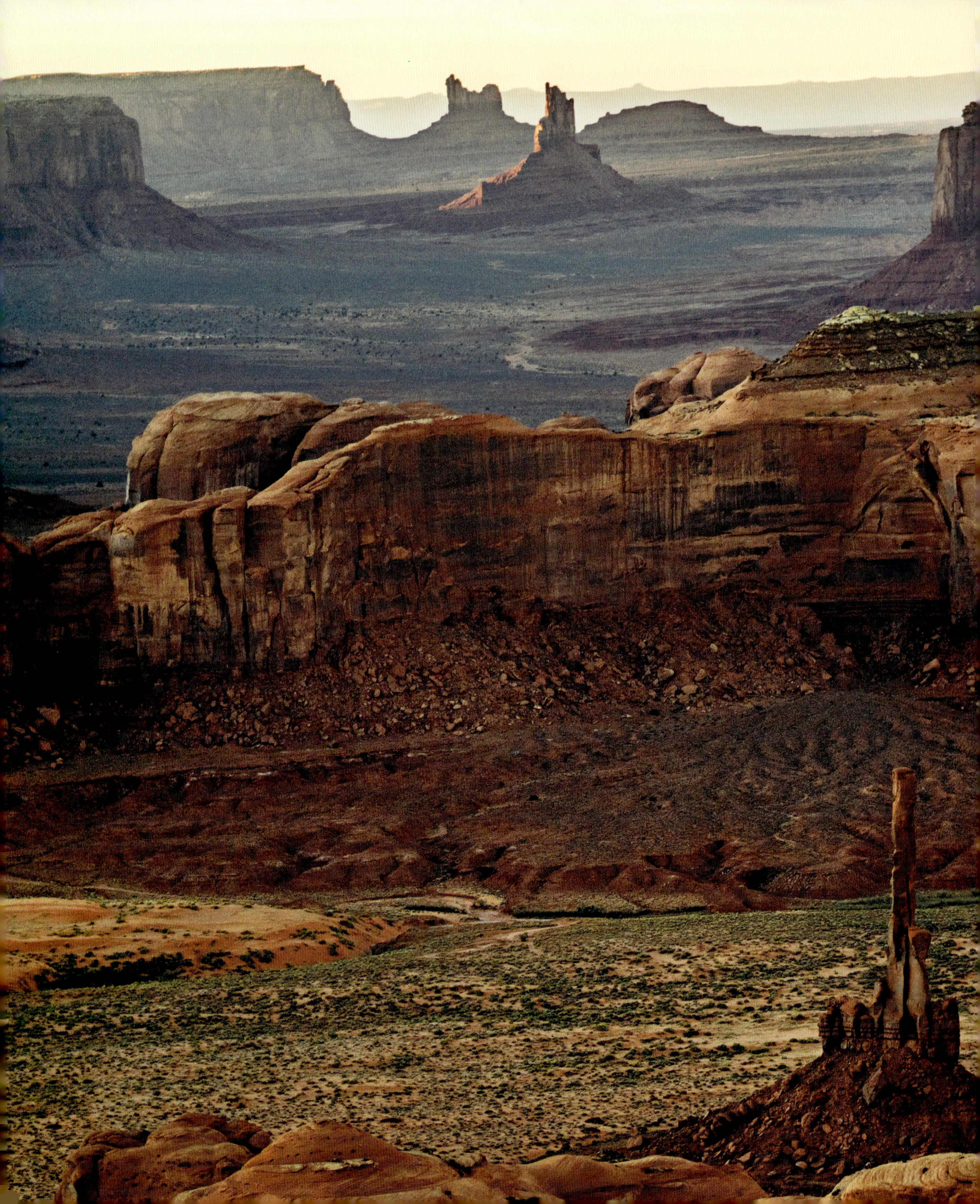

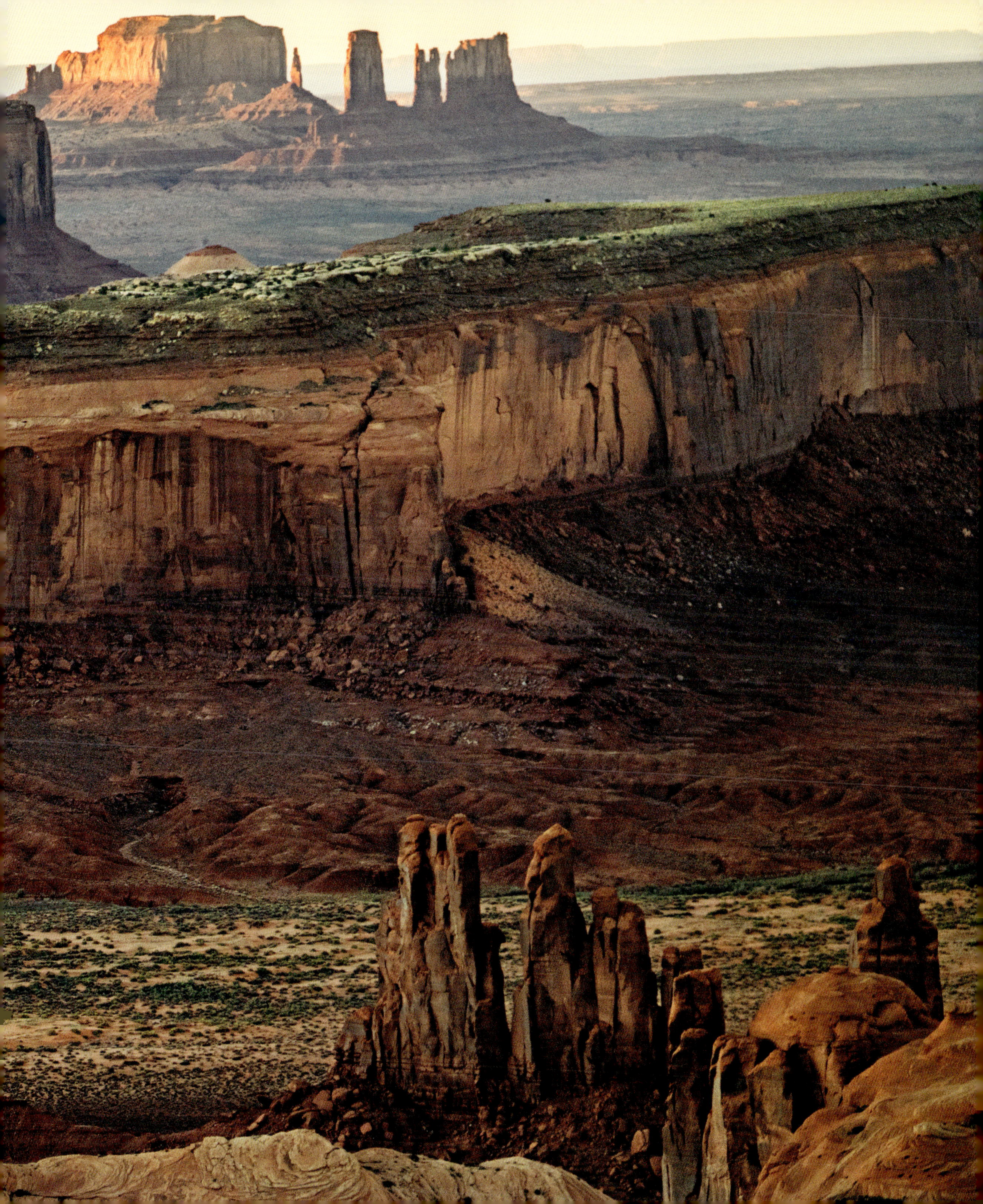

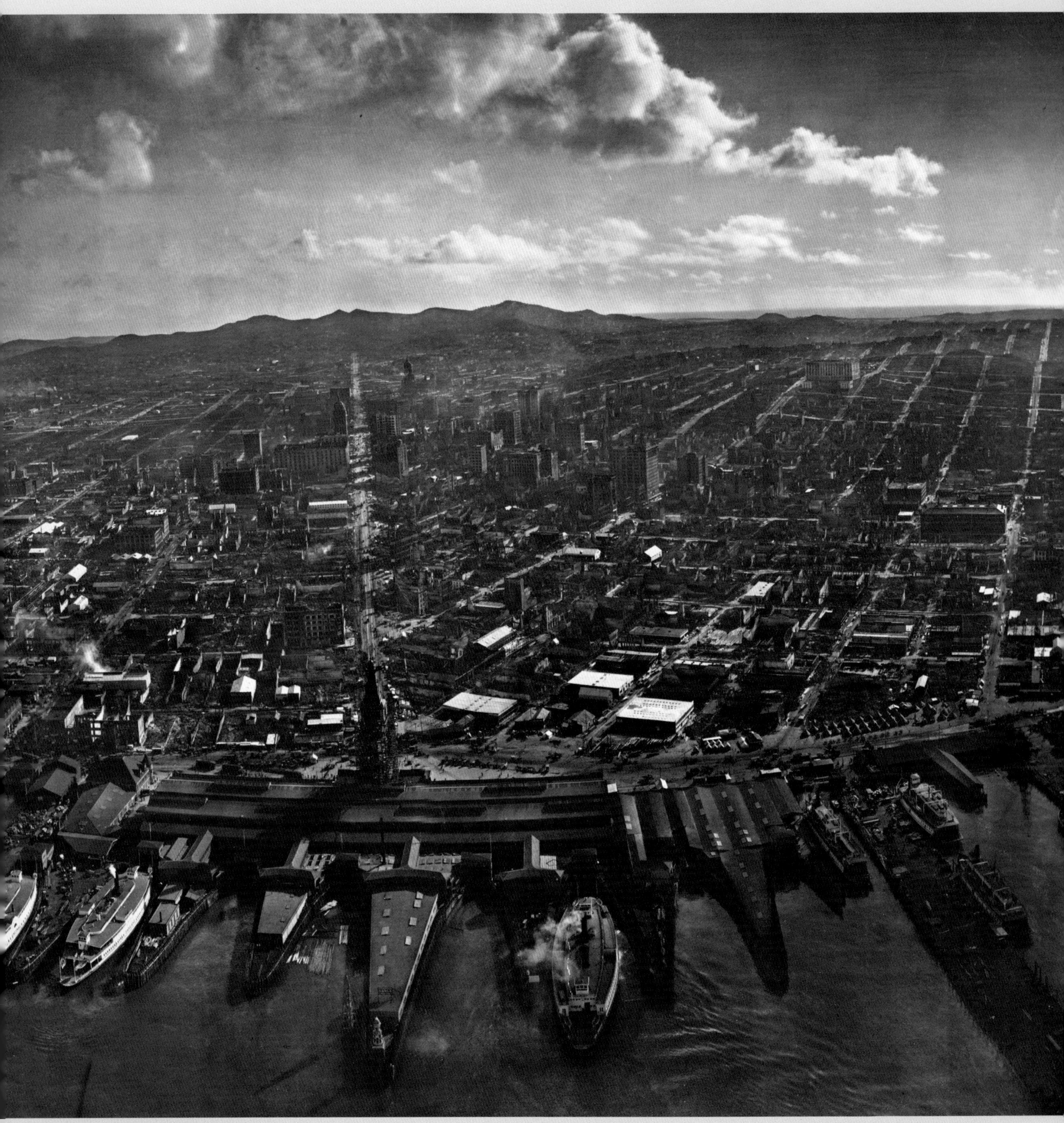

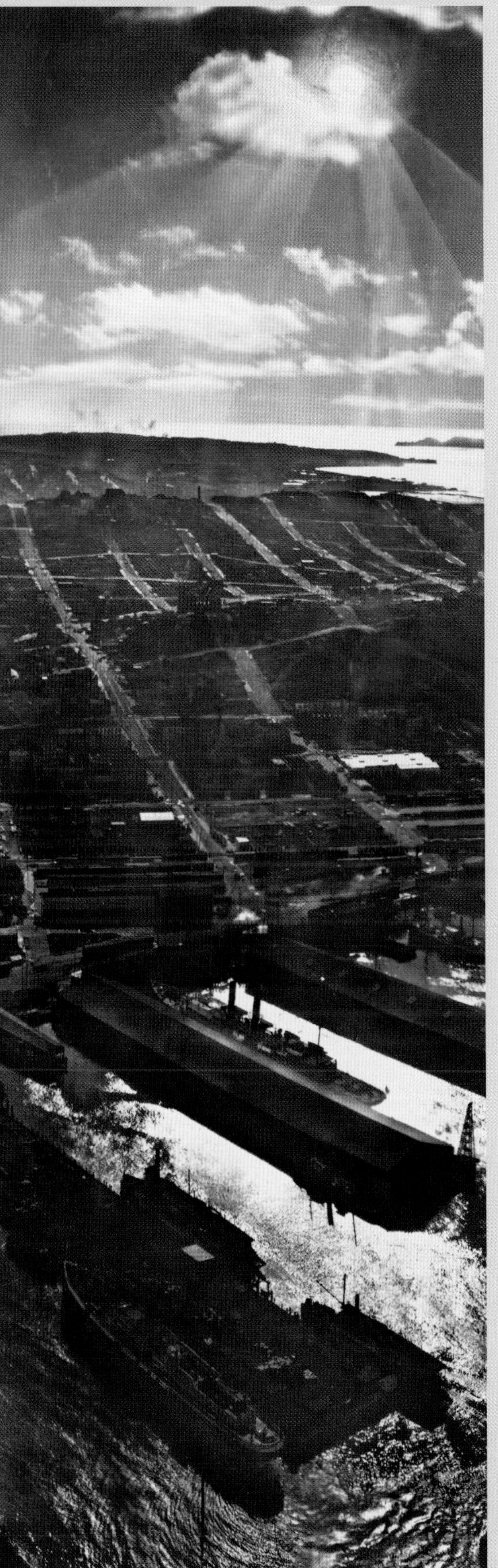

WHAT THE
KITES SEE

People had imagined seeing the world from above long before they unlocked the mysteries of flight. In the late 1700s, balloons gave humans their first glimpses of the aerial world four decades before the first picture was ever taken. It would be another 30 years before camera technology conquered the weight and exposure challenges inherent in making photos in flight. But as creative and technological advances pushed both disciplines forward, society clamored for more. A new scale of seeing had been unlocked, and it was destined to become accessible to everyone.

When the 1906 earthquake rocked San Francisco, George R. Lawrence was poised to capitalize on years of tinkering and development with his new aerial photography system. After surviving a couple balloon-related accidents and with airplanes just entering their infancy, he turned to an older, more established technology. Using a series of linked kites, he orchestrated this famous aerial panorama

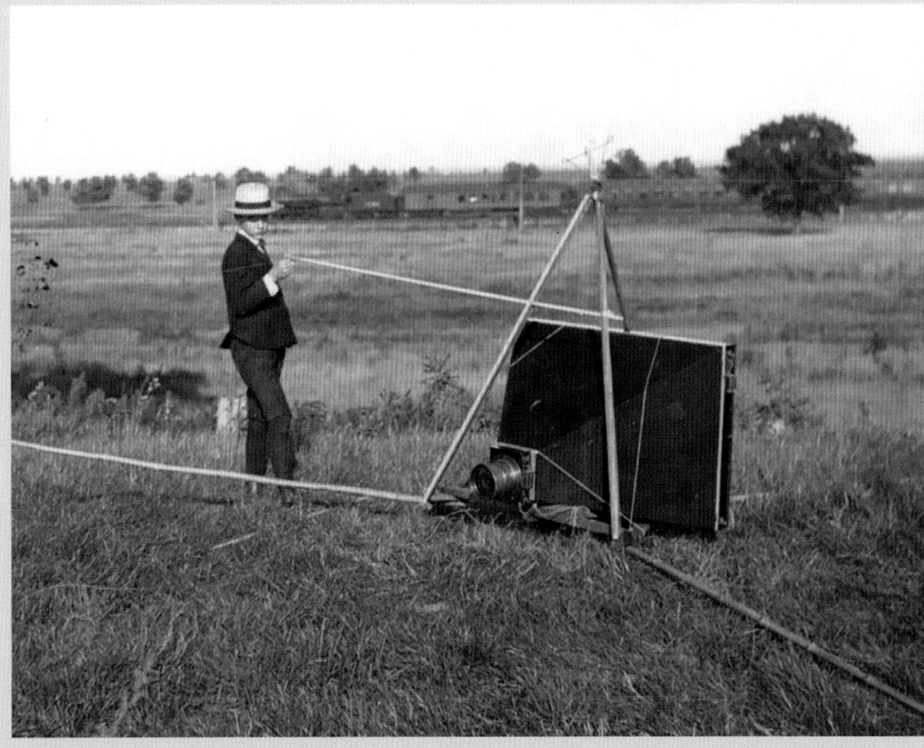

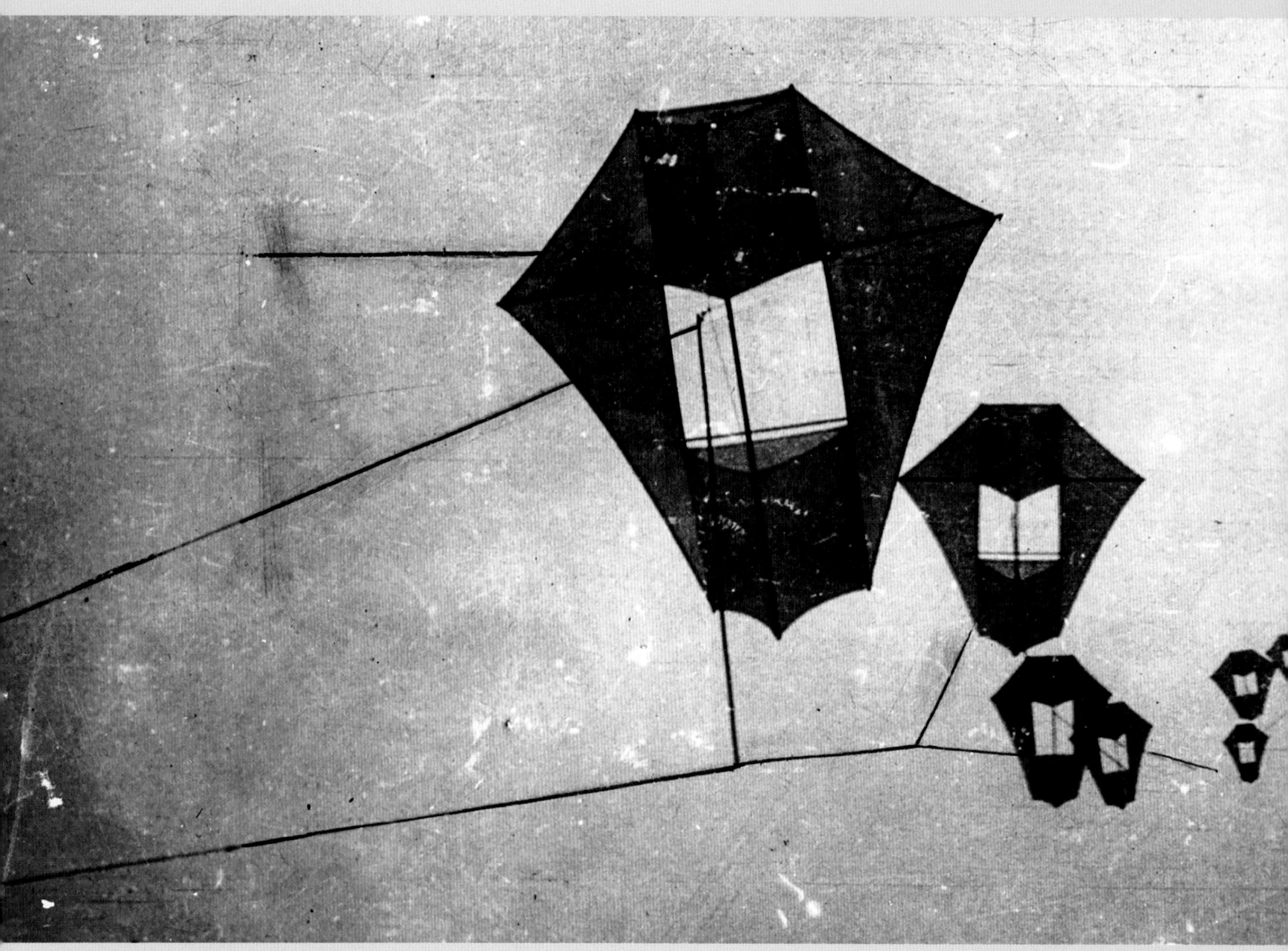

of San Francisco (pages 234–35). Captured with a custom-built 49-pound (22 kg) camera hoisted about 2,000 feet (600 m) into the air, this view of the scale of destruction became a sensation, selling $15,000 worth of prints (almost $500,000 today). His company's slogan, "The hitherto impossible in photography is our specialty," spoke to the confluence of technology and creativity behind this image.

Only 54 years later, the CIA had created a spy satellite capable of taking high-resolution photos of Earth's surface. This view (opposite, top) of the same part of San Francisco is a declassified image from the CORONA satellite program, which was primarily used to gather intelligence over the Soviet Union and other regions of the world. Relying on film cameras, the satellites would shoot a roll of film, then drop it down toward Earth, where, with luck and skill, the parachuting recovery capsule could be collected midfall by an airplane (opposite, bottom).

GEORGE R. LAWRENCE
George Lawrence used a train of kites to hoist his camera to the elevation desired for his aerial photographs.

Previous pages, left:
GEORGE R. LAWRENCE
From his "Captive Airship"—a kite carrying a camera—the photographer recorded the ruins of San Francisco after the 1906 earthquake and fire.

Previous pages, right:
CHICAGO HISTORY MUSEUM
Lawrence's son helped him rig the kite in Illinois.

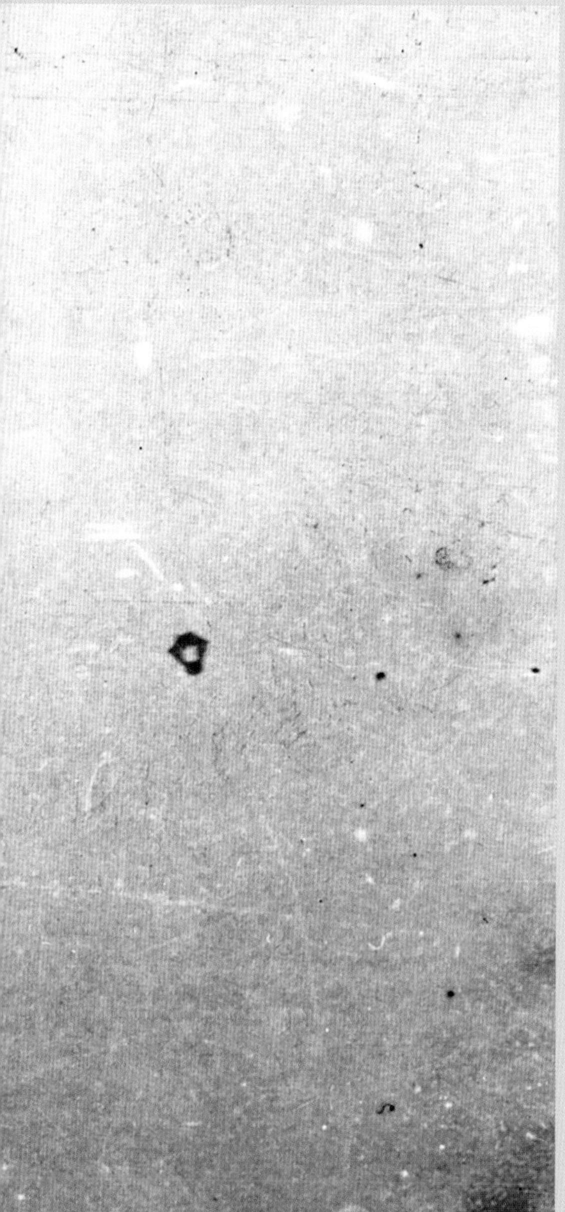

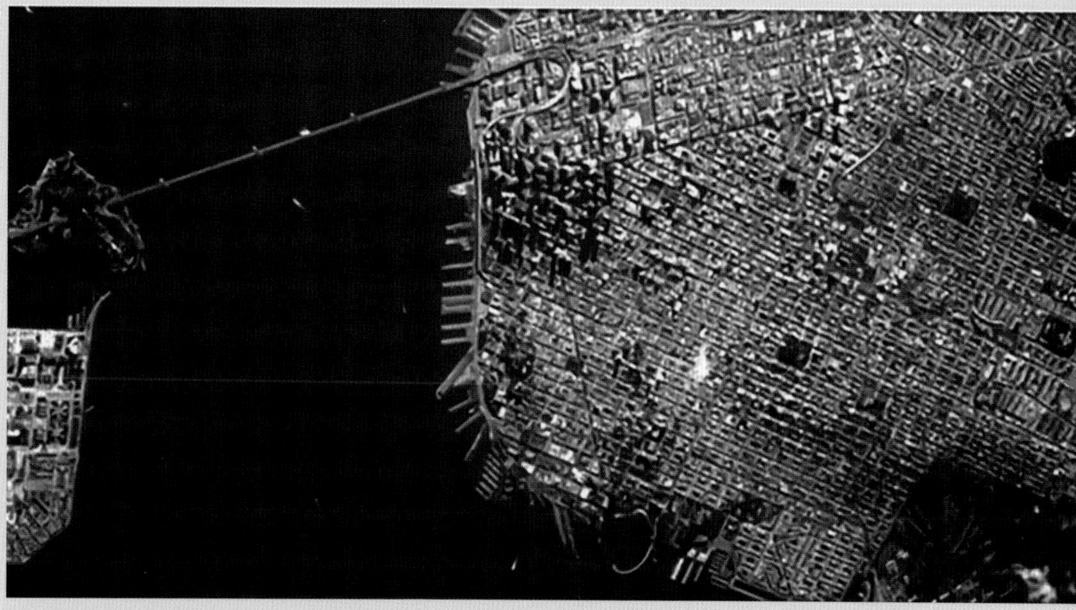

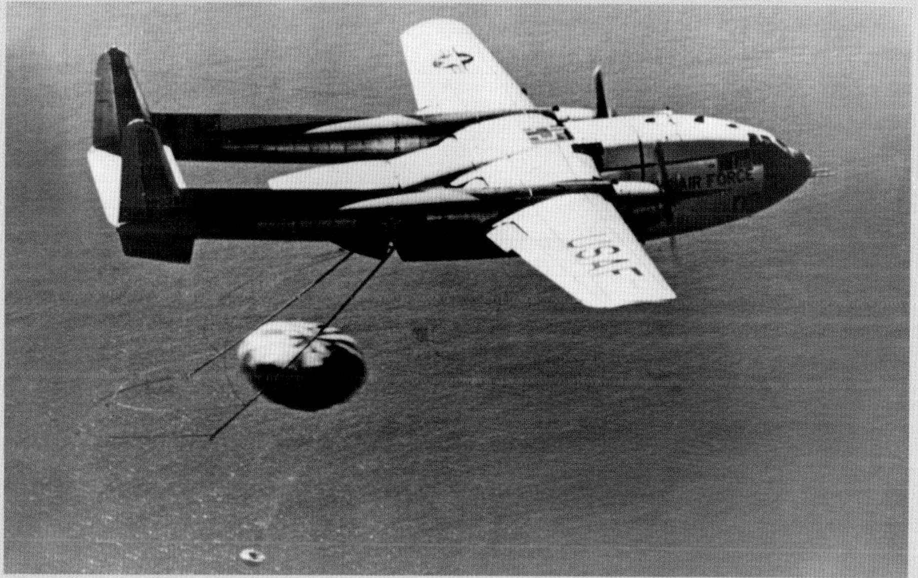

This was the dawn of a geoimaging revolution that now permeates our lives. These early images from the CORONA program were declassified in the 1990s, having long outlived their intelligence value. But now, they contain a treasure trove of information for anthropologists and ecologists. They show a world before modern agricultural and forestry practices spread across many regions, one with archaeological sites now demolished, or the limits of ecosystems long vanished.

It may come as a surprise that modern scientific researchers—myself included—still use kite photography to capture environmental patterns at certain scales. Kites save on batteries, handle cold temperatures well, and don't raise many eyebrows when going through customs in foreign countries. So while satellite-based imaging systems continue to unlock insights at planetary scales, so, too, do small digital cameras dragged around by simple, reliable, and easily transportable kites.

Top:
U.S. NATIONAL ARCHIVES
A mid-20th-century CORONA satellite, used primarily for military surveillance, captured this aerial view of San Francisco circa 1960.

Above:
U.S. AIR FORCE
C-119 "Flying Boxcar" aircraft caught film canisters as they parachuted down from spy satellites during the 20th century's Cold War.

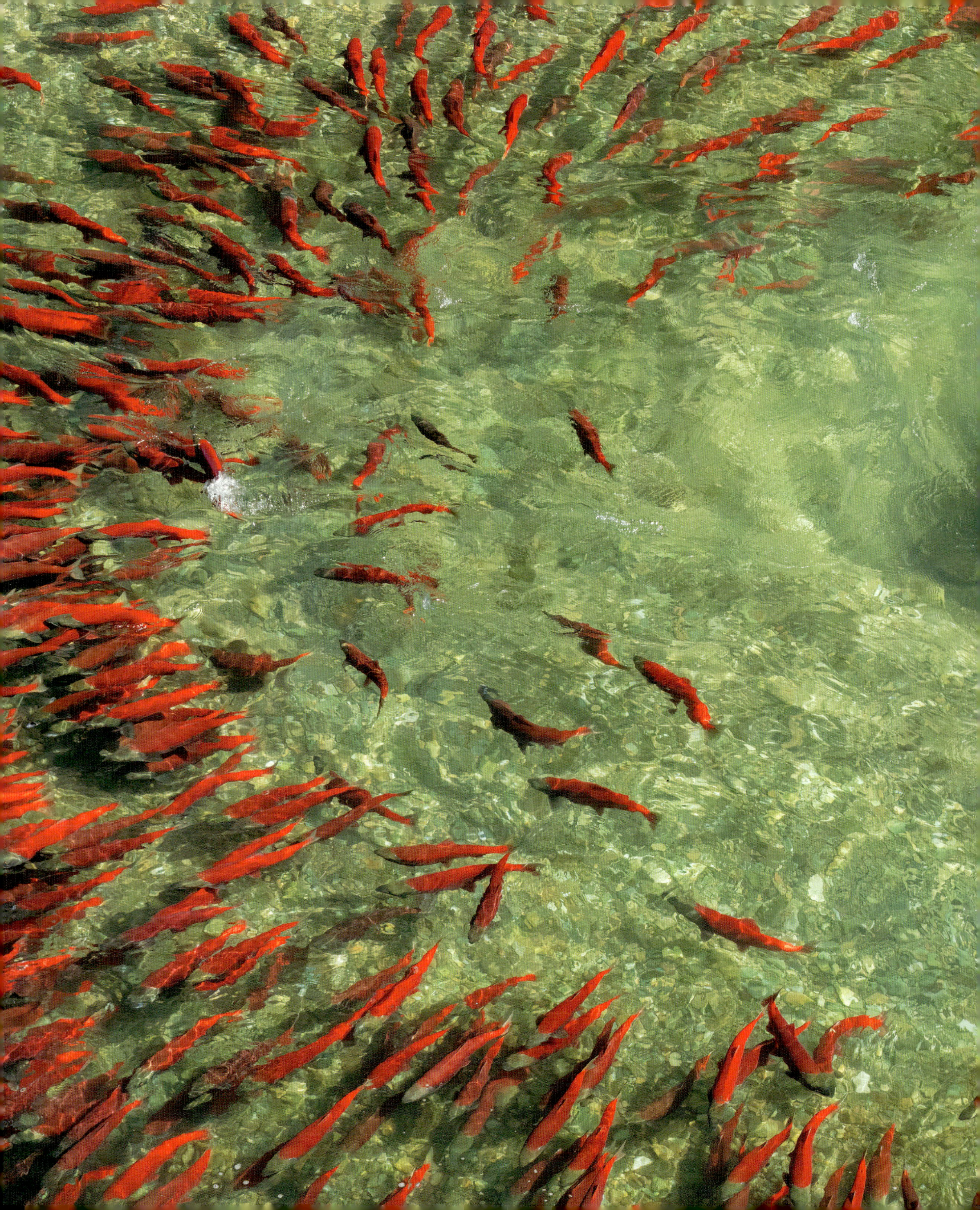

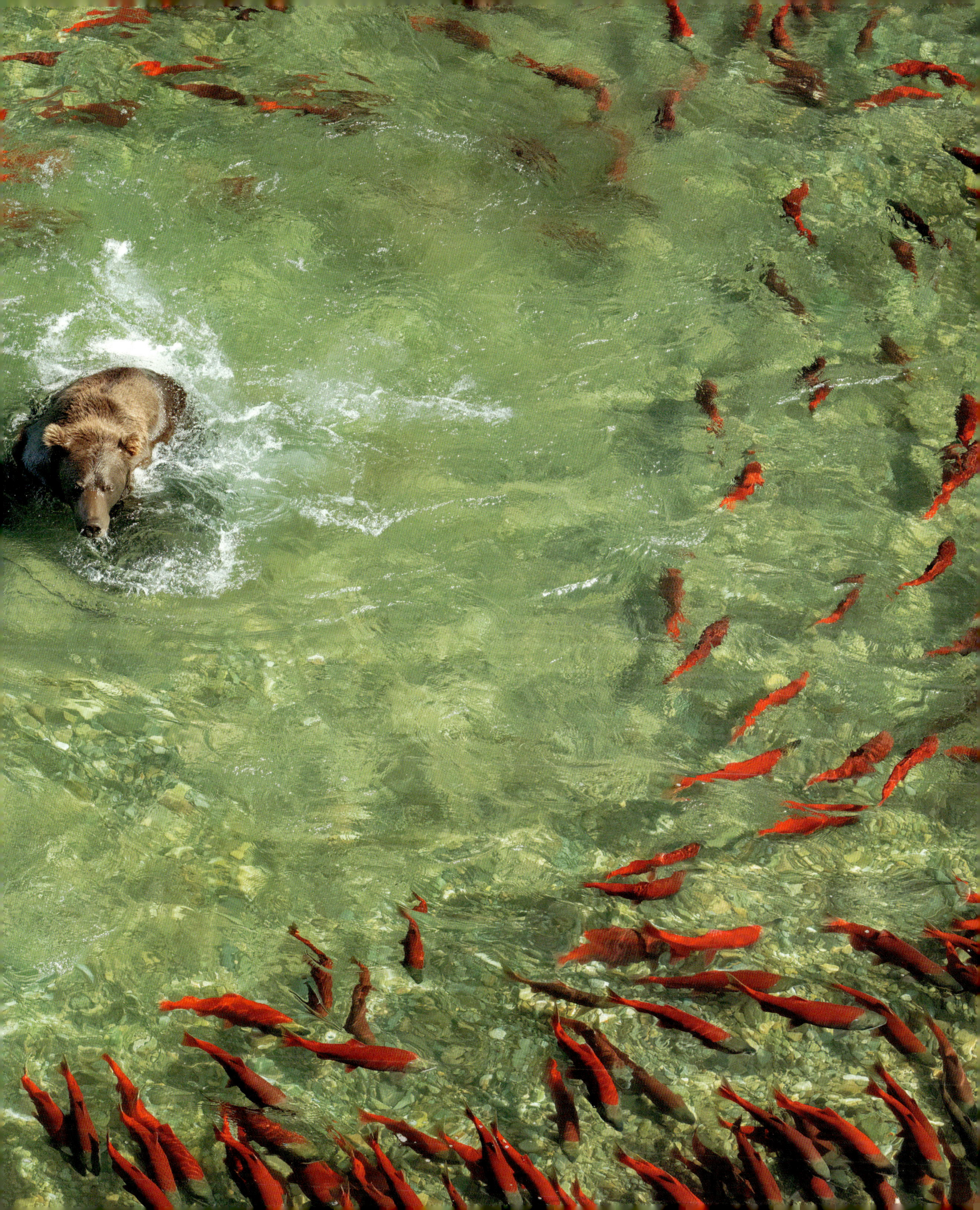

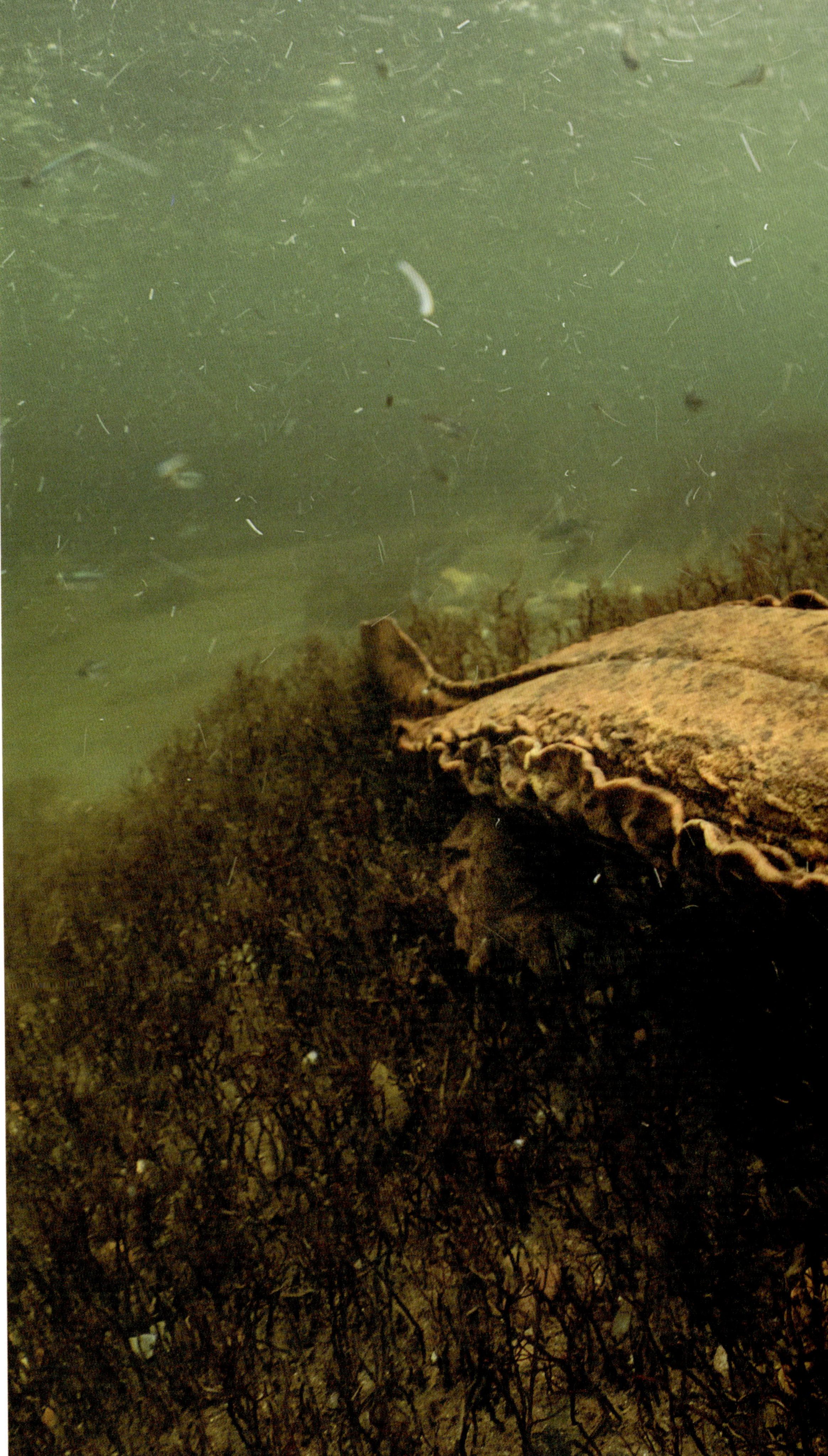

DAVID HERASIMTSCHUK
A hellbender grabs hold of its prey, a northern water snake, in murky Tennessee waters.

Previous pages:
BARRETT HEDGES
Sockeye salmon swim in all directions, escaping from a hungry brown bear in Alaska.

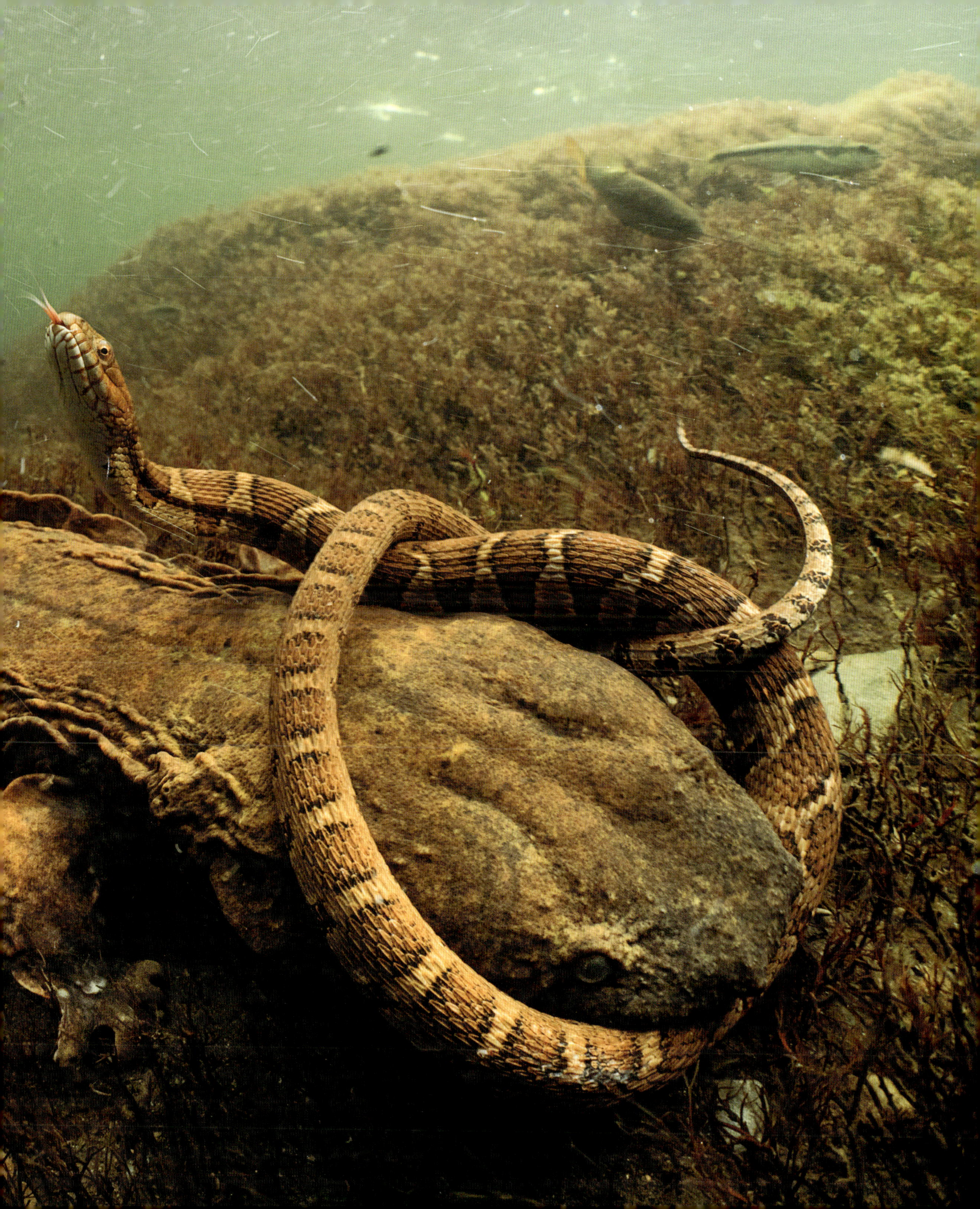

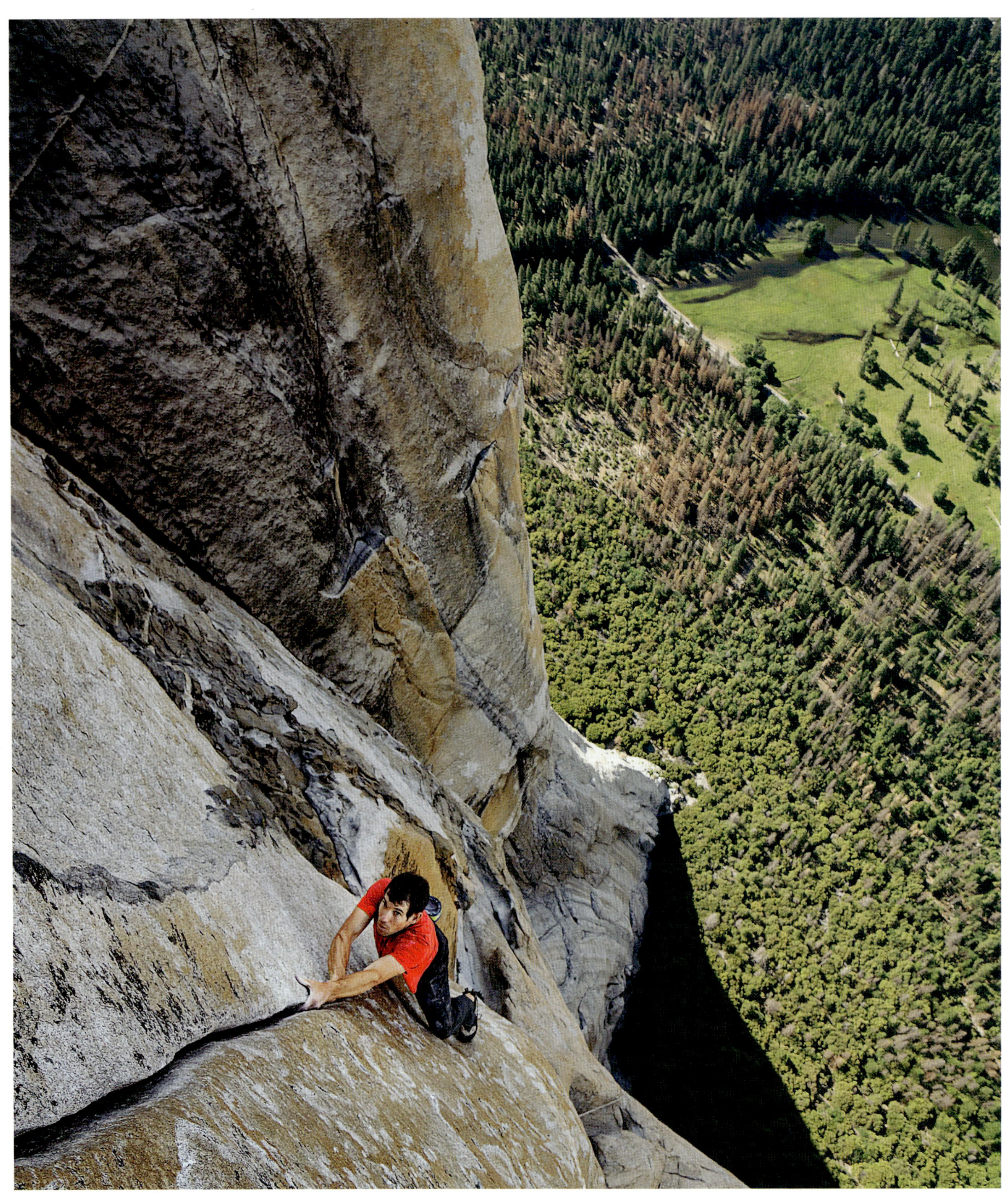

JIMMY CHIN
Alex Honnold free soloes up El Capitan, a sheer rock cliff in California's Yosemite Valley.

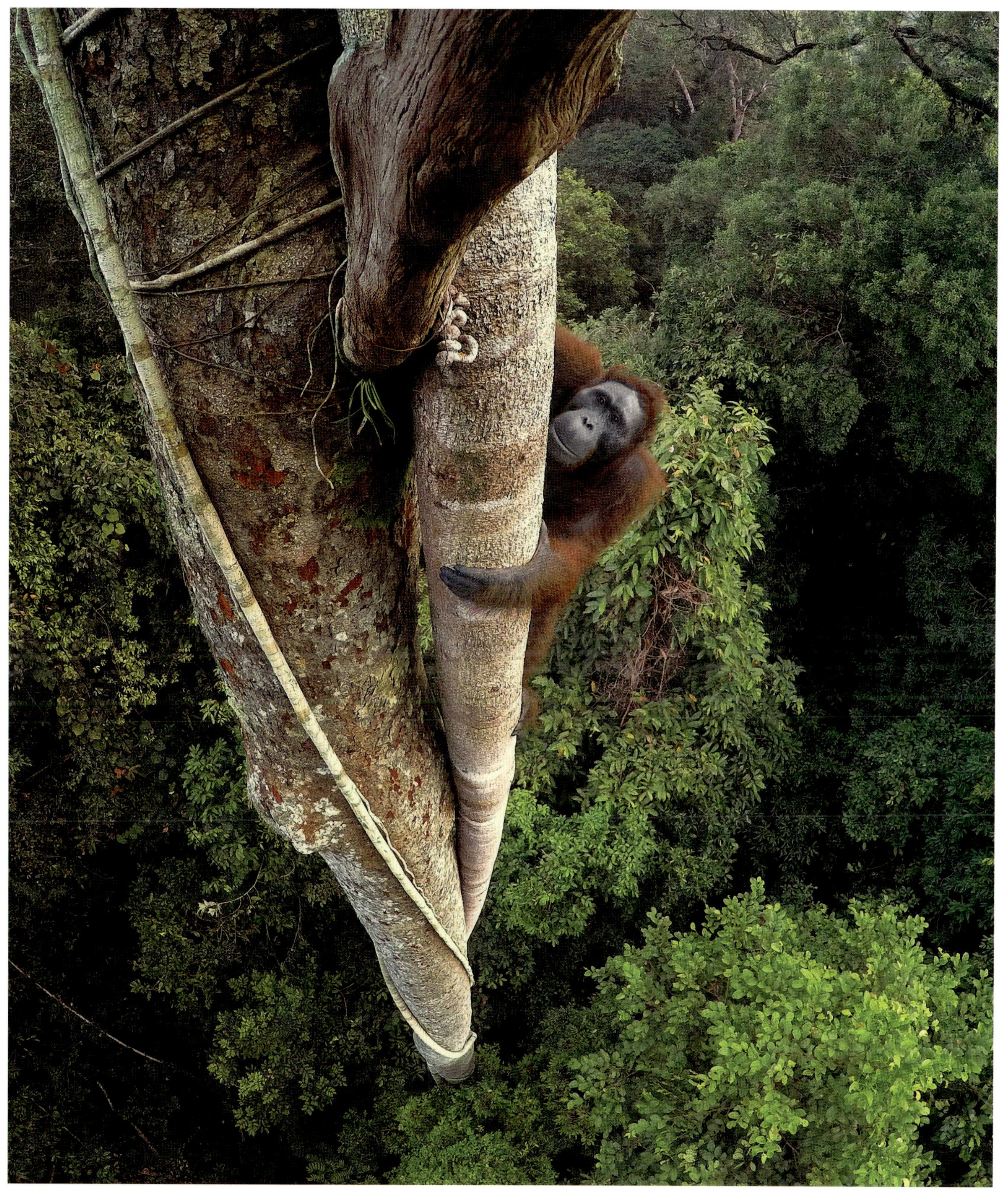

TIM LAMAN
An orangutan climbs up a strangler fig, tempted by its fruit, in Borneo's West Kalimantan Province.

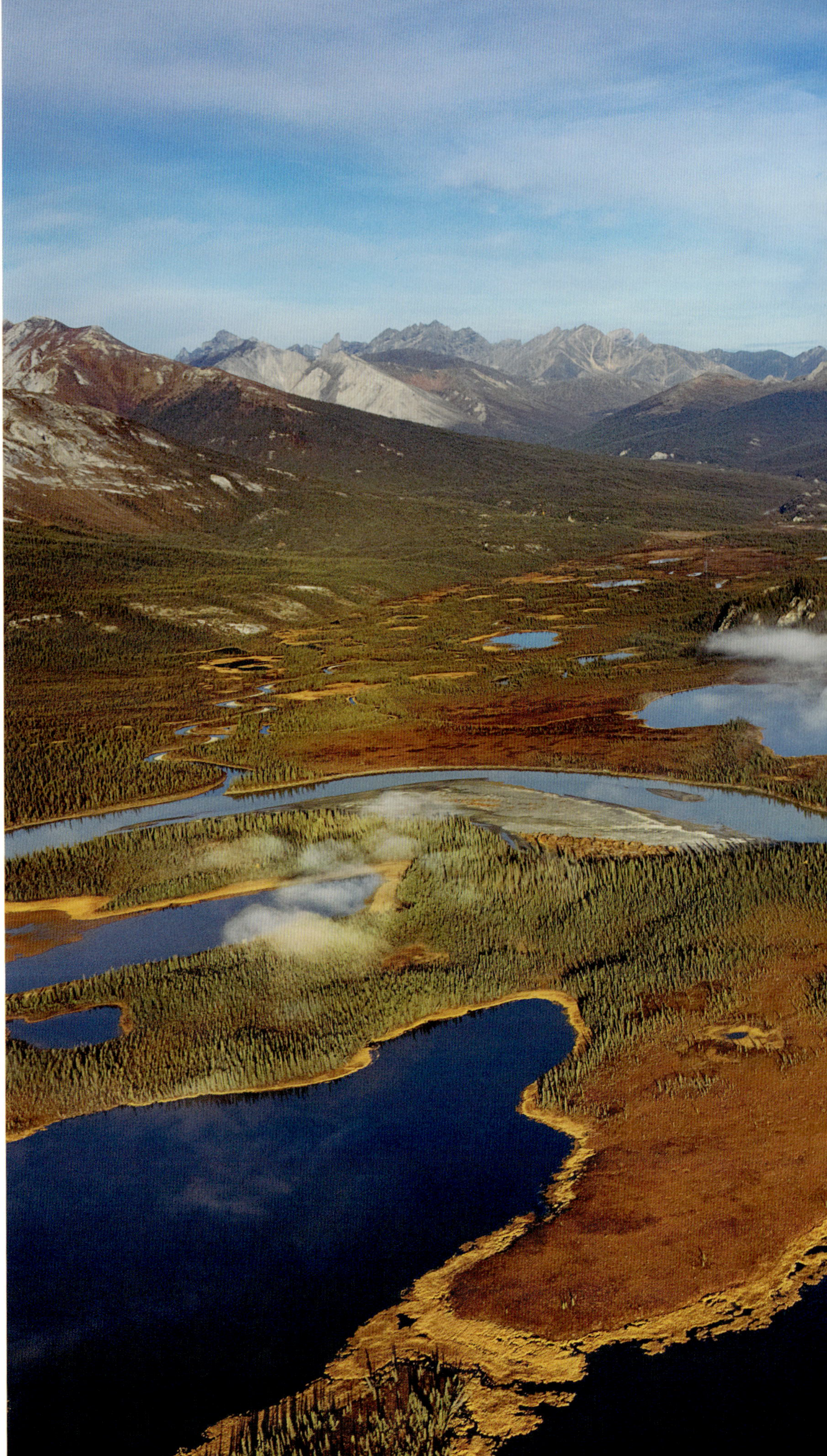

KATIE ORLINSKY
Alaska's Alatna River flows out of
the Brooks Range, its valley
offering wildlife a corridor for
movement north and south with
the seasons.

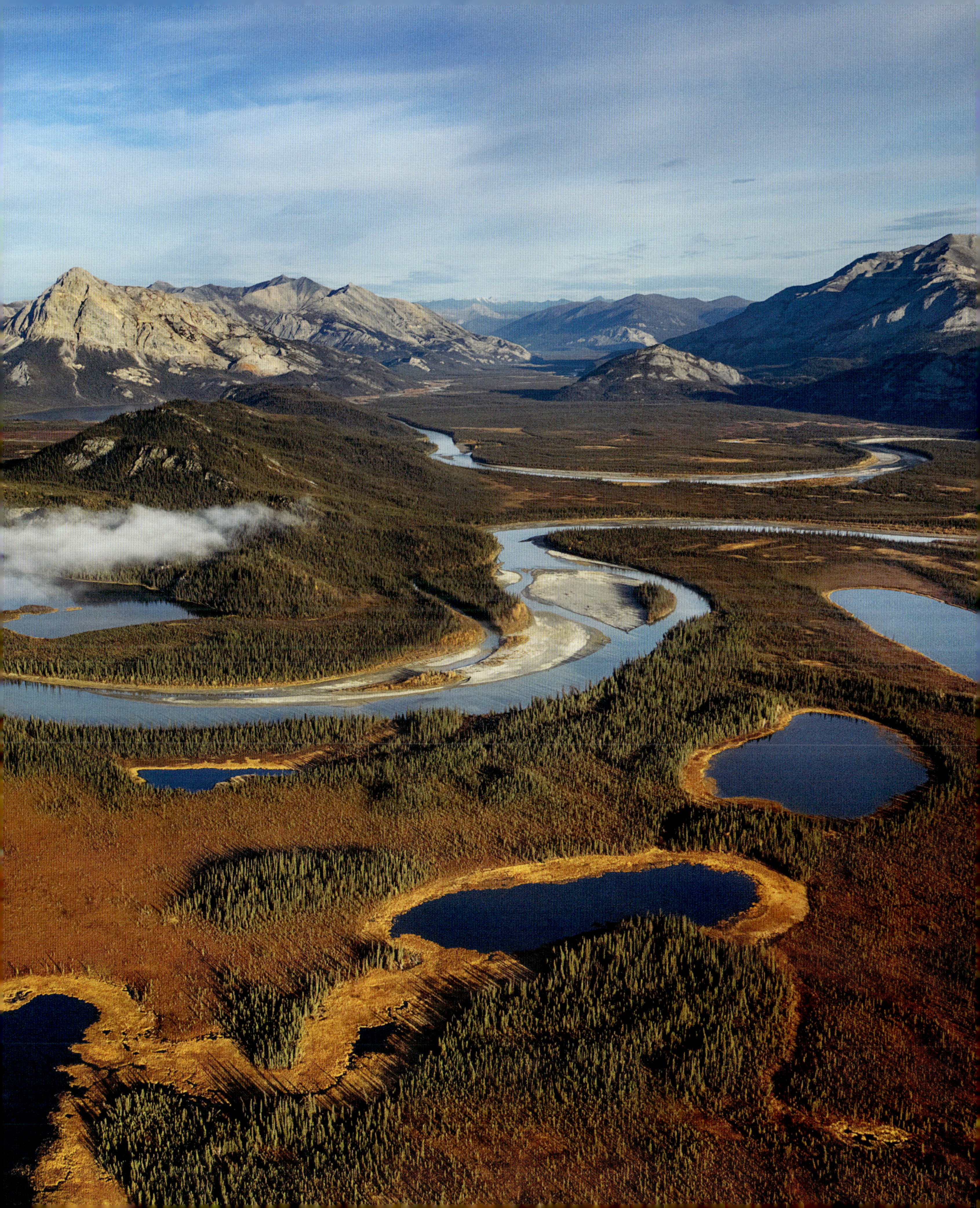

The enormous
complexity of the
world leaves me
little peace—curiosity
kills complacency.

~ANSEL ADAMS, *ANSEL ADAMS: AN AUTOBIOGRAPHY*

HENLEY SPIERS
A larval octopus jets through deep, dark waters.

Following pages:
OVERVIEW
Cargo ships and tankers await entry outside the port of Singapore, their colors dotting the deep blue of the South China Sea in this satellite image.

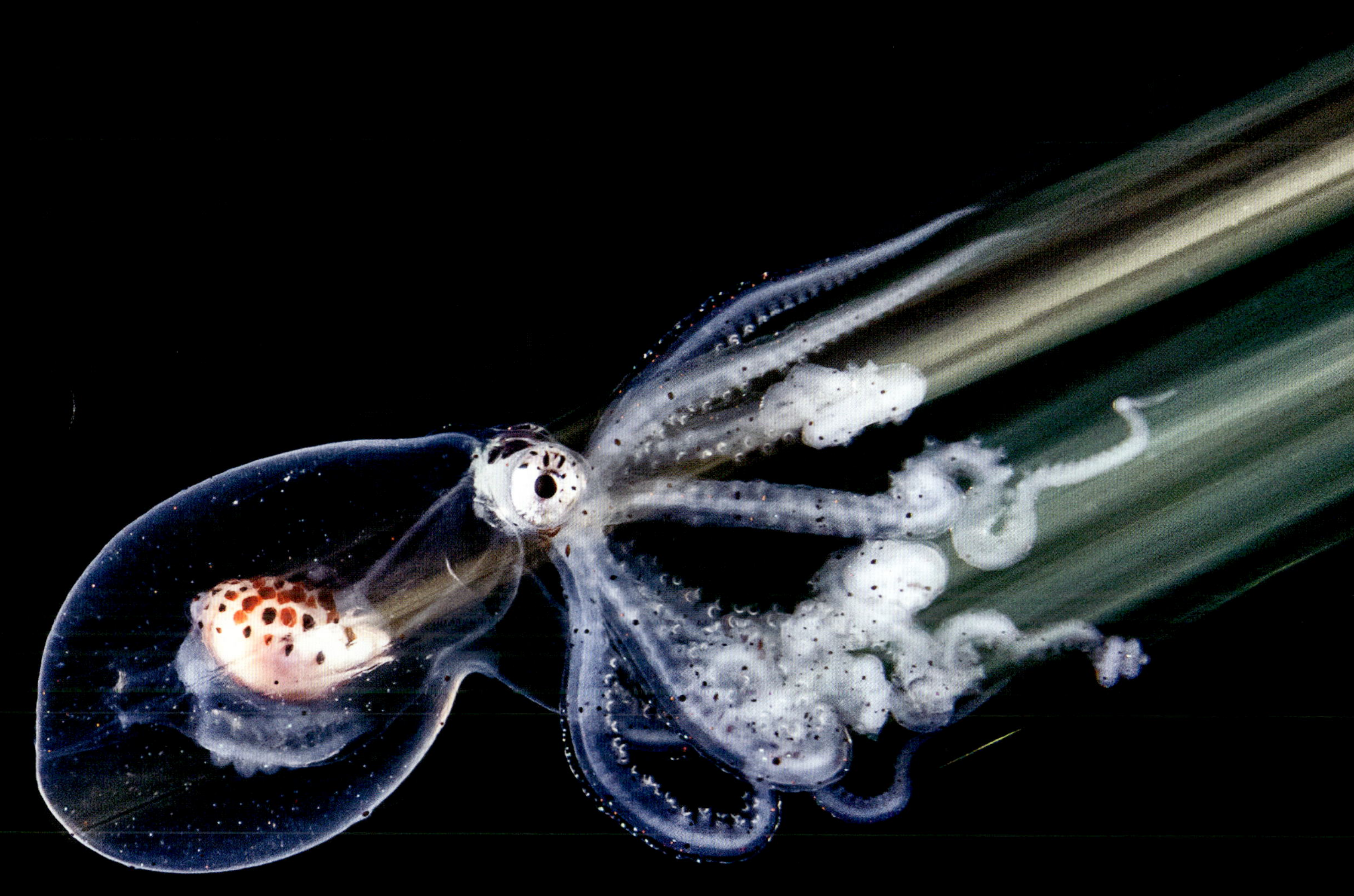

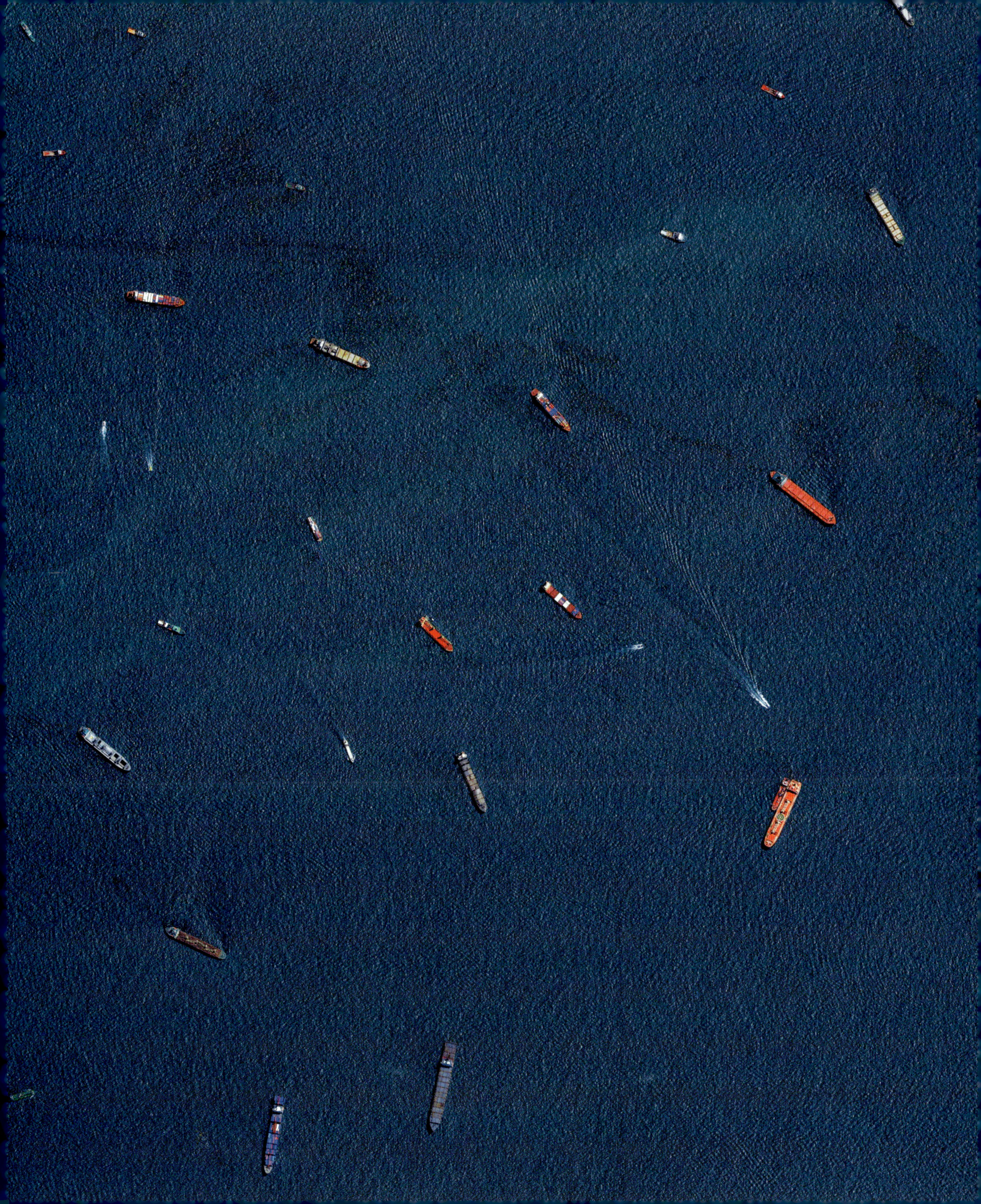

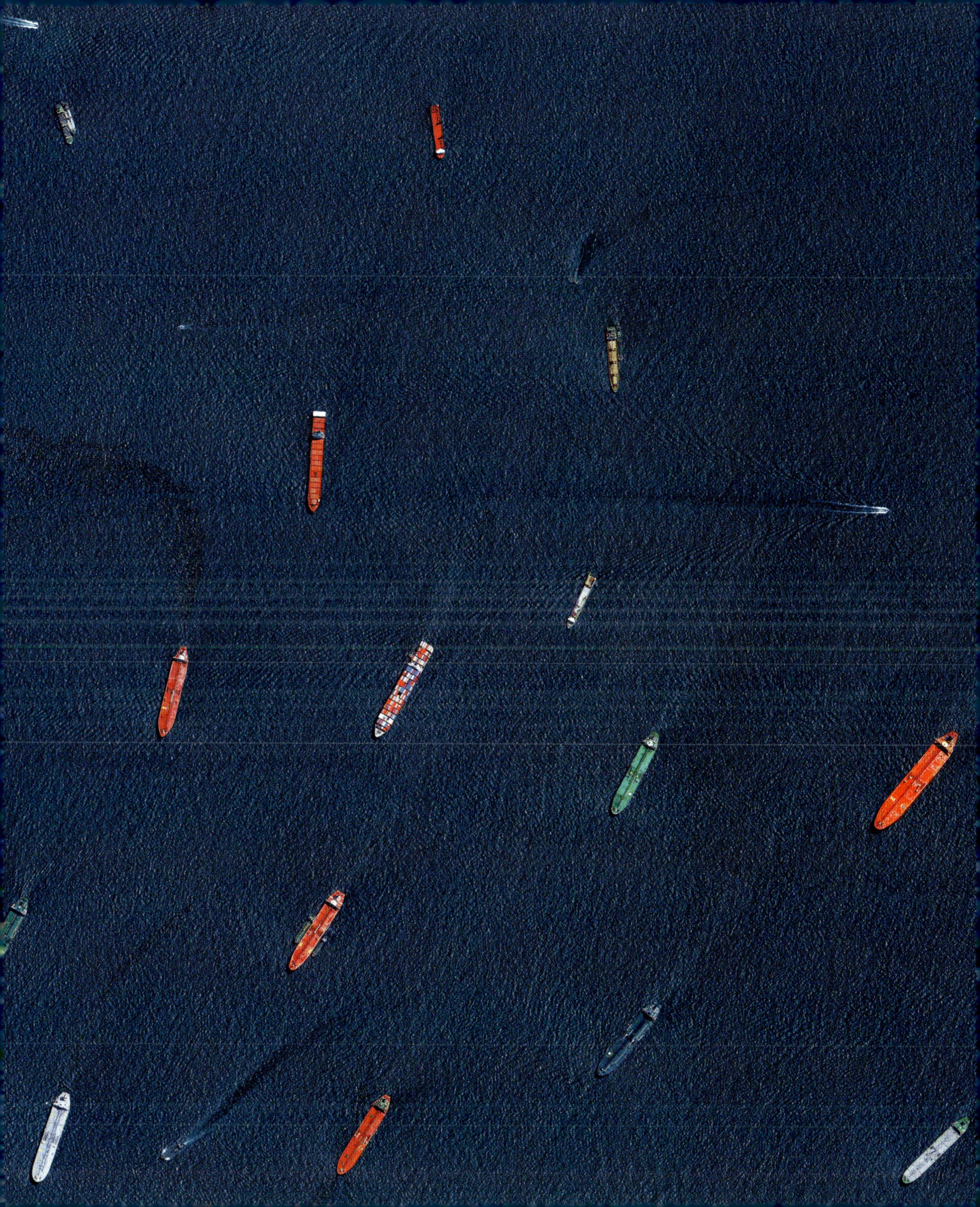

All architecture
is what you
do to it
when you
look upon it.

DAVID NADLINGER
Technology exposes the minuscule. Here, a single strontium atom becomes visible as it reradiates absorbed laser light.

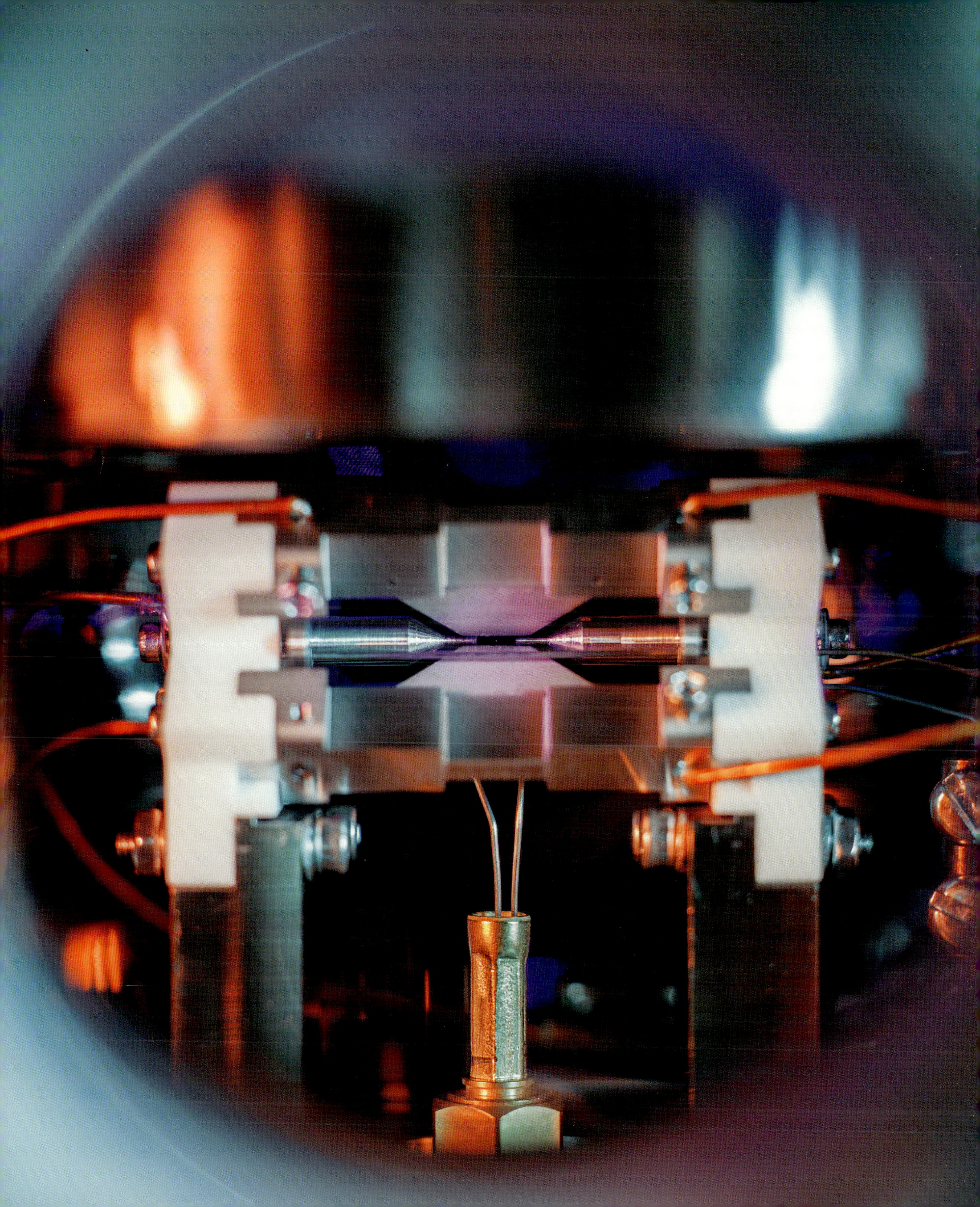

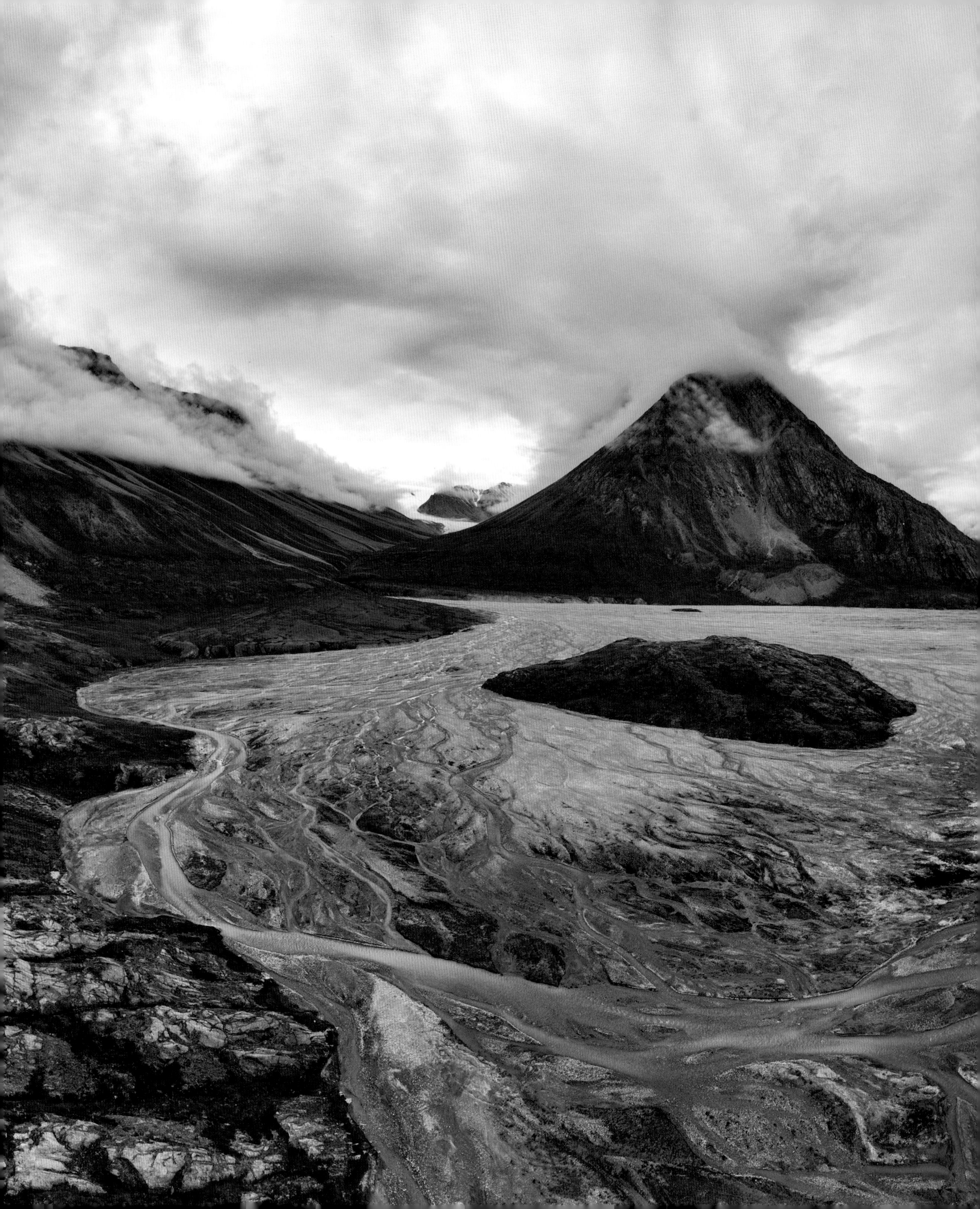

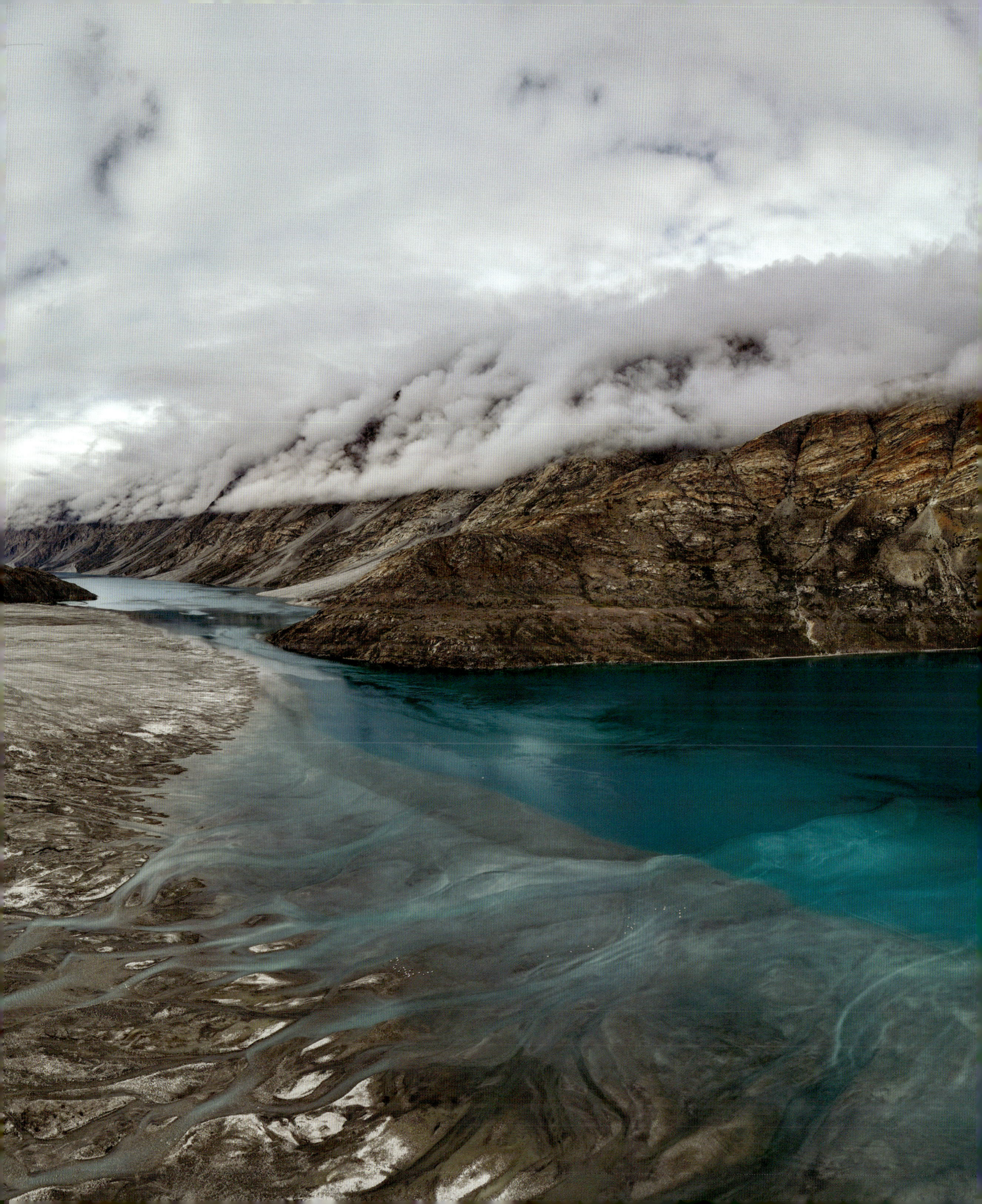

A 14th-century church tower is all
that remains visible after the
Italian government created Lake
Resia by flooding the Tyrolean
town of Curon.

Previous pages:
JEFFREY KERBY
As runoff slides from the
Greenland ice sheet, it forms this
delta at Röhss Fjord in
northeastern Greenland.

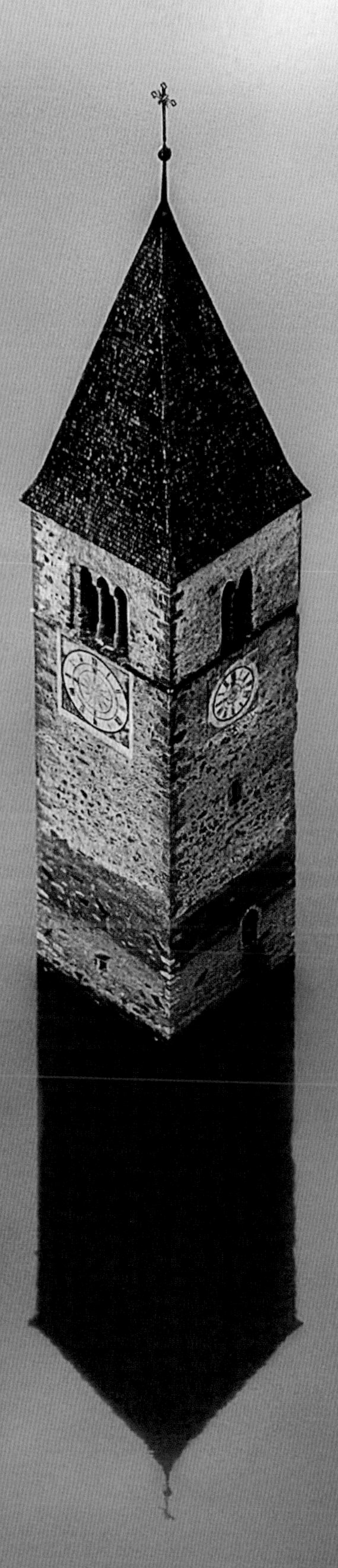

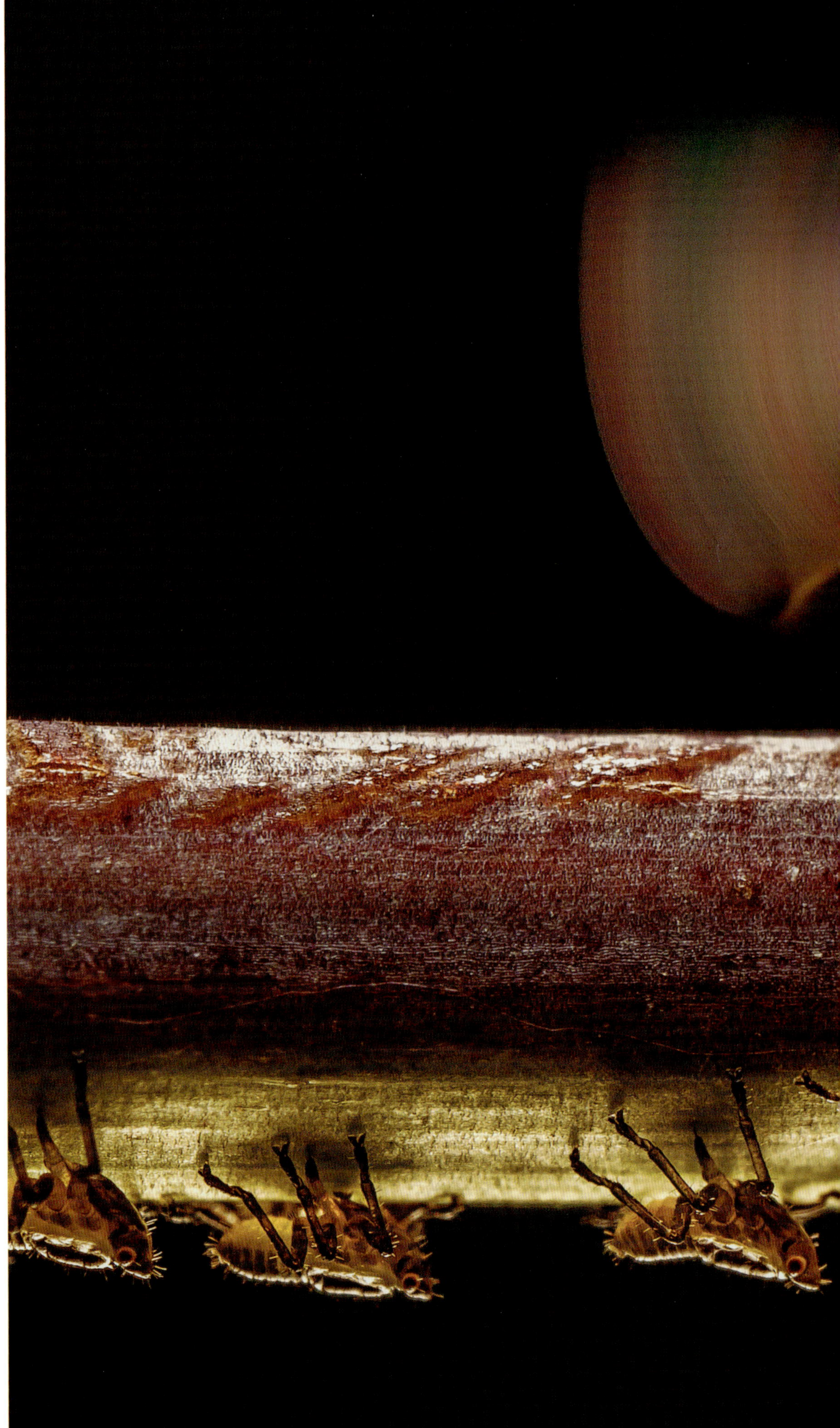

JAVIER AZNAR GONZÁLEZ DE RUEDA
In the Ecuadorean Amazon, a bee flaps its wings, warning treehopper nymphs of an intruder: the photographer.

256

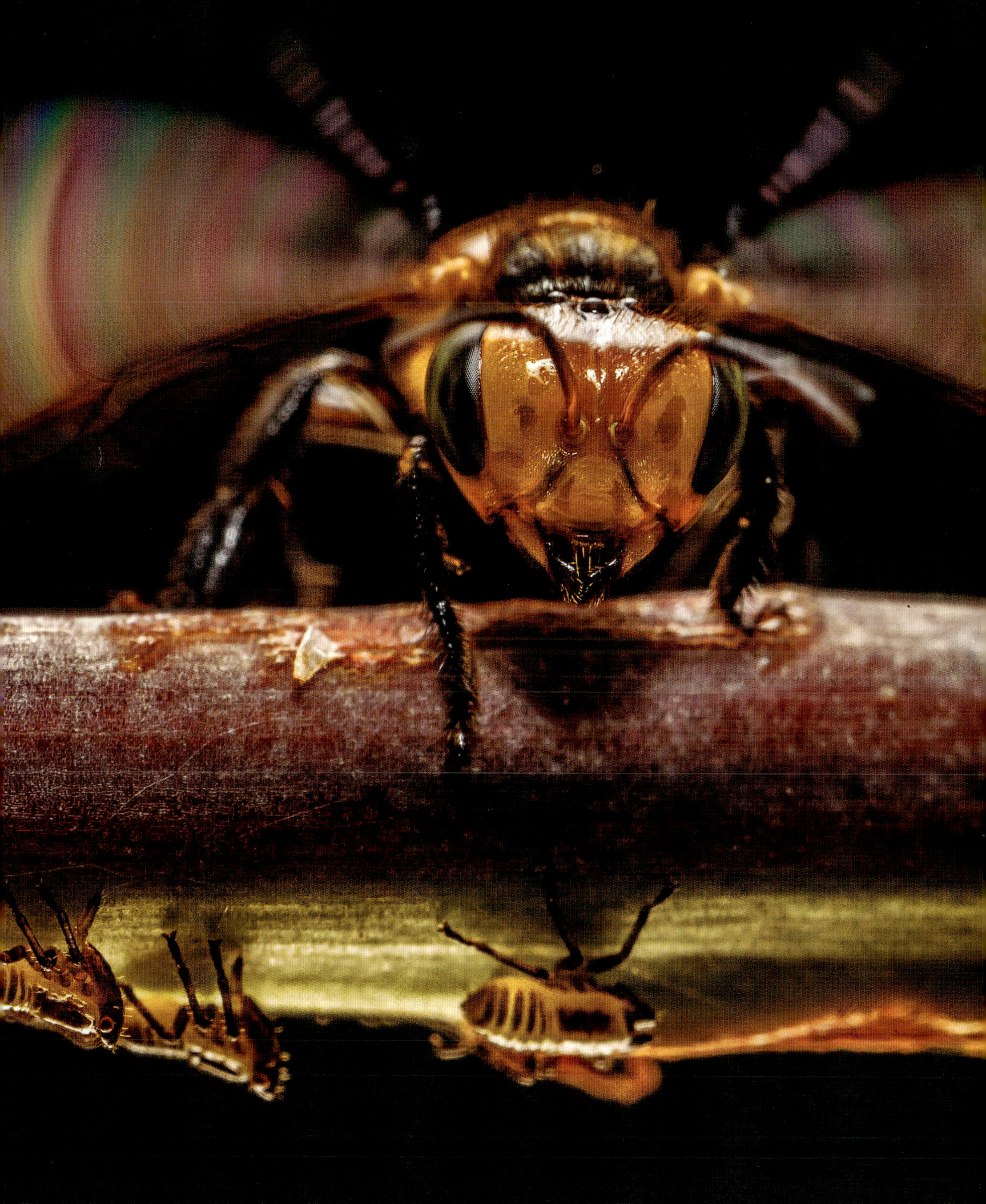

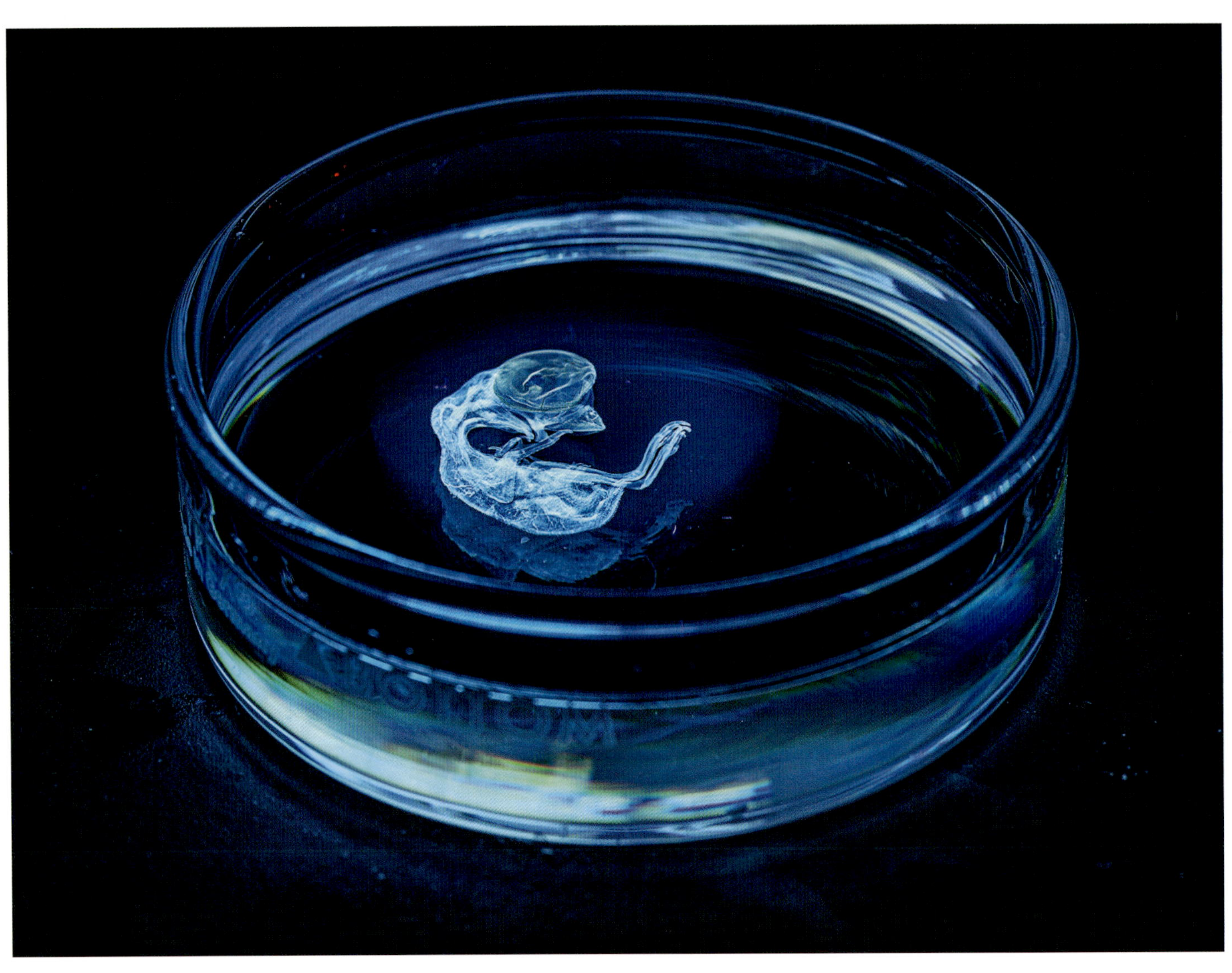

PAOLO VERZONE
Stained blue in a laboratory petri dish, a chicken embryo offers clues about the genetics of dinosaurs and their descendants.

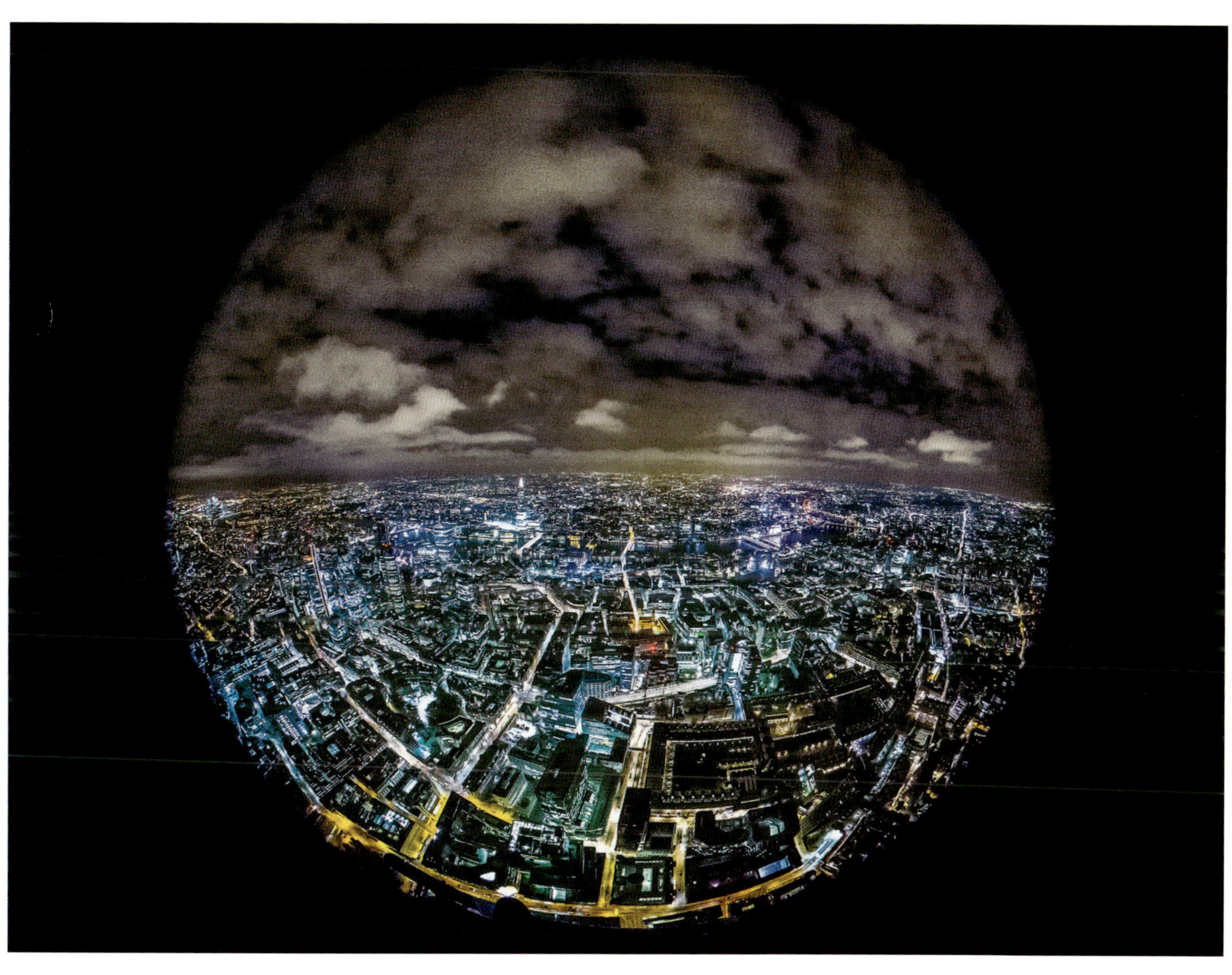

VINCENT LAFORET
Clouds above, bustle below: a fish-eye view of the London cityscape

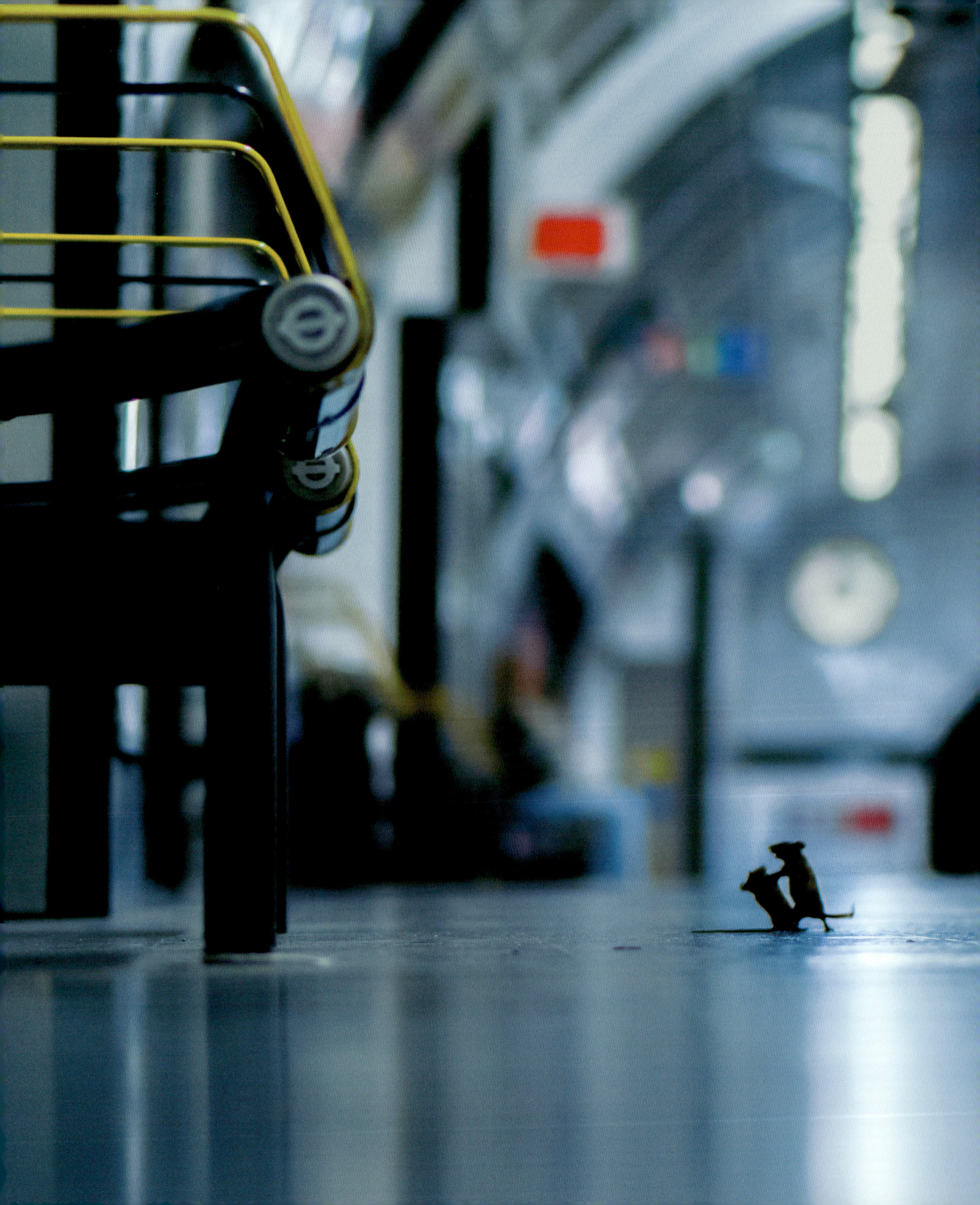

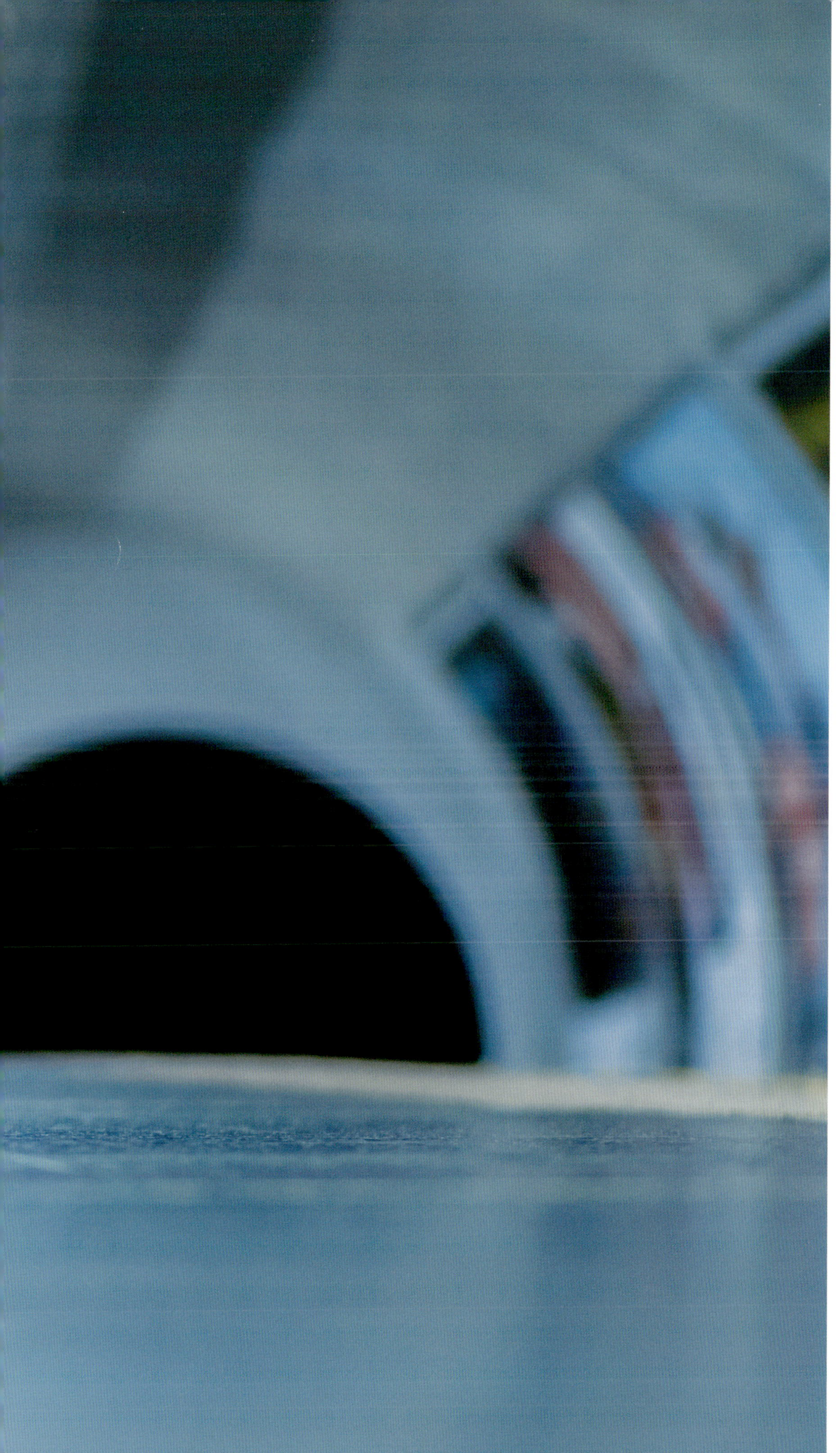

SAM ROWLEY
Mice skirmish over crumbs of
food dropped in a London
Underground stop.

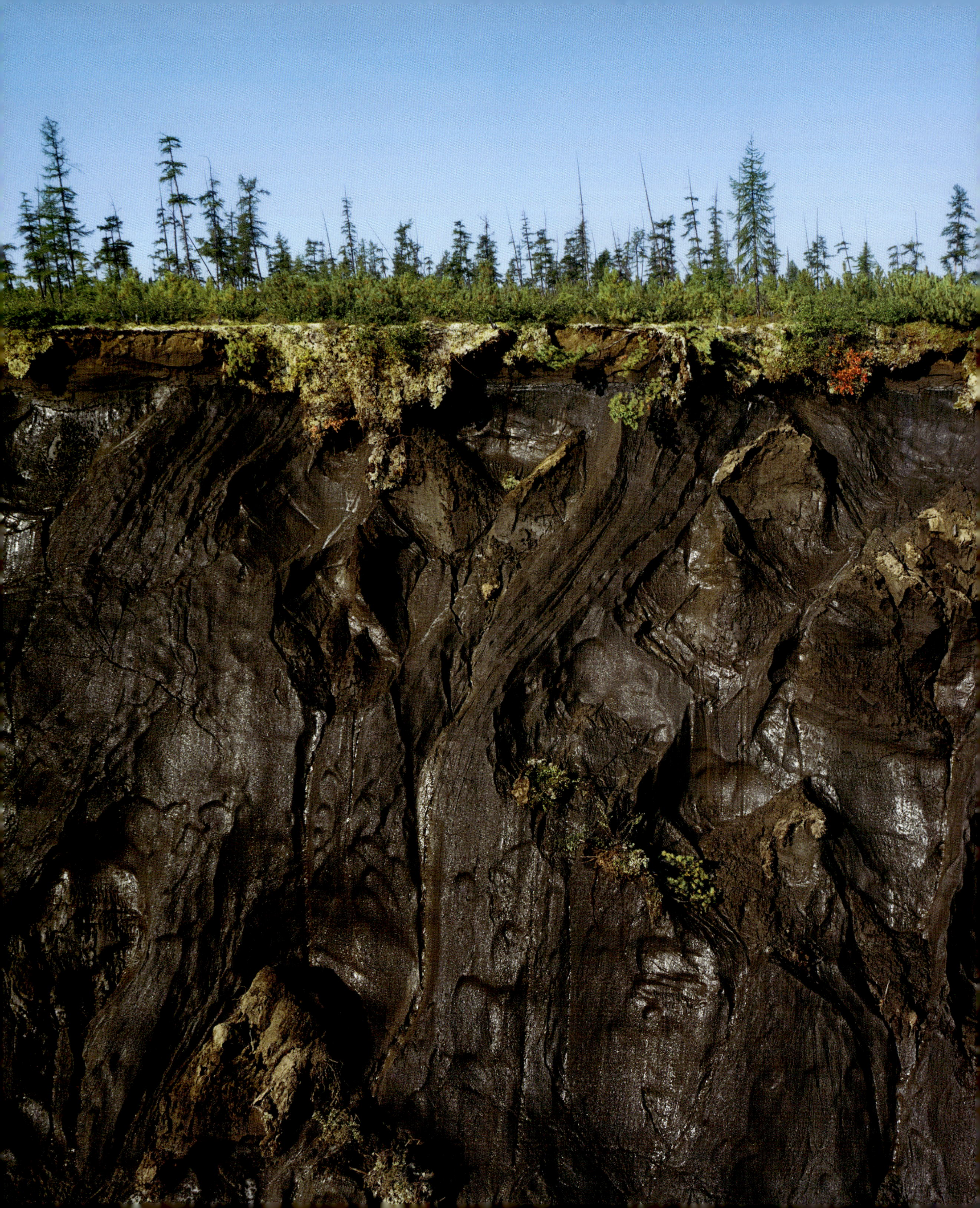

Structure brings
order to our perceptions.
It can both clarify them,
but also impose our
preconceptions on them.

~STEPHEN SHORE, "FORM AND PRESSURE"

KATIE ORLINSKY
Lumbering in the 1960s initiated Russia's Batagaika Crater, the world's biggest permafrost thaw slump,
revealing the depth of ancient organic matter compared with the slim layer of soil and forest above.

Following pages:
GURCHARAN ROOPRA
Flamingos wing over Kenya's Lake Magadi. The lake's swirls of color come from high concentrations of sodium carbonate.

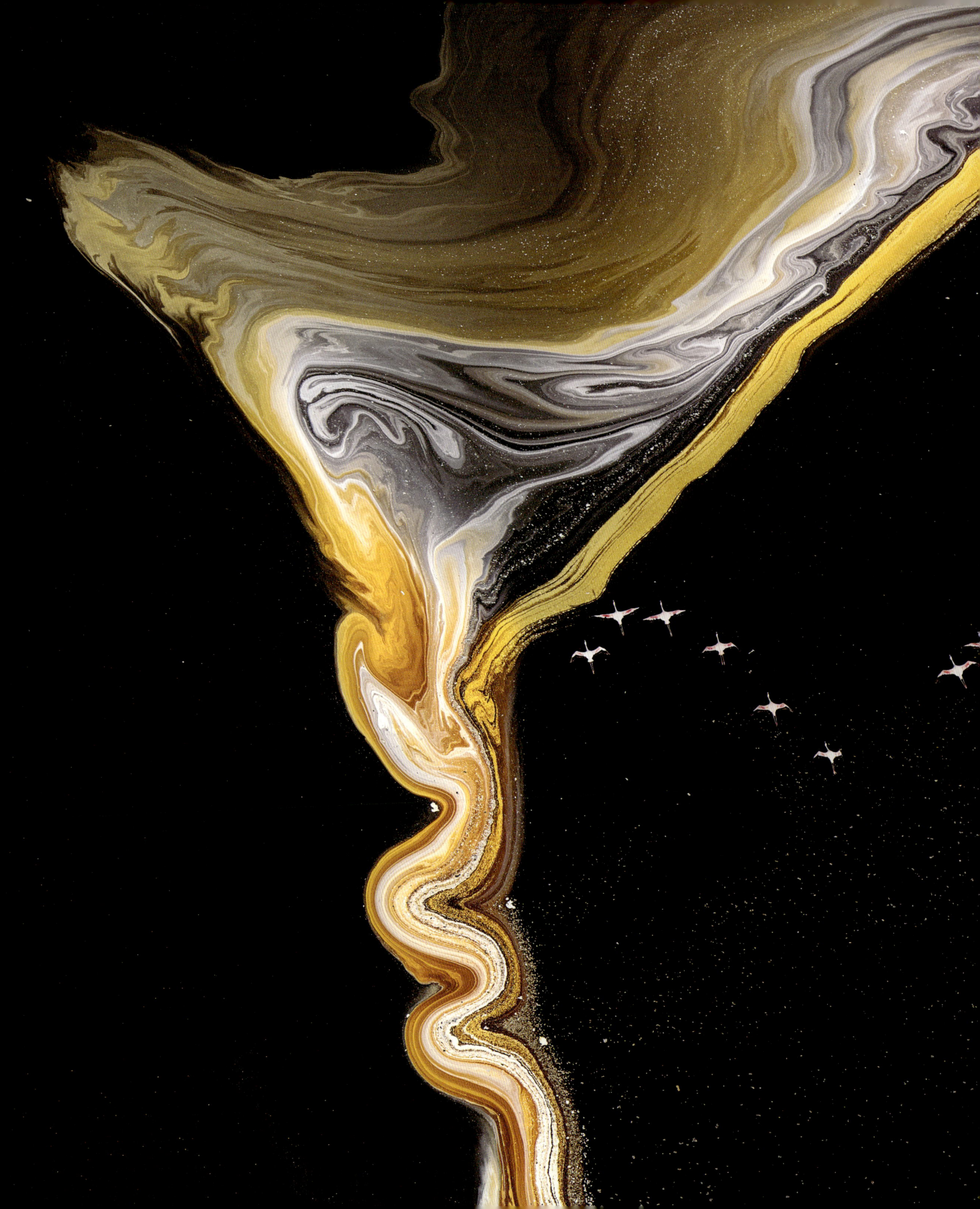

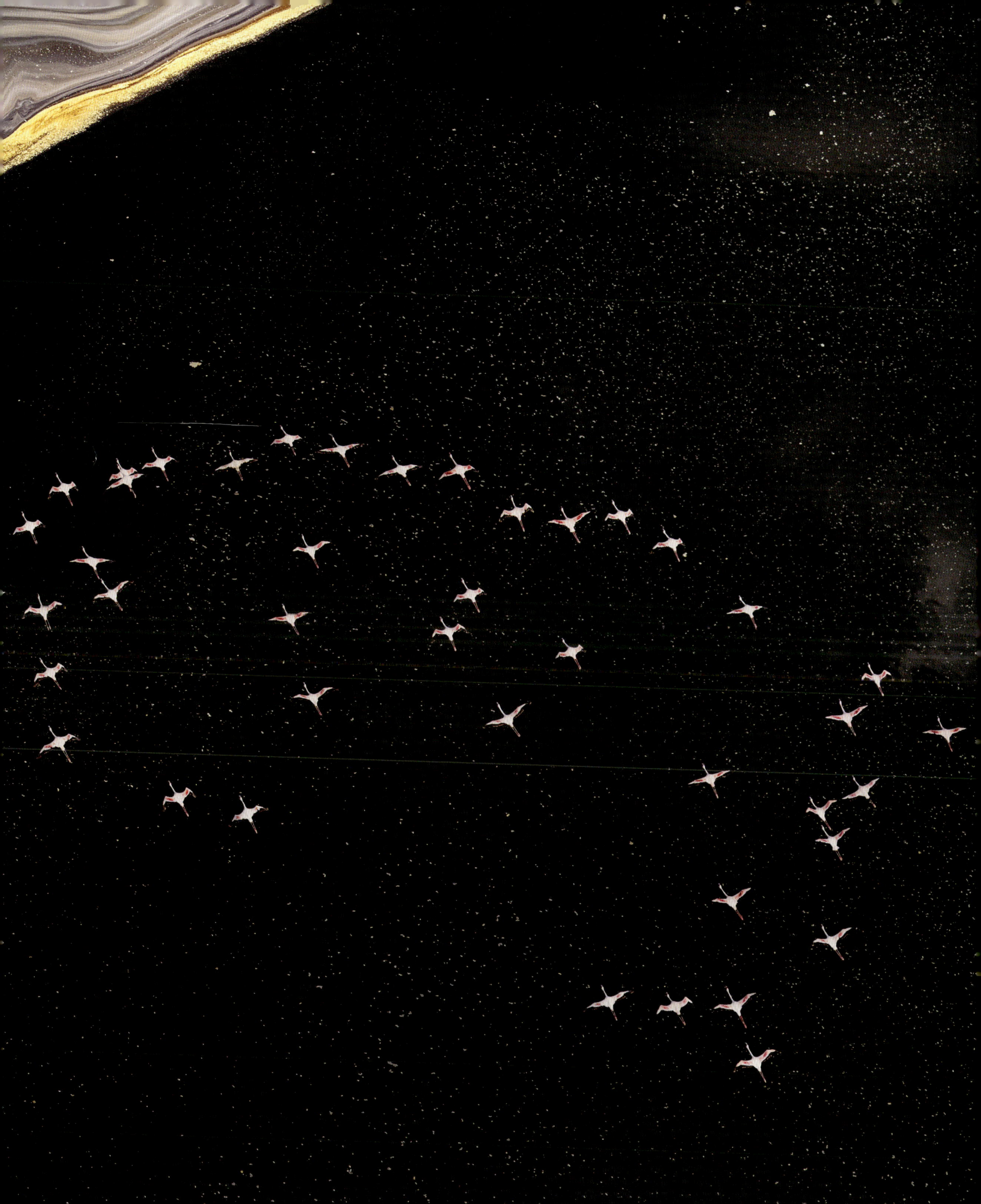

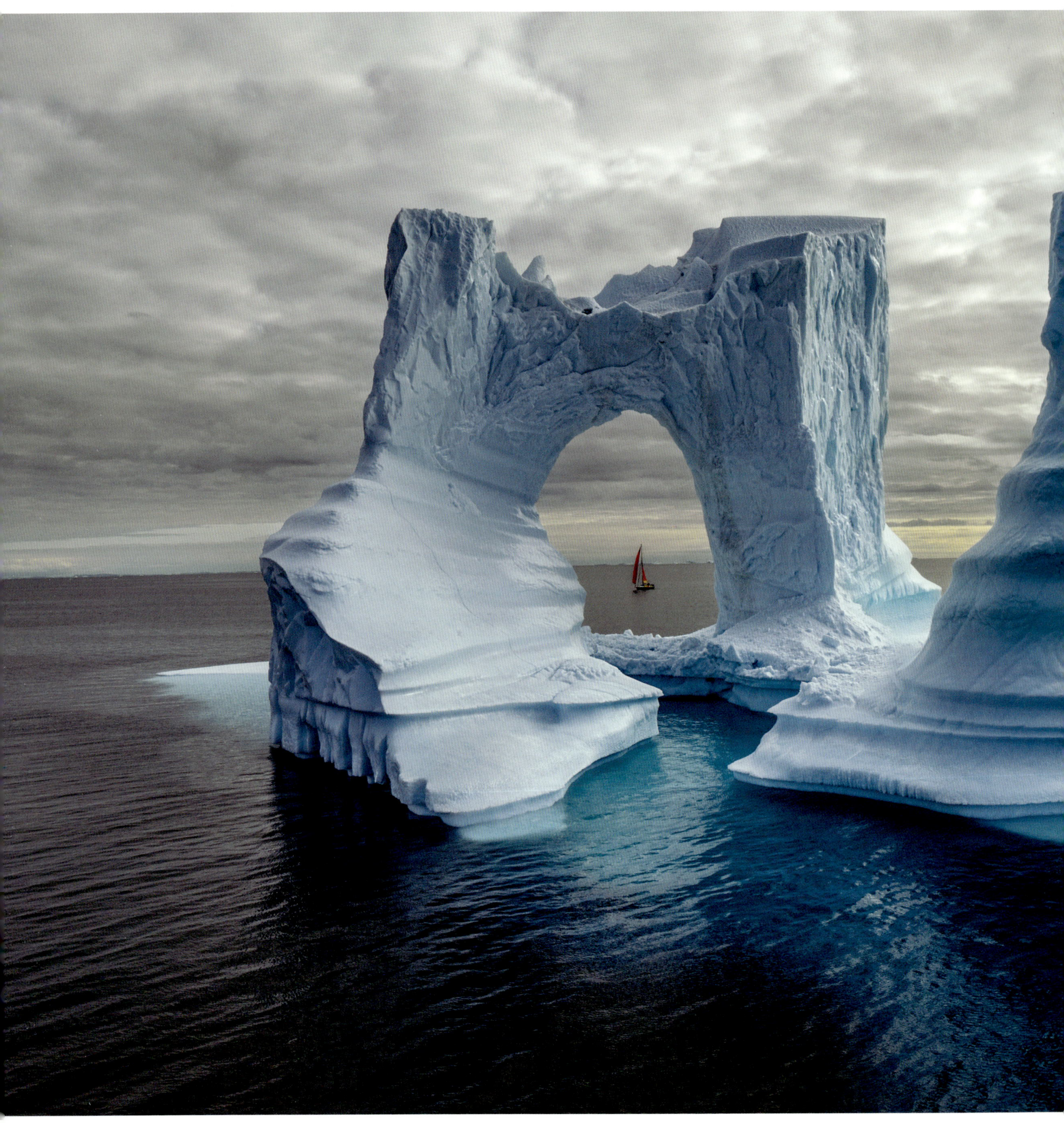

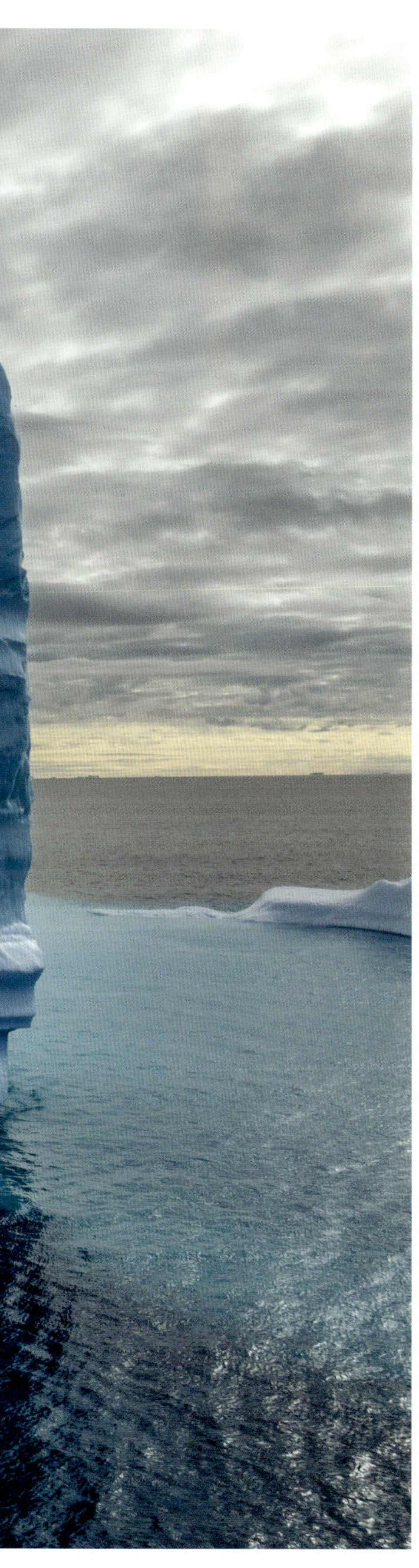

IN CONVERSATION WITH

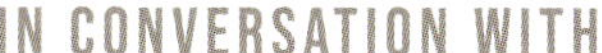

RENAN OZTURK

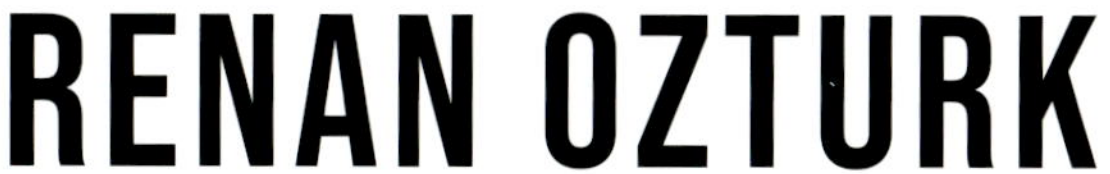

Renan Ozturk is an expedition climber, photojournalist, and documentary filmmaker. His early career as a landscape artist saw him lug canvases through national parks and the Himalaya, and his unique blend of climbing achievements and visual storytelling made him a National Geographic Adventurer of the Year in 2013. In recent years, his acclaimed work on the films *Meru* and *Sherpa* has garnered global attention. He is based in Colorado.

JEFFREY KERBY: You do a lot of things. You're a storyteller, you're a painter, you're a mountaineer, and you take exceptional photographs. Have photographs always been a tool for those pursuits, or are they a pursuit in and of themselves?

RENAN OZTURK: I never set out to be a photographer. I thought I was going to do alpine ecology, studying ravens in the mountains or something. In undergrad, the last class I took was an art class, and I was doing both artwork and climbing for a long time. At first, my friends would drop me off in the desert, and I would just walk the road until I found people that I could climb with, but then I started doing these bigger expeditions and landscape-based art around big mountains. That led into bigger opportunities for sponsored climbing expeditions, like on the North Face team and some early National Geographic stuff. I was just a climbing rigger on those, but then camera technology got a lot smaller and they started bringing cameras on those trips—things like *Meru,* for example. I was doing time-lapses and then taking the time-lapses and cutting them up with [the editing software] After Effects and flying cameras through them and

stuff like that. It was more video storytelling, and it took a while before I even focused on photos. That came later.

JK: How is doing photos different for you than setting up a video?

RO: It's a thousand times easier and more enjoyable. I mean, people will tell you how hard it is to, like, be there for the moment and find the whole story in a frame and all that bullshit, but if I'm totally honest, it's a pleasure. I'm still mainly hired to do video, so when I'm doing still assignments now, it gets hard to balance the two. With Nat Geo assignments, you're forced to be creative with stills, and seeing how aerial stills have become a staple is exciting. That was how I first thought I could bring unique stills to a project, because I really wasn't that great of a still photographer.

RENAN OZTURK
Framed by an iceberg, *Polar Sun* sails through Greenland's waters, tracking the route of Sir John Franklin, who died in his 1847 search for the Northwest Passage.

Following pages:
RENAN OZTURK
The breadth and magnificence of Mount Everest and environs can only be conveyed by stitching together multiple images of adjacent landscapes.

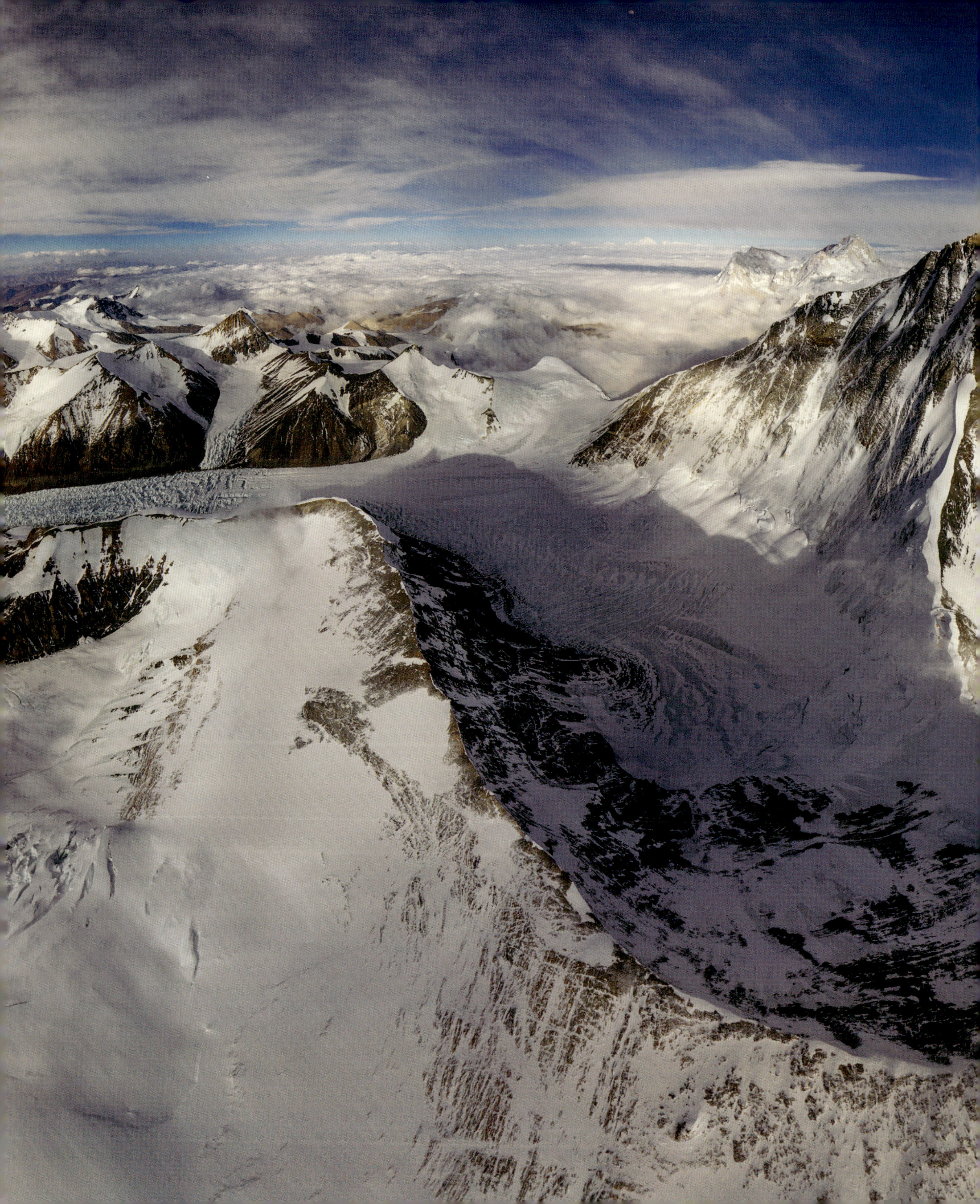

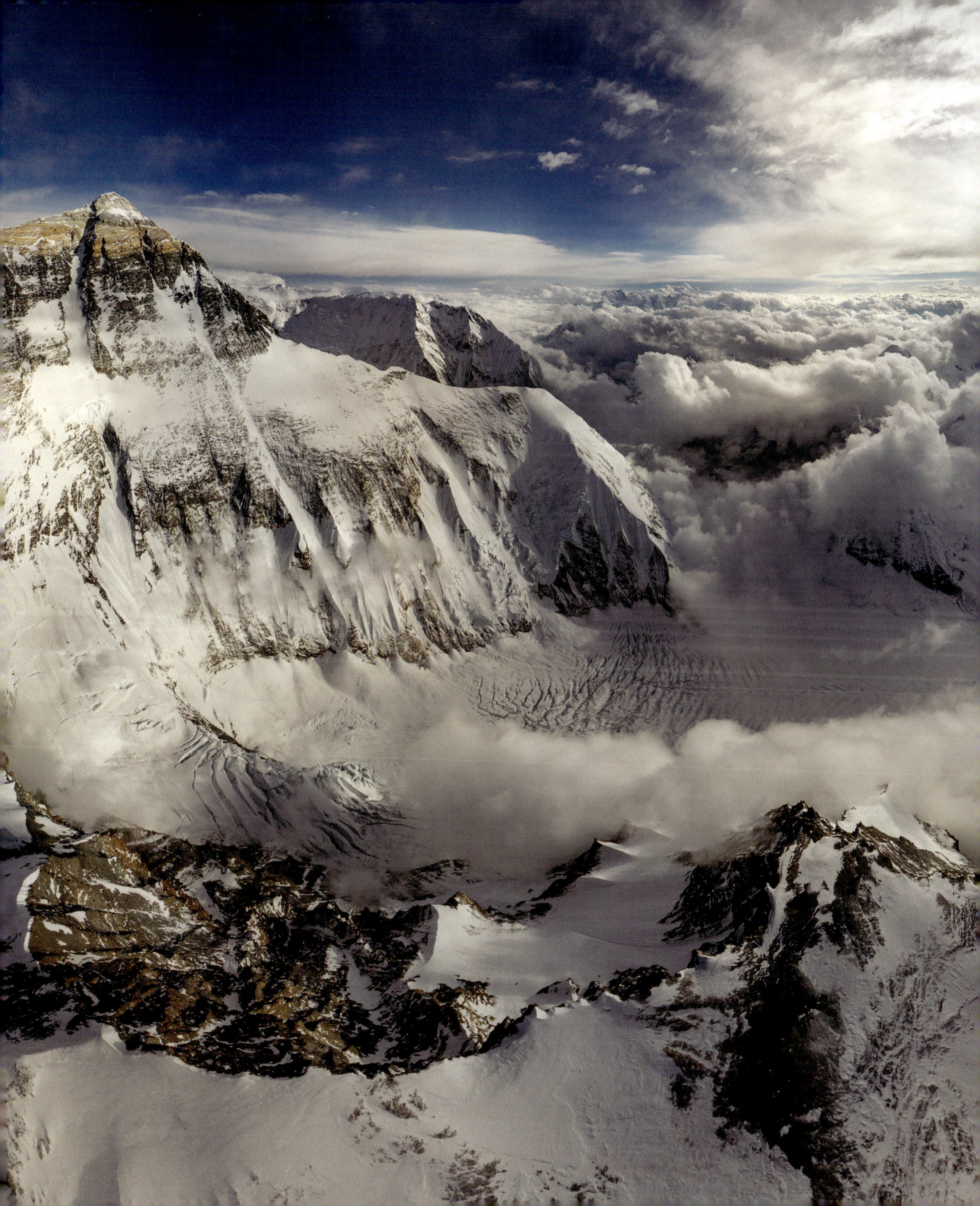

JK: When you go to a place, do you go in light, or go with everything you can carry?

RO: On the last story, I think we had 60- or 70-pound (27–32 kg) bags. I think the risk of loading up on gear is more worth it when you have the right camera in your hand and you're bringing back something that's new and different. That makes people feel empathy for a place or story. And counterintuitively, even though the reason I got into all this is because the cameras got small enough for me to take them on climbs, I'm now trying to take the most advanced *and* lightest-weight thing, which is an extremely difficult balance. Instead of just bringing the smallest drone, I'm training for a year with my team to see if, by our combined force, we can get the craziest tool in the craziest place and bring back something really special. That's where you really suffer hard carrying a lot of gear. A lot of people don't see behind the scenes, how a lot of this creative work comes down to logistics and, essentially, being very skilled luggage handlers in airports.

JK: Wasn't that relevant to your honey hunter story?

RO: Yeah. It was a video story about the last honey hunter. This man was a shamanistic honey hunter who was chosen in a dream to harvest hallucinogenic honey from these cliff faces, and he had to free solo the cliffs on handmade bamboo ropes. I thought I could just use my video aerial skills to shoot it, but because of all the batteries and stuff I wanted to bring, I almost got arrested in Dubai on the way to Nepal, and it became difficult to receive funding for the film portion of the project. Instead, I only had approval for a still assignment. But I had never shot a still assignment in my life. So I was calling around trying to figure out how to do it. It ended up with me totally free hanging from the cliff by a rope trying to get stills. There was no

way to face the subject. I was just spinning out of control. We figured out that if you had another person next to you, you could kick off them as ballast. I still think the whole thing sort of failed, but I guess hanging from a rope could still be considered an aerial still in a certain way. [*laughs*] Not as many drone options back then.

JK: Now we have lots of options. But are there shortcomings to shooting with a drone?

RO: I don't think you get the intimacy. You don't feel like you're there as much. I mean, you can get really close, but there's just something about the depth of field you get with the bigger cameras. With a drone, you're not getting that same look and amount of depth of information in your photo as when you're with your subject.

JK: The biggest camera I can think of is the Bradford Washburn camera.

RO: Brad Washburn was the original scale guy. His camera was developed for military use. I think it was a Fairchild K-22 with giant 8x10 plates. He saw the future in a lot of ways. For example, he was the first one to map Denali by flying over in planes, and I guess he would argue with Ansel Adams about the nature of landscape photography. He would always say you need a figure in there for scale, but Adams thought it should be more of a pure thing, that we should show nature without humanity. Now it's a little more commonplace to see figures in landscapes because we look at most media on phones through social media. As photographers we almost teach ourselves to avoid those kinds of shots now, because it's such a trope with Instagram and stuff.

JK: I think your shot of the arched iceberg uses scale very effectively. How did you get that shot?

RO: That iceberg was about 10 miles (16 km) off the coast of Disko Bay. We just saw it in the distance. I was kind of screwed at first trying to shoot this boat going through the region because it was such a big landscape. There was no real way for me to develop a sense of scale rather than using what I learned from climbing. The classic thing for climbing and shooting places like the Alaska Range is you get your colors to blend into the landscape. But if you want to see people in the landscapes, you put colorful jackets on the figures. So I got us some red sails for the boat on this Northwest Passage trip … You're probably laughing because that's a tourist thing to do.

JK: [*laughs*] I'm laughing because for my project this summer, I made everybody bring a red or an orange jacket so I can see them in the field. That's the Renan tip right there!

RO: Yeah, I mean, it's not rocket surgery. It's pretty simple. And the massive iceberg arch with the boat in there is one of the best shots from that entire Northwest Passage trip. Without the sails, the boat would've just blended in, and you wouldn't have a chance to do that shot journalistically. Some people might've changed the color of the sails in post, but that's where I draw the line.

JK: I wanted to touch on the Everest panorama. That was drone facilitated, but I know it wasn't easy. Can you tell me the story behind that photo?

RO: We were trying to find Sandy Irvine's body in the death zone above 26,000 feet (8,000 m), because that would rewrite the greatest feat in exploration, which is who first climbed Everest. [Irvine and mountaineer George Mallory disappeared on Everest in 1924. Mallory's body was found in 1999 with no definitive proof that either he or Irvine had summited; Irvine's body is yet to be found.] If you find Irvine's body, you probably find his camera and solve the mystery. Searching the death zone isn't very easy, so we thought we would use drone photogrammetry to do that. But we didn't know if drones were going to be able to fly that high. We did testing in a hyperbaric chamber so we could simulate flying at crazy altitudes. In those conditions, you have to either hack the drones to make them do things they're not allowed to do, or get permission from the manufacturer to unlock them.

We were doing a little bit of both. The Mavic [drone] launched from the North Col at 23,000 feet (7,010 m) and went up to summit altitude. On that particular drone, you couldn't affect the descent speed. So when you pressed down on the controller, it was practically falling out of the sky—like pretty insane, dangerously fast. Luckily, we didn't lose it.

It ended up being an amazing thing to capture Everest in that way. Essentially, we were doing 360-degree stitches— aside from directly above the drone, which is blue sky anyway—taking 27 photos in kind of an overlapping nature, creating a globe that you can fly around in and take rectangular pieces from. It's a great technique. Now we do them everywhere.

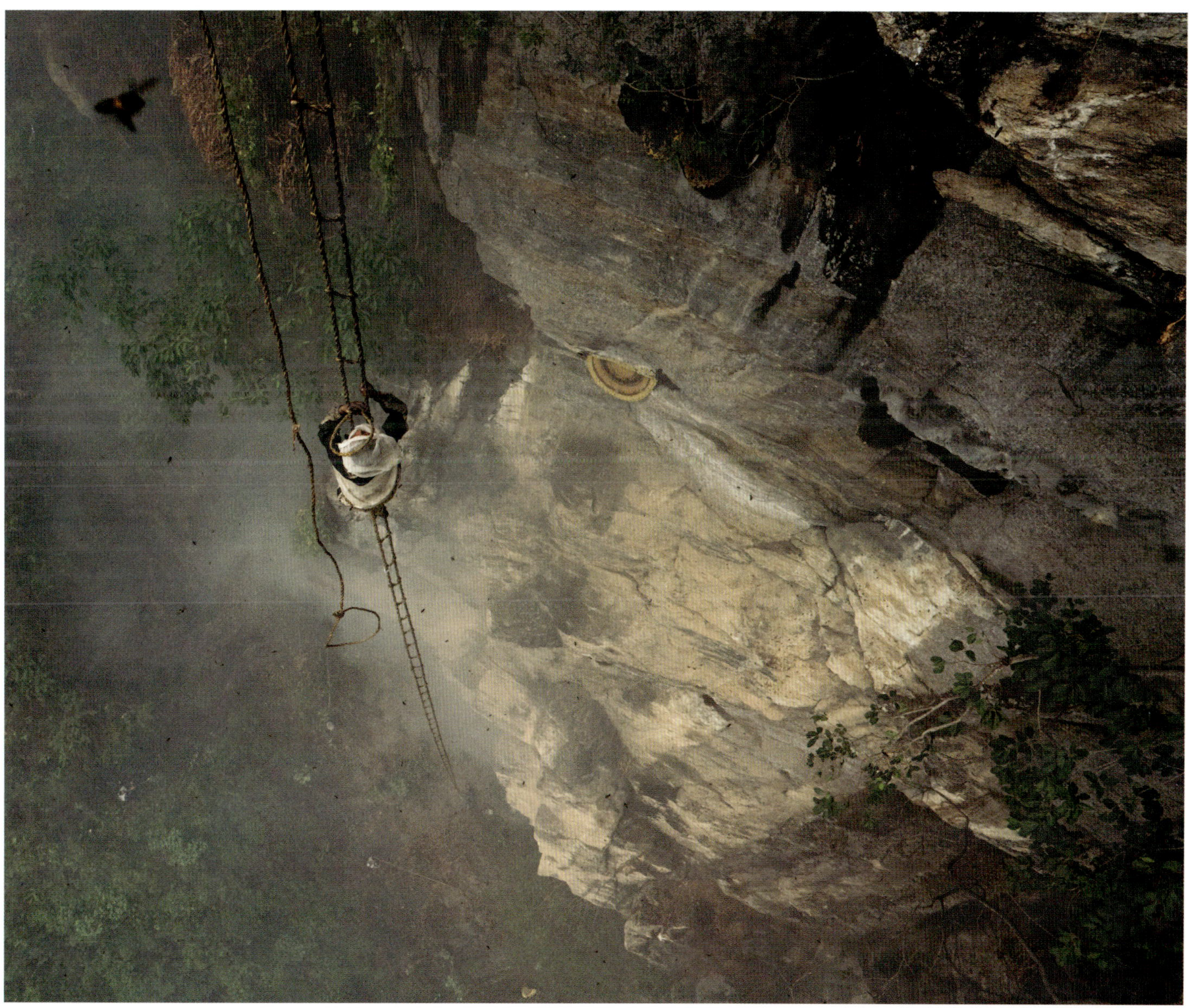

RENAN OZTURK
A honey hunter seems to dangle midair as he climbs a rope ladder to harvest hallucinogenic honey from cliffs in the jungles of eastern Nepal.

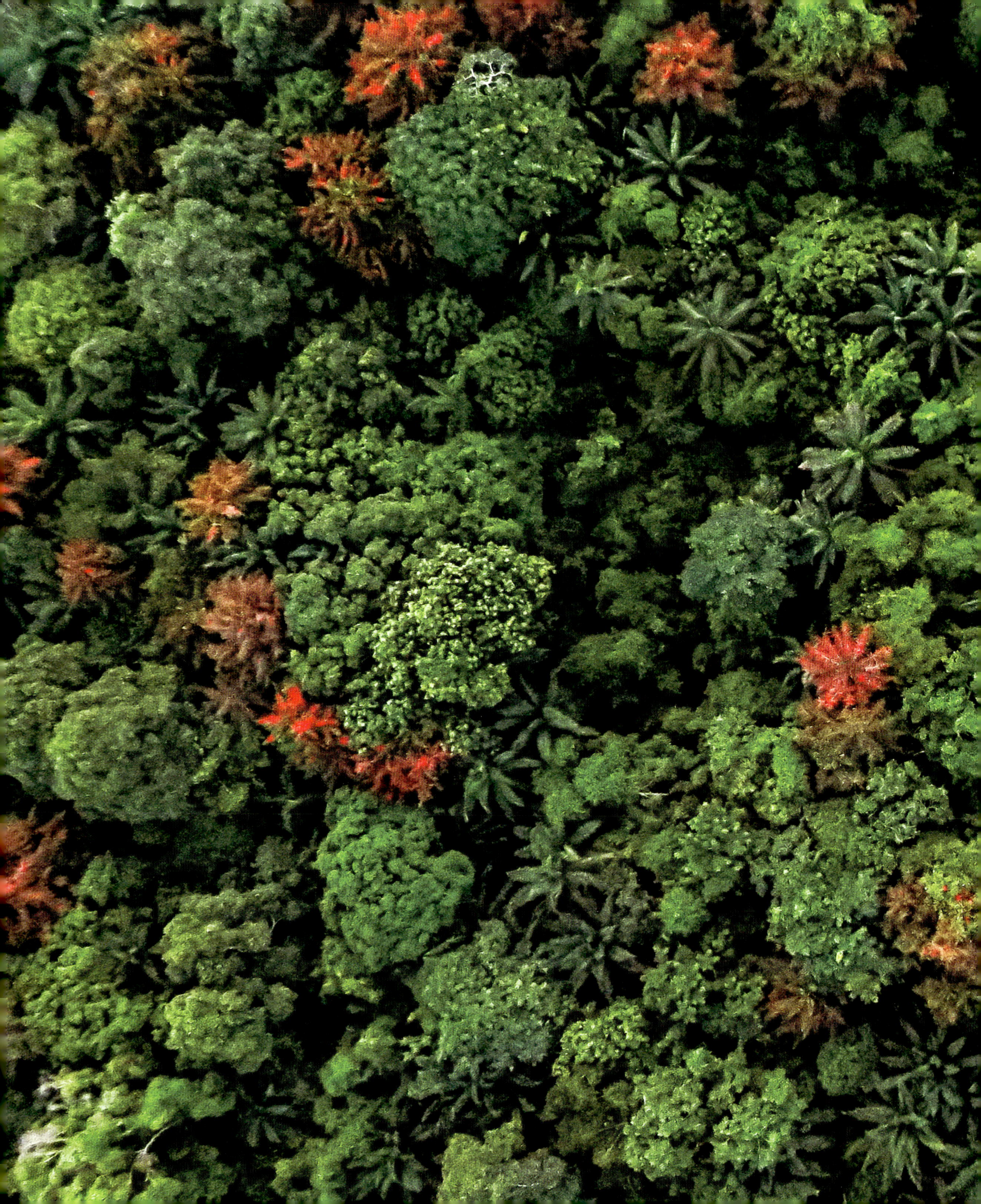

CHAPTER FOUR

TEXTURE

Nature accommodates itself
to every man's necessity.
If the eye is maimed ...
the touch becomes more
poignant and discriminating.

~HELEN KELLER, *THE WORLD I LIVE IN*

The forests of the Issa Valley in Tanzania resemble the African savanna from six million years ago, when early human ancestors took their first steps on two legs. This makes it an attractive place to study how large, intelligent primates like chimps behave, albeit in a very different setting than the dense forests of Gombe where Jane Goodall did her pioneering research.

Ironically, the sparse density of trees in the Issa Valley makes finding chimps to study much more difficult, because the animals tend to spread out over larger areas. In 2015, with National Geographic support, I joined teams from the Greater Mahale Ecosystem Research and Conservation project and Conservation Drones in western Tanzania. Our goal was to try to solve the problem of finding chimps by searching from above the treetops.

It can take weeks to survey an area like this by foot. Simply walking through the hilly, densely vegetated understory is slow, and it is hard work to clear a path. The chimps here are also shy of humans and will usually slip away from an area long before you know they're present. For our team, the easiest way to tell if chimps were in an area was to find their nests—beds made of branches and leaves that they make in the treetops. Even after chimps leave a location, their nests stay behind for a few weeks before they decay, providing a lingering clue of their presence.

We split into two groups. One walked the forest looking up into the canopy for nests, and the other flew drones above the trees, looking downward and snapping pictures. Both approaches had their challenges, and by comparing our results, we improved survey methodologies and even found a few nests.

But photos brought back by the drones revealed more than just signs of chimps. Looking through thousands of photos of anonymous trees for nests, the entire landscape began to take on abstract forms. At times I felt like I was looking down at macrophotos of moss and bryophytes, or a loosely woven but brightly colored carpet. The textures were busy and varied, and it became difficult to focus on any particular area or individual tree.

Looking down on the world from above can feel distant and detached, but textures have a unique ability to pull us in close. They trick our eyes into feeling rather than seeing. Sometimes this creates a pleasant sensation, other times it can make us cringe.

The photographers in this chapter take us through a full range of these feelings. Piotr Naskrecki captures the feel of cool, saturated earth as African catfish churn the mud of their habitat (pages 318–19). The ridged patterns of a mushroom captured by J. Fritz Rumpf (pages 320–21) simultaneously evoke the idea of waves and sand dunes while making us question what is up and what is down. Dasha Plesen photographs the mold she grows from bacteria collected from the air and surfaces around us, making us wonder what textures might be hidden in our next sneeze (page 311).

If textures allow us to feel with our eyes, what breadth and depth of those feelings can you find in these images? ■

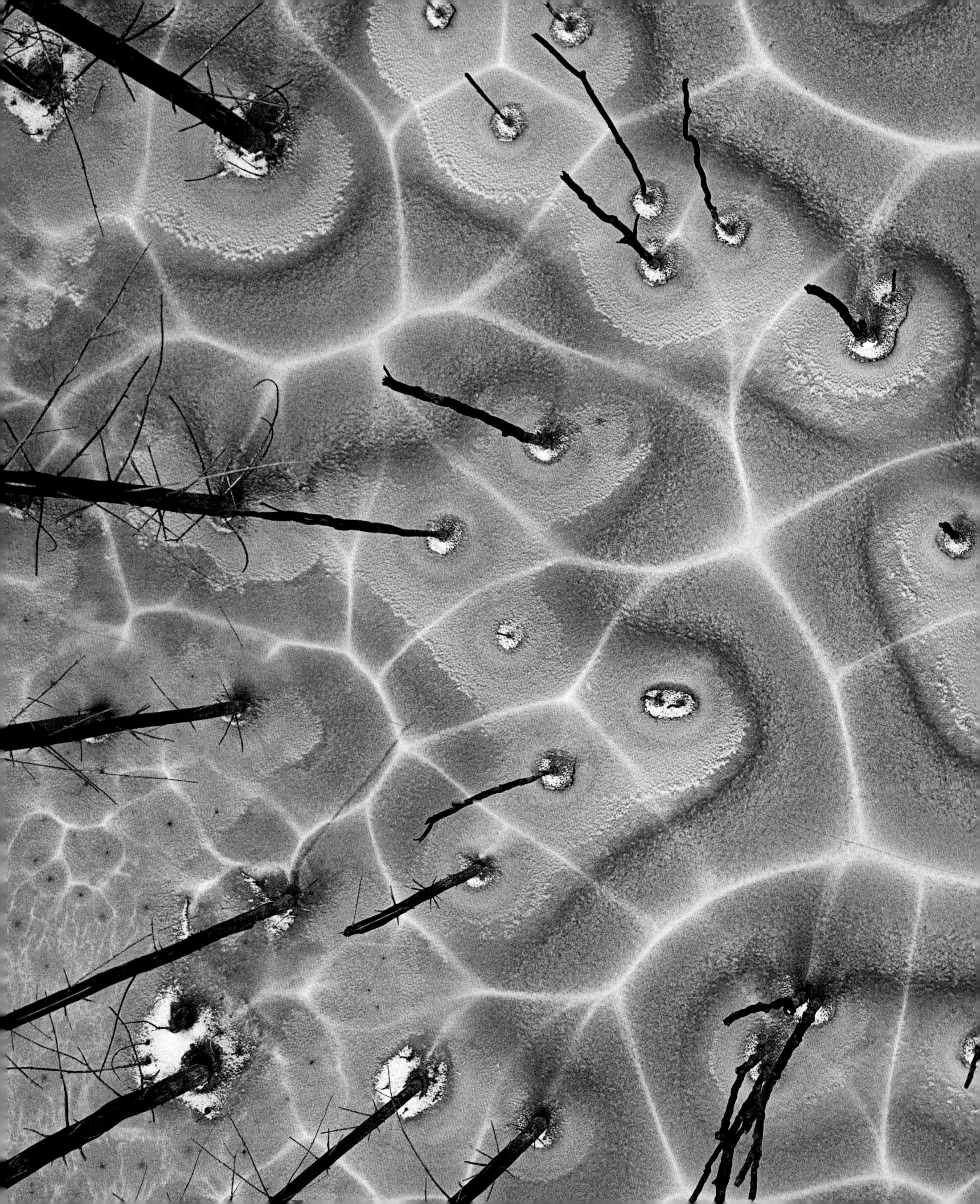

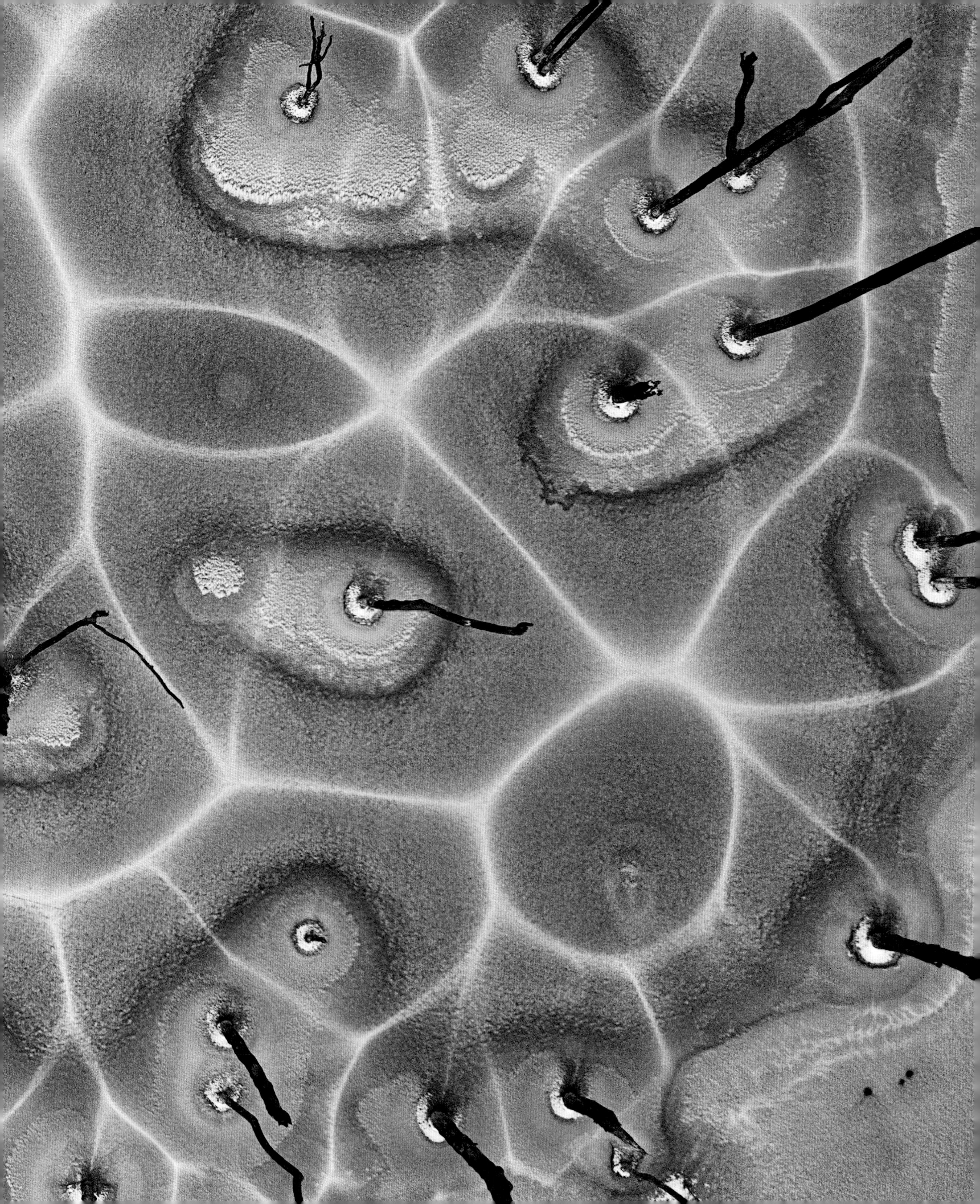

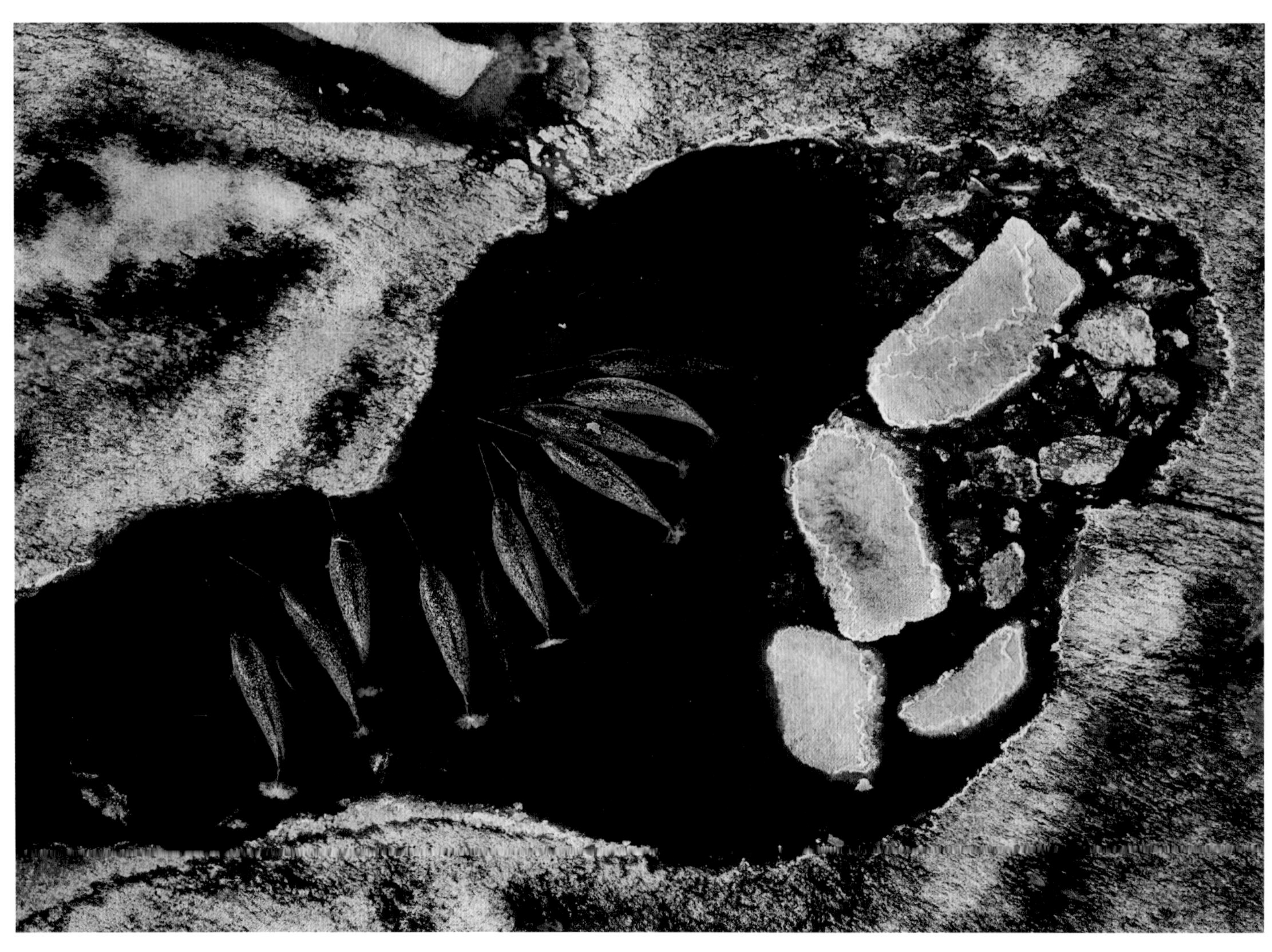

PAUL NICKLEN
Male narwhals cluster in meltwater, surrounded by the receding ice pack, in Canada's Admiralty Inlet.

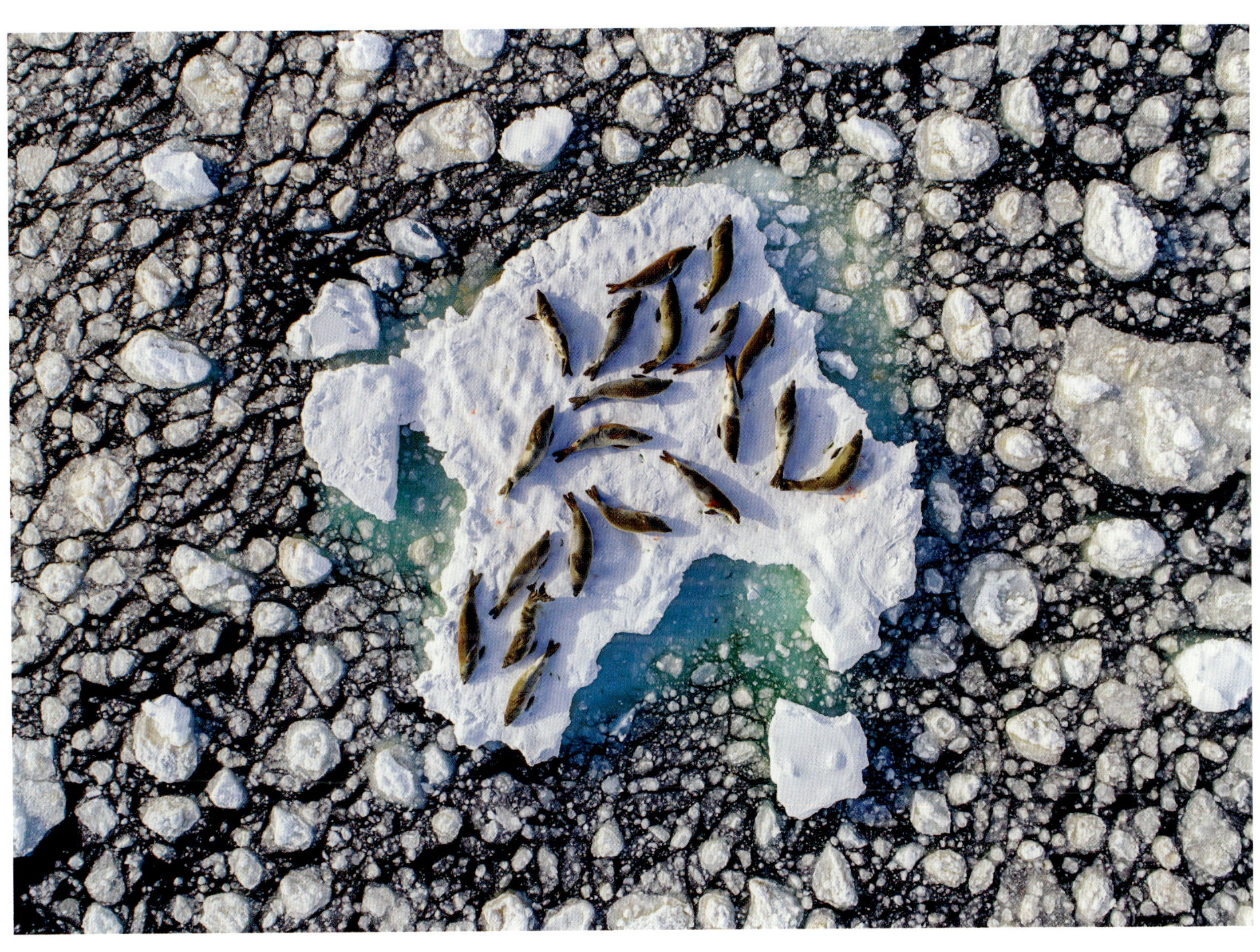

FLORIAN LEDOUX
Crabeater seals rest atop the ice after a night feed.

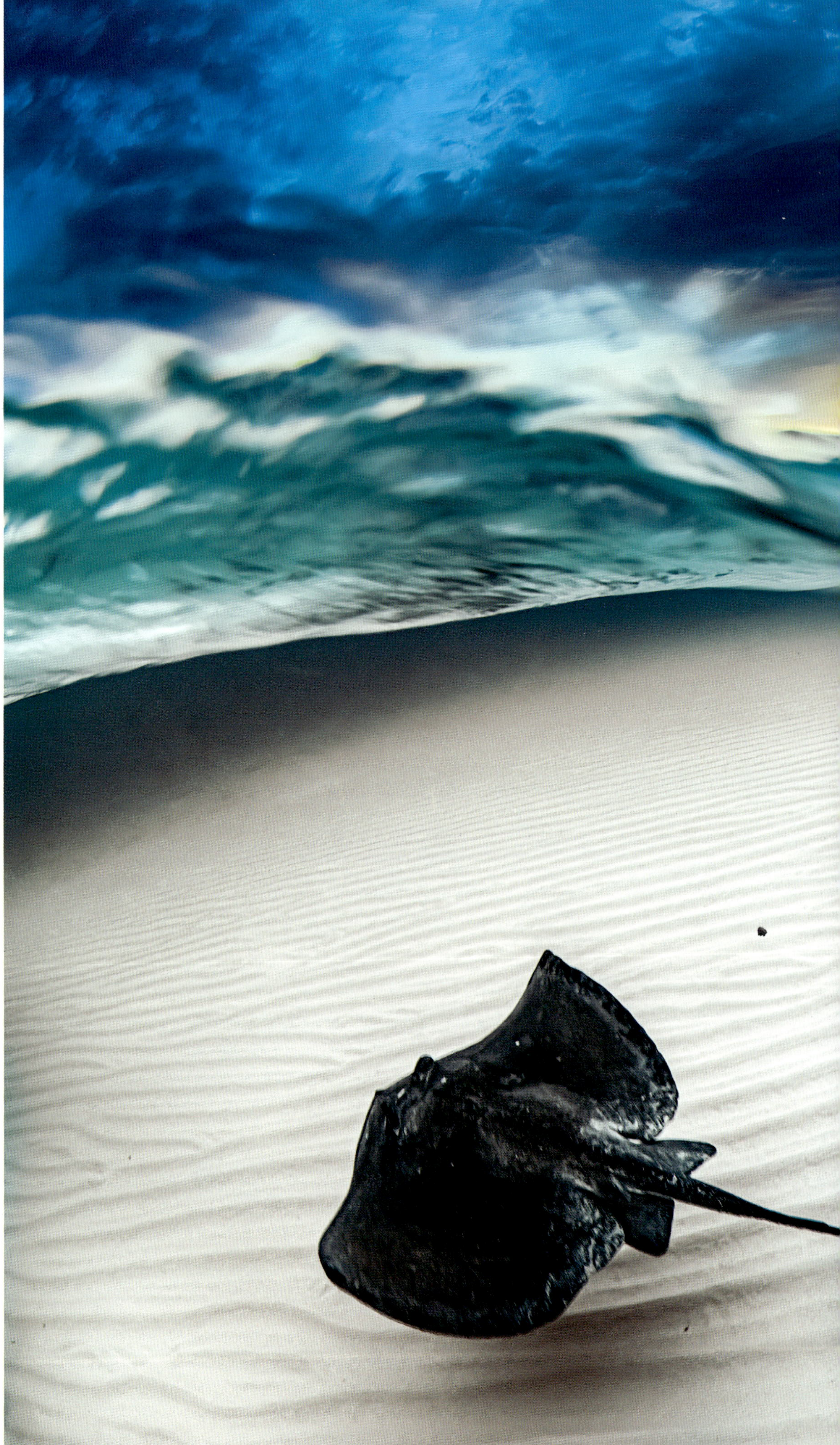

GREG SHERMAN
Southern stingrays glide over rippled white sand, the waves and sky another world above and beyond them.

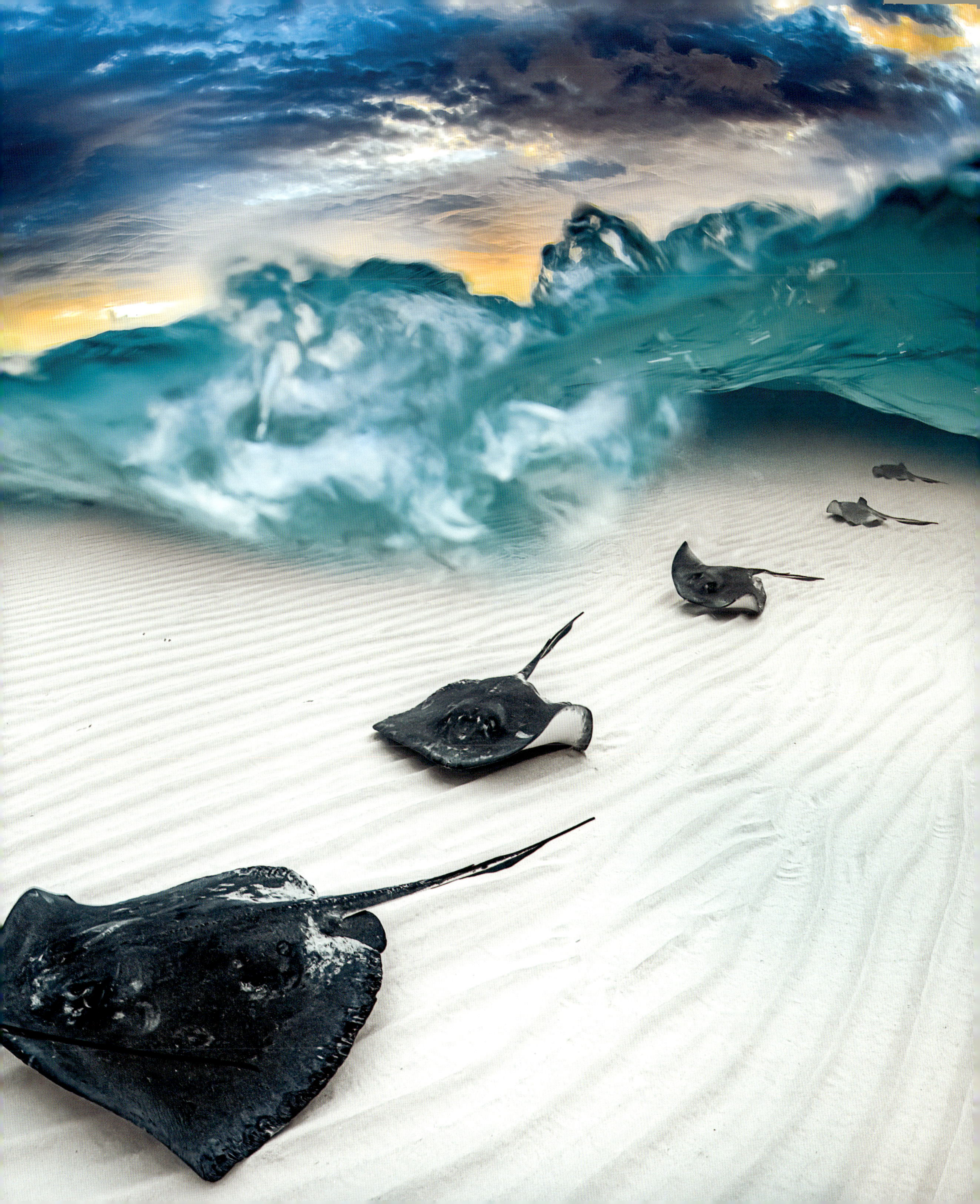

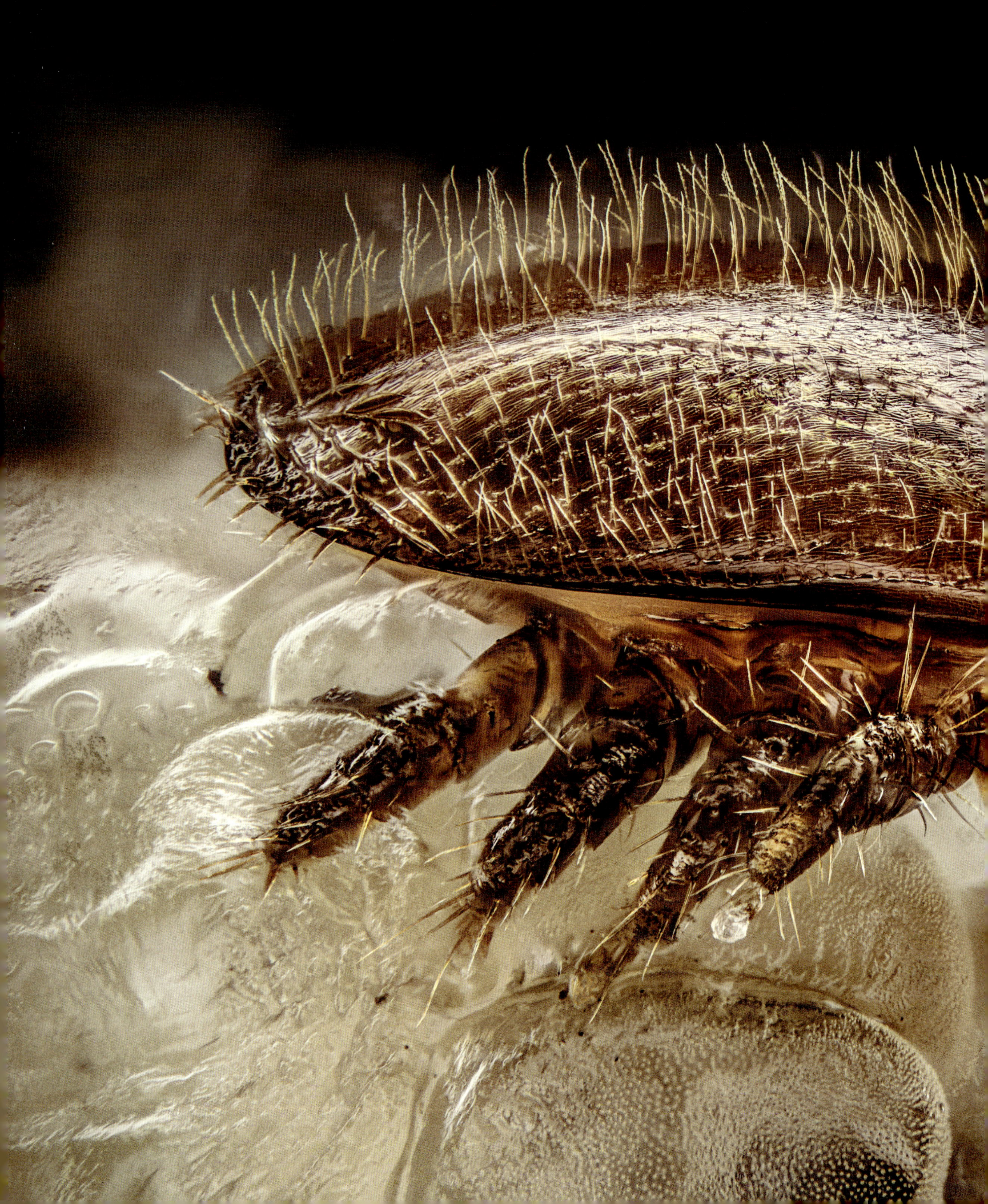

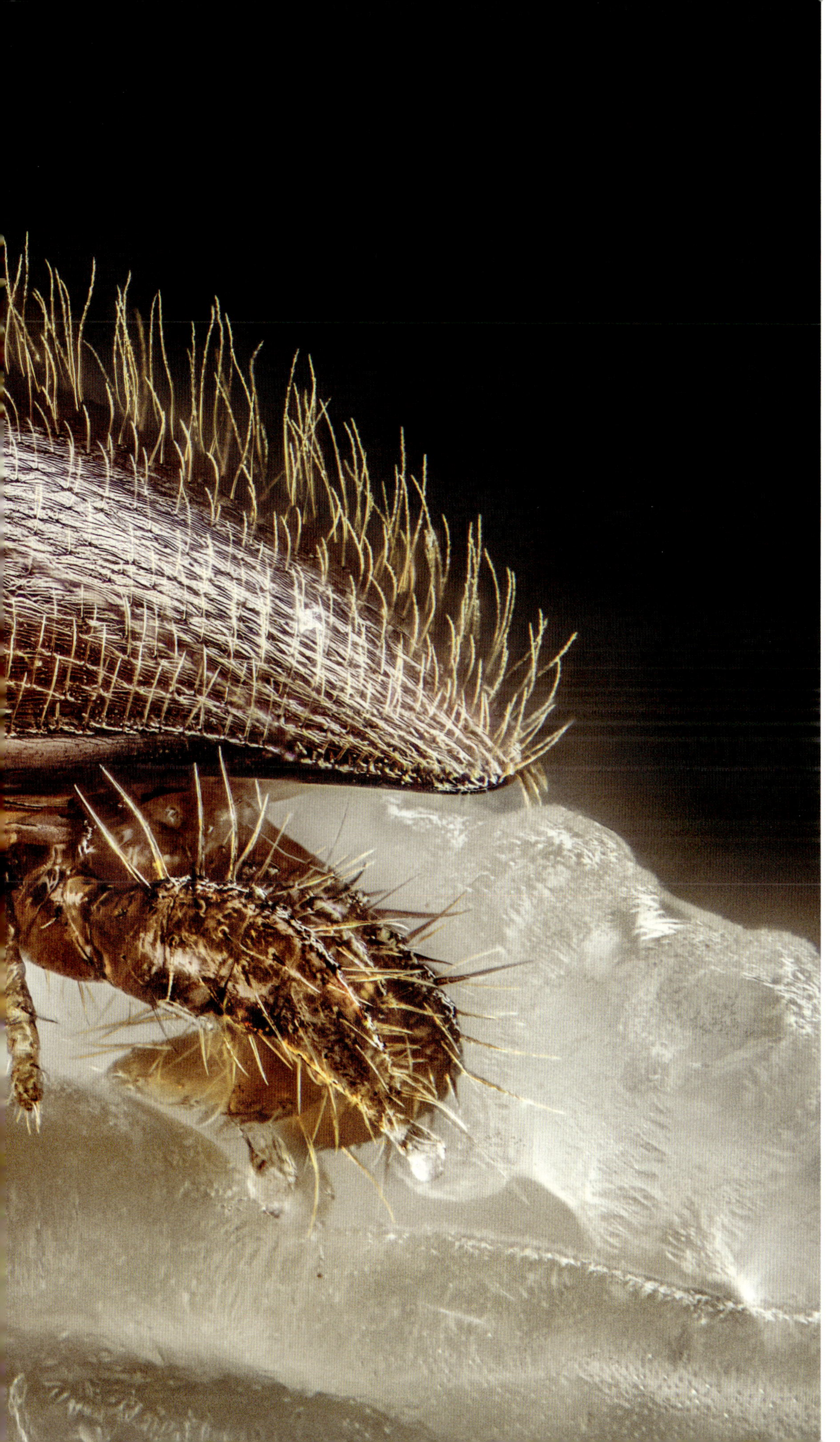

ANAND VARMA
A photographic technique called focus stacking brings this fuzzy Asian mite—no larger than a pinhead—into sharp clarity as the mite burrows into the gelatinous surface of a bee larva.

Nature can put on a thrilling show. The stage is vast, the lighting is dramatic, the extras are innumerable, and the budget for special effects is absolutely unlimited.

~YANN MARTEL, *LIFE OF PI*

KILIII YUYAN
Water trapped in chinks dug into a sandstone surface reflects the golden hue of the sun.

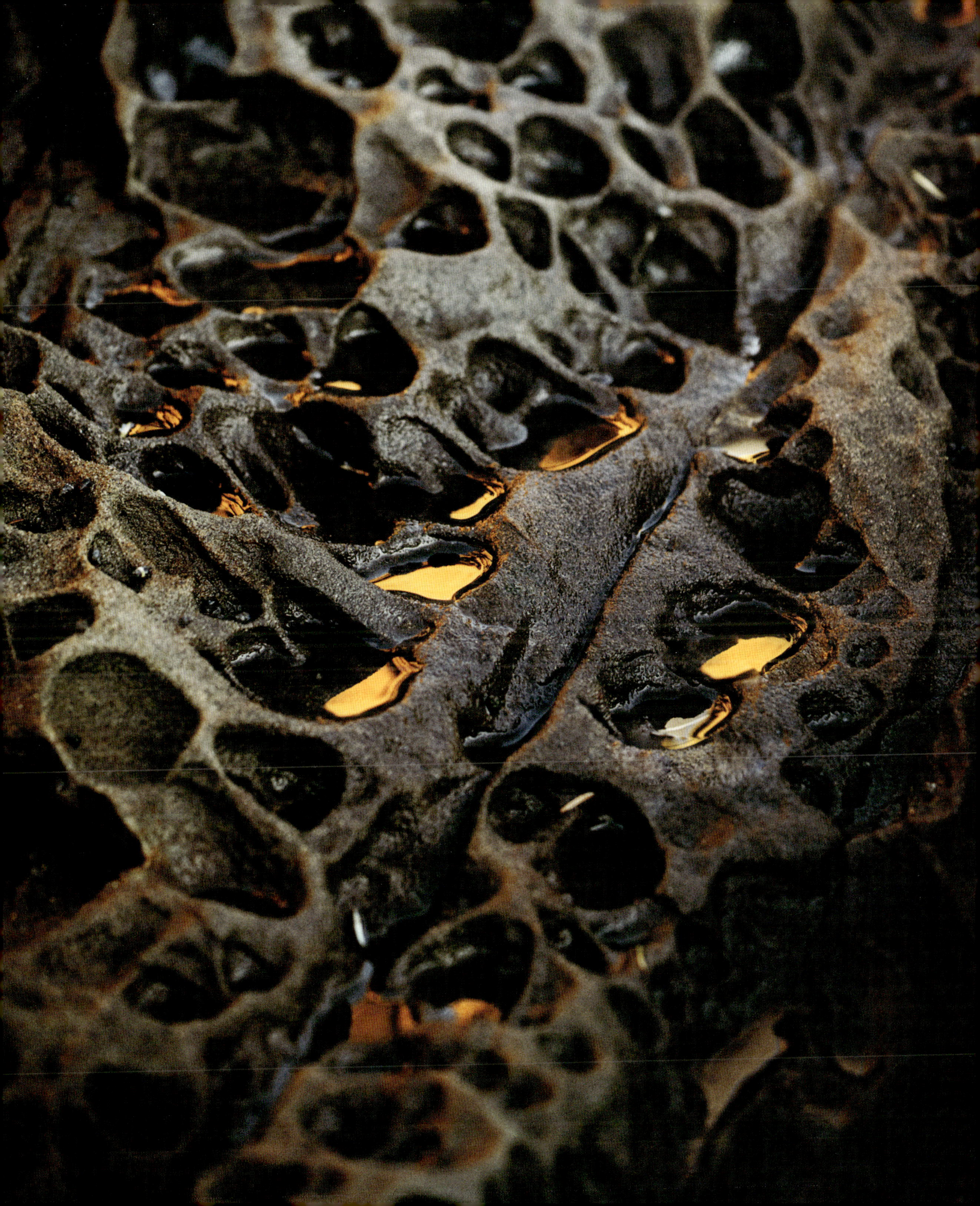

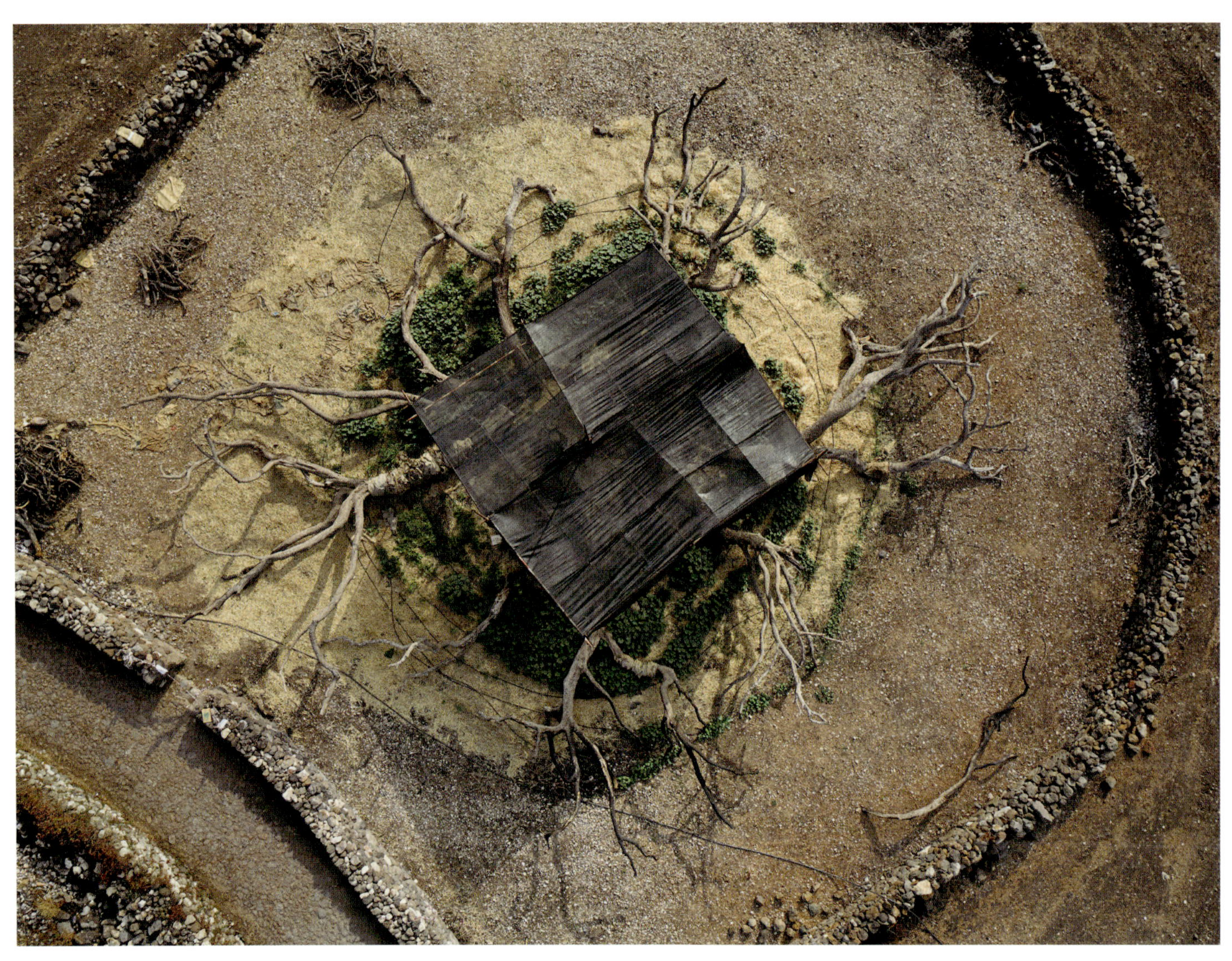

Victim of 2021 wildfires in west Sardinia, a thousand-year-old olive tree struggles to survive, protected by a tent designed to promote its revival.

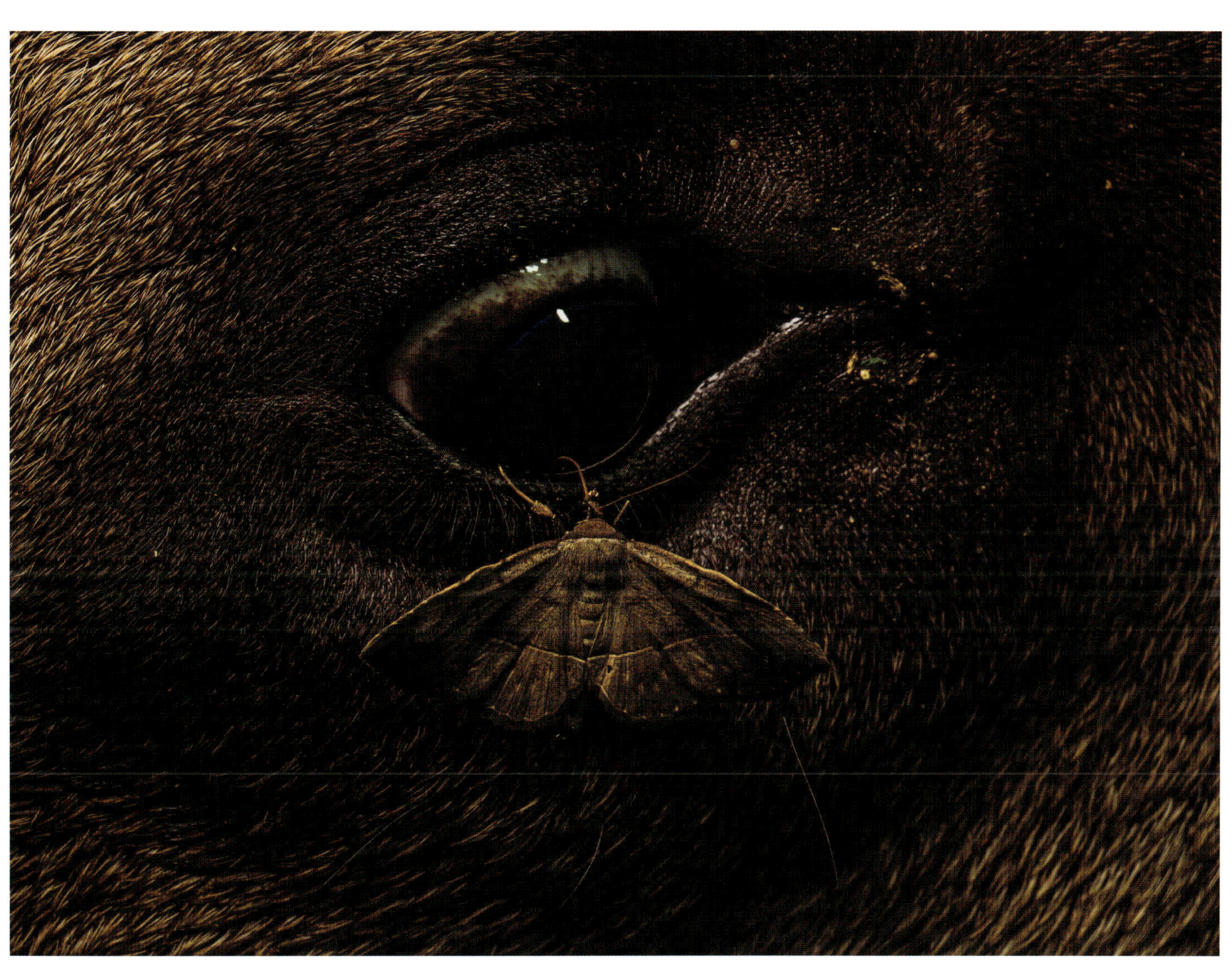

JAVIER AZNAR GONZÁLEZ DE RUEDA
A moth finds salt, essential for survival, by licking the tears of a tapir.

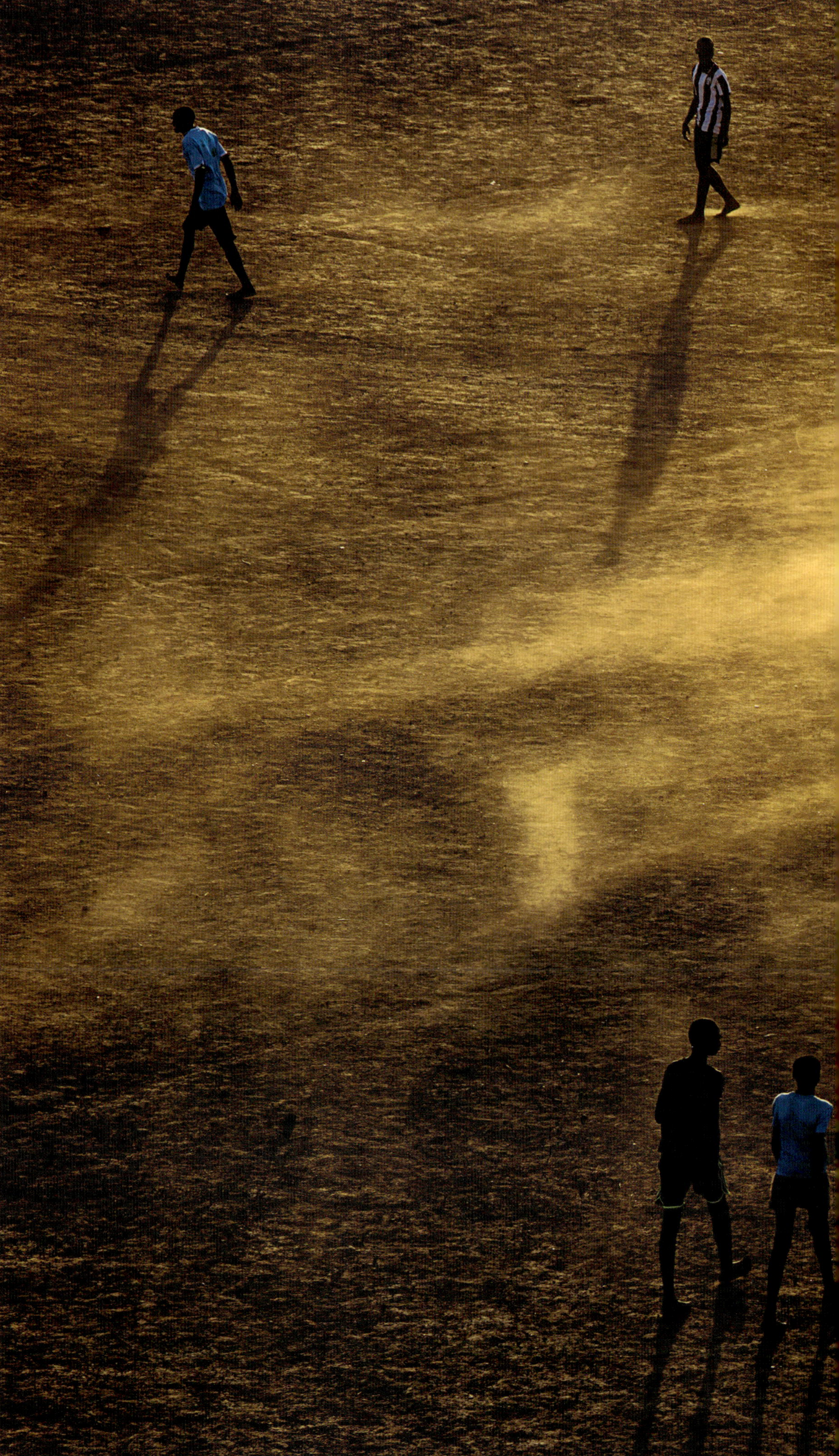

MICHAEL CHRISTOPHER BROWN
Boys stand tall, their evening
shadows even taller, as they play
football in the Kakuma Refugee
Camp in northwestern Kenya
near the borders of Uganda and
South Sudan.

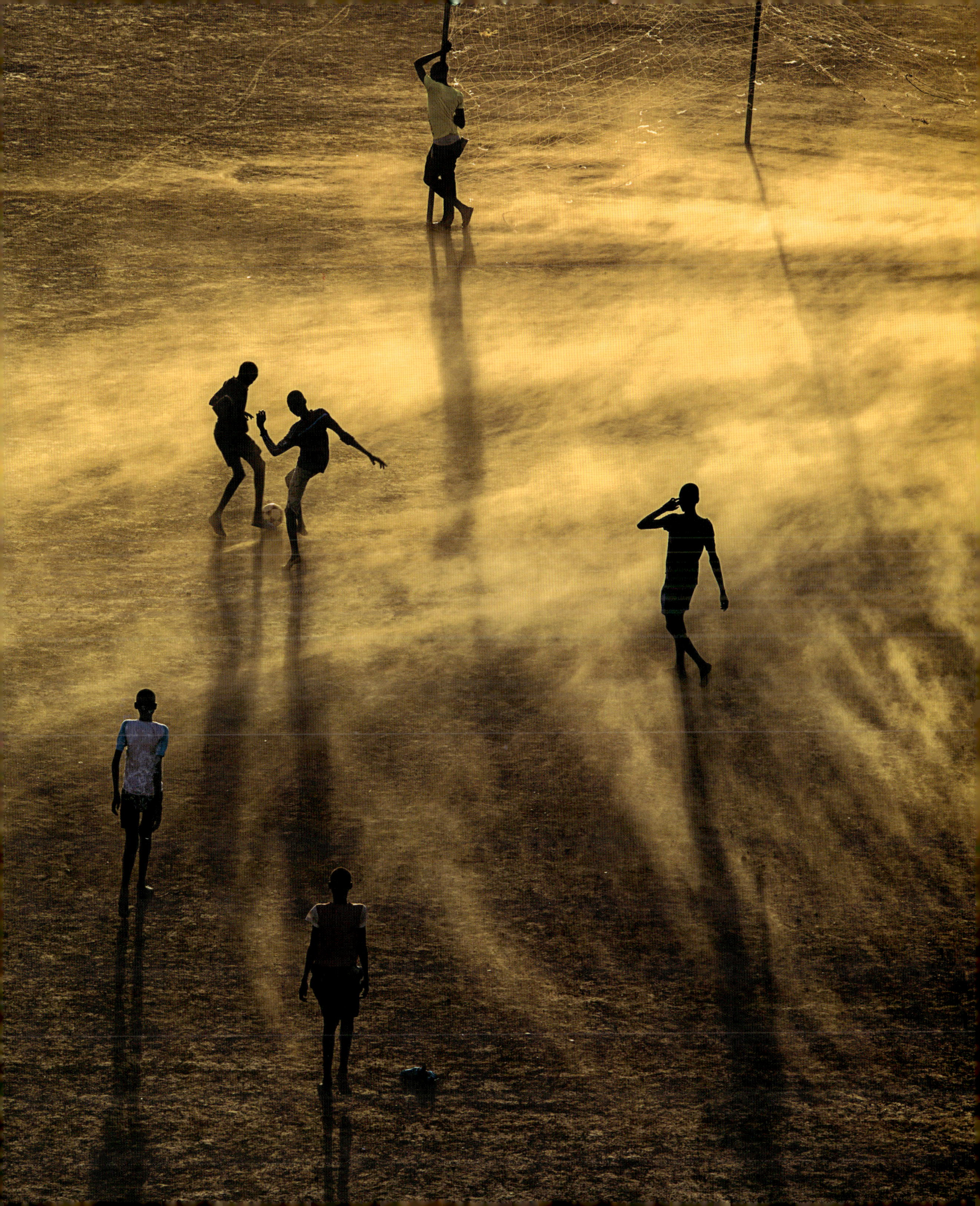

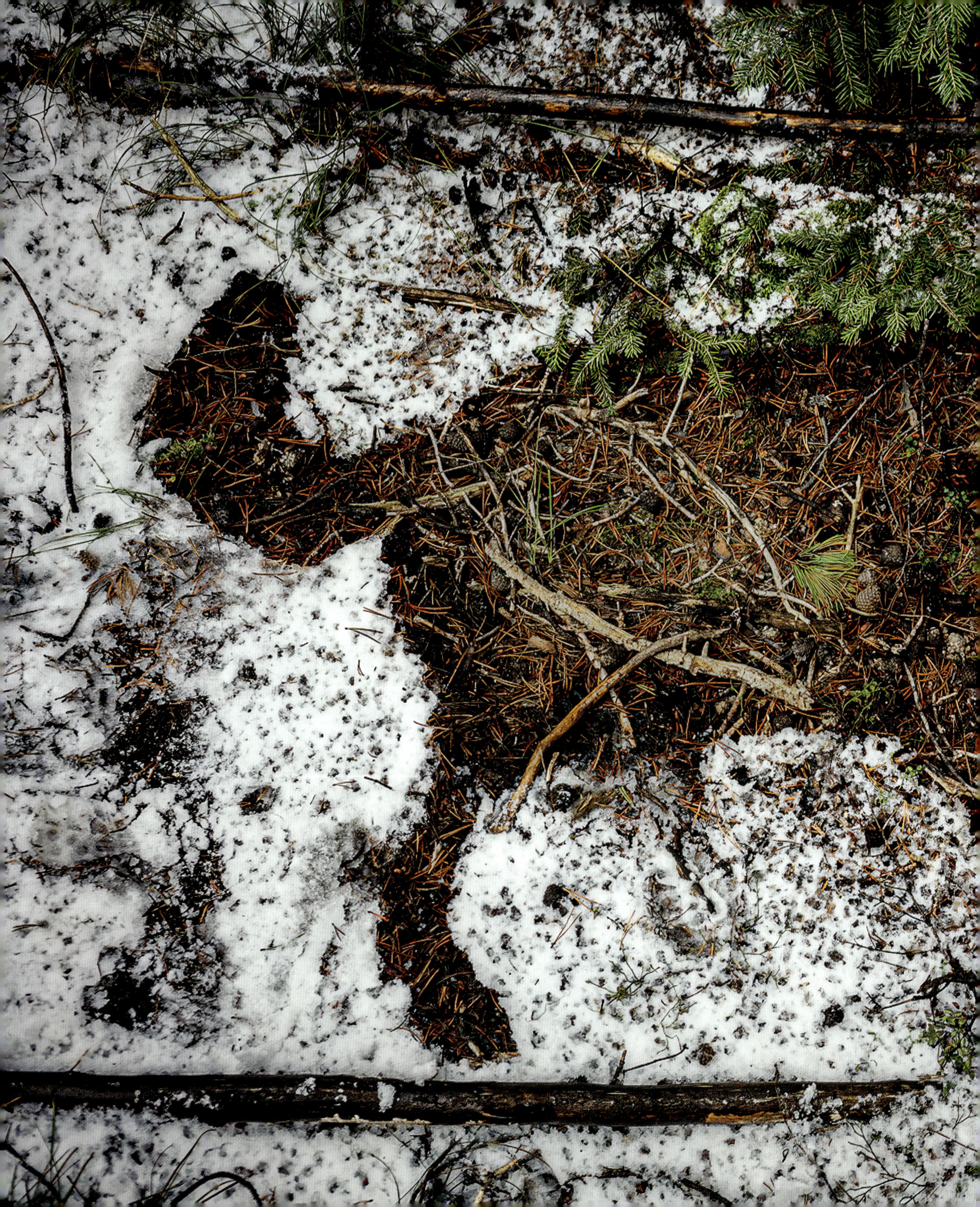

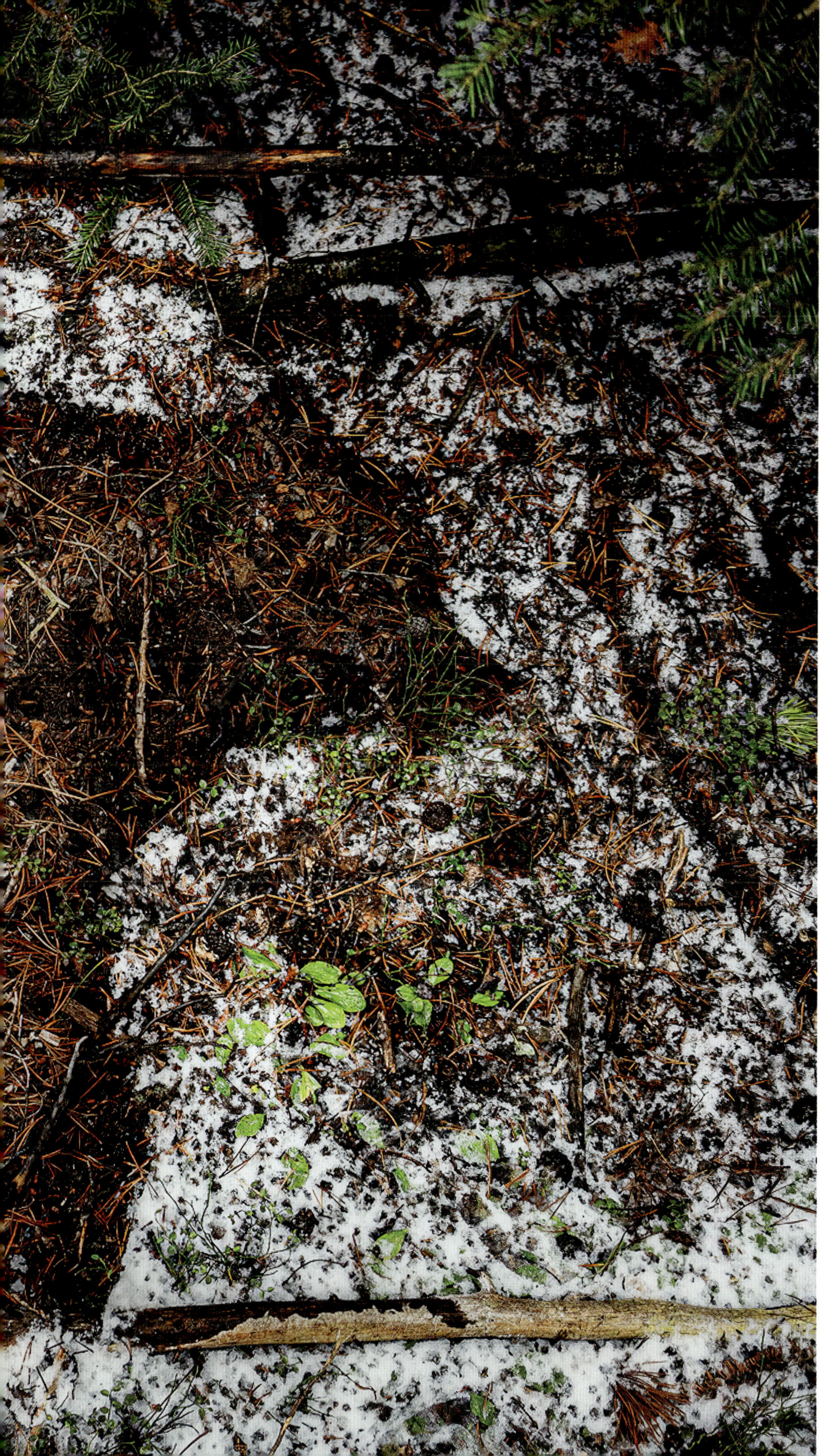

Rangers at Yellowstone National Park have removed a female wolf that died in the wild. Her silhouette remains, etched into snow-covered duff.

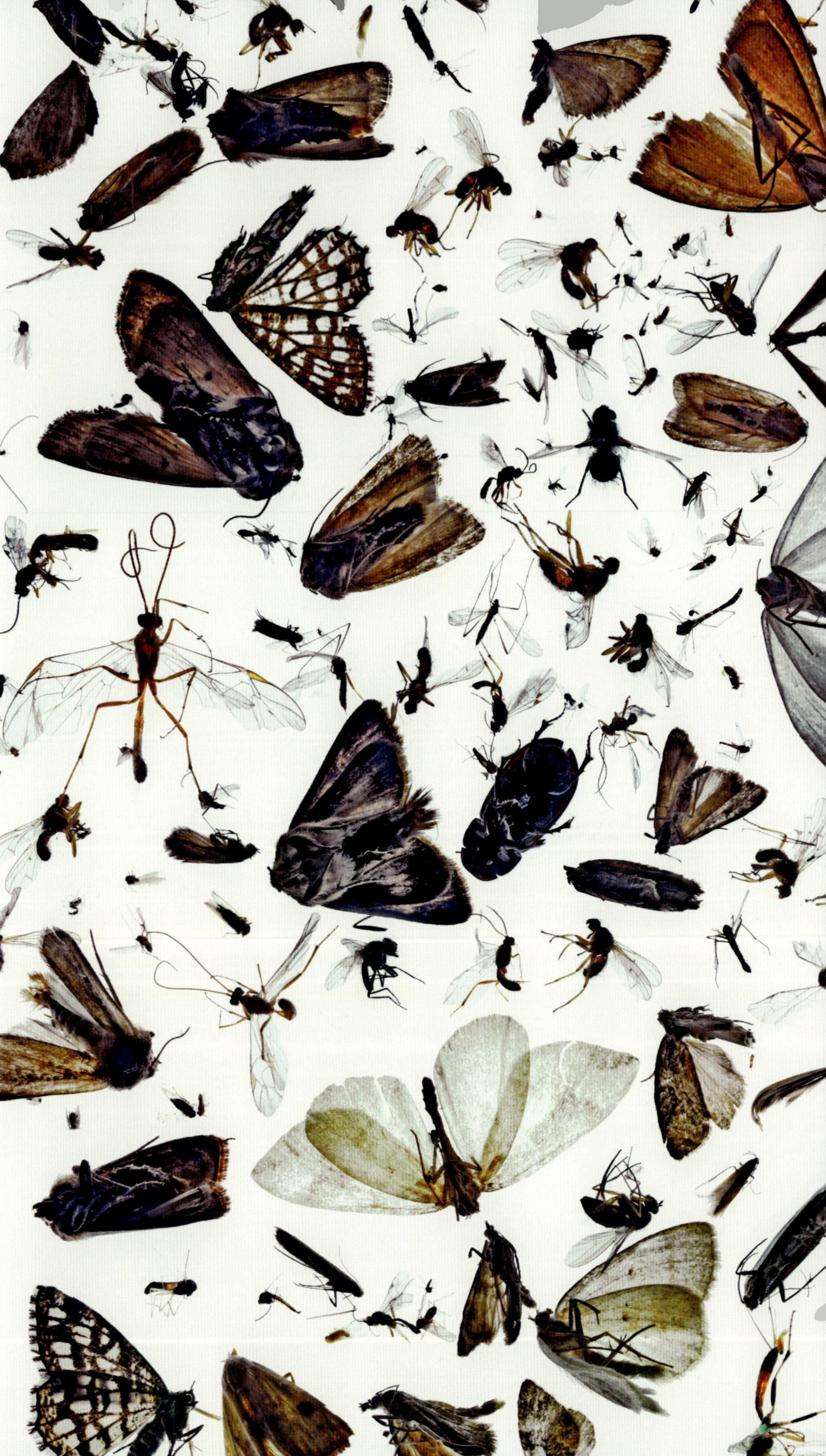

PÅL HERMANSEN
Attracted by night lights, which cost them their lives, a disorganized array of flying insects creates a tapestry of textures.

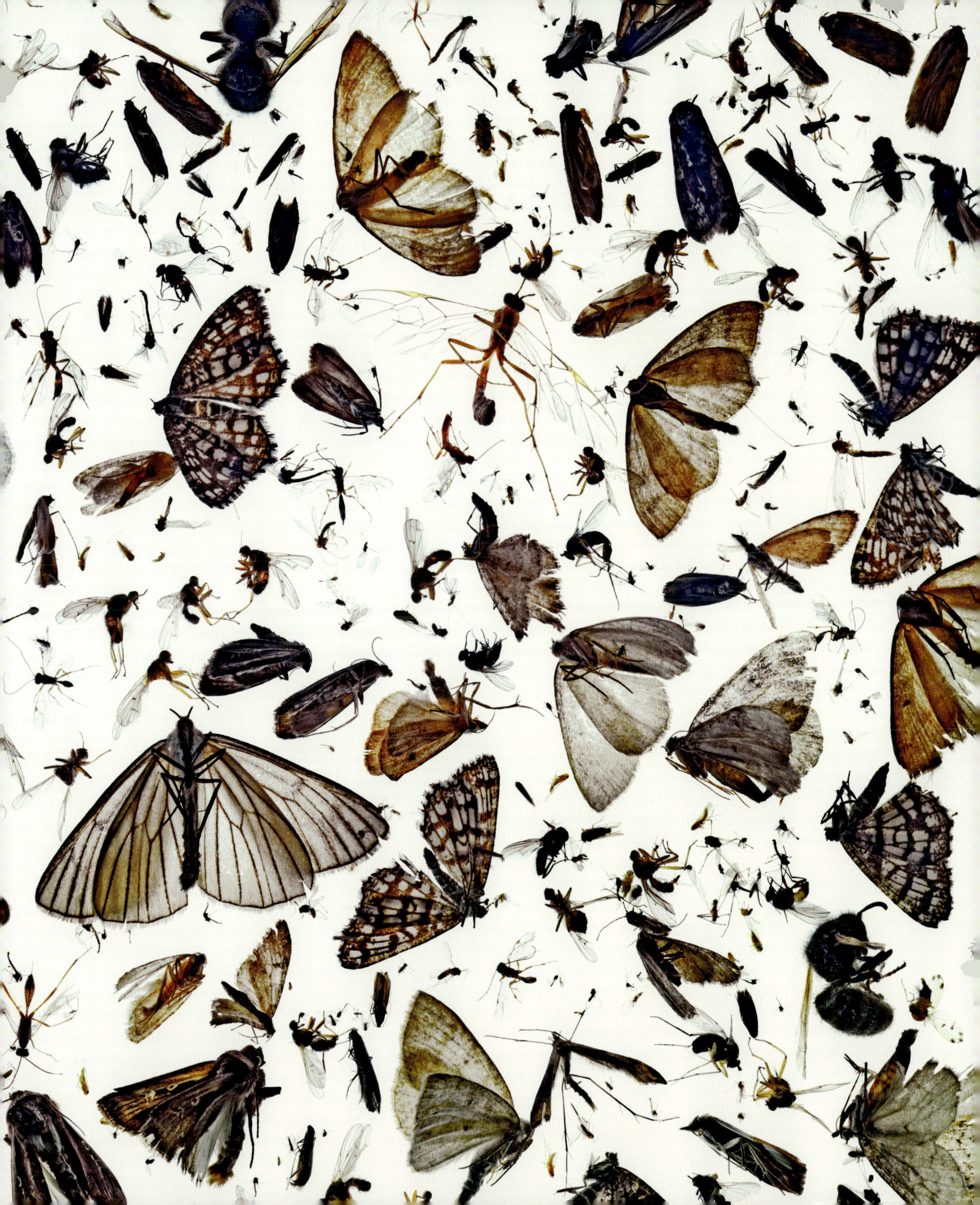

I had drifted o'er seas without ending, /
Under sinister grey-clouded skies /
That the many-fork'd lightning
is rending, / That resound with
hysterical cries

RYOTA KAJITA
Bubbles rise up and freeze inside a hole in the ice near Fairbanks, Alaska.

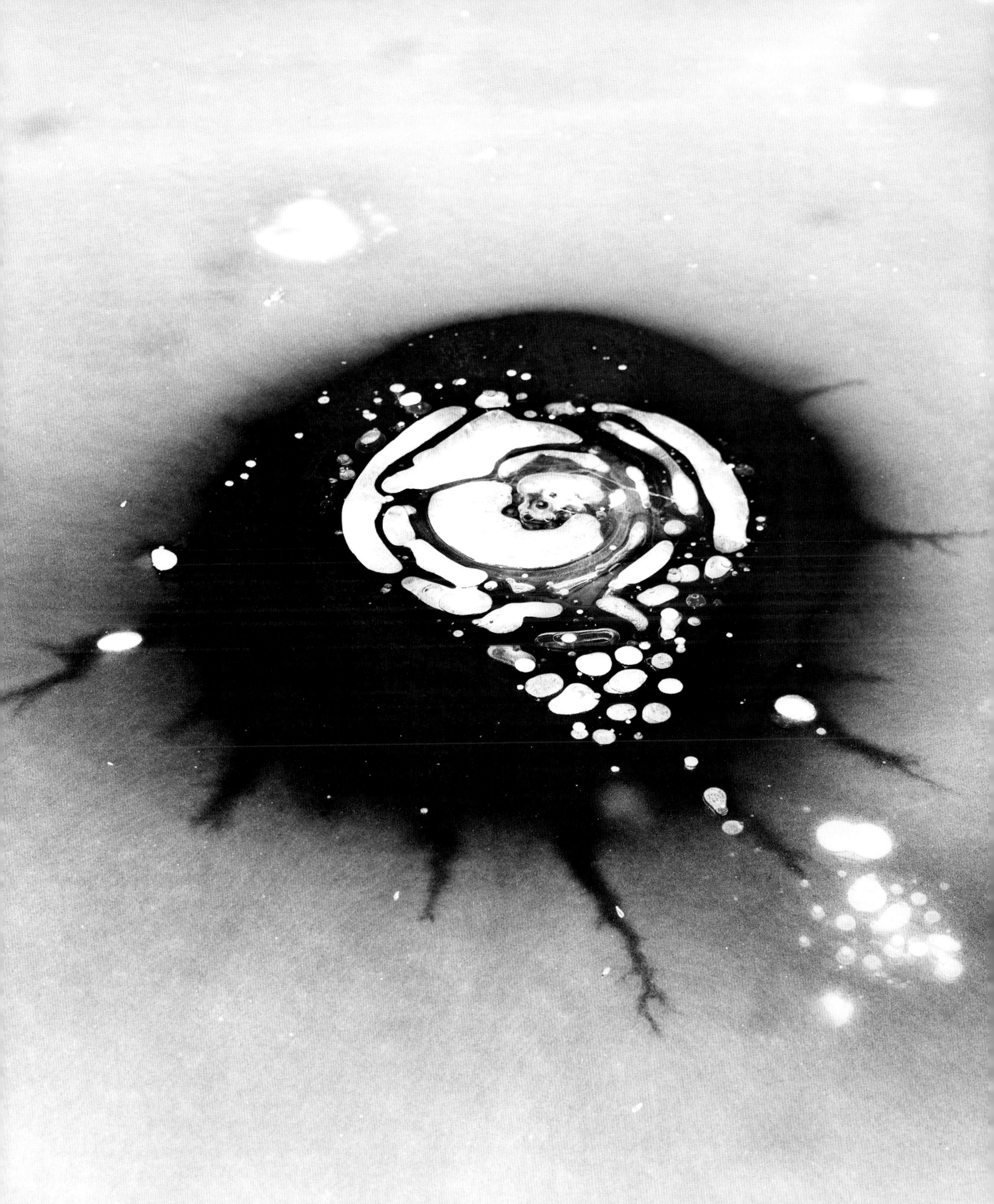

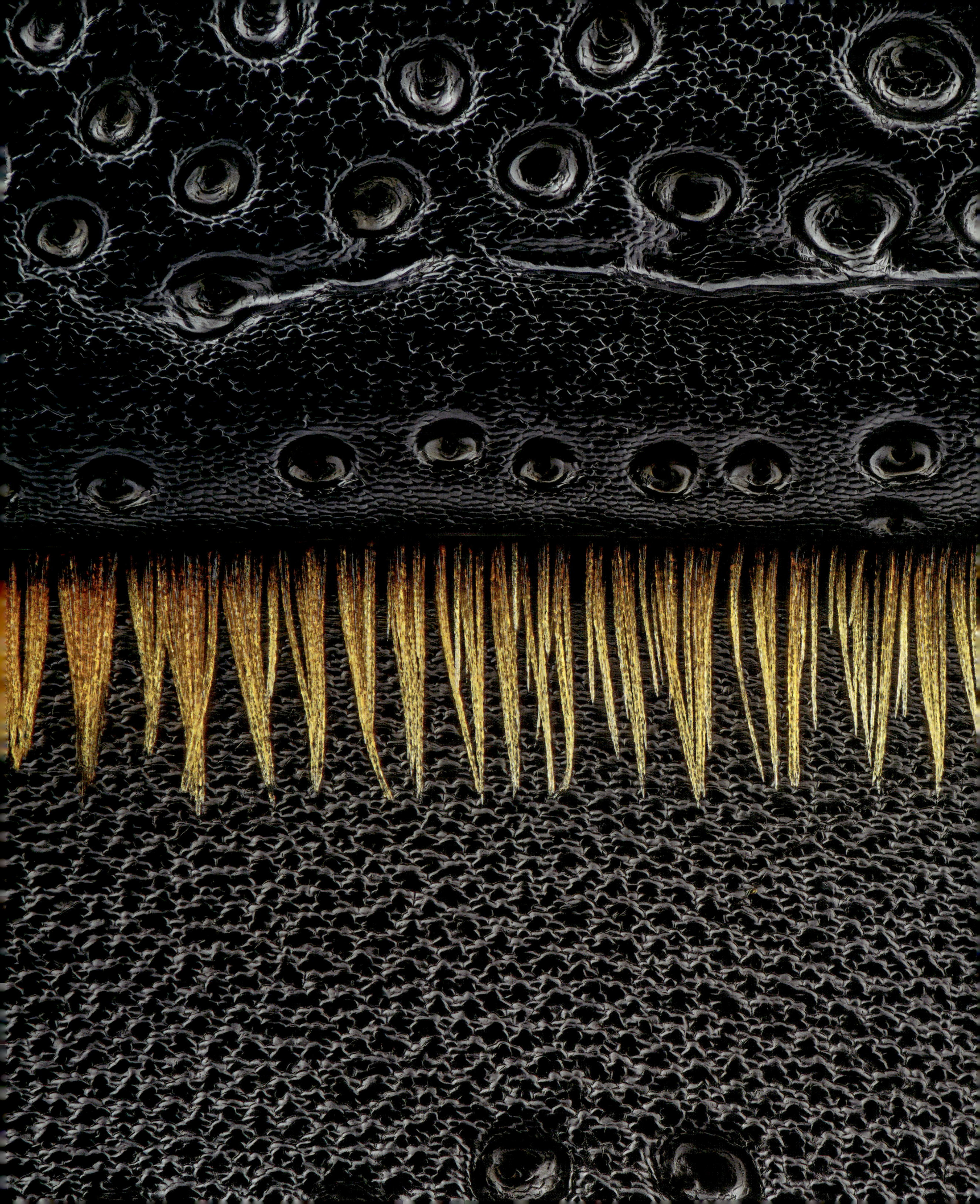

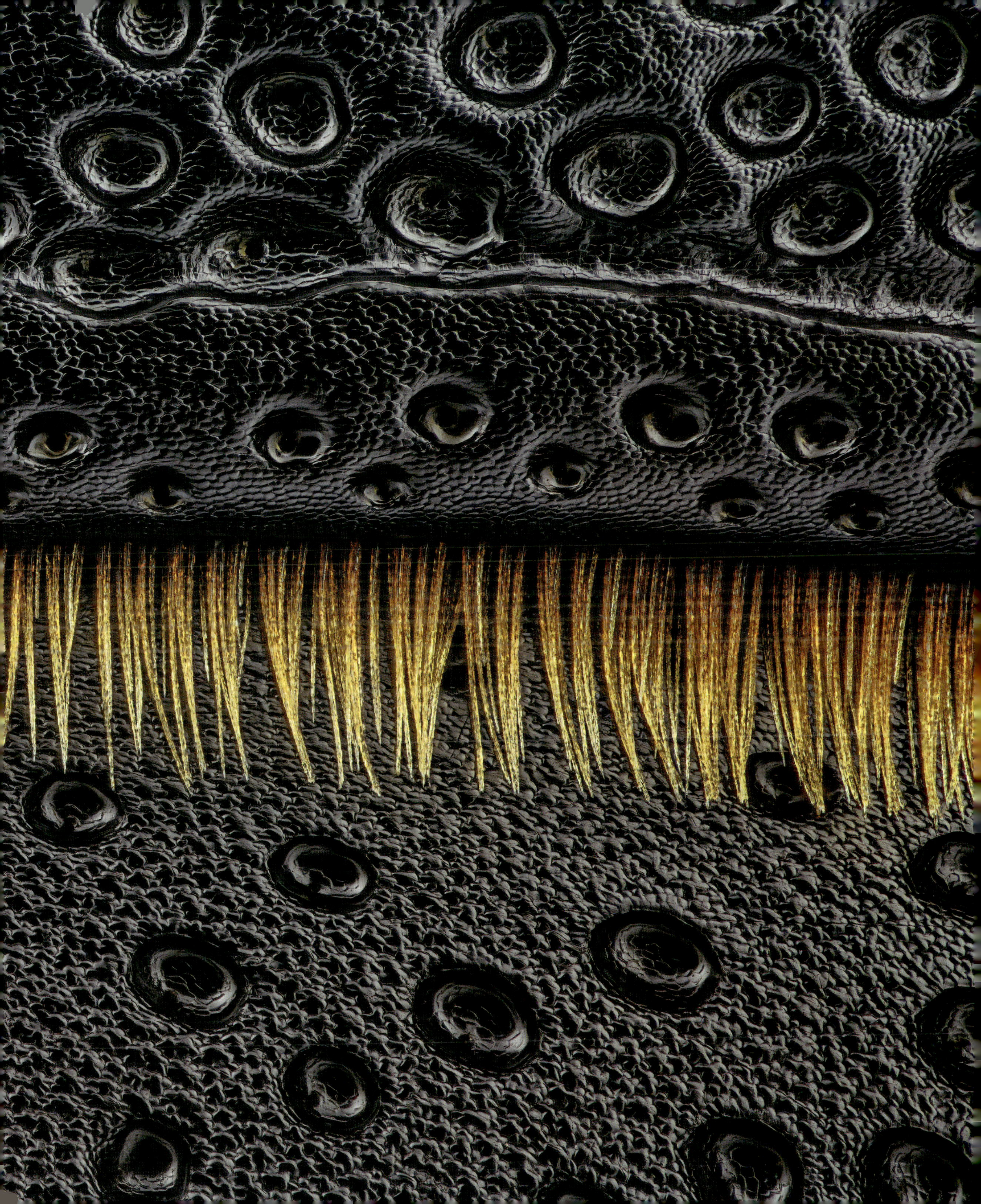

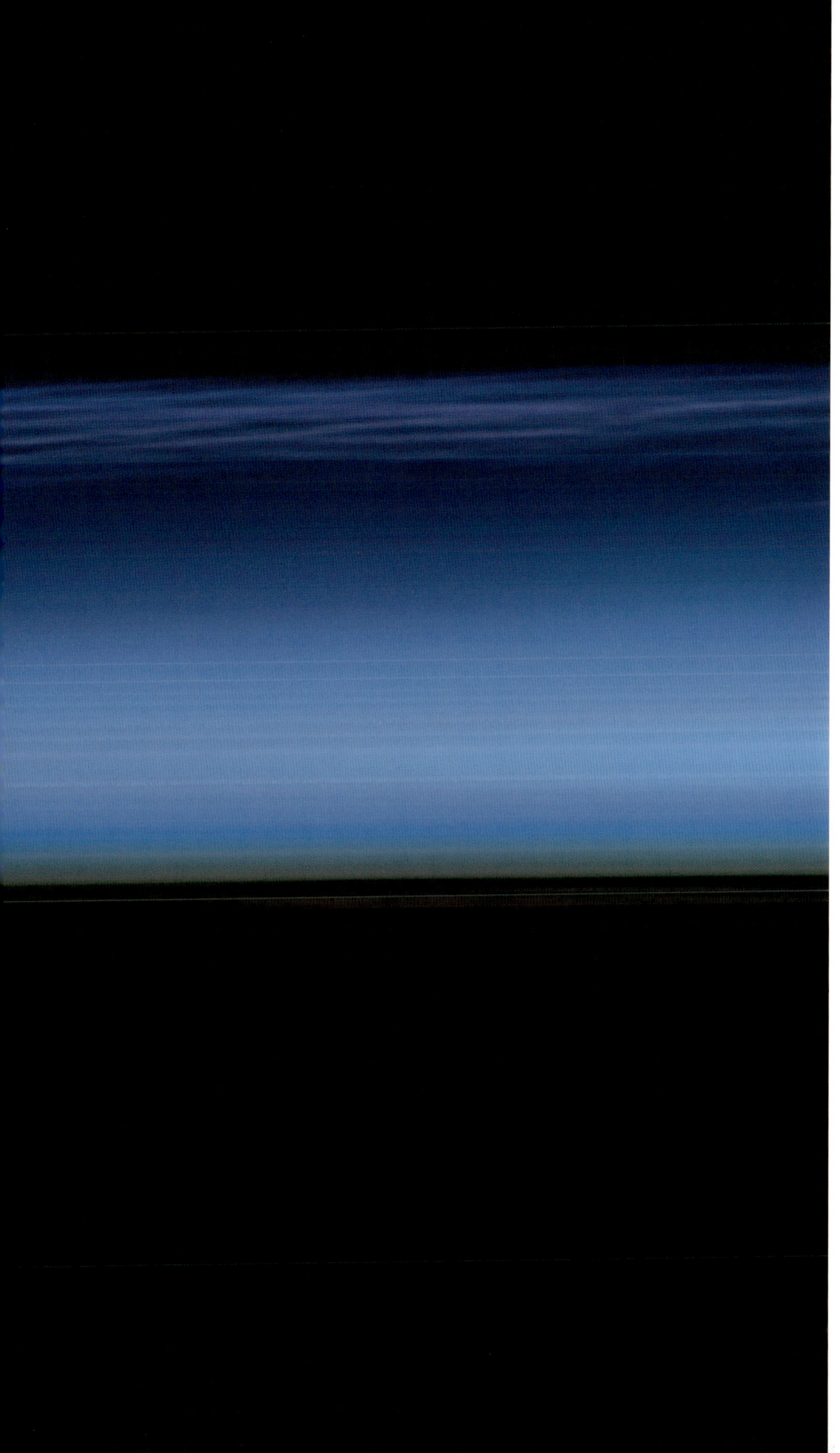

NASA–JSC
An image from the International Space Station captures rare polar mesospheric clouds, often called "noctilucent" for their ropy brilliance against the darkness of space.

Previous pages:
THORBEN DANKE
A stubble of fine hairs curtains the joint between the head and body of a stag beetle.

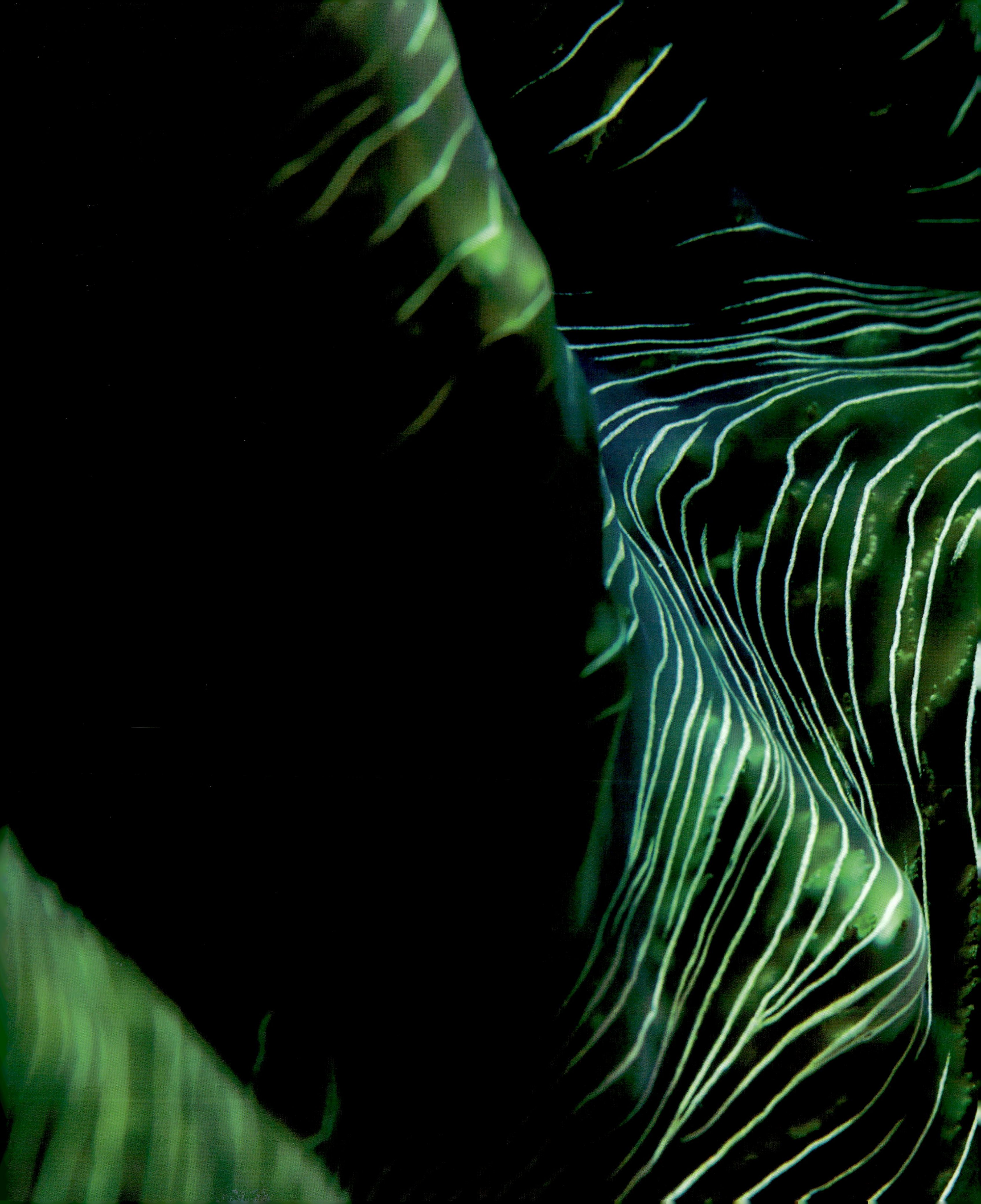

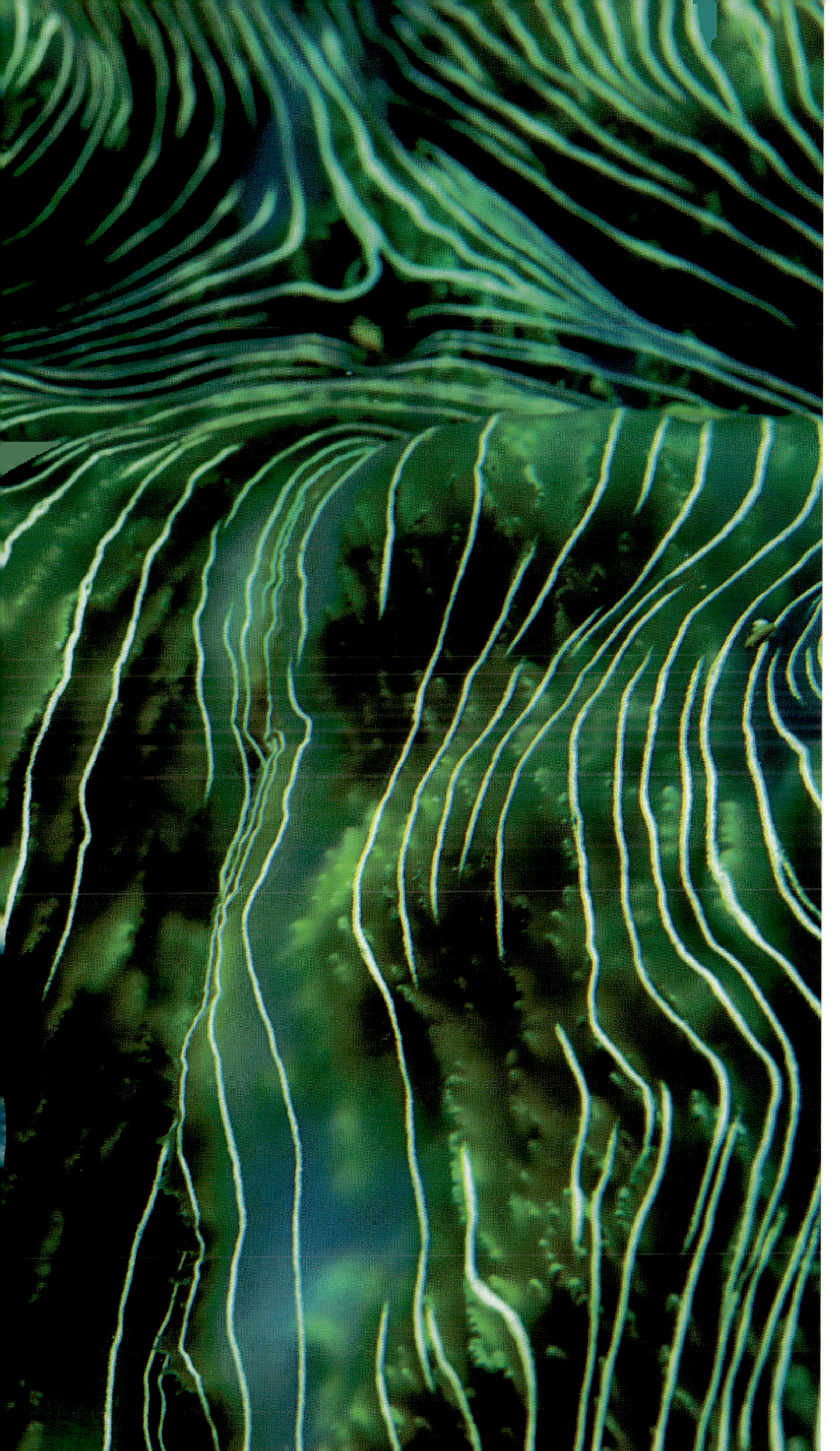

MATTIAS KLUM
Bends and curves stream across
the surface of a giant clam in the
Raja Ampat archipelago of
Indonesia.

Following pages:
BACHIR MOUKARZEL
Rectilinear geometries of human
architecture, including the famous
Rialto Bridge, contrast with the
natural curve of Venice's Grand
Canal.

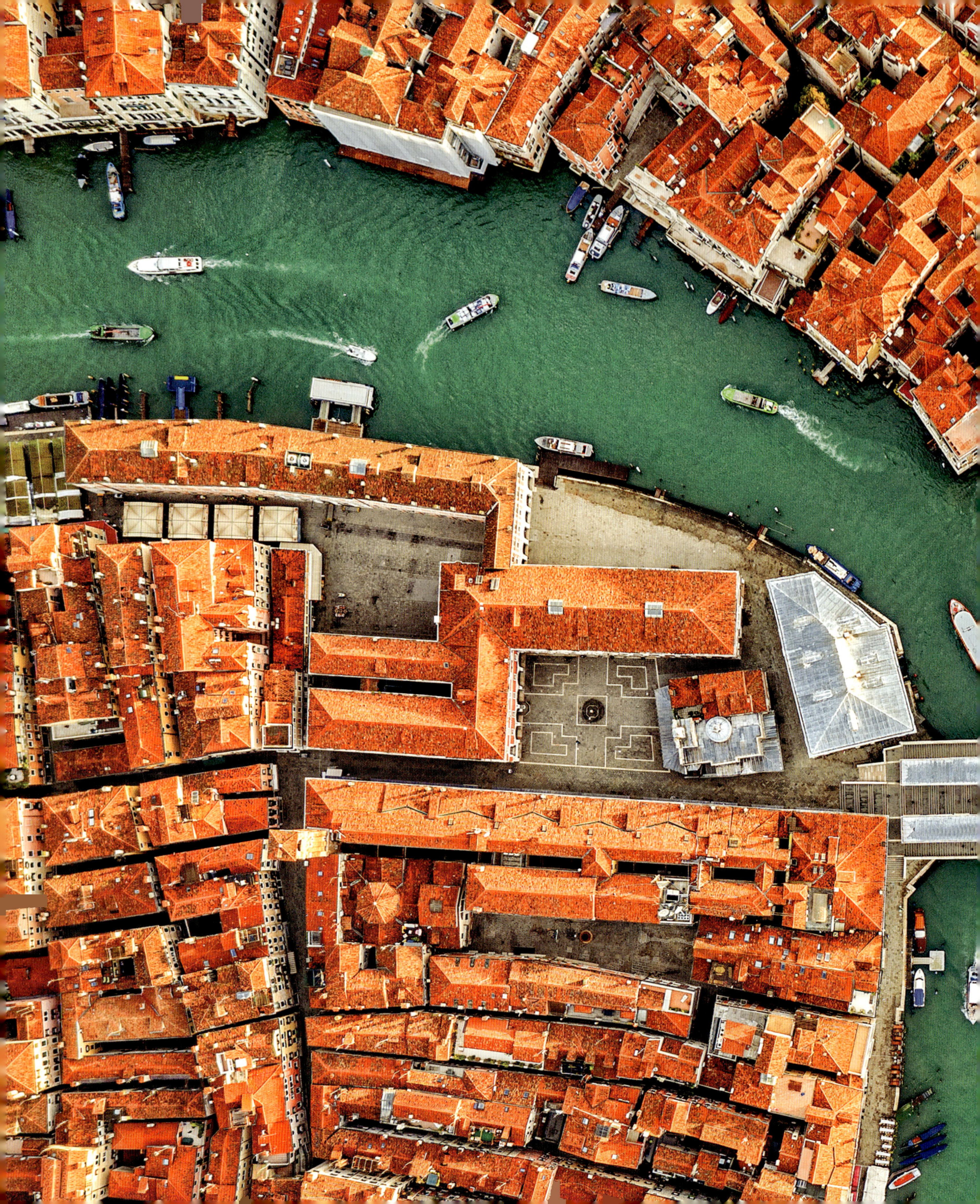

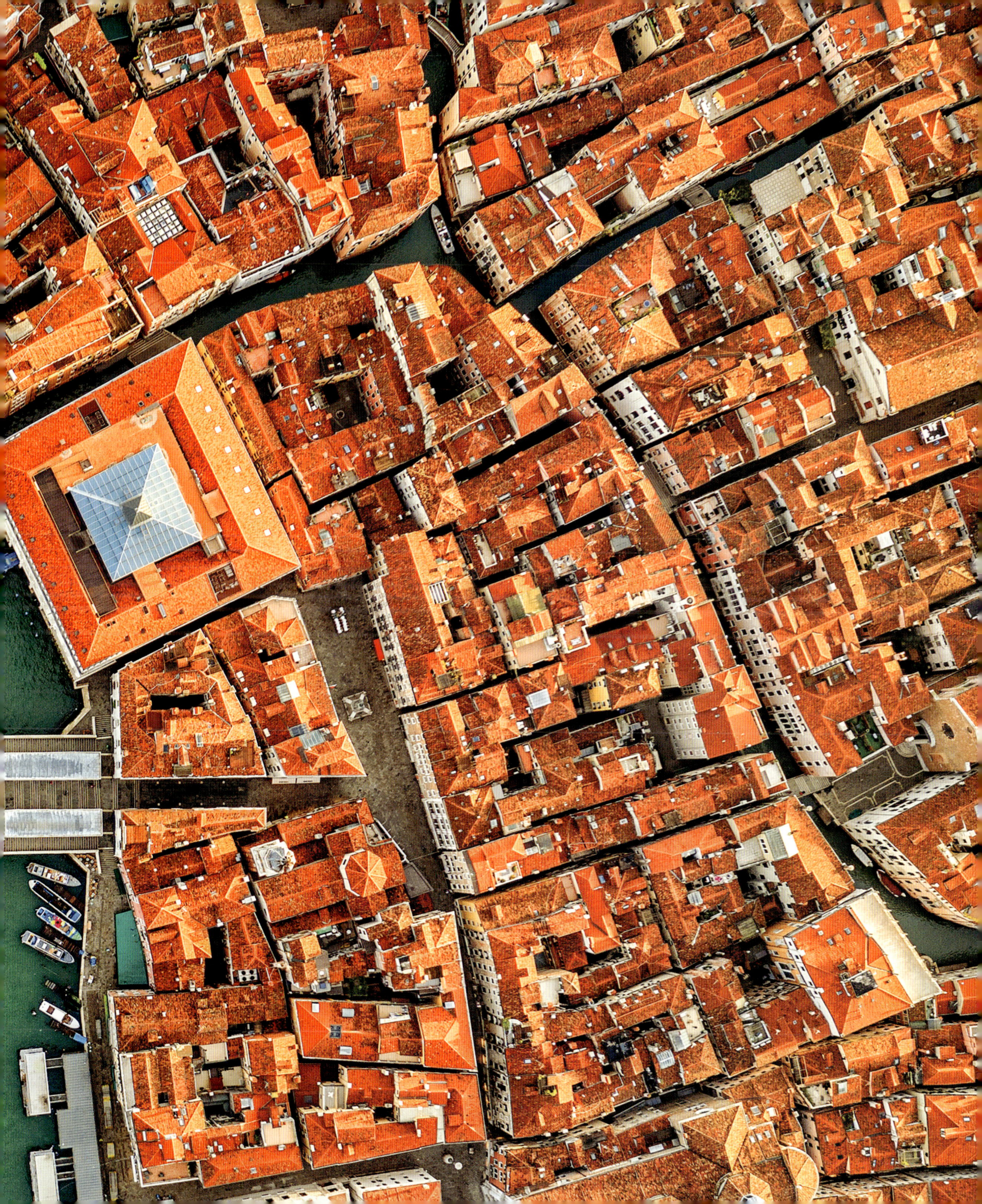

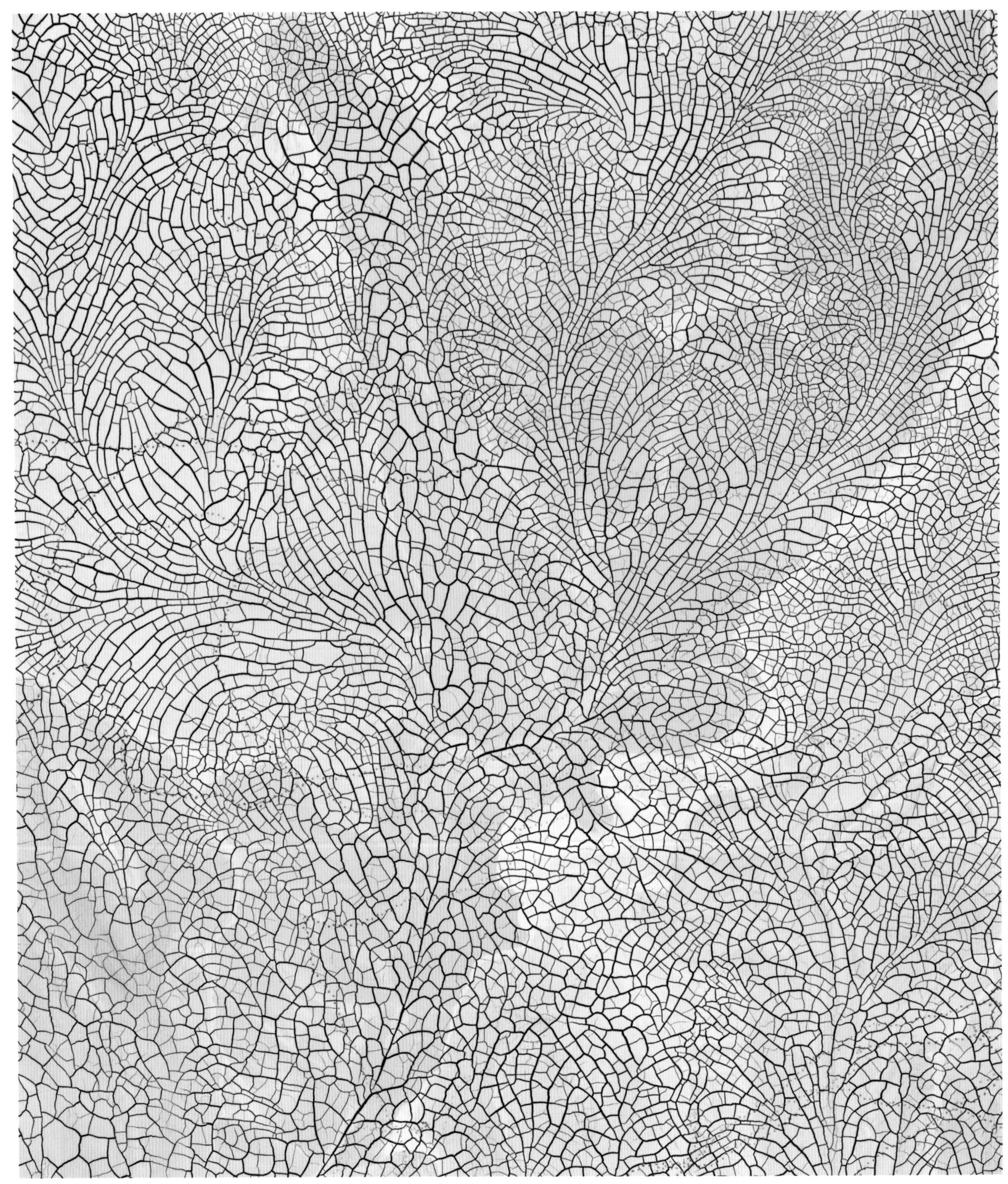

KACPER KOWALSKI
Cracks in ash created at Poland's Belchatów coal-fired power station

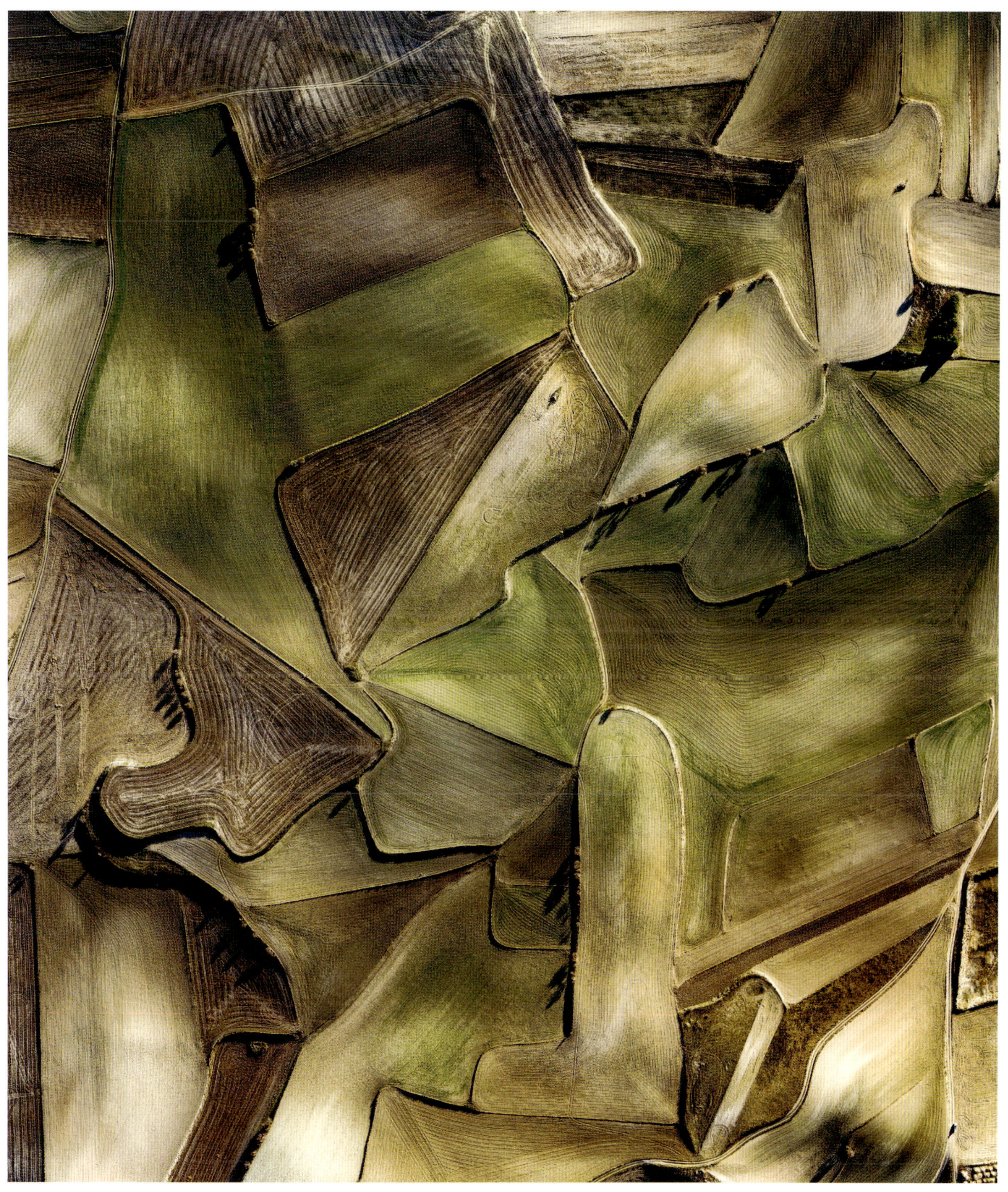

MILAN RADISICS
The farmers of Esquivias, Spain, long ago divided the terrain into resident polygons, seeking to level the land to capture precious rainfall.

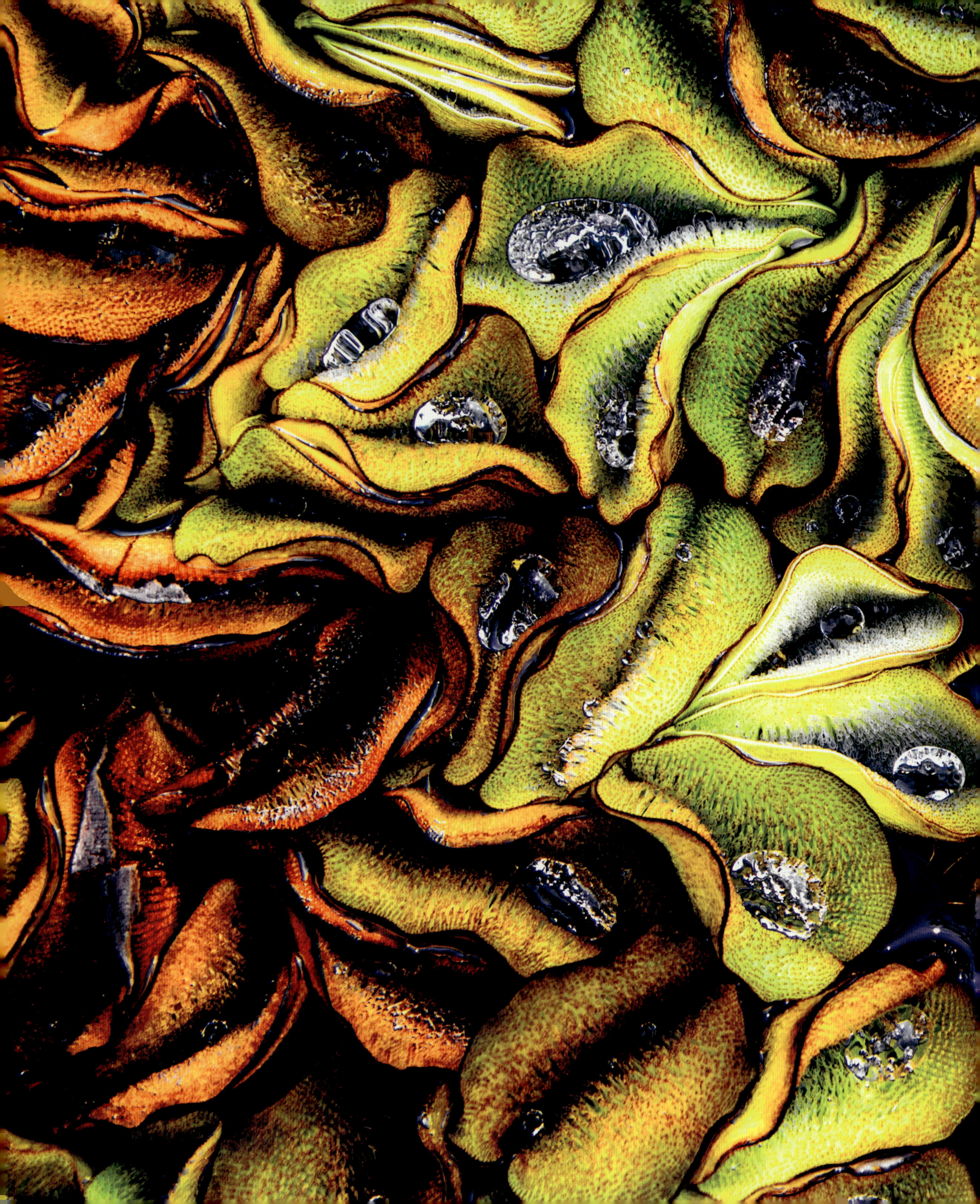

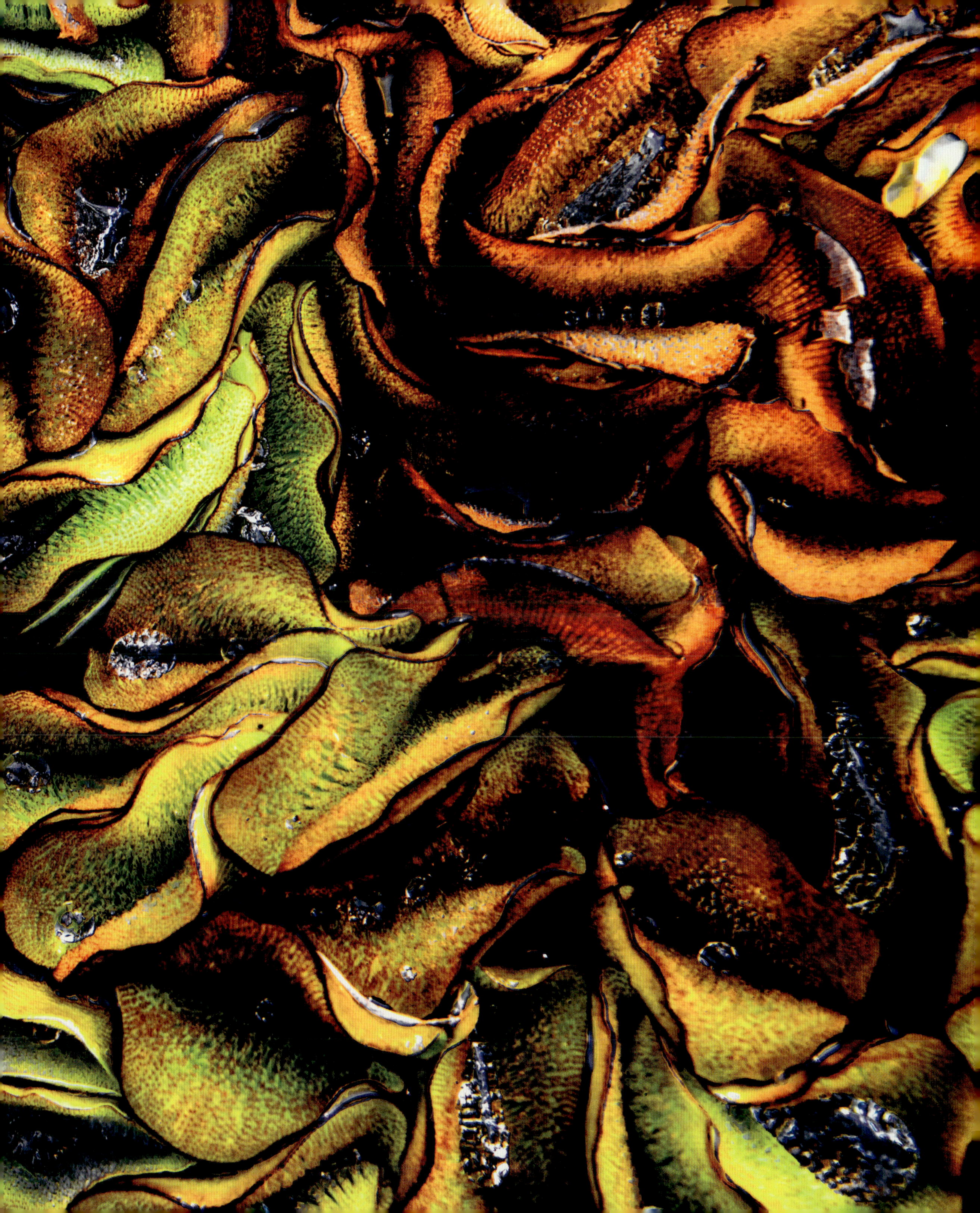

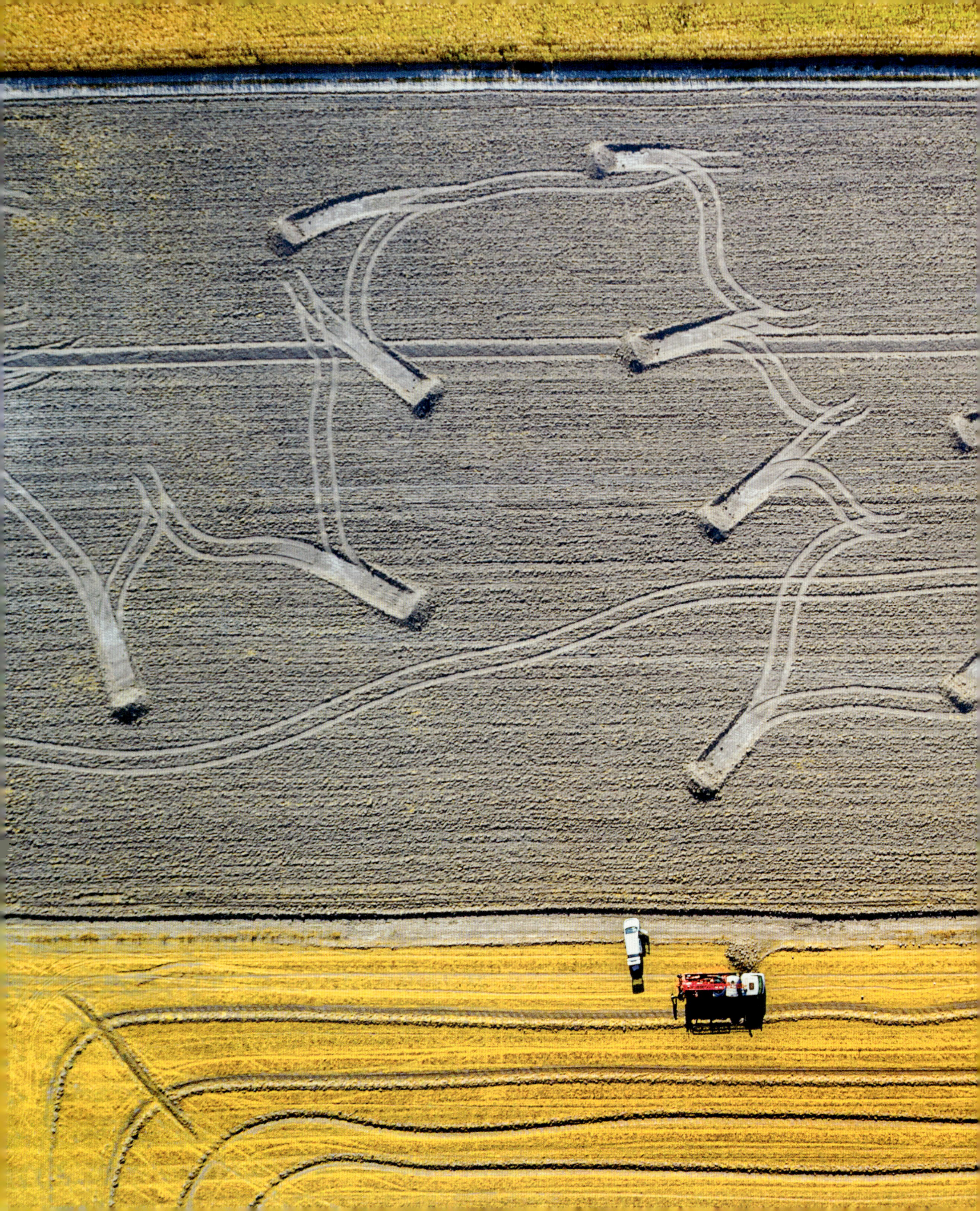

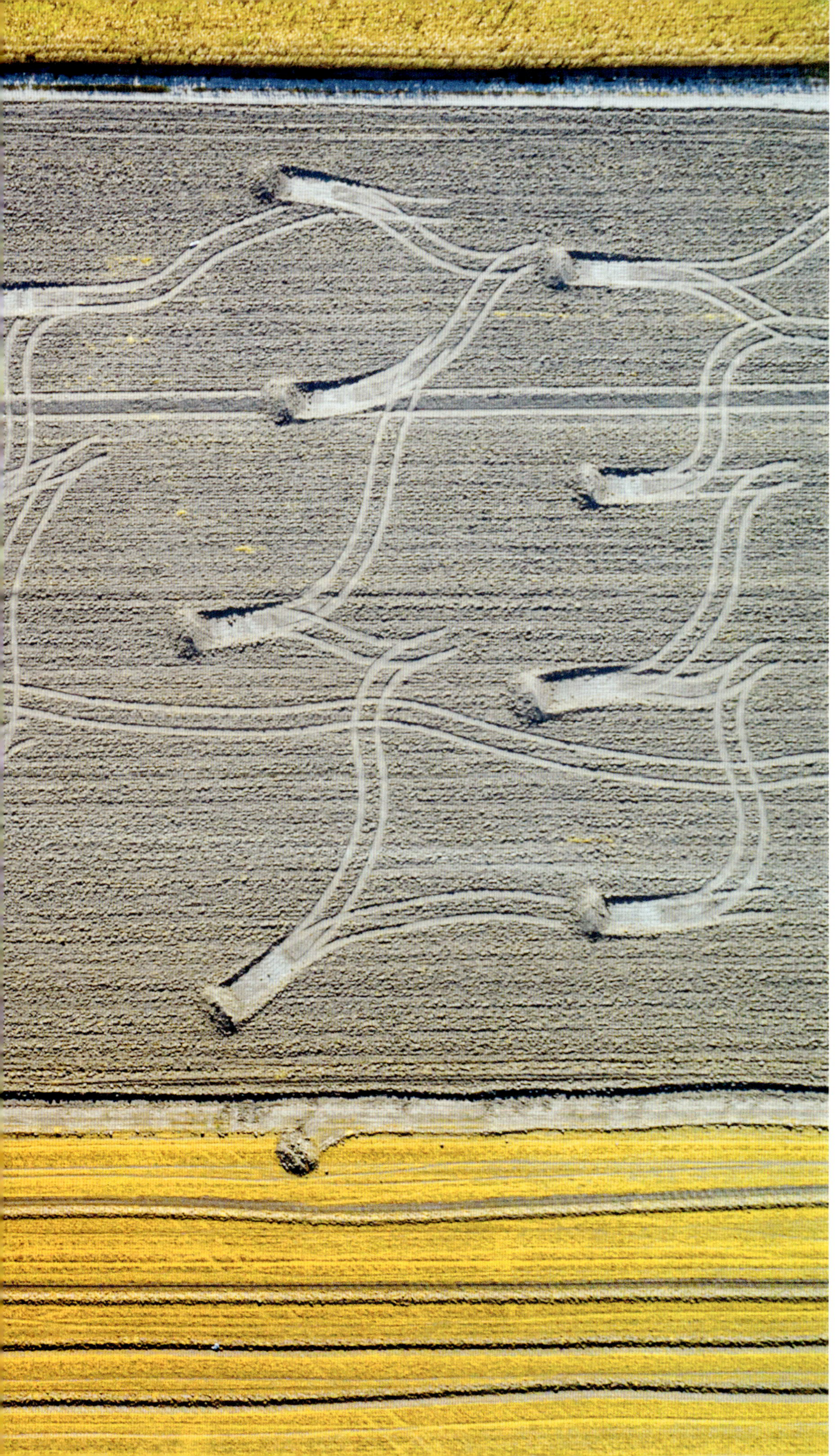

MUSTAFA BINOL
Digging deeper: Fields once fertile now require irrigation, to be provided by deeper wells being dug by heavy equipment.

Previous pages:
YINGTING SHIH
Like pearls in a crowd of verdant oysters, drops of water glisten in the folds of tiny pond-dwelling plants.

It is a narrow
mind which
cannot look at
a subject from
various points
of view.

DASHA PLESEN
By growing various types of mold in a petri dish, the artist creates a surprisingly beautiful tableau.

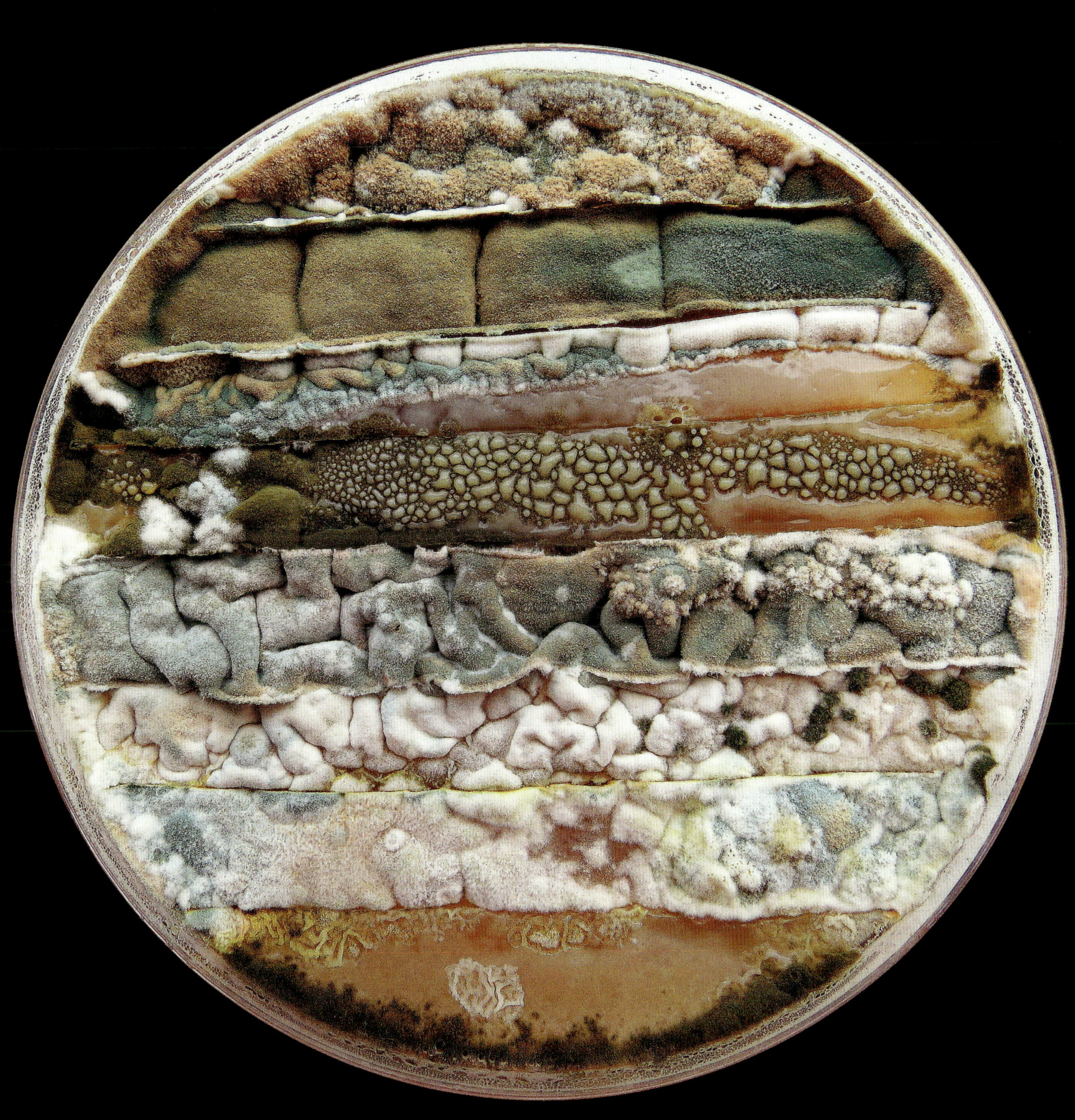

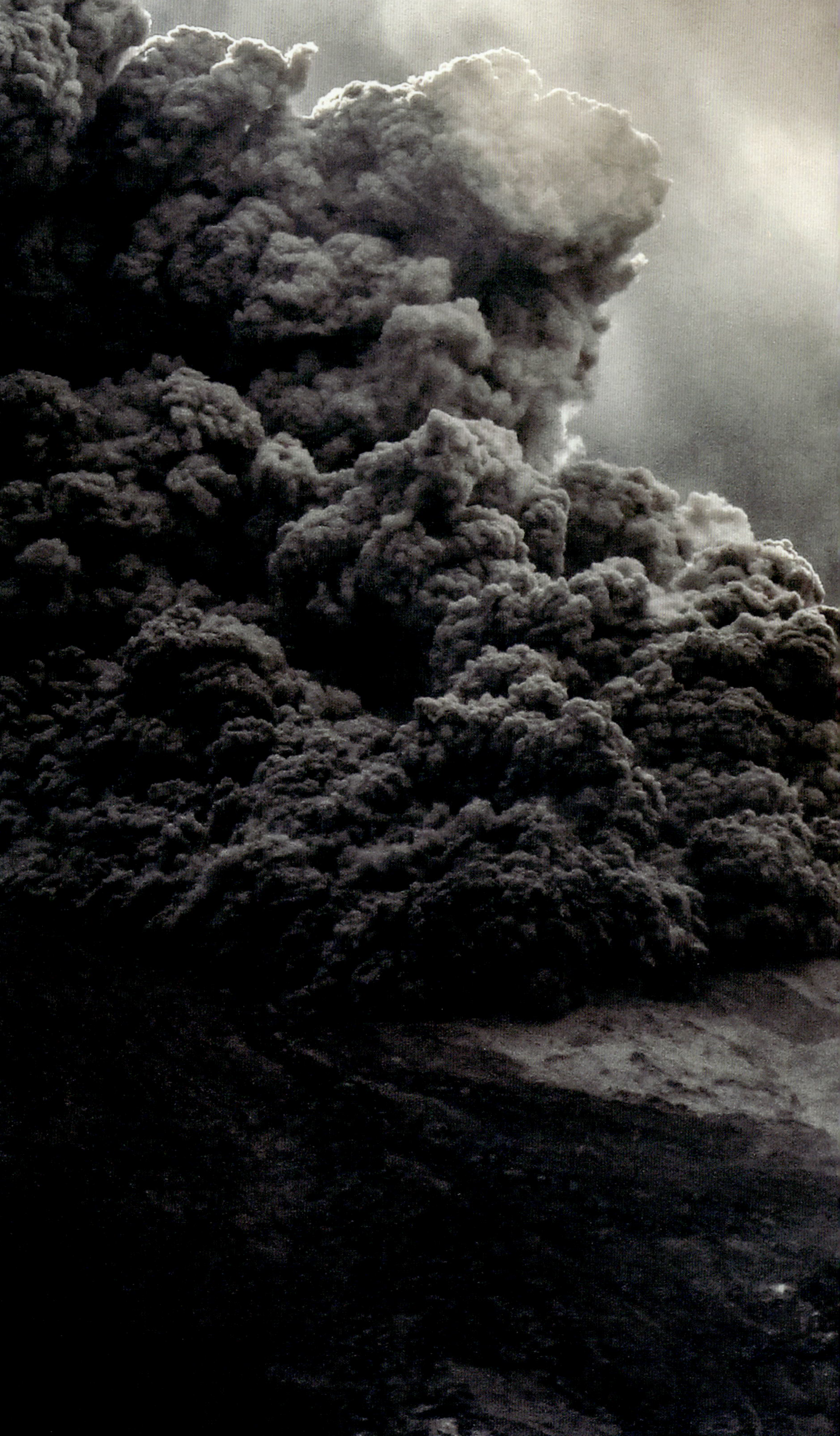

ALBERT IVAN DAMANIK
Volcanic effluent billows, flows, and fogs, emerging from Mount Sinabung near the village of Jeraya, North Sumatra, Indonesia.

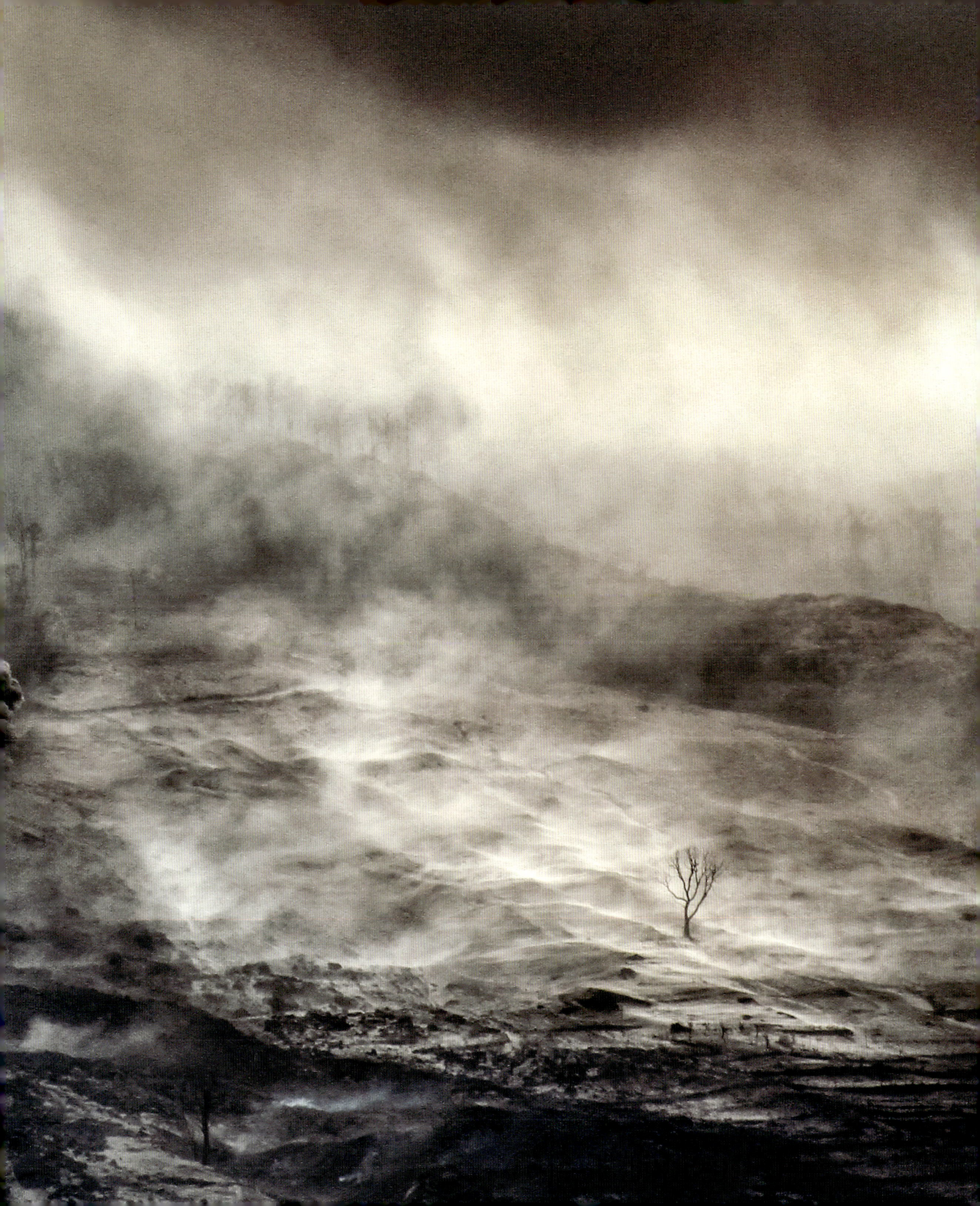

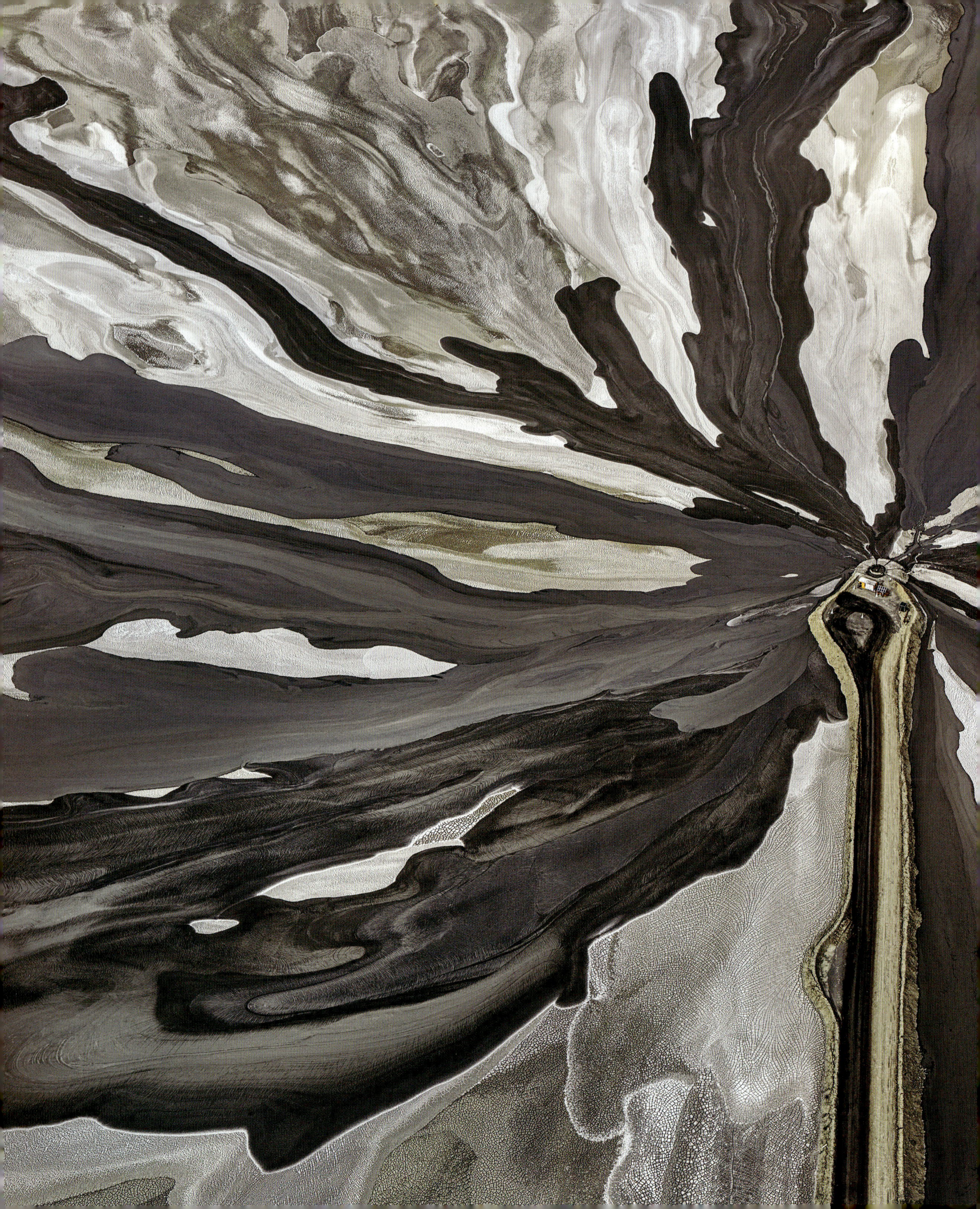

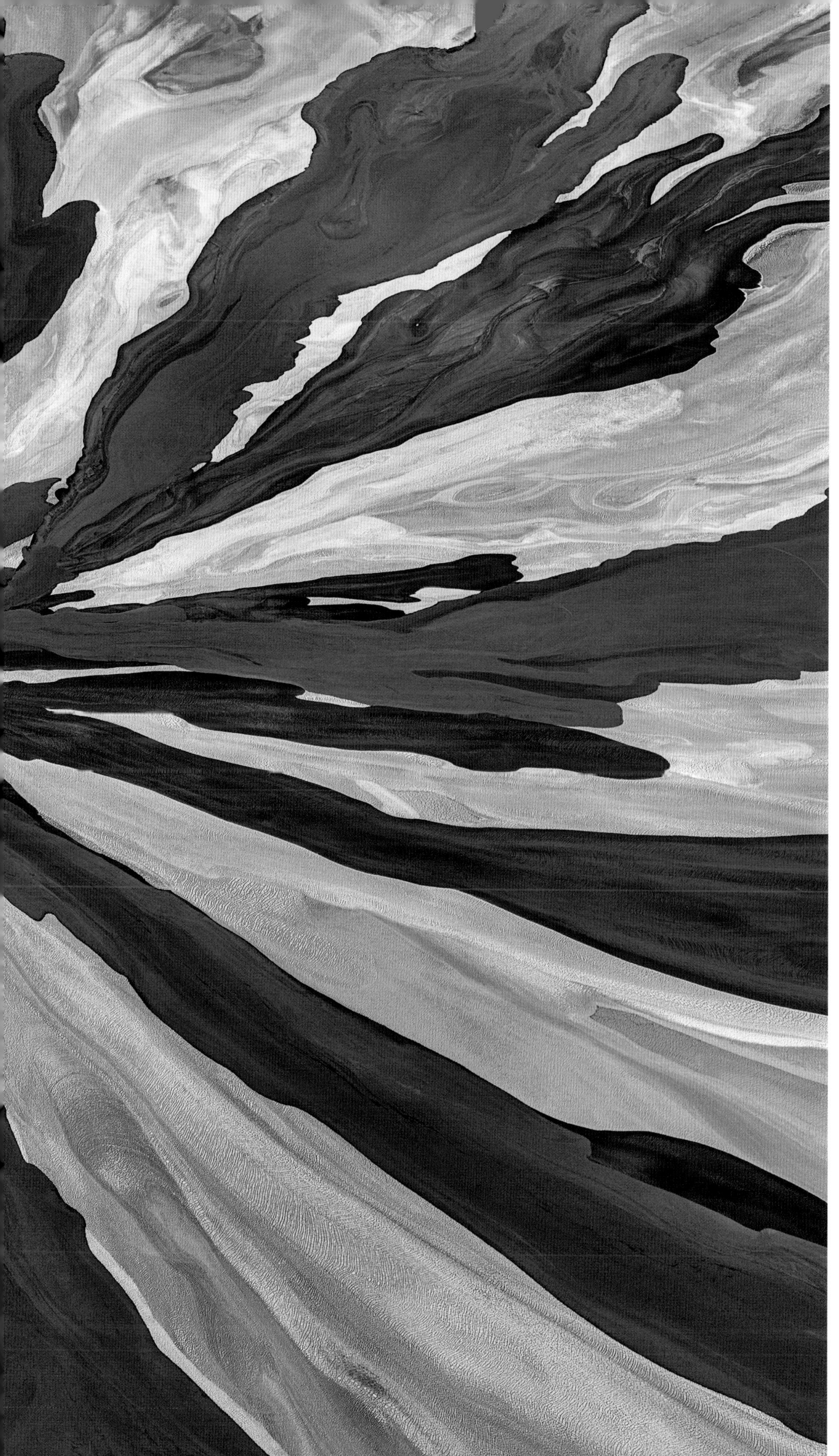

EDWARD BURTYNSKY
Tailings ponds radiate from a
diamond mine in South Africa.

315

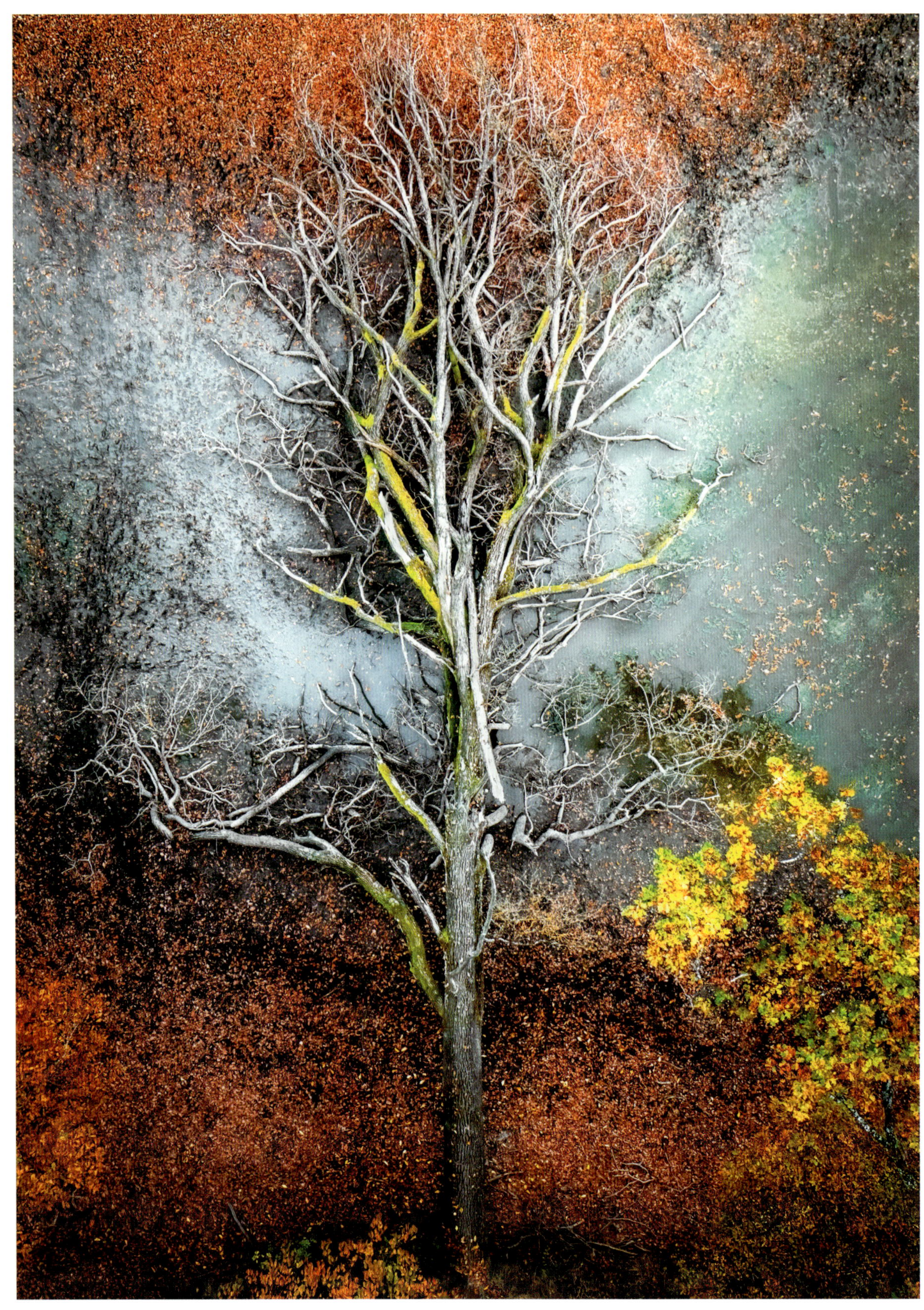

DANIEL FRANC

In South Bohemia, a fallen tree traverses autumnal colors and a pond deliberately emptied for winter.

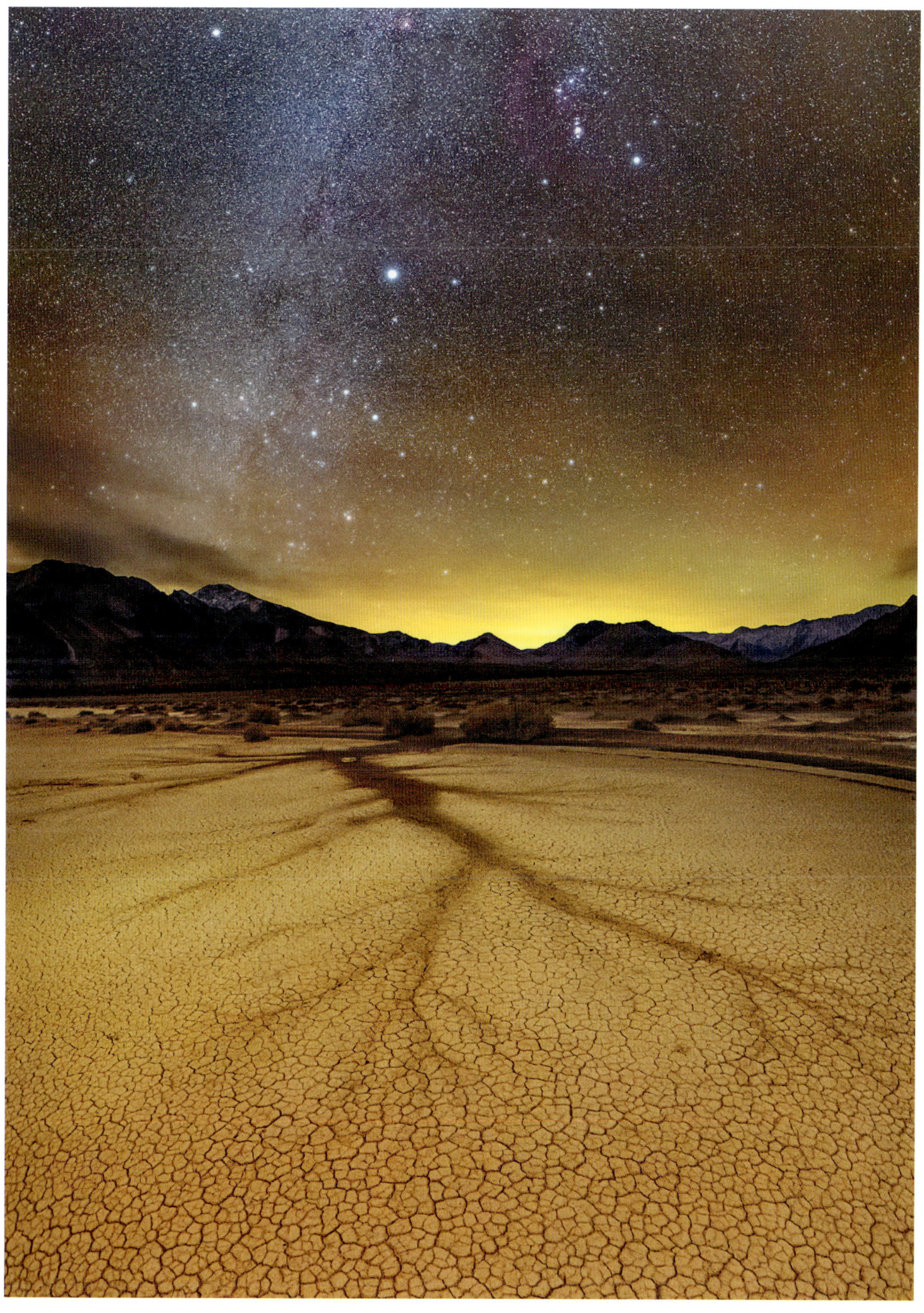

BABAK TAFRESHI
Stars above, cracks and crevices in a dried-up streambed below: a nighttime moment in California's Death Valley National Park

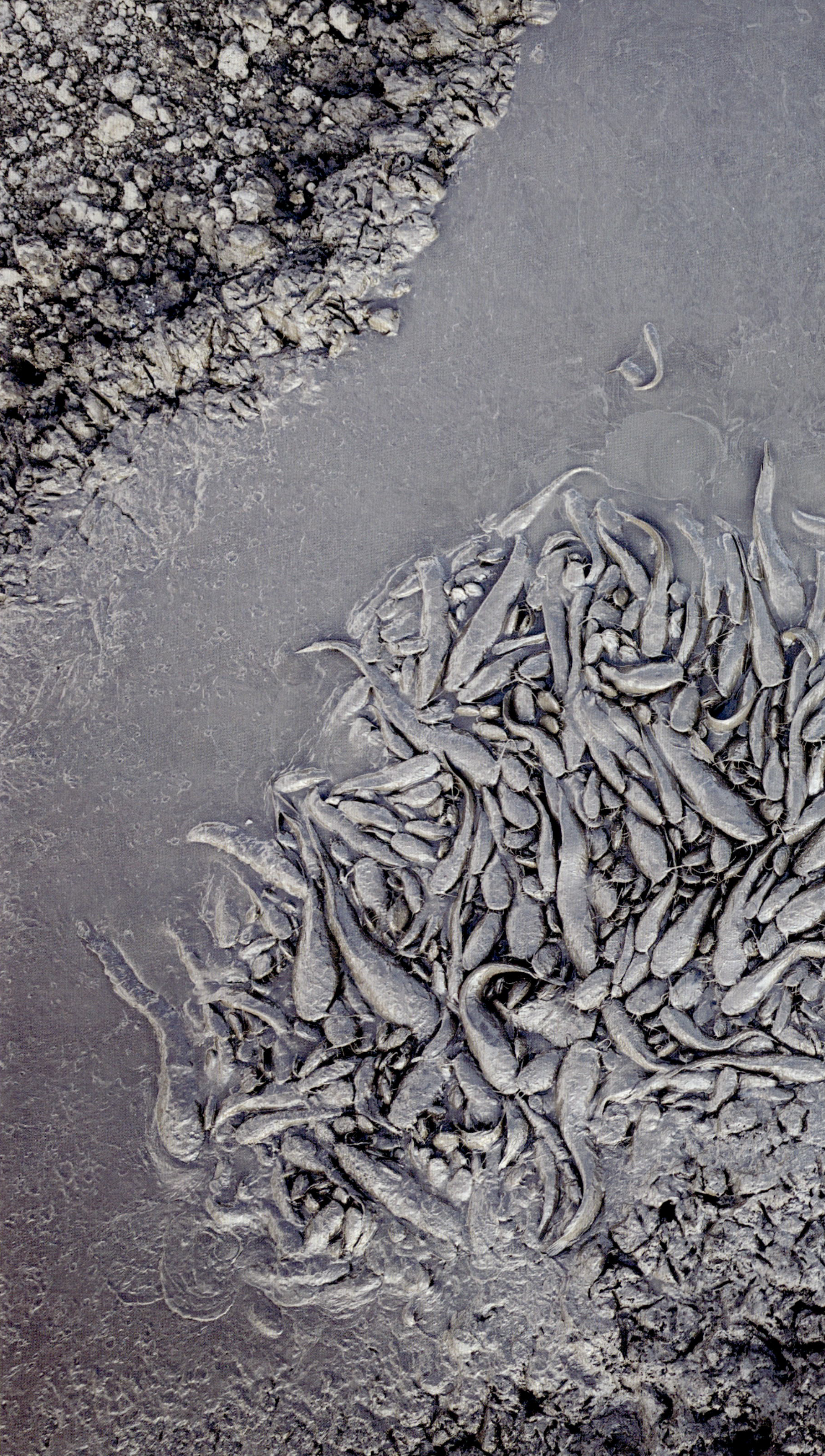

PIOTR NASKRECKI
African sharptooth catfish
scavenge the remains of a
waterbuck in the mud of
Mozambique's Gorongosa
National Park.

Following pages:
J. FRITZ RUMPF
Found in Arizona's White
Mountains, the ruffled gills of a
milk cap mushroom bruise blue,
typical of the species.

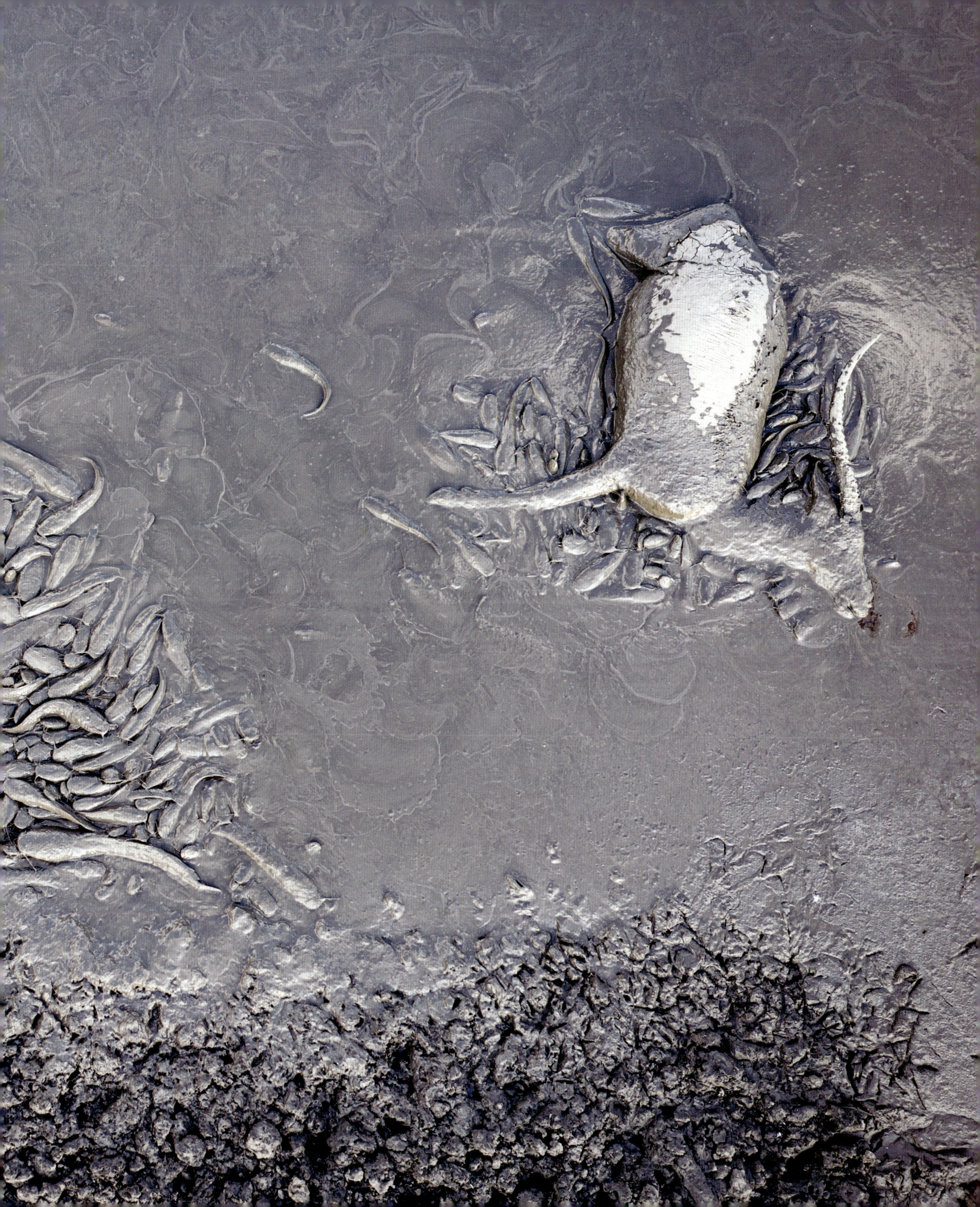

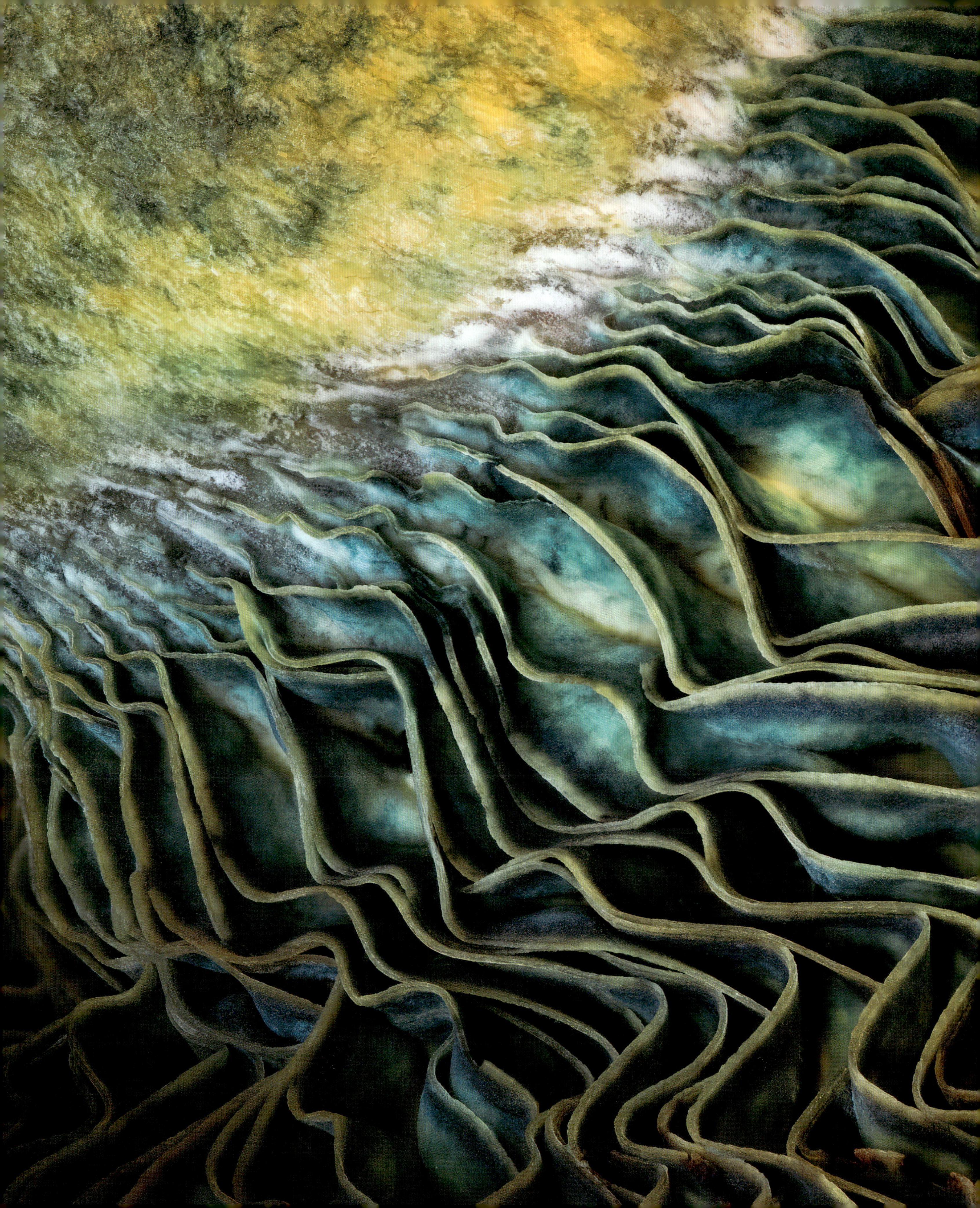

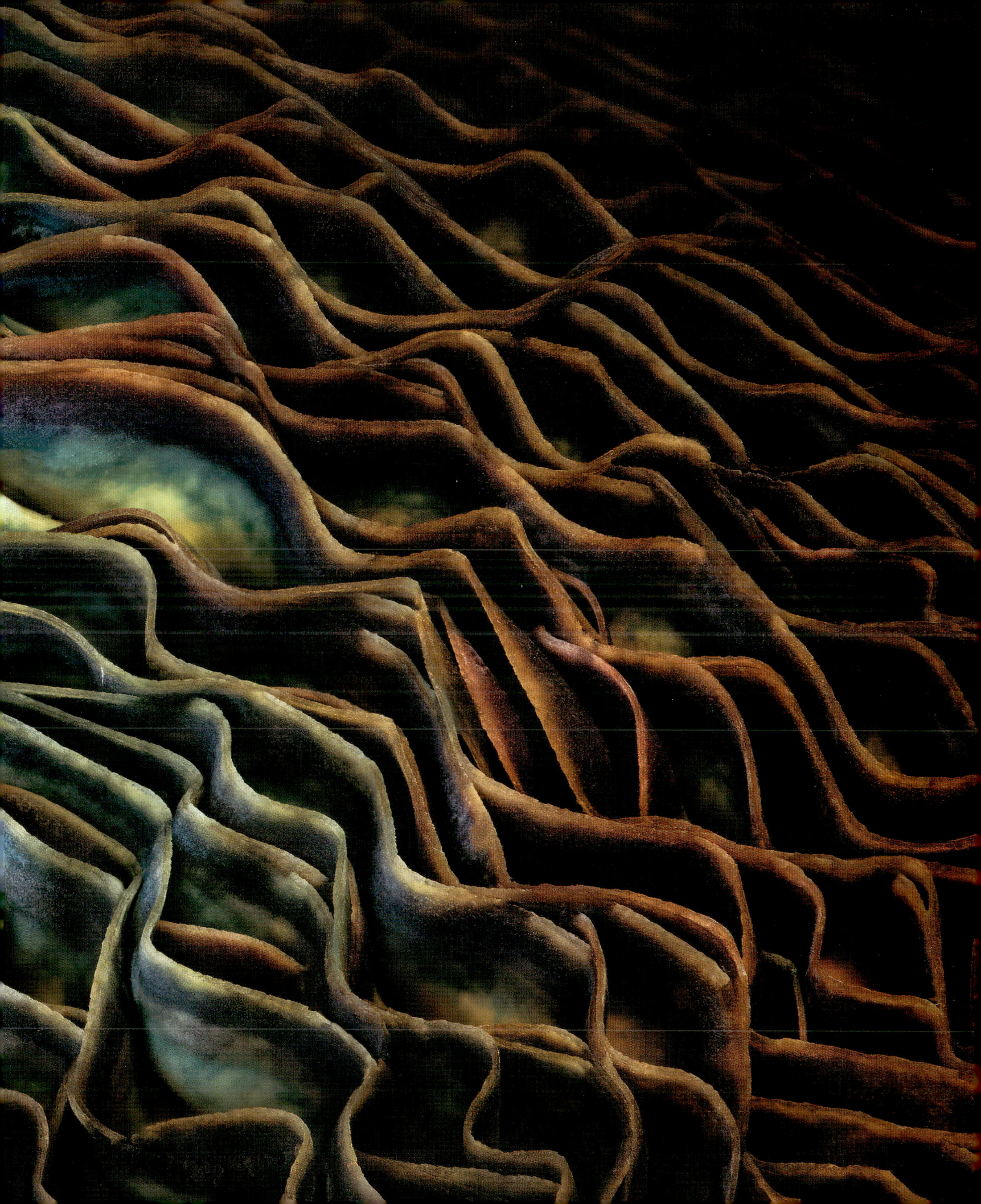

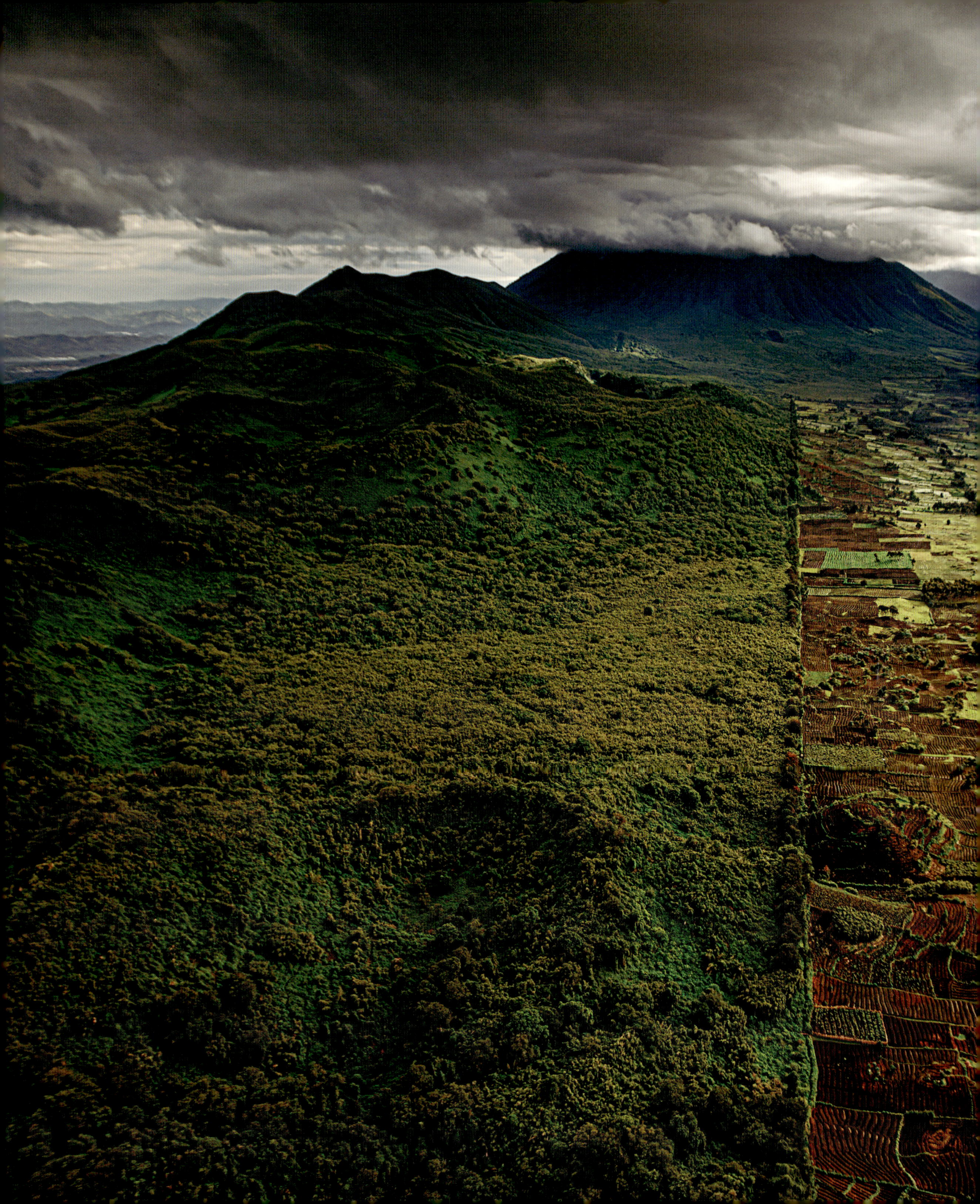

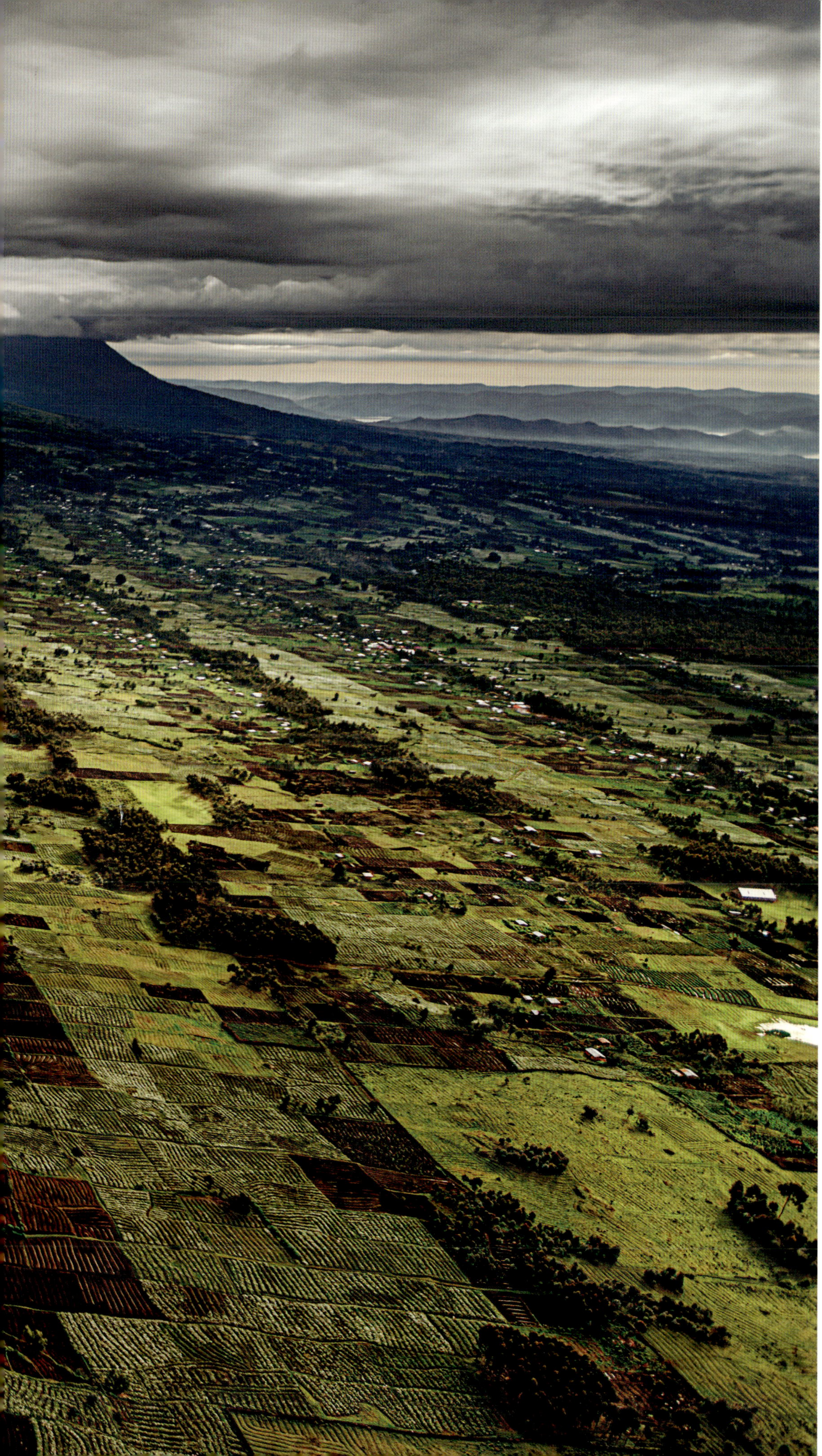

RONAN DONOVAN
Photographed from a helicopter, a clear divide separates the gorilla habitat of Volcanoes National Park from cultivated farmland in northern Rwanda.

I was something that lay under the sun and felt it, like the pumpkins, and I did not want to be anything more. I was entirely happy.

~WILLA CATHER, *MY ÁNTONIA*

DANIEL BELTRÁ
The Gulf of Mexico adopts an eerie glow in the aftermath of the BP Deepwater Horizon oil spill.

Following pages:
SOLLY LEVI
Impala shadows seem to frolic as the animals traverse a salt pan in the Namibian Kalahari.

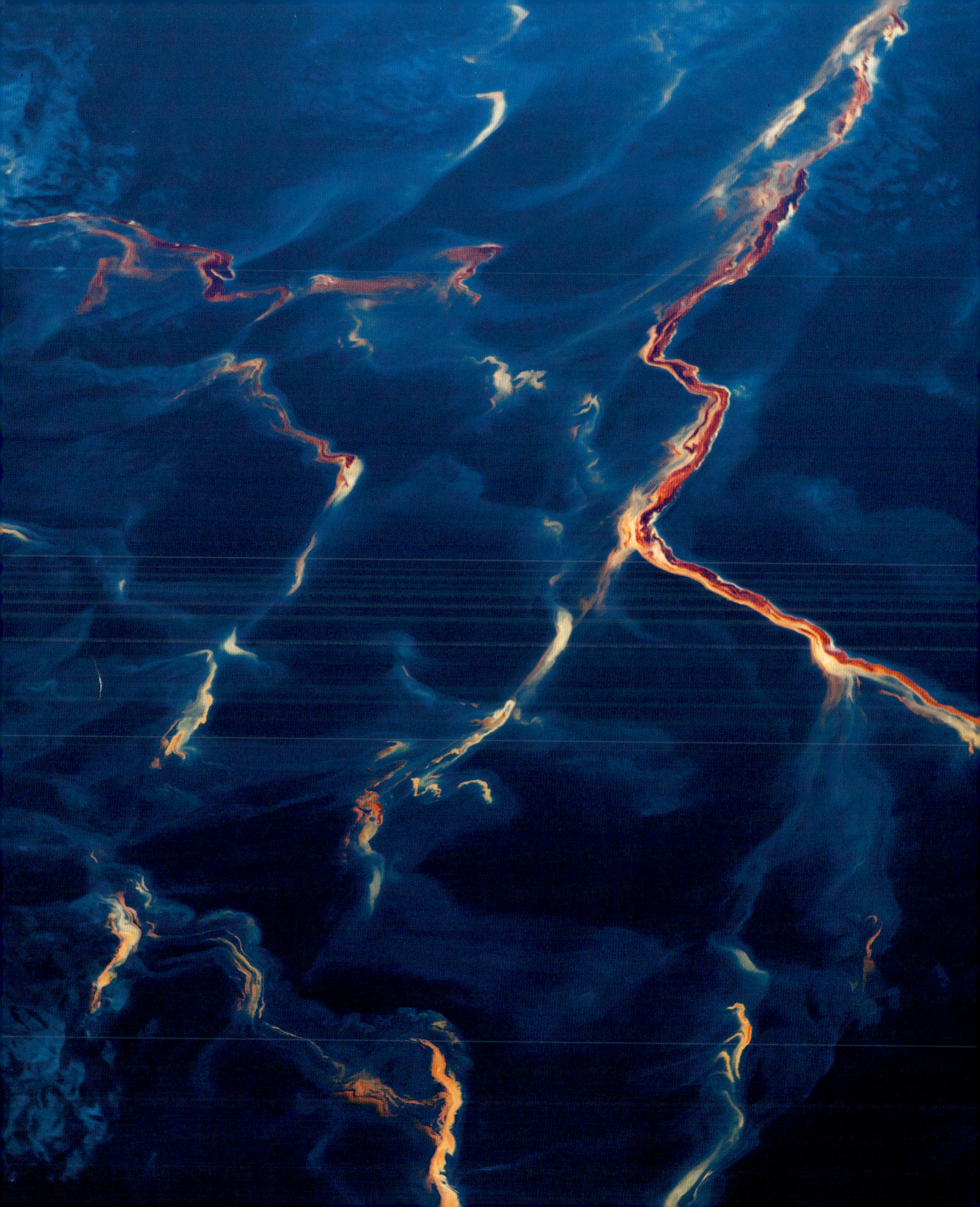

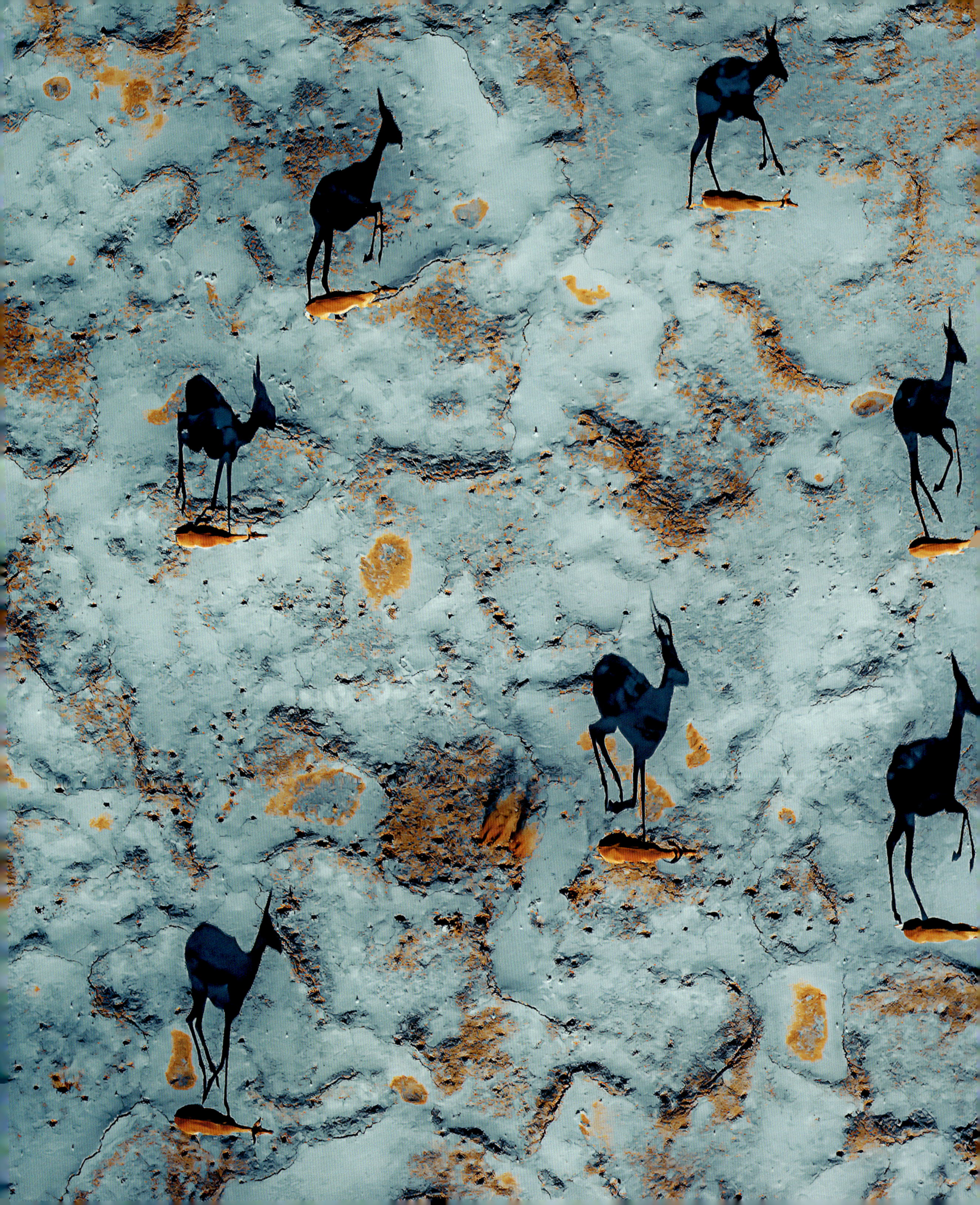

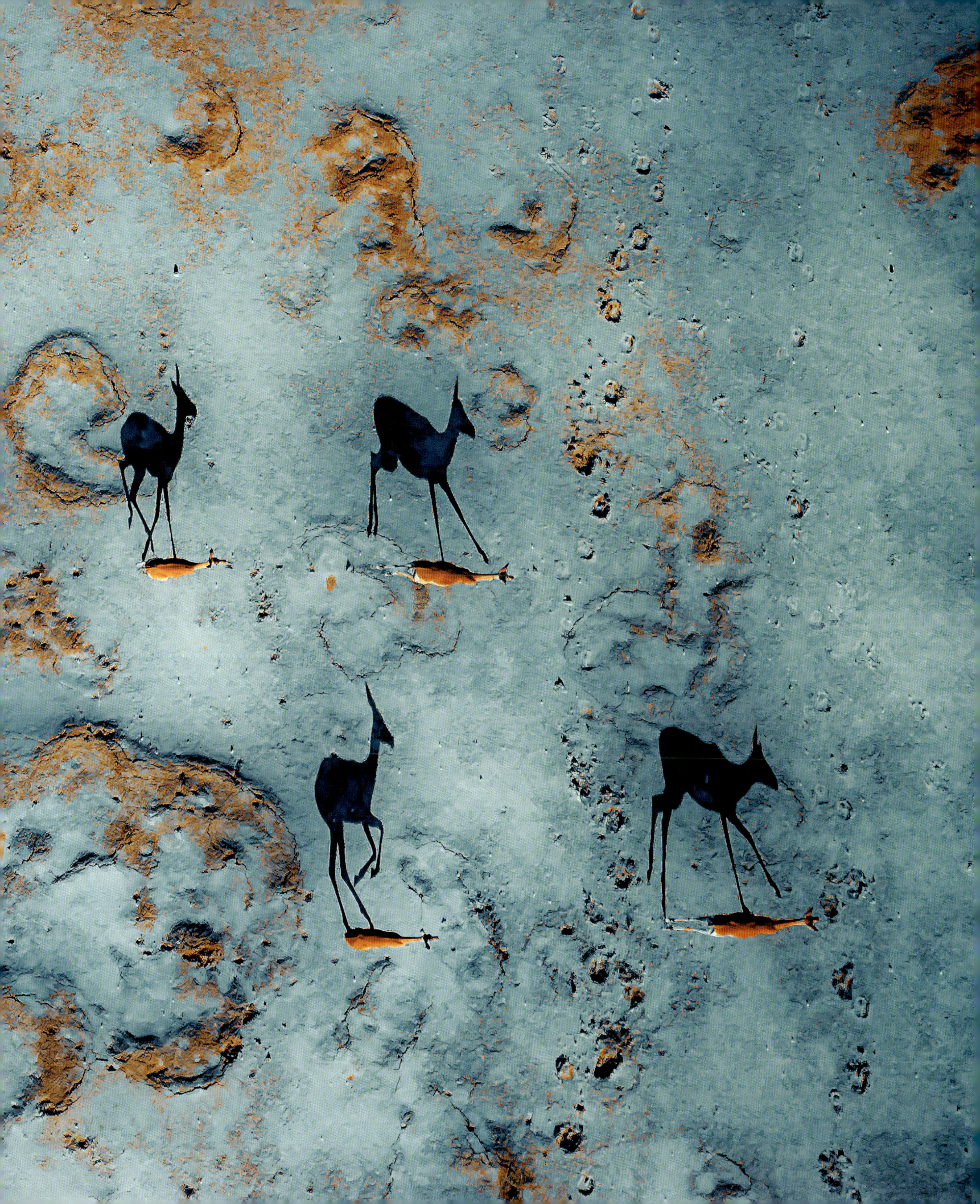

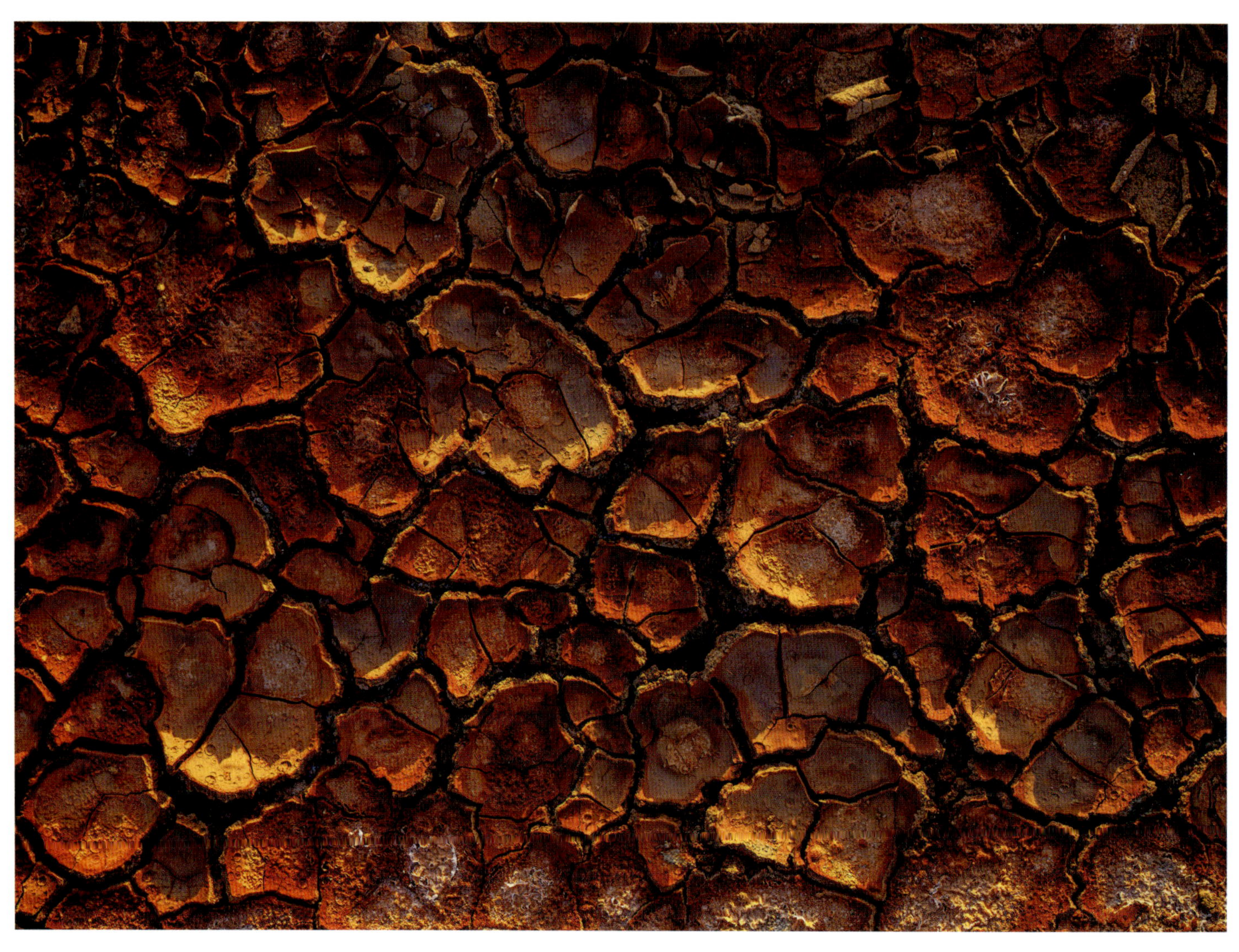

JAVIER AZNAR GONZÁLEZ DE RUEDA
Chunks of earth full of life, despite their desert look, characterize Spain's Mancha Húmeda,
a wetland dominated by tamarisk trees.

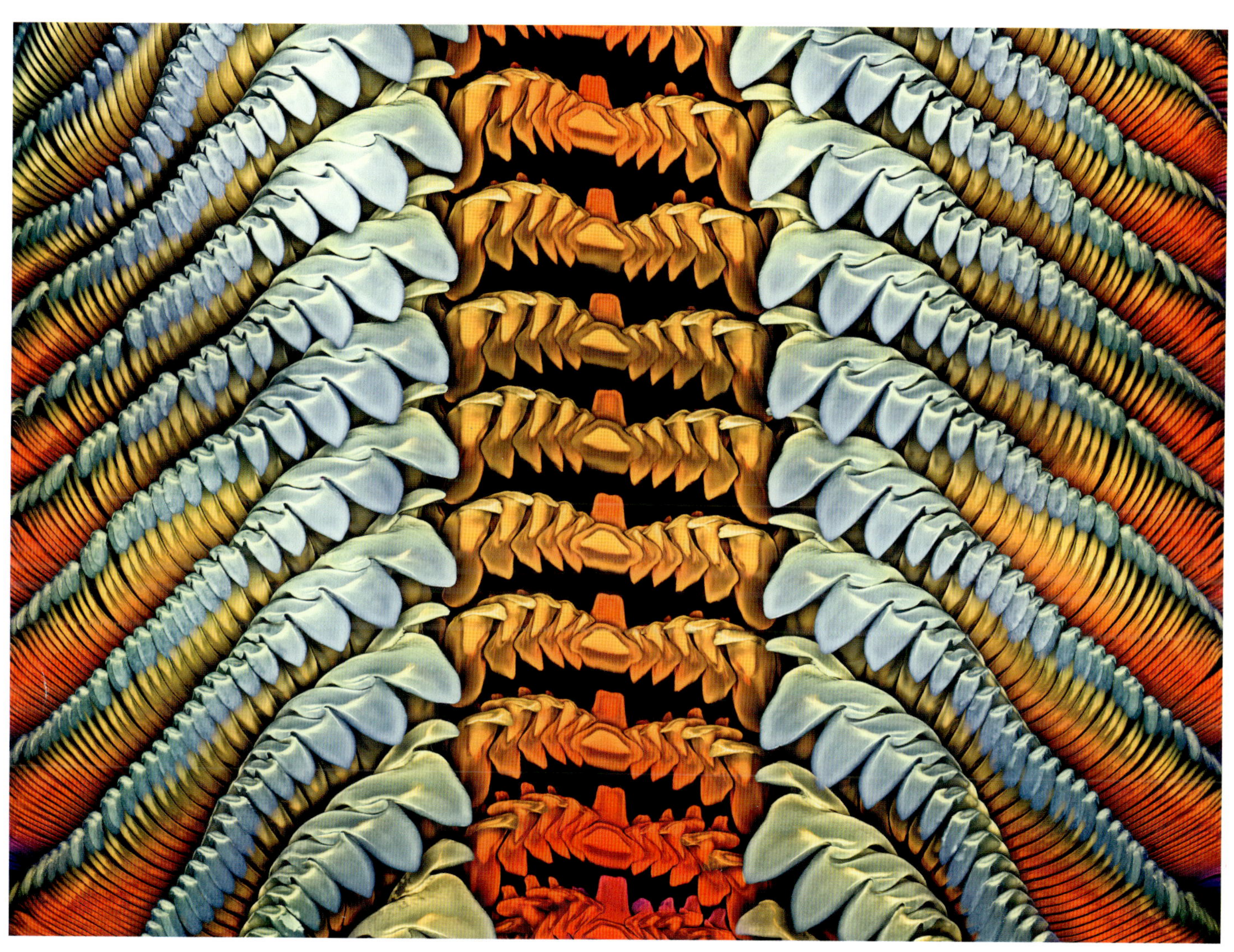

IGOR SIWANOWICZ
Intricate structures show how the radula, or rasping tongue, of a marine snail can scrape its chosen bits of food,
such as diatoms, off kelp and other algae.

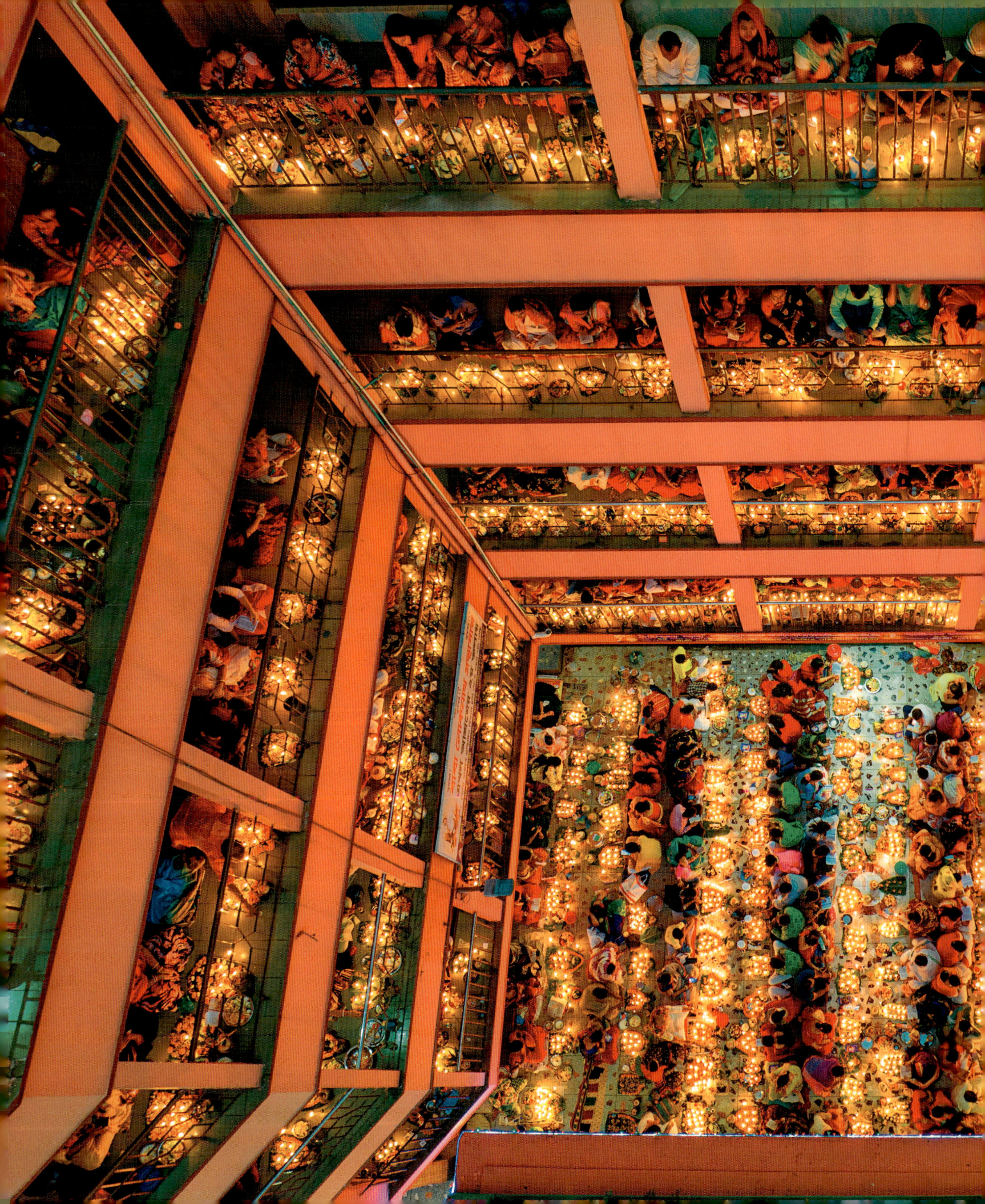

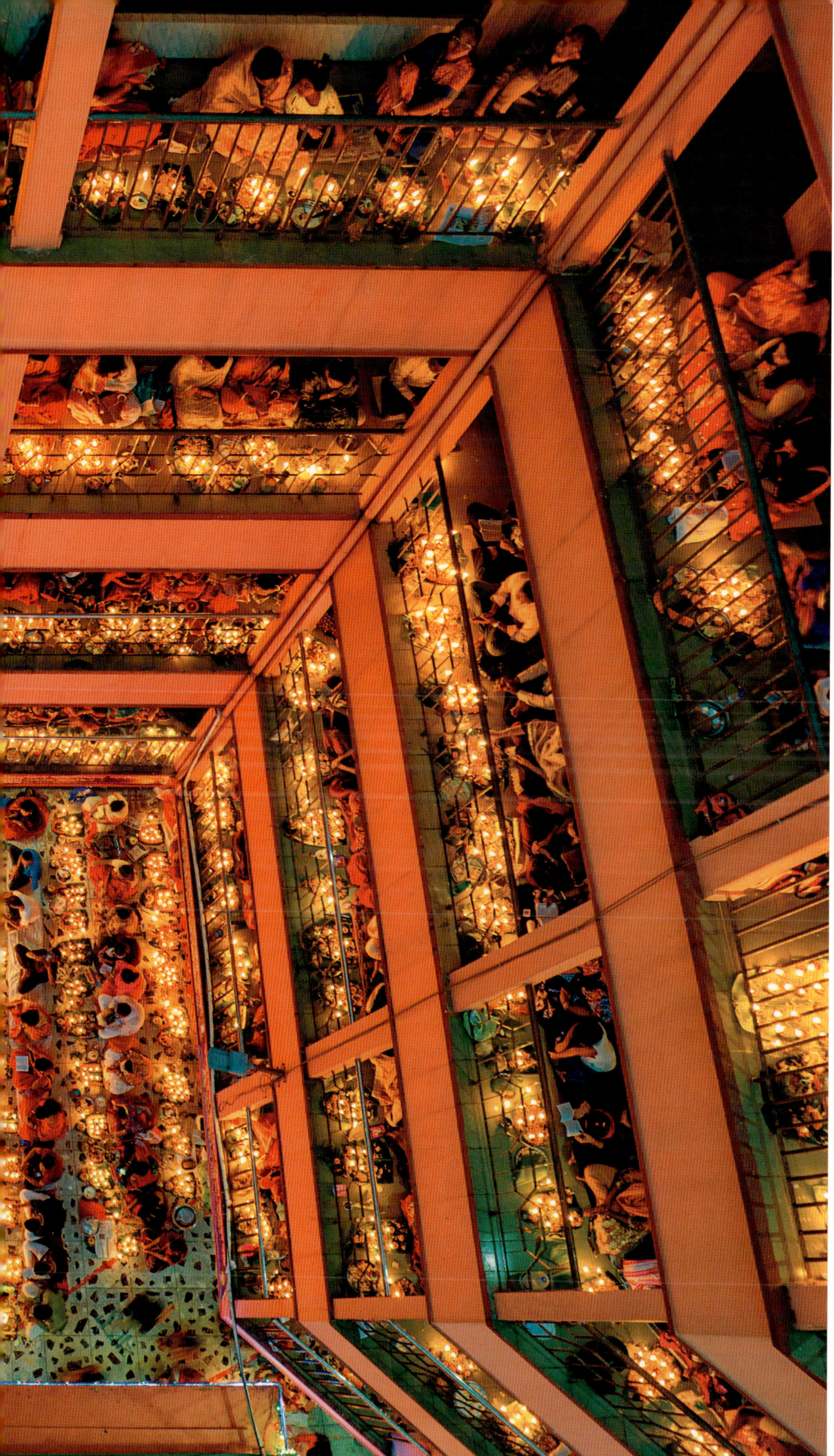

AZIM KHAN RONNIE
A top-down look shows devotees and their candles gathered for Rakher Upobash, an annual festival in honor of an 18th-century Hindu saint celebrated near Dhaka, Bangladesh.

Following pages:
JEFFREY KERBY
Just after a violent eruption, volcanic ash erodes the shoreline of Raikoke Island in eastern Russia.

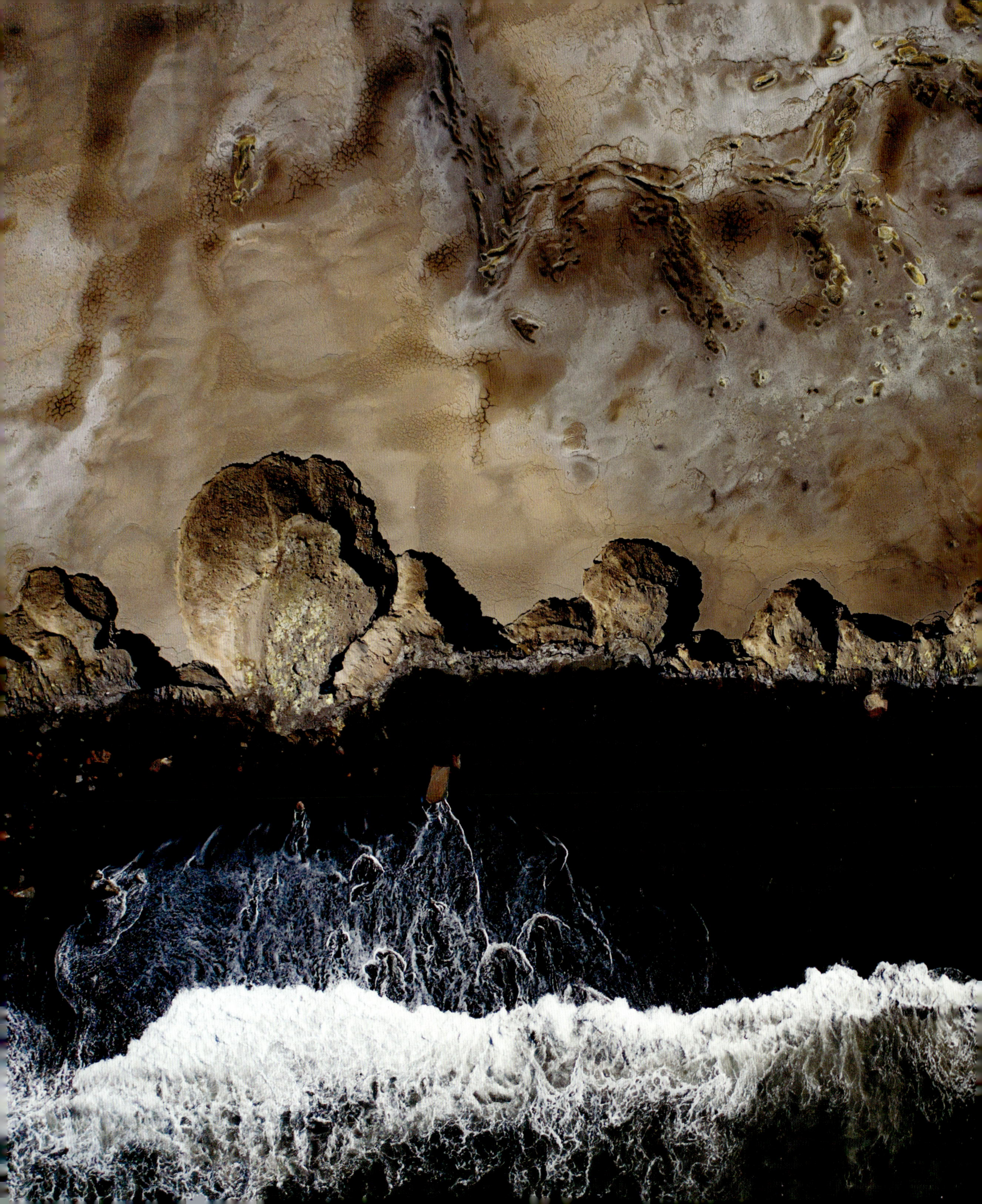

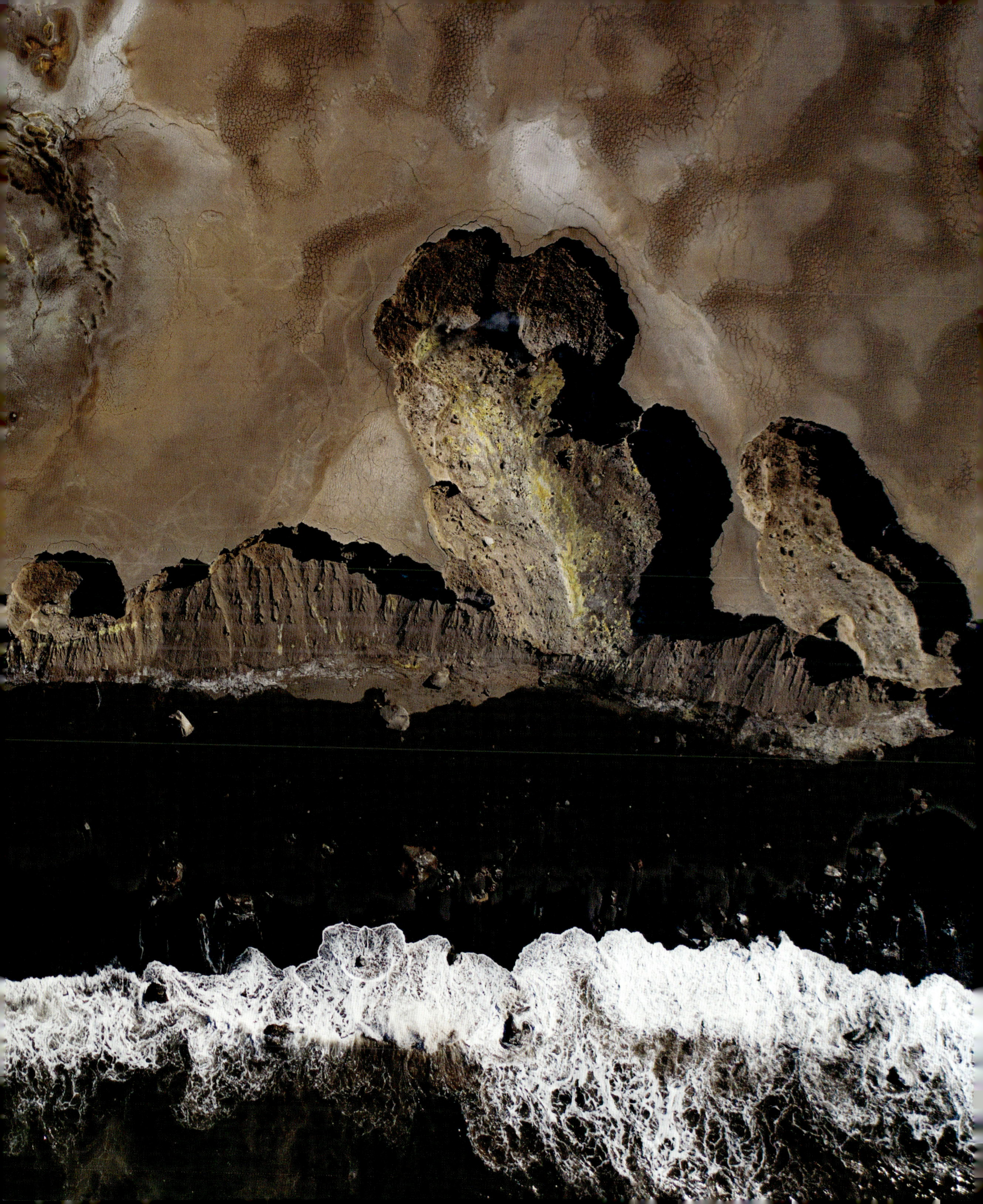

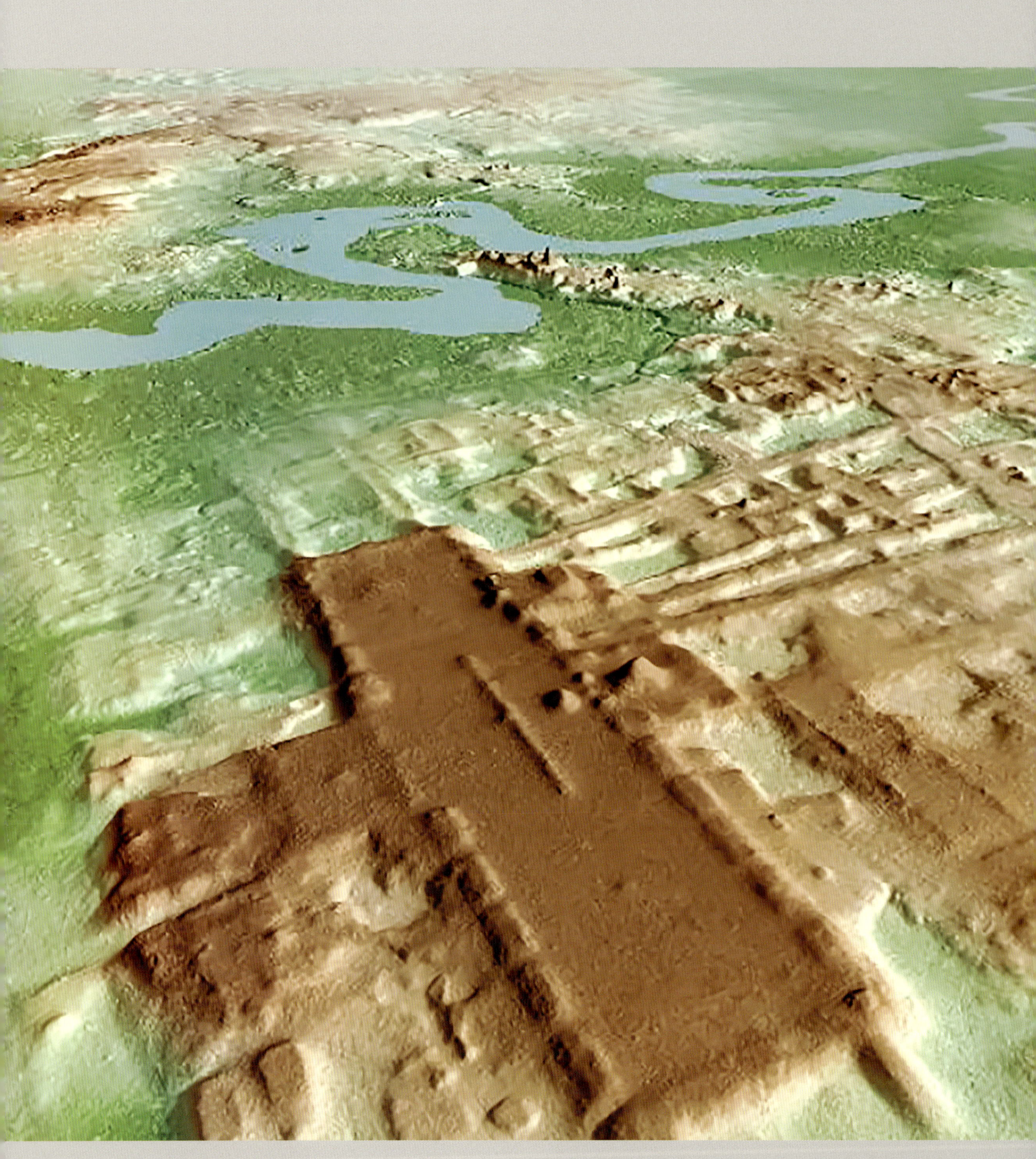

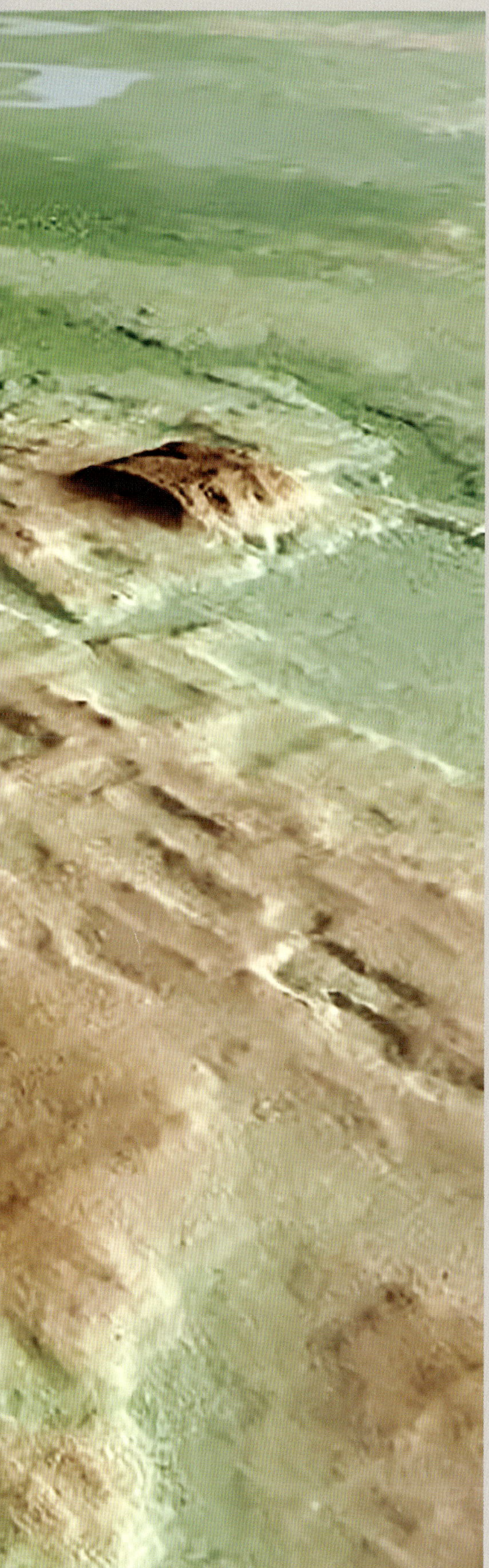

WHAT LOOKS DOWN AT US?

Sometimes texture itself becomes the medium of expression. More than a thousand years ago, people in what is modern-day Peru created hundreds of textured figures, shapes, and lines by digging shallow trenches in the Nasca Desert. The earthworks they created, collectively called the Nasca lines, stretch across 170 square miles (440 sq km) and include the figures of a monkey, a giant, a hummingbird, and many others. While some are visible from nearby hills, they seem designed for aerial viewing despite being created in a time when human flight was still well over a thousand years distant. Similar large earthworks have been found elsewhere in Peru, like the Paracas Candelabra, and in various regions of the Middle East. The original intentions of their makers are still debated, but despite some historical and oral reports, they remained out of global attention until pilots began flying over these regions in the 1920s and reporting back on what they saw. People have long modified the texture of the earth for a variety of reasons,

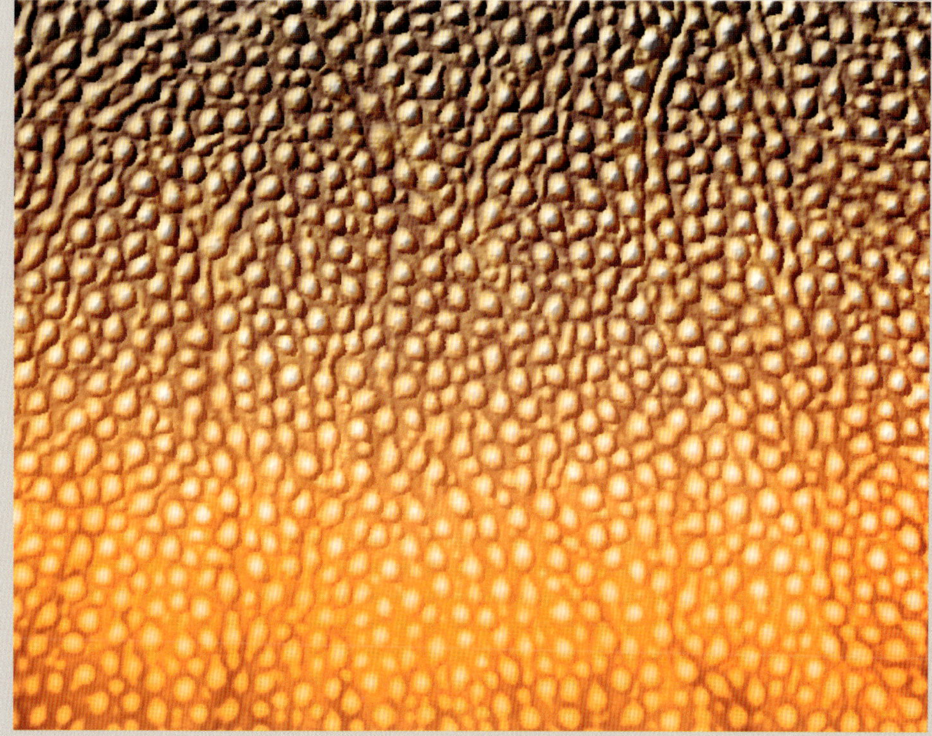

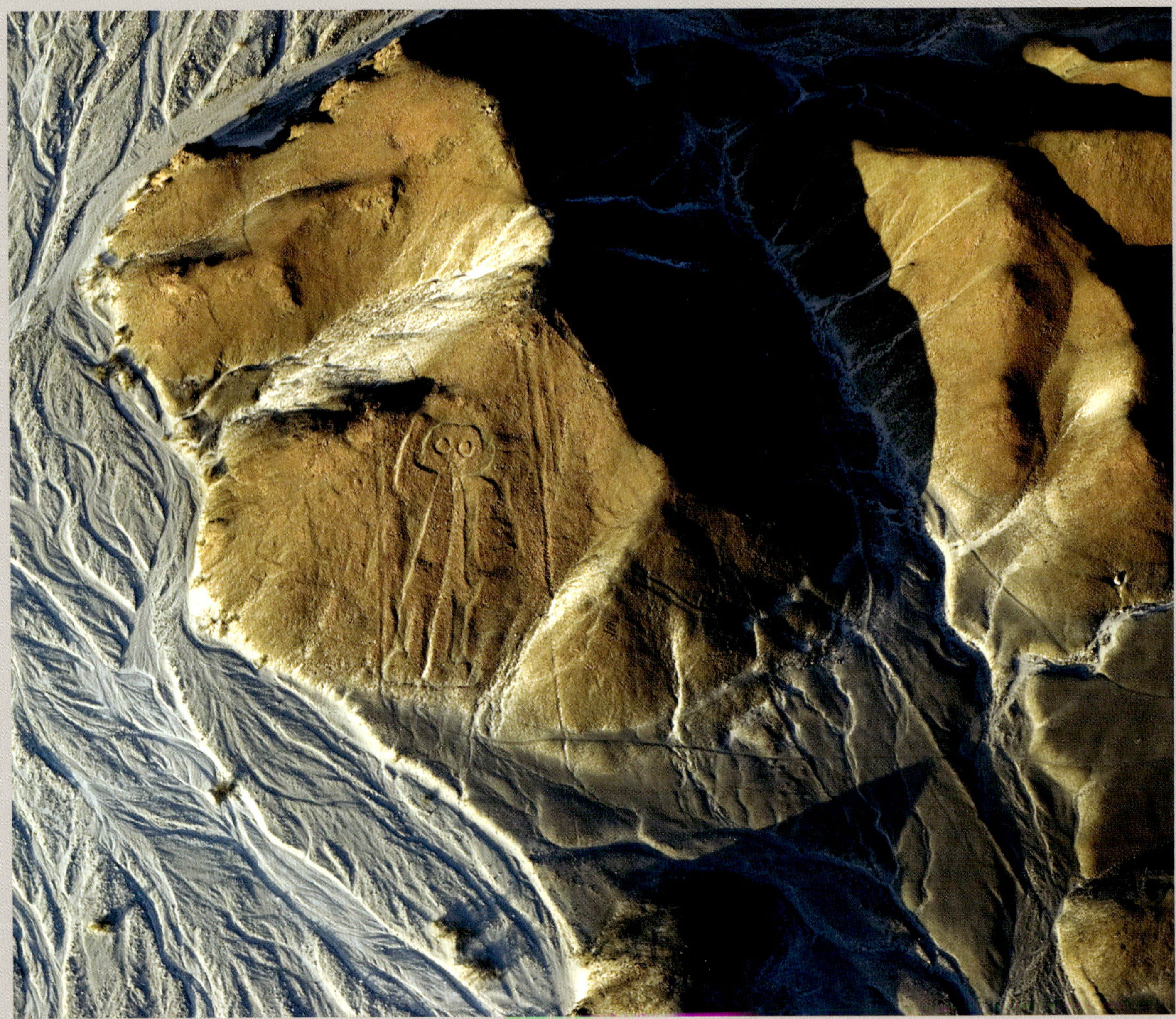

but sometimes it is simply to express something to a vantage point they knew they themselves would never see.

Recent advances in imaging capabilities are revealing textures of the planet's surface that no pilot could dream of seeing. Light Detection and Ranging, more commonly called lidar, is now widely used to explore the texture of Earth even in regions covered by dense vegetation. Planes carrying lidar systems send a huge number of laser pulses down toward the ground and then measure how they bounce off its surfaces. Computers then process these data into images that can effectively see through forest canopies, peer beneath tall grasslands, and see textures of the planet otherwise hidden from plain sight. This can be useful for mapping past river flows—which leave subtle but broad textural clues across landscapes, or even the structures of previously unknown civilizations hidden in forests. One recent study using lidar imagery gathered across the Amazon

TAKESHI INOMATA
Lidar technology reveals the forms of a 3,000-year-old Maya complex more than a third of a mile (0.5 km) across in Tabasco, Mexico.

WASHINGTON GEOLOGICAL SURVEY
Sometimes called a pimply prairie, these Mima mounds pock the land southwest of Olympia, Washington. Now part of a natural preserve, the mounds and their cause are still under study.

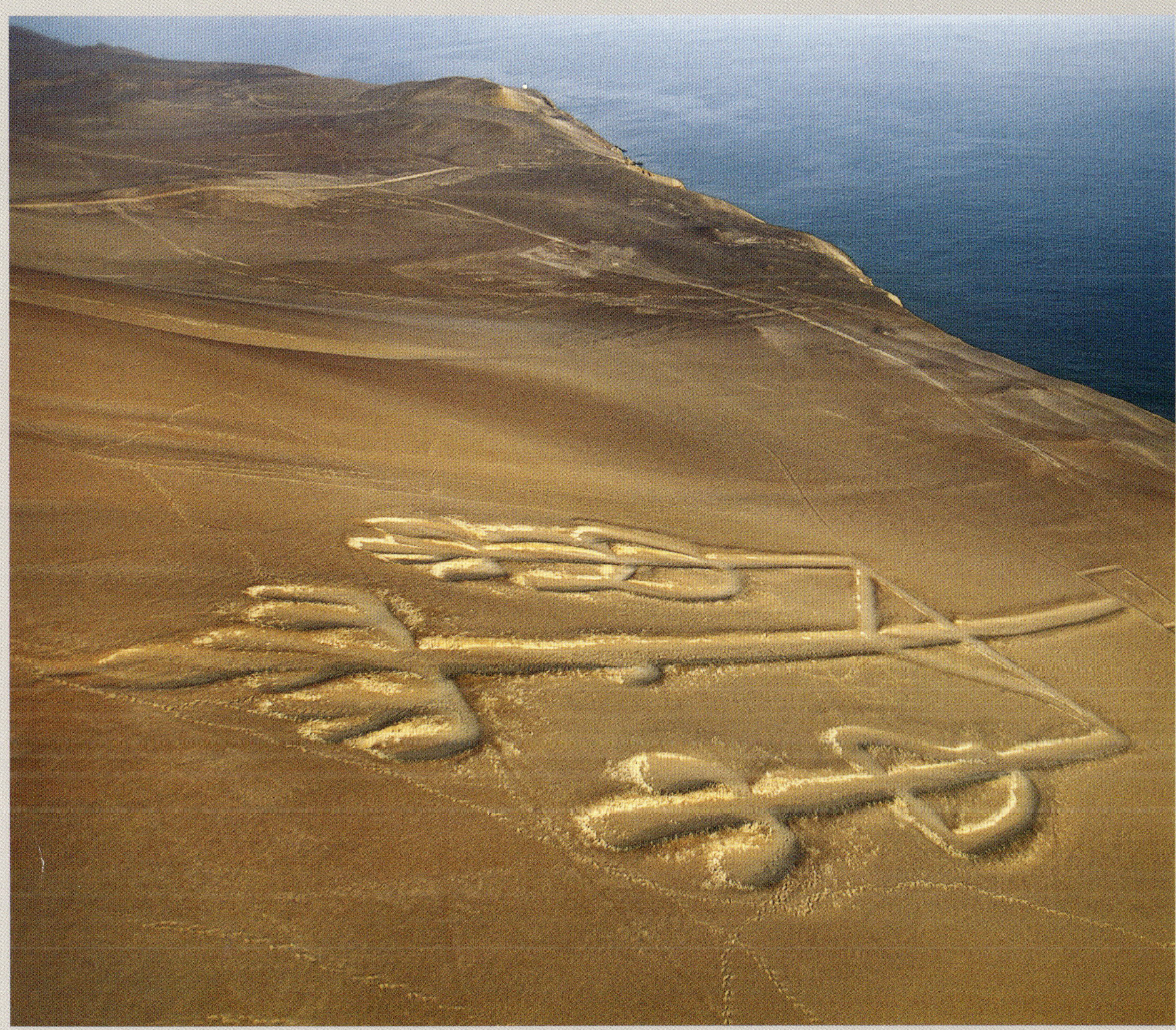

suggests there are tens of thousands of unreported pre-Hispanic earthworks in the region, many buried under tree canopies. Even unknown cities are being discovered, like the Maya city of Ocomtún, recently identified by textures revealed from lidar mapping in Mexico's Yucatán Peninsula.

The textures of our planet have been a canvas for human expression and natural processes from time immemorial. We do not know all the reasons why people, hundreds or thousands of years ago, cre-ated huge textural modifications like the Nasca lines that can only fully be taken in from above. But as we continue to modify the entirety of the planet's surface with our activities, modern imaging is reveal-ing works from the past that had long since been lost. There is great value in rediscovering these textures, even as we struggle to make sense of and appreciate those we already know. They are all part of our human story and our desire to be seen from above.

GEORGE STEINMETZ
Like the more famous Nasca lines, this geoglyph (nicknamed the Paracas Candelabra) has an estimated age of two millennia. It overlooks the Pacific from a Peruvian peninsula.

Opposite:
FABERFOTO-IT
The giant—more recently dubbed the astronaut—is one of many fascinating Nasca line earthworks created some 2,000 years ago in Peru.

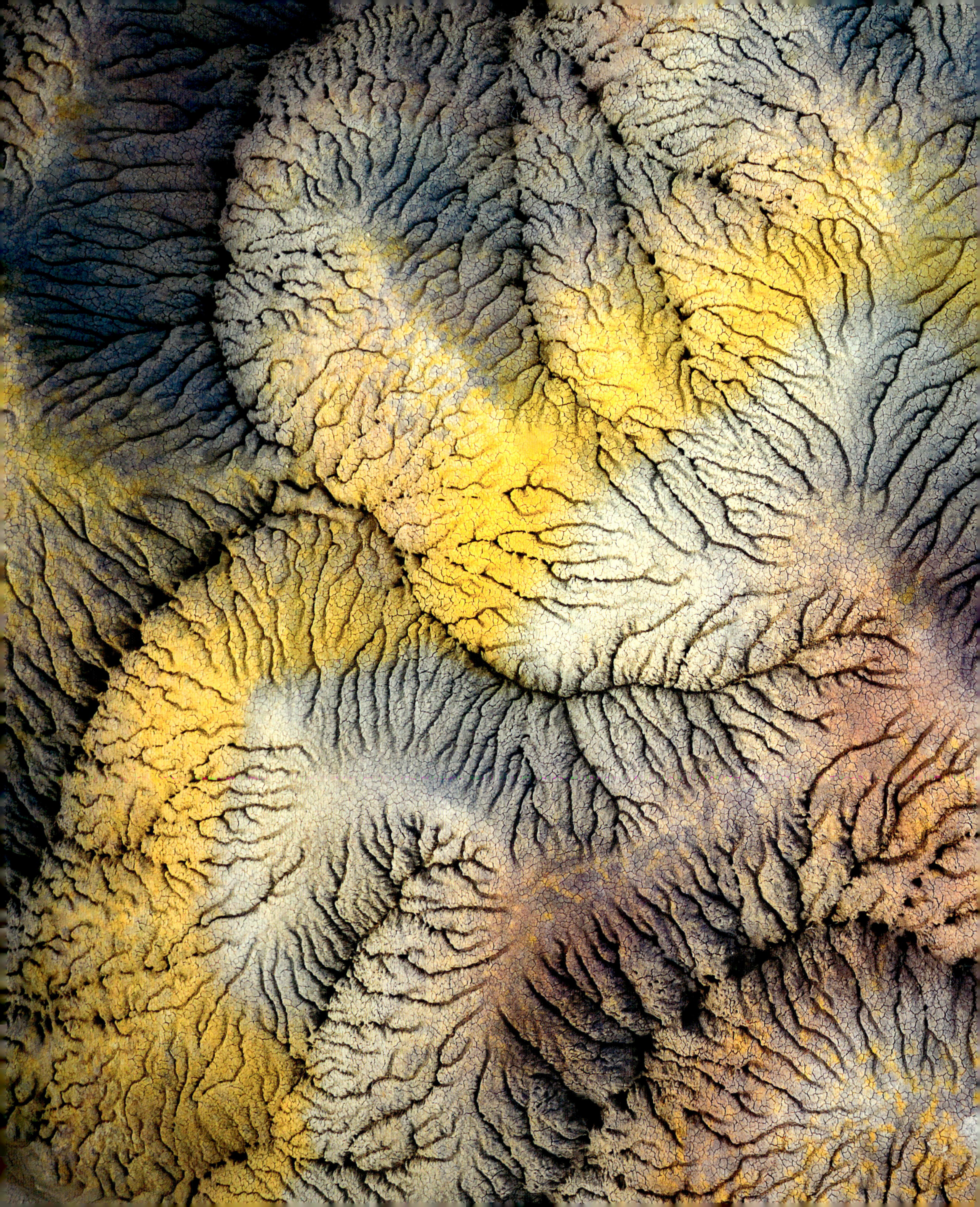

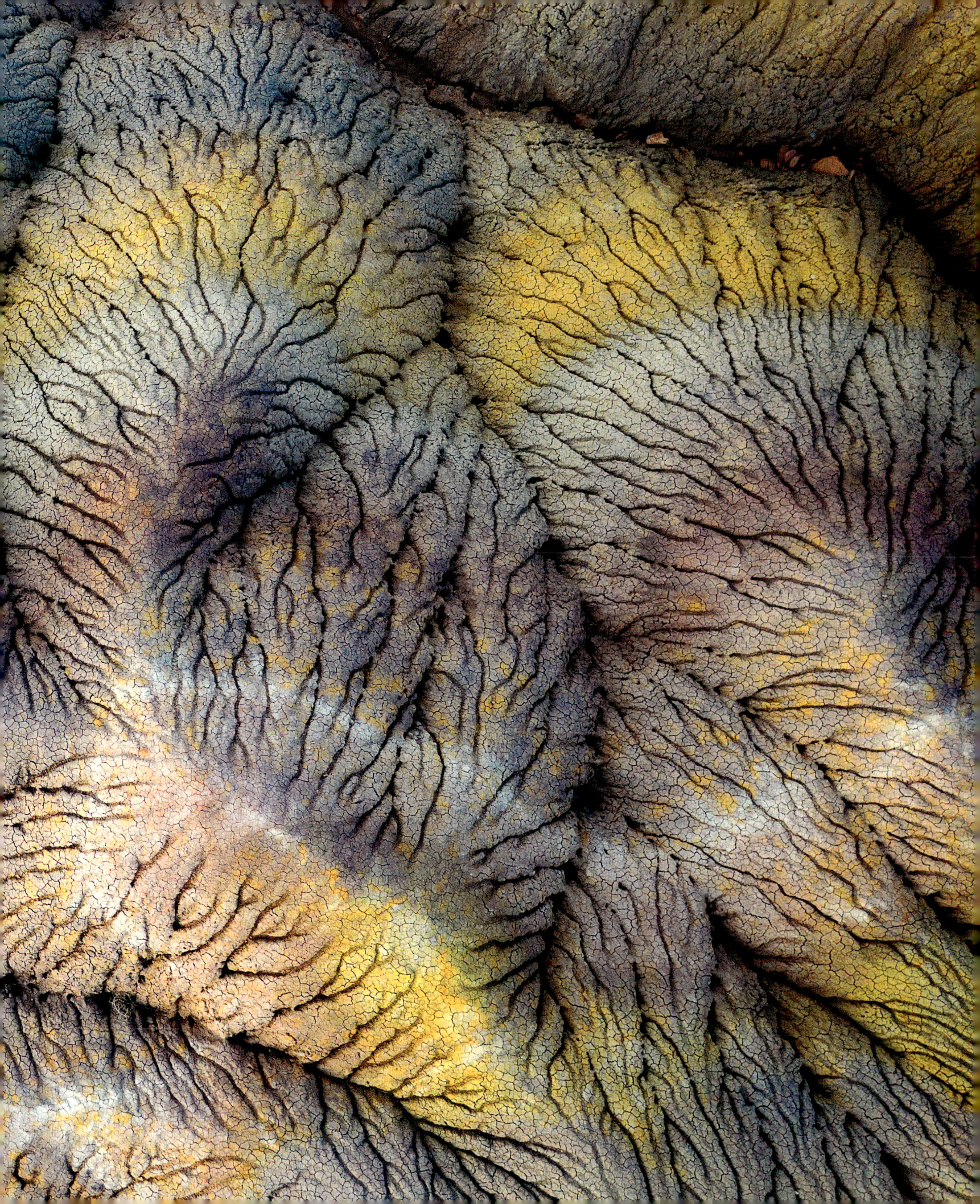

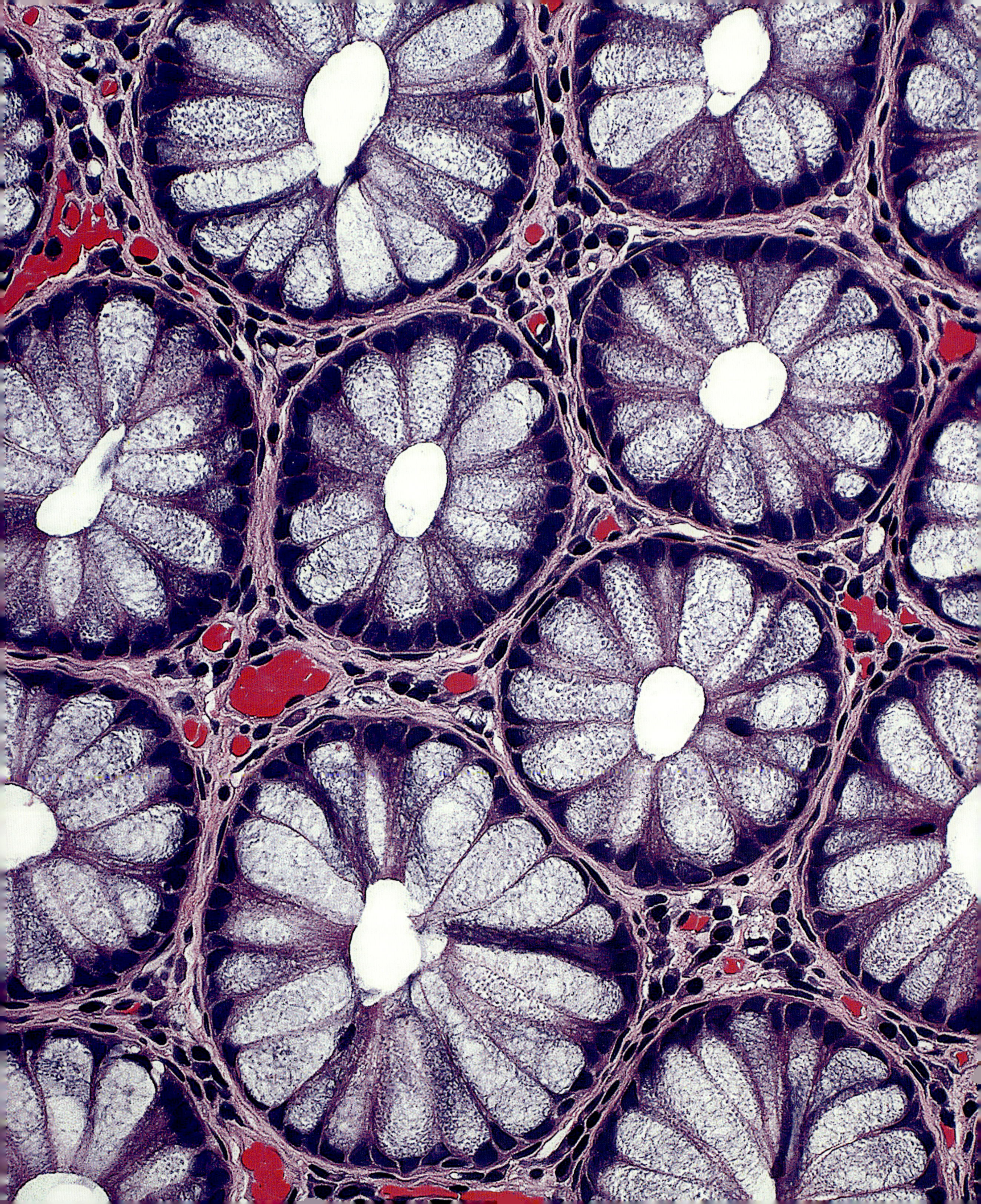

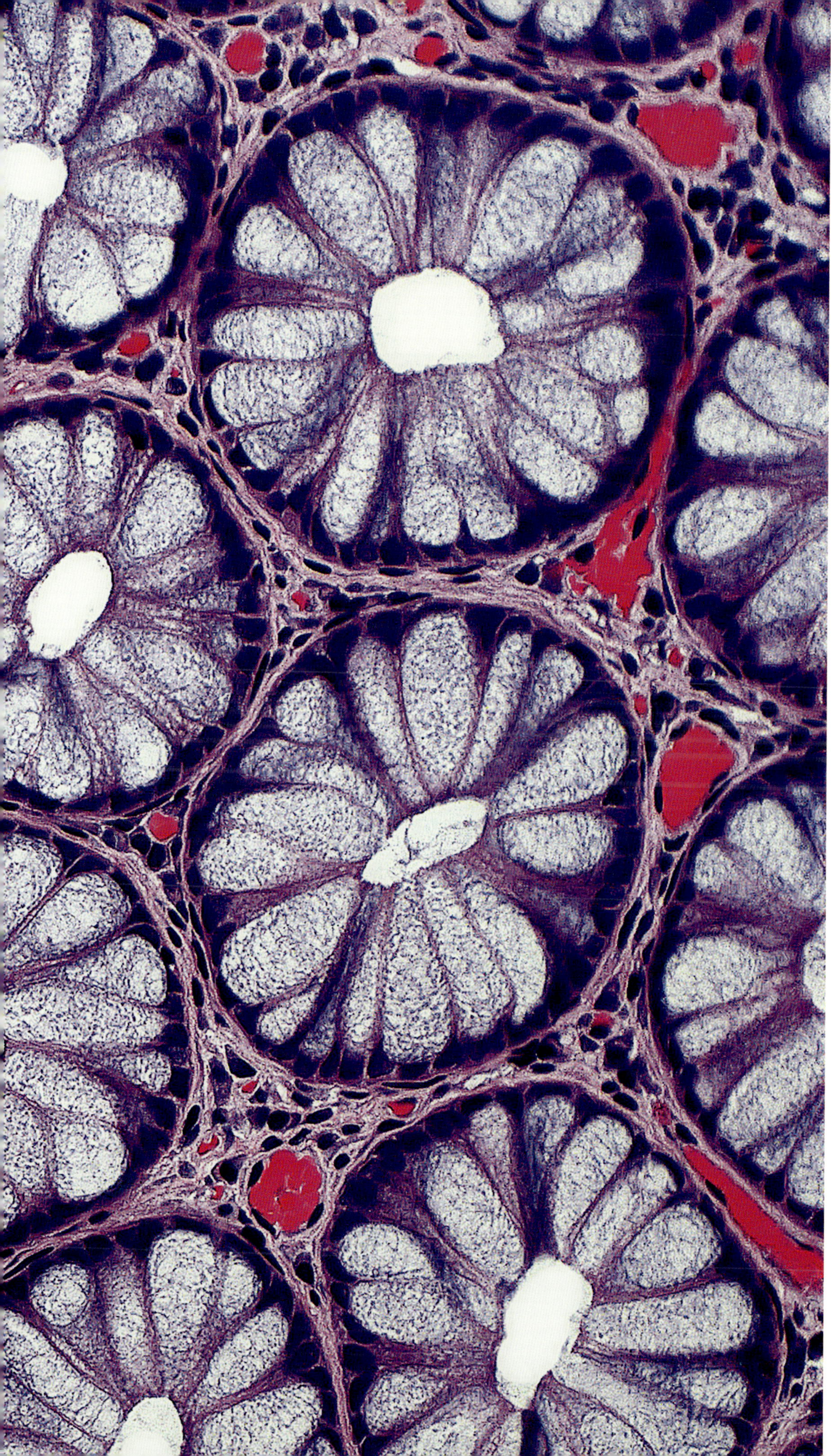

ZIAD EL-ZAATARI
Epithelial crypts—protected
locations in the human colon
where new lining cells
can form—here magnified
and in cross section

Previous pages:
DAVID SWINDLER
Ridges and valleys undulate
through the topography of
Arizona's Vermilion Cliffs
National Monument.

I lingered round them,
under that benign sky ...
and wondered how anyone
could ever imagine unquiet
slumbers for the sleepers
in that quiet earth.

~EMILY BRONTË, *WUTHERING HEIGHTS*

LORENZO POLI
A pool of water snakes through glacial ice in Norway.

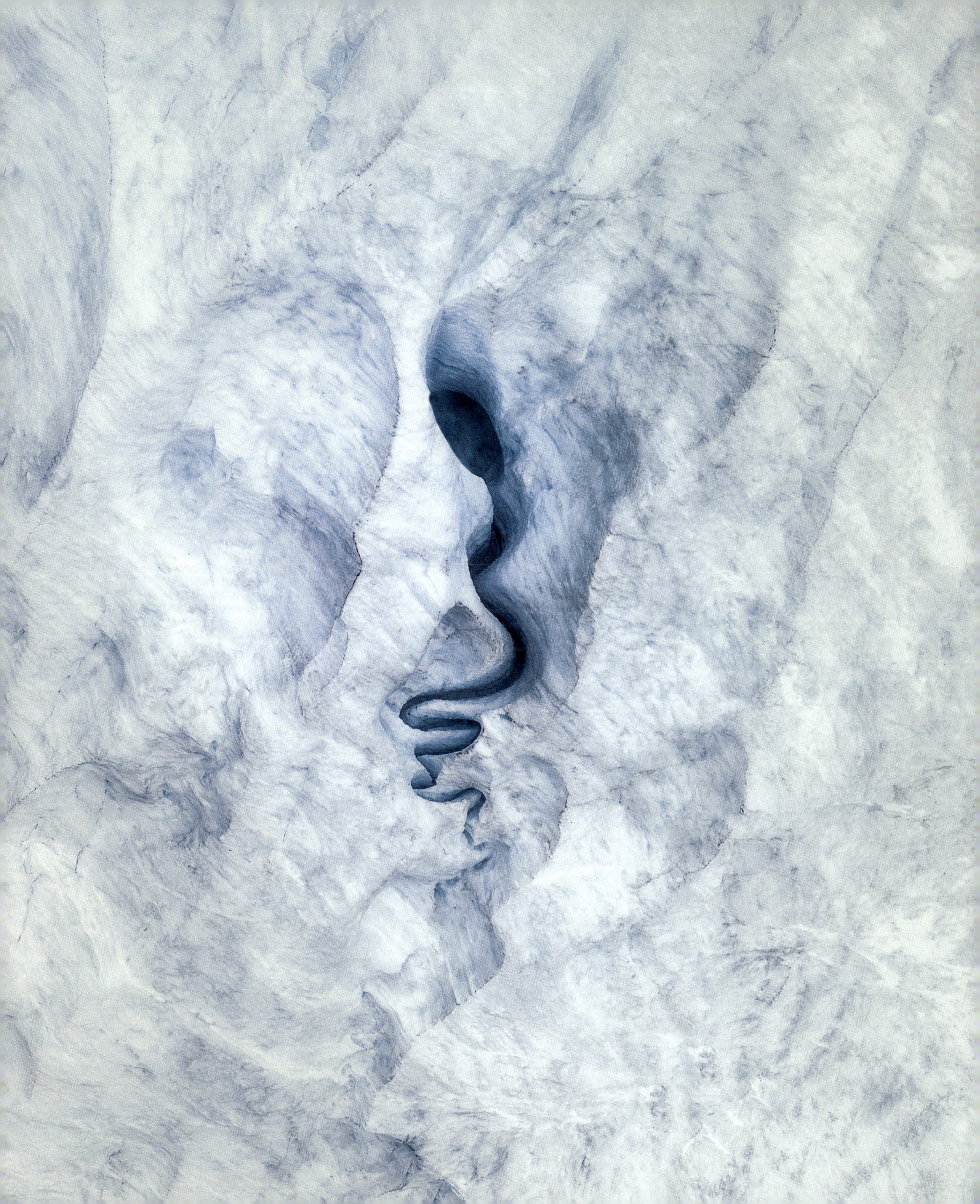

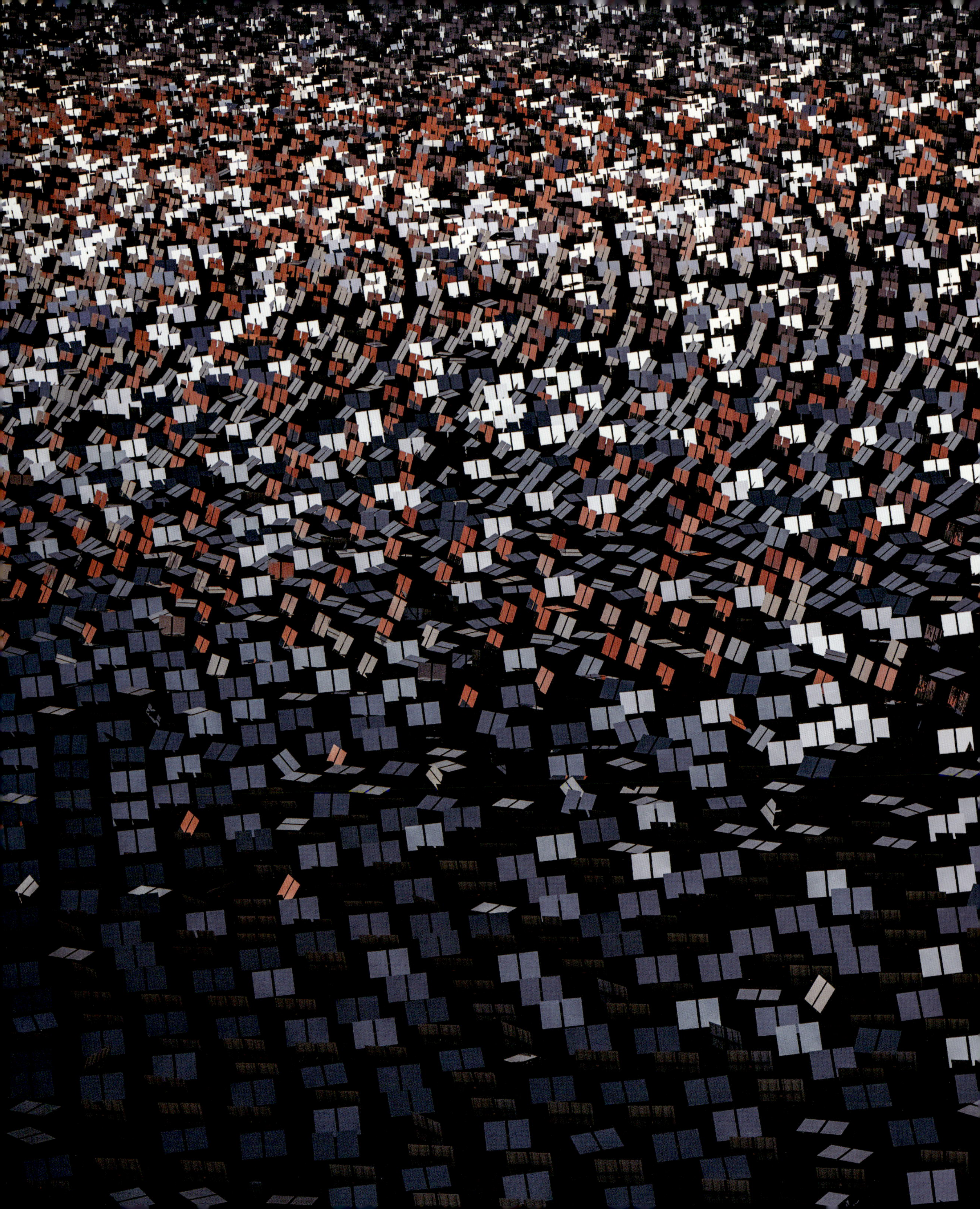

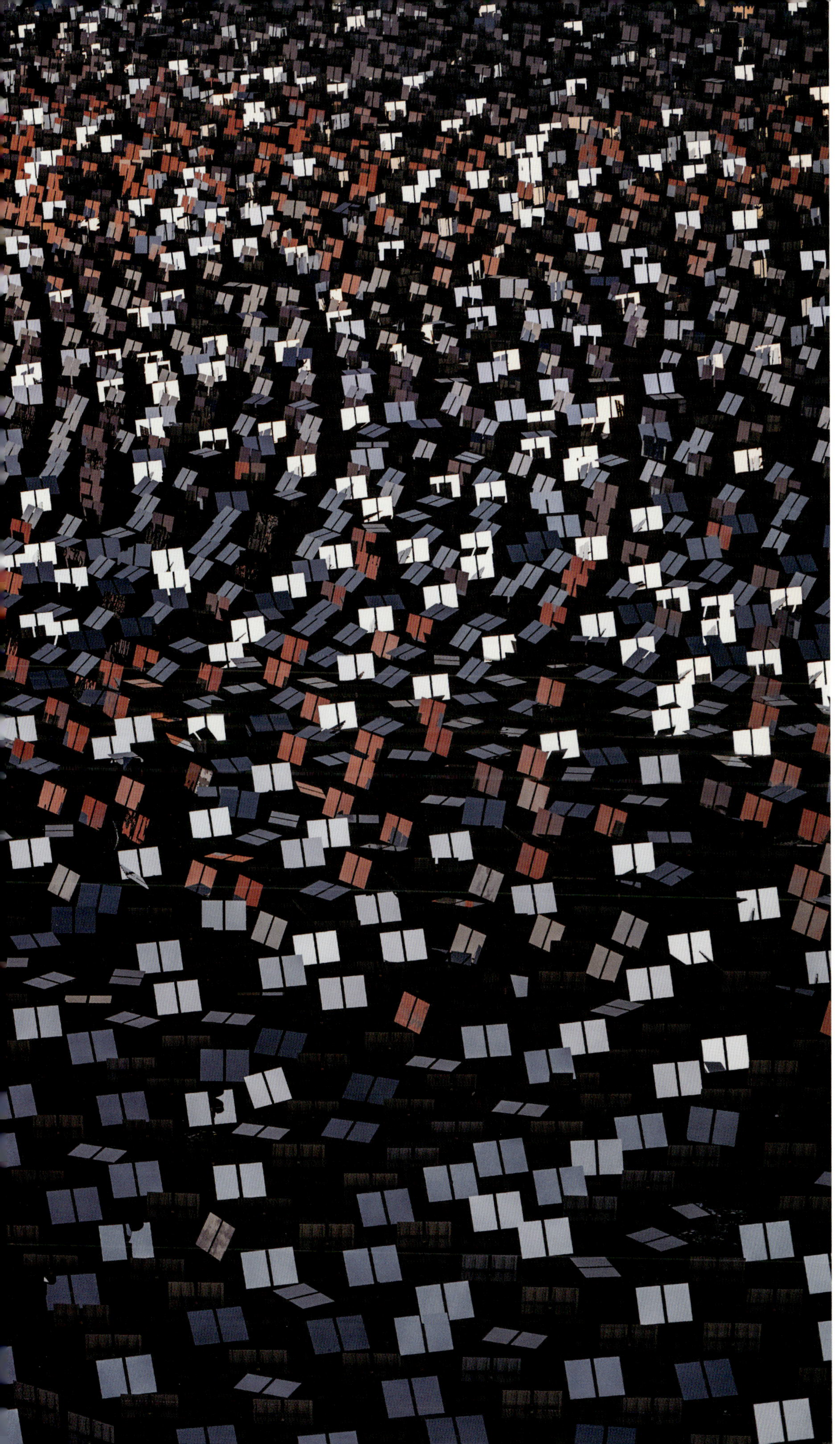

TOM HEGEN
A massive array of solar panels
in the Ivanpah Solar Electric
Generating System in California
collects energy from the sun.

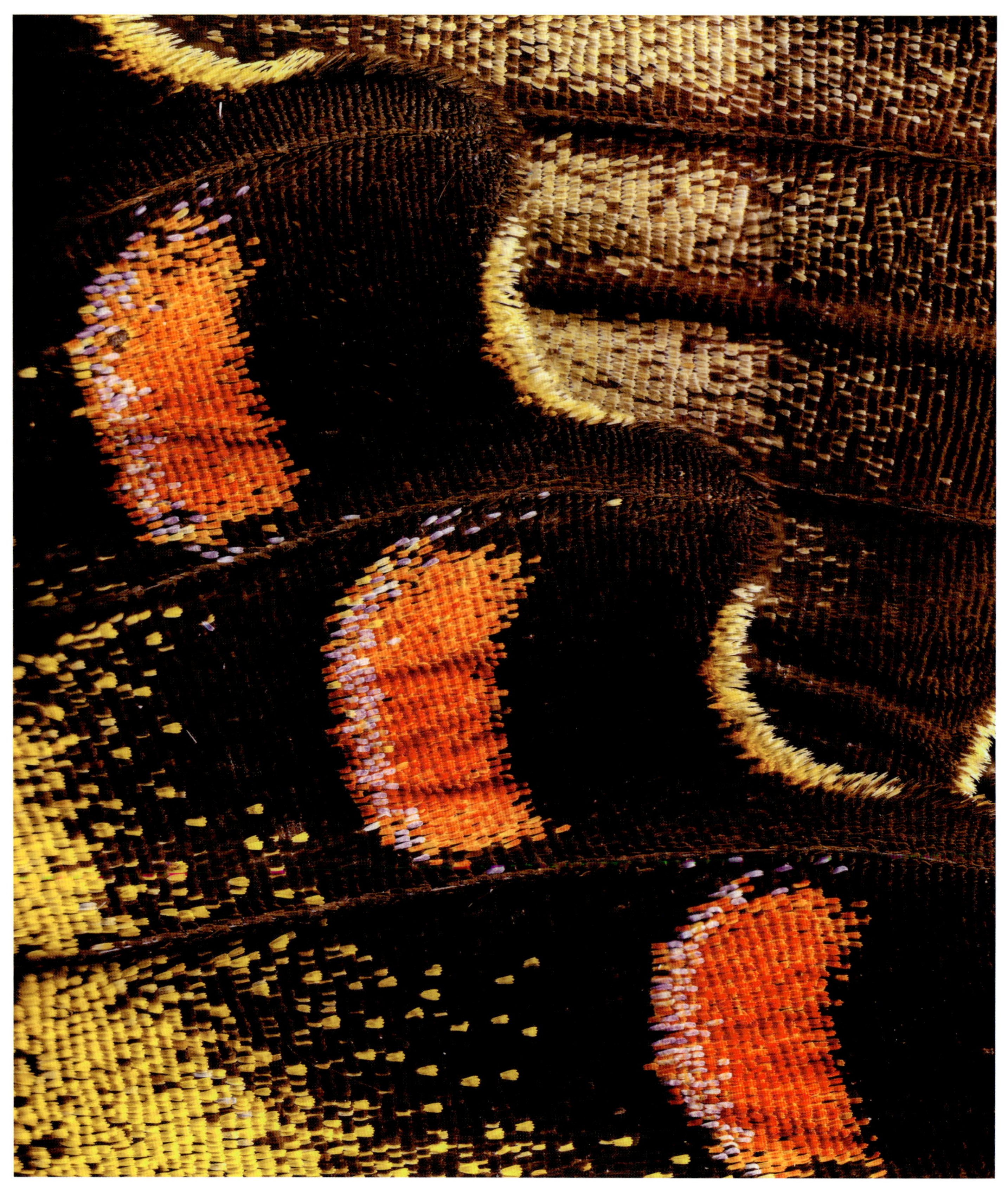

CHRIS PERANI
Tiny scales shimmer on the wing of a butterfly.

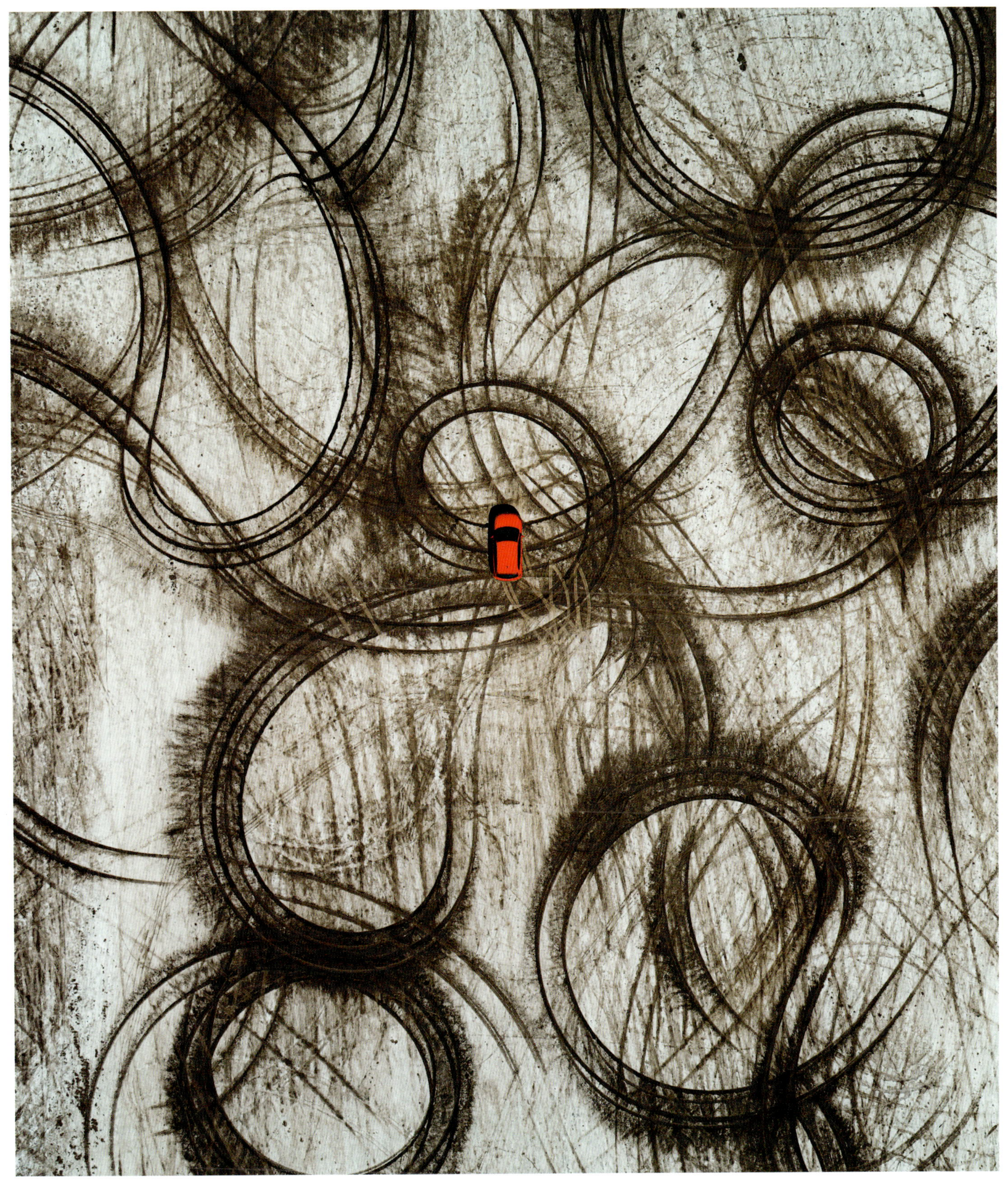

JP AND MIKE ANDREWS
Shapes in the sand: A bright red vehicle leaves tire-track swoops on a beach.

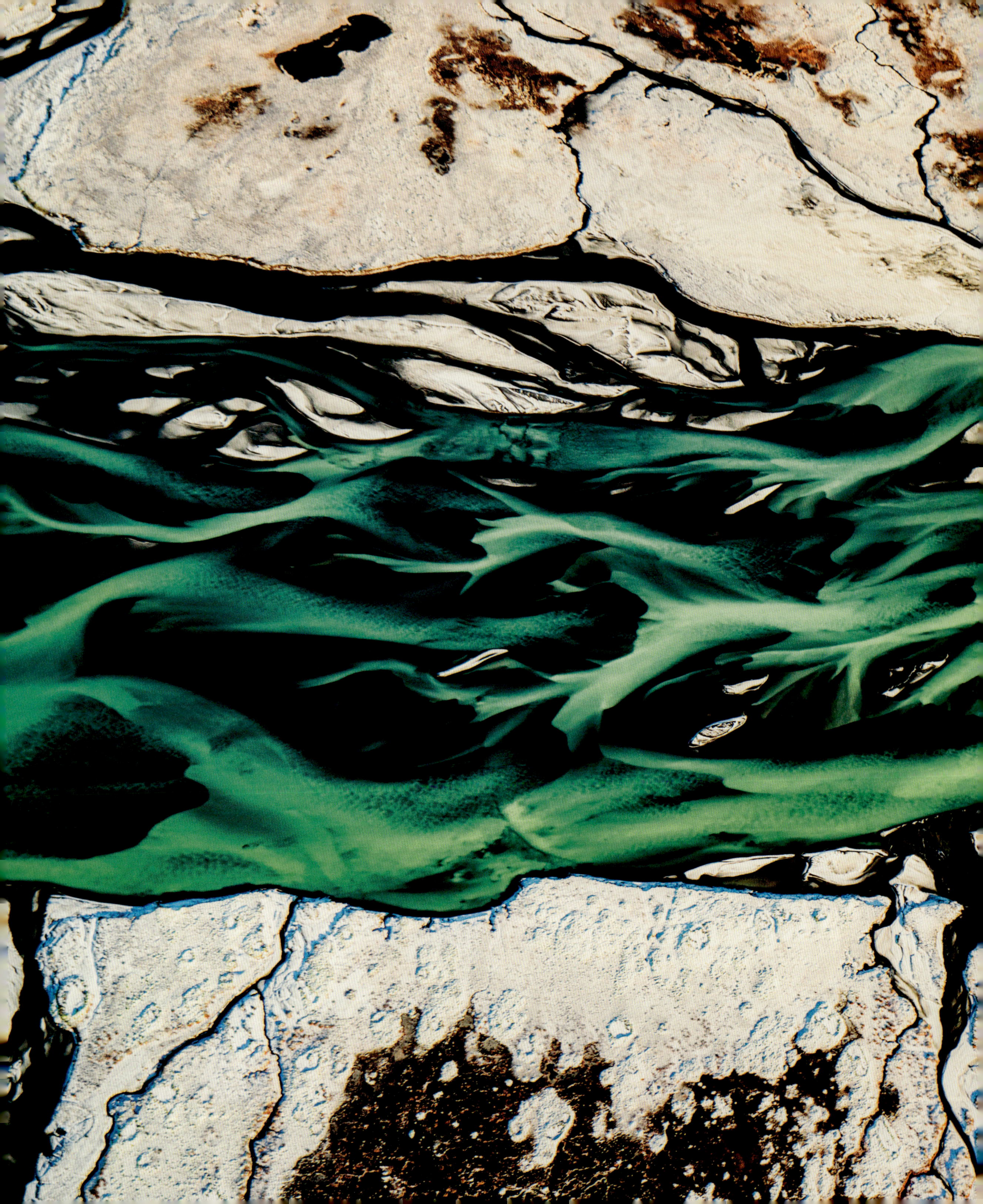

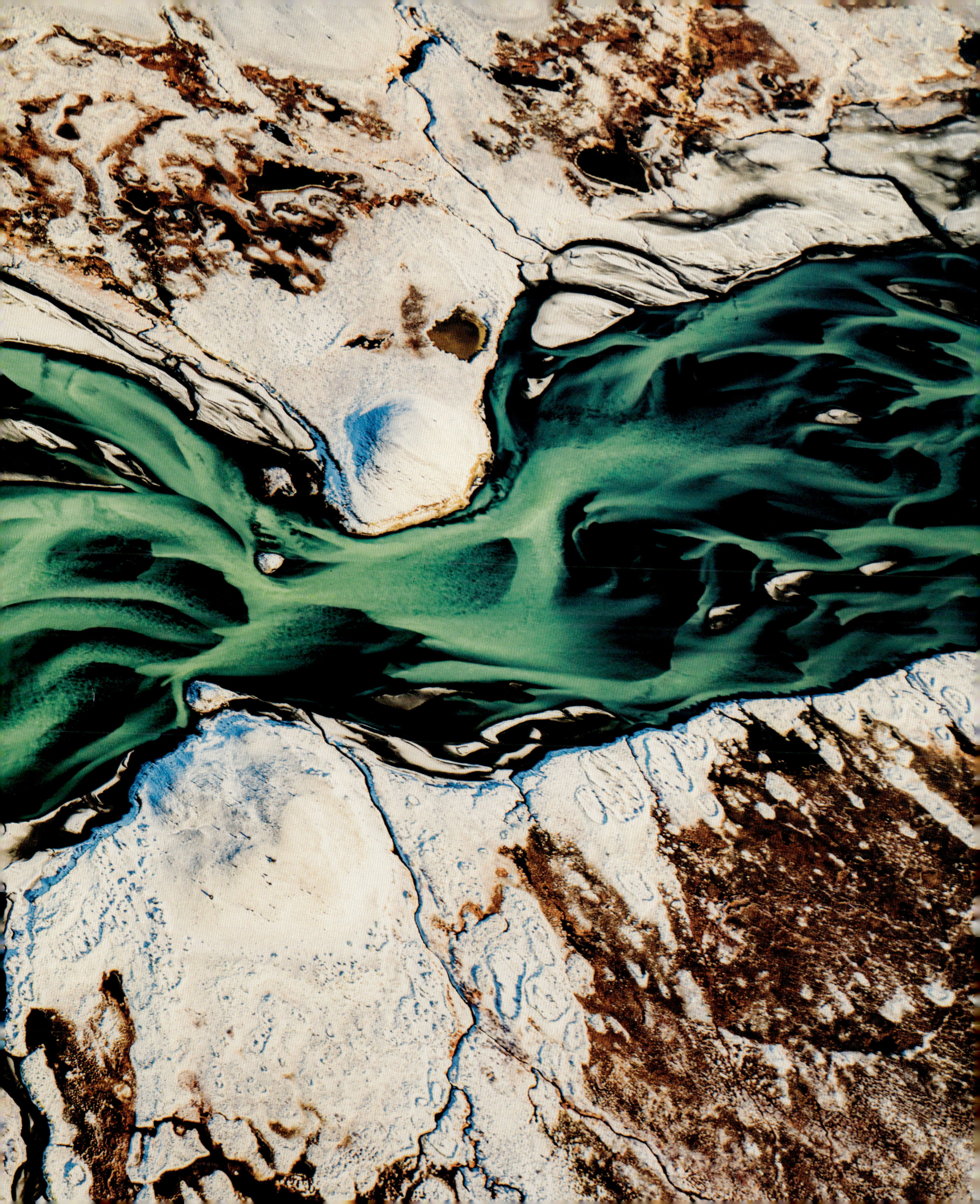

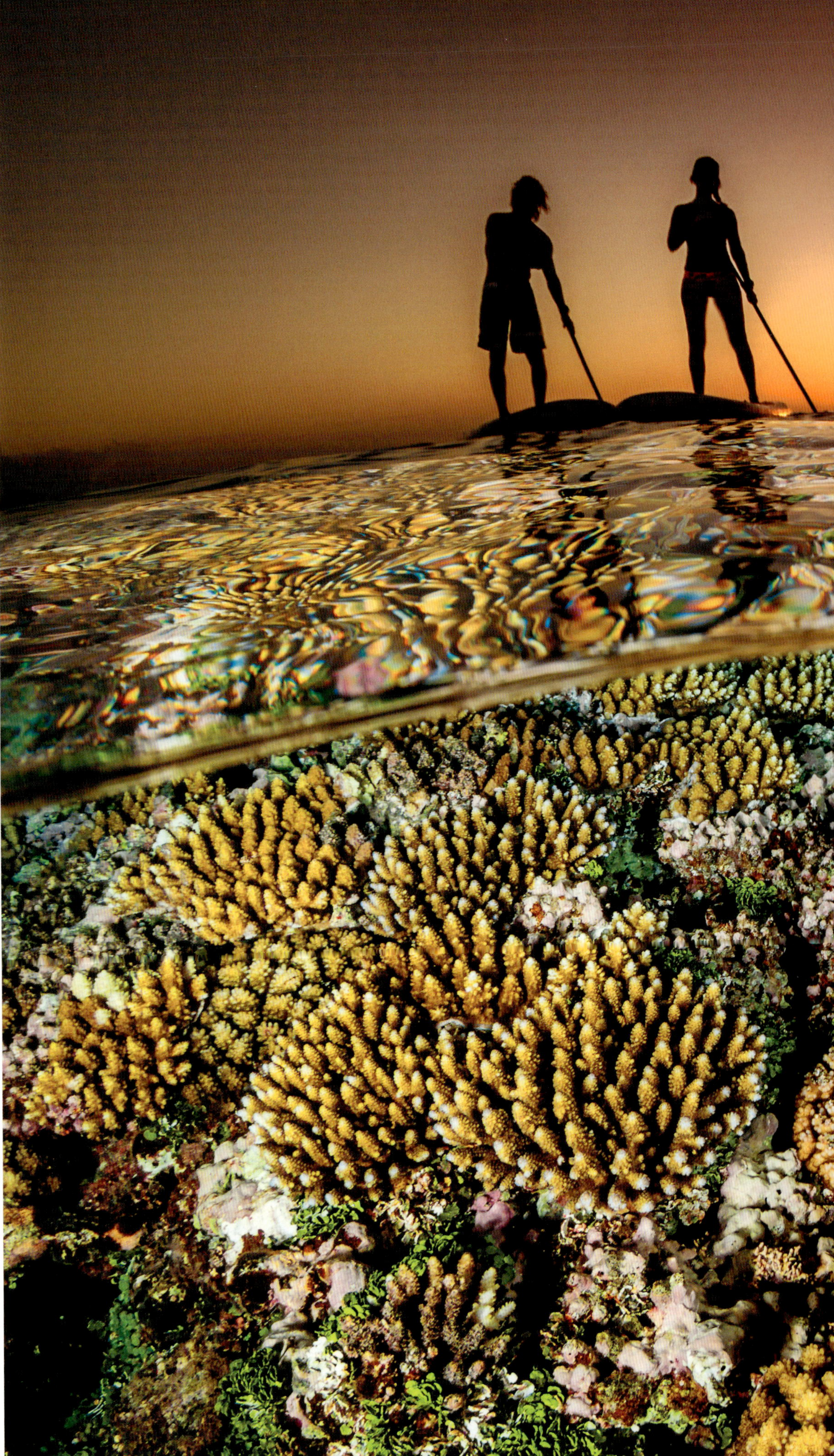

GRANT THOMAS
Silhouetted paddleboarders
glide over a dense coral forest.

Previous pages:
CHRIS BURKARD
Strands of silt and ice streak
through a river, transecting
Iceland's Hofsjökull glacier.

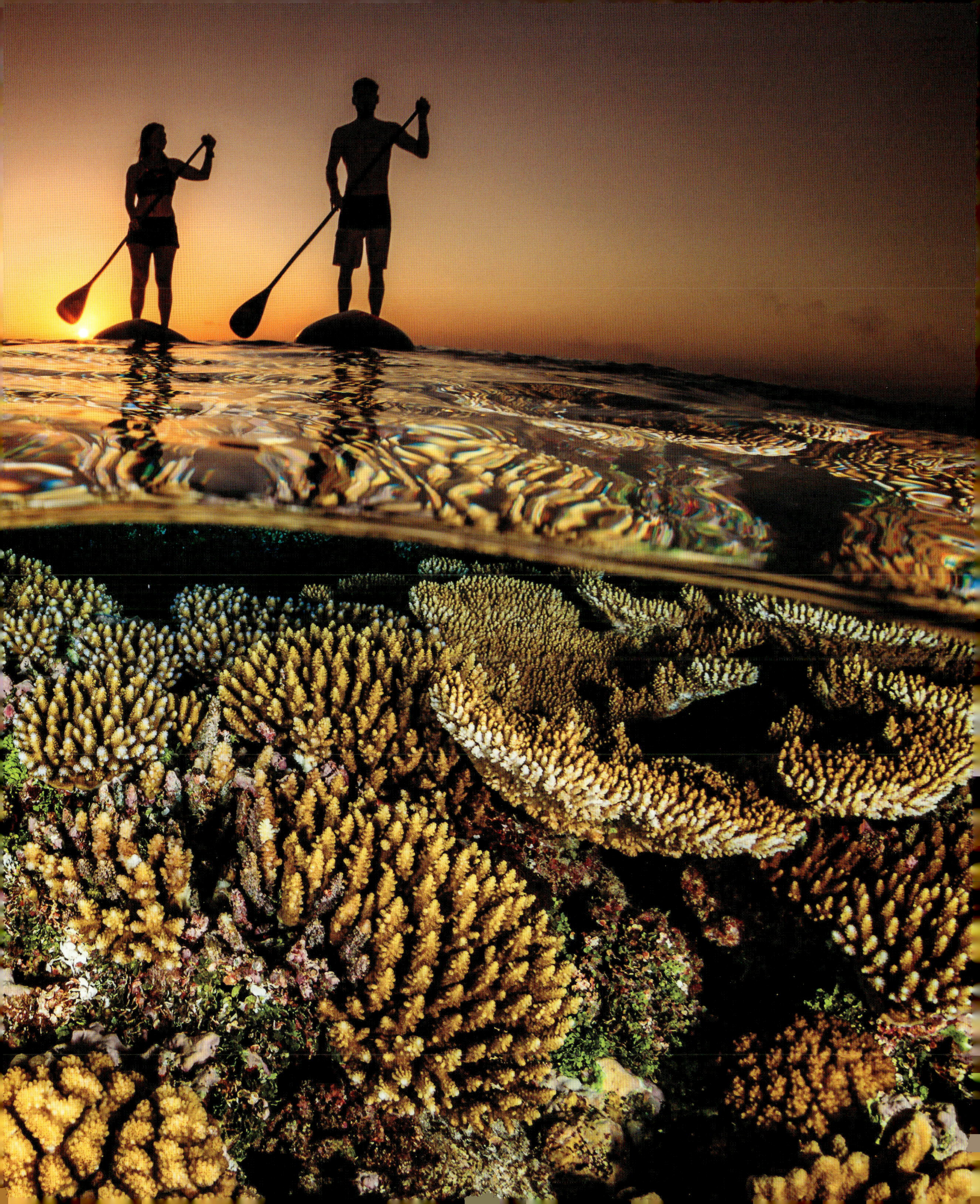

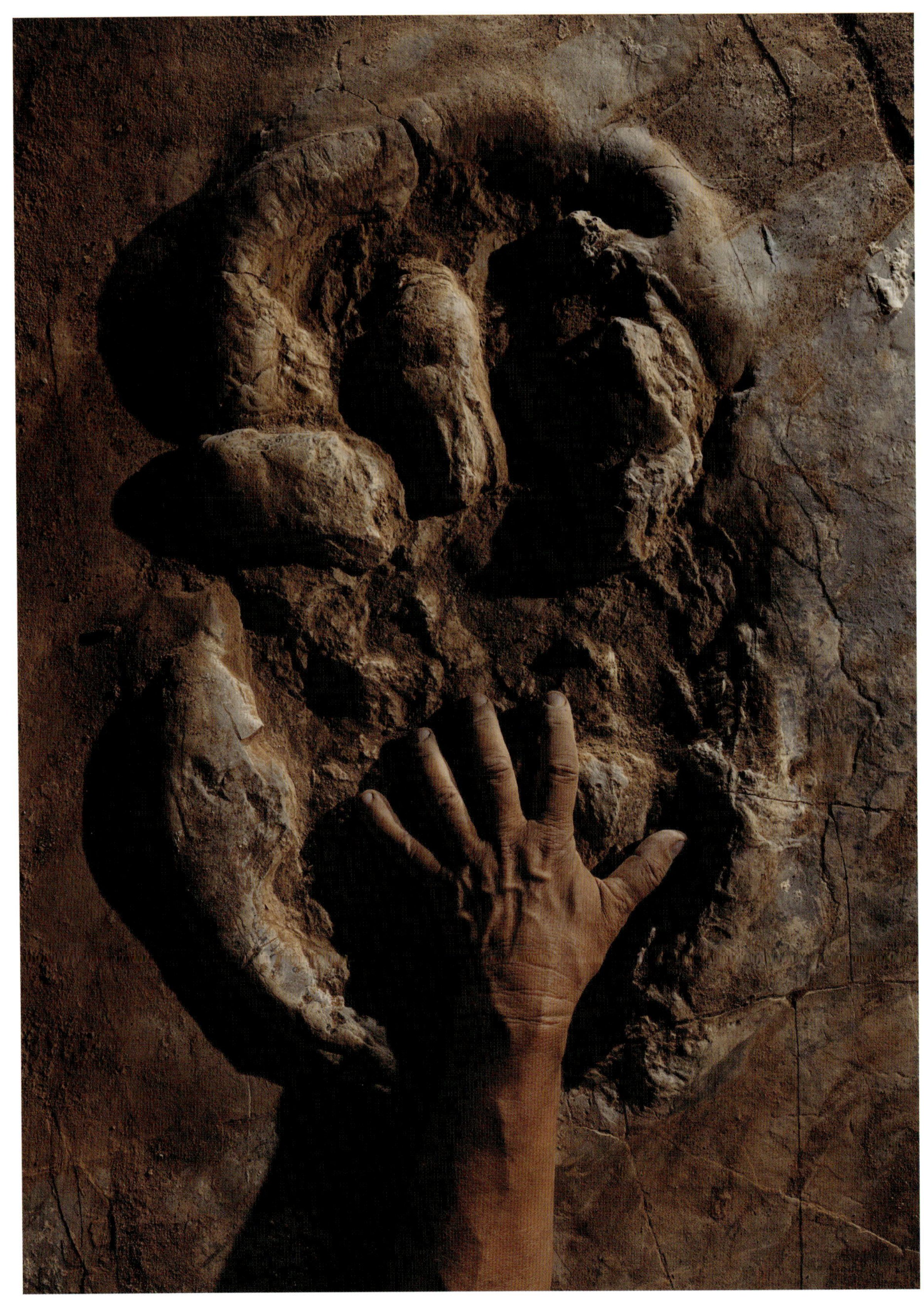

Reaching out and touching the prehistoric past, a human hand meets a sauropod footprint in the Sahara in Niger, Africa.

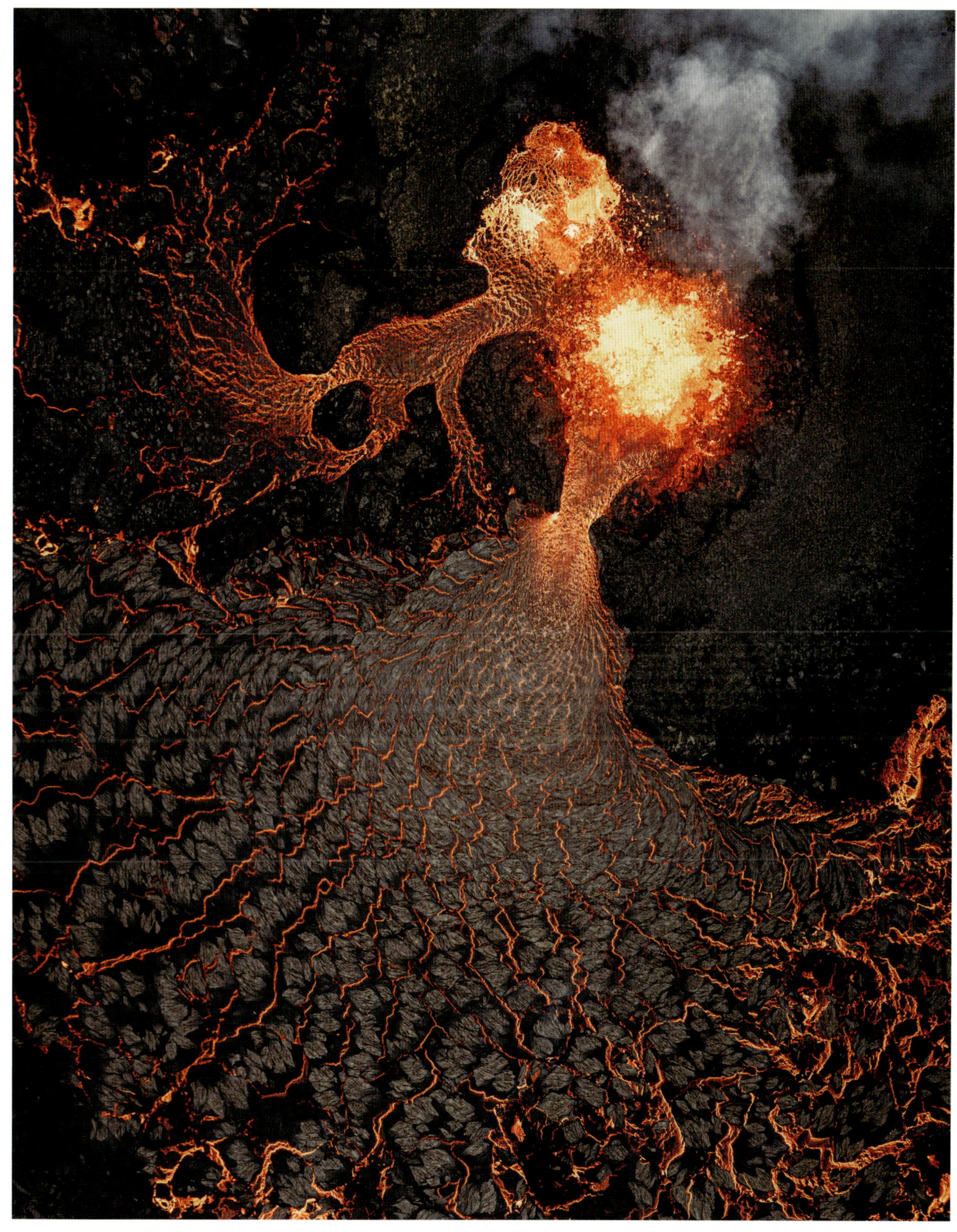

Iceland's Fagradalsfjall volcano erupts, causing bursts of light and rivulets of lava.

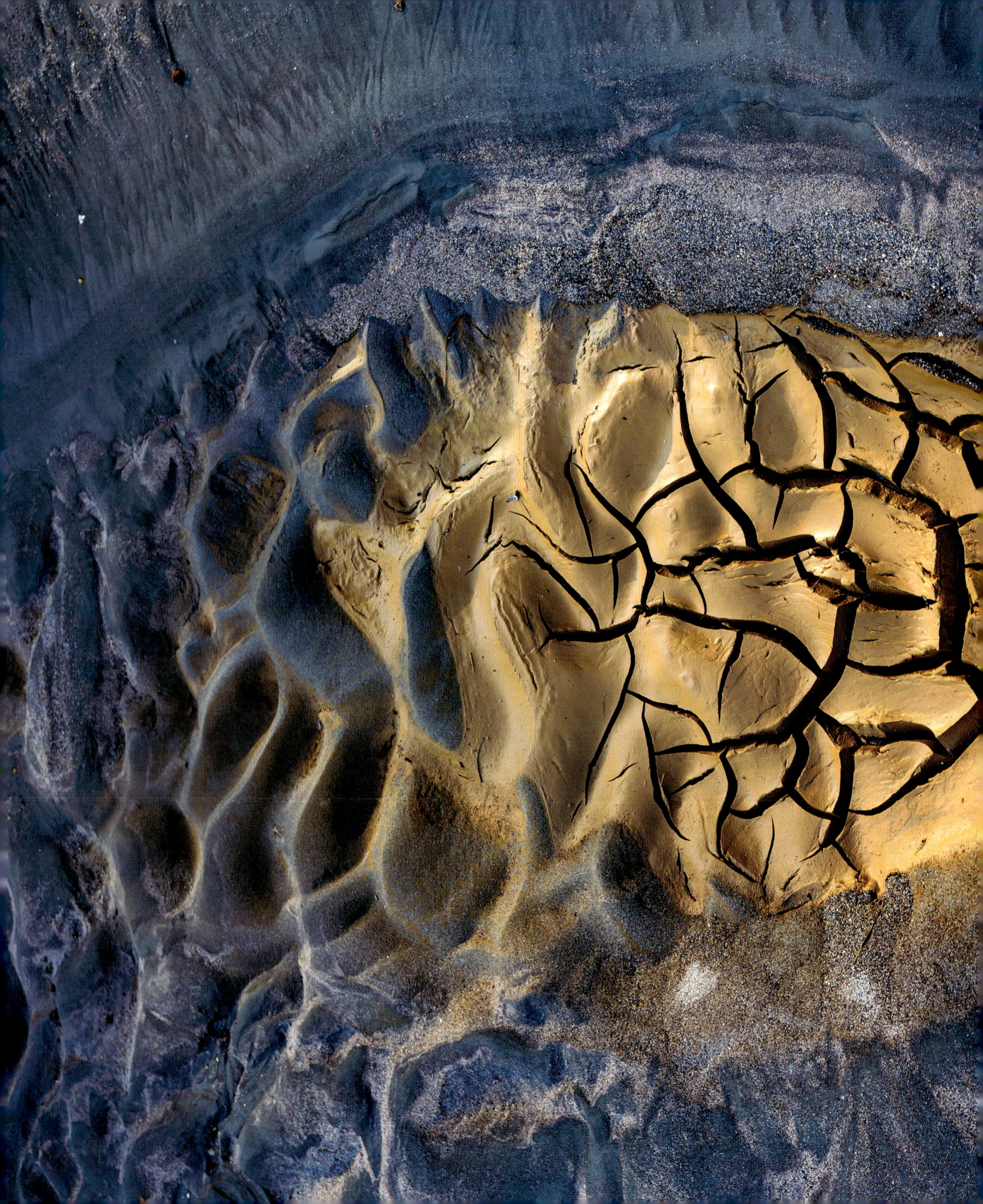

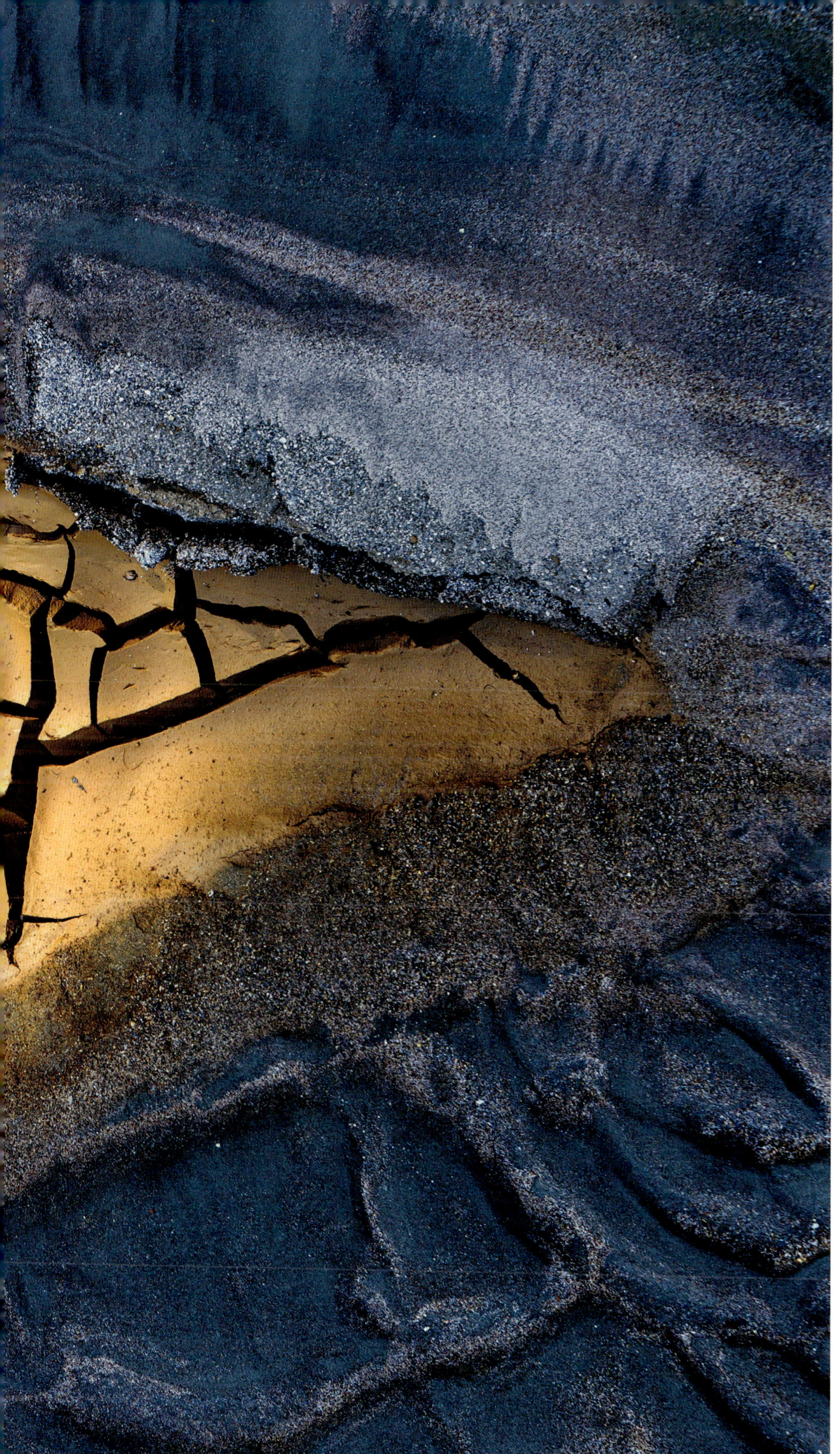

JUAN JESÚS GONZÁLEZ AHUMADA
The iron red waters of Spain's Rio Tinto—Stained River—contribute their color to sediment nearby, dry, cracked, and unearthly.

Following pages:
MAC STONE
Not the moon but a crescent-shaped oil sheen, the only clue telling us that we are looking down at old-growth cypress and tupelo, reflected in a South Carolina swamp

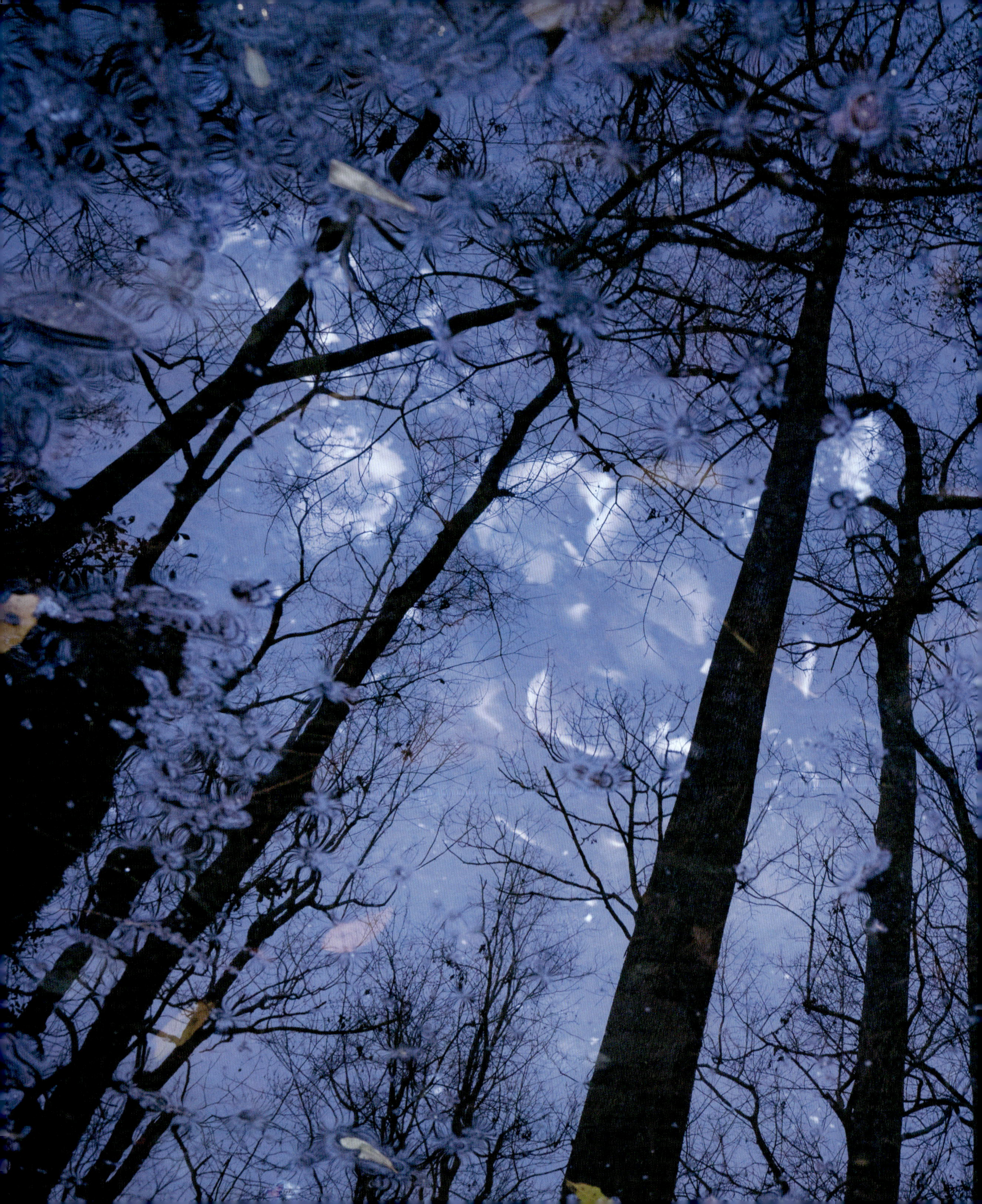

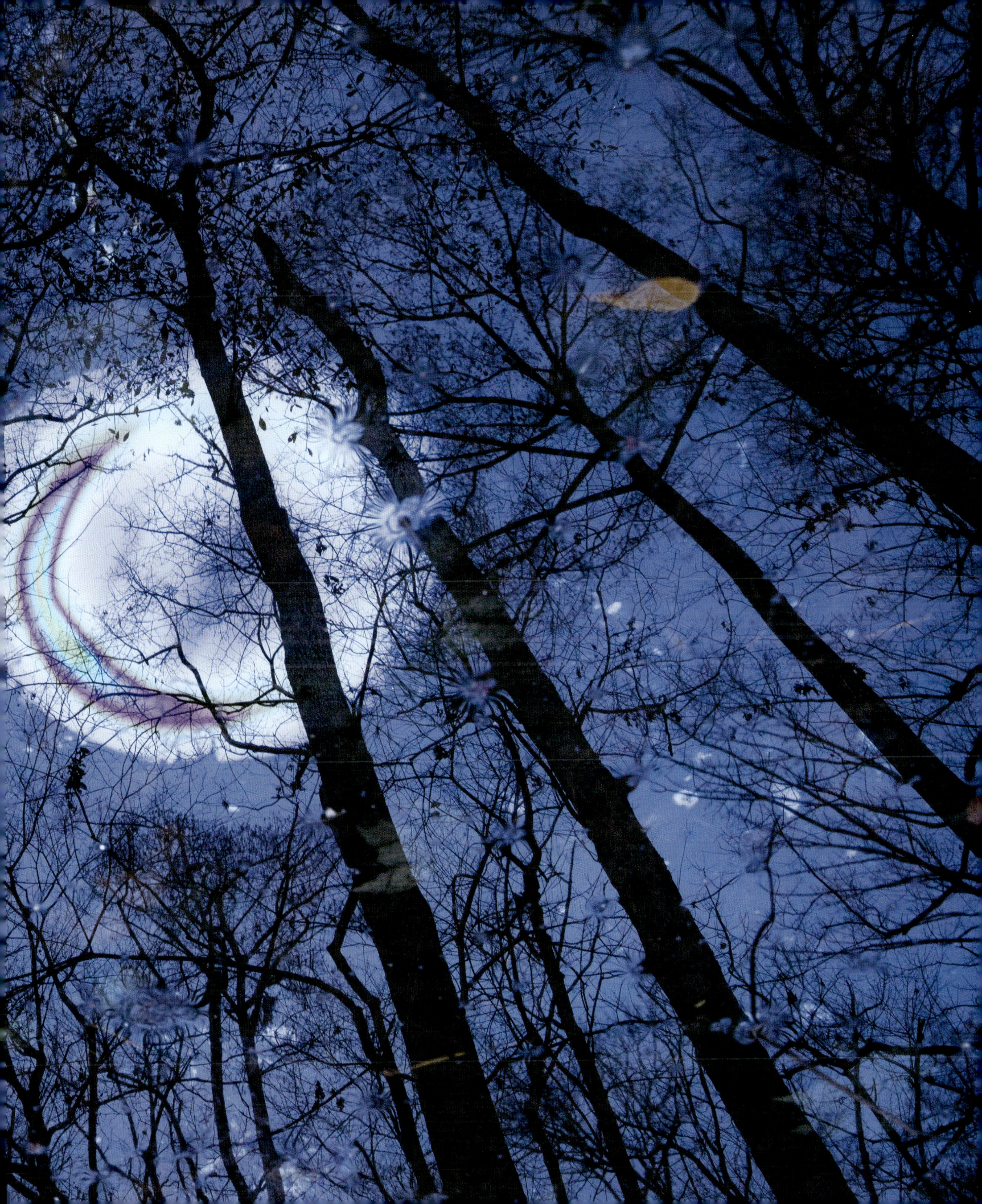

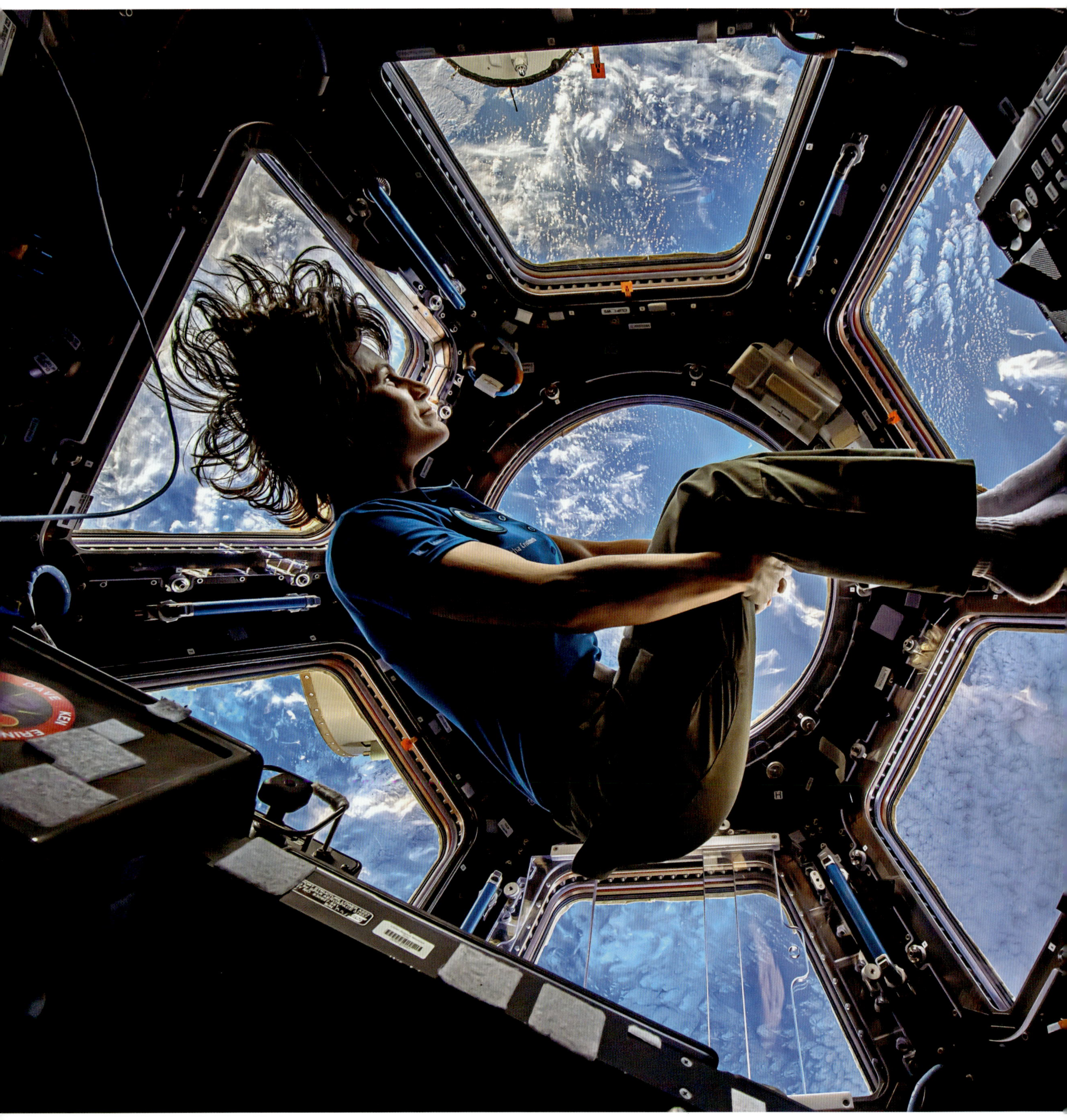

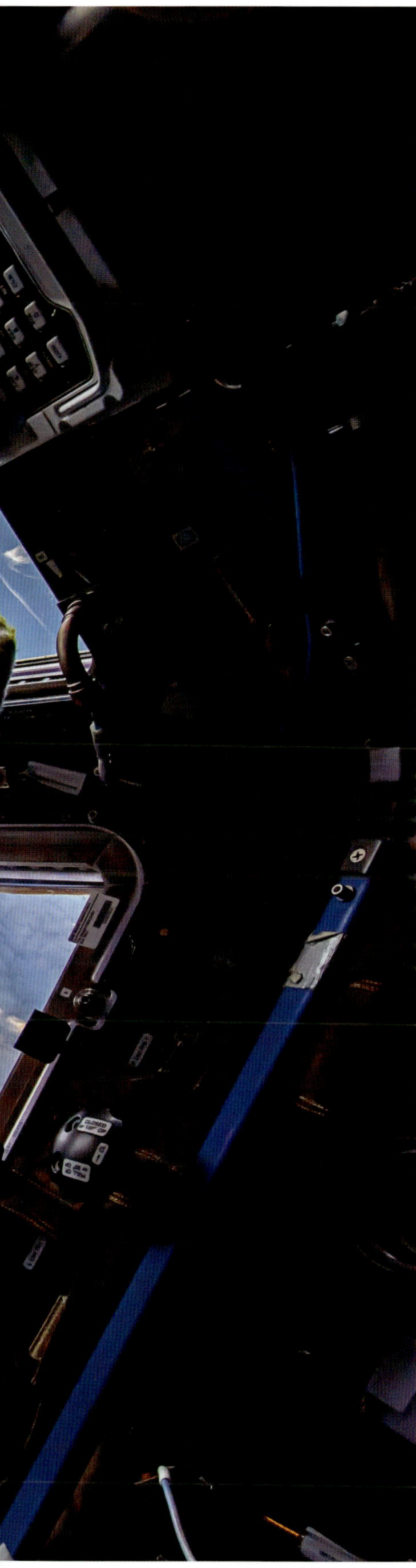

SAMANTHA CRISTOFORETTI

Samantha Cristoforetti, born in Milan, earned her fighter pilot wings in the Italian Air Force in 2006 and was selected as a European Space Agency astronaut in 2009. She became the first Italian woman in space on her first mission in 2014, when she also set the record for the longest uninterrupted space flight by a European astronaut (200 days). During her second mission, in 2022, she completed her first space walk and commanded the International Space Station.

JEFFREY KERBY: Did you take up photography early in life, or did your interest evolve over time?

SAMANTHA CRISTOFORETTI: I've been a little bit interested in photography and curious about learning the basics of it over the years, but I never invested in the expensive camera equipment that you need to do things seriously. When I was preparing for my first mission, all of a sudden I got all this really cool equipment that was made available to me for the flight. And so I started checking out the cameras. In space, photography is a very natural thing to do because there's not a lot of pastimes on the space station, and when you see all these things from the window, you want to capture them and share them. Maybe in hindsight, we should probably do less photography and spend more time just enjoying the view [*laughs*], but it's like, *Oh, my gosh, this is so cool.* For somebody like me who has not spent years fine-tuning their photography skills, it feels easy, because all this amazing equipment you have is so easy to handle due to the microgravity. You can take an 800-millimeter lens, and it's just floating! I don't have the issue of, you know, *How do I hold it?* or *What's the proper technique?*

I basically don't do any photography on Earth because I don't have all that cool equipment available and it's just, like, *whatever* [*laughs*].

JK: Was the 800-millimeter lens your biggest reach?

SC: There's a doubler. You can go to 1600, but I'm not a big fan of this. I tried to use it at night to get really cool city shots, but for smaller cities I think 400 is a good lens. Some people really like the 1600. Scott Kelly was up with me on my first mission and he did a lot with the 1600 because he was looking for details in cities, like football stadiums and things like that. I like the shorter lens, especially out of the cupola, where you can capture the big picture and the curvature of Earth and that kind of stuff. For me, if you go too long, they look like pictures you could take from an

---

SAMANTHA CRISTOFORETTI
Samantha Cristoforetti floats in the International Space Station, a view of Earth visible through its seven-windowed cupola.

Following pages:
SAMANTHA CRISTOFORETTI
Nighttime lights outline the boot shape of Italy, with the islands of Corsica, Sardinia, and Sicily nearby.

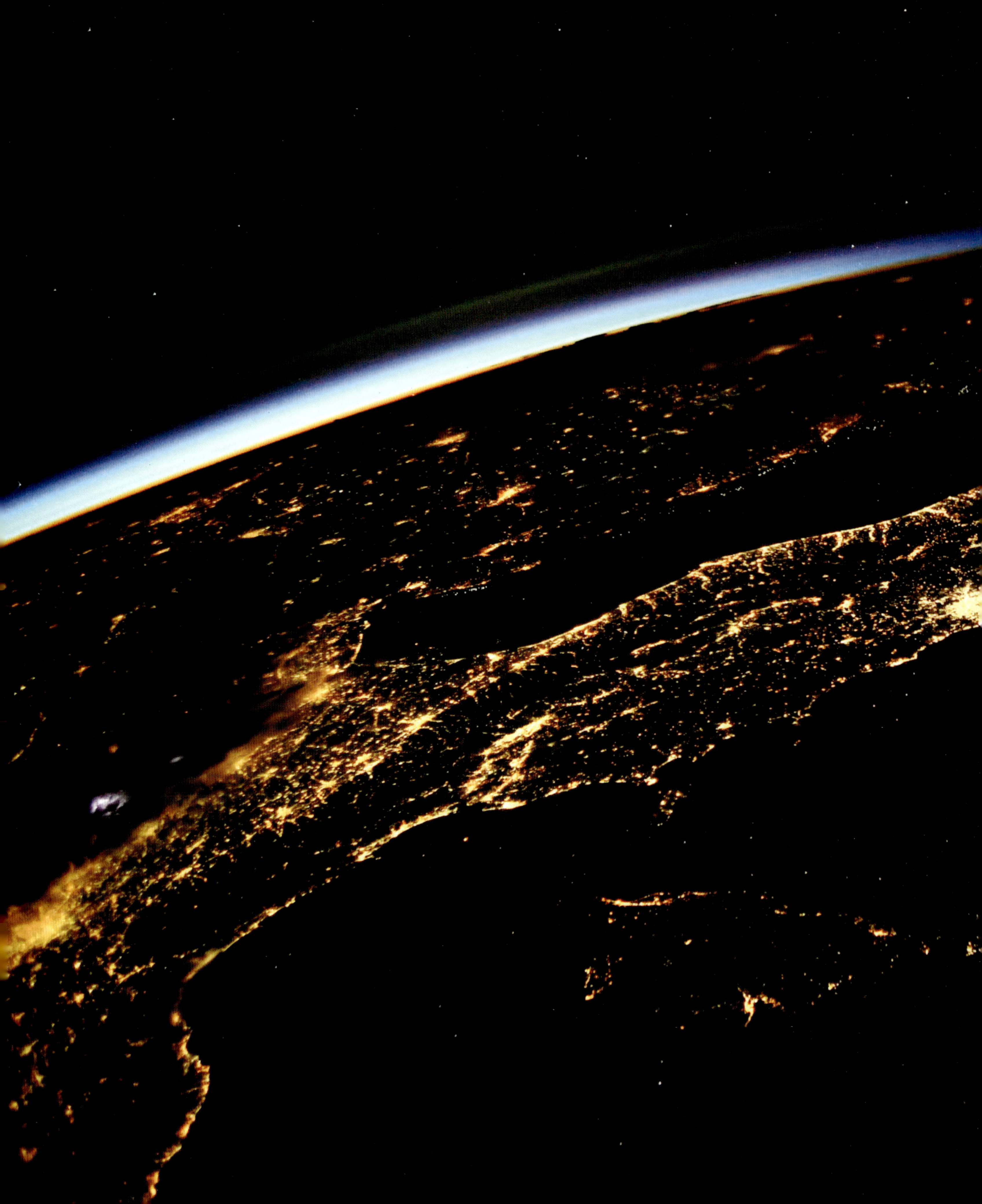

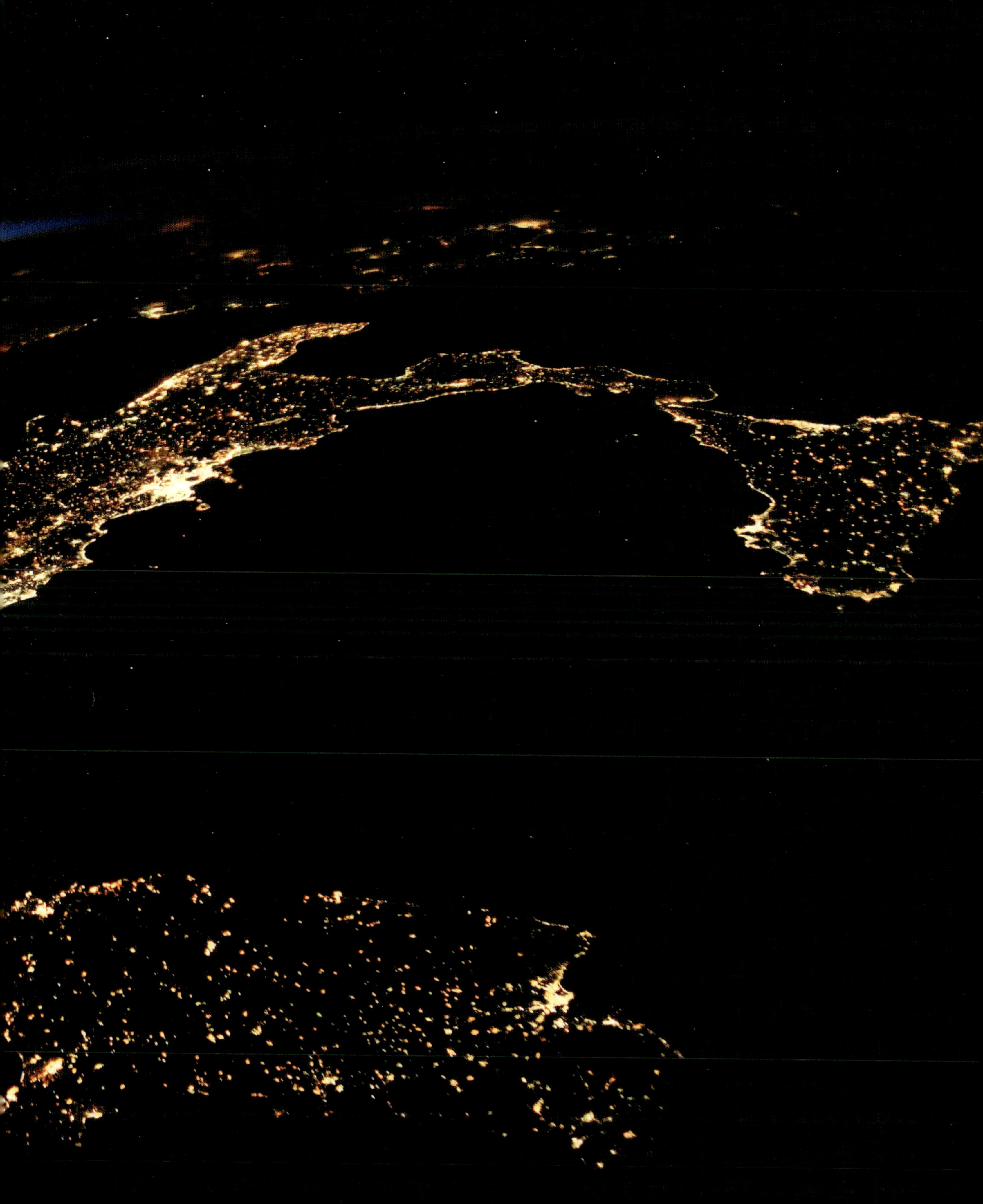

airplane. I mostly want them to look like pictures that you're taking from space.

JK: I'm very curious about the cupola area. I've only seen the iconic pictures of it. How do you get there, and are there other places you can take pictures from as well?

SC: The cupola is special because it has the side picture. So if you want to see Earth with the horizon and the stars, then you have to go to the cupola. The main window is pointing down toward Earth, but there's also the six windows all around that give us that side view. There's other windows that in some ways are better for pictures, though. The cupola windows unfortunately have a pretty bad optical quality, so long lenses work very badly and the pictures become really blurry—although it's gotten a little bit better. It's not the windows themselves, but they have scratch panes that really degrade the optical properties. There are other windows that are more intended for science photography and stuff, and those have really good optical qualities. One is in the lab and it's just a round window that looks straight down. So if you want to take the city-light pictures that I talked about, for example, with the 400 millimeter lens, you would go there.

JK: Did you have any training on how to find places on Earth from the space station, or is that something you learned on the job?

SC: There's a big community in the astronaut world that comes from the military, and so, when you fly combat airplanes, you are trained to find and recognize targets. Funnily enough, it's a skill that translates well to finding your photography targets on the space station. You have a bit of a trained eye. Of course, the perspectives are different and you have to get used to the scale of things, but it's pretty much the same skill. Earth is big, of course—you're not going to know in detail every place—but especially the places that you're more interested in, you

start to become familiar and understand its features, be it your hometown, or your family's, whatever. Most of the targets I was looking for on my first flight were the UNESCO heritage sites. On the second mission, I had this project of taking pictures of glaciers and a few personal places, like family-related and friends-related things.

JK: When you get a list like that, do you map it out before you get up there? Or do you wait for certain patterns or light? I would guess you get a lot of sunsets.

SC: We have a software program—it's not the most user-friendly, but it works—where you can submit to NASA a list of your targets before you fly. You can categorize them, like your glaciers, your UNESCO sites, islands, volcanoes, and NASA puts them into the software in a personal folder for you. Then [during a flight] the targets appear on the map camera, and the software can calculate when the next pass is. It will tell you the azimuth [a measurement determining the direction of a celestial object from the observer]—if it's going to be near or off to the side—and it has a weather model so you can have an idea if it's going to be cloudy or not. In space, you're worried about the clouds if you want to take pictures of Earth.

JK: The clouds in your images carry such interesting textures from space. Do you see other interesting textures from that vantage point that you don't see from the ground?

SC: You're looking for patterns and things like that. Certainly the deserts are very particular, but also the more humanized landscapes. If you fly over the Great Plains in North America, for minutes and minutes you see all those squares of the crops. There's a lot of that. In desert areas, you've got the typical yellowish color, and then this pattern of circles that are green from the irrigation systems. In Southeast Asia, some of the fishing boats are green

dots. I've been told they use these very strong, greenish—well, from orbit they look green—lights to attract a special type of fish. And sometimes it's through this thin layer of cloud, so you've got these layers of clouds and then from beneath it all, these green dots popping through. It's pretty amazing.

In the Middle East and North Africa, you see sometimes the oil wells, I think, where they burn whatever gases escape, and so you see those dots of flames scattered in irregular patterns, especially if it's a dark night without the moon. It's pitch-black desert, but then you see these dots of fire.

JK: How have people responded to the pictures that you've captured or shared?

SC: It's amazing. We post some on social media, and they always draw lots of attention. You have thousands of people who are really excited about seeing pictures from space. I notice the interest is very much mediated by the personal connection. I'm Italian, and in European countries, astronauts are usually quite well known. When there's a mission, a lot of people know about it and follow the astronauts.

JK: I just found out that someone in my office here in Denmark has a brother, Andreas Mogensen, who's up in space right now. So I'm feeling the Denmark excitement of having an astronaut.

SC: No kidding! What are the chances of that? That's fantastic. I remember coming back from my first mission, and one of the things that people told me when I met them was, *Oh, we miss your pictures so much.* And my answer was—maybe I'm too rational, I'm an engineer—but I'm like, *Well, there's astronauts out there right now, and they're also taking pictures. Why are you missing our pictures?* They're like, *Oh, no. That's not the same. We want your pictures.* And it's not that my pictures are any better than anyone else's. It's just this personal connection to what I do.

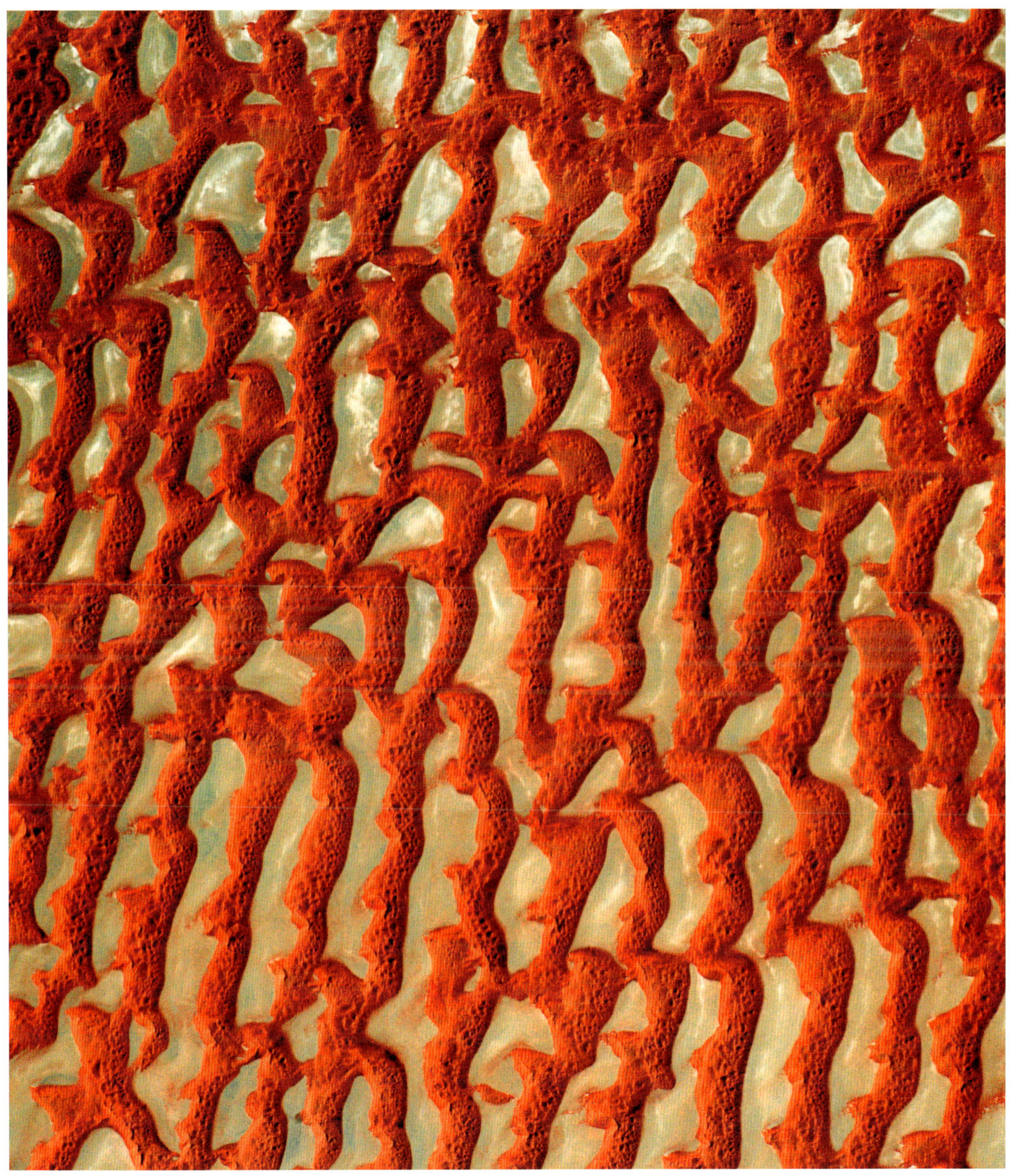

SAMANTHA CRISTOFORETTI
Dunes and swales ripple across Oman's Rub' al-Khali—Earth's second largest expanse of sand, after the Sahara.

ACKNOWLEDGMENTS

I am thankful for the support of the National Geographic Society across numerous projects and expeditions. Kaitlin Yarnall, Katia Andreassi, Rebecca Martin, all my grant officers, and the Explorer programs team past and present—you have opened so many doors, righted many ships, and created an incredible community.

Thank you to everyone at National Geographic Books, including Lisa Thomas, Elisa Gibson, Adrian Coakley, Susan Hitchcock, Sanaa Akkach, Tyler Daswick, Becca Saltzman, and Meredith Wilcox. Sanaa, your abilities and enthusiasm turned the layout process into the most enriching education.

Special thanks to Acacia Johnson, Robbie Shone, Renan Ozturk, and Samantha Cristoforetti for the fascinating conversations.

To my innumerable collaborators and colleagues—no project happens in isolation. Special thanks to the editorial staff at *National Geographic* magazine; to Peter Fashing, Nga Nguyen, Vivek Venkataraman, and all involved with the Guassa Gelada Research Project; to everyone at the Arctic Research Centre at Aarhus University and the staff at the Aarhus Institute of Advanced Studies; to the teams at Conservation Drones, the Greater Mahale Ecosystem Research and Conservation project, and the Jane Goodall Institute; to Vladimir Burkanov and the crew from the Kurils; and to Brian Buma, Aka Simonsen, Kim Young, and Alejandra Borunda (let it snow!). Anand Varma, your advice and friendship are invaluable to me and so many others.

To my parents, Janet and Steve, and to my brother, Micky, thank you for your unwavering love and support, even when I'm on the other side of the world.

And finally, to Jess. You inspire me. Thank you for your endless love and encouragement.

ILLUSTRATIONS CREDITS

Front cover: A wedding party arrives at Bled Island in Lake Bled, Slovenia (Tobias Hägg/Airpixelsmedia).

Back cover: Melt water flows away from the Greenland ice sheet into Röhss Fjord in Northeast Greenland National Park (Jeffrey Kerby).

2-3, Getty Images; 18, Panos Pictures; 28-9 and 30-1, Amazing Aerial Agency; 33, Barry Webb FRPS; 38, Boyan Ortse - @boyanoo; 39, Amazing Aerial Agency; 51, Björn Ewers, @studyo_314; 62-3, image by Overview, source imagery © Maxar; 64-5, Adobe Stock; 68-9, Nature Picture Library; 72-3, Yousef Al Habshi/UAEmacro; 78-9, National Geographic Image Collection; 90-1, image by Overview, source imagery © Maxar; 100-1, Panos Pictures; 106, image by Overview, source imagery © Maxar; 112, Amazing Aerial Agency; 118 and 119, Amazing Aerial Agency; 120-1, AirPano LLC/ Amazing Aerial Agency; 123, National Geographic Image Collection; 130-1, National Geographic Image Collection; 131, Dave Wells, Prevailing Wind Productions; 141, Adobe Stock; 146-7, Sysaworld/Getty Images; 150, Nature Picture Library; 151, Amazing Aerial Agency; 158, National Geographic Image Collection; 159, Debbie E Photos - Debbie Stevens; 166, Getty Images; 172, Martin Oeggerli, made with support from School of Life Sciences, FHNW, Switzerland; 175, Nature Picture Library; 176-7, Chin Leong Teo - @teochinleong78; 179, Amazing Aerial Agency; 183, Amazing Aerial Agency; 188-9, National Geographic Image Collection; 193, National Geographic Image Collection; 198-9, Science Source; 202-3, Science Source; 208, David Fairs/New Light Visuals; 210-1, @earthbyoren - Oren Alon; 212-3, National Geographic Image Collection; 214-5, image by Overview, source imagery © Nearmap 218-9, Tendance Floue/MNHN; 220-1, Reuters/Redux; 225, Stocksy; 226-7, National Geographic Image Collection; 232-3, Renan Ozturk, Expedition Studios; 234-5, Library of Congress Prints and Photographs Division, #ppmsca-07823; 235, Chicago History Museum, ICHi-011050 (National Geographic edit); 236-7, Chicago History Museum, ICHi-011047; George R. Lawrence, photographer; 240-1, David Herasimtschuk/Freshwaters Illustrated; 242-5, National Geographic Image Collection; 248-9, image by Overview, source imagery © Maxar; 251, David Nadlinger, University of Oxford; 258, National Geographic Image Collection; 262, National Geographic Image Collection; 266-71, National Geographic Image Collection; 278, National Geographic Image Collection; 282-3, National Geographic Image Collection; 292-3, Nature Picture Library; 296-7, Thorben Danke/sagaoptics; 298-9, NASA/ISS Crew Earth Observations experiment and Image Science & Analysis Laboratory, Johnson Space Center; 302-3, Amazing Aerial Agency; 304, Panos Pictures; 305, Milan Radisics, Water. Shapes. Earth; 311, Shutterstock; 314-5, © Edward Burtynsky, courtesy Sundaram Tagore Gallery and Howard Greenberg Gallery, New York; 317, National Geographic Image Collection; 329, Igor Siwanowicz, Janelia Research Campus of the HHMI; 330-1, Amazing Aerial Agency; 334-5, TNS/ABACA-PRESS/Alamy Stock Photo; 335, Washington State DNR; 336, Shutterstock; 347, Abstract Aerial Art/Getty Images; 353, Stills; 358-9, ESA/NASA-S.Cristoforetti/R. Rossi; 360-1, ESA/NASA; 363, ESA/NASA; 366, Renan Ozturk, Expedition Studios.

ABOUT THE AUTHOR

Jeffrey Kerby is a photographer and ecologist whose work has taken him from New Hampshire to Denmark to his current residence in Cambridge, England, where he works at the Scott Polar Research Institute at the University of Cambridge. He has participated in 12 National Geographic Society projects, leading four of them. His first *National Geographic* magazine assignment focused on gelada monkeys and community conservation initiatives in the Ethiopian Highlands, and his most recent was documenting the search for the world's northernmost flower in northern Greenland. He holds a Ph.D. in ecology focused on Arctic regions, and he actively works in the sciences using drone, time-lapse, and satellite imagery to better understand the interactions between living creatures and their environment.

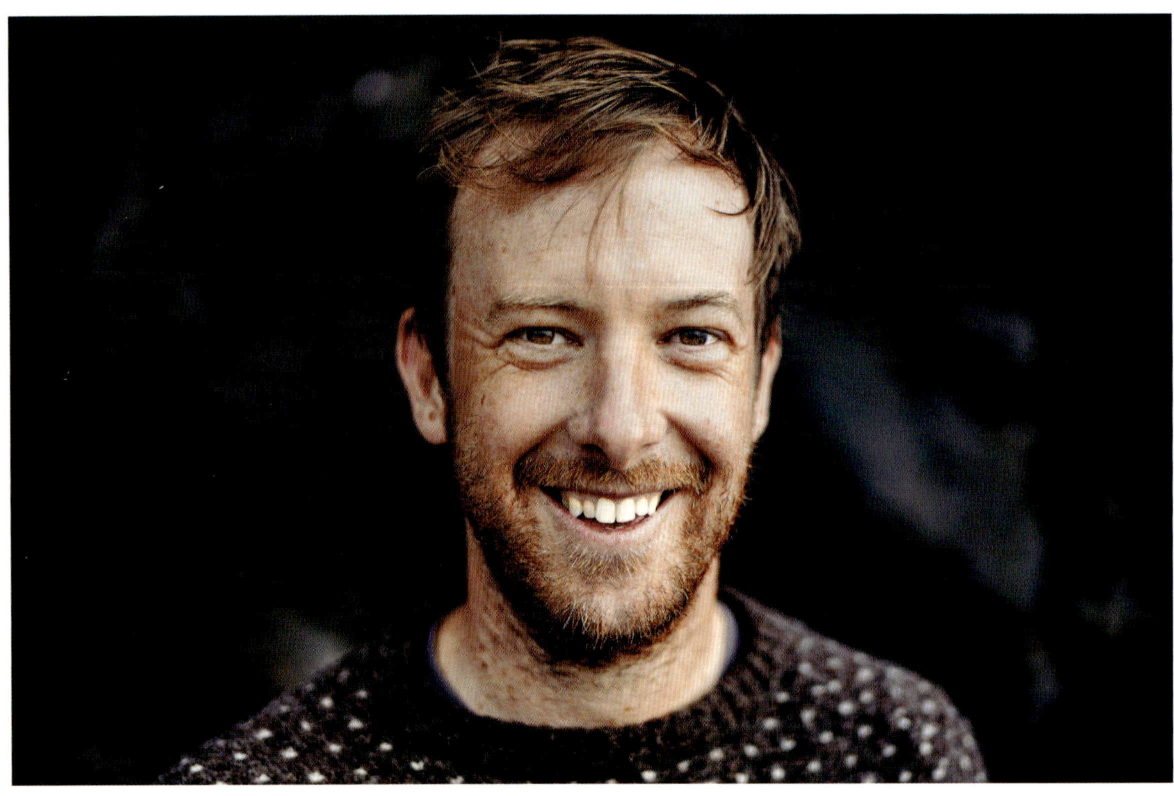

Since 1888, the National Geographic Society has funded more than 14,000 research, conservation, education, and storytelling projects around the world. National Geographic Partners distributes a portion of the funds it receives from your purchase to National Geographic Society to support programs including the conservation of animals and their habitats.

Get closer to National Geographic Explorers and photographers, and connect with our global community. Join us today at nationalgeographic.org/joinus

For rights or permissions inquiries, please contact National Geographic Books Subsidiary Rights: bookrights@natgeo.com

ISBN: 978-1-4262-2340-2
Printed in China
24/PPS/1

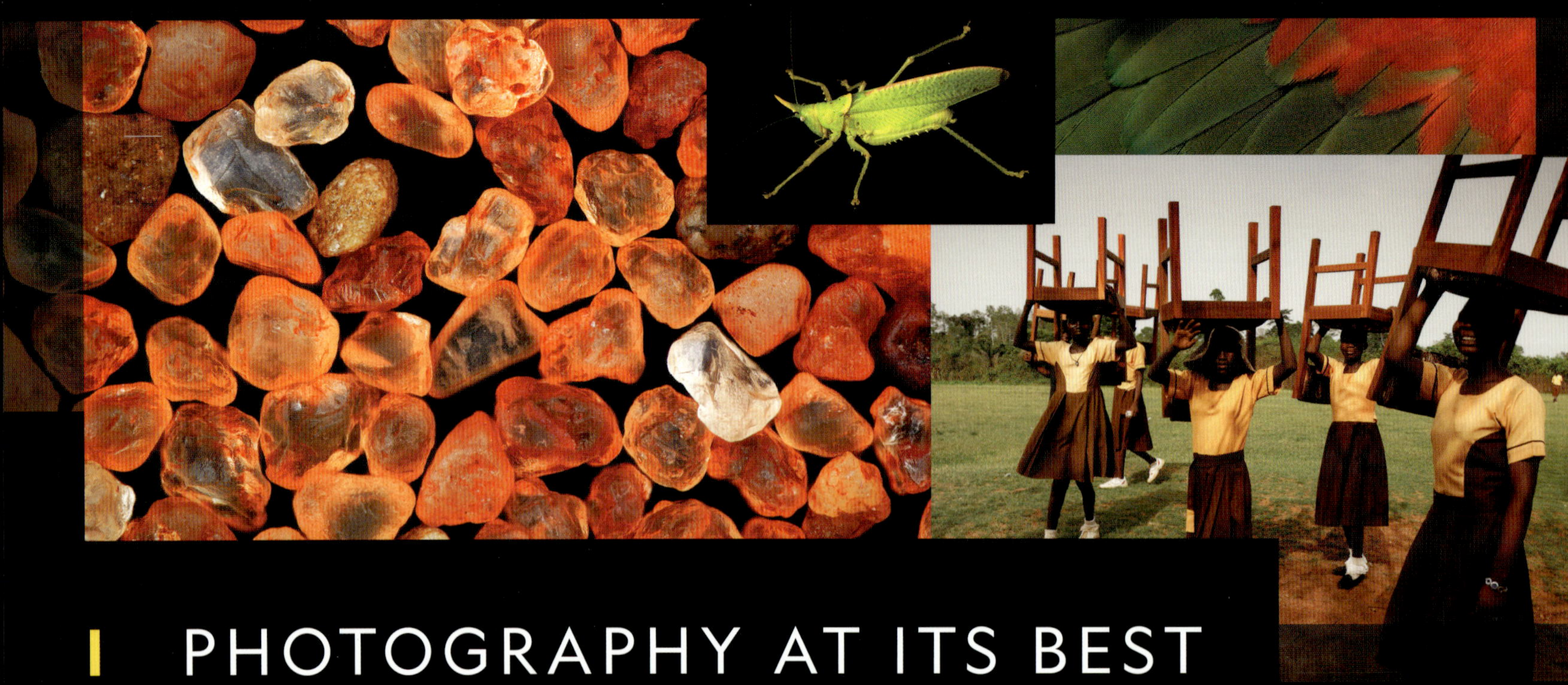

PHOTOGRAPHY AT ITS BEST

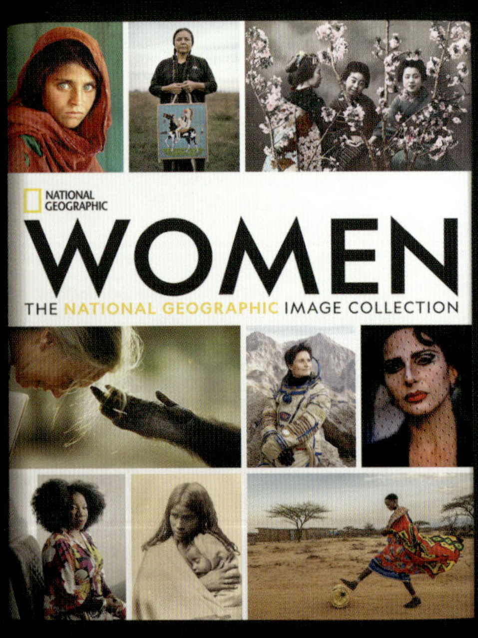

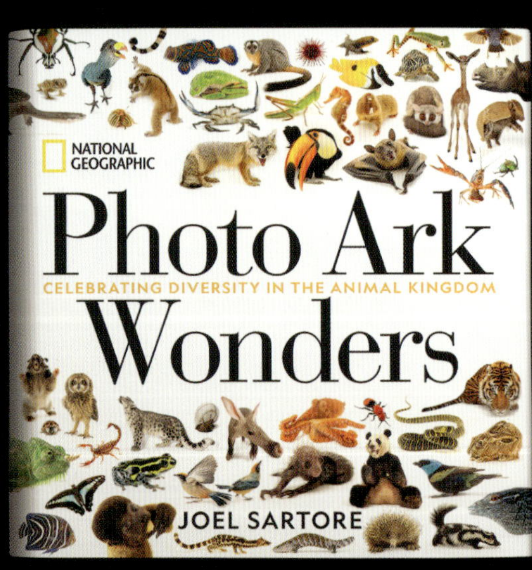

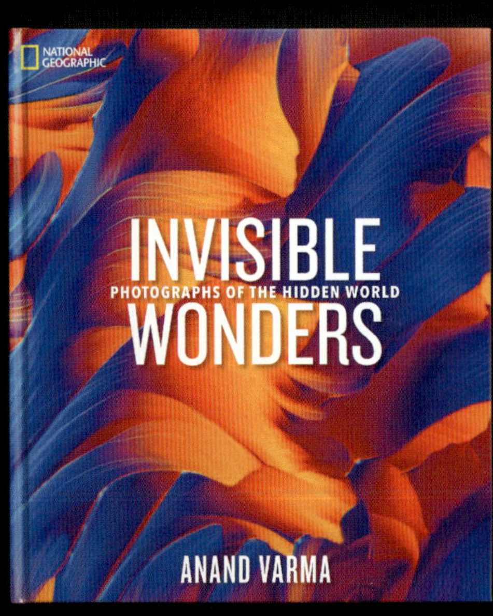

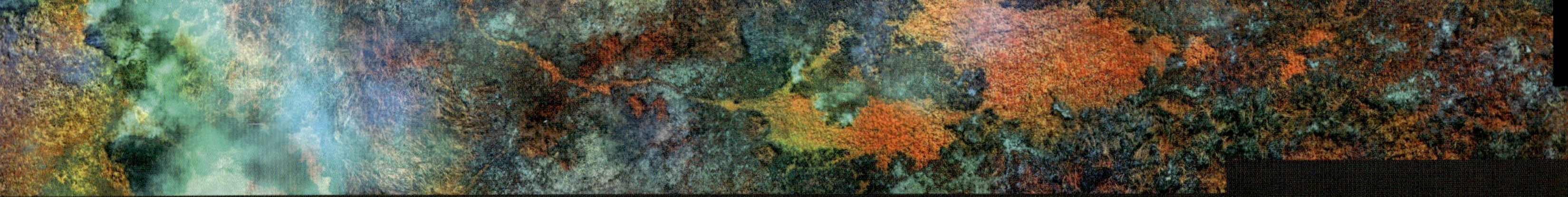

AVAILABLE WHEREVER BOOKS ARE SOLD

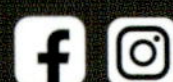 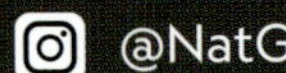 @NatGeoBooks

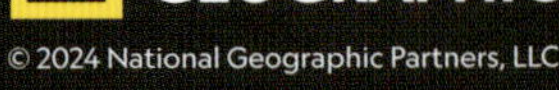

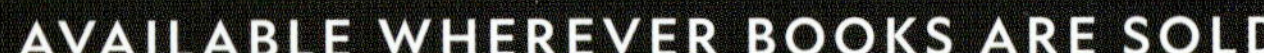